FOLK LORE NOTES

FOLK LORE NOTES

Vol. I — Gujarat
Vol. II — Konkan

Compiled from Materials Collected by
A.M.T. Jackson

Vol. I

FOLKLORE OF GUJARAT

R.E. Enthoven

ISBN : 978-93-5324-425-5 (Set)

ISBN : 978-93-5324-426-2 (HB)

First Published, 1914 (Vol. I)

Published, 2020

Published by

Facsimile Publisher
12 Pragati Market
Ashok Vihar, Ph-2
Delhi-110052
E-mail: books@facsimilepublisher.com

Printed at: G. Print Process, Delhi.

Folklore of Gujarat
Author: A.M.T. Jackson

FOLK LORE NOTES.

VOL. I—GUJARAT.

COMPILED FROM MATERIALS COLLECTED BY

THE LATE A. M. T. JACKSON, INDIAN CIVIL SERVICE.

R. E. ENTHOVEN, C.I.E., I.C.S.

BRITISH INDIA PRESS, MAZGAON BOMBAY.

1914.

INTRODUCTION.

THE circumstances attending the murder of Mr. A. M. T. Jackson in Nasik in December 1909 led to the raising of a small subscription among his friends, to be devoted to a memorial in some shape or form, showing the respect and affection with which he was regarded in Western India. A large part of the fund then raised was expended on the purchase of his valuable library, which now forms a part of the collection owned by the Bombay Branch of the Royal Asiatic Society. It was subsequently decided that the balance could not be better spent than in defraying the cost of publishing certain folklore materials which he had collected and intended, at the time of his untimely death, to publish in the pages of the *Indian Antiquary*. These materials were the result of an enquiry set on foot by him about the year 1900. His plan of operation was to forward, through the agency of the Education Department, Crooke's list of folklore questions to schoolmasters in various parts of the Presidency. The question paper is given below ; the replies form the raw material from which these notes have been compiled. For convenience they are divided into two series : Gujarat and the Konkan.

I desire at the outset of these introductory remarks to explain that, when at the request of the memorial committee I undertook the task of seeing these notes through the press, I did not contemplate any critical handling of the materials found in the papers made over to me. I had neither the leisure nor the knowledge to carry out Mr. Jackson's intention, *i. e.*, to edit the notes carefully with such criticisms and comparisons as his ripe scholarship would have suggested. I make no claim, therefore, to have effected more than to have rescued from the wastepaper basket a number of replies to questions regarding the beliefs of the people in Gujarat and the Konkan. The notes as now presented doubtless contain much that is trivial, and possibly many inaccuracies ; but among them students of folklore may on the other hand discover material of real value—such as they are, they will, I trust, repay careful study, and perhaps serve one day to form the basis of a further and more comprehensive examination of the folk-lore of the Bombay Presidency—an examination which should not be too long deferred, for the old practices and beliefs are yearly tending to decay and vanish in contact with the spread of education. The field for enquiry is wide and rich, but workers fail to come forward ; and meanwhile the old beliefs and practices slowly disappear. On the subjects with which these notes deal, much information of value has already been collected and recorded by another oriental scholar, the late Sir James Campbell, K.C.I.E., and will be found partly in the pages of the Bombay Gazetteer, and partly in the notes on the Spirit Basis of Belief and Custom which he published from time to time in the *Indian Antiquary*. The present notes carry striking confirmation of Sir James Campbell's theory regarding the extent to which beliefs and religious practices in this country can be traced to the desire to propitiate spirit presences. It may be remarked that Campbell's work in the domain of Indian folk-lore does not seem to have received the notice that it deserves in the works of writers on folk-lore generally, possibly because so much of it is buried in the pages of the Bombay Gazetteer or in scattered numbers of the *Indian Antiquary.* The notes would amply repay the labour of republication, with a summary and suitable index. They deal very fully with spirit worship and possession, witchcraft and magic, and the evil eye. They differ from the present notes in being to a large extent comparative, assembling under the various heads of ancestor worship, spirit haunts, spirit possession, exorcism, etc., kindred beliefs from all parts of the world. Doubtless his work to no small extent suggested to Mr. Jackson the line of enquiry which is contained in the question paper. From the materials accumulated by these two scholars a comprehensive study of the folk-lore of western India may one day be compiled.

The notes illustrate very fully the common beliefs in unseen presences causing mischief of various kinds. They illustrate the common methods of protection by propitiation, of spirit and disease scaring, and of avoidance of the effects of the evil eye. A full list will be found (pp. 126-130) of the lucky and unlucky omens besetting the undertaking of various acts, and much information is recorded regarding lucky and unlucky numbers, and spirit scaring names which has not, so far as I am aware, been made public before. Ceremonies for exorcising spirits that have possessed human beings are given in some detail. There will also be found an account of the interpretation commonly put on such natural phenomena as the rainbow, an eclipse, thunder, lightning, meteors, comets, &c.

Many examples are given of the beliefs regarding the means for securing successful pregnancy. The trees and animals worshipped in the country side are described, with the ceremony that is held to be suitable in each case. An unusually interesting belief is that which attributes to a certain lake in Gujarat the power to transform males into females and vice versa (see p. 39). The curing of diseases by the wearing of magic threads and the application of *mantras* or holy verses is also dealt with in some detail. Finally a list is given of the shrines of the country side with the tradition regarding the holy man in whose honour and to whose memory they have been erected. They are for the most part worshipped alike by Hindu and Musalman.

In conclusion, I would refer once more to the fact that no attempt has been made to edit critically the information embodied in these notes. In the scanty leisure available after official demands on my time have been met, it has only been possible to see the materials through the press as they stood, after translation. The task has been greatly lightened by the generous assistance received from R. B. P. B. Joshi who undertook the preparation of the whole of the MSS. of the Konkan series. I am also greatly indebted to Mr. G. M. Kalelkar for many arduous hours of work on the compilation of the Gujarat papers. To both these gentlemen my cordial thanks are due for their co-operation. If the publication of these materials serve to stimulate interest in the subject of Indian folk-lore, they will not have been printed in vain. Such as they are, they will, I trust remain as a small tribute to the memory of an oriental scholar, of no mean merit, of whose services India was deprived in so untimely a manner.

R. E. ENTHOVEN.

QUESTIONS ON FOLKLORE.

By W. CROOKE, Late of the Indian Civil Service.

Author of the Popular Religion and Folklore of Northern India.

I. NATURE POWERS.

1. Give any indications of the connection of the worship of the Deota or minor local deities with the lower races, as, for instance, where the village deity is served by a priest drawn from the lower castes.

2. Give any current beliefs about sun worship. How and at what periodical feasts is the worship conducted and what form of ritual is adopted?

3. Give any customs of moving round temples or sacred objects in the course of the sun in the heavens: cases in which women after childbirth are exposed to the sun: conception believed to be caused by exposure to the rays of the sun: the use of the Swastika as an emblem.

4. Give any legends or customs connected with moon worship: the spots on the surface of the moon: the moon as a healer of disease: the custom of drinking the moon's rays: any ceremonies at new or full moon.

5. Give any legends and rites connected with eclipses.

6. Similarly for star worship; superstitions connected with the rainbow; the milky way.

7. Rites connected with worship of the earth mother: sacred things not to fall on earth: occasions when people sleep on the earth.

8. Superstitions connected with thunder and lightning.

9. Popular belief regarding earthquakes.

10. Collect instances of and ritual for worship of sacred rivers; springs; waterfalls; water spirits and goblins: prejudice against saving drowning people: ceremonies at digging and dedication of wells; well water as a cure for disease: instances of sacred lakes: palaces under the water.

11. Instances of sacred mountains and legends connected with them: dread of climbing mountains.

12. Name any deities supposed to control the weather, and describe the modes of causing or averting rain, of checking storms and hail.

13. Give instances of any rites in which women alone take part or from which they are excluded: any rites in which the worshipper must be nude.

14. Are there any sacred stones which are believed to influence the rain?

15. Note any superstitions in connection with aerolites and meteors.

II. THE HEROIC GODLINGS.

16. Describe the ritual and any legends or superstitions connected with the worship of Hanumān, Bhīmsen, Bhishma.

17. Name and describe the local deities most generally worshipped in your neighbourhood. What legends are connected with them; who are their priests; what offerings and on what occasions are offerings made to them?

18. How is the local deity of a new settlement selected and installed?

19. What local deity is considered responsible for crops and cattle? When and how is he worshipped?

20. Describe the worship of Bhairon or Bhairava, Ganesa, the Matris or Mothers, the deities of the jungle, those who assist parturition.

III. DISEASE DEITIES.

21. Describe the worship of any deities who are believed to have the power of averting or causing disease, such as cholera, small pox, fever, etc.

22. Is epidemic disease attributed to witchcraft, and, if so, what precautions are taken? Give particulars of observances in connection with cattle disease.

23. What methods are in vogue for the exorcism of disease? Give examples of any rural charms used for this purpose.

24. Is dancing used in exorcism? If so, give instances of religious dances.

25. What are the position and functions of the village sorcerer and how is he appointed?

26. Give examples of the offering of rags, coins, etc., at sacred trees, wells, etc.

27. Give any methods of transferring disease to another person.

28. Give instances of the use of scapegoats.

IV. THE WORSHIP OF ANCESTORS AND SAINTS.

29. Give instances of worship of ancestors: the belief that spirits are mortal and that the spirits of the dead are re-born in children.

30. Give instances of miracle-working tombs, and of saints who have been deified in modern times.

31. Give instances of Muhammadan saints whose worship has been adopted by Hindus.

32. Give the rural methods in vogue for the cure of barrenness.

V. THE WORSHIP OF THE MALEVOLENT DEAD.

33. What are the current beliefs as to the cause of dreams and the omens derived from them?

34. Is it considered possible for the soul to leave the body temporarily? If so, give instances.

35. What is the popular conception of the character and functions of the Bhut or disembodied soul?

36. What beliefs are current as to the state of the soul after death; the path to the other world: the condition of souls in the other world: the possibility of the soul returning thence?

37. What belief is current as to the souls of those dying by a sudden or violent death?

38. What are believed to be the appearance and habits of the Bhut?

39. In what way do spirits enter or leave the body?

40. What is the current theory regarding sneezing and yawning?

41. What is known of the Rakshasa or malevolent demon?

42. Name and describe any other varieties of malignant spirits.

43. Do any evil spirits go about headless?

44. What special evil spirits infest burial or cremation grounds, and what are the other haunts of such spirits?

45. Does any special class of evil spirit infest mountains, jungles, trees?

46. What fiends attack the young mother and her child?

47. What belief prevails as to the spirits of those killed by tigers or other wild beasts?

48. What form does the ghost of a woman dying at childbirth or during her menses assume?

49. Is there any belief that the father has to take special precautions at the birth of his child?

50. Is there any belief in a connection of the bat or owl with spirits of the dead?

51. Describe the evil spirits which haunt ruins and guard buried treasure: or occupy caves and mines.

VI. THE EVIL EYE AND THE SCARING OF GHOSTS.

52. Describe the belief in the Evil eye and the modes of evading it.

53. Does the belief in giving opprobrious names to children prevail, and if so, how is it accounted for?

54. Can you give instances of change of sex?

55. Illustrate the value of the following protection against evil spirits—iron and other metals: coral and shells : precious stones: blood: incense: spittle: salt: water: grain: colours: grasses: tattooing: leather: garlic: glass.

56. Describe the amulets generally used.

57. Illustrate the sacred circle as a protective.

58. Illustrate the belief in omens, numbers, lucky and unlucky days.

59. What means are adopted to help the spirit to the other world, to prevent it from returning and to secure its good-will to the survivors?

60. Illustrate the prevalence of earth burial and cremation: the customs of shaving the hair: placing food or other articles for the use of the dead.

61. Does the spirit reappear in the form of insects and animals?

62. Are the earthen vessels of the household broken at death : if so, why? Describe rites connected with mourning.

63. What spirits are benevolent?

64. Illustrate the belief in tree spirits.

65. What spirits are special protectors of crops and cattle?

66. What spirits are invoked to frighten children?

VII. TREE AND SERPENT WORSHIP.

67. Name any sacred groves in your neighbourhood and describe any prejudice against cutting trees.

68. Are any trees specially connected with any local deity or saint?

69. Name any trees which receive particular respect or devotion and note any legends or superstitions in connection with them.

70. Does the custom of marrying a bride or bridegroom to a tree prevail? Any instances of marriage to a god: religious prostitution.

71. Give instances of snake worship and shrines of serpent deities: of deified snake heroes.

72. Does the belief prevail that snakes guard treasure? Give details.

73. What snake festivals are observed? Describe the ritual.

74. What is the village treatment of snake-bite?

75. The snake has a jewel in his head: he is connected with the rainbow: he has a palace under the water: he weds mortal girls: he protects the household—illustrate these beliefs.

VIII. TOTEMISM AND FETISHISM.

76. Can you quote any beliefs which are suggestive of Totemism? Are any clans named after or do they claim descent from animals or plants? What animals are treated with special respect by particular tribes? Do special castes refuse to eat any special food?

77. Are any local deities specially associated with animal worship?

78. Illustrate the worship of stocks and stones. Is any respect shown to perforated stones?

79. Are there any modern survivals of human sacrifice?

80. Are fetish stones supposed to cure disease or to be the abode of spirits?

81. Are any fetishes peculiar to particular families or castes?

82. Is special respect shown to the corn sieve, the winnowing basket, the broom, the rice pounder, the plough?

83. Give instances of fire worship. Is the sacred fire maintained in any shrine? Is fire made by friction for special rites.

IX. ANIMAL WORSHIP.

84. Illustrate from local examples the worship or respect paid to the horse, ass, lion, tiger, dog, goat, cow, buffalo, antelope, elephant, cat, rat and mouse, squirrel, bear, jackal, hare, crow, fowl, dove and pigeon, swan, and other birds, alligators, fish and insects, and give any legend or superstition in connection with them.

X. WITCHCRAFT.

85. How far does the belief in witches and their powers prevail? Do they appear as animals and have they special haunts and seasons?

86. What ordeals are used to test a witch and what means to guard against her witchcraft?

XI. GENERAL.

87. Describe the rural ceremonies in connection with ploughing, sowing the various crops, reaping and harvesting.

88. Rites intended for the protection of cattle: to ensure sunshine, and favourable weather: to scare noxious animals or insects: to protect special crops: illustrate these from local custom.

89. Are there any rites in which secrecy and silence are essential?

90. Describe the observances at the Holi.

91. Give details of any rites performed when boys or girls attain puberty.

TABLE OF CONTENTS.

CHAPTER IV.

The worship of ancestors and saints.

CHAPTER V.

The worship of the malevolent dead.

CHAPTER VI.

The evil eye and the scaring of ghosts.

CHAPTER VII.

Tree and Serpent worship.

CHAPTER VIII.

Totemism and Fetishism.

CHAPTER IX.

Animal worship.

CHAPTER X.

Witchcraft.

CHAPTER XI.

General.

THE FOLKLORE OF GUJARAT

NATURE POWERS

CHAPTER I

BESIDES the higher-grade deities, whose worship is enjoined and treated of in the Shāstras and Purānas, numerous other minor deities, none of whom however find a place in the Scriptures, are worshipped by the lower classes. The principle underlying the whole fabric of the worship of these minor deities, who for the most part are the spirits of dead ancestors or heroes, has more in it of fear for their power of harming than of love for their divine nature. All untoward occurrences in domestic affairs, all bodily ailments and unusual natural phenomena, inexplicable to the simple mind of the villager, are attributed to the malignant action of these nameless and numerous spirits, hovering over and haunting the habitations of men.[1] The latent dread of receiving injuries from these evil spirits results in the worship by the low-class people of a number of *devas* and *mātās*, as they are called. The poor villager, surrounded on all sides by hosts of hovering spirits, ready to take offence, or even to possess him, on the smallest pretext, requires some tangible protector to save him from such malign influences.[1] He sets up and enshrines the spirit that he believes to have been beneficent to him, and so deserving of worship, and makes vows in its honour, often becoming himself the officiating priest. Each such deity has its own particular *thānak* (*sthāna*) or locality. Thus there is hardly a village which has not a particular deity of its own. But in addition to this deity, others in far off villages are generally held in high esteem.[1]

There are a number of ways in which these lower-class deities can be installed. Their images are made either of wood, stone, or metal.[2] No temples or shrines are erected in their honour.[3] An ordinary way of representing them is by drawing a trident, (*trishūl*, a weapon peculiar to god Shiva) in red lead and oil on an upright slab of stone on a public road, on any dead wall, on the confines of a village, or a mountain side, or a hill top, in an underground cellar, or on the bank of a stream.[1] Some people paint tridents in their own houses. The *trishūl*, or trident, may also be made of wood, in which case its three points are plastered with red-lead and oil and covered with a thin coating of tin.[5] Sometimes carved wooden images in human shape, daubed over with red-lead and oil, are placed in a small wooden chariot or in a recess about a foot square. In some shrines two brooms or whisks of peacock's feathers are placed on either side of the image.[6] A slight difficulty overcome or a disease remedied by a vow in honour of any of these deities offers the occasion for an installation, and in all future emergencies of the same kind similar vows are observed. A *mātā* installed to protect a fortress or a street is called a Gadheri Mātā, and the worshippers of a fortress, or street, mother are known as Pothias.[7] At the time of installation flags are hoisted near the dedicated places. A troop of dancers with jingling anklets recite holy verses, while the *bhuva*, exorcist-priest, performs the ceremonies. Generally installations are frequent during the

[1] Khan Bahadur Fazlullah and Mr. K. D. Desai.
[2] Mr. D. K. Pandya, Schoolmaster, Dhhank.
[3] The Deputy Educational Inspector, Gohelwad.
[4] Mr. N. D. Vora, Schoolmaster, Rajpara.
[5] The Deputy Educational Inspector, Gohelwad.
[6] Mr. M. D. Vyas, Shastri, Bhayavadur.
[7] Mr. K. P. Joshi, Schoolmaster, Limbdi.

Navarātra* holidays when, if no human-shaped image is set up, a *trishūl* at least is drawn in red-lead and oil.[1] Some of these evil deities require, at the time of their installation, the *balidān* (sacrifice or oblation) of a goat or a he-buffalo. Also, when a spirit is to be exorcised, the symbol of the familiar spirit of the exorcist is set up and invoked by him.[1] After the installation, no systematic form of worship is followed in connection with them.[2] Regular forms are prescribed for the *real* gods of the Purānas. But upon these the low-caste people are not authorised to attend.

Still, in practice there are two forms of worship : ordinary or *sāmānya-pūjā* and special or *vishesha-pūjā*.[3] Ordinary worship is performed by bathing the deity—which can be done by sprinkling a few drops of water over it—burning a ghi, or an oil, lamp before it, and by offering a cocoanut and a pice or a half-anna piece. The last is taken away by the *bhuva*, or priest, who returns generally half or three-quarters of the cocoanut as a *prasād* of the god.

There are no particular days prescribed for such worship, but Sundays and Tuesdays would seem to be the most favoured.[4] On such days, offerings are made for the fulfilment of a vow recorded in order to avoid a *bādhā*, or impending evil. In the observance of this vow the devotee abstains from certain things, such as ghi, butter, milk, rice, juvar, betelnut till the period of the vow expires. When a vow is thus discharged, the devotee offers flowers, garlands, incense, food or drink according to the terms of his vow.[4] The *dhūpa*, *i.e.*, burning incense of *gūgal* (balsamodendron) is one of the commonest methods of worship.

The days for special worship are the Navarātra holidays, the second day of the bright half of Āshādh, the ninth month of the Hindu Calendar,[5] Divāsā[6] or the fifteenth day of the dark half of Āshādh, and Kālī-chaudas[7] or the fourteenth day of the dark half of Āshvin, the last month ; besides other extraordinary occasions when a spirit has to be exorcised out of a sick person.

The Navarātra days are said to be the most auspicious days for devī-worship. People believing in the power of the mātās observe fast on these days. Most of them at least fast on the eighth day of the Navarātra known as Mātā-ashtamī, taking only a light meal which consists of roots, as a rule, especially the suran (Amorphophallus campanulatus), and of dates and milk.[8] On the Navarātra days red-lead and oil are applied to the images of the devis, and a number of oblations, such as loaves, cooked rice, *lāpsi*†, *vadān*‡ and *bāklā*§ are offered.[9] The utmost ceremonial cleanliness is observed in the preparation of these viands. The corn is sifted, cleaned, ground or pounded, cooked, treated with frankincense, offered to the gods and lastly partaken of before sunset, and all these operations must be performed on the same day; for the offerings must not see lamp-light.[10] Girls are not allowed to partake of these offerings. All ceremonies should be conducted with much earnestness and reverence ; otherwise the offerings will fail to prove acceptable to the mātās or devis.[10]

On Mātā-ashtamī and Kālī-chaudas devotees sometimes offer rams, goats or buffaloes as victims to the devis or devas in addition to the usual offerings of *lāpsi*, *vadān* and *bāklā*.[10] The night of Kālī-chaudas is believed to be so favourable for the efficacious

*The first nine days of Āshvin, the last month of the Gujarat Hindu Calendar, known otherwise as Mātānā dāhadā-mātā's days. The influence of the mātās is very strong in these days.

1 Mr. K. D. Desai.

2 Mr. M. D. Vayas, Shastri, Bhayavadur.

3 The Deputy Educational Inspector, Gohelwad.

4 Mr. K. D. Desai.

5 Mr. N. D. Vora, Schoolmaster, Rajpara.

6 Mr. B. K. Dave, Schoolmaster, Kotda-Sangani.

7 Mr. N. D. Vora, Schoolmaster, Rajpara.

8 Mr. K. D. Desai.

† *Lapsi* is coarse wheat-flour fried in ghi and sweetened with molasses or sugar.

‡ Vadān-bean flour—generally of gram or peas—is allowed to remain in water with spices until the paste acquires a sufficient degree of consistence, when it is rolled into small biscuit-sized balls and fried in oil.

§ *Bāklā* are small round flat cakes of dry boiled beans.

9 Mr. N. D. Vora, Schoolmaster, Rajpara.

10 Mr. N. M. Dave, Schoolmaster, Sānkā.

recitation (*sādhana*) of certain *mantras*, mysterious incantations possessing sway over spirits, that *bhuvas* (exorcists) leave the village and sit up performing certain rites in cemeteries, on burning-ghats, and in other equally suitable places where spirits are supposed to congregate.[1]

On Divāsā, the last day of Āshādh, the ninth month, low-caste people bathe their gods with water and milk, besmear them with red-lead and oil, and make offerings of cocoanuts, *lāpsi*, *bāklā* of *adād* (Phanseolus radiatus) or *kansār**. Particular offerings are believed to be favoured by particular deities : for instance, *khichdo* (rice and pulse boiled together) and oil, or *tavo* (flat unleavened loaves) are favoured by the goddess Meldi, boiled rice by Shikotar and *lāpsi* by the goddess Gātrād.[2]

On these holidays, as well as on the second day of the bright half of Āshādh the devotees hoist flags in honour of the spirits, and play on certain musical instruments producing discordant sounds. Meanwhile *bhuvas*, believed to be interpreters of the wills of evil spirits, undergo self-torture, with the firm conviction that the spirits have entered their persons. Sometimes they lash themselves with iron chains or cotton braided scourges.[3] At times a *bhuva* places a pan-full of sweet oil over a fire till it boils. He then fries cakes in it, and takes them out with his unprotected hands, sprinkling the boiling oil over his hair. He further dips thick cotton wicks into the oil, lights them and puts them into his mouth and throws red-hot bullets into his mouth, seemingly without any injury.[4] This process secures the confidence of the *sevakas* or followers, and is very often used by *bhuvas* when exorcising spirits from persons whose confidence the *bhuvas* wish to gain. A bowl-full of water is then passed round the head of the ailing person (or animal) to be charmed, and the contents are swallowed by the exorcist to show that he has swallowed in the water all the ills the flesh of the patient is heir to.[4]

In the cure of certain diseases by exorcising the process known as *utār* is sometimes gone through. An *utār* is a sacrificial offering of the nature of a scapegoat, and consists of a black earthen vessel, open and broad at the top, and containing *lāpsi*, *vadān*, *bāklā*, a yard of *atlas* (dark-red silk fabric), one rupee and four annas in cash, pieces of charcoal, red-lead, *sorro* (or surmo-lead ore used as eye-powder), an iron-nail and three cocoanuts.[4] Very often a trident is drawn in red-lead and oil on the outer sides of the black earthen vessel.[5] The *bhuva* carries the *utār* in his hands with a drawn sword in a procession, to the noise of the jingling of the anklets of his companions, the beating of drums and the rattling of cymbals. After placing the *utār* in the cemetery the procession returns with tumultuous shouts of joy and much jingling of anklets.[6]

Sometimes *bhuvas* are summoned for two or three nights preceding the day of the *utār* ceremony, and a ceremony known as *Dānklān-beswān* or the installation of the *dānklā*[7] is performed. (A *dānklā*† is a special spirit instrument in the shape of a small kettle-drum producing, when beaten by a stick, a most discordant, and, by long association, a melancholy, gruesome and ghastly sound—K. B. Fazlullah).

Many sects have special deities of their own, attended upon by a *bhuva* of the same order.[8] The *bhuva* holds a high position in the society of his caste-fellows. He believes himself to be possessed by the devi or mātā whose attendant he is, and declares,

[1] Mr. N. M. Dave, Schoolmaster, Sanka.

* Kansār is coarse wheat-flour cooked in three times as much water, sweetened with molasses or sugar, and taken with ghi.—B. L. Dave, Schoolmaster, Kotda-Sangani.

[2] The Deputy Educational Inspector, Gohelwad.

[3] Mr. G. K. Dave, Schoolmaster, Sultanpore.

[4] Mr. N. D. Vora, Schoolmaster, Rajpara.

[5] Mr. B. K. Dave, Schoolmaster, Kotda-Sangani.

[6] Mr. N. D. Vora, Schoolmaster, Rajpara.

[7] Mr. Girijashankar Karunashankar, Schoolmaster, Songadh.

[8] Mr. Jagannath Hirji, Schoolmaster, Chok.

† A *dānklā* is otherwise known by the name of *dāg-dudioon*.

while possessed by her, the will of the mātā, replying for her to such questions as may be put to him.[1] The devis are supposed to appear in specially favoured *bhuvas* and to endow them with prophetic powers.[2]

The following is a list of some of the inferior local deities of Gujarat and Kathiawar :—

(1) Suro-pūro.—This is generally the spirit of some brave ancestor who died a heroic death, and is worshipped by his descendants as a family-god at his birthplace as well as at the scene of his death, where a pillar (pālio) is erected to his memory.[3]

(2) Vachhro, otherwise known by the name of Dādā (sire).—This is said to have been a Rajput, killed in rescuing the cow-herds of some Chārans. who invoked his aid, from a party of free-booters.[4] He is considered to be the family-god of the Ahirs of Solanki descent, and is the sole village-deity in Okha and Baradi Districts.[5] Other places dedicated to this god are Padānā, Aniālā, Taluka Mengani,[6] Khajurdi, Khirasarā and Anida.[7] He is represented by a stone horse, and Chārans perform priestly duties in front of him.[8] Submission to, and vows in honour of, this god, are believed to cure rabid-dog-bites.[9]

(3) Sarmālio commands worship in Gondal, Khokhāri and many other places. Newly-married couples of many castes loosen the knots tied in their marriage-scarves as a mark of respect for him.* Persons bitten by a snake wear round their necks a pieee of thread dedicated to this god.[9]

(4) Shītalā is a goddess known for the cure of small-pox.—Persons attacked by this disease observe vows in her honour. Kālāvad and Syādlā are places dedicated to her.[9]

(5) Ganāgor.—Virgins who are anxious to secure suitable husbands and comfortable establishments worship this goddess and observe vows in her honour.[9]

(6) Todāliā—She has neither an idol nor a temple set up in her honour, but is represented by a heap of stones lying on the village boundary—Pādal or Jāmpā. All marriage processions, before entering the village (Sānkā) or passing by the heap, pay homage to this deity and offer a cocoanut, failure to do which is believed to arouse her wrath. She does not command daily adoration, but on occasions the attendant, who is a Chumvāliā Koli, and who appropriates all the presents to this deity, burns frankincense of *gugal* (balsamodendron) and lights a lamp before her.[10]

(7) Buttāya also is represented by a heap of stones on a hilloek in the vicinity of Sānkā. Her worshipper is a Talabdia Koli. A long season of drought leads to her propitiation by feasting Brāhmans, for which purpose four pounds of corn are taken in her name from each threshing floor in the village.[10]

(8) Surdhan.—This seems to have been some brave Kshatriya warrior who died on a battlefield. A temple is erected to his memory, containing an image of Shiva. The attending priest is an Atit.[10]

(9) Ghogho.—This is a cobra-god worshipped in the village of Bikhijada having a Bajana (tumbler) for his attending priest.[10]

(10) Pir.—This is a Musalman saint, in whose honour no tomb is erected, the special site alone being worshipped by a devotee.[10]

(11) Rancki is represented by a heap of stones, and is attended upon by *chamārs* (tanners). Her favourite resort is near the Dhedvādā (*i.e.*, a quarter inhabited by sweepers). A childless Girasia is said to

[1] Mr. Jethabhai Mangaldas, Schoolmaster, Gondal.

[2] Mr. Nandlal Kalidas, Schoolmaster, Chhatrāsā.

[3] Mr. D. K. Pandya, Schoolmaster, Dhbank.

[4] Mr. H. R. Pandya, Schoolmaster, Khirasarā.

[5] Mr. L. G. Travadi, Schoolmaster, Upleta.

[6] Mr. D. K. Pandya, Schoolmaster, Dhbank.

[7] Mr. H. R. Pandya, Schoolmaster, Khirasarā.

[8] Mr. L. G. Travadi, Schoolmaster, Upleta.

[9] Mr. D. K. Pandya, Schoolmaster, Dhbank.

* Two pieces of cloth, a shouldercloth and a scarf are cast over the bridegroom and the bride, and they are tied together by a knot. It is the unloosening of this tie which is here referred to.—Mr. K. D. Desai.

[10] Mr. N. M. Dave, Schoolmaster, Sānkā.

have observed a vow in her honour for a son, and a son being born to him, he dedicated certain lands to her ; but they are no longer in the possession of the attendants.[1]

(12) Hanuman.—On a mound of earth there is an old worn-out image of this god. People sometimes light a lamp there, offer cocoanuts and plaster the image with red-lead and oil. A *sādhu* of the Māragi sect, a Koli by birth, acts as *pujari*.[1]

(13) Shaktā (or shakti).—This is a Girasia goddess attended upon by a Chumvāliā Koli. On the Navarātra days, as well as on the following day, Girasias worship this goddess, and if necessary observe vows in her name.[1]

(14) Harsidh.—Gāndhavi in Bardā and Ujjain are the places dedicated to this goddess. There is a tradition connected with her that her image stood in a place of worship facing the sea on Mount Koyalo in Gandhavi. She was believed to sink or swallow all the vessels that sailed by. A Bania named Jagadusā, knowing this, propitiated her by the performance of religious austerities. On being asked what boon he wanted from her, he requested her to descend from her mountain-seat. She agreed on the Bania promising to offer a living victim for every footstep she took in descending. Thus he sacrificed one victim after another until the number of victims he had brought was exhausted. He then first offered his four or five children, then his wife and lastly himself. In reward for his self-devotion the goddess faced towards Miani and no mishaps are believed to take place in the village.[2]

(15) Hinglaj.—This goddess has a place of worship a hundred and fifty miles from Karachi in Sind, to which her devotees and believers make pilgrimage.[2]

In the village of Jāsdān, in Kathiawar, there is an ancient shrine of Kālu-Pīr in whose memory there are two sepulchres covered with costly fabrics, and a large flag floats over the building. Both Hindus and Musalmans believe* in this saint, and offer cocoanuts, sweetmeats and money to his soul. A part of the offering being passed through the smoke of frankincense, burning in a brazier near the saint's grave in the shrine, the rest is returned to the offerer. Every morning and evening a big kettle-drum is beaten in the Pīr's honour.[3]

Other minor deities are Shikotār, believed by sailors to be able to protect them from the dangers of the deep;[4] Charmathvati, the goddess of the Rabarīs ;[5] Macho, the god of the shepherds ;[5] Meldi, in whom Vaghries (bird-catchers) believe ;[6] Pithād, the favourite god of Dheds ;[7] Dhavdi, who is worshipped by a *hajām* (barber) ;[8] Khodiar ;[9] Géla,[9] Dādamo,[9] Kshetrapāl,[9] Chāvad,[10] Mongal,[10] Avad,[10] Pālan,[10] Vir

[1] Mr. N. M. Dave, Schoolmaster, Sānkā.

[2] Mr. D. K. Pandya, Schoolmaster, Dhhank.

* The tendency to fraternise as much in belief as in nationality is a notable feature of Indian life. The saying goes :—Hindu Musalmān ék Rām bijó Rehmān. The Hindu and Musalman are not far apart, one is the follower of Rām, the other of Rehmān (the most compassionate—a Kuranic name of Allah). Again says another proverb : The Hindu and Musalmān are as closely connected as the breast and the skirt of a garment (Hindu né Musalmān moli dāman jo vehevār). The Hindu pays homage to the Pīr, the Muslim repays the compliment by holding some of his Hindu brother's lower class deities, such as Vaital and Kāli and Ambā, in awe. The Hindu worships and breaks cocoanuts before the Moharram *taazias*—the Musalman responds by showing a sneaking sort of a regard for the Holi, whom he believes to have been a daughter of the patriarch Abraham. This reciprocal good fellowship in time of political agitation, like those of the Indian Mutiny, results in the " chapati ", or unleavened bread loaf, being considered a symbol to be honoured both by Muslim and Hindu ; and in more recent times, as during the plague troubles in Allahabad and Cawnpore, shows itself in the Muslim garlanding the Hindu on a holiday, and the Hindus setting up sherbat-stalls for Musalmans on an Id day.—Khan Bahadur Fazlullah.

[3] Mr. J. N. Patel, Schoolmaster, Jasdan.

[4] Mr. Jaggannath Hirji, Schoolmaster, Chok.

[5] Mr. Nandlal Kalidas, Schoolmaster, Chhatrāsā.

[6] Mr. O. A. Mehta, Schoolmaster, Lakhapadar.

[7] Mr. N. J. Bhatt, Moti Marad.

[8] Mr. J. D. Khandhar, Sayala.

[9] Mr. N. M. Dave, Sanka.

[10] Mr. N. D. Vora, Rajpara.

Vaital,[1] Jālio,[1] Gadio,[1] Paino,[1] Parolio,[1] Sevalio,[1] Andhario,[1] Fulio[1] Bheravo,[1] Ragantio,[1] Chod,[2] Gātrad,[2] Mammai and Verai.[3] There are frequent additions to the number, as any new disease or unusual and untoward incident may bring a new spirit into existence. The installation of such deities is not a costly concern,[4] and thus there is no serious check on their recognition.

The sun, the beneficent night-dispelling, light-bestowing great luminary, is believed to be the visible manifestation of the Almighty God,[5] and inspires the human mind with a feeling of grateful reverence which finds expression in titles like *Savitā*, Life-Producer, the nourisher and generator of all life and activity[6].

He is the chief rain-sender[7]; there is a couplet used in Gujarat illustrative of this belief. It runs:—"Oblations are cast into the Fire : the smoke carries the prayers to the sun; the Divine Luminary, propitiated, responds in sending down gentle showers." "The sacred smoke, rising from the sacrificial offerings, ascends through the ethereal regions to the Sun. He transforms it into the rain-giving clouds, the rains produce food, and food produces the powers of generation and multiplication and plenty. Thus, the sun, as the propagator of animal life, is believed to be the highest deity.[7]"

It is pretty generally believed that vows in honour of the sun are highly efficacious in curing eye-diseases and strengthening the eyesight. Mr. Damodar Karsonji Pandya quotes from the Bhagvadgītā the saying of Krishna:

प्रभास्मि शशिसूर्ययोः

"I am the very light of the sun and the moon.*" Being the embodiment or the fountain of light, the sun imparts his lustre either to the bodies or to the eyes of his devotees. It is said that a Rajput woman of Gomātā in Gondal and a Brahman of Rajkot were cured of white leprosy by vows in honour of the sun.[8] Similar vows are made to this day for the cure of the same disease. Persons in Kathiawar suffering from ophthalmic disorders, venereal affections, leucoderma and white leprosy are known to observe vows in honour of the sun.[9]

The Parmār Rajputs believe in the efficacy of vows in honour of the sun deity of Māndavrāj, in curing hydrophobia.[10]

Women believe that a vow or a *vrat* made to the sun is the sure means of attaining their desires. Chiefly their vows are made with the object of securing a son. On the fulfilment of this desire, in gratitude to the Great Luminary, the child is often called after him, and given such a name as Suraj-Rām, Bhānu-Shankar, Ravi-Shankar, Adit-Rām.[11]

Many cradles are received as presents at the temple of Māndavrāj, indicating that the barren women who had made vows to the deity have been satisfied in their desire for a son, the vows being fulfilled by the present of such toy-cradles to the sun. In the case of rich donors, these cradles are made of precious metal.[12]

At Mandvara, in the Muli District of Kathiawar, the Parmār Rajputs, as well as the Kāthis, bow to the image of the sun, on their marriage-day, in company with their newly-married brides.[12] After the birth of

[1] Mr. N. D. Vora, Rajpara. [2] The Deputy Educational Inspector, Gohelwad.
[3] Mr. G. K. Dave, Sultanpore. [4] Mr. K. D. Desai. [5] Mr. D. K. Pandya, Dhhank.
[6] Mr. K. D. Desai. [7] Mr. M. D. Vyas, Schoolmaster, Bhayavadur.
* Cf. Allaho núr-us-samáwátiwal ard, mathalo nurihi-ka miskatin bihá nusbáh—Koran.
Allah ! He is the light of the Heavens and the Earth. The likeness of His Light being similar to a lamp in a glass.—Fazlullah Latfullah.
[8] Mr. Jethabai Mangaldas, Schoolmaster, Gondal ; and Damodar Karsonji, Schoolmaster, Dhhank.
[9] Mr. B. K. Dave, Schoolmaster, Kotda-Sangani. [10] Mr. N. M. Dave, Sanka.
[11] Mr. N. D. Vora, Rajpara. [12] Mr. N. M. Dave, Sanka.

a son to a Rajputani, the hair on the boy's head is shaved for the first time in the presence of the Māndavrāj deity,* and a suit of rich clothes is presented to the image by the maternal uncle of the child.[1]

The sun is सर्वसाक्षी the observer of all things and nothing can escape his notice.[2] His eye is believed to possess the lustre of the three Vedic lores, *viz.*, Rigveda, Yajurveda and Sāmaveda, and is therefore known by the name of वेदत्रयी. The attestation of a document in his name as Sūrya-Nārāyana-Sākshi is believed to be ample security for the sincerity and good faith of the parties.[3] Oaths in the name of the sun are considered so binding that persons swearing in his name are held to be pledged to the strictest truth.[4]

Virgin girls observe a *vrat*, or vow, called the '*tili-vrat*' in the sun's honour, for attaining अखंड सौभाग्य—eternal exemption from widowhood. In making this *vrat*, or vow, the votary, having bathed and worshipped the sun, sprinkles wet red-lac drops before him.[5]

According to Forbes's Rāsmālā, the sun revealed to the Kāthis the plan of regaining their lost kingdom, and thus commanded their devout worship and reverence. The temple named Suraj-deval, near Thān, was set up by the Kāthis in recognition of this favour. In it both the visible resplendent disc of the sun and his image are adored.[6]

People whose horoscopes declare them to have been born under the *Sūrya-dashā*, or solar influence, have from time to time to observe vows prescribed by Hindu astrology.[7]

Cultivators are said to observe vows in honour of the sun for the safety of their cattle.[8]

The following are some of the standard books on sun-worship:—

(1) Aditya-hridaya—literally, the Heart of the Sun. It treats of the glory of the sun and the mode of worshipping him.

(2) Brihadāranyakopanishad and Mandula-Brahmans—portions of Yajur-veda recited by Vedic Brahmans with a view to tender symbolic as well as mental prayers to the sun.

(3) Bibhrād—the fourth chapter of the Rudri.

(4) A passage in Brāhman—a portion of the Vedas, beginning with the words स्वयंभूरसि Thou art self-existent—is entirely devoted to Sun-worship.[9]

(5) Sūrya-Purāna—A treatise relating a number of stories in glorification of the sun.

(6) Sūrya-kavacha.[10]

(7) Sūrya-gīta.

(8) Sūrya-Sahasranama—a list of one thousand names of Sūrya.[11]

It is customary among Hindus to cleanse their teeth every morning with a wooden stick, known as *dātan*† and then to offer salutations to the sun in the form of a verse which means: "Oh God, the *dātans* are torn asunder and the sins disappear. Oh the penetrator of the innermost parts, forgive us our sins. Do good unto the benevolent and unto our neighbours." This prayer is common in the mouths of the vulgar laity.[12]

Better educated people recite a shloka, which runs: "Bow unto Savitri, the sun, the observer of this world and its quarters, the eye of the universe, the inspirer of all energy, the holder of a three-fold person-

* A similar custom is observed in Gujarat. Unfortunate parents, who have lost many children, vow to grow the hair of their little children, if such are preserved to them, observing all the time a votive abstinence from a particular dish or betelnut or the like. When the children are 3 or 5 or 7 years old, the vow is fulfilled by taking them to a sacred place, like the temple of Ranchhodji at Dakor, to have their hair cut for the first time. This vow is known as bābari in Southern Gujarat.—K. D. Desai.

[1] Mr. N. M. Dave, Sanka. [2] Mr. Jethabhai Mangaldas, Gondal. [3] Mr. K. D. Desai.

[4] Mr. N. M. Dave, Sanka. [5] The Deputy Educational Inspector, Gohelwad.

[6] Mr. M. M. Rana, Barton Female Training College, Rajkot.

[7] Mr. G. K. Dave, Schoolmaster, Sultanpore.

[8] Mrs. Raju Ramjee Kanjee, 2nd Assistant, Girls' School, Gondal.

[9] Mr. D. K. Pandya, Dhhank. [10] Mr. M. M. Rana, Rajkot.

[11] Mr. Girijashankar Karmeashankar, Schoolmaster, Songadh.

† The Hindus use the tender sprigs of the Nim or Babul trees for tooth-brushes. After they have done duty as brushes they are cloven into two and the tenderest part is used as a tongue-scraper.—Khan Bahadur Fazlullah. [12] Mr. N. M. Dave, Sanka.

ality (being an embodiment of the forms of the three gods of the Hindu Trinity, Brahma, Vishnu and Maheshvar)—the embodiment of the three Vedas, the giver of happiness and the abode of God.[1]

After his toilet a high-caste Hindu should take a bath and offer morning prayers and *arghyas* to the sun.[2] The *Trikāla-Sandhyā* is enjoined by the Shāstras on every Brahman, *i.e.*, every Brahman should perform the *Sandhyā* thrice during the day: in the morning, at mid-day and in the evening. The *Sandhyā* is the prayer a Brahman offers, sitting in divine meditation, when he offers three *arghyas* to the sun and recites the Gāyatrī mantra 108 times.[3]

The *arghya* is an offering of water in a spoon half filled with barley seeds, sesamum seeds, sandal ointment, rice, and white flowers. In offering the *arghya* the right foot is folded below the left, the spoon is lifted to the forehead and is emptied towards the sun after reciting the Gāyatrī mantra.[4] If water is not available for offering the *arghyas*, sand may serve the purpose. But the sun must not be deprived of his *arghyas*.[5]

The Gāyatrī is the most sacred mantra in honour of the sun, containing, as it does, the highest laudations of him.[5] A Brahman ought to recite this mantra 324 times every day. Otherwise he incurs a sin as great as the slaughter of a cow.[6] Accordingly a Rudrākshmālā, or a rosary of 108 Rudrāksh beads, is used in connecting the number of Gāyatrīs recited.[7] It is exclusively the right of the twice-born to recite the Gāyatrī. None else is authorised to recite or even to hear a word of it. Neither females nor Shūdras ought to catch an echo of even a single syllable of the Gāyatrī mantra[8].

A ceremony, called Sūryopasthān, in which a man has to stand facing the sun with his hands stretched upwards at an angle towards the sun, is performed as a part of the *sandhyā*.[9]

Of the days of the week, Ravivar, or Sunday is the most suitable for Sun worship[10]. Persons wishing to secure wealth, good-health and a happy progeny, especially people suffering from disorders caused by heat and from diseases of the eyes, barren women, and men anxious for victory on the battlefield, weekly observe vows in honour of the sun, and the day on which the vow is to be kept is Sunday.[11] It is left to the devotee to fix the number of Sundays on which he will observe the *vrat*, and he may choose to observe all the Sundays of the year.[12] On such days the devotees undergo ceremonial purifications by means of baths and the putting on of clean garments, occupy a reserved clean seat, light a ghi-lamp and recite the Aditya-hridaya-pātha, which is the prescribed mantra for Sun worship.[13] Then follows the Nyāsa, (न्यास) in the recitation of which the devotee has to make certain gestures (or to perform physical ceremonials). First the tips of all the four fingers are made to touch the thumb as is done in counting. Then the tips of the fingers are made to touch the palm of the other hand. Then one hand is laid over the other. Then the fingers are made to touch the heart, the head, the eyes, and the hair in regular order. The right hand is then put round the head and made to smite the left.[13] An *ashtadala* or eight-cornered figure is drawn in *gulal*,

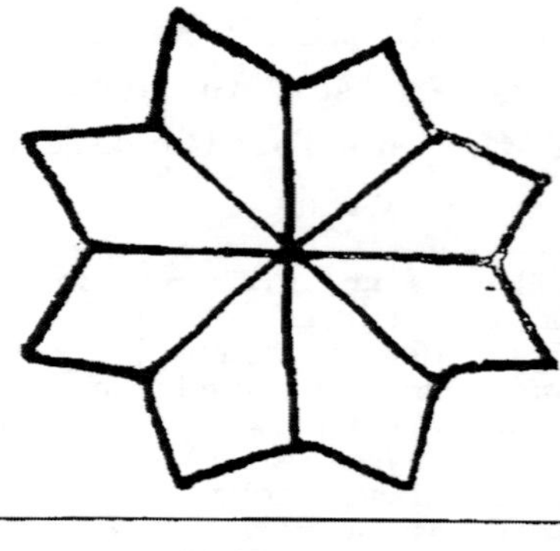

[1] Mr. N. M. Dave, Sanka.
[2] The Deputy Educational Inspector, Gohelwad.
[3] Mr. K. D. Desai.
[4] Mr. Jethalal Anūpram, Schoolmaster, Aman.
[5] The Deputy Educational Inspector, Gohelwad.
[6] Mr. K. D. Desai.
[7] Mr. N. D. Vora, Rajpara.
[8] Mr. K. D. Desai.
[9] Mr. M. D. Vyas, Shastri, Bhayavadur. [10] Mr. K. P. Joshi, Limbdi, and L. D. Mehta, Mota Devalia.
[11] Mr. N. D. Vora, Rajpara, and Mr. B. K. Dave, Kotda-Sangani. [12] Mr. B. K. Dave, Kotda-Sangani.
[13] Mr. Nandlal Kalidas, Schoolmaster, Chhatrāsā

(red powder) and frankincense, red ointment and red flowers are offered to the sun.[1] Durvā grass is also commonly used in the process of Sun-worship.[2]

Sometimes a hexangular figure is drawn

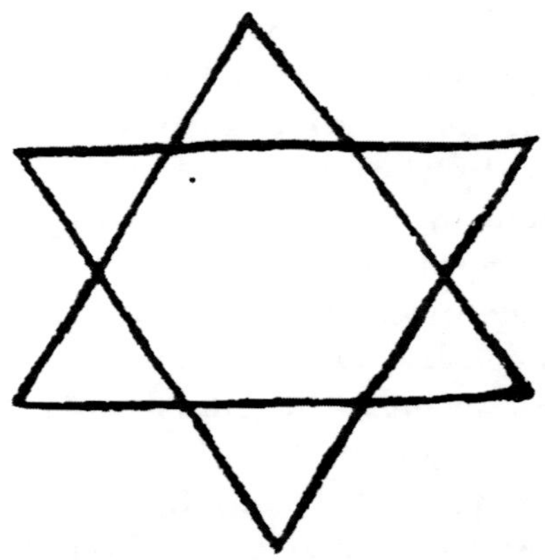

instead of the *ashtadal*, a copper disc is placed over it and the sun is worshipped by Panchopachar or the five-fold ceremonials.[3] Of all ceremonials a namaskār is especially dear to the sun.[4] It is said :—

नमस्कारप्रियो भानुर्जलधाराप्रियः शिवः ।
परोपकारप्रियो विष्णुर्ब्राम्हणो भोजनप्रियः ॥

A namaskār or bow is dear to the sun; a stream of water (pouring water in a small stream over Shiva's idol) is dear to Shiva: benevolence to Vishnu and a good dinner to a Brahman.[4]

In observing vows in the sun's honour on Sundays, the following special foods are prescribed in particular months :[5]—

(1) In Kārtika, the first month, the devotee is to take only three leaves of the Tulsi or the holy basil plant.

(2) In Mārgashīrsha, the devotee may only lick a few pieces of candied sugar.

(3) In Pausha, the devotee may chew three stalks of green darbha grass.

(4) In Māgha, a few seeds of sesamum and sugar mixed together may be swallowed.

(5) In Phālguna, a consecrated draught of curds and sugar may be drunk.

(6) In Chaitra, people should break their fasts with a little ghi and molasses.

(7) In Vaishākha, the only satisfaction allowed to those observing the *vrat* is to lick their own palms three times.

(8) In Jyeshtha, the fast is observed simply on three *anjalis* or palmfuls of pure water.

(9) In Ashādha, three chillies may be eaten.

(10) In Shrāvana, only cow-urine and molasses are tasted.

(11) In Bhādrapada, cow-dung and sugar are partaken of.

(12) In Āshvina, the application of chandan (sandal wood) either in the form of an ointment or of powder.

Only a few very pious and enthusiastic devotees observe all Sundays in the above manner. In average cases, the devotee allows himself rice, ghi, sugar, milk, *i. e.*, white food, the restriction being only as to colour.[5]

People observing vows in honour of the sun take food only once during the day, and that too in *bājas* or dishes made of *khākhara* (or palāsh) leaves. This is considered one of the conditions of worship, there being some mysterious relation between Sūrya and the *khākhara*.[6]

If the Pushya Nakshatra happens to fall on a Sunday, the worship of the sun on that day is believed to be most efficacious in fulfilling the desires of the devotees.[7]

Of the days of the month, the seventh day of both the bright and the dark halves of each month[8] and the Amāvāsyā day, *i. e.*, the last day of a Hindu calendar month,[9] are set apart for Sun-worship. The ceremonies of the worship are the same as those on Sundays. In fact, in almost all the observances in connection with the sun the same ceremonials are to be gone through. Very often a Brahman recites the pātha direct-

[1] Mr. K. P. Joshi, Schoolmaster, Limbdi.
[2] Mr. G. K. Bhatt, Songadh.
[3] Mr. B. K. Dave, Schoolmaster, Kotda-Sangani.
[4] Mr. Girijashankar Karunashankar, Schoolmaster, Songadh.
[5] Mr. Nandlal Kalidas, Schoolmaster, Chhatrasa.
[6] The Deputy Educational Inspector, Gohelwad.
[7] Mr. D. K. Shah, Charadavah.
[8] Mr. K. P. Joshi, Limbdi.
[9] Mr. N. D. Vora, Rajpara.

ing his hosts or hostesses to perform certain ceremonial gestures. On the last of the number of days which the devotee has decided to observe, the *vrat* is celebrated and Brahmans are feasted. This celebration of the *vrat* is known as *vratujavavun*.[1]

The special occasions for Sun-worship are the Sankrānti days and the solar eclipses.

In each year there are twelve Sankrānti days on which the sun moves from one sign of the zodiac to another. Sun-worship is performed on all these Sankrāntis, but Makara-Sankrānti, which falls on the 12th or 13th of January, is considered the most important.[2] The Uttarāyana-parvan falls on this day, *i. e.*, the sun now crosses to his northern course from his southern, and the time of that Parvan is considered so holy that a person dying then directly attains salvation.[3] On this day, many Hindus go on a pilgrimage to holy places, offer prayers and sacrifices to the sun, and give alms to Brahmans in the shape of sesamum seeds, gold, garments and cows.[4] Much secret, as well as open, charity is dispensed,[5] grass and cotton-seeds are given to cows, and *lāpsi** and loaves to dogs.[5] Sweet balls of sesamum seeds and molasses are eaten as a *prasād* and given to Brahmans, and dainties such as *lāpsi* are partaken of by Hindu households, in company with a Brahman or two, who are given dakshinā after the meals.[6]

On solar eclipse days, most of the Hindu sects bathe and offer prayers to God. During the eclipse the sun is believed to be combating with the demon Rāhu, prayers being offered for the sun's success. When the sun has freed himself from the grasp of the demon and sheds his full lustre on the earth, the people take ceremonial baths, offer prayers to God with a concentrated mind, and well-to-do people give in alms as much as they can afford of all kinds of grain.[7]

The Chāturmās-vrat, very common in Kathiawar, is a favourite one with Hindus. The devotee, in performing this *vrat*, abstains from food on those days during the monsoons on which, owing to cloudy weather, the sun is not visible. Even if the sun is concealed by the clouds for days together, the devout votary keeps fasting till he sees the deity again.[8]

Barren women, women whose children die, and especially those who lose their male children, women whose husbands suffer from diseases caused by heat, lepers, and persons suffering from ophthalmic ailments observe the vow of the sun in the following manner.[9] The vows are kept on Sundays and Amāvāsyā days, and the number of such days is determined by the devotee in accordance with the behests of a learned Brahman. The woman observes a fast on such days, bathes herself at noon when the sun reaches the zenith, and dresses herself in clean garments. Facing the sun, she dips twelve red karan flowers in red or white sandal ointment and recites the twelve names of Sūrya as she presents one flower after another to the sun with a bow. † On each day of the *vrat*, she takes food only once, in the shape of *lāpsi*, in *bajas* of khākharā or palāsh leaves; white food in the form of rice, or rice cooked in milk is sometimes allowed. She keeps a ghi-lamp burning day and night, offers frankincense, and sleeps at night on a bed made on the floor.[10]

People who are declared by the Brahmans to be under the evil influence (dashā) of Sūrya, observe vows in the sun's honour and go through the prescribed rites on Sundays. Such persons take special kinds of food and engage the services of priests to recite

[1] Mr. K. D. Desai. [2] Mr. G. K. Bhatt, Schoolmaster, Songadh. [3] Mr. N. J. Bhatt, Moti-Murad.
[4] Mr. Ranchhodji Becher Pandya, Shastri, Jelpur, Sanskrit Pāthashālā. [5] Mr. M. M. Rana, Rajkot.
* Wheat flour fried in ghi with molasses. [6] Mr. K. D. Desai. [7] Mr. M. M. Rana, Rajkot.
[8] Mr. K. D. Desai. [9] Mr. N. D. Vora, Schoolmaster, Rajpara.
† The names are: 1 Āditya, 2 Divākar, 3 Bhāskar, 4 Prabhākar, 5 Sahasrānshu, 6 Trilochan, 7 Haritāshva, 8 Vibhāvasu, 9 Divākrit, 10 Divādarshātmaka, 11 Trimūrti, 12 Sūrya.
[10] Mr. N. D. Vora, Rajpara.

holy texts in honour of the sun. If all goes well on Sunday, Brahmans, Sādhus and other pious persons are entertained at a feast. This feast is known as *vrat-ujavavun*. Some persons have the sun's image (an ashtadal) engraved on a copper or a golden plate for daily or weekly worship.[1]

On the twelfth day after the delivery of a child, the sun is worshipped and the *homa* sacrifice is performed.[2]

If at a wedding the sun happens to be in an unfavourable position according to the bridegroom's horoscope, an image of the sun is drawn on gold-leaf and given away in charity. Charity in any other form is also common on such an occasion.[2]

A Nāgar bride performs sun-worship for the seven days preceding her wedding.[3]

In Hindu funeral ceremonies three *arghyas* are offered to the sun, and the following mantra is chanted[4] :—

आदित्यो भास्करो भानु रविः सुर्यो दिवाकरः ।
षण्नाम स्मरेन्नित्यं महापातकनाशनम् ॥

It means—one should ever recite the six names of the Sun, Aditya, Bhāskar, Bhānu, Ravi, Surya, Divākar, which destroy sin.

The sun is also worshipped on the thirteenth day after the death of a person, when *arghyas* are offered, and two earthen pots, containing a handful of raw *khichedi*—rice and pulse—and covered with yellow pieces of cotton are placed outside the house. This ceremony is called *gadāso bharvo*.[4]

Rajahs of the solar race always worship the rising sun. They also keep a golden image of the sun in their palaces, and engage learned Brahmans to recite verses in his honour. On Sundays they take only one meal and that of simple rice (for white food is most acceptable to the sun).[5]

Circumambulations round images and other holy objects are considered meritorious and to cause the destruction of sin.[6] The subject has been dwelt on at length in the Dharmasindhu-grantha, Vratarāja, and Shodashopachāra among the Dharma-Shāstras of the Hindus.[7]

The object round which turns are taken is either the image of a god, such as of Ganpati, Mahādev or Vishnu[8] or the portrait of a *guru*, or his footmarks engraved or impressed upon some substance, or the *agnikunda* (the fire-pit),[9] or the holy cow[10], or some sacred tree or plant, such as the Vad (banyan tree), the Pipal (ficus religiosa),[11] the Shami (prosopis spicegera), the Amba (mango tree), the Asopalava tree (Polyalthea longi folia),[12] or the Tulsi (sweet basil) plant.

It is said to have been a custom of the Brahmans in ancient times to complete their daily rites before sunrise every morning, and then to take turns round temples and holy objects. The practice is much less common now than formerly.[13] Still, visitors to a temple or an idol, usually are careful to go round it a few times at least (generally five or seven). The usual procedure at such a time is to strike gongs or ring bells after the turns, to cast a glance at the *shikhar* or the pinnacle of the temple, and then to return.[14]

Women observing the *chāturmās-vrat*, or the monsoon vow, lasting from the eleventh day of the bright half of Ashādh (the ninth month) to the eleventh day of the bright half of Kārtik (the first month) first worship the object, round which they wish to take turns, with *panchāmrit* (a mixture of milk, curds, sugar, ghi and honey). The number of turns may be either 5, 7, 21 or 108. At each turn they keep entwining a fine cotton thread and place a *pendā** or a *bantāsā*† or a betel-leaf or an almond, a cocoanut, a fig or some

[1] Mr. G. K. Dave, Sultanpur.
[2] Mr. H. M. Bhatt, Schoolmaster, Ganod.
[3] Mr. Girijashankar Karunashankar, Schoolmaster, Songadh.
[4] Mr. H. M. Bhatt, Schoolmaster, Ganod.
[5] Mr. Chhaganlal Motiram, Wala Taluka.
[6] Mr. R. B. Pandya, Jetpur Sanskrit School.
[7] Mrs. Raju Ramjee Kanjee, Girls' School, Ganod.
[8] Mr. D. K. Pandya, Schoolmaster, Dhhank.
[9] Mr. R. B. Pandya, Jetpur Sanskrit School.
[10] Mr. J. D. Khandhar, Sayala.
[11] Mr. D. K. Pandya, Dhhank.
[12] Mr. N. D. Vora, Rajpara.
[13] Mr. D. K. Pandya, Schoolmaster, Dhhank.
[14] Mr. N. D. Vora, Schoolmaster, Rajpara.
* Milk and sugar ball.
†A sugar cake.

other fruit before the image or the object walked round. These offerings are claimed by the priest who superintends the ceremony.[1] When a sacred tree is circumambulated, water is poured out at the foot of the tree at each turn.[2]

During the month of Shrāvan (the tenth month) and during the Purushottama (or the intercalatory) month, men and women observe a number of vows, in respect of which, every morning and evening, they take turns round holy images and objects.[3]

People observing the *chāturmās-vrat* (or monsoon vow), called Tulsi-vivāha (marriage of Tulsi), worship that plant and take turns round it on every eleventh day of both the bright and the dark halves of each of the monsoon months.[3] The *gautrat-vrat* (gau= cow) necessitates perambulations round a cow, and the *Vat-Sāvitri-vrat* round the Vad or banyan tree. The banyan tree is also circumambulated on the Kapilashashthi day (the sixth day of the bright half of Mārgashīrsha, the second month) and on the Amāvāsyā or the last day of Bhādrapada (the eleventh month).[4]

Women who are anxious to prolong the lives of their husbands take turns round the Tulsi plant or the banyan tree. At each turn they wind a fine cotton thread. At the end of the last turn, they throw red lac and rice over the tree and place a betelnut and a pice or a half-anna piece before it.[5]

The *Shāstras* authorise four *pradakshinās* (or perambulations) for Vishnu, three for the goddesses, and a half (or one and a half)[6] for Shiva.[7] But the usual number of *pradakshinās* is either 5, 7, 21 or 108. In taking turns round the image of Vishnu, one must take care to keep one's right side towards the image, while in the case of Shiva, one must not cross the *jalādhari** or the small passage for conducting water poured over the Shiva-linga.[7]

Sometimes in *pradakshinās* the votary repeats the name of the deity round which the turns are taken while the priest recites the names of the gods in Shlokas.[8] Sometimes the following verse is repeated.[9]

पापोऽहं पापकर्माऽहं पापात्मा पापसंभवः ।
त्राहि मां पुण्डरीकाक्ष सर्वपापहरो भव ॥
यानि कानि च पापानि जन्मांतरकृतानि च ।
तानि तानि विनश्यन्तु प्रदक्षिणपदेपदे ॥

'I am sinful, the doer of sin, a sinful soul and am born of sin. O lotus-eyed One! protect me and take away all sins from me. Whatever sins I may have committed now as well as in my former births, may every one of them perish at each footstep of my *pradakshinā*.'

The recitation and the turns are supposed to free the soul from the *pherā* of *lakh-choryasi*†. Alms are given many times to the poor after *pradakshinās*.[10]

The reason why *pradakshinās* are taken during the day is that they have to be taken in the presence of the sun, the great everlasting witness of all human actions.[11]

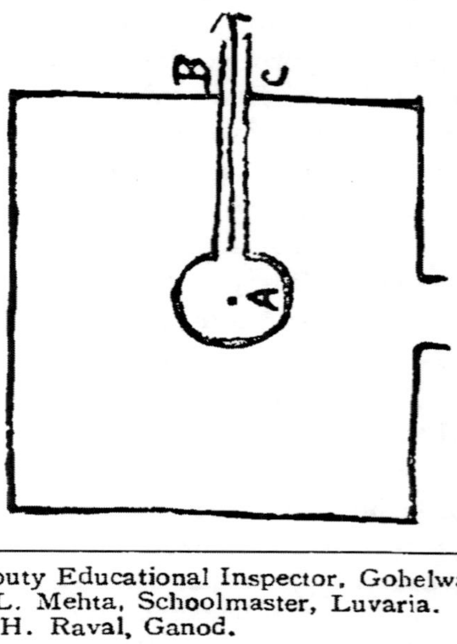

[1] Mr. N. D. Vora, Schoolmaster, Rajpara.
[2] The Deputy Educational Inspector, Gohelwad.
[3] Mr. D. K. Pandya, Dhhank.
[4] Mr. P. L. Mehta, Schoolmaster, Luvaria.
[5] Mr. Jeram Vasaram, Schoolmaster, Jodia.
[6] Mr. M. H. Raval, Ganod.
[7] Mr. H. M. Bhatt, Ganod.

* See figure above. *A* shows Shiva's image: the arrow-head, the jalādhari which a person is not to cross. He is to return from the point *B* in his first round and from the point *C* in his half turn. Thus *B C* remains uncrossed. The circle round *A* shows the Khāl, place wherein god Shiva is installed.—K. D. Desai.

[8] Mr. G. K. Dave, Sultanpore.
[9] The Deputy Educational Inspector, Gohelwad.

† Hindus believe that a soul has to go through a lakh and eighty-four thousand transmigrations before it attains final emancipation. The cycle of 1,84,000 births is called the *phera* of *lakh—choryasi*.—K. D. Desai.

[10] Mr. N. M. Dave, Sānkā.
[11] Mr. D. K. Pandya, Schoolmaster, Dhhank.

As all seeds and vegetation receive their nourishment from solar and lunar rays, the latter are believed in the same way to help embryonic development.[1]

The heat of the sun causes the trees and plants to give forth new sprouts, and therefore he is called 'Savita' or Producer.[2] Solar and lunar rays are also believed to facilitate and expedite delivery.[3] The medical science of the Hindus declares the Amāvāsya (new-moon day) and Pūrnima (full-moon day) days—on both of which days the influence of the sun and the moon is most powerful—to be so critical for child-bearing women as to cause, at times, premature delivery.[4] Hence, before delivery, women are made to take turns in the sunlight and also in moonlight, in order to invigorate the fœtus, thus securing that their delivery may be easy. [The assistance rendered by solar rays in facilitating the delivery is said to impart a hot temperament to the child so born, and that by the lunar rays a cool one.][5] After delivery, a woman should glance at the sun with her hands clasped, and should offer rice and red flowers to him.[6] Sitting in the sun after delivery is considered beneficial to women enfeebled by the effort.[7] It is a cure for the paleness due to exhaustion,[8] and infuses new vigour.[9]

The Bhils believe that the exposure of a new-born child to the sun confers upon the child immunity from injury by cold and heat.[10]

The practice of making recently delivered women sit in the sun does not seem to be widespread, nor does it prevail in Kathiawar. In Kathiawar, on the contrary, women are kept secluded from sunlight in a dark room at the time of child-birth, and are warmed by artificial means.[11] On the other hand, it is customary in many places to bring a woman into the sunlight after a certain period has elapsed since her delivery. The duration of this period varies from four days to a month and a quarter. Sometimes a woman is not allowed to see sunlight after child-birth until she presents the child to the sun with certain ceremonies, either on the fourth or the sixth day from the date of her delivery.[12]

A ceremony called the Shashthi-Karma is performed on the sixth day after the birth of a child, and the Nāmkaran ceremony—the ceremony of giving a name—on the twelfth day. The mother of the child is sometimes not allowed to see the sun before the completion of these ceremonies.[13] Occasionally, on the eleventh day after child-birth, the mother is made to take a bath in the sun.[14]

Exactly a month and a quarter from the date of delivery a woman is taken to a neighbouring stream to offer prayers to the sun and to fetch water thence in an earthen vessel. This ceremony is known as Zarmāzaryan.[15] Seven small betel-nuts are used in the ceremony. They are carried by the mother, and distributed by her to barren women, who believe that, by eating the nuts from her hand, they are likely to conceive.[16]

[1] Mr. D. K. Pandya, Dhhank.
[2] Mr. N. M. Dave, Sānkā.
[3] Mr. N. D. Vora, Rajpara.
[4] Mr. D. K. Pandya, Schoolmaster, Dhhank.
[5] Mr. Jethalal Anupram, Schoolmaster, Ainan.
[6] Mr. R. B. Pandya, Jetpur Sanskrit School.
[7] Mr. D. K. Pandya, Schoolmaster, Dhhank.
[8] Mr. N. J. Bhatt, Moti-Murād.
[9] Mr. N. D. Vora, Rajpara.
[10] Mr. D. K. Shah, Schoolmaster, Charadwa.
[11] Mr. K. P. Joshi, Schoolmaster, Limbdi.
[12] Mr. Nandlal Kalidas, Schoolmaster, Chhatrāsa.
[13] Mr. Chhaganlal Motiram, Schoolmaster, Wala Talu.
[14] The Deputy Educational Inspector, Goholwad.
[15] Mr. B. K. Dave, Kotda-Sangani, and the Schoolmaster, Movaiyam.
[16] Mr. K. D. Desai.

In difficult labour cases, *chakrāvā* water is sometimes given to women. The *chakrāvā* is a figure of seven cross lines drawn on a bell-metal dish, over which the finest white dust has been spread. This figure is shown to the woman in labour : water is then poured into the dish and offered her to drink.[1] The figure is said to be a representation of Chitrangad.[2] It is also believed to be connected with a story in the Mahābhārata.[3] Subhadrā, the sister of god Krishna and the wife of Arjuna, one of the five Pāndavas, conceived a demon, an enemy of Krishna. The demon would not leave the womb of Subhadrā even twelve months after the date of her conception, and began to harass the mother. Krishna, the incarnation of god, knowing of the demon's presence and the cause of his delay, took pity on the afflicted condition of his sister and read chakrāvā, (Chakravyūha). a book consisting of seven chapters and explaining the method of conquering a labyrinthine fort with seven cross-lined forts. Krishna completed six chapters, and promised to teach the demon the seventh, provided he came out. The demon ceased troubling Subhadrā and emerged from the womb. He was called Abhimanyu. Krishna never read the seventh chapter for then Abhimanyu would have been invincible and able to take his life. This ignorance of the seventh chapter cost Abhimanyu his life on the field of Kuru-kshetra in conquering the seven cross-lined labyrinthine forts. As the art of conquering a labyrinthine fort when taught to a demon in the womb facilitated the delivery of Subhadrā, a belief spread that drinking in the figure of the seven cross-lined labyrinthine fort would facilitate the delivery of all women who had difficulties in child-birth.[3]

The figure *Swastika* (literally auspicious), drawn as shown below, is an auspicious

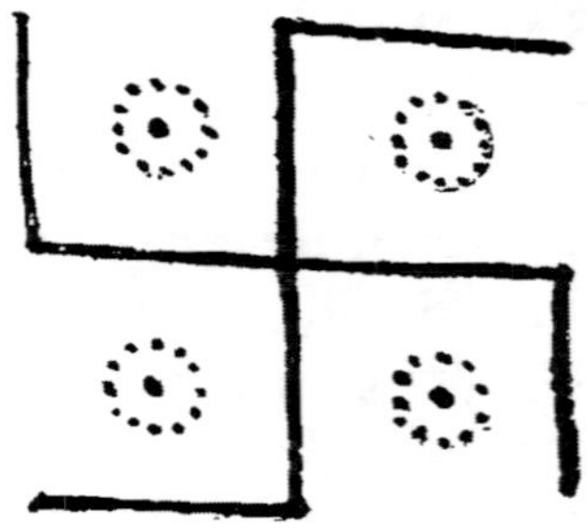

sign, and is believed to be a mark of good luck and a source of blessings. It is one of the sixteen line-marks on the sole of the lotus-like feet of the god Ishwar, the Creator of the Universe.[4] The fame of the good effects of the Swastika figure is said to have been first diffused throughout society by Nārad-Muni, as instructed by the god Brahma.[5]

Various conjectures have been made concerning the origin of this figure. The following explanation is found in a work named Siddhāntsar. The Eternal *Sat* or Essence, that has neither beginning nor end nor any maker, exhibits all the religious principles in a *chakra* or a wheel-form. This round shape has no circumference ; but any point in it is a centre ; which being specified, the explanation of the whole universe in a circle is easy. Thus the figure ⊙ indicates the creation of the universe from *Sat* or Essence. The centre with the circumference is the womb, the place of creation of the universe. The centre then expanding into a line, the diameter thus formed represents the male principle, *linga-rūp*, that is the producer, through the medium of activity in the great womb or *mahā-yoni*. When the line assumes the form of a cross, it explains the creation of the universe by an unprecedented combination of the two distinct natures, animate and inanimate. The circumference being

[1] Mr. R. B. Pandya, Jetpur Sanskrit School.
[2] Mr. D. K. Shah, Charadwa.
[3] Mr. K. D. Desai.
[4] Mr. D. K. Pandya, Schoolmaster, Dhhank.
[5] Mr. N. D. Vora, Schoolmaster, Rajpara.

removed, the remaining cross represents the creation of the world. The Swastika, or Sathia, as it is sometimes called, in its winged form (卍) suggests the possession of creative powers by the opposite natures, animate and inanimate.[1]

Another theory is that an image of the eight-leaved lotus, springing from the navel of Vishnu, one of the Hindu Trinity, was formerly drawn on auspicious occasions as a sign of good luck. The exact imitation of the original being difficult, the latter assumed a variety of forms, one of which is the Swastika.[2]

Some people see an image of the god Ganpati in the figure. That god being the master and protector of all auspicious ceremonies has to be invoked on all such occasions. The incapacity of the devotees to draw a faithful picture of Ganpati gave rise to a number of forms which came to be known by the name of Swastika.[3]

There are more ways than one of drawing the Swastika, as shown below, but the

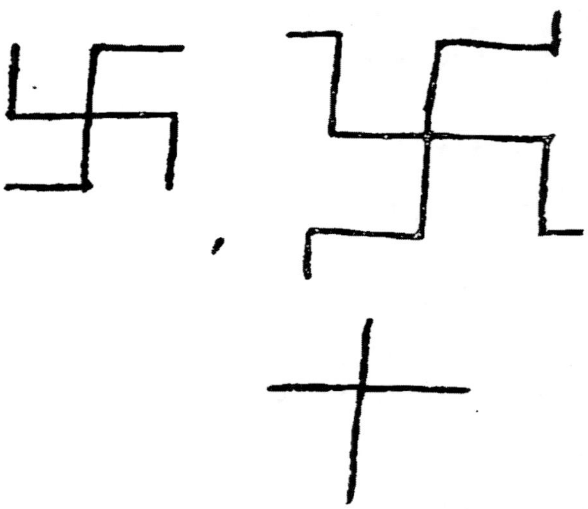

original form was of the shape of a cross. The first consonant of the Gujarati alphabet, *ka*, now drawn thus ક, was also originally drawn in the form of a cross (+). Some persons therefore suppose that the Swastika may be nothing more than the letter ક (*ka*), written in the old style and standing for the word *kalyān* or welfare.[4]

Though the Swastika is widely regarded as the symbol of the sun, some people ascribe the figure to different deities, *viz.*, to Agni,[5] to Ganpati,[6] to Laxmi,[7] to Shiva,[8] besides the sun. It is also said to represent Swasti, the daughter of Brahma, who received the boon from her father of being worshipped on all auspicious occasions.[9] Most persons, however, regard the Swastika as the symbol of the sun. It is said that particular figures are prescribed as suitable for the installation of particular deities: a triangle for one, a square for another, a pentagon for a third, and the Swastika for the sun.[10] The Swastika is worshipped in the Ratnagiri district, and regarded as the symbol as well as the seat of the Sun-god.[11] The people of the Thana district believe the Swastika to be the central point of the helmet of the sun; and a vow, called the *Swastika-vrat*, is observed by women in its honour. The woman draws a figure of the Swastika and worships it daily during the Chaturmās (the four months of the rainy season), at the expiration of which she presents a Brahman with a golden or silver plate with the Swastika drawn upon it.[12]

A number of other ideas are prevalent about the significance of the Swastika. Some persons believe that it indicates the four directions;[13] some think that it represents the four *mārgas*—courses or objects of human desires—*viz.*, (1) Dharma, religion; (2) Artha, wealth; (3) Kām, love; (4) Moksha, salvation.[14] Some again take it to be an image of the ladder

[1] Mr. N. J. Bhatt, Schoolmaster, Moti-Murād.

[2] Mr. K. P. Joshi, Schoolmaster, Limbdi.

[3] Mr. H. R. Pandya, Schoolmaster, Khirasarā.

[4] Mr. Girijashankar Karunashankar, Schoolmaster, Songadh.

[5] Mr. D. K. Pandya, Schoolmaster, Dhhank.

[6] Mr. H. R. Pandya, Khirasarā.

[7] Mr. D. K. Shah, Charadwa.

[8] The Schoolmaster, Chank, Kolaba.

[9] Mr. D. K. Shah, Charadwa.

[10] Mr. N. M. Dave, Sānkā.

[11] The Schoolmaster, Pendhur, Ratnagiri.

[12] The Schoolmaster, Anjār.

[13] Mr. Jethabhai Mangaldas, Schoolmaster, Gondal.

[14] Mr. Girijashankar Karunashankar, Schoolmaster, Songadh.

leading to the heavens.[1] Others suppose it to be a representation of the terrestrial globe, and the four piles of corn placed in the figure, as shown below (p. 16) represent the four mountains, Udayāchala, Astāchal, Meru and Mandārāchala.[2] The Swastika is also believed to be the foundation-stone of the universe.[3]

The Swastika is much in favour with the gods as a seat or couch, and as soon as it is drawn it is immediately occupied by some deity.[4] It is customary therefore to draw the Swastika on most auspicious and festive occasions, such as marriage and thread ceremonies, the first pregnancy ceremonies and the Divali holidays.[5] In the Konkan the Swastika is always drawn on the *Antarpāt*, or the piece of cloth which is held between the bride and the bridegroom at the time of a Hindu wedding.[6] And at the time of the Punyāha-wāchan, a ceremony which precedes a Hindu wedding, the figure is drawn in rice and is worshipped.[6] Throughout the Chāturmās some persons paint the auspicious Swastikas, either on their thresholds or at their doors, every morning.[7]

On the sixth day from the date of a child's birth, a piece of cloth is marked with a Swastika in red lac, the cloth is stretched on a bedstead and the child is placed upon it.[8] An account of this ceremony is to be found in the treatises Jayantishastra, Jātakarma, and Janakālaya.[8]

Before joining the village-school, little boys are made to worship Saraswati, the goddess of learning, after having installed her on a Swastika, in order that the acquisition of learning may be facilitated.[9]

A Brahman host, inviting a party of brother-Brahmans to dinner, marks the figure one (१) against the names of those who are eligible for dakshinā, and a Swastika against the names of those who are not eligible. These latter are the *yajamāns* or patrons of the inviting Brahman, who is himself their *pūjya, i. e.*, deserving to be worshipped by them. A *bindu* or dot, in place of the Swastika, is considered inauspicious.[10]

The Swastika is used in calculating the number of days taken in pilgrimage by one's relations, one figure being painted on the wall each day from the date of separation.[10]

It is said that the Swastika when drawn on a wall is the representation of Jogmāya. Jogmāya is a Natural Power, bringing about the union of two separated beings.[11]

The Jains paint the Swastika in the way noted below and explain the figure in

the following manner:—The four projectors indicate four kinds of souls: *viz.*, (1) Manushya or human, (2) Tiryach or of lower animals, (3) Deva or divine, (4) Naraki or hellish. The three circular marks denote the three Ratnas or jewels, *viz.*, (1) Jnān or knowledge, (2) Darshana or faith, (3) Charita or good conduct; and the semicircular curve, at the top of the three circles, indicates salvation.[12]

[1] Mr. L. D. Mehta, Motā Devāliā.
[2] The Schoolmaster, Ganod.
[3] The Schoolmaster, Agashi and Arnālā,
[4] Mr. T. D. Khāndhār, Schoolmaster, Sayala.
[5] Mr. Girijashankar Karunashankar, Songadh.
[6] The Schoolmaster, Mith-bāo, Ratnagiri.
[7] Mr. D. K. Pandya, Schoolmaster, Dhhank.
[8] Mr. Jetbalal Anupram, Schoolmaster, Aman.
[9] Mr. M. H. Raval, Vanod.
[10] Mr. D. K. Pandya, Dhhank.
[11] Mr. Girijashankar Karunashankar, Songadh.
[12] Mr. K. D. Desai

Every Jain devotee, while visiting the images of his gods, draws a Sathia (Swastika)[1] before them and places a valuable object over it. The sign is held so sacred that a Jain woman has it embroidered on the reticule or *kothali* in which she carries rice to holy places.*

'I am the very light of the sun and the moon,' observes Lord Krishna in his dialogue with Arjuna,[2] and the moon also receives divine honours like the sun. Moon-worship secures wealth, augments progeny, and betters the condition of milch-cattle.[4] The suitable days for such worship are the second and the fourth days of the bright half of every month (Dwitīya or Bīj and Chaturthi or Choth, respectively) and every full-moon day (Purnima or Punema). On either of these days the devotees of Chandra (the moon) fast for the whole of the day and take their food only after the moon has risen and after they have seen and worshipped her.[4] Some dainty dish such as *kansār*,† or plantains and puris,‡ is specially cooked for the occasion.

A sight of the moon on the second day of the bright half of every month is considered auspicious. After seeing the moon on this day some people also look at silver and gold coins for luck,[5] The belief in the value of this practice is so strong that, immediately after seeing the moon, people refrain from beholding any other object. Their idea is that silver, which looks as bright as the moon, will be obtained in abundance if they ook at a silver piece immediately after seeing the moon.[6] Moon worship on this day is also supposed to guarantee the safety of persons at sea.[7] In the south, milk and sugar is offered to the moon after the usual worship, and learned Brahmans are invited to partake of it. What remains after satisfying the Brahmans is divided among the community.[8] On this day, those who keep cattle do not churn whey nor curd milk nor sell it, but consume the whole supply in feasts to friends and neighbours.[8] The Ahirs and Rabaris especially are very particular about the use of milk in feasts only: for they believe that their cattle are thereby preserved in good condition.[9]

The fourth day of the dark half of every month is the day for the observance of the *chaturthi-vrat* (or *choth-vrat*). This *vrat* is observed in honour of the god Ganpati and by men only. The devotees fast on this day, bathe at night after seeing the moon, light a ghi lamp, and offer prayers to the moon. They also recite a *pāth* containing verses in honour of Ganpati, and, after worshipping that god, take their food consisting of some specially prepared dish. This *vrat* is said to fulfil the dreams of the devotees.[10]

The day for the *chaturthi-vrat* in the month of Bhādrapad (the 11th month of the Gujarati Hindus) is the fourth day of the bright half instead of the fourth day of the dark half,[11] and on this day (Ganesh

[1] Mr. Girijashankar Karunashankar, Songadh.

* The Swastika is found at Pompeii and in the Greek 'key' pattern. It is also found on Persian and Assyrian coins and in the Catacombs at Rome. It is to be seen on the tomb of the Duke of Clarence, who was drowned in a butt of Malmsey wine, at Tewkesbury, and occurs in Winchester Cathedral, where it is described as the fyle-foot.—R. E. E.

[2] Mr. D. K. Pandya, Schoolmaster, Dhhank. Compare a similar idea in the Kurān in the chapter An Nur (the Lights): "Allah is the Light of the Heavens and the Earth. The semblance of his light is the nyche wherein there is a light."—K. B. Fazlullah.

[3] Mr. J. A. Jani, Schoolmaster, Aman.

[4] Mr. N. D. Vora, Schoolmaster, Rajpara; and Mr. B. K. Dave, Schoolmaster, Kotda-Sangani.

† Kansār is coarse wheat flour sweetened with molasses and cooked in water until the whole quantity of water is absorbed and taken with ghi.

‡ Puris are cakes of fine wheat flour, fried in ghi.

[5] Mr. D. K. Pandya, Dhhank.

[6] Mr. K. D. Desai.

[7] Mr. D. K. Pandya, Dhhank.

[8] The Schoolmaster, Rajpara.

[9] Mr. K. P. Joshi, Limbdi.

[10] Mr. G. K. Bhatt, Songadh.

[11] Mr. K. P. Joshi, Limbdi, and B. K. Dave, Kotda-Sangani.

Chaturthi[*]) the moon is not worshipped. The very sight of her is regarded as ominous, and is purposely avoided.[1] The story is that once upon a time the gods went out for a ride in their respective conveyances. It so happened that the god Ganpati fell off his usual charger, the rat, and this awkward mishap drew a smile from Chandra (the moon). Ganpati, not relishing the joke, became angry and cursed Chandra saying that no mortal would care to see his face on that day (which happened to be the fourth day of the bright half of Bhādrapad). If any one happens to see the moon even unwittingly on this day, he may expect trouble very soon.[2] There is one way, however, out of the difficulty, and that is to throw stones on the houses of neighbours. When the neighbours utter abuse in return, the abuse atones for the sin of having looked at the moon on the forbidden night. The day is therefore called (in Gujarat) *Dagad-choth*, *i. e.*, the Choth of stones.[3]

On the fourth day of the dark half of Phālgun (the 5th month of Gujarati Hindus) some villagers fast for the whole of the day and remain standing from sunset till the moon rises. They break their fast after seeing the moon. The day is, therefore, called *ubhi* (*i.e.*, standing) *choth*.[4]

Virgins sometimes observe a vow on Poshi-Punema or the full-moon day of Pausha (the 3rd month of the Gujarati Hindus). On this day a virgin prepares her evening meal with her own hands on the upper terrace of her house. She then bores a hole through the centre of a loaf, and observes the moon through it, repeating while doing so a verse[†] which means : O Poshi-Punemadi, *khichadi* (rice and pulse mixed together) is cooked on the terrace, and the sister of the brother takes her meal.[5] The meal usually consists either of rice and milk or of rice cooked in milk and sweetened with sugar, or of *kansār*. She has to ask the permission of her brother or brothers before she may take her food ; and if the brother refuses his permission, she has to fast for the whole of the day.[6] The whole ceremony is believed to prolong the lives of her brothers and her future husband. The moon is also worshipped at the time of *griha-shānti*, *i. e.*, the ceremonies performed before inhabiting a newly-built house.[7]

If the moon is unfavourable to a man born under a particular constellation, on account of his occupying either the 6th, the 8th or the 12th square in a *kundali*[‡] (see below)

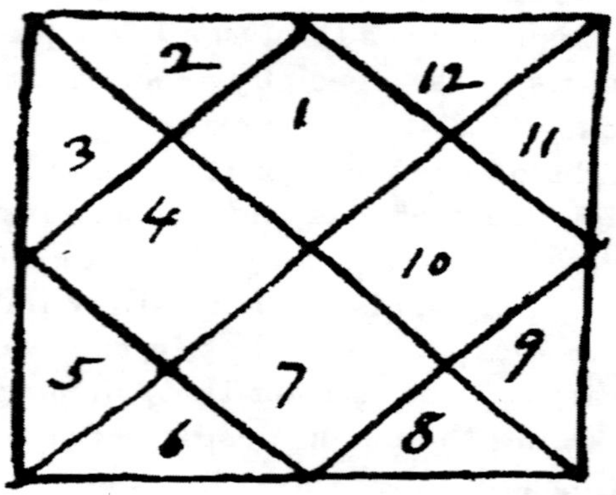

prayers are offered to the moon ; and if the occasion is a marriage, a bell-metal dish, full of rice, is presented to Brahmans.[8]

* All observers of the *Chaturthi-vrat* worship the god Ganpati on this day, and offer him one thousand trifoliate sprouts of dūrva (cynodon dactylon). The dish specially prepared for the occasion is *Golana-lādu*—sweet-balls of wheat flour fried in ghi and mixed with molasses.—Mr. N. M. Dave, Sānkā.

1 Mr. N. M. Dave, Sānkā.

2 The Deputy Educational Inspector, Gohelwad.

3 Mr. K. D. Desai.

4 The Schoolmaster, Vanod.

† The original is—
Poshi Poshi Punemadi,
Āgāshe rāndhi khichadi,
jame bhāini benādi.

5 The Schoolmaster, Kotda-Sangani and The Schoolmaster, Jodia.

6 Mr. R. B. Pandya, Jetpur Sanskrit School.

7 Mr. L. D. Mehta, Schoolmaster, Mota-Devalia.

‡ A Kundali is an astrological diagram of the position of planets at any particular time. The numbers in the diagram change their positions according to the position of planets at any given time.—Mr. D. Desai.

8 Mr. Chhaganlal Motira, Wala Taluka.

The appearance of the moon and the position of the horns of her crescent at particular times are carefully watched as omens of future events. Cultivators believe that if the moon is visible on the second day of the bright half of Āshādh (the 9th month of Gujarati Hindus), the sesamum crops of that season will be abundant; but if the moon be hidden from sight on that day, the weather will be cloudy during the whole of Āshādh, and will prove unfavourable to vegetable growth.[1] If the moon appears reddish on a Bīj day (or the second day of the bright half of a month), and if the northern horn of the crescent be high up, prices in the market are believed to rise; if, on the other hand, it is low, it prognosticates a fall in prices. If the two horns are on a level, current prices will continue.[1]

Similarly, the northern horn of the crescent, if it is high up on the Bīj day of Āshādh, augurs abundant rainfall; if it is low, it foreshadows a season of drought.[2]

If the moon presents a greenish aspect on the full-moon day of Āshādh, excessive rains may be expected in a few days; if on that day she rises quite clear and reddish, there is very little hope of good rains; if she is partly covered by clouds when she rises and then gets clear of the clouds, and then again disappears in the clouds in three *ghadis*,* three *pohors*,* or three days, rain is sure to fall.[3]

If on the 5th day of the bright half of Chaitra, the moon appears to the west of the Rohini constellation, the prices of cotton are believed to rise; if to the east, they are said to fall; and if in the same line, the current rates are believed to be likely to continue.[4]

The Bīj (2nd day) and the ninth day of Āshādh (the 9th month of the Gujaratis and the 4th month of the Hindus of the Deccan) falling on a Sunday is a combination that foretells excessive heat. If they fall on Wednesday, intense cold is said to be the result. Their occurring on a Tuesday, threatens absence of rains, and on a Monday, a Thursday or a Friday, foreshadows excessive rainfall.[5]

Thunder on Jeth-Sud-Bīj, or the second day of the bright half of Jyeshtha, is a bad omen and threatens famine.[6]

The spots on the moon have given rise to numerous beliefs, mythological as well as fanciful. One of them is that they are the result of a curse, pronounced by the sage Gautama on Chandra. Indra, the god of rain, was infatuated with the charms of Ahalyā, the wife of Gautama, and with the help of Chandra laid a cunning plot to gain his ignoble object. Accordingly, one night, Chandra set earlier than usual, when Indra assumed the form of a cock and crowed at midnight in order to deceive Gautama into the belief that it was dawn, and therefore his time for going to the Ganges to perform his religious services. The trick was successful, and the holy sage being thus got rid of, Indra assumed the form of Gautama himself and approached Ahalyā, who was surprised to see her husband (as she thought) so quickly returned. The wily god allayed her suspicions by explaining that it was not yet time for the morning ceremonies, and thus enjoyed the favours due to her husband. Gautama, in the meanwhile, finding the water of the Ganges cool and placid, and discovering that it was not yet dawn, returned to his hermitage. On reaching home he detected the treachery of Indra, who tried to escape in the disguise of a tom-cat. The exasperated sage then cursed Indra, Chandra and his wife: Indra to have a thousand sores on his person, Ahalyā to turn into a stone, and Chandra to have a stain on his fair face.[7]

Another mythological story is that Daksha Prajāpati, the son of Brahmā, gave all his

[1] Mr. N. M. Dave, Sānkā.

[2] The Schoolmaster, Khāndhār.

* One *ghadi* is equal to 24 minutes and one *pohor* (prahara) lasts for three hours.

[3] Mr. M. P. Shah, Schoolmaster, Zinzuwada.

[4] Mr. N. M. Dave, Sānkā.

[5] Mr. M. P. Shah, Schoolmaster, Zinzuwada.

[6] Mr. N. M. Dave, Sānkā.

[7] The Schoolmasters of Dhhank, Rajpara and Limbdi

twenty-seven daughters in marriage to Chandra, who was inspired with love for one of them only, named Rohini, the most beautiful of them all. The slighted twenty-six sisters complained to their father, Daksha, of Chandra's preference for Rohini. Daksha in anger cursed Chandra to be attacked by consumption (which is supposed to be the reason of the waning of the moon) and his face to be marred by a stain.[1]

The curse of Gautama and the curse of Daksha are also supposed to be reasons of the waxing and the waning of the moon.

Another belief regarding the moon-spots is that when the head of Ganpati was severed by Shiva's trident, it flew off and fell into the chariot of the moon. The spots are either the head itself[2] or are due to drops of blood fallen from the flying severed head.[3]

The spots are also said to be explained by the fact of the image of god Krishna or Vishnu* residing in the heart of the moon who, as a devotee of Vishnu, holds his image dear to his heart.[4]

The moon is often called *mrigānka* (*lit*. deer-marked) and *mriga—lānchhana* (*lit* deer-stained); and a further explanation of the spots in this connection is that the moon-god took into his lap a strayed deer, out of compassion, and thus his lap became stained.[5] Jains believe that in the nether parts of the moon's *vimān* or vehicle, there is an image of a deer whose shadow is seen in the spots.[6]

Some persons declare the spots to be a *shami* tree (*prosopis spicigera*).[7] The belief of the masses in Gujarat is said to be that the spot on the moon's disc is the seat of an old woman, who sits spinning her wheel with a goat tethered near her.[8] If the droppings of the goat were to fall on earth, departed souls would return to the earth.[9]

It is said that a child and a tree are never seen to grow except during the night. Such growth is therefore held to be due to lunar rays.[10] As all trees, plants, etc., thrive owing to the influence of the moon, the moon-god is called the lord of herbs. The moon is also a reservoir of nectar and is called *Sudhākar, i. e.,* one having nectarine rays.[11] As the lord of herbs, the moon-god is supposed to have the power of removing all diseases that are curable by drugs, and of restoring men to health.[12]

Persons suffering from white leprosy, black leprosy, consumption and diseases of the eyes are believed to be cured by the observance of the *Bij* and *Punema* vows.[13] Consumption in its incipient and latter stages is also said to be cured by exposure to the rays of the moon.[14] Constant glimpses of the moon add to the lustre of the eyes.[15] On the *Sharad-Punema*, or the 15th day of the bright half of Ashvin (the last month of the Gujaratis and the 7th month of the Deccani Hindus), tailors pass a thread through their needles in the belief that they will thereby gain keener eyesight.[16]

A cotton-wick is exposed to the moon on Sharad-Punema, and is afterwards lighted in oil poured over the image of Hanūmān. The soot, which is thus produced, if used on the Kali-chaudas day—the fourteenth day of the dark half of Ashvin—is said to possess much efficacy in strengthening the eyesight and also in preserving the eyes from any disease during the ensuing year.[17]

Sweetened milk or water is exposed to moonlight during the whole of the night of

[1] The Schoolmaster, Rajpara. [2] The Schoolmaster, Dadvi. [3] The Schoolmaster, Lilapur.

* Throughout the Hindu Scriptures, Vishnu and his incarnations are described as being of *Shyama-varna* or dark complexion.—Mr. K. D. Desai.

[4] The Schoolmaster, Dadvi. [5] The Deputy Educational Inspector, Halar. [6] Mr. K. P. Joshi, Limbdi.

[7] The Schoolmaster, Lilapur. [8] Mr. Nandlal Kalidas, Chhatrasa. [9] Mr. M. P. Shah, Zinzuwada.

[10] The Mistress of Rajkot Civil Station Girls' School. [11] Mr. Nandlal Kalidas, Chhatrasa.

[12] Rao Saheb Shelke and the Shastri of Bhayavadur. [13] The Schoolmaster, Rajpara.

[14] The Schoolmaster, Dhhank. He refers to the books Vratarāj and Pathyapathya on this point.

[15] The Deputy Educational Inspector, Halar; and the Schoolmaster of Chauk, Kolaba.

[16] The Schoolmaster, Jodia. [17] The Schoolmaster, Kolki.

Sharad-puncma (the full-moon day of Ashvin) in order to absorb the nectarine rays of the moon, and is drunk next morning. Drinking in the rays of the moon in this manner is believed to cure diseases caused by heat as well as eye-diseases, and it similarly strengthens the eyesight and improves the complexion.[1] Sugar-candy thus exposed and preserved in an air-tight jar is partaken of in small quantities every morning to gain strength and to improve the complexion.[2] The absorption of the lunar rays through the open mouth or eyes is also believed to be of great effect in achieving these objects.[3]

Once upon a time the gods and demons, by their united efforts, churned the ocean and obtained therefrom fourteen *ratnas* or precious things.* These were distributed among them. Lakshmi, the *kaustubha* jewel, the Shārnga bow and the conch-shell fell to the share of Vishnu, and the poison, *Halāhal visha*, was disposed of to Shiva. Only two things remained, *sudhā*, or nectar, and *surā* or liquor. To both gods and demons the nectar was the most important of all the prizes. A hard contest ensuing between them for the possession of it, the demons, by force, snatched the bowl of nectar from the gods. In this disaster to the gods, Vishnu came to their help in the form of Mohini—a most fascinating woman—and proposed to the demons that the distribution of the immortalising fluid should be entrusted to her. On their consent, Vishnu or Mohini, made the gods and the demons sit in opposite rows and began first to serve the nectar to the gods. The demon Rāhu, the son of Sinhikā, fearing lest the whole of the nectar might be exhausted before the turn of the demons came, took the shape of a god and placed himself amongst them between Chandra (the moon) and Sūrya (the sun). The nectar was served to him in turn, but on Chandra and Sūrya detecting the trick, the demon's head was cut off by Vishnu's discus, the *sudarshana-chakra*. Rāhu however did not die: for he had tasted the nectar, which had reached his throat. The head and trunk lived and became immortal, the former being named Rāhu, and the latter Ketu. Both swore revenge on Chandra and Sūrya. At times, therefore, they pounce upon Chandra and Sūrya with the intention of devouring them. In the fight that ensues, Chandra and Sūrya are successful only after a long contest, with the assistance of the gods, and by the merit of the prayers that men offer.[4]

The reason of the eclipse is either that Chandra and Sūrya bleed in the fight with Rāhu and their forms get blackened[5]; or that the demon Rāhu comes between the two luminaries and this earth, and thus causes an eclipse[6]; or because Rāhu obstructs the sun and the moon in their daily course, and this intervention causes an eclipse[7]; or because Rāhu swallows the sun and the moon, but his throat being open, they escape, their short disappearance causing an eclipse.[8]

Besides the mythological story, there is a belief in Gujarat that a *bhangi* (scavenger or sweeper), creditor of the sun and the moon, goes to recover his debts due from them, and that his shadow falling against either of them causes an eclipse.[9]

---

1 The Schoolmasters of Rajpara, Limbdi, and Ibhrampur.

2 Mr. K. D. Desai.

3 The Shastri of Jetpur, Pathashala.

* The following Sanskrit verse mentions all of them: —

लक्ष्मीः कौस्तुभपारिजातकसुरा धन्वंतरिश्चन्द्रमा ।
गावः कामदुहः सुरेश्वरगजो रम्भादिदेवाङ्गनाः ॥
अश्वः सप्तमुखो विषं हरिधनुः शंखोऽमृतं चांबुधेः ।
रत्नानीह चतुर्दश प्रतिदिनं कुर्वन्तु वो मंगलम् ॥ १ ॥

Rao Saheb P. B. Joshi.

4 The Schoolmasters of Jodia, Dhhank, Songadh, Rajpara, and Limbdi.

5 The Schoolmaster of Khirāsara.

6 Mr. D. K. Pandya, Dhhank.

7 Mr. Laxmichand Hemji, Vasāwad.

8 Mr. G. K. Bhatt, Songadh.

9 Mr. K. P. Joshi Limbdi.

A third explanation of the eclipse is that the sun and the moon revolve round the Meru mountain, and the shadow of the mountain falling upon either of them causes an eclipse.[1]

It is believed amongst Hindus that eclipses occur when too much sin accumulates in this world.[2] Most Hindus regard an eclipse as ominous, and consider the eclipse period to be unholy and inauspicious. The contact of the demon Rāhu with the rays of the sun and the moon pollutes everything on earth. Great precautions therefore become necessary to avoid pollution.[3] A period of three *pohors** (*prahars*) in the case of the moon, and of four in the case of the sun, before the actual commencement of an eclipse, is known as *vedha*, *i. e.*, the time when the luminaries are already under the influence of the demon. During this period and during the time of an eclipse people observe a strict fast. Anyone taking food within the prohibited period is considered *sutaki* or ceremonially impure, as if a death had happened in his family.[4] An exception is, however, made in the case of children, pregnant women and suckling mothers who cannot bear the privation of a strict fast. From the beginning of an eclipse to its end, everything in the house is believed to be polluted, if touched.[4]

As the sun and the moon are believed to be in trouble during an eclipse, people offer prayers to God from the beginning of the *vedha* for their release. It is the custom to visit some holy place on an eclipse-day, to take a bath there, and to read holy passages from the Shāstras. Some people, especially Brahmans, sit devoutly on river-banks and offer prayers to the sun.[4] Much secret as well as open charity is given at the time of an eclipse. But the receivers of charity during the actual period of an eclipse are the lowest classes only, such as *bhangis*, *mahārs* and *māngs*. When an eclipse is at its full, these people go about the streets giving vent to such cries as *āpódān chhuté chānd* (give alms for the relief of the moon!).[5]

Among the gifts such people receive are cotton clothes, cash, grain such as sesamum seeds, *udad*, pulses, and salt.[6] The gift of a pair of shoes is much recommended.[7] Sometimes a figure of the eclipsed sun or moon is drawn in *juari* seeds and given away to a *bhangi*.[8]

Although the period of an eclipse is considered inauspicious, it is valued by those who profess the black art. All *mantras*, incantations, and *prayogas*, applications or experiments, which ordinarily require a long time to take effect, produce the wished for result without delay if performed during the process of an eclipse.[9]

If a man's wife is pregnant, he may not smoke during the period of an eclipse lest his child become deformed.[10] Ploughing a farm on a lunar-eclipse day is supposed to cause the birth of Chāndrā-children, *i. e.*, children afflicted by the moon.[10]

After an eclipse Hindus bathe, perform ablution ceremonies, and dress themselves in clean garments. The houses are cleansed by cowdunging the floors, vessels are rubbed and cleansed, and clothes are washed, in order to get rid of the pollution caused by the eclipse.[11] Unwashed clothes of cotton, wool, silk or hemp, according to popular belief, do not become polluted.[11] The placing of *darbha* grass on things which are otherwise liable to pollution is also sufficient to keep them unpolluted.[12]

Brahmans cannot accept anything during the impious time of an eclipse, but after it

[1] Mr. K. P. Joshi, Limbdi.
[2] Mr K. D. Desai.
[3] Mr. Laxmichand Hemji, Vasāwad.
* A *pohor* or *prahar* is equal to three hours.
[4] Mr. D. K. Pandya, Dhhank.
[5] Mr. Khan Bahadur Fazlullah.
[6] The Schoolmasters of Jodia and Songadh.
[7] Mr. K. D. Desai.
[8] Mr. N. D. Vora, Rajpara.
[9] Mr. G. K Bhatt, Songadh.
[10] Mr. K. D Desai.
[11] The Schoolmaster of Jodia.
[12] Mr. D. K. Pandya, Dhhank.

is over, alms are freely given to them in the shape of such costly articles as fine clothes, gold, cattle and the like.[1]

After an eclipse Hindus may not break their fast till they have again seen the full disc of the released sun or the moon. It sometimes happens that the sun or the moon sets *gherāyalā* (while still eclipsed), and people have then to fast for the whole of the night or the day after, until the sun or the moon is again fully visible.[2]

There is a *shloka* in the *Jyotish-Shāstra* to the effect that Rāhu would surely devour Chandra if the *nakshatra*, or constellation of the second day of the dark half of a preceding month, were to recur on the Purnima (full-moon day) of the succeeding month. Similarly, in solar eclipses, a similar catastrophe would occur if the constellation of the second day of the bright half of a month were to recur on the Amāvāsya (the last day) of that month.[3] The year in which many eclipses occur is believed to prove a bad year for epidemic diseases.[4]

The Jains do not believe in the Hindu theory of *grahana* (or the eclipse).[5] Musalmans do not perform the special ceremonies beyond the recital of special prayers; and even these are held to be supererogatory.[6]

With the exception that some people believe that the stars are the abodes of the gods,[7] the popular belief about the heavenly bodies seems to be that they are the souls of virtuous and saintly persons, translated to the heavens for their good deeds and endowed with a lustre proportionate to their merits.[8] And this idea is illustrated in the traditions that are current about some of the stars. The seven bright stars of the constellation *Saptarshi* (or the Great Bear) are said to be the seven sages, Kashyapa, Atri, Bhāradwāj, Vishwāmitra, Gautama, Jāmadagni and Vasishtha, who had mastered several parts of the *Vedas*, and were considered specialists in the branches studied by each, and were invested with divine honours in reward for their proficiency.[9] Another story relates how a certain hunter and his family, who had unconsciously achieved great religious merit, were installed as the constellation *Saptarshi** (or the Great Bear). A hunter, it is narrated in the *Shivarātri-māhātmya*, was arrested for debt on a *Shivrātri*† day, and while in jail heard by chance the words 'Shiva, Shiva' repeated by some devotees. Without understanding their meaning, he also began to repeat the same words, even after he was released in the evening. He had received no food during the day, and had thus observed a compulsory fast. In order to obtain food for himself and his family, he stationed himself behind a *Bel*‡ tree, hoping to shoot a deer or some other animal that might come to quench its thirst at a neighbouring tank. While adjusting an arrow to his bowstring,

[1] Mr. D. K. Pandya, Dhhank.

[2] Mr. K. D. Desai.

[3] Mr. D. K. Shah, Charadwah.

[4] Mr. T. D. Khandhar, Sayala.

[5] The Schoolmaster, Jodia.

[6] Khan Bahadur Fazlullah.

[7] Mr. M. M. Rana, Barton Female Training College, Rajkot.

[8] Mr. Nandlal Kalidas, Chhatrasa, and Mr. M. M. Rana, Barton Female Training College, Rajkot.

[9] Mr. Motichand Vasanji Doshi, Kāluwad.

* I believe the name of the constellation is wrongly given : it ought to be Mriga. One of the stars in this group, known as 'Sirius', in Western astronomy, is often called Vyādha (*i. e.*, the hunter).—Mr. K. T. Gupte.

The Mrig constellation is also said to represent the goddess Saraswati, who had assumed the form of a gazelle in order to escape the amorous grasp of Brahmā, her father. While the deer in the Mrig constellation is Saraswati, the Ardra constellation is Mahādev who had followed to chastise Brahma, who also is seen as the Brahma constellation.—Mr. N. M. Dave, Sānkā.

† The thirteenth day of both the bright and dark halves of a month, sacred to the worship of god Shiva.

‡ The three-leaf-clusters of this tree are loved by the god Shiva if put upon his image.—Mr. K. D. Desai.

he plucked some leaves out of the thick foliage of the tree and threw them down. The leaves, however, chanced to fall on a *Shiva-linga* which happened to stand below, and secured for him the merit of having worshipped god Shiva with Bel-leaves on a *Shivrātri* day. He was also all the while repeating the god's name and had undergone a fast. The result was that not only were his past sins forgiven, but he was placed with his family in heaven.[1]

Similarly, Dhruva, the son of king Uttānapād, attained divine favour by unflagging devotion, and was given a constant place in the heavens as the immovable pole-star.[2]

According to Hindu astrology, there are nine *grahas** or planets, twelve *rāshis*† or signs of the zodiac, and twenty-seven *nakshatras*‡ or constellations. Books on astrology explain the distinct forms of the *nakshatras.* For instance, the Ashvini constellation consists of two stars and presents the appearance of a horse. It ascends the zenith at midnight on the *purnima* (the 15th day of the bright half) of Ashvin (the first month of the Gujarati Hindus). The constellation of Mrig consists of seven stars, four like the legs of a sofa and three others under them in a line. All these twenty-seven groups of stars reach the zenith at midnight on particular days in particular months; and the months of the Hindu calendar are named after them.[3]

All planets influence the life of a person, one way or the other, according to their position in the heavens at the time of his birth. A *kundali, i. e.,* a figure like the one

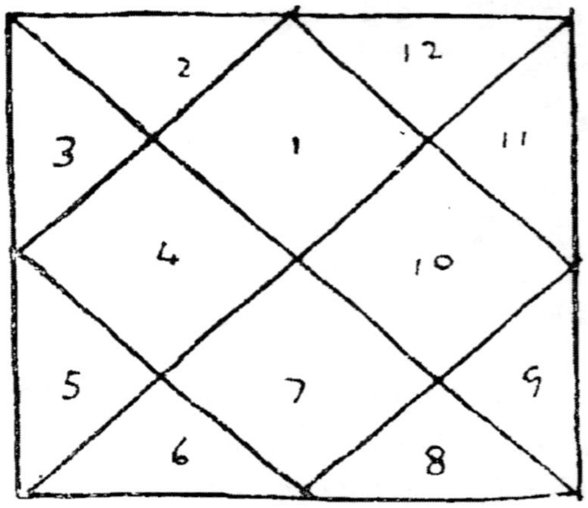

shown here, is drawn by astrologers to illustrate the respective positions of the planets. The twelve squares of the diagram represent the twelve signs of the zodiac, and the positions of the planets in different squares influence persons in different ways. Ravi (the Sun), Budha (Mercury) and Shukra (Venus) occupy one *rāshi* for one month; Chandra (the Moon) occupies a *rāshi* for 135 *ghadis*,¶ *i. e.,* two days and a quarter; Mangal (Mars) for one month and a half; Guru (Jupiter) for thirteen months; Shani (Saturn) for two years and a half, and Rāhu for a year and a half. This is their normal and ordinary motion. But if they take an abnormal course and move either too fast or too slow, they finish their revolution through a *rāshi* within a shorter or a longer period.[4]

If the planet Guru (Jupiter) occupies either the 1st, 3rd, 4th, 6th, 8th, 10th, or 12th, square of a *kundali*, it is said to bring about a rupture with friends, pecuniary wants, and an increase in the number of enemies.[5]

[1] Mr. D. K. Pandya, Dhhank.

[2] Mr. N. M. Dave, Sānkā.

* The nine *grahas* are, Ravi (the Sun), Chandra (the Moon), Mangal (Mars), Budha (Mercury), Guru (Jupiter), Shukra (Venus), Shani (Saturn), and Rāhu and Ketu.

† The names of the twelve *rāshis* are:—1 Mesha (Aries), 2 Vrishabha (Taurus), 3 Mithun (Gemini), 4 Karka (Cancer), 5 Sinha (Leo), 6 Kanyā (Virgo), 7 Tulā (Libra), 8 Vrishchika (Scorpio), 9 Dhanu (Sagittarius), 10 Makara (Capricornus) 11 Kumbha (Aquarius), 12 Mīna (Pisces).

‡ The following are the twenty-seven *nakshatras*:—1 Ashvinī, 2 Bharanī, 3 Kritikā 4 Rohinī, 5 Mrig, 6 Ardra, 7 Punarvasu, 8 Pushya, 9 Āshlesha, 10 Magha, 11 Pūrvā-phālguni, 12 Uttara-phālguni, 13 Hasta, 14 Chitrā, 15 Swāti, 16 Vishākha, 17 Anurādha, 18 Jyeshthā, 19 Mūl, 20 Pūrvāshādha, 21 Uttarāshādha, 22 Shravana, 23 Dhanishtha, 24 Shatatārakā, 25 Pūrvābhādrapada, 26 Uttarābhadrapada, and 27 Revati.

[3] Mr. D. K. Pandya, Dhhank.

¶ One *ghadi*=24 minutes.

[4] Mr. Motechand Vasanji Doshi, Kālāwad.

[5] The Schoolmaster, Dadvi.

If Shani (Saturn) occupies the 1st, 2nd, 4th, 5th, 7th, 8th, 9th, or the 12th square in a man's *kundali*, it causes despondency of mind, family quarrels, imminent injuries from foes, and pecuniary wants.[1]

The presence of Mangal (Mars) in the 3rd, the 6th, or the 11th square is auspicious.[1]

Of the nine planets, Budha, Guru, and Chandra are benevolent, Mangal and Ravi are neither benevolent nor baneful; and Shani, Rāhu, and Ketu are downright malevolent.[2] Each planet has a story connected with it concerning its benevolence or malevolence, and showing also the way to secure its propitiation. For instance, the malevolence of Shani drove King Vikrama to unknown countries, and subjected him to grave calamities. On the advice of a wise man, however, he observed the Saturday-vows and thus overcame his difficulties.[3]

When a planet is unfavourable to a person, it has to be propitiated by vows, and the person who is under its evil influence often lays upon himself the obligation of abstaining from particular articles of food or from wearing certain articles of clothing for a certain number of days.[4] Particular days of the week are set apart as appropriate for the worship of particular planets, and, on such days, the person keeping the vow observes a fast and worships the planet through the medium of a Brāhman.[5] For instance, *vrats* or vows are observed on Tuesdays in honour of Mangal (Mars), when an image of the planet, engraved on a golden dish, is worshipped, and the person observing the vow takes food consisting of wheat only, and that too, only once during the day. This mode of fasting is followed for a number of consecutive Tuesdays prescribed by an astrologer; and on the last Tuesday, when *pūrnāhuti** is offered, Brāhmans are feasted and *dakshina* is given to them. A piece of red cloth and some corn are used in the installation of the planet; these and the golden engraving are carried away by the priest.[3]

Similarly, in propitiating Rāhu and Ketu the same ceremonies are gone through: only, instead of wheat, *mug* (Phasolcus mungo) is eaten by the devotee. In the same way Shani (Saturn) is said to favour the diet of *adād* (or lentils): Guru (Jupiter) inclines to *chana* (or gram), while Shukra (Venus) favours *cholā* (dolichos sinensis).[3]

Certain forms or figures, called *mandals*, are favoured by particular *grahās*, and are drawn in their honour in worshipping them. Different things, too, are given in charity in honour of different planets.[6]

All the nine *grahas* and the twenty-seven nakshatras are worshipped on the occasion of the *Griha-Shanti* ceremony, which is performed before occupying a newly erected building.[2]

It is considered inauspicious to hold a marriage ceremony while Shukra (Venus) is invisible. In such a case, however, the ceremony may be performed after setting up and worshipping a small golden image of the planet.

Of the stars, the constellation of *saptarshi* is perhaps the one most often worshipped. Its worship forms a part of the ceremonies performed on the occasion of investing boys with the sacred thread[7] and also of the ceremonies of marriage. The worship of the *saptarshi* on marriage occasions is believed to be an attestation of the marriage, and to secure the benign care of the *saptarshi* for the couple. The form of worship is sometimes as follows: a red and white piece of

[1] The Schoolmaster of Dadvi.
[2] N. M. Dave, Sānkā.
[3] M. H. Raval, Vanod.
[4] Hirji Monji, Ganod.
[5] N. D. Vora, Rajpara.
[6] Gangaram Tribhowandas, Lilapur.
[7] D. K. Pandya, Dhhānk.

* *I. e.*, a handful of rice, ghi, cocoanuts, and some other objects are cast into the fire as an offering.

cloth is stretched on the ground, bearing an image of the *saptarshi* over it; wheat and rice are scattered over the cloth, a ghi-lamp is lighted, and red lac and flowers are offered to the image.[1] Another form of worship is to mark seven red-lac-dots on a *pātla* or a wooden stool, and to place seven pice and seven betel-nuts thereon. After worshipping the seven pice, the bridal pair are made to take four turns round the stool, touching the stool with their great toes at every turn. A proverb runs to the effect that, whatever may happen to the couple, still the seven pice of *satpati* (*i. e.*, the ceremony described) are secure.[2] A third process is to form seven small piles of *kamod*,* on each of which, successively, the bride places her right foot while the bridegroom removes each pile one by one.[3]

The fifth day of the bright half of Bhādrapad (the eleventh month of the Gujarati Hindus) is observed as a day of worship in honour of the *saptarshi* group. People observe a fast on that day. Brāhmans set up seven *chāts*† in honour of the seven sages, adding an eighth in honour of Arundhatī, the wife of Vasishtha, and worship them by *shodashopachār* (*i. e.* sixteen-fold ceremonial). The worship is said to secure felicity for departed souls.[4]

The *saptarshi* are also annually worshipped by Brāhmans on cocoanut-day (the 15th day of the bright half of Shrāvan) on the occasion of changing their sacred threads. Hindu seamen also worship the constellation on the same day.[5]

In the performance of the *Nīl-parvān* ceremony, which is held to propitiate the spirits of departed ancestors, and which requires a calf and a heifer to be married, an entertainment being simultaneously given to one hundred and eight Brāhmans, and on the occasion of Vastu or the ceremonies performed before or at the time of occupying a newly-built house, burnt offerings and worship are offered to the *saptarshi*.[6]

Every Brāhman must offer *arghyas*‡ to, and worship, the *agastya* constellation, in a hut of *darbha*§ and *kāsada*,§ within seven days from the date of its appearance. Failure to make this offering brings pollution on him for seven months, and disqualifies him from performing any of the rites or ceremonies prescribed by the Shastras.[6]

Married couples are made to look at the Pole star immediately after the Hymenal knot is tied by the priest, in the hope that they may be as long-lived or as inflexible or unmoved by the ups and downs of life.[2]

The twelfth day after the death of a person, known as *Tārā-bāras* (or the star-twelfth) is kept as the day of star-worship by the relatives of the deceased, when one member of the family observes a fast on that day in honour of the deceased, and takes food only after worshipping the stars at night. It is customary on this day to give up the use of bronze vessels and to give them away in charity.[7]

Just as persons carrying or accompanying a corpse to the cemetery are considered *sutaki* (under ceremonial impurity), so those who witness this rite are also considered unclean : but they are purified by a sight of the stars.[8]

Young girls watching the starry sky at night recite a verse which means, "I worshipped the star-spangled firmament first and

[1] K. P. Joshi, Limbdi.
[2] R. B. Pandya, Jetpur Sanskrit Pathashālā.
[3] The Schoolmaster of Khirasarā.
[4] D. K. Pandya, Dhhānk, and N. M. Dave, Sānkā.
[5] B. K. Dave, Kotda-Sangani.
[6] Jairam Vasaram, Jodia.
[7] Kalyanji Bhaishankar, Kolki, and R. B. Pandya, Jetpur.
[8] G. K. Bhatt, Songadh.
* A superior kind of rice.
† Twisted braids of *darbha* grass.
‡ *Arghya* is an offering of water in a spoon filled with barley seeds, sesamum seeds, sandal ointment, rice, and flowers.
§ Two varieties of sacred grass, used in thatching roofs.

then my lover Ābhlā dabhlā Kankunā dābhlā* — "Ye stars! blind the prowling thief and seize him if he tries to steal away, and your blessings on my lord confer!"[1]

The *Rohini* and *Krittika* constellations, popularly known as Gadli, are supposed to indicate the rise and fall in the cotton-market.[2]

The dimmest star of the *saptarshi* group foretells the death of a person within six months from the date on which it becomes invisible to him.[3] Again, if a man cannot perceive the *saptarshi* or the galaxy in the sky, it is considered such a bad omen that his end is believed to be near at hand.[4]

The rainbow is believed to be the bow of Indra,† the god of rains, and is therefore called '*Indra-dhanushya.*' We see it when Indra draws his bow to release the rains from the rākshasas (demons);[5] or, when successful in bringing down rain, Indra manifests his glory by drawing a bow;[6] or when in the struggle for supremacy between Summer and the rainy season, Indra draws his bow to defeat Summer.[7]

It is also believed that when Rāmchandra, the hero of the *Rāmāyana*, adjusted an arrow to the bow of Shiva, to compete for the hand of Sītā in the swayamvara (or maiden's-choice marriage) celebrated by her, the bow was split into three pieces, which ever since present themselves as rainbows in the sky.[8]

The rainbow is popularly regarded as an indication of good or bad rainfall according as it appears at particular hours and in particular directions. If a rainbow appears in the east a speedy rainfall is expected; if on the other hand it is seen in the west, rainfall is apprehended to be distant.[9] Some people, however, believe the contrary, *i.e.*, they regard the appearance of a rainbow in the west as an indication of good rains, and in the east as a sign of scarce rainfall.[10] Perhaps both ideas are reconciled by a third belief according to which the appearance of a rainbow in a direction facing the sun, indicates the proximity of rain.[11]

If a rainbow is seen at sunset or sunrise just before the commencement of rain the fall of rain will be excessive; but if it appears after rainfall, the rain will probably cease.[12] According to some persons the appearance of a rainbow in the morning portends a drought.[13] There is, however, a popular saying to the effect that were the *kachbi, i. e.*, the rainbow, to be seen at sunrise in the west, it foretells great floods before nightfall.[7]

The sight of a rainbow is sometimes regarded as a bad omen. Some believe that it shortens a man's life and brings misfortunes to him.[4] Others believe that it is calamitous to a man's relations by marriage, especially to the mother-in-law, who is sure to lose her power of hearing.[14] People sometimes clash earthen vessels against one another to avert the evils which are to be feared from a rainbow.[15] It is also said that the sight of the whole of the rainbow is a good omen:

1 Odhowji Avichal, Lākhāpadar.
2 Talakshi Dharamsi, Khandhar.
3 The Deputy Educational Inspector of Gohelwad.
4 Harji Monji, Ganod.
5 L. D. Mehta, Mota Devalia.
6 Nandlal Kalidas, Chhatrāsā.
7 N. M. Dave, Sānkā.
8 The Schoolmaster of Pālānvār.
9 D. K. Pandya, Dhhank.
10 K. P. Joshi, Limbdi.
11 The Schoolmaster of Luvaria.
12 Mr. Kalyanji Bhaishankar, Kolki.
13 The Schoolmaster of Khandhar.
14 Mr. R. B. Pandya, Jetpur.
15 Mr. M. M. Rana, Barton Female Training College, Rajkot.

* Meaningless terms.

† Indra has full sway over the twelve meghas (or clouds), of which Shāmaghana is the greatest. Indra directs them to pour down waters in whatever regions he likes. At the time of the deluge he lets loose all the twelve meghas under the lead of Shāmaghana and thus brings about the destruction of this world.—N. D Vora, Rajpara.

but the sight of a part, however large, is inauspicious.[1]

According to the *Purānas*, the milky way or *ākāsh-ganga* is the celestial River Ganga which was brought down by Bhagīrath to the earth.[2] King Sagar once performed an *ashwa-medha*[*] sacrifice, when, according to custom, he let loose a horse, and sent his sixty thousand sons with it. Indra, jealous of the growing power of Sagar, stole the horse and concealed it in the hermitage of Kapila, when the sage was deeply absorbed in religious meditation. The sixty thousand sons of Sagar followed it to this asylum, where they taunted and insulted the sage, believing him to be the thief. Kapila, who was ignorant of the theft, opened his long-closed eyes in anger, emitting sparks of flame from them, and destroyed the sons of Sagar together with the whole of their army. Bhagīrath, the grandson of Sagar, propitiated the sage, and on his advice practised religious austerities in honour of Shiva for the purpose of bringing down the River Ganga from heaven. Through the kindness of God Shiva, Bhagīrath was at last successful in bringing the celestial river down to this world; and with the water of the river he revived the sons of Sagar. The River Ganga (*i. e.*, the Ganges) in this world is therefore also known by the name of Bhāgirathi. It is this heavenly river which we see as the milky way.[3] Like the sacred Ganges on the earth, the River Ganga in the celestial regions is held in great respect by the gods[4] and purifies the heavenly bodies, just as the earthly Ganges washes away the worst sins of mortals.[1]

Some people, however, believe the milky way to be the track by which the holy Ganges descended from heaven to earth.[5]

Another belief is that the God Vishnu, at the time of his Vāman (or Dwarf) incarnation, touched the *ina* (*i. e.*, the Egg) in his third footstep and thus caused a flow of waters, which is known as *ākāsh-ganga*.[6] Some suppose the milky way to be a ladder leading to the heavens.[7] Astrologers call it *Vatsa*, a fictitious creature with numerous horns, mouths, and tails.[8] According to another belief, the milky way consists of two *rekhās*—lines—one of sin and the other of good and meritorious actions. The length of one line compared to the other betokens the predominance of good or evil as the case may be.[9] The milky way is also supposed to be the track left by the *rath* or car of Rāmachandra.[10]

Ākāsh-ganga or the milky way is said to consist of one crore and eighty lacs of stars.[11] If a man cannot perceive the milky way in the sky, his end is believed to be near at hand.[12]

The Musalmāns declare the milky way to be the track formed by the footstep of the horse of the Prophet Muhammad, on the occasion of his night-journey to Heaven.[7]

[1] Mr. D. K. Shah, Charadwah.

[2] Mr. Jairam Vasaram, Jodia, and B. K. Dave, Kotda-Sangani.

[3] Mr. Vallabh Ramji, Mendardā.

[4] Mr. N. D. Vora, Rajpara.

[5] Mr. Nandlal Kalidas, Chhatrasa.

[6] Mr. Jethalal Anupram, Aman.

[7] Mr. Jairam Vasaram, Jodia.

[8] Mr. N. M. Dave, Sānkā.

[9] Mr. D. K. Pandya, Dhhank.

[10] Mr. K. B. Fazlul'ah.

[11] Mr. G. K. Bhall, Songadh.

[12] Mr Hirji Monji, Ganod.

[*] When a king desired to be *Chakravarti*—Sovereign of all India—he used to perform a horse-sacrifice, and a horse was let loose with a copper-plate fastened to its head with the name of the king engraved upon the plate. The horse moved in front followed by the king's army. Those who were not willing to acknowledge the suzerainty of the king challenged his army by seizing the horse. Such a horse-sacrifice, if successfully completed, threatens the power of Indra, who is therefore said to be very jealous and to create obstacles to the performance of such sacrifices—K. D. Desai.

The occasion for earth-worship most frequently arises when anything is to be built upon its surface. At the time of setting the *manek-stambha*, or the first pillar of a marriage-bower or a bower for a thread-ceremony,[1] before commencing the construction of wells, reservoirs, and tanks[1] and in laying the foundation-stone of a house, a temple, or a sacrificial pit,[2] or of a street, a fortress, a city, or a village,[3] or of any constructive work raised upon or made under the ground, certain ceremonies, called *khat-muhūrt* or *khat-puja*, are performed. The earth-mother is then worshipped in the manner prescribed in the *Shastras*, to propitiate her against interruptions in the completion of the work undertaken. The owner or the person interested in the new construction pours a little water on the earth where the foundation-pit is to be dug, sprinkles red lac and *gulal* (red powder), places a betel-nut and a few precious coins, and digs out the first clod of earth himself.[4] Some of the things offered to the earth at the time of *khat-puja* are *panchāmrit*,* betel-nuts, betel-leaves, *pancharatna* (or the five kinds of precious things, namely, gold, silver, copper, coral, and pearls), a bowl and green garments.[2] Under the influence of particular *rāshis* (signs of the zodiac), particular corners of the building under construction are required to be dug in the *khat-muhūrt* ceremonies.[3] For instance, a little digging in the north-west corner is believed to be favourable to the constructor who happens to be under the influence of *Sinha* (Leo), *Kanya* (Virgo) and *Tula* (Libra): in the north-east corner, if under the influence of *Vrishchika* (Scorpio), *Dhanu* (Sagittarius) and *Makar* (Capricornus): in the south-east corner if under the sway of *Kumbha* (Aquarius), *Min* (Pisces) and *Mesha* (Aries): in the south-west corner in the case of *Vrishabh* (Taurus), *Mithun* (Gemini) and *Kark* (Cancer).[3] After the worship of the earth-mother, sugar or molasses is distributed among neighbours, bystanders and relatives, in token of the auspiciousness of the occasion.[5] An image of Ganpati is worshipped in a copper-dish, this is buried underground, and a brick is laid on it when starting the work of construction.[3] In setting up the *manek-stambha* on marriage occasions, a small earthen bowl is filled with milk, curds, turmeric, *dūrvā*-sprouts† and *mag* seeds (phasoleus mungo), and buried in the ground after being sprinkled over with red lac and rice.[6]

The ceremonies appertaining to *khat-muhūrt* are treated of at length in a book called *Dharma-sindhu*.[7] They are believed to secure durability of construction.[4]

On the *Dasarā*‡ day or the 10th day of the bright half of Ashvin (the last month), Rājās go out in state with their ministers and subjects to worship the earth-mother and the holy *shami* tree (prosopis spicegera). A wetted plot of ground is first dug over with pikes, *javālā* (tender wheat plants) and

[1] Mr. N. D. Vora, Rajpara.

[2] Mr. D. K. Pandya, Dhhank.

[3] Mr. N. M. Dave, Sānkā.

[4] Mr. Talakshi Dharashi, Sayala.

[5] The Schoolmaster of Dadvi.

[6] Mr. Jairam Vasaram, Jodia.

[7] The Schoolmaster of Gondal Taluka

* A mixture of milk, curds, ghi, honey and sugar.

† Dūrvā is a kind of sacred grass.

‡ On the Dasarā holiday, which is also known as *Vijayādashmī*, Hindus take special dishes, dress themselves in their best garments and go out of towns and villages to worship the earth-mother and the holy *shami*, with *javālā* stalks, a few of which are inserted in the folds of their head-dress as auspicious tokens. In towns, and big cities a procession is formed, conducted by some city magnate or a native chief riding an elephant. They go in state to the place of worship, and after the completion of the worship a goat or a he buffalo, preferably the latter, is killed, and a salvo of three to seven or more cannon is fired. People then return home and prostrate themselves before their elders, and receive from them a handful of candied sugar, a betel-nut and leaf, with blessings for long-life and prosperity. Such blessings are considered likely to prove effective.—K. D. Desai.

shami leaves are then mixed with the muddy earth, and small balls of the mixture are made. A pice and betel-nut are placed in each ball, and they are presented to the worshipper as a mark of good luck. Travellers carry such balls with them on their journeys for luck. Kings carry the same to obtain success on the battle-field. The Pāndavas had such balls with them on the field of Kurukshetra when they obtained a victory over the Kauravas.[1] The balls are also used as *pastānā*.* The *javālā* in the balls are taken out and allowed to grow in an earthen vessel filled with clay and manure till they reach a span in heigth, when they are taken up and used.[2]

Earth-worship is performed before burying treasure underground, and also when a marriage-procession, at the time of returning, reaches the limits of the bridegroom's village.[3]

In some places, virgins worship the plot of ground on which the *Holi* is lighted, for about ten or twelve days after the *Holi* holiday.[4]

Another occasion for earth-worship is the third day of the bright half of Chaitra (the sixth month), on which day Vishnu saved the earth in his Varāha (or Boar) incarnation, when it was being carried to the nether regions by the demon Shankhāsur.[5]

On the eighth day of the bright half of Māgh and also of Āshvin (the fourth and the last month respectively), *naivedya* (an oblation of food) is offered to the earth-mother, and is then used as her *prasād* (gift). No cooked food is allowed to fall on the ground on this day: even the leavings after meals are given away to cows.[6]

When any ceremony is to be performed on the earth's surface, as much of the spot as is required for the ceremony is cleansed by watering it and plastering it with cow-dung. A betel-nut and a pice are then placed on it as the *Chādā* or rent of the spot.[7]

On those occasions when *dakshina* is given to Brāhmans outside the village limits, worship of the earth-mother is performed by pouring milk on the ground, and by placing seven betel-nuts and seven single copper-pieces thereon.[8]

Some ambitious Brāhmans dig earth from near the roots of a banyan tree after offering prayer to the earth, and out of it, make an image of *Parthishwar*—Lord of the Earth— hoping thereby to obtain wealth. The same ceremony, if observed near the roots of a pipal tree (ficus religiosa), is believed to confer wealth and male issue.[2]

When Vishnu killed the demons Madhu and Kaitabha, the earth was strewn with their flesh and marrow (*meda*). Therefore the earth is called *medini*, and for the same reason is unclean, and no holy objects are allowed to touch it.[9] Another explanation is that the earth was rendered unclean because blood was shed on its surface in the combat of the demon Vritrāsur with the god Indra.[10]

The things polluted by a contact with the earth are either objects which are to be

[1] Mr. N. D. Vora, Rajpara.
[2] Mr. Jairam Vasaram, Jodia.
[3] Mr. H. M. Bhatt, Ganod.
[4] Mr. Talakshi Dharashi, Sayala.
[5] Mr. B. K. Dave, Kotda-Sangani.
[6] Mr. Nandlal Kalidas, Chhatrāsā, and the Schoolmaster of Jāsdān.
[7] The Schoolmaster of Pātanvāv.
[8] The Schoolmaster of Sultanpur.
[9] Mr. Laxmichand Hemji, Vasāvad.
[10] Mr. Madhowji Tulsiram, Movaiya.

* Some Hindus, when intending to go on a journey, consult an astrologer as to the *muhūrt* or auspicious hour for setting out. If they do not happen to leave their place at the prescribed moment, they put a *pasrānā*—some of the articles to be carried by them in their journey—such as a suit of clothes or a box, in a neighbour's house as a token of their having set out at the stated time.—K. D. Desai.

dedicated to gods, such as sandal-wood ointment, *panchāmrit*,* the leaves of the *bel* tree (Aegle marmelos), *tulsi* leaves (leaves of the holy or sweet basil plant), betel-leaves and flowers ;[1] or objects which are sacred because of their having been dedicated to the gods, including *tīrtha*[2] or water used in bathing the images of gods† ; or things which are by nature so holy that it is improper to place them on the bare earth ; for instance, images of deities, water of the sacred Ganges or the Jumna,[3] any holy writ,[4] a conch-shell and even gold.[5] Cooked food also deserves respect, as it supports the lives of men, and it is sinful in a Hindu to let it lie on the bare ground. Any irregular conduct in this respect arouses the wrath of the Annadeva (or the food, deity).[6]

It is, however, maintained by some that the reason why certain things, such as materials of worship, are not allowed to touch the earth, is that the earth itself being a deity, such things would be dedicated to this deity by a contact with the earth and would thus become incapable of any further use, as things that are dedicated to one deity cannot again be offered to another.[7]

During the course of the recitation of mantras (holy hymns) in honour of Vishnu and Mahādeva ; on the occasion of offering prayers to the *grahas* (planets) for their propitiation ; and on occasions like *Vishnu-yāga*,‡ *Mahārudra*,‡ *Shatachandi*, *Gayatrī-purashchara*§ and *Brāhmana-varana*‖ the devotee or the sacrificer and the priest sleep on *darbha* grass or on clean woollen blankets, spread on the bare ground.[1]

Other occasions for sleeping on the floor are the days of the observance of certain *vrats* or vows ; such as, the *Divāsa* or the 15th day of the dark half of Āshādh (the ninth month), the *Jamnāshtami* or the 8th day of the dark half of Shrāvana (the tenth month), the days of *Goatrad*, a *vrat* lasting from the 11th day to the 15th day of the bright half of Bhādrapad, Mahāshivarātri or the 14th day of the dark half of Māgh, the Ekādashi day or the 11th day of both the bright and dark halves of a month,[4] the *Navrātra* days or the first nine days Ashvin, eclipse days, and the day of *Jāgran* or the 15th day of the bright half of Āshādh,[6] besides, sometimes, the whole of the months of Shrāvana and the Purushottam or intercalary month ; and the *chāturmās*, *i. e.*, the four months of the rainy season.[8]

A Brāhman in his *brahmacharya* (or the period of his life which, according to the *Shāstras*, should be devoted to the acquirement of learning, and which commences from the date of his being invested with the sacred thread and terminates at the age of twenty-three) and a widow are not allowed by the *Shāstras* to sleep elsewhere than on beds made on the ground.[4]

Women, while in menstruation, sleep on the floor for four days.[2] Some women, when they are separated from their husbands, also sleep in this fashion.[8]

A dying person, two or three minutes before his death, is placed on the ground, which

[1] Mr. N. D. Vora, Rajpara.
[2] The Schoolmaster of Lilapur.
[3] Mr. Jairam Vasaram, Jodia.
[4] Mr. D. K. Pandya, Dhhank.
[5] Mr. K. D. Desai.
[6] The Schoolmaster of Dadvi.
[7] The Schoolmaster of Gondal Taluka.
[8] Mr. M. M. Rana, Barton Female Training College, Rajkot.

* A mixture of milk, curds, ghi, honey, and sugar.

† Such objects are taken in a plate and thrown over a *tulsi* (or sweet basil) plant.—K. D. Desai.

‡ Sacrifices in honour of Vishnu, Mahādev and the goddess Chandi, respectively.—K. D. Desai.

§ A form of devotion requiring the recitation of the *Gayatri-mantra* a hundred thousand times with certain symbolic ceremonies.—K. D. Desai.

‖ The appointment of duly authorised Brāhmans to perform religious ceremonies.—K. D. Desai.

is first purified with cow-dung-plaster.[1] For ten days after a death, the members of the deceased's household and his relatives sleep on beds spread on the bare ground.[2] If the demise be very affecting, the nearest relatives sleep on the floor for periods which may extend to three months, six months, or even for a year, and sometimes the penance lasts for their whole lives.[1]

It is customary, among some sects, not to allow the *sātharā*—*i. e.*, the spot lately occupied by a corpse in the house—to be *suna* or unoccupied for a single night. Someone must sleep on the spot for twelve consecutive days from the date of demise.[3]

Pilgrims,* after pilgrimage, abandon sensual pleasures, take their meals only once every day, and sleep on the floor.[1] It is customary to sleep always on the ground while in holy places. Devotees, ascetics, *sādhus*, and their disciples sleep on the ground.[2]

The God Indra has twelve *meghas* or clouds under his control, and he directs each of them to pour out their waters wherever he likes. When in the least irritated in the execution of his orders, Indra's voice is heard in this world in thunder-claps which rise to a terrible pitch if the deity becomes downright angry.[1] Thunder is also said to be the loud laughter of Indra when in a happy mood.[4]

Another belief is that during the rainy season, Indra plays *gedi-dāndā*†, and the strokes given to the *gedi* in the course of the game, produce what we call thunder;[5] or, that the clouds are god's footballs, and thunder is produced by his foot striking them, while at play during the rainy season.[2] Some believe thunder to be due to the loud sounds produced by various musical instruments which are played upon the occasion of the marriage-ceremony of Indra.[6] According to others, thunder is produced by the cannon of Indra;[7] or, as some again say, by the trumpetings of *Airāvat*, the elephant of Indra[8]; or, we hear thunder when Indra draws his bow and adjusts an arrow to the bow-string, in order to bring about the fall of rain.[9]

A further belief attributes thunder to the very rapid pace of the chariot of Bhagwān.[10] Some people, however, say that it is produced when Bhīma (one of the five Pāndavas) wields his prodigious club or bludgeon.[11] In the opinion of others, Vidyut or Tanyatun, the offspring of Lambā, the daughter of Daksha, and the wife of Dharmarāj thunders in the rainy season.[12] It is also suggested that the god of rains shakes the heavens and thus produces thunder.[3] The *Shāstras*, it is said, declare that thunder is caused by the sounds of the *dundubhi*—or

[1] Mr. M. M. Rana, Rajkot.
[2] Mr. D. K. Pandya, Dhhank.
[3] Mr. Jairam Vasaram, Jodia.
[4] Mr. L. I. Joshi, Surela.
[5] Mr. K. P. Joshi, Limbdi.
[6] Mr. N. D. Vora, Rajpara, or of Bhagwan, according to Jairam Vasaram, Jodia.
[7] Mr. N. M. Dave, Sānkā.
[8] Mr. N. D. Vora, Rajpara.
[9] The Shastri of Jetpur, Pathashala.
[10] The Schoolmaster of Pāolānvav.
[11] Mr. G. K. Dave, Sultanpur.
[12] The Schoolmaster of Rajkot Girls' School.

* Intending pilgrims sometimes impose such self-denials upon themselves, vowing abnegation from particular articles of food or wear till they have performed their pilgrimage. Some renounce the use of ghi, some of milk, others of betel-leaf or nut, others swear not to wear a turban or a dupatta—till they are given the merit of a pilgrimage.—Khan Bahadur Fazlullah.

† This game, much resembling the English boys' game of Tip cat, is also known as *gilli-dānda*. The *gedi* or *gilli* is a small piece of wood, two or three inches in length, an inch or less in diameter and sometimes tapering at both ends. The *dānda* is a small round stick, of the same thickness and a foot or more in length, by which the *gedi* is played. There are two sides to the game as in cricket, though not composed of a definite number of players. There are a number of ways in which the game can be played.—K. D. Desai.

kettledrums—beaten by the gods in delight at the sight of rain.[1] There is also a popular belief in the Surat district that an old hag causes thunder either when she grinds corn or when she rolls stones in the clouds.[2]

The prevalent belief about lightning seems to be that it is the girl whom Kansa tried to dash against a stone, but who escaped and went up to the sky. Kansa, the tyrant king of Mathura, was informed by a heavenly voice, by way of prophecy, that a son would be born to his sister who would cause his destruction. Kansa thereupon confined his sister Devaki and her husband Vasudeva in prison, loaded them with fetters, and kept the strictest watch over them. He took from Devaki, and slew, every child of hers as soon as it was born. In this way he disposed of her first six children. On the seventh occasion, however, on which Devaki gave birth to a son named Krishna, a girl was born at the same hour to Nanda in Mathura; and Vasudeva secretly interchanged the two children in spite of the vigilance of Kansa. When Kansa knew of his sister having been delivered, he seized the infant girl and tried to dash her against a stone. The little one immediately flew away to the skies, where she still dwells in the form of *Vijli* or lightning.[3]

The *Shāstras* describe *Vijli* as the distinctive weapon of Indra, just as *pashupatākā* is peculiar to Shiva and the *Gāndīva* bow to Arjuna.[4]

Other beliefs about lightning are that *Vijli* is the sister of Megharāja, the god of rains, and appears to announce his approach:[5] that *Vijli* is a goddess who rests upon winds, fire, and rains:[6] that *Vijli* is but the thunderbolt of Indra:[7] that lightnings are the flashes of the bright weapon of Indra:[8] that lightning is the lustre of the fireworks and the lamps lighted by the gods in honour of the nuptials of Indra:[9] that lightning is produced by the sparks caused by the friction of the *gedi* and the *dāndā* of Indra when the god plays the game.[10] *Vijli* is also known as Saudāmini, *i. e.*, one residing on Mount Sudāma.[11]

The occurrence of thunder and the appearance of lightning on particular days and in particular directions are regarded as signs of the abundance or scarcity of rain during the season.

Thunder during the Rohini *nakshatra** is a bad omen: it foreshadows either a famine,[12] or a *Boterun, i. e.*, complete cessation of rains for seventy-two days after the thunder-claps are heard.[8] According to another view, if the Rohini *nakshatra* lasts for a fortnight and if the sky is clear during the period and yet lightning and thunder occur, a *Boterun* will be the consequence; but if lightning and thunder were to accompany the clouds in the same *nakshatra*, heavy and plentiful rains may be confidently expected.[13] Lightning without clouds in the same *nakshatra* is believed to be the cause of what is popularly called Rohinī-*dāzi, i.e.*, the burning heat of Rohini.[14]

Some persons expect a *Boterun* after *kadakas* or crashing thunder. Others apprehend a famine if they hear thunder on the second day of the bright half of Jyeshtha (the eighth month).[8]

[1] Mr. H. M. Bhatt, Ganod.
[2] Mr. K. D. Desai.
[3] The Schoolmasters of Dhhank, Sanka, Limbdi, and Sultanpur.
[4] Mr. M. M. Rana, Rajkot.
[5] The Schoolmaster of Lilapur.
[6] The Schoolmaster of Charadwa.
[7] The Schoolmaster of Surela.
[8] Mr. N. M. Dave, Sanka.
[9] Mr. N. D. Vora, Rajpara.
[10] The Schoolmaster of Kolki.
[11] The Schoolmaster of Gondal.
[12] Mr. D. K. Pandya, Dhhank.
[13] Mr. B. K. Dave, Kotda-Sangani.
[14] The Schoolmaster of Dadvi.
* *i.e.*, the period for which the Rohini *nakshatra* lasts.

Thunder or lightning in the Hasta* *nakshatra* foretells good harvests and a prosperous year.[1] Thunder in the same *nakshatra* is believed to muzzle the jaws of serpents and other noxious creatures, and to achieve this object, also, *a sāmelu* (or a log of wood) is struck against a *mobhārā* (or a hollow stone used for threshing corn).[2] If thunder is not heard during this *nakshatra*, mosquitoes and other insects and vermin are believed to be likely to multiply.[3]

If thunder is heard during the Ārdrā *nakshatra*, the rainfall will be delayed for a month.[4]

Lightning is commonly seen on the second and the fifth day of the bright half of Āshādh, and is considered a sign of good rainfall, while its absence indicates a probable scarcity of rain.[5] Its appearance on the fifth day of Āshādh is believed by some to foretell an early fall of rain.[1] Since the rainfall, and therefore the state of the crops during the ensuing year, are suggested by lightning on this day, corn-dealers settle a rise or fall in the price of corn according as lightning is or is not seen on that occasion.[6]

Thunder in the east predicts a speedy fall of rain.[1] If flashes of lightning are seen in the north-east or the north, rain will fall within three days.[1] Lightning in the south-east or the south foretells extreme heat.[7]

Long-continued thunder shows that the rainfall is distant. Similarly, continued flashes of lightning intimate danger to the lives and property of people.[7] Sudden thunder portends an immediate cessation of rain.[1] Thunder or lightning out of season threatens calamity to the country.[8]

Vijli or lightning is said to be fettered on the fifth day of the bright half of Āshādh—(or, as some say, on the second day of Shrāvan)[2]—after which date no apprehensions of its destructive powers need be entertained.[9] Till then, however, it is free and is likely to injure those persons† who have not cut or shaved their hair from their birth.[10]

The occurrence of lightning is believed to cause the delivery and sometimes even the death of pregnant women.[11]

Any period marked by the occurrence of lightning is considered inauspicious.[12]

The Puranas speak of fourteen worlds—the seven *swargas* (celestial regions) and the seven *pātāls* (nether regions)‡. Underneath the seventh *pātāl*§ lies Shesha (the divine cobra) who supports all the fourteen worlds on one of his one thousand hoods. On account of the heavy burden, the serpent-god sometimes gets tired, and tries to change his position. The result of the movement is an earth-quake.[9] According to another version, an earthquake occurs when Shesha changes

[1] Mr. D. K. Pandya, Dhhank.
[2] Mr. N. M. Dave, Sānkā.
[3] Mr. B. K. Dave, Kotda-Sangani.
[4] The Schoolmaster of Luvaria.
[5] The Schoolmaster of Dadvi.
[6] The Schoolmaster of Songadh.
[7] Talakshi, Dharashi, Sayala.
[8] Mr. L. H. Jadow, Vasawad.
[9] Mr. M. M. Rana, Rajkot.
[10] Mr. G. K. Dave, Sultanpur.
[11] The Schoolmaster of Charadwa.
[12] Mr. Jairam Vasaram, Jodia.

* The Hasta *nakshatra* generally commences at the end of Bhādrapad or the beginning of Ashvin and lasts for a fortnight. The rains during this period, which are required for the rabi crops, are so much esteemed that each drop of them is said to be worth a drop of ghi. People store the *hathio-varshād* or the rain water of Hasta in reservoirs for drinking purposes, believing it to be very pure and digestive.—K. D. Desai.

† Among the Hindus it is customary for those whose children do not live to keep their children unshaved for a certain number of years, after which the children are taken to a holy place and shaved there for the first time. The temple of Ranchhodji at Dākor is a favourite place for such ceremonies.—K. D. Desai.

‡ The seven nether worlds are Atāl, Vital, Sutal, Talātal, Mahātal, Rasātal, and Pātāl.

§ In an ocean, as some say—D. K. Pandya, Dhhank.

his posture in sleep,[1] or is the result of a hair falling from the body of Shesha.[2] Some people say that ordinarily Shesha does not feel the weight of the fourteen worlds on his head; he bears the load as if it were only a single sesamum seed. But when too much sin accumulates in any of the regions, the burden becomes unbearable for him: he begins to shake under it, and an earthquake occurs.[3]

Some believe that there is a tortoise under the divine cobra who supports the world:[4] others go further, and add a frog below the tortoise:[5] and it is said that the slightest motion on the part of either the tortoise or the cobra is the cause of an earthquake.

Another belief is that earthquakes occur whenever there is tyranny or injustice on the part of a king, or whenever immorality spreads in society, because the earth is unable to bear the sin, and trembles at the sight of it.[6]

According to a different opinion, the earth is supported by the *Pothia* or the favourite bull of Shiva on one of his horns. An earthquake is caused whenever he transfers the earth from one horn to another in order to relieve the former from the constant pressure of the burden.[7]

There is also a belief that deities of some strange species reside in the nether regions, and the earth is shaken whenever these beings fight among themselves.[5]

According to the Varāha-sanhita, an earthquake is always the precursor of some unprecedented calamity.[8] The prevalent belief in the popular mind seems to be that an earthquake is the result of immorality and sin, and further that it forebodes some dire calamity, such as famine, pestilence, an outbreak of fire, a revolution, or a great war.[9] The phenomenon is, therefore, regarded with great fear; and when it occurs, people endeavour to avoid the contingent evils by such meritorious acts as the giving of alms, and generally by leading a virtuous life.[10]

The most popular of the holy rivers are the Ganges, the Jumna (or Jamuna), the Narbadā, the Saraswati (near Sidhpur), the Kāveri, the Godāvari, the Gandaki, the Sarayu, the Dāmodari, the Sindhu (or Indus), the Mahānad, the Gomati (near Dwārka), the Brahmaputra, the Sābarmati, the Ghels (near Gaddheda), the Tungabhadra, the Suvarnabhadrā, the Bhadrashitā, the Jambuvati, the Phalaku (or Phalgu), the Kaushiki, the Tāmraparni, the Sita and the Alakanandā. Any point where three rivers meet is also a sacred place. Most of the holy rivers are the subject of many traditions, and books have been written to celebrate their merits.

The Ganges, the Jumna, and the Godāvari are said to be the holiest of all rivers.[9] There are a number of beliefs about the origin of the Ganges. One of them is that the Ganges is the stream caused by King Bali washing the feet of Vāman (the Dwarf incarnation of Vishnu).[11] Another story relates that the god Brahma was exhausted by overwork at the time of the marriage of Shiva and Pārvati. The gods, therefore, created water from their own lustres, and gave it to Brahma in a gourd, to be used in a similar contingency. When Vishnu in his *Vāman avatār* (or Dwarf incarnation) bestrode the heavens with a single step, Brahma washed his toe in the water from this gourd. A stream was thus created called Swarga-ganga

[1] Mr. Jethalal Devji, Bantwā.
[2] Mr. G. K. Bhatt, Songadh.
[3] Mr. D. K. Pandya, Dhhank, and Mr. M. M. Rana, Rajkot.
[4] The Deputy Educational Inspector of Gohelwad.
[5] Mr. Jairam Vasaram, Jodia.
[6] Mr. K. P. Josi, Limbdi, and Mr. Raju Ramjee Kanjee Pathak, Girls' School, Gondal.
[7] Mr. J. K. Upaddhyaya, Pātanvão.
[8] Mr. Raju Ramjee Kanjee Pathak, Gondal.
[9] Mr. D. K. Pandya, Dhbank.
[10] Mr. K. D. Desai.
[11] Mr. M. M. Rana Rajkot.

and brought down to the earth by Bhagīrath, the grandson of Sagar. When the Ganges fell from the heavens, it was supported and held fast by God Shiva in his *jatā* or matted hair. It was released by his loosening the hair, and in its course, inundated the sacrificial ground of King Jahnu. The latter, being angry, drank up its waters. On the entreaties of Bhagīrath, he released the stream by tearing off his thigh.* The river then flowed to the spot where the sixty thousand sons of Sagar were burnt to ashes; and it is said by some that one of the sixty thousand was saved at the end of each year up to the year 1955 of the Samvat era (corresponding to A. D. 1899), by the end of which period all the sixty thousand had attained salvation. From the earth the Ganges went to the nether regions. Thus flowing in the heavens, on the earth and in the Pātāl, the Ganges is called Tripathaga (*i. e.*, flowing in three courses). In its divine form, the Ganges is the wife of Shiva. Owing to the curse of Brahma, she was born in human form in this world and was married to Shantanu, by whom she became the mother of Bhishma, the heroic uncle of the Kauravas and the Pāndavas.[1]

It is customary among Hindu pilgrims, when they visit Kāshi (Benares) to take with them copper-vessels filled with *Gangājal* (water of the Ganges), and to worship the Gangā when they reach their homes after the pilgrimage. A figure is drawn in seven different kinds of corn; the bowl is placed on it; *abil gulāl* (red powder), frankincense, and *naivedya* (an oblation of food) are offered; a ghi lamp is lighted: a Brahman woman is dressed as Uma, the wife of Shiva, and Brahmans are entertained at a feast, *dakshina* being given to them.[2]

The water of the Ganges, as well as that of the Jumna, is believed to be so pure that it cannot be affected by microbes, even if kept for years in the house. This quality is believed to be a manifestation of its divine nature. It is further called *patit-pāvan* (lit. purifier of the fallen), and exculpates the sinful from their sins, either by a single draught or by bathing in it.[3] *Gangājal* is kept in most Hindu families, a draught of it taken by a dying person being believed to secure *moksha* or eternal salvation for the soul.[4]

A vow is observed by women, in honour of the Ganges, for the first ten days of the month of Jyeshtha. On these days they rise early in the morning and bathe in the holy waters of the Ganges.[5]

Sometimes ghi lamps are placed upon the waters of the Ganges or the Jumna, and vessels of metal, pice, and cocoanuts are cast into the stream. At such a time, when many people are standing on the banks offering prayers with folded hands, or engaged in the *arati*,† the river presents a very picturesque scene, the numerous lights being reflected in the water.[6]

The Jamuna or Yamuna is the daughter of the Sun, and the sister of Yama, the god of Death. The banks of the Jumna are well known as the scene of the amorous sports of God Krishna.[7] The story of the defeat of the demon Kāliya Nāg who was ejected from the Jumna by Krishna is well-known.

[1] Mr. M. M. Rana, Rajkot.

[2] The Schoolmaster of Lilapur.

[3] Mr. D. K. Pandya, Dhhank.

[4] The Schoolmaster of Kolki.

[5] The Schoolmaster of Upleta.

[6] The Schoolmaster of Kolki and the Shastri of Jetpur Pathashala.

[7] Mr. N. M. Dave, Sanka.

* The river is, therefore, regarded as his daughter, and is called Jahnavi.

† The waving of lights to and fro before an object of worship.

It is said that those who have bathed in the Jumnā or have once tasted its water, need not be afraid of Yama, the god of Death.[1] It is considered meritorious among the Hindus to bathe the image of god Shiva in water from the holy Jumnā or the Ganges or the Godāvari.[2] There is a popular *shloka* in honour of the Jumnā which runs:—"Victory to thee! Oh Yamunā, flowing through the Madhu-vana (the Madhu woods), the bearer of shining waters, the companion of Jāhnavi, the daughter of Sindhu, the ornament of the enemy of Madhu (*viz.*, Krishna), the appeaser of Mādhava, the dispeller of the danger of Gokal, the destroyer of the sins of the world, the giver of intellect, the scene of the amorous sports of Keshava. Victory to thee! O remover of difficulties, purify me."[3]

The banks of the Godāvari are known as the site of the hermitage of Gautama. When the planet Brihaspati (Jupiter) enters the Sinha-rāshi (the constellation Leo)* the holy Ganges goes to the Godāvari, and remains there for one year. During that year, all the gods are believed to bathe in this river. Thousands of pilgrims visit Nasik to offer prayers to the Godāvari, and after bathing in the river, give alms to Brahmans. Similarly, on the Kapilāshashti day, on which six *jogs* or conjunctive incidents occur simultaneously, the virtue of all *tīrthas* or holy places is believed to be concentrated in the Godāvari at Nasik.[3]

The mere sight of the Narbadā has the same effect as a bath in the Ganges or the Jumnā.[4] It is said that the Narbadā is the image of Shiva, and that fragments of the stony bow of Shiva are to be found in its bed.[5] The stones in the bed of this river have the same sanctity as the images of god Shiva.[6] *Shāligram* stones, which are worshipped as the images of Vishnu, are found in this river.[6] It is an act of high merit among Hindus to take a *pradakshinā* round the Narbadā, *i. e.*, to travel along the banks of the river, inhabited as the region is by many *Sādhus* and other holy persons.[7] Ashvatthāmā, the immortal son of Drona, is believed to reside on the banks of this river and to pay occasional visits to the Bhils in the neighbourhood.[7] The *Shukla-tīrtha*, situated on the Narbadā, is visited by numerous pilgrims, and a fair is held there on every sixtieth year.[7]

The sage Kapila instructed his mother Devahūti with divine knowledge on the banks of the Saraswati. Since then, the river is held sacred and funeral ceremonies—*Shrāddhas*—are performed on its banks in honour of departed female ancestors.[5] Similarly *Shrāddhas* in honour of male ancestors are performed at the confluence of the Ganges, the Jumnā, and the Saraswati at Allahabad † [8]

Of the Gandaki it is said that it contains as many *shankars* (images of Shiva) as there are *sankars* (stones). The *shāligram* stone is found in this river also. The Saryu is sacred as the scene of the childish sports of Rāmachandra, the hero of the *Rāmāyana*. On the banks of the Phalaku or Phalgu, Rāmachandra performed *Shrāddha* ceremonies in honour of his father Dasharath.[5]

1 Mr. B. K. Dave, Schoolmaster Kotda-Sangani.
2 The Schoolmaster of Dadvi.
3 Mr. D. K. Pandya, Schoolmaster Dhhank.
4 The Schoolmaster of Upleta.
5 The Schoolmaster of Luvaria.
6 Mr. L. D. Mehta, Mota Devalia.
7 Mr. K. D. Desai.
8 The Schoolmaster of Jodia.

* This happens every twelfth year. The year of *Sinhastha* i. e. the year when Brihaspati stands in the Sinha-rāshi, is the only one in which marriages among the Kadvâ Kunbis take place; and for this reason the smallest children in the community, sometimes even those who are in the womb, are married in this year.—Mr. M. M. Rana, Rajkot.

† The Saraswati is believed to be present, but invisible at this spot.

4

A bath in the waters of a holy river washes away the sins of the bather.[1] It is also meritorious to repeat the names of the several holy rivers.[2] The performance of *Shrāddha* ceremonies on the banks of a holy river secures the felicity of deceased ancestors in heaven.[1] At the time of performing *Shrāddhas* at a holy place, Hindus shave their moustaches, bathe in the sacred waters, and then go through the necessary ceremonies, in the course of which *pindas* are offered to the *Pitars* (spirits of dead ancestors). Brahmans are feasted after the ceremonies, and *dakshinā* is given to them.[3] *Tarpan* or an offering of water with flowers, ointment, red lac, cocoanuts, and betel, is frequently made to the river on the banks of which the ceremonies are performed.[4] The bones of a deceased person, left unburnt after cremation of the body, are gathered together and thrown into holy rivers such as the Ganges, the Jumnā, and the Godāvari, for the purification of his soul.[5]

When heavy floods threaten a village or a city with serious injury, the king or the headman should go in procession to propitiate the river with flowers, cocoanuts, and other offerings in order that the floods may subside.[6] A story is related of the occurrence of heavy floods in a village in the Jatalpur taluka, when a certain lady placed an earthen vessel (ordinarily used for curdling milk), containing a ghi lamp, afloat on the floods, whereupon the waters were at once seen to recede.[7]

Besides the holy rivers, there are numerous *kunds* or sacred pools which are regarded with equal reverence, and in which a bath has the same efficacy for destroying sin. Similarly, they are equally suitable places for the performance of *Shrāddha* ceremonies. These *kunds* are the subject of numerous beliefs, and each of them has a certain *māhātmya* or peculiar merit of its own. Six miles to the east of Dwārkā, near the seacoast, there is a *kund* called Pind-tārak, where many persons go to perform the *Shrāddha* and the Nārāyan-bali ceremonies. They first bathe in the *kund*: then, with its water, they prepare *pindas*, and place them in a metal dish: red lac is applied to the *pindas*, and a piece of cotton thread wound round them; the metal dish being then dipped in the *kund*, when the *pindas*, instead of sinking, are said to remain floating on the water. The process is believed to earn a good status for the spirits of departed ancestors in heaven.[1] It is further said that physical ailments brought on by the *avagati*—degradation or fallen condition—of ancestors in the other world, are remedied by the performance of *Shrāddha* on this *kund*.[8]

The Dāmodar *kund* is situated near Junāgadh. It is said that if the bones of a deceased person which remain unburnt after his cremation are dipped in this *kund*, the soul of that person obtains *moksha* (or final emancipation).[1]

There is a *vāv* or reservoir on Mount Girnār, known as Rasakūpikā-vāv. It is believed that the body of a person bathing in it becomes as hard as marble, and that if a piece of stone or iron is dipped in the *vāv*, it is instantly transformed into gold. But the *vāv* is only visible to saints and sages who are gifted with a supernatural vision.[9]

Kāshīpuri (Benares) contains a *vāv* called Gyān-vāv, in which there is an image of Vishweshwar (the Lord of the universe, *i.e.*, Shiva). A bath in the water from this *vāv* is believed to confer upon a person the gift of divine knowledge.[1]

[1] Mr. D. K. Pandya, Dhhank.
[2] Mr. D. K. Shah, Charadwah.
[3] The Schoolmasters of Dhhank, Vanod, and Kolki.
[4] Mr. M. R. Raval.
[5] The Schoolmaster of Dadvi.
[6] The Schoolmaster of Limbdi Taluka.
[7] Mr. K. D. Desai.
[8] Mr. Jairam Vasaram, Jodia.
[9] Mr. D. K. Pandya, Dhhank, and the Headmistress of Gondal Girls' School.

In the village of Chunval, a few miles to the north of Viramgām, there is a *kund* known as Loteshwar, near which stands a *pipal* tree. Persons possessed by ghosts or devils, are freed from possession by pouring water at the foot of the tree and taking turns round it, remaining silent the while.[1]

A bath in the Mān-sarovar near Bahucharāji is said to cause the wishes of the bather to be fulfilled. There is a local tradition* that a Rajput woman was turned into a male Rajput of the Solanki class by a bath in its waters.[1]

There is a *kund* called Zilāka near Zinzuwādā with a temple of Naleshwar Mahādev near it. The *kund* is said to have been built at the time of King Nala. It is believed locally that every year, on the 15th day of the bright half of *Bhādrapad*, the holy Ganges visits the *kund* by an underground route. A great fair is held there on that day, when people bathe in the *kund* and give alms to the poor.[2] There is also another *kund* close by, known as Bholava, where the river Saraswati is believed to have halted and manifested herself on her way to the sea.[3]

There is a *kund* in Baladāna near Wadhwan, dedicated to Hol, the favourite *mātā* of the *Chārans*. In this *kund*, black or red *gagar bedinus*—pieces of cotton thread—are sometimes seen floating in the water. They appear only for a moment, and sink if any one endeavours to seize them. The appearance of black pieces forebodes famine: but the red ones foretell prosperity.[4]

In Bhadakon near Chudā there is a *kund* called Garigavo. The place is celebrated as the spot of the hermitage of the sage Bhrigu and a fair is held there annually on the last day of *Bhādrapad*.[4]

Persons anxious to attain heaven, bathe in the Mrigi *kund* on Mount Girnār; and a bath in the Revati *kund*, which is in the same place, confers male issue on the bather.[5] There is also a *kund* of the shape of an elephant's footprint *Pagahein* on Mount Girnār. It never empties and is held most sacred by pilgrims.[6] People bathe in the Gomati *kund* near Dwārkā and take a little of the earth from its bed, for the purification of their souls.[7] In the village of Bābarā, Babhruvāhan, the son of Arjun, is said to have constructed several *kunds*, all of which are believed to be holy.[6]

The Lasundra *kund* near Lasundra in the Kaira District[8] and the Tulsi-shyāma *kund* on Mount Girnār[9] contain hot waters. There is also a hot *kund* called *Devki-unai*, about thirty miles to the south of Surat.[8] There the waters remain hot throughout the whole of the year, except on the fifteenth day of the bright half of *Chaitra*. On this day, the waters cool, and people can bathe in the *kund*. Many pilgrims visit the place on this occasion, to offer money, cocoanuts, and red lac to the *unai mātā*, whose temple stands near the *kund*. It is said that King Rāma built this *kund* while performing a local sacrifice, and brought water up from the pātāl (nether regions) by shooting an arrow into the earth.[10]

Other holy *kunds* are: the Bhīm *kund*, the Gomukhi-gangā, and the Kamandalu *kund* on Mount Girnār near the temple of Bhimnāth Mahādeo; the Rādhā *kund*, the Lalita *kund*, and the Krishna-sarovar in Dwārkā; the Rāma-sarovar, the Sītā *kund* and the Devki-unai *kund* in Ayodhya (Oudh): [11] and the Suraj *kund*[12] and the Hanumāndhāra[13] *kund* on Mount Girnār.

[1] The Schoolmaster of Kolki.
[2] Mr. M. H. Raval, Vanod.
[3] Mr. M. S. Shah, Zinzuwādā.
[4] Mr. N. M. Dave, Sānkā.
[5] The Shastri of Jetpur Pathashala.
[6] Mr. L. D. Metha, Mota Devalia.
[7] The Schoolmaster of Khirasarā.
[8] The Schoolmaster of Lewaria.
[9] Mr. Jairam Vasaram, Jodia.
[10] Mr. K. D. Desai.
[11] Mr. N. D. Vora, Rajpara.
[12] The Schoolmaster of Moti Murad.
[13] The Schoolmaster of Gondal Taluka.
* See P. 42.

Waterfalls are not very familiar to the people of Gujarāt. There is a belief, however, that barren couples obtain issue if they bathe in a waterfall, and offer a cocoanut.[1]

If a river source issues from an opening, in the shape of a *go-mukh* (cow's-mouth), the stream is called *dhodh*, and is considered as sacred as the holy Ganges. A bath in such a *dhodh* has the same efficacy for absolving persons from their sins.[2]

When a person dies an accidental death and before the fulfilment of his worldly desires, his soul receives *avagati* (*i.e.*, passes into a degraded or fallen condition), and it is not released from this state till *Shrāddhas* have been duly performed in its name, and the objects of its desire dedicated to it with proper ritual. The same fate befalls those souls which do not receive the funeral *pindas* with the proper obsequies. Such fallen souls become ghosts and goblins,* and are to be found where water is, *i. e.*, near a well, a tank, or a river.[3]

Those who meet death by drowning become goblins, residing near the scene of their death, and are a source of danger to all who approach the water; for instance, in Monāpuri and Sāsai, there are two *ghunas* (mysterious watery pits) haunted by *bhuts* (ghosts) which take the lives of one or two buffaloes every year.[4] *Mātās* † and *Shankhinis* also haunt wells, springs, and tanks and either drown, or enter the persons of those who go near their resorts.

Persons who are possessed in this manner, can be freed by *bhuvas*,† who give them a magic thread to wear.[5]

There is a *vāv* called *Nīlkanth vāv* near Movaiya, in which a Pinjari (a female cotton-carder) is said to have been drowned, and to have been turned into a ghost, in which form she occasionally presents herself to the people.[6]

Another ghost haunts an old *vāv*, called Madhā, in Vadhwān and drowns one human being every third year as a victim. But a male spirit named *Kshetrapāl* resides in the *kotha* (or entrance) of the *vāv*, and saves those who fall near the entrance. A person is, however, sure to be drowned if he falls in any other part of the *vāv*.[7] A ghost also resides in the *vāv* at Hampar near Dhrāngadhrā and terrifies the people at times.[7]

The goddess Rainadevi resides in water, and is worshipped by virgins on the fifteenth day of the bright half of *Āshādh*, when they grow *javārās* (tender wheat-plants) in an earthen vessel and present them to her, remaining awake for the whole of the night to sing songs in her honour.[2]

Daryā-Pir, the patron of Luvānās (merchants) and Khārvās (sailors), resides in the sea ; and vows are observed in his honour by these people on the second day of the bright half of every month, when they pass a little water through his sieve.[8]

[1] The Shastri of Jetpur Pathashala. [2] Mr. K. D. Desai.

[3] D. K. Pandya, Dhhank; the Shastri of Jetpur Pathashala and the Schoolmaster of Limbdi Taluka.

[4] Mr. L. D. Mehta, Mota Devalia.

[5] The Schoolmaster of Limbdi Taluka and the Shastri of Jetpur Pathashala.

[6] The Schoolmaster of Movaiya. [7] N. M. Dave, Sānkā.

[8] The Schoolmaster of Kolki.

* There are several species of *bhuts* and *prets*—ghosts and goblins—thus, for instance, *Jalachar*, i. e., those who live in water ; *Agnichar*, i. e., those found in fire ; *Bhuchar*, i. e., those hovering on the earth ; *Gaganachar*, i. e., those moving in ethereal regions, *Manushyachar*, i. e., those moving among men ; *Khagachar* or those moving among birds, and *Pashuchar*, i. e., those living among beasts. N. D. Vora, Rajpara.

† *Vide* page 1.

It is well known that a drowning person clings fast to anyone who tries to save him, and endangers the lives of both himself and his saviour.[1] It is also believed by some people that the messengers of Varuna (the lord of all waters) seize those persons who bathe in a river earlier than the usual hour in the morning; and the act of saving a drowning person thus deprives Varuna of his victim, and brings down the wrath of that deity.[2]

Sometimes, for the sake of *moksha*, a person takes *samādhi* (*i. e.*, drowns himself with a religious motive) in a holy river, such as the Ganges or the Jumnā. In such a case the relatives and other persons refrain from interference, and do not try to rescue the person.[1]

When a well is to be dug, an expert is first called to select a likely spot on which to dig. A Brahman is then consulted as to the auspicious hour on which the work of digging should be commenced.[3] For this purpose, Tuesdays and those days on which the earth sleeps are to be avoided. The earth is supposed to be asleep on the following six days in every month, namely: the 1st, the 7th, the 9th, the 10th, the 14th and the 24th days following a *sankrānti* (*i. e.*, the day on which the sun crosses from one constellation to another). Excluding these days, a date is generally fixed on which the *Chandra-graha* (or the planet moon) is favourable to the constructor of the well.[4]

On the appointed day, the expert, the constructor of the well, the Brahman priest, and the labourers go to the place where the well is to be dug, and an image of the god Ganpati—the protector of all auspicious ceremonies—is first installed on the spot and worshipped with *panchāmrit*.*[5] A green coloured piece of *atlas* (silk cloth), about two feet long, is then spread on the spot, and a pound and a quarter of wheat, a cocoanut, betels, dates and copper coin are placed on it. A copper bowl containing some silver or gold coins and filled with water, is also placed there; the mouth of the bowl is covered with the leaves of the Ashoka tree (*Jinesia Asoka*) and a cocoanut is placed over the leaves. After this, the priest recites sacred hymns and asks his host to perform the *khāt*† ceremonies.[6] Among favourite offerings to Ganpati and the earth in the course of worship and in the performance of the *khāt* ceremonies are: curds, milk, honey, molasses, cocoanuts, *dhanā* (a kind of spices), leaves of *nāgarvel* (a kind of creeper) and red lac.[3] The expert who is called to choose a proper site for the well offers frankincense and a cocoanut to the spot, and lights a lamp thereon. After the *khāt* ‡ ceremonies are over, the host distributes sugar or molasses among the by-standers, and offers a sum of money to the expert, who usually refuses it, asking the host to spend it in charity. Those who accept money give away a part of it in alms to the poor.[3]

Sometimes, to secure the unobstructed completion of the work, the god Ganpati and the goddess Jaladevi are installed and worshipped daily, till water appears in the well.[4] Some people, however, install the goddess Jaladevi after the appearance of water, when a stone is taken out from the bottom of the well and is plastered with red lead to represent the goddess and is ceremoniously worshipped. When the construction of the well is complete, *vāstu*, i. e., the ceremony in vogue after the completion of a new building, or *jalotsava* (the water-festival) is celebrated, Brahmans being entertained at a feast, with *dakshinā* given.[7]

[1] N. D. Vora, Rajpara.
[2] The Schoolmasters of Vanod and Kolki.
[3] D. K. Pandya, Dhhank.
[4] H. M. Bhatt, Ganod.
[5] The Schoolmasters of Dhhank and Pātanvāv.
[6] The Schoolmaster of Dadvi.
[7] The Shoolmasters of Ganod and Dadvi.
* A mixture of milk, curds, ghi, honey and sugar.
† *Vide* page 29.
‡ Rich persons use silver or golden spades and hoes when turning up the first clod of earth.

The water of the Krukalas well in the island of Shankhodwār is believed to cure fever and diseases caused by morbid heat. A draught of the water of the Gomukhi-gangā near Girnār, makes one proof against an attack of cholera.[1]

The water of a *gozarā* well (*i. e.*, a well which is polluted on account of a person being drowned in it) cures children of bronchitis and cough.[2]*

There is a well near Ramdorana, of which the water is effective against cough,[3] and the water of the Bhamaria well near Vasāwad possesses the same virtue.[4]

The water of the Mrigi *kund* near Junāgadh remedies leprosy.[3]

The Pipli well near Zālāwād and the Detroja-vāv near Kolki are well-known for the stimulative effect of their waters on the digestion.[5]

If a dark stone is found in the course of digging a well, the water of that well is believed to have medicinal properties.[6]

The birth of a child under the *mul nakshatra* endangers the life of its father: but the misfortune is averted if the child and its parents bathe in water drawn from one hundred and eight wells.[1] Such water, if swallowed, is said to cure *sanipāt* or delirium.[7]

In the island of Shial there is a *vāv* called Thān-*vāv*, where mothers, who cannot suckle their children for want of milk, wash their bodices. When they afterwards wear these bodices, these are believed to be able to cause the due secretion of milk.[8]

The most famous of the sacred lakes are Pampa†, Bindu‡, Pushkar and Sāmbhar near Ajmere, Mān-sarovar near Bahucharāji, Nārāyan-sarovar in Cutch, Rāvanrhad in the Himālayas, and Rāmarhad. The following popular myth is related about Mān-sarovar.

Two kings once agreed that the two children that should first be born to them should marry each other. But it happened that both the kings had daughters. One of them, however, concealed the fact, and gave out that the child born to him was a son. So that when the children attained a marriageable age, they were married to each other according to the agreement.

But the wife found out the secret when she went to stay with her supposed husband, and disclosed it to her parents, who invited the counterfeit son-in-law to their house with the object of ascertaining the truth. The alleged son, however, suspected the design and fled, with a mare and a bitch. On arriving near Mān-sarovar, the animals went into the lake in order to refresh themselves, when there was an immediate transformation; and the bitch and the mare came out a horse and a dog. On observing this miracle, their mistress followed their example and was also turned into a male. The story is still sung by girls in a *garabi* (song) during the *Navarātra* holidays.[9]

There is a belief that the ancient golden city of Dwārkā, the capital of god Krishna, still exists in the sea, although it is invisible to the eyes of mortals.[6] A story is told of a man named Pipo Bhagat, who, once perceiving a golden bowl floating in the sea, plunged into the water and saw the golden palaces of Dwārkā and god Krishna resting therein. It is said that he returned with the tide and related his experience to several people.[10]

1 B. K. Dave, Kotda, Sangani.
2 The schoolmasters of Limbdi and Chhatrasa.
3 The Schoolmaster of Upleta.
4 The schoolmaster of Mota Devalia.
5 The Schoolmaster of Kolki.
6 D. K. Pandya, Dhhank.
7 The Schoolmaster of Pātanvāv.
8 G. K. Bhatt, Songadh.
9 Jairam Vasaram, Jodia.
10 The Shastri of Jetpur, Pathashala.

* It is a common practice to bring a small circular piece of an earthen vessel from the neighbourhood of such a well and to hang it by a piece of string round the neck of a child to cure it of *hadakhi-udharas* or strong cough.—K. D. Desai.

† Pampa is described in the *Rāmāyana* as being situated in the Dandaka forest, *i. e.*, in the Deccan. and seems to be the modern Hampi in Bellary district.

‡ Perhaps the one in Sidhpur—K. T. G.

Similarly, the golden Lanka of Rāvan is still believed to exist under the sea, ruled over by Bibhishan, the brother of Rāvan, and visible only to the eyes of saints and holy persons.[1] It is a common belief that the nether regions are inhabited by a species of semi-divine beings, half men and half serpents, called Nāgs, who possess magnificent palaces under the water.[2] The story of Kāliya Nāg, who resided at the bottom of the Jumnā and was driven from that place by Krishna, is well known.[3] There are a number of mythological traditions in the *Purānas* of kings and princes having visited these palaces in watery regions, and of their having brought back beautiful *Nāgakanyās* (daughters of Nāgs) therefrom.[4] For instance, Arjuna married a *Nāgakanyā* named Ulupi when he was living in exile with his brothers. He also stayed for some time with the Nāgs.

Ghosts and demons sometimes inhabit palaces under the water. Deep waters, unfrequented by men, are the favourite resorts of such beings.[5]

The god Varuna resides in the waters, and is said to have once carried off Nand (the adoptive father of Krishna) to his watery abode, for having bathed in the Jumnā before dawn.[3]

Kālindi, the daughter of the king of the Kalingas, practised religious austerities in a palace under the waters of the Jumnā with the object of securing a suitable husband. Krishna, on being informed of this by Arjuna, went to the place and married her.[6]

There is a story in the *Purānas* that a king, named Nandrāj, used to bury his treasures in the sea with the assistance of a *mani* (jewel) which furnished a safe passage through the water. The *mani* was in the end burnt by the queen of Nandrāj and the treasure still lies hidden in the waters of the sea.[7]

It is narrated in the fourth chapter of *Bhāgvat-purān* that the ten thousand sons of Prachetas used to reside in palaces built under water.[8]

Mountains are held to be sacred in a variety of circumstances; thus, some are valued for possessing medicinal drugs : some are revered as the birthplaces of the gods, or as the residences of saints : some for possessing many *tīrthas* (holy spots) : some because they were visited by Rāma or the Pāndavas : some serve as guardians of the four quarters : and some contain the sources of holy rivers.

Both the important ranges of the Presidency, the Sahyādri and the Sātpuda, are subjects of veneration in the popular mind. The Himālayas, the Vindhyā Mountains, and the Nilgiris command special respect. Other sacred mountains are Girnār and Shetrunja in Kāthiāwār, Mount Ābu, Pāvāgad near Baroda, Brahmagiri Ārāsur, Tryambak near Nasik, Koyalo, Govardhan near Mathurā, Revatāchal near Dwārka, and Hinglaj in Sind.

It is said that in ancient times there were deep miry ditches where Girnār and Ābu stand at present. One day a cow belonging to the sage Vasishtha fell into one of them and was found by Kacha, the son of Brihaspati, after a long search. When the incident was brought to the notice of Vasishtha, he requested Meru (a mythical mountain) to send his two sons Girnār and Ābu to occupy and fill the ditches. Girnār required sixty-eight *tīrthas* to accompany him; and the boon was granted by the gods.[9]

---

1 The Schoolmasters of Dadvi and Kolki.
2 D. K. Pandya, Dhhank.
3 H. M. Bhatt, Ganod.
4 The Schoolmaster of Kolki.
5 Jairam Vasaram, Jodia.
6 The Schoolmaster of Khirasara.
7 N. M. Dave, Sānkā.
8 The Deputy Educational Inspector of Hālār.
9 The Schoolmasters of Dhhank, Moti Parabadi, and Luvaria.

Girnār is one of the seven great mountains which once possessed wings.[1]* It is also known as the place where the sage Dattātraya performed religious austerities.[2] The place is so holy that any person dying within a radius of twelve *gaus*† from it is believed to attain *moksha*.[3] A visit to the temples on Girnār absolves one from all sins; and taking a turn round Girnār and Shetrunja is said to bring good fortune.[4] Bhagwān manifests himself to those who ascend the Bhairavajaya summit on Girnār. There is a rock on this mountain of which it is said that those who cast themselves from it directly attain heaven.[5]

Pāvāgad is known for the temple of Mahākāli Mātā. It is said that King Patai once propitiated her by austerities, and on being desired to demand a boon, asked the goddess to accompany him to his palace. The goddess was highly incensed at this request, and promptly destroyed him.[5]

Hanūmān, the monkey-god, once promised to take the Mountain Govardhan to meet Rāma. It is well known how the monkey allies of Rāma constructed a bridge of rocks across the sea to Laṇkā, and how Hanūmān supplied the requisite material by fetching huge mountains. Whilst engaged on this work, he was one day carrying the Govardhan mountain to the site of the bridge, when Rāma issued an order that all monkeys who were fetching mountains should deposit their burdens at the spot where they stood at the moment of the order. Hanūmān could not disobey the order of his lord, and he had accordingly to drop the Govardhan mountain near Mathurā. In order to fulfil Hanūmān's promise, however, Vishnu held the mountain over his head for seven days, at the time of his Krishna incarnation.[5]

It is said that the inhabitants of the districts round Govardhan formerly revered and adored Indra. But Krishna condemned this custom, and introduced the worship of Govardhan. Indra was exasperated at this conduct, and poured tremendous rains on Gokal in order to drown Krishna and his followers. But Krishna held up the Govardhan mountain on his little finger and sheltered all his people under its cover. The mountain was supported in this manner for seven days, by the end of which the rains subsided and Indra confessed himself vanquished. Even now Vaishnavas form an image of Govardhan out of mud and worship it on the *Janmāshtamī* day (*i.e.*, the eighth day of the dark half of Shrāvan).[6]

The Oshama Hill near Pātanvāv (in the jurisdiction of Gondal) is noted for the beautiful temples of Tapakeshwar Mahādev, and Mātari Mātā. It is said that Bhīma‡ the second of the five Pāndavas, first met the giantess Hidimbā, on this hill.[7] The charcoal-like stones which are dug out in numbers from this hill are believed by the people to have been blackened by the blood of the giant Hidimb, the brother of Hidimbā who was killed by Bhīma.[8]

[1] The Schoolmaster of Chhatrasa.
[2] The Schoolmaster of Lilapur.
[3] The Shastri of Jetpur, Pathashala.
[4] The Schoolmaster of Kolki.
[5] The Schoolmaster of Lilapur.
[6] The Schoolmasters of Kotda-Sangani, Vanod, and Luvaria.
[7] The Schoolmaster of Ganod.
[8] The Schoolmaster of Pātanvāv.

* All mountains once possessed wings and caused much havoc when they flew about. So Indra clipped their wings with his thunderbolt and they are lying motionless since.—K. D. Desai.

† Three-fourths of a *gāu*=one mile.

‡ After the conflagration of Lakshabhuvan, the Pāndavas escaped to the Hidimba forest. There one day, in his excursions, Bhīma came across the giantess Hidimbā sitting on a see-saw. On her offering to marry him if he succeeded in swinging her see-saw, he is said to have swung it so high in the skies that she could even see the stars during daytime.—K. D. Desai.

Mount Shetrunja (or Shatrunjaya) possesses numerous Jain shrines and attracts thousands of pilgrims every year. The hearts of all pilgrims are believed to be purified from the moment they come within six miles of the mountain.[1]

Mount Abu possesses the temple of Ambā Mātā where Krishna's hair was clipped for the first time.[2] Tryambak is known for the temple of Tryambakeshwar and the source of the holy Godāvari.[3] About Revatāchal, it is said that the mountain was golden in ancient times.[4] In the Vindhya Mountains is situated the famous temple of Omkār Mandhātā.[5] The hermitage of Kākbhushundi in the Nilgiris was visited by Rāma when he listened to the religious stories read out by that sage. The sage Agatsya also is said to have resided in these mountains.[6]

The temple of Hinglaj stands on a hill, which is situated at a distance of eighteen days' journey by road from Karachi. The Mātā is ministered to by a Musalman and the place is mostly visited by *Atits, Bāvās, Khatris, Chhipās, Mochis*, and other low-caste Hindus. On occasions the doors of the temple spontaneously open, and after the devotees have visited the *Mātā*, they again shut in the same mysterious manner.[5]

As the abode of Shiva and as containing the sources of the holiest of rivers, the Himālayas are the most sacred of all mountains, and possess many holy places of pilgrimage, such as Badrinārāyan, Kedārnāth, Hardwār, etc. Badrinārāyan is the favourite resort of those who have relinquished the world and who only wish to meditate on the Divine Being. The sages Nara and Nārāyan are said to have peformed religious austerities in this place, and eighty-eight thousand *rishis* (sages) are believed to be similarly occupied there to-day. Owing to the excessive cold, the place is extremely difficult to reach. Pilgrims carry burning hearths with them to protect themselves against cold. Besides, it is necessary to cross the Pathar-nadi (or stony river), of which the water, if touched, turns one into stone. The method of crossing this river is to suspend *sikāns* or slings above its water and to swing from one sling to another.[7]

A hill called Swargārohan is believed to be twenty miles to the north of Badrikedārnāth and is said to lead to heaven. In ancient times the Pāndavas had repaired to this place in order to do penance for the sin of having killed their kinsmen in the Great War. But when they tried to ascend to heaven by the Swargārohan Hill, only Yudhishthir and his faithful dog were able to reach their goal: the rest were frozen in the snow.[7]

Mount Kailāsa, the abode of Shiva, is supposed to be situated in the northern part of the Himālayas. The mountain is described as always covered with verdure and full of beautiful gardens and of palaces made of jewels, with roads paved with golden dust and *sphatika-mani* (crystal stone).[7] It is said that Rāvan, the king of Lankā, once uprooted this mountain and held it on the palm of his hand, in order to display his prowess. The demon Bhasmāsur, who was enamoured of the goddess Pārvati, is said to have performed the same feat in order to frighten Shiva.[3]

Another mythical mountain is Meru, which is supposed to occupy the centre of the earth.* The sun, the moon, and all the planets revolve round this mountain, and it therefore plays an important part in the causation of day and night. For night falls on one side of the earth when the sun goes

[1] The Shastri of Jetpur Pathashala.

[2] The Schoolmaster of Lilapur.

[3] The Schoolmaster of Ganod.

[4] R. B. Dave.

[5] The Schoolmaster of Jodia.

[6] The Schoolmaster of Luvaria.

[7] M. M. Rana, Rajkot.

* The earth is believed to be flat like a dish and to consist of seven large islands, which are compared to the seven petals of a lotus.

to the other side of Meru; and the day begins when the sun emerges from that side of the mountain. Meru is sixty-eight thousand *yojans** in height, and penetrates the earth to the depth of sixteen thousand *yojans*. Its eastern side appears white, the southern is yellow, the western is black, and the northern red. The mountain is also believed to consist of gold and gems. The Ganges, in her fall from the heavens, is said to have descended first on the top of this mountain and then to have flowed in four streams in four directions. The southern stream is known as the Ganges; the northern, in Tartary, is called Bhadrasoma; the eastern is the same as the Sitā; and the western is named Chax or the Oxus. The top of this mountain is believed to be inhabited by gods, *gandharvas* (celestial musicians) and *rishis* (sages).[1] According to the *Yoga-vāsishtha*, there is a *kalpa-vriksha*† on the Lalmani summit of Meru, where a *rishi* named Bhushundkāk is engaged in devotional prayers since time immemorial.[2] The Purānas declare that Vaivaswat Manu, the first man, resided near Meru, and that his descendants migrated to Ayodhyā to found there a kingdom which was afterwards ruled over by Rāma.[1]

It is believed by some people that mountain-tops are inhabited by a class of recluses, called Aghori-bāvās, who devour human beings.[3] The Kālikā hill near Girnār is believed to be frequented by *Joganis* (female harpies) who take the lives of visitors to the hill, and it is said that none who visits the place is ever known to return.[4] Persons who visit the temple of Kālikāmātā on Mount Girnār always lose one of their party, who falls a victim to the goddess.[5]

The changes in the seasons are attributed by some to Brahma, Vishnu, and Mahesha (Shiva), the gods of the Hindu Trinity. Brahma sends down the rains and produces corn, grass, etc., Vishnu protects and nourishes the harvests in winter, and Shiva causes the heat of the summer.[6] There is also a belief that these three gods go down in turns to the *pātāl* (nether regions) and stay there for four months. Vishnu descends on the eleventh day of the bright half of Āshādh, and on that day the rainy season begins. When Vishnu comes up and Shiva takes his place, people experience the cold of winter: but as this god always keeps a *dhuni*‡ burning near him, the waters under the surface of the earth, such as those in the wells, remain hot during this period. Such waters are cooled when Shiva returns and Brahma goes down to the *pātāl*: but the return of Shiva causes summer on the earth.[7]

According to another belief, the sequence of the seasons is controlled by the sun-god.[8] There are six *ritus* or seasons; and the changes in the *ritus* depend upon the position of the sun in the twelve *rāshis* or signs of the Zodiac.[9] Each *ritu* lasts for a period of two months, during which time the sun travels through two *rāshis*. *Vasant-ritu* is the period which the sun takes to pass through the *Min* (Pisces) and *Mesha* (Aries) *rāshis*. *Grishma-ritu* corresponds to the time during which the sun passes through *Vrishabha* (Taurus) and *Mithun* (*Gemini*). During *Varshā-ritu* the sun moves through the signs *Karka* (Cancer) and *Sinha* (Leo), and during *Sharad-ritu* through *Kanyā* (Virgo) and *Tulā* (Libra). *Hemant-ritu* is the time which the sun takes to travel through

[1] M. M. Rana, Rajkot.
[2] D. K. Pandya, Dhhank.
[3] The Schoolmaster of Limbdi.
[4] The Schoolmaster of Upleta.
[5] The Schoolmasters of Dhhank and Sānkā.
[6] The Schoolmaster of Zinzuwādā.
[7] The Schoolmaster of Mendarda.
[8] The Schoolmasters of Dhhank and Gondal Taluka.
[9] The Shastri of Jetpur,
* One *yojan*=eight miles.
† A magic tree, supposed to grant all desires.
‡ Fire used for the purposes of smoking.

Vrishchika (Scorpio) and *Dhanu* (Sagittarius). *Shishir-ritu* occurs when the sun stands in the *Makar* (Capricornus) and *Kumbha* (Aquarius) *rāshis*.[1]

Indra (the god of rain), Varuna (the lord of all waters), Vāyu (the god of wind), Agni (the god of fire), and the moon-god are also believed by some to have power over the seasons.[2]

The belief is as old as the *Vedas* that demons sometimes obstruct the fall of rain, and confine the waters of the clouds. It is Indra who fights with them and breaks through their castles by means of his thunderbolt, sending down showers of rain for the benefit of his worshippers. So, whenever there is an unusual drought, people still invoke the aid of this god, and celebrate a festival in his honour, called *Ujjani* or *Indramahotsava*. *Homas** are performed to propitiate the god, and Brahmans are entertained at a feast. Sometimes the festival is celebrated outside the village, where people go in large parties to dine together. The usual dish on such an occasion is *Meghlādu* or sweet balls of wheat-flour fried in *ghi*.

Another favourite ceremony supposed to cause rain to fall is the submersion of the image of Shiva in water, by blocking up the *khāl* or passage in the *Shiva-linga* by which water poured over the image usually runs off.[2] This ceremony is known as *Jala-jātrā*. *Rudrābhisheka*, or the ceremony of pouring water in a constant stream over the image of Shiva for eleven consecutive days and nights, is sometimes performed with the same object.[3]

Sometimes the assistance of Shringhi *rishi* is invoked to bring about a fall of rain. The *rishi* is installed in water, mantras are recited, and prayers are offered before a sacrificial fire. This ceremony, called *Parjanya-shānti*, is said to have been performed within recent years in Bombay, and to have been successful in bringing rain.[4]

It is also said that rainfall can be caused by singing a song or a sacred hymn to the *malār* tune. There is a tradition that the well-known saint Narsinha Mehta once sang this tune on the occasion of the celebration of the first pregnancy of his daughter, and the performance was immediately followed by a shower of rain. Rain, which is brought down in this manner, can be put a stop to by singing to a different tune.[5]

Low-caste women have recourse to the following expedient to bring rain. Five or six of them place a quantity of muddy earth on a wooden stool, which is carried by one of them. The lump of mud is covered with leaves of the *Gidotān* or *Tindotān* creeper, and is called *mehulo* or *meghalo*. The whole party then sing songs, and visit every house in the village. A bowl of water is poured over the *mehulo* and the women receive some corn for their trouble.[6]

Some believe that when the worship of the village-gods is neglected and when the people grow corrupt, ill-treat the saints and are given to the killing of cows and Brahmans, Yama, the God of Death, directs his colleagues, Indra and Varuna, to threaten the world with a drought. The rainfall returns only when the people revert to righteous ways, and after Indra and Varuna have been conciliated by offerings.

The lower classes of the people believe a prolonged cessation of rain to be due to the wrath of local minor deities, aroused by the neglect of their worship. In such a contingency, therefore, they prepare *bāklan*† of

[1] K. D. Desai.
[2] N. D. Vora, Rajpara.
[3] D. K. Pandya, Dhhank.
[4] The Schoolmaster of Ganod.
[5] The Schoolmaster of Upleta.
[6] The Deputy Educational Inspector of Gohelwad and K. D. Desai.
* Offering oblations to gods by throwing *ghi* into the consecrated fire.
† A flat round loaf, about two to four inches in diametre, prepared from the flour of *uḍad*.

udad (lentils), *lāpsi*,* *vadān*† and other dishes, and offer them to the local gods for their propitiation.[1]

To stop an incessant fall of rain, people often observe the *Āladrā* vow. The *patel* or headman issues a proclamation that on a particular day none should cook, or churn whey, or fetch water, or wash clothes, or attend to any of the multifarious household duties; but that all should pass the day in prayer. A complete cessation from toil in favour of earnest devotion to divine powers are the peculiar features of this vow. People do not abstain from food: but food must be prepared on the previous day. If the rains do not cease in spite of this vow, but threaten the village with inundation, the headman leads a procession to the confines of the village and makes an offering to the waters.[2]

In some places a spinning wheel, sometimes specially constructed of human bones,[3] is turned by a naked person in the reverse direction to the usual one, with the object of causing the cessation of immoderate rainfall.[4]

A cessation of rains is also believed to be brought about by offering an oblation to the god Kasatia, and by the observance of the vow called *Kasatia gānth* (or tying the knot of Kasatia). The vow lasts for three weeks, and those who observe it do not partake of anything except rice[5] (or, according to others, *jirān*, a kind of spice[6]).

Some persons attribute a heavy fall of rain to the wrath of Indra, and offer ceremonious prayers to appease that god.[7] In some places people engage the services of magicians to restrain the fall of rain.[8] Farmers sometimes brand the rain by casting burning sparks upon it in order to stop an incessant fall.[9] Vows in honour of *samudra* (the ocean) are also observed with the same object.[3]

In the changing circumstances of life, women more readily have recourse to religious vows for the fulfilment of their wishes than men. This fondness of women for vows has brought into vogue a number of *vrats* or religious observances which are practised by women only. *Gangigor* or *Ganāgor*, *Vat-Sāvitri*, *Molākat*, *Goutrāt*, *Alavana* or *Alunda*, *Eva-vrat*, *Tulsi-vrat* *Umā masheshwar-vrat*, and *Surya-vrat* are instances of such vows.[1] The *Molākat-vrat* is observed by virgins from the eleventh to the fifteenth day of the bright half of *Āshādh*.[10] The *Goutrāt-vrat* is believed to secure male progeny, as well as long life to the husband. It is observed on the fourth day of the dark half of *Shrāvana*, on which day women fast till the evening, and then take food after worshipping a cow.[11] The object of the *Eva-vrat* (or *Jiva-vrat*) is to secure eternal exemption from widowhood, the day for this vow being the last day of *Āshādh*. It is then necessary to observe a fast till the evening; and the only food allowed is a preparation of wheat, taken at nightfall.[12]

On the fourth day of the dark half of *Shrāvan*, women observe a *vrat* called *Bol-choth*. In the morning the woman worships

[1] K. D. Desai.

[2] M. M. Rana, Rajkot.

[3] The Deputy Educational Inspector of Gohelwad.

[4] D. K. Pandya, Dhhank.

[5] The Shastri of Jetpur Pāthashālā, and the Schoolmaster of Vanod.

[6] The Schoolmaster of Mota Dewalia. According to him, the same vow is also observed to bring about a rainfall.

[7] The Schoolmaster of Ganod.

[8] The Schoolmaster of Vanod.

[9] The Shastri of Jetpur Pāthashālā.

[10] The Schoolmaster of Jodia.

[11] The Schoolmaster of Zinzuwâdâ.

[12] The Schoolmaster of Mendarda.

* Coarse wheat-flour fried in *ghi* and sweetened with sugar or molasses.

† Bean-flour, generally of gram or peas, is allowed to remain in water with spices, until the paste acquires a sufficient degree of consistency, when it is rolled into small biscuit-sized balls and fried in sweet oil.

a cow and her calf (which must both be of the same colour), applies a little cotton to the horns of the cow, and makes an auspicious mark on the foreheads of both with red lac. She then places an offering of betel and rice before the cow, takes four turns round the pair, and whispers in the ears of the cow the words *tārun satya mārun vritya* (your truth and my devotion). A Brāhman then recites the legend of the *vrat.**

After narrating this story, the Brahman takes the betel and other things placed before the cow. The woman then returns home and takes food for the first time during that day, the meal consisting of loaves of bājrā-flour and some preparation of *mag* (*phaselus mungo*). Some women take *ghi* and *khir* : but any preparation of cow's milk is strictly forbidden. Similarly, there is a prohibition against using things which have been cut by a knife or scissors.[1]

The worship of the goddess Rāndal is a favourite *vrat* with Gujarati women. A bower is erected for the installation of the goddess, and a *bājat* or a wooden stool is placed therein. A piece of fine cloth is spread on the *bājat*, and a figure is drawn in seeds of corn. A *kalasio* or bowl, with a cocoanut on it, is placed over the figure. The cocoanut has two eyes painted on it in black collyrium and a nose in red lac, and is decorated with rich clothes and ornaments to represent the goddess Rāndal. Ghi lamps are kept constantly burning before the goddess for three consecutive days and nights. An invitation is sent to the neighbouring women, who bring offerings of ghi to the goddess, and dance in a group at night to the accompaniment of melodious *garabis* (songs).[2] Sometimes, if a child is ill, or some misfortune is apprehended, *gorānis*, *i.e.*, a certain number of unmarried girls and unwidowed women, are invited to a feast in honour of Rāndal.

On the *Nāgapanchami* day, *i.e.*, the 5th day of the bright half of *Shrāvan*,† women draw an image of a *nāg* (cobra), and worship it with sprouts of *bājrā*. In some places it is the custom to avoid all food but *khichedi*‡ on this day.

The *wad* (the banyan tree) is worshipped on the first day of the dark half of *Shrāvan.* On that day the woman wears a necklace of fifteen leaves of this tree and prepares a dish called *navamuthium.*§ A *dorā* or piece of string is also worn on the person to ward off evil.[3]

Rishi-panchami,‖ *Gauri-pujan*, *Shitalāi-pujan*, *Shili-sātem* are holidays observed only by women. On the *Rishi-panchami* day only *niar*¶ rice is allowed to those who observe the *vrat.*[4]

Besides the observance of *vrats*, there are other ceremonies, auspicious as well as inauspicious, in which women alone can take part. Only women are concerned with all those ceremonies which are gone through on the birth of a child. On the twelfth day after birth, a name is given to the child by its aunt The ceremony of making an auspicious mark on the throne of a king is performed by an unwidowed woman or an unmarried girl.[5]

1 The Schoolmaster of Jodia.

2 The Schoolmasters of Vanod and Kolki.

3 The Schoolmaster of Surel.

4 The Schoolmaster of Jasdan.

5 Mr. M. M. Rana, Rajkot.

* The story tells how a woman and her daughter-in-law, intending to observe this vow, killed and cooked a calf by mistake ; covered with shame, they locked themselves up in their house, and refused admission to the neighbours, to whom they confessed their crime. On searching for the remains of the calf, the neighbours discovered that it had been miraculously restored to life.—R. E. E.

† Some observe the *Nāgapanchami* on the fifth day of the bright half of Bhādrapad.

‡ A mixture of rice and pulse treated with spices and cooked in water.

§ A preparation of nine handfuls of wheat.

‖ *Vide* Page 24.

¶ A kind of rice grown without ploughing.

At the time of a marriage, women make the auspicious mark on the forehead of the bridegroom and carry a *lāman-divo** to fetch *ukardi.** For nine days preceding the date of marriage the bride and the bridegroom are besmeared with *pithi* or yellow turmeric powder, when auspicious songs are recited by a party of women invited to witness the ceremony. When the bridegroom reaches the entrance of the marriage bower, he is welcomed there by his mother-in-law, who carries him on her hip to his seat in the marriage booth.[1]

It is necessary to make certain marks on the corpse of a woman, and these marks are made by women only.[2] Similarly, women alone take part in the ceremony of getting a widow's hair shaved on the ninth day after her husband's death.[3]

The *Shāstras* have enjoined the worship of certain higher-grade deities, and have prescribed certain ceremonials for the purpose. But women are not authorised to make use of these ceremonies. The reason is that the *Shāstras* regard women as inferior to men and do not grant them the privileges given to the latter. They are not allowed to learn the *Vedas* nor can the *Gāyatri-mantra* be taught to them. The result is that women are not qualified to perform the ceremonial worship of such higher-grade deities as Vishnu, Shiva, Durgā, Ganpati, and Hanumān;[4] similarly the sacrificial rites of *Vishnuyāg, Shaktiyāg, Ashvamedha, Rājayajna,* and *Gāyatri-purashcharan* can only be performed by men.[5]

It is the duty of men only to worship the *shami* tree (*prosopis spicegera*) on the *Dasarā* day, and the *Hutāshani* fire on the day of *Holi.*[5]

Women are not allowed to worship the god Kārtikey, who is said to shun women, and to have pronounced a curse against all who visit his image.[5]

The fifteenth day of the bright half of *Chaitra* is the anniversary of the birth of Hanumān, and a *vrat* called *Hanumān-jayanti* is observed on this day. This *vrat,*[6] as well as the *Ganesh-chaturthi-vrat*[7] are meant only for men.

The ceremonies of *Shrāddha*† and the *Baleva*[8] ceremonies can be performed by men only. The duty of giving *agni-sanskār*[1] to corpses, *i.e.*, of performing the necessary rites at a funeral, is also laid on men.

People who practise the art of attaining mastery over spirits and fiends, usually remain naked while they are engaged in the performance of their mysterious rites. There are many branches of this black art: for instance, *Māran,*[9] *Uchchātan,*[10] *Lamban, Vashīkaran,*[11] *Mohan,*[12] *Stambhan,*[13] *etc.*, and although the *meli vidyā* (sacrilegious art) is not held in respect by high-class Hindus, it is popular among the lower

[1] The Schoolmaster of Ganod.

[2] Mr. M. M. Rana, Rajkot.

[3] The Schoolmaster of Zaramā-Zāravā.

[4] The Schoolmaster of Kolki and the Head-Mistress of Rajkot Civil Station Girls' School.

[5] Mr. K. D. Desai.

[6] The Shastri of Jetpur Pāthashālā.

[7] The Schoolmaster of Surel.

[8] Mr. N. M. Dave, Sanka.

[9] The art of taking the life of a person by means of a magical process called *muth-māravi.* The victim of this process suddenly vomits blood and loses his life, unless the evil influence is counteracted by another sorcerer.—B. K. Dave, Kotda Sangani.

[10] Causing a person to leave his business by making him disgusted with it, by means of magical spells.

[11] The art of so influencing the conduct of a person as to bring him perfectly under control.

[12] Bewildering an enemy by means of magical charms.

[13] The suppression of any force or feeling by magical means.

* The mother of the bride, accompanied by other women who sing songs on the way, carries an iron lamp to the village-boundary, and from that place the party bring earth to erect the altars on which sacrificial fires are burnt. The lamp is called *lāman-divo* and the earth which is brought is called *ukardi.*—K. D. Desai.

† *Vide* question 10.

classes. There is a belief that knowledge of this art dooms a person to hell ; but it secures to those who master it a position of much importance, and therefore finds many followers. The art consists in the knowledge of certain mysterious incantations, which enable a person to influence the spirits and to bring about certain results through their agency. Not only has every person when learning this art, to remain naked, but all those who make *prayogas* or experiments in it afterwards must observe the same precaution. The night of *Kāli-chaudas* or the 14th day of the dark half of *Āshvin*, is considered to be the most favourable time for the *sādhan* or accomplishment of this secret art of remaining naked.[1] On this day, it is the custom of those who exercise the art, to go stripped to a cemetery in the dead of night, and to cook food in a human skull as an offering to the spirits residing in the neighbourhood. On the same night, some sorcerers, after stripping themselves, are said to ride round the village on some mysterious conveyance.[2]

A practice is noted among low-class people of performing a *sādhana* before the goddess Jhāmpadi for the sake of progeny. The man who performs the *sādhana*, has first to go naked to a cemetery on a Sunday night, and to fetch therefrom the ashes of a corpse. At the time of the *sādhana*, the man takes his seat on a corpse, fills a *madaliun* or hollow bracelet with the ashes brought from the cemetery, and puts it on his arm above the elbow [3]

Dhobis, *Mālis*, *Vālands* and other low-caste people remain naked while worshipping Bhairav.[4] In the performance of the *anushthān* (propitiation) of such deities as Kāl-Bhairav,[5] Batuk,[5] Mani,[6] Griva,[6] *etc.*, the devotees keep their persons uncovered. The worshippers of the goddess Jakshani also remain naked when they attend upon her.[7]

Persons who practise the art of curing men from the effects of serpent-bites by means of incantations, have to sit naked under water in order to gain efficacy for their *mantras*.[4]

Followers of the *Devi-panth*, *Shakti-panth* and *Aghori-panth* sects remain naked while worshipping or offering victims to their gods.[8] *Vāma-mārgis* worship a nude image of the goddess *Digambarā*.[3]

The hook-shaped instrument, known as *ganeshio*, which is used by thieves in boring a hole through the walls of a house, is sometimes prepared by a blacksmith and his wife on the night of *Kāli-chaudas*, both being naked at the time. Instruments prepared in this fashion are believed to secure success for the thief, who scrupulously sets aside the first booty acquired by the help of the *ganeshio* for the blacksmith as a reward for his services. He does not grudge the reward however large the booty may be.[2]

In making dice according to the directions of *Ramalashāstra*, the workers should remain naked.[7]

There is a belief that granulations in the eyes of a child are cured if the maternal uncle fetches naked the beads of the *Arani* tree, and puts a circlet of them round the neck of the child.[9]

If a person uncovers himself on hearing the screech of an owl, and then ties and unties seven knots in a piece of string, repeating the process twenty-one times, the piece of string is believed to possess the virtue of curing *Taria Tāv* or periodical fever.[10] Another remedy for the same ailment is to go to a distance of three miles from the village and there to eat food which has been cooked in a state of nudity.[1]

[1] Mr. K. D. Desai.
[2] The Schoolmaster of Ganod.
[3] Mr. N. M. Dave, Sānkā.
[4] The Schoolmaster of Moti Murad.
[5] Mr. B. K. Dave, Kota Sangani.
[6] Mr. N. D. Vora, Rajpara.
[7] Mr. D. K. Pandya, Dhhank.
[8] The Schoolmasters of Dhhank and Songadn.
[9] The Deputy Educational Inspector of Gohelwad.
[10] The Schoolmasters of Upleta and Aman.

In the preparation of Nargudikalpa* or Gujakalpa*, some drugs have to be procured by a naked person.[2]

It is considered meritorious by some persons to rise early in the morning and to bathe naked on the Makar Sankrānti day.[3]

A Brahman boy must be naked at the time of the peformance of his thread investiture ceremony. After the ceremony, the maternal uncle of the boy presents garments to him, which he thereupon puts on.[4]

In Gujarat, for the most part, the people seem to be unacquainted with the belief that certain stones possess the virtue of influencing the rain. Some persons however attribute this quality to the stones on such sacred mounts as Girnār, Ābu, and Pāvāgadh.[5] There is a point called Tonk, on mount Girnār, of which it is said that rain is certain to fall whenever anyone succeeds in climbing it.[6] There is also a common belief that *arasi* marble if heated has influence over rain.[7]

It is a common practice to submerge the image† of Shiva in water with the object of bringing rain. Similarly the image† of the goddess Harshadh is sometimes bathed when rain is desired.[8] The *bhuva* or the *bhui*, *i.e.*, the male and the female attendants of the goddess are at the same time given a bath, and an offering of *Khir*‡ is made to the goddess.[8]

There are two goals which a pious Hindu tries to attain by leading a life of purity and virtue, *viz.*, (i) *moksha* or final emancipation, merging into the Eternal Spirit, and (ii) *swarga* (heaven or paradise) where meritorious persons enjoy pure pleasures unalloyed by earthly cares. The stars are the spirits of so many righteous persons who are translated to *swarga* for their good actions, and are endowed with a lustre proportionate to their individual merits. But every moment of enjoyment in *swarga* diminishes the store of merit: and those whose whole merit is thus exhausted, on receiving their proportionate share of pleasures, must resume their worldly existence. The Bhagavad-gītā says: "क्षीणे पुण्ये मर्त्यलोकं विशन्ति" *i.e.*, "they enter the mortal world when their merit is expended." Meteors are believed to be spirits of this description who fall from their position as stars, to live again on this earth.[9]

Another explanation of meteors is that they are the sparks produced when the *vimāns* (or vehicles) of celestial people clash against each other.[10]

Meteors are also held to be the *agār* or *charak* (*i.e.*, excreta) dropped either by a curious water-bird,[2] or by Garud, the favourite eagle, and vehicle of Vishnu,[11] or by a fabulous bird Anal.[12] The latter is said to fly at an immeasurable height from the surface of the earth, and to take food only once a day.[12] It is almost impossible to catch the *charak* when it falls to earth: but if ever it can be secured, the application of it to the eyes of a blind man will restore his eyesight. It also furnishes an effective remedy for leprosy, and gives a golden lustre to the body of a person suffering from that disease.[11]

Some declare that meteors are stars which fall owing to the curse of Indra, and subsequently assume the highest human form on earth.[1]

---

1 Mr. Nandlal Kalidas, Chhatrasa.
2 The Schoolmaster of Āman.
3 The Deputy Educational Inspector of Halar.
4 Mr. K. D. Desai.
5 The Shastris of Jetpur and Bhayavadar.
6 The Shastri of Jetpur Pāthashālā.
7 The Schoolmaster of Chok.
8 The Schoolmaster of Pātanvāv.
9 Mr. K. D. Desai and the Schoolmaster of Dhhank.
10 The Schoolmaster of Jodia.
11 The Schoolmaster of Ganod.
12 The Schoolmasters of Dhhank and Ganod and the Mistress of Rajkot Civil Station Girls' School.

* Name of a medicinal preparation.

† But the virtue of influencing rain belongs to the *Shiva linga* and to the idol of Harshadh, not because they are made of any particular kind of stone, but because they represent certain deities.

‡ Rice cooked in milk and sweetened with sugar.

It is also said that the stars descend to earth in human form when sins accumulate in the celestial world.[1]

The influence of meteors on human affairs is treated at length in the *Varāhasanhitā*.[2] The phenomenon is popularly regarded as an evil omen : it is supposed to portend devastation by fire, an earthquake, a famine, an epidemic, danger from thieves, and storms at sea.[3] The appearance of a bright shooting star is supposed to foretell the death of some great man;[4] and on beholding one, it is customary to repeat the words 'Rām Rām'* several times.[5] A shower of meteors is believed to presage some civil commotion or a change in the ruling dynasties.

Some persons, however, regard the appearance of meteors as auspicious or baneful, according to the *mandal* or group of stars, from which they are seen to fall. Meteors from the *Vāyu-mandal*, (or the group of stars known by the name of Vāyu) portend the breaking out of an epidemic : those from *Varuna-mandal*, are believed to be favourable to human happiness; if they fall from *Indra-mandal*, they forebode danger to all kings; those from *Agni-mandal*, threaten war between nations.[6]

During the monsoons, rain is believed to fall in that direction in which a meteor is seen to shoot.[7] A meteor in the west is ominous to kings, and if it falls into the sea, it forebodes evil to the dwellers on earth.[8]

The appearance of a comet is believed to portend some dire calamity to the king and the nation.[8] It is said that if a heavenly body is seen, *chhogālo*,† *chhogālā* kings (*i.e.*, great and celebrated kings) are in danger of their lives.[9] A comet is also believed to threaten all tailed animals with destruction.[9]

1 The Schoolmaster of Sayala. Perhaps it is the accumulation of sin in this world that brings down the saints of heaven in human form. The earth is unable to bear too much sin and would soon come to an end if the balance between virtue and sin were not maintained. It is for this purpose that saints are born in this world and add to the store of merit on earth, by preaching righteousness to people and by leading a virtuous life.—K. D. Desai.

2 The Schoolmaster of Ganod. 3 The Schoolmasters of Rajpara, Vasawad, Upleta, and Khirasara.

4 The Schoolmasters of Pātanvāv and Sultānpur. 5 The Schoolmaster of Sultanpur.

6 The Schoolmaster of Charādwā. 7 The Deputy Educational Inspector of Gohelwad.

8 The Schoolmaster of Jodia. 9 The Schoolmaster of Songadh.

* It is an act of merit to repeat the name of Rām, the seventh incarnation of Vishnu. As the death of a righteous person is due to the growth of sin in this world, people utter the name of Rām in order to atone for that sin. The name is repeated as long as the shooting star is visible. Vaishnavas recite the name of Krishna.—K. D. Desai.

It is also said that the name of Rām or Krishna is repeated, because the falling star enters the Court of God Bhagwān.—The Schoolmaster of Lākhāpadar.

† (*I.e.*) with a tail. *Chhogā* is the end of a turban, which is allowed to hang down the back.

CHAPTER II.

HEROIC GODLINGS

SEVERAL stories, in addition to the legend of the Rāmāyana, are related of the birth of the god Hanumān. Dasharatha, king of Ayodhyā, being childless, once performed a sacrifice with the hope of thereby obtaining male issue. On the completion of the ceremony a heavenly being rose out of the sacrificial fire and presented the king with a celestial preparation, called *pāyas*, which he directed the king to give to his wives if he desired a son. The king divided the divine gift among his three queens ; but the share of one of them was snatched away by an eagle. It was dropped into the hands of Anjani; who was herself childless, and was practising austerities for the sake of obtaining son. On partaking of the *pāyas*, Anjanī conceived, and the son born to her was afterwards known as the god Hanumān.

Another story relates how Anjani was one of those persons who helped Indra in his evil designs on Ahalyā, the wife of Gautama. She had on that account been cursed by Gautama, and threatened with the birth of a fatherless child. To prevent the curse from taking effect, Anjanī buried herself in the ground as far as her waist, and began to observe religious austerities in the hope of propitiating Shiva. The latter was pleased with her devotion, and sent her a *mantra* through Nārada, who was ordered to deliver it in her ear. Vāyu, the god of wind, forced the *mantra* into her womb, and she conceived a son named Hanumān. This son had the form of a monkey, because, at the time of conception, Anjanī happened to behold a monkey, named Keshi, on a neighbouring tree.

Hanumān is a *chiranjīva*, *i.e.*, one of those seven * persons who are to live for ever and are therefore considered to be immortal. He is represented as possessed of miraculous strength, and his body is *vajramaya*, *i.e.*, adamantine. When Sītā was carried off by Rāvana, it was he who crossed the sea and brought news about her to Rāma. When Ahi and Mahi, two cousins of Rāvana, carried off Rāma and Lakshmana by magic and decided to offer them as victims to their favourite goddess Panoti, Hanumān entered the temple of Panoti, crushed her under his feet, and released Rāma and Lakshmana. Hence he is known as the conqueror of Panoti. After the death of Rāvana, Hanumān was left to guard the kingdom of Lankā, which was conferred by Rāma on Bibhīshana, the brother of Rāvana.[1]

Hanumān is an incarnation of one of the eleven Rudras,† [2] is a *brahmachāri* (*i.e.*, one who has taken the vow of celibacy), a powerful and benevolent deity, and a giver of many blessings. At the same time, he is considered to be the master-deity of all *bhuts*, *prets*, *pishāchas*, (ghosts, goblins, fiends), of *dākans* (witches), *shakans*, *chudel*, *vantri*, of the forty-nine *virs* (male

[1] K. D. Desai, from the answers of various Schoolmasters.
[2] The Schoolmaster of Vasavad.

* The following couplet mentions all of them :

अश्वत्थामा बलिर्व्यासो हनुमांश्च बिभीषणः ।
कृपः परशुरामश्च सप्तैते चिरजीविनः ॥

† A group of gods supposed to be inferior manifestations of Shiva, who is said to be the head of the group.

fiends), of the fifty-two *vetāls*, of *yakshas* and *yakshinis* and of all evil spirits in general, who are believed to obey his commands.[1] Vows are observed in honour of Hanumān if a person is possessed by a *bhut* or a *pret*, or if he is seared by a *jhapat* (sudden encounter) with a devil, or if he happens to step inadvertently within the *kundalan** of an *utār*. Persons who are possessed by evil spirits are exorcised by the *bhuvas* by reciting the *zanzira mantra* in honour of Hanumān.[2]

Kāli-Chaudas, *i. e.*, the 14th day of dark half of Ashvin† is considered to be the most favourable day for practising the black art; and the god Hanumān is accordingly worshipped with much ceremony by *bhuvas* on that day.[1]

All *bhuts*, *prets* and spirits are thus believed to obey the commands of the god Hanumān. In the course of a *sādhana* (*i. e.* the process of procuring the fulfilment of certain desires through the favour and by the agency of spirits) the latter are conjured in the name of Hanumān, so that the *sādhana* may not prove inefficacious. For this purpose the *Hanumān raksha mantra* is repeated one hundred and eight times before the image of the god, the devotee remaining standing all the time. A lamp of clarified butter is also lighted, and frankincense is burnt. The *mantra* runs as follows:—'Om namo Hanumān bālā ghatapīdam, pānikā rakhavālā, lohaki kothadi, bajarkā tālā, deva-dānava-kumār, nikal Hanumān āsan, Mahādev bāsan, Hanumān hathēla, bajarkā khīlā.' It is neither pure Sanskrit, nor Gujarāti, nor Hindustāni, but roughly it means:—'Bow to the young Hanumān, the tormentor of *ghata*, the guardian of water, the iron-safe, the lock of *vajra*, the son of the gods and the demons. Take your seat, the receptacle of Mahadev, O stubborn god, O Nail of adamant.' After the repetition of the *mantra*, four nails are driven into the four corners of the seat of the votary, and it is believed that the *sādhana* is thus rendered sure of success.[3]

The god Hanumān is sometimes worshipped when a serious epidemic is to be warded off. The usual mode of propitiating him in such cases, and also in exorcising spirits, is to pour red lead and oil over his image, to make an offering of *udad* seeds (*Phaseolus radiatus*) and molasses, and to invest the image with a wreath of one hundred and eight flowers of *ānkadā*‡ or of as many leaves or berries of the same plant.[4]

The influence of the god is believed to be so powerful in some places that it is said that a *bhut* or a *pishācha* is at once exorcised from the body of a person who observes certain ceremonies there. In some places the mere sight of the image of the god has the same effect, and it is believed that ghosts shriek and fly from the bodies of possessed persons, if these visit the images of Hanumān. In Kodolia, about half a mile to the west of Lilapur in Gujarāt, there is a temple of Hanumān where persons suffering from fever go on a Saturday, and take a meal before 2 p. m. at which time the god goes out to graze his cows. This proceeding is believed to work a cure in cases of fever and is called *anagah*.[5] A mere glance at the temple of Hanumān at Khandia and

[1] The Schoolmaster of Rajpara.

[2] The Schoolmaster of Dadvi.

[3] The Schoolmaster of Limbdi Taluka.

[4] The Deputy Educational Inspector, Prānt Hālār.

[5] The Schoolmaster of Lilapur.

* *Kundalan* is the circle formed round the *utār* by a *bhuvā*, after he has placed the *utār* in a cemetery or over a crossway.—The Schoolmaster of Dadvi.

† This is the day to learn such arts as that of *muth*, *chot*, *māran*, *etc.*, i.e., the art of doing bodily injuries by means of magic even to persons who are at a distant place. The process is gone through in a cemetery at the dead of night.—The Schoolmaster of Rajpara.

‡ A poisonous plant, the leaves of which are used in fomenting in cases of palpitation and of stomach troubles.—The Deputy Educational Inspector, Prānt Hālār.

Saranghur, or of that image which is known as 'Bhīd-bhanjan,' is sufficient to drive out evil spirits from the bodies of possessed persons.[1] The same virtue is attributed to the images of Hanumān at Bhurakhia, near Lathi and at Nariana, near Dhrangadhra, in Jhalavar,[2] Kathiawar.[2]

There are certain peculiar conjunctions of planets, which if they appear in a person's horoscope, always bring him misfortunes. In such circumstances, the person is said to be under the influence of *panoti*.* Such influence lasts for a period varying from one year to seven years and a half.[3] When the planet Shani (Saturn) enters the 1st, 11th, or the 12th *rāshi* in relation to a person, the latter is said to be 'affected by *sādāsāti-panoti*, i.e., *panoti* extending over seven years and a half.[4] The *panoti* enters the life of such a person with feet either of gold, silver, copper or iron : and in most cases the result is disastrous. If the *panoti* affects the head of a person, he loses his wits ; if it affects the heart, it takes away his wealth ; when it affects the feet, it brings bodily ailments. In order to counteract the evil effects of *panoti*, people worship Hanumān as the god who crushed the malignant goddess Panoti under his feet. On Saturdays red lead and oil, *adad*, molasses are offered to the image of the god.[3] Frankincense is burnt, a lamp is lighted, and a wreath of *ānkadā* flowers is sometimes dedicated.[5] A fast is observed on such days ; and sometimes the services of a Brahman are engaged to recite verses in honour of the god.[4]

There is a belief that Hanumān cries out once in twelve years, and those men who happen to hear him are transformed into *hijadās* (eunuchs).[3]

Oil which has been poured over the image of Hanumān and caught in a vessel is called *naman*. It is sometimes carried in a *vātki* (a small metal cup) and is burnt to produce *anjan* (*i. e.*, soot used as collyrium). This *anjan* is believed to improve the eyesight, and to protect a person from the influence of evil spirits.[2] There is a saying in Gujarāti that *Kāli-chaudasno ānjyo, ane koine na jāy gānjio'*, i. e., a person using *anjan* on Kālichaudas day cannot be foiled by anyone.[6]

Of the days of the week, Saturday is the most suitable for the worship of Hanumān. Of all offerings, that of red lead and oil is the most acceptable to him.[6] When Hanumān was carrying the Drona mountain to the battlefield before Lankā, he was wounded in the leg by an arrow from Bharata, the brother of Rāma. The wound was healed by the application of red lead and oil, and hence his predilection for these things.[2] It is also said that after the death of Rāvana and at the time of the coronation of Bibhīshana, Rāma distributed prizes to all his monkey followers, when nothing was left for Hanumān except red lead and oil.

Mostly *Ānkadā* flowers are used in worshipping Hanumān, but sometimes *Karan* flowers also are made to serve the purpose.[2] The favourite dishes of Hanumān are *maliddā*†, *churamā*‡ and *vadān*.§ [6] The usual *naivedya* is *malidda* of *Savāpāti*, i.e., of wheat weighing about six pounds and a quarter and *vadān*.[7]

Bhīma the second of the Pāndavas was begotten from Kunti by Vāyu, the god of

[1] The Schoolmaster of Songadh.
[2] The Schoolmaster of Ganod.
[3] The Schoolmaster of Jodia.
[4] The Schoolmaster of Sanka.
[5] The Schoolmaster of Dadvi.
[6] K. D. Desai.
[7] The Schoolmaster of Rajpara.

* The *panoti* cannot affect anybody who has an elder male relative living, *i. e.*, it influences only the eldest male member of a family.—K. D. Desai.

† A sweet preparation of wheat flour fried in ghi.

‡ Sweet balls of wheat flour fried and afterwards soaked in ghi.

§ Small biscuit-sized cakes of pulse flour treated with spices and fried in oil—K. D. Desai.

wind, and hence was called Vāyusuta. From his childhood he was possessed of miraculous strength, and had a voracious appetite. Every day he consumed 12 *kalashis** (or 192 maunds) of corn, and as much oil as is yielded by 13 *ghānis*.* He also required a maund and a quarter of betelnuts after each dinner. These habits had procured him the name of Vrikodara, *i.e.*, wolf-bellied. He played a very important part in the Great War, and on the last day of the battle smashed the thigh of Duryodhana with his ponderous mace. In his early days he killed several demons including Baka and Hidimba.[1]

Bhīma never took food without first worshipping Mahādev. On one occasion no temple of Shiva could be found within easy distance, and in a rage, Bhīma turned his bowl upside down and set it up as Mahādev. Such was the first installation of Bhīmanāth Mahādev revered to this day by all Hindus.[1]

Once upon a time Bhīma obstructed the stream of a river by laying himself across it, when the river rose to the banks and submerged a temple of Shiva near by. Shiva thereupon assumed the form of a lion and pretended to chase Pārvatī in the guise of a cow. Bhīma, in his true Kshatriya spirit, instantly rose from the water in order to save the cow from the lion. But the latter gave Bhīma a blow on the shoulder with one of his paws, and instantly transformed himself into a sage. After Bhīma had fruitlessly searched for the lion for a long time, he was informed by the sage that it was he, Shiva, who had assumed the form of a lion in order to rouse him from his position across the river. Shiva then favoured him with a boon that the half of his body which had received the blow would be turned into *vajra* (adamant). On Bhīma's request a further boon was granted to him that he should in future be able to digest as much as he could eat without suffering discomfort. Hence the proverb: *Bhīma khāve shakuni aghe*.[2]

It is said that Bhīma once played at *navateri* (lit. nine and thirteen), *i.e.*, he flung into the sky nine elephants with his right hand and thirteen with his left. The corpses of these animals were afterwards brought down to earth by Shukamuni to expiate king Janmejaya's sin of *Brahmahatyā* (Brāhman-slaughter).[2]

In his whole life-time Bhīma is said to have fasted only on one day, which happened to be the eleventh day of the bright half of Jyeshtha and is now called *Bhīma-agiāras*. On this day people who desire to be cured of dyspepsia observe a strict fast, taking neither food nor water, and pass their hands over their bellies repeating the name of Bhīma and also offer cocoanuts to his image.[3] On the night of *Bhīma-agiāras*, persons who are anxious to obtain health, wealth and victory over their enemies, bathe the image of Bhīma in water and *panchāmrit*† and worship it according to the prescribed ceremonies.[4]

In some places there are *vāvs* (or tanks) called Bhīma-vāvs which are said to have been formed by the strokes of Bhīma, when playing *gilli-dandā*.[5]

There are huge images of Bhīma on Mount Pālitānā.[6] There are many places in different parts of India which possess such images and which are believed to have been visited by the Pāndavas during their exile from Hastinapur. The Pāndavas never attained the status of gods and there is no systematic form of worship for them.[1]

---

[1] K. D. Desai.

[2] The Schoolmaster of Aman.

[3] The Shastri of Jetpur Pāthashālā.

[4] The Schoolmaster of Rajpara.

[5] The Schoolmaster of Kolki.

[6] The Schoolmaster of Ganod.

* A *ghāni* is that quantity of oil seeds which is put in at one time to be crushed in an oil mill.

† A mixture of milk, honey, curds, sugar and ghi.

Bhīshma, the uncle of the Kauravas and the Pāndavas, was an incarnation of one of the Ashtāvasus* and was the son of king Shantanu by Ganga. The stories about Bhīshma are chiefly derived from the Mahābhārat, and need not be repeated here. He is not regarded as a god and does not receive systematic worship.[1]

A fast is observed on the eighth day of Māgh, the anniversary of the death of Bhīshma. A *dorā* (a knotted piece of string) tied in the name of Bhīshma is believed to cure fever.[2] The *Yantra* (a mystical formula or diagram) of Bhīshma is sometimes drawn on a piece of paper, water is poured over it, and the water is offered to women in labour to drink, as likely to expedite delivery. Bhīshma-worship is supposed to facilitate the observance of the *Brahmacharya-vrat* (the vow of celibacy) and to bestow heroism and learning.[3] Bhīshma is credited with having composed the well-known poem, Bhīshmastavarāj, which recites the glory of Krishna and shows the way to attain salvation.[4]

There is a large temple of Ganpati near the eastern gates of Dhhank. It is said that this Ganpati informed a goldsmith, by appearing in a dream, that he was buried in a particular spot, and promised that a son would be born to him if he raised a temple in honour of the god. The goldsmith satisfied the wishes of the god and was soon relieved from the repeated taunt of the *vānziāpanā* (*i. e.*, the barrenness of his wife).[5]

The following tradition is connected with a place, about a mile from Dhhank, called Dhhank-ni Fui. Dhhank was in ancient times a great city and was known as *Preh Pātan*†. Once a *bāvā* (recluse), named Dhundhalimal, came to reside with his *chelā* (disciple) in a cave on a neighbouring hill. Every day the *chelā* went about the city begging alms for himself and his *guru*; but nobody except a poor *kumbhāran* (a potter-woman) ever gave him anything. So the *chelā* was obliged to cut and sell fuel in order to obtain means of subsistence, although he did not mention this fact to his *guru*. One day the *guru* noticed the growing baldness of his disciple and on being questioned about it, the latter had to admit his difficulties in earning a livelihood. The next day the *bāvā* decided to test the charity of the neighbourhood, and went on a begging round in person. He moved about the city from door to door, crying aloud *ālek ālek*, but nobody except the *kumbhār* woman offered him so much as a handful of flour. He then addressed the latter thus:—"Girl, this city is sinful and will shortly meet with destruction. Fly, therefore, instantly with your family and never turn your face towards the city in your flight". Having thus warned the only righteous person in the city, the *bāvā* returned to his cave where, after reciting an incantation in high exasperation, he pronounced a terrible curse for the destruction of the city 'Let Pātan be buried and let *māyā*‡ be reduced to *māti* (dust).' A whirlwind at once arose and destroyed the whole city. The *kumbhāran* had already fled with her children; but she unfortunately happened to look back in her flight, in spite of the warning, and she and her children were all turned into stones. In this form she can be seen even to-day, with two of her children on her shoulders and leading the other two.

1 Mr. K. D. Desai.

2 The Shastri of Jetpur Pāthashālā.

3 The Schoolmaster of Rajpara.

4 The Schoolmaster of Charadwa.

5 The Schoolmaster of Dhhank.

* The Vasus are a class of deities, eight in number, and are often collectively called Ashtāvasus.

† *Vide* Bombay Gazetteer, Vol. VIII, page 414.

‡ *Māyā*, in philosophy, means the illusion, by virtue of which, one considers the unreal universe as existent and distinct from the supreme spirit. Here it means the effect of *māyā*, the unreal splendour of the world, in fact phenomena opposed to the noumenon.

To the south of the same village on the banks of a small lake are situated the temples of Hinglaj Mātā and Kāmdev Mahādev. If there is a prospect of a drought in any year, the people of the village make an offering of *lāpsi* to the former deity in order to bring about a fall of rain. About two miles from Dhhank there is a temple of Vikani, in whose honour vows are observed for the cure of fractured bones of men and animals. Brāhmans are feasted at the temple of Hanumān at Timbo, four miles away from Dhhank. At a distance of about two *khetarvās* (fields) there is the shrine of Ashabi-pir where Mussalmāns feast *fakirs* and other co-religionists of theirs.[1]

Besides the above there are the temples of Shankar Tapakeshwar Mahādev and Mungeshwar Mahādev near the hill mentioned in the paragraph above and the temples of Pipaleshwar Mahādev and Rāmchandraji, to the south of Dhhank. There are also temples erected in honour of *suttees* known as Nomalmātā, Hulmātā, etc.[1]

The river Vinu meets the Bhādar, at a place two miles to the east of Ganod, and the Moja also joins the Bhādar a little further to the east. Hence the spot is called *Traveni* (a confluence of three rivers) and is regarded as holy. The beautiful temple of Baraneshwar Mahādev is situated here. Vows for feasting a certain number of Brāhmans, are observed in honour of this deity.[2]

The celebrated shrine of Husen-pir is situated in the vicinity of Ganod, and is much revered by the Khoja community, who hold a fair there on every *Āso-sud-bij*, i. e. the second day of the bright half of Āshvin. The fair lasts for seven or eight days, when Khojas from Bombay and even Zanzibar visit the place. A large building, the Khojakhana, is set apart to the west of the shrine for the *sabhā* (or meeting). The largest fair was held in *samvat 1940* (1884 A.D.), when H. H. the Agashah paid a visit to the shrine. There is a large gathering of people at the place every *bij* day.[2]

Husen-pir was a native of Kadi and a Saiyed by birth. In his youth, with his father's permission, he decided to remain unmarried, and took to travelling. In the course of his wanderings he halted for a week on the spot where his shrine stands at present, and was so charmed with the place, that he asked the owner of it, a Rabāri, Almora by name, for permission to reside there always. The Pīr was accompanied by two followers of the Mujāvar fakir sect. The present Mujāvar attendants at the shrine are descended from them, and stand in the 12th or the 15th degree of descent.[2]

One evening (it was the 5th day of the dark half of Bhādrapad) the Pīr accompanied by his two followers went to the Bhādar to offer the evening prayers. After the prayers were over, he told his followers that a flood was soon coming in the river, and asked both of them to leave him and return with their horses. One of them left the place as directed: but the other placed his head on the Pīr's lap and was drowned along with his master in the flood, which came down as if in obedience to the Pīr's words. Before dying the Pīr granted a boon to the Mujāvars that their line of descent would never fail for want of their heirs, and that their heirs would always be his attendants.[2]

The same night the Pīr informed the Khojas of Keshod and Kutiana that his corpse and that of his Mujāvar follower lay unburied at a particular spot. The Khojas, accompanied by the Rabāri Almora, visited the place in the morning and made ready to carry the corpses to Junāgadh. They found to their astonishment that the corpses could not be removed. Almora then recollected the request of the Pīr, and told the Khojas of his favourite place. The corpses were then carried to their present place of rest, and all efforts of the Khojas to proceed further

[1] The Schoolmaster of Dhhank.

[2] The Schoolmaster of Ganod.

proved unavailing. At that time there was a village called Keralun about a mile from the present site of Ganod. It is, however, uninhabited and in ruins and its site is now known as the *timbo* of Keralun. The Khojas erected a shrine over the place where the Pīr was buried, and the tombs of his relatives were afterwards erected in the vicinity. Vows observed in honour of the Pīr having proved fruitful in many cases, the Pīr's fame spreads wider every day. The Gondal Durbar has granted a *wādi* (a piece of land) for the maintenance of the Mujāvar family, who also receive the things that are offered to the Pīr. The Khojas consider it a merit to dedicate a portion of their earnings to this Pīr. People of all castes from Ganod offer one *kori** at the time of the marriage of a girl at their house. The knots of the marriage-scarves of newly-wedded couples are untied here, and the ceremony of shaving children for the first time is also performed in the presence of the Pīr. The usual offering to the Pīr consists of *churamu* and *kansār* : some people, however, offer a goat or a ram and call it *pānechednāriel*.[1]

There is a hollow log of wood on the boundary of Lath, a sub-village of Gondal and a mile to the South of Ganod. Long ago a fakir, while accompanying a band of outlaws *bārvatias*, was killed in a scuffle and was buried here. A *bābul* tree grew over his tomb, and came to be known afterwards as Lakkad Pir (the wooden Pir). The tree after a time withered till its stem was reduced to a small log with a hole in the centre. People observe vows in honour of this Pir for the cure of cough and bronchitis in children. After recovery, the children are made to pass through this *bākān* or hole and an offering of *kansār* is made to the Pīr. It is not only the Musalmāns who observe vows in the Pīr's honour : Hindus also have the same strong faith in him.[1]

Nearly twelve miles from Vanod lies the temple of Bechrā Mātā, who is the patron goddess of the Pāvaiyā sect. A male buffalo is offered to her as a victim on the 15th day of the bright half of every month. Near the temple there is the holy *kund* of Mānsarovar, the legend about which has already been related in these notes†

The village of Dādvi possesses the shrine of Mangalshā Pīr. Friday is the day for special worship of the Pīr, when dainties and cocoanuts are offered, and a flag is hoisted. Frankincense is burnt every evening.[2] There is also a temple of Māchho, the goddess of the Bharvāds, who offer her *lāpsi* and cocoanuts on every *bij* day. They also light a ghi lamp and lop off the ears of a goat or a ram, and offer the blood to the goddess.[2]

In Kolki a *bāvā* of the Bharvād caste named Hado Bhagat is said to have set up the images of all the gods in a certain temple. It is believed that he possessed miraculous powers. His decendants do not sell goats to Kasāis (butchers[3]).

There is a temple of Khodiār Mātā in Chok. The goddess is worshipped by Atits, who offer her *lāpsi* on every Dasarā day. There is also a temple of Hanumān, where the Khākhis bring an offering to the god every Saturday.[4]

In the village of Motā Devaliā are the temples of Bholānāth, Mahādev and Pipaleshwar Mahādev. Both the deities are worshipped by Atits, who perform the ceremony with the usual materials of frankincense, a ghi-lamp, cooked food, and who also blow a conch. It is said about Pipaleshwar Mahādev that none can stay at night in the temple. Once a Brāhman, who insisted on passing the night there, was hurled to a

[1] The Schoolmaster of Ganod.

[2] The Schoolmaster of Dadvi.

[3] The Schoolmaster of Kolki.

[4] The Schoolmaster of Chok.

* *Kori* may mean either a new garment or an unused earthen jar.

† See p. 42 *Supra*.

distance of two fields. There is also a temple of Swāmi-Nārāyan and three temples of Thākorji where the ceremony of worship is performed every morning and evening in the usual way with frankincense, a ghi lamp, and *ārati*. The shrine of Nilā-Pīr on the village boundary is revered alike by Hindus and Musalmans.[1]

In the vicinity of Chhatrasa, there is a temple of Kishordās Hanumān. On *Kāli-Chaudas* day the people of the village offer *churamu* and *vadān* to the god. The shrine of Gebalashā Pīr is situated two miles away from Chhatrasa, on the boundary line between that village and Kalānā. Sweet-balls, or sometimes only molasses, are offered to this Pīr on the fulfilment of vows observed in his name. Near the village gates lies the shrine of Daudshah, of whom it is said that he deprives thieves of their eye-sight, if they try to enter Chhatrasa. In the Vishnu-mandir, *annakūt** is offered to Vishnu by the attendant priest, on the first day of the bright half of Kārtik.[2]

A temple of Khodiar Mātā surrounded by Pandari creepers is to be seen on the way from Mojidad to Sanka. The Thakor of Limbdi used to kill a goat before the goddess during the Navarātra holidays; but an offering of *lāpsi* is now substituted for the goat. There is another temple of the same goddess on the way to Zābālā where she is worshipped by the Bhadkavā Durbar. The attendants at both places are Atits, and the usual offering consists of *lāpsi* and *khir*.† At a place near the boundary-line between Mojidad and Ayarda, Swāmi-Nārāyan Bhagwān and Sahajānand Swāmī are said to have bathed in the company of Hanumān in the river Vansal. The Brahmachāris‡ of the Swāmi-Nārāyan sect hold a fair there and offer prayers to Hanumān on the 15th day of the dark half of Bhādrapad.[3]

Every marriage-procession on its way to and from the place of marriage has to offer a new earthen jar to such field-deities as Dādmokhodiar, Lālo, Hardās, etc. Failure to do so arouses the wrath of these deities and brings disasters to the married couple. The only form of worship in use for these deities is to apply red lead and oil to their images. Seven kinds of corn, *viz*. *adād* (phaseolus radiatus), *mag* (phaseolus mungo), *kalathi*, *math*, *chanā* (gram), wheat and *juvari* are mixed and cooked together and the preparation which is called *khichdi* is offered to the deities at sunset. If the deities are not propitiated in this manner, they are believed to do harm to the people of the village.[4]

On a hill near the village of Patanvav there is a temple of Mātāji, where a ghi lamp is kept constantly burning at the cost of the Gondal Durbar. In Patanvav itself there is a shrine of Ahabā Pir attended upon by a fakir. At the approach of the monsoons, all the villages offer *lāpsi* to Mātāji and *churamu* to the Pīr.[5]

In Paj, near Sultanpur there is a shrine of Gebansha Pīr surrounded by a number of *bābhul* trees; and it is said that if a person were to cut any of the trees, he would meet with death or at least fall ill. There is a cobra deity, called Khetalo, near Sultanpur whose *gors* (attendant priests) are Nāgmagā Brahmans. It is believed that this deity confers once on each generation of the *gors*, as much wealth as would suffice for the life-time of all men of that generation.[6]

1 The Schoolmaster of Mota Devalia.

2 The Schoolmaster of Chhatrasa.

3 The Schoolmaster of Mojidad.

4 The Shastri of Jetpur, Pāthashālā.

5 The Schoolmaster of Patanvav.

6 The Schoolmaster of Sultanpur.

* An offering of all sorts of dainties and vegetables.

† Milk and rice boiled together and sweetened with sugar.

‡ *I. e.* persons who have taken the vow of celibacy.

There is a temple of Hadmatio Hanumān about half a mile to the west of Luvaria. A *Kanbi* of the Dhani tribe once, while pursued by robbers, took shelter behind the image of Hanumān, and vowed that he and his descendants would discharge priestly duties towards the god if he escaped safely out of the difficulty. The god protected him in his danger, and his descendants are now the recognised attendants at the temple.[1]

The village of Aman possesses the holy tomb of Davalshah Pīr. This Pīr lived in the 15th century and was a native of Ahmedabad. He had come to serve in the Amaran *thāna*, when he was killed in a battle. A tomb was built over his body, and he soon came to be regarded as a Pīr. His name became famous when a blind Bharvād regained his eye-sight through his favour. The Pīr also gave a son to a Bania from Ahmedabad who visits the tomb every year in a black suit. Once a Miana killed a cow and took refuge at the shrine of this Pīr: but the shrine spontaneously caught fire and he was burnt with it. The present building was erected by the Bania, and the ladies of the Jamsaheb's court have supplied silver gates and copper railings to it. The Jamsaheb also presents *kinkhab* coverings for the tomb every year. On the night of the *Uras* (or the fair held in the Pīr's honour) sandalwood is burnt before the Pīr.[2]

Charadwa is well-known for the temple of Rājeshwari Mātā. King Prithwi Rāj Chohān suffered from white leprosy and was once going to Dwārkā, with the hope that residence in the holy city would cure him of his disease. On the way, one of his best bullocks suddenly fell. The animal was almost given up for dead when a young woman named Rājbāi, daughter of Udā Chāran, happened to pass by while carrying water in earthen pots. Rājbāi touched the bullock with one of her toes, and to the astonishment of all beholders, the animal at once got up. Prithwi Rāj got rid of his leprosy by the favour of Rājbāi, who granted him an additional boon that she would come to help him on another occasion if he remembered her and sought her assistance. Rājbāi then directed him to visit Dwārkā. Long after, king Prithwi Rāj, when he was at his own place, remembered her in a moment of distress, and she went there (in spirit) after giving instructions to her relatives not to dispose of her body, as she would return soon. But the relatives did not understand her, and before she had returned from Prithwi Rājā's place, her body was disposed of according to the usual manner. For this, Rājbāi cursed her relatives that one of their descendants in each degree would turn out a lunatic. In her memory a pillar was raised and an image set up, both of which are worshipped every morning and evening. Milk, sugar and cakes are offered to her every morning in a *thāl* or dish, and milk and sugar every evening. There is a festival in honour of Rājbāi during the Navarātra holidays.[3]

The temple of Swāmi-Nārāyan at Charadwa contains the images of Shrikrishna, Baldev Rādhā, Rāma, Lakshman and Sītā. The ceremony of *ārati* is performed before the images five times every day. The first is called *mangalārati* or the auspicious *ārati* and is performed early in the morning. The second is *Shangār (Shringār) ārati*, when night garments are taken off the images and new ones are put on for the day. The third, *Rājbhog ārati*, takes place at the time when dainties and cooked food are offered to the gods. The *Sandhyā ārati* follows the offering of milk, sugar and cakes to the gods in the evening. The last, *Pidhān ārati*, is performed at night, when night garments are substituted for the rich dresses of the day. There are five occasions during the year

[1] The Schoolmaster of Luvaria. [2] The Schoolmaster of Aman. [3] The Schoolmaster of Charadwa.

when a fair is held at this place: (1) the Annakūt fair on the first day of Kārtik; (2) Vasantapanchamī fair, on the fifth day of the bright half of Māgh; (3) Hutāshani or Holi fair, on the 15th day of the bright half of Phālgun; (4) Rāmanavamī fair, on the 9th day of the bright half of Chaitra, (5) Jamnāshtamī fair on the 8th day of the dark half of Shrāvan.[1]

To the north of Charadwa there is a field-goddess, named Motisāri Meldi Mātā, in whose honour persons who are afflicted by diseases take a vow of presenting a *tavā* (a cake fried in oil in a pan). There is also a serpent-god named Charmaria who receives an offering of *lāpsi* on every *Aso-sud-bij*, *i. e.*, the second day of the bright half of Ashvin.[1]

Besides these there are four temples of Shiva, one of Shaktimātā, one of Hanumānji and two Mahomedan Pīrs in the village.[1]

In Limbdi Taluka, there is a temple of Kālikā Mātā, in whose honour vows are observed by persons suffering from physical or mental afflictions. The attendant at the place is a Brahman, and the worshippers of the Mātā visit her temple on a Sunday or a Tuesday and offer sweetmeats or *lāpsi*. On the eighth day of Ashvin a *havan* is made (*i. e.*, offerings are burnt) before the goddess.[2]

Vows in honour of Khodiar Mātā are efficacious in the prevention of such epidemies as cholera. The Khiyado Māmo quells evil spirits, *bhūts* and *prets*. The Khodo Māmo cures such diseases as cough and bronchitis. In the temple of Rāmnāth, a *brahmabhoj*—a feast to Brahmans—is given on the last day of Shrāvan.[2]

Near the western gates of Zinzuwada is seen the celebrated shrine of Rājbāi Mātā. In old times Zinzuwada was only the *nehado** of a Bharvād called Zunzā. At that time the queen of the reigning prince of Pātan could not be delivered of a child even though two years had passed since the time of conception. Once while on tour the queen's party encamped near the *nehado* of Zunzā Bharvād. The latter, when he learnt of the queen's misfortune, said that the co-wives of the queen had bewitched her by the *kāman* art, *i. e.*, by passing an earthen pot round her and by burying the pot underground with a live frog hanging with its head downwards in it. He added that the queen would not be delivered unless the frog was brought out by some stratagem. He asked the queen and her followers to stay there for some time, and sent word to Pātan with a messenger that the queen was delivered of a son. The co-wives of the queen, dismayed at the unexpected news and at the futility of the *kāman* art, went to look at the buried frog, which instantly jumped out and at the same moment the pregnant queen gave birth to a son. As the child was brought to birth by the instructions of a *Siddha-purusha* (a magician), it was named Siddharāj. The town of Zinzuwada was built in memory of Zunzā Bharvād, and a temple of Rājbāi Mātā was erected in honour of the queen. A large lake named Sensāsar was also constructed in memory of Sensā, the brother of Zunzā.[3]

Soon afterwards people began to observe vows in honour of Rājbāi Mātā. The devotees of the goddess visit her temple every evening. All newly-married couples in the village offer salutations to the Mātā accompanied by hired musicians and a party of women who sing on the way to the shrine. A virgin walks in front of the party with an earthen pot and a cocoanut on her head. After the salutations, sweetmeats to the amount vowed for are distributed among all those who are present. Sometimes a woman who has observed vows for the sake of a son,

[1] The Schoolmaster of Charadwa.

[2] The Schoolmaster of Limbdi Taluka.

[3] The Schoolmaster of Zinzuwada.

* *Nehado* is the residence of Bharvāds or shepherds.

presents a silver umbrella to the goddess, of the value of one rupee and a quarter or five rupees and a quarter, on the birth of a son to her. Burnt offerings and *lāpsi* are presented to the goddess to protect the town from such misfortunes as cholera, plague, etc.[1]

There is a well-known place called Vāchhdā-solanki about eight miles from Zinzuwada. Once a Rajput boy, aged sixteen, was going round the marriage-altar at the time of his wedding, in the village of Kuar, when he heard a piteous cry from a distressed cowherd, whose cows were being carried away by freebooters. The boy immediately ran to rescue the cows; but he was killed in the encounter. A temple was built on that spot in his honour. There is a small *kund* near the temple, the water in which is believed never to dry up and to possess the quality of curing hydrophobia.

Goradia Hanumān lies three miles from Zinzuwada, and there is a tradition that there is a treasure hidden near by. Many vows are observed in honour of Dhamā Hanumān, whose place is at a distance of two miles from Zinzuwada.[1]

The holy *kund* of Zilānand is one mile from Zinzuwada. It is a custom of the neighbourhood to throw the bones of deceased persons into this *kund*, and a fair is held annually at the place on the last day of Bhādrapad. The Bhotāvo *kund* is one mile distant from Zilānand *kund*: the bottom of this *kund* presents a bluish appearance, and the water always remains hot. It is said that there are sulphur mines below.[1]

A princess of Marwar used to worship five gods: Sumaria Ganesh, Kanaknath, Ratneshwar Mahādev, Nāgnāth and Hanumān; and she had taken a vow never to take food before she had worshipped all of them. The gods followed her everywhere in all her tours, but they had made one condition, that they would stop if she looked behind at them on the way. The princess happened to look back at Ganpati on the ridge of Sumaria near Keshia, three miles to the east of Jodia. So Ganpati would not leave Sumaria, and was installed there as Sumaria Ganesh. The same happened to Ratneshwar near Badānpur; to Kanaknāth, at a place midway between Kanakpuri (the modern Kunad) and Badanpur; and to Hanumān, near Kunad. In the same manner, Nāgnāth was installed near the Balambha gate of Jodia. The old town of Kanakpuri was buried by an earth-quake, and the image Kunadia Hanumān was found among its ruins.

The attendants of Sumaria Ganesh are Atīts. A fair is held there on the 4th day of Vaishākh, when thousands of Dheds flock to the place. The usual offering to the god consists of sweet balls. Kanaknāth is attended upon by Atīt Bāvās who share among themselves whatever is offered to the god. Shaivas hold a fair here on the 8th day of the dark half of Shrāvan.

The devotees of Kunadia Hanumān observe *anagh* (vulgarly called *anagodha*) at his place on Saturdays. They cook their food there and make offerings to the god before partaking of it, fasting afterwards for the day. The *anagh* is observed in the month of Mārgashīrsha. The attendants of this god are Khākhi Bāvās.[2]

One mile to the north-west of Jodia, towards the sea, there is a stone image of a horse set up on a pedestal, known as Rāval Pīr. A heroic Girāsia of the Dāl sect, named Rāval, was once shipwrecked while on an expedition from Cutch, and is said to have landed at the spot where Rāval Pīr stands at present. He received a hearty reception at the hands of the then ruling prince of Jodia (who was a Khavās) and was installed in the Durbār as Nana Rāval Pīr.

On the second day of the bright half of Āshādh (which is the new year's day

[1] The Schoolmaster of Zinzuwada.

[2] The Schoolmaster of Jodia.

according to the Halari year) Hindus offer *lāpsi* to Rāval Pīr as also on each Monday in the month of Bhādrapad. On occasions of popular distress, such as the breaking out of cholera or when the rains stop for days together, the *bhuwās* at the place, who are Dāl Rajputs, receive the *pedi* (a small heap of *lāpsi*) on behalf of the Pīr, and being possessed, declare the will of the Pīr as to when rain may be expected or when an epidemic will be warded off. Persons who are anxious for the success of their undertakings observe vows in honour of the Pīr which may cost them anything from a single pice to twenty-five rupees. At the shrine of Nānā Rāval Pīr, huge kettledrums are beaten and the ceremony of *ārati* is performed every morning and evening.[1]

The present site of Lilapur was formerly uninhabited, and the village stood nearly one mile off. Once the goddess Bhavānī directed the *patel* of the village in a dream to reside on the present site, and promised him that he would be always happy and that none of his descendants for seven generations would die of cholera. In testimony of the reality of the dream a box of red lac, a cocoanut, a reel of red thread—called *nādāsādi* and *chunadi*—were found under the patel's pillow. The village was then removed to its present site. The descendants of the patel are called Yadodā. The Mātā chose to take a Bharvād to be her attendant. On the 15th day of the bright half of Shrāvan offerings are burnt before the Mātā, when the attendant *bhuvā* has to offer sweetmeats worth five rupees. Every Bharvād family spends a rupee and a quarter every third year in honour of the Mātā.

During the famine of the year 1895 Samvat era (=1839 A. D.) the *bhuvā* was thinking of leaving the Mātā in order to escape from starvation, when the goddess appeared in a dream to him, and told him that he would find half a rupee every morning in the temple until he saw and partook of the new harvest. In the month of Shrāvan, he happened to partake of some new seeds and the coin could not be found as usual after this, although the new harvest was not quite ready till three months afterwards. At the entreaties of the *bhuvā*, however, the Mātā again told him in a dream that he would find a silver anklet, weighing 60 *tolas*, on the *bhogavā* (village boundary) of the village of Shiyani. A number of vows are observed in honour of this goddess with various motives.[2]

The Shakta Mātā in the western part of the same village prevents the Joganīs or female fiends from spreading contagious diseases.[2]

The Surdhans near the gates of Lilapur represent two heroes who were killed in an encounter with freebooters in the *Samvat* year 1836 (1780 A. D.). The knots of the marriage-scarves of the descendants of the Surdhans are untied before them, and any of their female descendants visiting the images without a veil on their faces, are subjected to serious calamities.[2]

About ten years ago Unād Bhagat and Jivā Bhagat of Paliad were one day walking together, when Unād Bhagat collected seven stones and placing them one over the other, said to Jivā Bhagat that he was constructing a *pālio, i. e.*, a tomb for Jivā. Immediately Jivā died, and Unād had to carry out what was merely meant in jest. Some rooms are built at the expense of the Jasdan Durbar, and a *pujāri* daily offers worship to Jivā Bhagat. A fair is also held in his honour on the second day of Bhādrapad.[3]

About two miles from Jasdan in the village of Bakhalvad there is a temple of Āvad Mātā. The latter represents the queen of one of the rulers of Jasdan. On every Vijayā-dashamī, *i. e.*, the 10th day of the

[1] The Schoolmaster of Goda. [2] The Schoolmaster of Lilapur. [3] The Schoolmaster of Jasdan.

bright half of Ashvin, the prince of Jasdan goes to visit the image in a procession, offers *lāpsi* to Āvad Mātā, and then a feast is celebrated. Formerly it was the custom to kill a buffalo before the goddess on this day: but only *lāpsi* is now offered instead. It is usual to take some wine also on this occasion.[1]

On the Chitalia hill, two miles from Jasdan, there is a temple of Shitalā, the goddess of small-pox, where children who have lately recovered from that disease are taken to offer salutations to the goddess. Silver images of human eye, milk, sugar, curds, grapes, cocoanuts, a sheet of blank paper, and a number of other things are presented to the goddess on such an occasion. Some persons vow to visit the goddess with a burning hearth on their heads. Such vows are discharged on a *sātem, i. e.*, the 7th day of the bright or the dark half of a month. On Shili Sātem, the 7th day of the dark half of Shrāvan, there is a large gathering of people at the place.[1]

The village-gods of Upleta are Kaleshwar, Pragateshwar, Somnāth, Nīlkanth, Dādmo and Khetalio. Pragateshwar is said to have emerged from the earth of his own accord and is therefore called *Swayambhu* (self-existent). The same is said about Nīlkanth and Somnāth also. The temple of Dādmo lies a little away from Upleta. Persons suffering from cough observe vows in his honour and partake of parched gram. There is a *devi* near Pragateshwar before whom a sacrifice is performed on the 9th day of the bright half of Ashvin, and cakes, bread, *khichdi* and *khir* are offered.[2]

In Gondal there is a temple of Gondalio Nāg and one of Nāgnāth Mahādev. Pure milk is the usual offering made to both the deities. Gondalio Nāg is installed in Durbārgadh and is white in appearance. Newly married couples of high class Hindus untie the knots of their marriage-scarves before this deity. In the Durbārgadh there are tombs of seven *ghoris* with whose assistance the first king of Gondal is said to have won his crown. There is also a family goddess of the Bhadeja Rajputs in Gondal known as Ashāpuri, a vow in whose honour is believed to fulfil all desires.[3]

There is a female spirit named Meldi in Movaiya who is worshipped by *bhuvās* on the 14th day of the dark half of Ashvin. On that day they heat oil in an iron pan and take out cakes from the burning oil with unprotected hands. A goat and a cock are also sacrificed on this occasion, and the meat is partaken of in order to win the favour of the goddess.[4]

There is a *bedā* tree near Movaiya about which the following story is told. Long ago there was a *kanbi* (farmer) in Movaiya who used to see a boy moving in front of him with an uncovered head whenever he was ploughing his field. One day the *kanbi* lopped off the hair from the boy's head who followed him to his home, entreating him to return the lock of hair. The *kanbi* however did not heed him, and concealed the lock of hair in a jar containing gram. The boy then served the *kanbi* as a field-boy, when one day he was asked by his master to take gram out of the jar for sowing. The boy, who was a *bhut*, found his lock of hair there, and when once he had obtained it, he took a very heavy load of gram to the *kanbi* and bade him good-bye. But before the boy had fled with his lock of hair, the *kanbi* begged of him a boon that a *bedā* tree should grow in his field, where vows could be observed in honour of the *bhut*.[4]

The villagers in Sayala accompanied by several *bhuvās* and by musicians who beat the *dhols* and the *dānklān* go outside the village

[1] The Schoolmaster of Jasdan.

[2] The Schoolmaster of Upleta.

[3] The Schoolmaster of Gondal Taluka and the Head Mistress of girls' school, Gondal.

[4] The Schoolmaster of Movaiya.

to visit the temple of Khodiār Mātā on the 15th day of the bright half of Shrāvan. The *bhuvās* wind a piece of cotton-thread round the village, and sometimes pour out milk or water in the same place in order to secure its safety from any epidemic. On the same occasion four divers, who are generally healthy young athletes, are presented with an earthen pot each and are made to stand in the village-tank till the water reaches to their necks. They are asked to dive simultaneously in the water at a signal from the headman of the village, and to get out immediately. Each of them is named after one of the four months of the rainy season and the amount of water in the pot of each is supposed to indicate the amount of rain which would fall in the respective months of the next year. After leaving the water the divers break the pots on the spot, and the fragments are taken away by the people, to be kept in their jars of corn, in the belief that they will bring prosperity in the ensuing season. The four divers are then made to run a race on the *maidan*, and he who wins the race gets a small plough and a cocoanut as a prize. The winner is called *hālino-jityo*, and it is believed that he will be successful in all his undertakings.

On the same day the *bhuvās* place a small four-wheeled chariot of the Mātā outside the village, and it is believed that the chariot carries off the plague, cholera and similar diseases with it. Such ceremonies are performed in most of the villages on the Balev holiday (*i. e.*, the Nārel-Purnimā day, or the 15th day of the bright half of Shrāvan).[1]

The foundation of a new settlement is carried out in various ways. A series of unusual accidents befalling the residents of a village makes them doubtful of the security of their residence, and produces a desire to move to a safer home. Very often on such occasions the *bhuvās* or exorcists are possessed by the Devis, or Mātās, and declare the will of the gods regarding a new settlement. Sometimes a change of home is recommended tot he villagers in a dream: sometimes a heavenly voice is said to direct the change, in addressing one of the villagers.[2]

An astrologer has first to be consulted as to the auspicious date on which the boundaries of the new settlement should be marked out. Three or four days before the delimitation, learned Brahmans are sent to purify the chosen site by the recitation of sacred mantras.[3] On the appointed day the headman of the village leads a procession to the site, and performs the ceremony of installing the village gods. It is said that, at the time of founding a new settlement, it is necessary to install and worship the *panch-deva* or the five deities, namely, Hanumān, Ganpati, Mahādev, Vishnu and Devi. Hanumān is installed at the village-gates, and is propitiated with an offering of *churmu* and *vadān*. The images of Ganpati and Vishnu are set up in a central place in the village, temples being built for them in due course. Mahādev is generally installed on the village-boundary, and has a temple built for him afterwards. Devi may be set up anywhere: her installation is not permanent nor does she receive systematic worship.[4] But more generally only Ganpati, Hanumān and Mātā are installed on this occasion.[5] Occasionally other deities, such as the Earth, Shesh Nāg,[*] the Navagrah (the nine planets), the pole-star and Kshetrapāl are also worshipped.[6]

The village-gates are fixed after the ceremony of installation, and a *toran*—a string of *āsopālav* leaves (Jonesia asoka) with a cocoanut in the centre—is fastened across them

[1] The Schoolmaster of Sayala.
[2] K. D. Desai.
[3] The Schoolmaster of Khirasara.
[4] The Schoolmaster of Chhatrasa.
[5] The Schoolmasters of Jodia and Khirasara.
[6] The Schoolmaster of Rajpara.
[*] The celebrated serpent of one thousand heads who supports all the worlds.

near the top.[1] Here the ceremony of *khāt-muhurt** is performed[2] and afterwards the headman, accompanied by a Brahman, who recites mantras, either winds a cotton-thread besmeared with red lac round the village or pours a stream of milk *dhārāvādi* along the village boundaries.[3] The headman has further to perform the *homa* at the gates of the village, when a company of Brahmans recite holy passages in honour of Hanumān and Mātā. At the time of the completion of the *homa,* when the *āhuti* (an oblation of ghi) is thrown on the fire, all persons present offer cocoanuts to the sacrificial fire.[4]

In some places it is usual to worship the newly chosen site itself, and then to drive into the ground a wooden peg besmeared with red lac, called the *khili* (peg) of Shesh Nāg, which is first ceremoniously worshipped with red lac, sandal-ointment and rice.[5]

After these ceremonies, the villagers are at liberty to build their own houses within the new settlement. When the houses are complete and ready for habitation, it is necessary to perform the ceremony known as *vāstun* (or *graha-shānti*) for the propitiation of the nine planets. Both the day of installing the gods and the day of *vāstun* ceremony, are observed as festivals, at which Brahmans are feasted, and *lāpsi, churmu* and *kansār* are offered to the gods.[6]

The new settlement may be named after the deity whose advice brought about the move or after the headman. It is sometimes named after the particular incident which drove the people to seek their new home.[6]

A failure of the harvest is in most cases due to the irregularity of the rains. It is therefore ascribed to the displeasure of Indra, the god of rain, and Varuna, the god of water. The mode of propitiating these gods has already been described.

Sometimes a cessation of rains is attributed to the wrath of the village-gods, whereupon the festival of *Ujāṇi* is celebrated in order to appease them. One day, preferably a Sunday, all the inhabitants go outside the village, and rich viands are cooked to be offered to the village-gods. At the same time, the headman performs a *homa* sacrifice and the dainties are partaken of after the villagers have thrown cocoanuts into the sacrificial fire.

In similar circumstances people sometimes seek the protection of the gods Annadeva, Annapūrṇā, and Kriyā Bhaudai. Six *dokdās*† or six pice are collected from every house in the village to make what is called a *chhakadi,* and the whole amount is then bestowed in charity in the name of the above-named deities.[7]

Rain during the Ashleshā and Maghā nakshatras‡ is destructive to the crops, and is a sign of the wrath of Indra, who should be appeased with sacrificial offerings.[8]

Diseases among cattle are believed to be brought on by the wrath of minor deities such as Shitalā Mahākāli[9] or the sixty-four Joganis.[10]§ The *bhuvās,* when they are

[1] The Schoolmasters of Chhatrasa and Rajpara.

[2] The Shastri of Jetpur Pāthashālā.

[3] The Schoolmasters of Khirasara, Jetpur and Rajpara.

[4] The Schoolmasters of Chhatrasa and Jetpur

[5] The Schoolmaster of Jodia.

[6] K. D. Desai.

[7] The Schoolmaster of Chhatrasa.

[8] The Shastri of Jetpur Pāthashālā.

[9] The Schoolmaster of Kotda-sangani.

[10] The Schoolmaster of Dadvi.

* Vide Chapter I., p. 29.

† 100 *dokdās*=1 rupee.

‡ The time taken by the sun to move through the constellations Ashleshā and Maghā, which is approximately the month of August.

§ Generally the same ideas prevail regarding diseases of cattle as in the case of human ailments. *Dorās* or magical threads and slips of paper are often used in cases of fever. In epidemics like cholera pollution is believed to be at the root of the evil. Bhangis are engaged to prepare images of corn to keep off the disease, and they forfeit their homesteads and property if the epidemic is not checked thereby. —*The Schoolmaster of Barton Female Training College, Rajkot.* (These images represent evil spirits presiding over particular diseases. Certain oblations are offered to these evil spirits, and after the recital of certain incantations they are either burnt or buried.)

possessed, declare to the people which particular deity is exasperated, whereupon that deity is conciliated either by offering dainties or a goat or a ram, or by the observance of *Ujāṇi.* A *dhārāvādi*—a stream of milk—is poured on to the ground adjoining the village side, and *toraṇs* of *āsopālav* leaves (Jonesia asoka) are fastened on the doors of the offended deity's temple.[1] It is also customary to place *baklān* and *vadān* at a spot where three roads meet in order to propitiate the evil spirits, who frequent such places.[2]

Small-pox is supposed to be the result of the displeasure of the goddess Shitalā. In all cases of small-pox the victim is left to suffer, the only remedy being the observation of vows in honour of the angry goddess. Different things are dedicated to the goddess according as the disease affects one part of the body or another; and they are usually offered on a Sunday or a Tuesday. The usual offering consists of *kulera,** a *tāv* (a sheet of paper), fried *juvāri*, fried gram, and other articles varying according to the symptoms.[3]

To ward off this disease the women of the village sometimes prepare cakes, *gānthiās,*† etc., on the sixth day of a month, the preparations being partaken of on the next day, when no fresh food is to be cooked.[4]

Kharavā affects the hoofs of cattle, in which it produces irritation; it is generally due to worms in the hoofs. A *jantra* (a mystical arrangement of words) of the twelve names of Mahāvir (the great warrior, *i. e.* Arjun) is written on a piece of paper, and tied round the neck of the diseased animal, fastened over the gates through which the cattle pass, or suspended over the street by which the cattle go out to graze.[5] The *jantra* is as follows:—

Shrisakhā	Dhanurdhāri	Gājidhanā ‡	Krishna-sakhā.
Dhananjaya	Lalanlārkhā ‡	Kapidhwaj.	Jayahari.
Gudākesh	Pitabhavā ‡	Narsinh	Pārth.

Sometimes the paper on which the *jantra* is written is placed in a hollow bamboo stick which is then fastened over the gates.[6] The *jantra* is believed to have the power to cure the disease.

Muvā-keshibi causes saliva to flow continuously from the mouths of animals. A *gagarbediun* (a piece of leather thong or a piece of black wood, on which magic spells have been cast) is suspended over the village gates or is tied to the neck of the animal, in the case of this disease occurring.[7]

In such diseases as *kharavā, sunaku, motu-dukh* (lit. the great malady), *valo, pet-tod,*§ *Bandhāi-javan,*‖ a *jantra* is tied by a piece of indigo-coloured cloth or by a piece of thread of the same colour, round the neck of the animal, and is also fastened over the village-gates. A *toraṇ* is prepared of the ears of *juvāri* corn with a cocoanut in the centre, and after magical incantations have been pronounced over it, is suspended over the village-gates. All animals passing under the *toraṇ* are believed to be proof against the disease.

1 The Schoolmaster of Dadvi.
2 The Schoolmaster of Mota-Devalia.
3 The Schoolmaster of Dhank.
4 The Schoolmaster of Kolki.
5 The Schoolmaster of Dhank.
6 The Schoolmaster of Ganod.
7 The Schoolmaster of Kolki.

* Small round cakes of wheat flour sweetened with molasses and fried in ghi.

† A preparation of fine gram flour treated with spices, which after being made into a thick paste, is passed through a sieve into boiling oil.

‡ Shrisakhā, Gājidhanā and Pitabhavā are most probably corruptions of Shrishasakhā, Gāndivadhanvā and Prithābhava respectively; Lalanlārkhā perhaps of Lalāma narākhya.

§ A disease which causes severe pain in the stomach of the affected animal.

‖ A disease which stiffens the limbs of animals and renders them incapable of any movement.

But if this is not successful in checking the course of the disease, it is usual to swallow the *chelans** of Mungi Mātā (the Dumb Mother). For this purpose the *bhuvās* of the Mātā, who are Bharvāds, are invited to the stalls of the affected cattle, where they recite magic incantations amidst tumultuous shouts and yells. After this they are fed with rice, ghi and sugar, this latter process being called 'swallowing the *chelans* of the Mātā.'[1]

In event of this process being of no avail in restraining the disease, the headman of the village in the company of his wife performs a *homa* sacrifice in the places dedicated to the Mātās, and offers an *āhuti*—a sacrificial oblation—when all the villagers dedicate cocoanuts to the sacrificial fire.[2]

Sometimes the wrath of the god Gorakhdev is supposed to be responsible for cattle-diseases. A bunch of the leaves of a poisonous medicinal plant *ānkdo* is passed seven times over the body of the ailing animal with the prayer 'May Gorakhdev be pleased,' and a cocoanut is dedicated to the god.[3]

Another method of checking cattle-disease is to bury the corpse of an animal which has died thereof near the village-gates. It is believed that this puts a stop to any further deaths among cattle from the same disease.[4]

When such a disease as *shili* (small-pox), *sakharado*, or *kharavā* prevails largely among cattle, a belief gains ground that the Dheds (who flay the dead cattle and sell their hides) have poisoned the drinking water of the cattle in order to increase their earnings.[5]

The god Kāl-bhairav was brought into existence by the fury of god Shiva, when he, being extremely angry with Brahmā, cut off the fifth head of the latter. Kāl-bhairav is the leader of all *bhuts* (ghosts) and *dākans* (witches), and resides at Kāshi (Benares) by the order of Shiva. His favourite haunt is a cemetery. His image is always represented as fierce and ugly.[6]

It is said that this god once entered the mouth of Gorakhnath and performed religious austerities in that strange abode. Although Gorakhnath was nearly suffocated, he could only persuade Kal-bhairav to come out by extolling his glory and by conferring on him the leadership of all *bhuts* and the guardianship of the Kotvālu fortress at Kāshi.[7]

Kāl-bhairav does not command worship on any auspicious occasion. On the other hand, he is much revered by persons who practise the black art. On *Kāli-chaudas* day his devotees worship him in a cemetery, offer an oblation of *baklan*, and recite magic incantations till late at night.[8]

The offerings favoured by Kāl-bhairav are *khir*,† cakes of wheat flour, sugar and *vadān*.‡[9] The sacrifice of a live animal is also acceptable.[10] The offering after presentation to the god, are given to black dogs.

Pregnant women in order to secure a safe delivery sometimes vow to abstain from ghi till they have offered an oblation to Kāl-bhairav.[11]

1 The Schoolmaster of Kolki.

2 The Schoolmaster of Kolki.

3 The Shastri of Jetpur Pāthashālā.

4 The Schoolmaster of Ganod.

5 The Schoolmaster of Ganod.

6 The Schoolmaster of Moti Murad.

7 The Schoolmaster of Chhatrasa.

8 The Schoolmaster of Jodia and Dodiala.

9 The Schoolmaster of Aman.

10 The Schoolmaster of Patanvav.

11 The Shastri of Jetpur Pāthashālā.

* The word *chela* in ordinary language means a pancake (*pudalo*) of wheat or gram, sweet or salt, and it is a favourite oblation to Mātā. So the word *chelan* may have come to be used for any oblation to Mātā and the expression swallowing the chelans may mean partaking of the oblation or offering of the Mātā.

† Milk and rice boiled together and sweetened with sugar.

‡ Vide page 48.

The following lines are often repeated in honour of this god[1]:—

भुक्तिमुक्तिदायकं प्रशस्तचारुविग्रहम् ।
भक्तवत्सलं स्थितं समस्तलोकविग्रहम् ॥
निष्क्वणन्मनोज्ञहेमकिंकिणीलसत्कटिम् ।
काशिकापुराधिनाथ कालभैरवं भजे ॥ १ ॥

(I worship Kāl-bhairav, the giver of food and of salvation, of auspicious and comely appearance, who is kind to his devotees.)

Ganpati or Ganesh, about whose origin the traditional legends prevail, is represented with four hands, in one of which he holds a *kamandalu* (a gourd), in the second a *lādu* (or a sweet-ball), in the third a *parashu* (or an axe), and in the fourth a *jap-māl* (or a rosary). He is sometimes called Dundalo (lit., big-bellied) because of his having a protuberant belly. He puts on a yellow garment and rides a mouse. His brother is Kārtik-swāmi who rides a peacock. His favourite dish consists of *lādus* or sweet-balls of wheat-flour fried in ghi and sweetened with molasses. Siddhi and Buddhi are the two wives of Ganpati. Before their marriage their father Vishwarupa had made a promise that he would bestow the hands of both on whomsoever circumambulated the whole Earth within one day. Ganpati reasoned that a cow and a mother are equal in merit to the Earth and by passing round the former, he got the hands of both. Ganpati is said to be the fastest writer of all, so that the sage Vyāsa secured his services as a scribe, at the instance of Brahmā, in writing the Mahābhārat. When Rāvan had conquered all the gods and made them serve in his household, Ganpati had to become a cowherd and to look after cows and goats.[2]

On *Vaishākh sud choth*, known as Ganpati *choth*, i. e., the fourth day of the bright half of Vaishākh, Ganpati is ceremoniously worshipped with red lead, red flowers, milk, curds, honey, etc. The image of the god is besmeared with red lead and ghi, and the remnant of this ointment is applied to the doors and windows of the house.[3] Sweet-balls of wheat-flour fried in ghi and sweetened with molasses are first dedicated to Ganpati and are afterwards partaken of as the god's gift.[4]

The people of Mahārāshtra observe Ganpati *choth* on the 4th day of the bright half of *Bhādrapad*, when an earthen image of Ganpati is made and worshipped with twenty kinds of leaves.[5]

It is a custom among the Vaishnavas to draw an image of Ganpati in those vessels which are to be used for cooking food at the time of performing the obsequies of a deceased Vaishnava.[6]

The Mātrikās are sixteen in number, and are worshipped on such auspicious occasions as a *yajna* (*i. e.*, a sacrifice), a wedding, or the ceremony known as *vāstu*.[7] Their installation consists in painting the following marks with red lac on the back walls of a house.

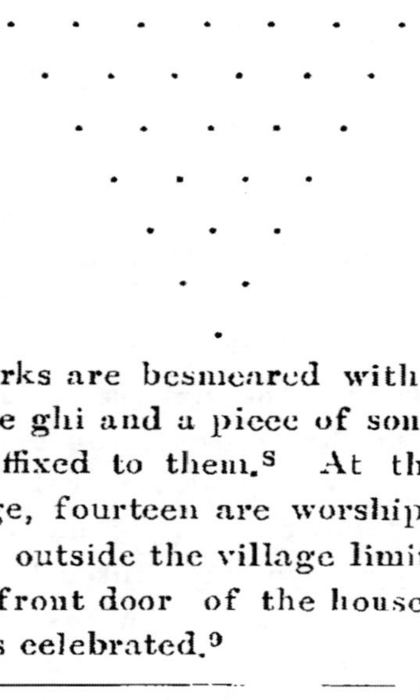

The marks are besmeared with molasses, and a little ghi and a piece of some precious metal is affixed to them.[8] At the time of a marriage, fourteen are worshipped in the house, one outside the village limits, and one near the front door of the house where the wedding is celebrated.[9]

[1] The Schoolmaster of Dhhank.
[2] The Schoolmaster of Barton Female Training College, Rajkot.
[3] The Schoolmaster of Kolki.
[4] The Schoolmaster of Dhank.
[5] The Schoolmaster of Dhhank.
[6] The Schoolmaster of Jasdan.
[7] The Schoolmaster of Aman.
[8] The Schoolmaster of Dhhank.
[9] The Schoolmaster of Aman.

The Mātrikās or Mātās are worshipped during the Navarātra holidays also. On this occasion small *morias* or earthen bowls with a hole in the centre of each, are plastered with *khadi* (red or green earth) and *kāyā*; and young girls carry them on their heads with burning lamps from door to door. At each house they receive oil for the lamp and a handful of corn. On the last day, *i. e.*, on the ninth day, all the bowls are placed on the special site dedicated to the Mātās. The songs, which are also accompanied by dancing, are called *garabi* or *garabā*.[1]

The Mātrikās are also supposed to be the *grahas* or planets which influence the life of a child in the womb, and their worship is believed to bring about an easy delivery.[2]

There is also a family goddess of the name of Mātrikā. In worshipping her, seven round spots are painted on a wall with red lac, and ghi is poured over them in such a manner as to form five small *relās* (streams). A mixture of molasses and ghi is then applied to these spots with a piece of *ādāchh* (red cotton yarn). By this process the devotee secures the motherly regard of the goddess.[3]

One of the deities which preside over child-birth is Randal Mātā or Rannā Devi, who is said to be the wife of the Sun.[4] In order to secure an easy delivery, pregnant women take a vow that they will invite one or more *lotās* (bowls) of this Mātā. The process of "inviting the *lotās*" is as follow:—

The tufts round the shell of a cocoanut are pulled out, the nut is besmeared with chalk, and marks representing two eyes and a nose are painted on it. (Or the nut is so placed that the two spots on its surface represent eyes, and the pointed tuft of fibres between them serves the purpose of a nose). A bowl is placed on a piece of cloth stretched on a wooden stool, and the cocoanut is placed over the bowl. It is then dressed in elegant female attire, and a ghi lamp is kept constantly burning near it. This completes the *sthāpan* or installation of Randal Mātā. Women bow down before this representation of the Mātā, and sing melodious tunes in its presence. On the morning of the following day, the image is carried to the temple of the village Mātā, the cocoanut is deposited there, and the garments are brought home. The cocoanut is subsqnently taken by the Brahman attendant of the Mātā.

On the day of the installation it is customary to invite five *gorāṇis** (married women whose husbands are living) to a feast of *khir* and cakes. On the next day, when the Mātā is sent away, three virgins are entertained with rice, sugar and milk.[5]

In some communities a custom prevails of "inviting the *lotās* of the Mātās" on the occasion of the first pregnancy of a woman. On the day on which the *lotās* are to be invited, the pregnant woman takes a bath early in the morning, and calls upon thirteen *gorāṇis*, whom she invites to dinner by marking their foreheads with red lac. A Brāhman is called to set up the Mātās, whose installation takes place in the same manner as that of Randal. The piece of cloth spread on the wooden stool is required to be green. When the *gorāṇis* sit down to the dinner, the pregnant woman washes their right toes with milk and swallows that milk as *charanāmrit* (lit. the nectar of the feet). The *gorāṇis* are required to taste a morsel of some preparation of milk before they begin their meal. At night, a company of women dance in a circle round the Mātās, singing songs. Next morning a *bhuvā* is called, who declares the will of the Mātās. On receiving a satisfactory reply from the *bhuvā*, the party disperses.[6]

[1] The Schoolmaster of Zinzuwada.
[2] The Schoolmaster of Ganod.
[3] The Schoolmaster of Sanka.
[4] The Schoolmaster of Sanka
[5] The Schoolmaster of Anandpur.
[6] K. D. Desai.
* Also known as *surāsaṇis*.

The goddesses Bahucharāji (or Bechrāji) and Ambāji are sometimes worshipped for the sake of safety during childbirth. The ceremony of Nāndi-Shrāddha which was performed when Rāma was born is sometimes gone through at the birth of a child.[1]

The deities of the forest reside in groves of trees or near the *Piludi* tree, to which their devotees must go in order to fulfil their vows.[2] These deities do not receive any formal worship. But they are noted for the cure of certain diseases, and the groves which they haunt are frequently visited by afflicted persons. These deities are installed in those places where they have manifested their powers.[3]

There is a belief that if unmarried persons touch *sindur* or red lead, a cobra deity of the forest, Kshetrapāl, takes them in marriage. But the danger can be averted by vowing to dedicate *khichaḍi,* red lead, a *dokado** and some fruit to this god at the time of marriage.[4]

[1] The Schoolmaster of Jodia.

[2] The Schoolmaster of Kolki.

[3] Mr. K. D. Desāi.

[4] The Schoolmaster of Kolki.

* A ball of molasses and sesamum seeds mixed together.

CHAPTER III.

DISEASE DEITIES.

Such diseases as cholera and small-pox are believed to be brought on by the wrath of the Mātās or Devis caused by neglecting to offer the usual oblations. In order to propitiate them, Brāhmans are engaged to recite the *Chandipāth* and to offer *havans* (sacrificial offerings). Very often the festival known as *ujani* is observed, in which all the villagers go outside the village to take their meals, and return home in the evening after witnessing the *āhuti* (the offering of cocoanuts to the sacrificial fire).*

Another belief personifies the diseases as *malin* or evil spirits who are fond of human prey. To ward them off, a *dhārā-vādi*, or stream of milk, is poured out in the village or a magic thread is passed round. The chariot† of the Mātā is driven through the village with the same object.[1]

There is a popular tradition that in ancient times cholera was subjugated by king Vikrama, and was buried underground. Once upon a time the British excavated the place in the belief that treasure was concealed there, and thus cholera was released. After many soldiers had fallen victims, the disease deity was at last propitiated by an oblation, and was handed over to the Bhangis (or scavengers) [2]

This association of the Bhangis with cholera is present in most of the beliefs current about the disease. There is a story that once upon a time a number of students had put up in a house by which a Bhangi was in the habit of passing frequently. He daily used to hear the students reciting the sacred texts and this produced in his mind the desire to become a Sanskrit scholar. For this purpose, having concealed his low birth, he went to Benares and by diligent study, soon became a *pandit*. He even married a girl of high caste. But his imposture being at last discovered, he burnt himself to death, and his ashes gave rise to the disease known as cholera.[3]

At the present day, if the epidemic breaks out, the Bhangis are often suspected in some way or other of having brought it about. It is said that they make statues of the flour of *adad* (phaseolus radiatus) and after piercing them with needles and pins, either throw them into the wells which are daily used by the villagers ‡ or bury them in a spot over which the people frequently pass. The whole affair is managed very secretly and at the dead of night. The slightest rumour of such proceedings causes a tumult in the village, and the Bhangis are then in danger of being severely handled by the enraged villagers.[4]

---

1 The Schoolmaster of Luvaria.

2 The Schoolmaster of Jodia.

3 The Schoolmaster of Kotda-Sangani.

4 The Schoolmasters of Jodia, Dadvi, and Songadh.

* *Vide* Question 19.

† A small wooden car five or six inches long is covered over with a piece of cotton cloth and the wooden image of a Mātā—Khodiār or Kālkā—besmeared with red lead is placed upon it. This *rath* or chariot of the Mātā is then passed through the village on the shoulders of a low-caste person, who begs corn from door to door and afterwards places the image at the gates of the neighbouring village. From thence it is removed by the people of that village to the next village and so on till it reaches the sea.—Mr. K. D. Desāi.

‡ Sometimes the statues of *adad* flour are besmeared with red lead and afterwards are boiled in dirty water. The whole of this preparation is then thrown into wells, the waters of which are used for drinking in the village.—The Schoolmaster of Songadh.

Another method by which the Bhangis are supposed to bring about cholera is to sprinkle the blood of a black cow on the image of Hanumān. The god is deeply offended at the insult, and in consequence spreads cholera in the neighbourhood. For this reason, offerings are burnt before Hanumān in order to stop an epidemic of cholera.[1]

Bhangis are also supposed by some to accomplish the same result by the help of *malin* or evil deities who are first gratified by the offering of victims.[2] One of such deities is Rāmdepir, to whom *bali-dān* (offering of a victim) is made by the people, through the medium of Bhangis, for the prevention of cholera.[2]

An outbreak of cholera offers a good opportunity to the Bhangis, who extort dainties and small sums of money from the people. Persons attacked by cholera often seek the services of a Bhangi and promise him liberal gifts if they are cured. The latter generally treats his patients by tying a magical thread round their elbows.[3]

It is said that the Bhangis have to present an offering to their *malin* or evil goddess every third year, and that, in so doing, they kill a black animal before the goddess. They then place an iron pan full of sesamum oil on the fire, and suspend the body of the animal above it. It is believed that as many human beings will fall victims to cholera as the number of the drops of blood that fall from the body of the animal into the iron pan.[4]

Another deity whose wrath is supposed to be responsible for the breaking out of cholera is Mahāmāri Devi.[5] The worshippers of this goddess are Bhangis. She is believed to send forth cholera when her oblations are stopped,[6] and her favour is regained by renewing the offer of these oblations. Sometimes the *Navachandi* sacrifice is performed at the principal village-gates, and the *chandipāth* is recited at the other gates. A number of Brāhmans and virgins are also feasted, and presented with garments. A magic cotton thread is passed round the village and a *dhārā-vādi*, or stream of milk, is poured out. The *bhuvās* go round the village playing upon the harsh unpleasant *danklan*. A goat is then taken to the temple of the Mātā, and the *bhuvās*, after cutting out its tongue, dip their hands in its blood and strike them against the doors of the temple. The goat is then killed and Similar blood-marks are made upon every door in the village as well as on the village-gates, where an iron nail is driven into the ground with an incantation. A lime is then cut, and an oblation is offered to the Mātā. Such a process is believed to stop the progress of the epidemic.[6]

Other deities connected in popular belief with cholera are the goddesses Visuchikā[7] and Chandikā.[8] Visuchikā is conciliated by burnt offerings : the recitation of the *chandipāth* wins the favour of Chandikā. There is also a giantess named Karkatā who is supposed to be responsible for cholera. She is said to have sprung from the sweat on the forehead of Brahmā and to reside in the *chandra mandal* (or lunar sphere).[9]

One of the remedies adopted to stop an epidemic of cholera is to propitiate Shiva by the performance of *Rudrayāg*,* *Mahārudra*,* *Shatachandi*,* *Homahavan* and by bestowing gifts on Brāhmans and other holy

[1] The School Master of Dadvi.

[2] The School Master of Chhatrasa.

[3] The School Master of Jodia.

[4] The School Master of Mendarda.

[5] The School Master of Movaiya.

[6] The School Master of Vanod.

[7] The School Masters of Devalia and Vasavad.

[8] The Shastri of Jetpur Pathshala.

[9] The School Master of Charadwa.

* These are different sacrifices, the first two in honour of Shiva, the third in honour of the goddess Chandi.

men.[1] Sometimes vows are observed with the same object in honour of a minor local deity named Lala Hardev.[2] Another method of driving off the disease is to convey it to the body of a goat or a ram, or a he-buffalo, and to drive the animal out of the village.[3]

Small-pox is believed to be the act of the goddess Shitalā Mātā, who spreads the disease whenever she is desirous of having victims.[4] Thus, in cases of small-pox, the patient very often receives no medical treatment, the only remedies adopted being directed towards the propitiation of the Mātā.* A number of vows are taken in the Mātā's name, to be fulfilled after the patient has recovered. Many people accomplish their vows before the Shitalā Mātā at Kalavad in Jāmnagar. A vow to visit this place after the patient's recovery, and to abstain from certain things till the day of the visit, is taken by the mother of the affected person in case of a severe attack. But almost every village contains a temple of Shitalā Mātā, and those, who cannot go to Kalavad, vow in the name of the local Mātā.[4] One of such vows is to go to the temple of the Mātā with a burning hearth on the head.[4] Such a vow is generally undertaken by the patient's mother.

Ordinarily in a case of small-pox, the patient is not allowed to bathe till he is completely free from all traces of the disease. A bath is then given on a Sunday, a Tuesday, or a Thursday, with water which has been heated by being placed in the sun. An image of Shitalā Mātā is set up in the house near the water room, and the patient worships the image after the bath. The image is drawn in cowdung with two cotton seeds to represent the eyes. An offering of *kulera* † and curds is made to the goddess. Five virgins are invited to dinner, and are served with cold food. All the members of the household also partake of cold food. On the 7th or the 13th day of the bright half of a month the patient is taken to the temple of Shitalā Mātā, when a cocoanut is broken in the presence of the goddess. Half of the cocoanut is brought home, the other half being carried away by the Mātā's attendant. Some people place a new earthen vessel filled with water near the goddess. Silver eyes, which may be worth anything between half an anna and half a rupee, are dedicated to the Mātā.[4]

The first visit to the Mātā should take place on a Sunday or a Tuesday. The things vowed to the goddess are dedicated on this occasion. It is also necessary to go to the goddess again on the next Tuesday or Thursday after the first visit. This time only water and red lac are offered.[5]

During the course of the disease no low-caste person and no woman in her monthly course is allowed to cast his or her shadow on the patient.[4] The women in the house are prohibited from combing their hair, or churning curdled milk, or indulging in sexual intercourse. Such acts are believed to cause extreme displeasure to the Mātā, who then causes some limb of the patient to be affected. Branches of *nimb* leaves are suspended over the doors of the house, and also round the patient's bed. The same leaves are used to fan the patient.[4]

[1] The School Master of Ganod.
[2] The School Master of Dhānk.
[3] The School Master of Dadvi.
[4] The School Master of Jodia.
[5] Mr. K. D. Desāi.

* The patient is often entirely made over to the Mātā and is again purchased from her at a nominal price of a rupee and a quarter. —Mr. K. D. Desāi.

† A mixture of the flour of *bājri*, ghi, and molasses.

When a child suffers from the disease, it is often weighed against dates, which are first dedicated to the goddess, and then distributed amongst the poor.[1] The child is taken to bow down before the goddess after nine or ten days from the date of attack, and the mother of the child offers several things to the Mātā, among which are grapes, sugar, a pinch of flour, a small earthen bowl full of water, and a blank sheet of paper.[2]

Different things are dedicated to the goddess according as the disease affects one part of the body or another. For instance, flour of *bājrā* or *juvāri* is offered in case of bronchitis; silver models of the human eye when the disease affects the eyes; a *goras* (a black earthen vessel full of curds) in case of morbid heat; a piece of black paper, in high fever, and salt if there is an itching sensation.[3] The Mātā is said to live on cold food and to be very fond of things which have a cooling effect such as fruits, sugar, etc. The same things are given to the patient as food.[4]

To secure the protection of Shitalā Mātā for their children, women annually observe the vow of *shili sātem* on the 7th day of the dark half of *Shrāvan*. On this day the Mātā is said to visit every house and to roll herself on the hearth. No fire is, therefore, lighted in the hearth on this day: for if the Mātā comes and is scorched by the fire she is sure to bring misfortune on that household. For this reason, a number of dainties and all the food necessary for the day is prepared on the previous day. On the day of *shili sātem*, *juvāri* seeds are spread on the hearth, and after being sprinkled with red lac, a cowdung bowl containing a plant called *vaṇa* is placed upon them. The women of the house bathe with cold water and take only one meal during the day. They further abstain from sewing and embroidering during that day. Sometimes a Brāhman is engaged to recite the *Shitalā shloka* from a book called Rudrayāmal.[5]

The following legend is related of *shili sātem*. A certain woman once forgot to extinguish the fire in her hearth on *Rāndhan Chhetha* (lit. cooking sixth), *i. e.*, the day previous to *shili sātem*. On the next day, the Mātā was scorched in the stomach when she came to roll herself on the hearth. In extreme anger the goddess cursed the woman saying that her only son would be burnt to death; and immediately the boy died. In her anguish the unfortunate mother confessed her fault to a friend, who advised her to go to the jungle and entreat the Mātā to give back her son. She found the goddess rolling in distress under a *bābul* tree. The woman slowly approached her, and began to comb out the Mātā's hair. She then placed her son in the Mātā's lap and entreated the goddess to revive the boy. The Mātā felt much relieved by the woman's attentions and blessed her saying that her bosom should be as quiet as her own head. Immediately, at these words, the boy revived, to the intense joy of his mother.[6]

Women whose relatives have recovered from a dangerous attack of small-pox observe a vow on every *sātem*, *i. e.*, the 7th day of the dark half of every month. They first bathe with cold water and, after offering an oblation of *kulerā*, take their meals only once during the day. This food has to be prepared on the previous day.

Shitalā Mātā is described as riding an ass in a nude state with the half of a *supadun* (a winnowing fan) for an umbrella and with a swing in one hand, and a broom in the other.[7] But more usually the Mātā is represented by a mere trunkless head in

[1] The School Master of Jodia.

[2] The School Master of Sayala.

[3] The Deputy Educational Inspector of Hālār.

[4] The School Master of Zinzuvāda.

[5] The School Masters of Dhānk and Ganod.

[6] The School Master of Vanod.

[7] The School Master of Ganod.

stone, besmeared with red lead. This is said to be the head of Babhrivāhan, the son of Bhīma* the second of the Pāndavas by a Nāg mother. At the time of the Great War, he was sent by his mother from his residence in the *pātāl* (the regions below this world) to assist his father, and as he did not know the Pāndavas, he was asked to join the weaker side. On coming to the earth he first met with Krishna who took a promise from him to lop his own head off. In return, Krishna promised him that he would be immortal, invisible and worshipped by all, and the head was set up on the flag of the Pāndavas. This head began to trouble the Pāndavas after their victory, and could only be quieted by the promise of Krishna to have him recognised as a deity with unlimited powers. This head afterwards came to be known as the controller of small-pox. How the head of the male Babhrivāhan came to be identified with Shitalā Mātā, it is difficult to explain.[1]

There is a tradition that a Kunbi once recovered his eyesight, lost in an attack of small-pox, by worshipping Shitalā Mātā, and by vowing not to tie his lock of hair till his blindness was cured.[2]

It is said that the powderlike substance which falls from the scabs of small-pox cures cataract if applied to the eyes.[2]

Daksha Prajāpati once celebrated a great sacrifice, but did not invite his son-in-law Shiva. The latter was extremely enraged at the insult, and eight sorts of fever were in consequence produced by his breath at that time.[3] According to another story *zār* or fever was created by Shiva in order to assist the demon Bānāsur in his contest with god Krishna, and it can be cured by the recitation of a piece called Ushāharan, from the *Harivansha.*[4] Some persons attribute fever to the wrath of Vishnu, and declare that it can be avoided by the recitation of *Vishnusahasranāma.*[5] Others believe it to be due to the anger of Shiva, and say that it can be cured by pouring a stream of water over the image of Shiva by offering *bel* leaves (*Aegle marmelos*) to him, and by reciting the *Mrityunjaya mantra* in his honour.[6] Others again ascribe it to the displeasure of the gods Hari† and Har,† saying that the heat is caused by the wrath of Shiva.[7]

The following are some of the remedies adopted in cases of fever:

(i) The recitation of sacred hymns in honour of the gods.

(ii) The worship of Narsinh. ‡

(iii) Rudrābhishek—pouring a stream of water on the image of Shiva with the recitation of verses in his honour.

(iv) Drawing the *jantra* of Mrityunjaya (*lit.* Death-conquering, an epithet of Shiva) as shown below.

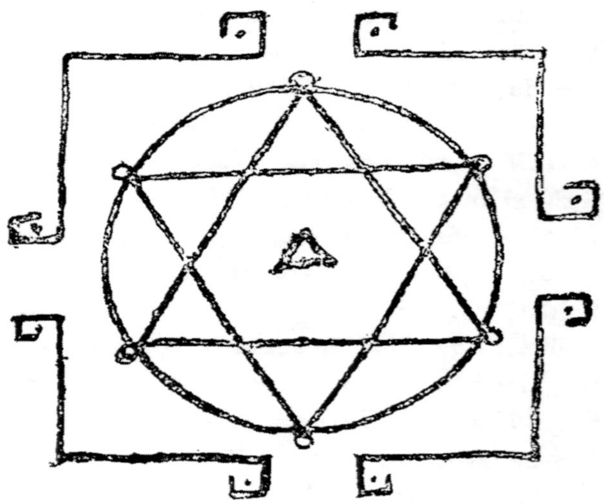

[1] Mr. K. D. Desāi.

[2] The School Master of Jodia.

[3] The School Master of Sanka.

[4] The Mistress of Rajkot, Civil Station Girls' School.

[5] The School Master of Ganod.

[6] The Shastri of Jetpur Pathshāla.

[7] The School Master of Charadwa.

* Babhrivāhan was not the son of Bhima, he was the son of Arjun by Chitrangadā, a princess of Manipur.

† Names of Vishnu and Shiva respectively.

‡ The half-man and half-lion incarnation of Vishnu.

(v) Tying a magic thread round the arm.[1] On a Sunday or a Tuesday a woollen thread or a piece of five-coloured silken thread is taken to a *bāvā* or a *jogi*, who mutters a few mystic words, and makes seven knots in the thread. The thread is treated with frankincense, and then tied round the arm.[2]

Periodical fevers are believed to be under the control of certain spirits. There is a story connected with almost every sort of fever, and it is believed that a person who listens to such a story is cured of fever.[3] The following legend is connected with *ekānterio*—intermittent fever occurring on alternate days. Once a Bania, on his way to a village, came across a banyan tree where he unyoked his bullocks and went to a distance to seek for water. Ekānterio (the spirit controlling intermittent fever) resided on this tree, and when the Bania had gone sufficiently far he stole from behind the tree and carried away the Bania's carriage together with his family. The Bania was much surprised to miss them on his return, but he soon found out the author of the trick, and pursued Ekānterio. That spirit however would not listen to the Bania's entreaties to return his carriage, and the matter was at last referred for arbitration to Bochki Bai. The latter decided in favour of the Bania, and confined Ekānterio in a bamboo tube. He was released on the condition that he would never attack those persons who listen to this story.[4]

There is a flower garden to the west of Jodia where there is a tree called *ghelun* (mad) tree. Vows in honour of this tree are believed to be efficacious in curing fever.[4]

It has been already said above that such epidemic diseases as cholera or the plague are often supposed to be the result of the sinister practices of the Bhangis. There is a belief that the Bhangis sometimes prepare an image out of the flour of *adad* (phaseolus radiatus) and pierce it with needles, and it is said that for every hole made in the image one human being falls a victim to some epidemic disease. Such an image is sometimes placed in an earthen vessel and buried underground in a public way so that every passer by treading on the spot where it is buried may be attacked by some disease. Or it is thrown into the well which is most used by village people, with the object that all persons drinking water from the well may perish by the disease.[5]

The Bhangis are also accused of causing an epidemic by means of boiling the ear of a buffalo and the flesh of an ox together in one vessel, it being believed that the virulence of the disease varies in proportion to the extent to which the boiling proceeds. This process is supposed to cause a disease among cattle also.[6]

Another belief is that the Bhangis charm seeds of *adad* and cloves by repeating magic incantations over them, and afterwards strew them on a highway in order that those who step on them may be attacked by cholera or some similar disease.[7] One motive suggested for such action is that they are thereby likely to receive their garments, which would be used for covering the bodies.[8] Also at the outbreak of such an epidemic, clothes, cocoanuts, ghi, molasses, wheat flour, etc., are offered by the people to the Bhangis, who in return give a *dorā*, a piece of thread, of black wool to be worn by the afflicted persons.[9]

But apart from such beliefs, the appearance of an epidemic is also attributed to other causes. There is the usual belief that it is caused by the diminution of virtue and the increase of sin among people and the

[1] The School Master of Dhānk.
[2] The School Master of Zinzuvāda.
[3] Mr. K. D. Desāi.
[4] The School Master of Jodia.
[5] Mr. K. D. Desāi.
[6] The Deputy Educational Inspector of Gohelwad.
[7] The School Master of Rajpara.
[8] The School Master of Jasdan.
[9] The School Master of Rajpara.

consequent wrath of the gods, who are only propitiated by the people again reverting to righteous ways and by the performance of sacrifices in their honour.[1]

There is also a belief that the sixty-four Joganis, when they are desirous of victims, cause baneful epidemics among mankind, the remedies in such a case being such as offering a goat or a he-buffalo to them, or the observation of an *ujāni* in their honour.

The following tale is related regarding an occurrence said to have taken place not long ago in the village of Verad. The headman of the village who was a Rajput by birth but who had lost his caste owing to irregular conduct with a woman, died of fever, and as he was an outcaste his body was buried instead of being cremated. Soon after, a number of persons in the same village happened to die of the same fever and the people conjectured that the late *patel's* corpse must be lying in its grave with its face downwards chewing the *khahan* (? perhaps *kaphan, i. e.* the cloth in which a corpse is wrapped). Many thought that the health of the village would not be restored until the corpse was replaced in the correct position with its face upwards and unless the *khapan* was taken out of its mouth. But none ventured to do so, being dissuaded by the fear of meeting with a worse fate.

But although they did not open the grave yet they arranged for certain vows to be taken in honour of the dead man, and that put a stop to the disease.[2]

Another story from the same place is that when small-pox once raged furiously in that village, the people of the place celebrated a magnificent feast of dainties prepared of wheat-flour, ghi, molasses, rice and pulse, and afterwards the Dheds of the village lopped off the head of a dead he-buffalo, burying it at the spot where the feast was held.[3]

The remedies adopted for the abatement of epidemic diseases have already been mentioned above, the most common being the winding of a cotton-thread, the pouring out of *dhārāvādi, i.e.*, milk, in the village, and the taking of the *rath* of the Mātā in a procession beyond the village boundary, the epidemic being supposed to be expelled in the *rath.* In the last case, after the *rath* has been taken to the neighbouring village, a charmed peg is sometimes driven into the ground near the village boundary to prevent the epidemic from crossing back again.[4]

Mention has already been made of the deities which protect the cattle and to whose displeasure diseases among cattle are attributed. It is said that such diseases are very common during the *vishi* of Shiva. A cycle of twenty years is called a *vishi,* three such cycles making a complete *samvatsar* of sixty years. Each of such *vishis* is presided over and named after each of the three gods of the Trinity, Brahmā, Vishnu and Shiva. The *vishi* of Brahmā is characterized by protection and creation, that of Vishnu by growth and that of Shiva by destruction, the last often bringing on such calamities as plague, famine and diseases among cattle.[5]

The following are some of the remedies practised by the village people in the case of certain cattle-diseases.

In the case of such diseases as *movā kharavā* or the like, there is a practice of burying a plough near one's gates, which is afterwards covered with dust gathered from three streets and is worshiped with a branch of a tree, a plate of iron and red lead. This ceremony has to be performed either on a Sunday or a Tuesday, and the man who performs it has to remain naked at the time.[6]

For the cure of *valo* (a disease in which the throat is inflamed), pieces of the stalk of *kukad-vel* (a kind of creeper) are tied

[1] The School Master of Kotda-Sangani.
[2] The School Master of Devalia.
[3] The School Master of Devalia.
[4] The School Master of Sanka.
[5] The School Master of Ganod.
[6] The School Master of Dhānk.

round the neck or the horns of the diseased animal and no other food except ghi and molasses is allowed to it for two or three days. A handful of salt is sometimes thrown on the back of the animal.[1] Sesamum oil is also said to work as a good medicine in the case of the same disease.[2]

Another remedy for the same disease is to pass a knotted bamboo stick with seven knots seven times over the back of the ailing animal.[3]

Ghi is sometimes used as a medicine in the case of small-pox. In the case of *shakario* or *kālo vā*, the animal is branded in the affected limbs. To one suffering from a stye in the eye an ointment prepared from the horn of a deer is applied, while a mixture of whey and salt is said to be useful in most eye maladies. The treatment for the swelling of the belly is a mixture of molasses, *ajamo* (ligusticum ajwaen) and *sanchal* (a kind of salt). To cure an animal of *khāpari* (a disease which affects milch-cattle), the milk of the affected animal is poured on *rāfdā* (a kind of jujube tree). If after delivery, some part of the embryo remains inside an animal, milk and molasses are given to expedite its removal.[4]

In the case of *kharavā* the ailing animal is made to move about in hot sand and is treated with salt, which is first fried on the fire of *Holi*. The remedy for the disease known as *kumbhava* is to give a dose of castor oil, *sanchal*, *ajamo* and hot water to the sick animal and also to tie a magic thread round its neck.[5]

A disease called *okarinu* (*i.e.*, vomitting) sometimes breaks out among sheep. In this case the shepherds separate all the affected animals from the herd and remove them to a distance. All the sheep which die of the disease are buried deep in a pit, which is guarded for several days, lest some other animals dig it up and let lose the buried epidemic by exposing the carcasses. It is believed that the contagion of this disease lies in the ears; and the ears of all the sheep in the herd are carefully watched if they bleed.[6]

The twin gods Ashivini Kumār are sometimes propitiated by means of an *anushthān* (the performance of religious austerities in their honour) in order that they may put a stop to a disease among cattle.[7]

It appears that dancing often forms a part of the process of exorcism. Frequently dancing is accompanied by the beating of cymbals and drums and other loud noises. A *mandalu* is convened at the house of the person who is to be exorcised *i. e.*, a number of *bhuvās* are invited to attend along with a number of low-caste drummers, and afterwards the ceremony of *utār* is gone through; the *utār* is then taken to a cemetery.[8]

Sometimes the beating of drums and cymbals is alone resorted to for expelling an evil spirit from the person of a patient. It is believed that this process is effectual in proportion to the degree of the intensity of the noise created.[9] The patient is asked to sit facing the east. The Bāval or Vāghri *i. e.*, the drummer, sits in front of him, and not only beats the drum as loudly as he can, but also sings hymns at the top of his voice in honour of his favourite goddess. In the meanwhile, the *bhuvā*, who is also in attendance, begins to be possessed, and discloses the fact by convulsive fits. After a while, the *bhuvā* suddenly stamps his foot furiously on the floor, and, seizing the patient by a lock of his hair, and perhaps even giving him a blow on the back, asks in a stern voice "Who art thou ? speak out at once why thou hast come or else I will burn thee to death."*

1 The School Master of Dhānk and the Shastri of Jetpur Pathshala.
2 The Shastri of Bhayavadur Pathashala.
3 The School Master of Zinzuwāda.
4 The Shastris of Jetpur and Bhayavadur.
5 The School Master of Wala Taluka.
6 The School Master of Anandpur.
7 The School Master of Kotda-Sangani.
8 The School Master of Zinzuwāda.
9 The School Master of Kotda-Sangani.

* All this of course is addressed to the evil spirit which is supposed to have possessed the patient.

The patient will then perhaps reply: 'Don't you know me? I am *chāran*', or I am *zāmbādi*, (a female spirit guarding the village gates) or *Vāgharan*† or *Purvaj* (the spirit of a deceased ancestor). Regarding the reason for possession, the evil spirit will give some such explanation as follows:—"Once upon a time the patient was taking a loaf and vegetables which he hid from me, and therefore I shall leave his person only with his life." The *bhuvā* will then say "life is precious and not so cheap as you think. If you want anything else, say so and leave this person." After a dialogue such as the above, the *bhuvā* and the spirit come to some compromise, and the *bhuvā* then leads a procession with the *utār* either to the village boundary or to a cemetery. The *bhuvā* then draws a circle on the ground with the point of a sword which he carries, and places the *utār* within the circle. He then slightly cuts the tip of his tongue with the edge of the sword, and spits blood into a fire lighted for the purpose. The smoke of this fire is supposed to carry the offering to the evil spirit. The *utār* is then taken away by the drummers, who share it secretly with the *bhuvā*. In the event of the patient deriving no benefit from this ceremony, the *bhuvā* advises the patient's relatives to repeat the process.[1]

The following ceremony is sometimes performed in order to ascertain whether a person is under the influence of an evil spirit or not. A *bhuvā* is invited to the patient's house in the company of drummers, and there he dances for some time amidst the din produced by the beating of the drums and by the loud recitation of hymns in honour of his favourite goddess. Afterwards a handful of grain is passed round the head of the patient and presented to the *bhuvā* for inspection. The *bhuvā* selects a few seeds from the grain and making certain gestures, offers them to the patient with either the words '*vācho*' or '*vadhāvo*'. In case the *bhuvā* says '*vācho*' and the number of seeds happens to be even, what he declared to be the cause of the patient's trouble is believed to be true. So also if the *bhuvā* says *vadhāvo* and the number of seeds proves to be odd. But in case the number of seeds proves to be odd when the *bhuvā* says '*vācho*', or even, when he says *vadhāvo*, then his explanation of the cause of the patient's trouble is not credited.

Sometimes Brāhmans instead of *bhuvās* are engaged to exorcise an evil spirit from the body of a sick person. A bellmetal dish, containing *adad* (phaseolus radiatus) wheat and *jowāri*, is placed on a copper jar and struck violently with a stick, called *velan*, so as to produce a loud noise. The patient, who is made to sit in front, begins to tremble and sometimes even to rave. The Brāhmans also create a loud noise and in a loud voice ask the patient who the evil spirit is and what it wants. The patient will then give out the name of some notorious *dākan* (witch) or of one of his deceased ancestors and will add that he desires a certain thing which he was used to get while in human form. The evil spirit is then propitiated by offering the things asked for and is requested to leave the body of the patient.[2]

The following are other methods of expelling an evil spirit from the body:—

Either *lobhān* i. e., incense powder, or chillies or even the excreta of dogs are burnt under the nose of the patient, who, overpowered, by the unpleasant odour, is supposed to give out the name of the evil spirit and also what the latter wants.

Water is charmed with incantations, and is either dashed against the patient's eyes or is given to him to drink.[3]

If the evil spirit possessing a patient is a *purvaj* i. e., the spirit of a deceased ancestor,

† Feminine of Vāghri belonging to the Vāghri caste.

[1] The School Master of Sānkā.

[2] The School Masters of Ganod, Vanod and Kolki.

[3] The School Master of Dadvi.

either *Nārāyan-bali Shrāddha* or *Nil-Parvani Shrāddha* or *Tripindi Shrāddha* is performed in order to propitiate it, and a party of Brāhmans is invited to dinner. In case the *purvaj* is a female, a cocoanut is installed in a *gokhalo* (a niche) in the wall to represent it, *ghi* lamps are lighted, and frankincense is burnt every morning before it. On the anniversary of the death of the *purvaj* a party of *gorānis* (unwidowed women) is invited to dinner.[1]

If a woman is believed to be possessed by a *dākan*, she is made to hold a shoe in her teeth and is taken to the village boundary, where the shoe is dropped, and a circle is drawn round it with water from a bowl carried by the party. The holding of the shoe by the teeth signifies a vow on the part of the *dākan* never to re-enter the person of the exorcised woman.[2]

The following are other occasions for religious dancing, namely during the *Nav-rātra* holidays (i. e. , the festival which commences from the lst day of the bright half of *Áshvin* and lasts for nine days); at the time of offering oblations to the village-gods; on the occasion of setting up a pillar in memory of a deceased person; at the time of the *Nilotsava** ceremony.

At the time when Randal the wife of Surya is installed and worshipped, a party of young women dance in a circle before the goddess to the accompaniment of *garabis*.[3]

The eighth day of the bright half of *Āshvin* is dedicated to the worship of the *Mātās* and *devis* (minor goddesses), and on this day, *bhuvās* have to dance each before his favourite *mātā*. This they have also to do on the lst day of the bright half of *Āshādh*. *Bhuvās* are also invited to dance on the *Diwāsā* day i. e., the last day of *Āshādh*.[3]

The *bhuvā* occupies a high place in the esteem of the village people, and commands much respect. In the first place, his position is that of a medium between the gods and goddesses on the one hand and human beings on the other.[4] He is the interpreter of the will of the gods, which he expresses to the public when in a state of trance. Besides he is believed to have power over the evil spirits which are visible to a *bhuvā* though cannot be seen by ordinary eyes.[5] He is the guardian of the village, his duty, being to protect the people from the malignant influence of the evil spirits.[5]

In the next place, it is also the office of the *bhuvā* to treat the sick. In cases when medicine is unavailing and where the malady is supposed to be the work of some evil spirit, the opinion of the *bhuvā* is sought by the relations of the patient and is given by the test of the scrutiny of grain.[6] When the sick person is found to be under the influence of a spirit, the common mode of exorcising is to take an *utār* to the cemetery. An image of a human being is prepared out of the flour of *adad* (phaseolus radialus) and is passed round the body of the sick person. The *bhuvā* then holds the image near his heart and stretches himself on a bier with the image on his bosom. In this condition the *bhuvā* is taken to the cemetery, and the evil spirit is believed to be driven by these means out of the patient's body.[7]

The *bhuvā* distributes *dorās* (magic threads) and anklets among the people. Such things are coveted for their efficacy in warding off the influence of evil spirits and are often sought after by people for their cattle as well as for

[1] The School Master of Limbdi Taluka. [2] Mr. B. K. Desāi.

* *Nilotsava* or *Nil-parnāvum* is a ceremony performed in honour of a young man, who has come to an untimely end. The chief part of the ceremony is the performance of the wedding of a bull-calf with a heifer. Sometimes a member of the deceased youth's family is possessed on such an occasion by the spirit of the deceased man and is believed to have then the power of correctly answering questions about future events, etc.—The School Master of Dhānk.

[3] The School Master of Devaliā. [4] The School Masters of Dhānk and Kotda Sangani.

[5] The School Master of Sanka. [6] The School Master of Dadvi.

[7] The School Masters of Dadvi and Kolki.

themselves.[1] The prosperity of the *dānklān-vagādnārs* (those who beat the drum) depends to a large extent on the success of the *bhuvā's* business, and for this reason, the drummers are often very good advocates of the *bhuvā* and take every opportunity of glorifying his powers and merits.

The respect which *a bhuvā* commands in this way is sometimes increased by the performance of such tricks as his putting lighted torches into his mouth, placing his hand in boiling oil, and similar performances.

But although there may be some *bhuvās* who profit by imposing upon the credulity of the villagers, there are many *bhuvās* who do not work with the expectation of any reward, and are only actuated by benevolent motives. Many of them honestly believe that at the time when they are thrown into a state of trance, the *mātās* or deities actually enter their bodies and speak their wishes through them as a medium.

In some villages, the office of the *bhuvā* is hereditary, and lands have been assigned to them in remuneration for their duty[2]. In addition to this religious calling, a *bhuvā* often follows some other profession as that of agriculture, weaving or spinning.[3]

The *bhuvā* generally belongs to some low caste and may be a Koli, Bharvād Rabāri, Vāghri or even a Chamār. The *bhuvās* are also known as *pothiās*. One good qualification for becoming a *bhuvā* is to possess the habit of throwing one's self into convulsive fits followed by a state of trance, especially on hearing the beating of a *dānklān* (drum). At such a time the *mātā* or *devi* is supposed to possess the person of the *bhuvā* and to speak out her wishes on being questioned. Some *bhuvās* are regularly possessed by some *devi* or *mātā* on every Sunday or Tuesday.[4]

A typical *bhuvā* has a braid of hair on his head, puts one or more iron or copper anklets round his leg or elbow, and makes a mark with red lead on his forehead. A *bhuvā* attending upon the goddess Meldi is generally[5] a Vāghri by caste and always wears dirty clothes. A Bharvād *bhuvā* has generally a silver anklet round his waist. A *bhuvā* has to observe a fast on all the nine days of the *Nav-rātras*. If a *bhuvā* happens to come across another *bhuvā* in convulsive fits or in a trance, he must need go into fits as well.

Generally speaking every *bhuvā* keeps an image of his favourite *mātā* in or near his own dwelling. Generally he erects a hut for the purpose and hoists a flag upon it. Near the image are placed a number of conch-shells and stones and brooms of peacock feathers. The deity is not systematically worshipped every day but receives adoration every Sunday and Tuesday. Sometimes the *bhuvā* has a disciple—a *sevaka*—who does the duty of dashing bell-metal cymbals at the time when the *bhuvā* throws himself in a trance.[6]

When a new *bhuvā* is to be initiated into the profession, he is made to sit before an image of the *mātā*, where he goes into convulsive fits while the *dānklān vagādnārs* beat the drums and loudly recite hymns in honour of the deity. Afterwards he is taken to a cemetery accompanied by the drummers and an expert *bhuvā*, where the latter marks out a square on the ground with the edge of a sword. The novice is asked to lie prostrate within the area thus marked out and to get up and lie again, doing the same four times, each time with his head towards each of the four quarters. The *bhuvā* who initiates the novice and who is thenceforth considered to be the *guru* or preceptor of the latter, ties a *rākhadi* (a piece of silk thread) round the elbow of the pupil.[7]

[1] The School Masters of Kotdā Sangni and Sanka.

[2] The School Master of Zinzuwādā.

[3] The School Master of Jodiā.

[4] The School Master of Sānka.

[5] The School Master of Dadvi.

[6] Mr. K. D. Desāi.

[7] The School Master of Pātanvāv.

Every *bhuvā* is required to propitiate his favourite goddess every third year, the ceremony which is then performed being called *Khad-Khadya-besādvi.* This is performed either during the *Nav-rātra* holidays or during the bright half of either the month of *Māgh* or *Chaitra.* All the *bhuvās* in the village are invited on the occasion, when there is *gānjā*-smoking or *bhāng*-drinking, partly at night. After the supper which follows this party, all the *bhuvās* gather together and go into convulsive fits till they are almost suffocated. Cocoanuts are then dedicated and cracked before the *mātā,* and the kernel is distributed among those present. The party then break up.[1]

It is believed by some people that the spirit of a Muhammadan saint. living or dead, dwells in such trees as the *Khijado,* i. e., *Shami* (Prosopis spicigera) and *Bāval,* i. e. , *Bābhul* (Acacia arabica). It is known by the name of *chitharia* that is , the ragged *Pir.* It is a common belief that if a mother fails to offer a rag or a piece of cloth to such a holy tree while passing by it, her children run the risk of falling ill. Women and ignorant people, therefore, make a point of offering rags to such trees whenever they happen to pass by them.[2]

According to another belief, travellers, in order to accomplish their journey safely, offer rags to such of the *Khijado, Bāval* or *Limdo* (Nim) trees as are reputed to be the residences of spirits, if they happen to be on their road.[3]

Some believe that both male and female spirits reside in the *Khijado, Bāval* and *Kerado* trees, and throw rags over them with the object of preventing passers by from cutting or removing the trees. Some pile stones round their stems and draw tridents over them with red lead and oil. If superstitious people come across such trees, they throw pieces of stones on the piles, believing them to be holy places, and think that by doing so they attain the merit of building a temple or shrine. A belief runs that this pile should grow larger and larger day by day, and not be diminished. If the base of such a tree is not marked by a pile of stones, rags only are offered; and if rags are not available, the devotee tears off a piece of his garment, however costly it may be, and dedicates it to the tree.[4]

Once, a child saw its mother offering a rag to such a tree, and asked her the reason of the offering. The mother replied that her brother, that is the child's maternal uncle, dwelt in the tree. Hence a belief arose that a *chithario* (ragged) uncle dwells in such trees. Others assert that the *chithario pir* dwells in such trees, and they propitiate him by offering cocoanuts and burning frankincense before it.[4]

There is a *Khijado* tree near Sultānpur which is believed to be the residence of a demon *māmo.* This demon is propitiated by the offerings of rags.

Some declare that travellers fix rags of worn out clothes to the trees mentioned above in order that they may not be attacked by the evil spirits residing in them. Another belief is that the spirits of deceased ancestors residing in such trees get absolution through this form of devotion. It is also believed that a goddess called *chitharia devi* resides in such trees, and being pleased with these offerings, blesses childless females with children, and cures persons suffering from itch of their disease. There is a further belief that ragged travellers, by offering pieces of their clothes to the *Khijado, Bāval* or *Kerado* trees, are blessed in return with good clothes.

Some believe that Hanumān, the lord of spirits, resides in certain trees. They call him *chithario* or ragged Hanumān. All passers by offer rags to the trees inhabited by

1 The School Master of Sānkā.

2 The School Master of Kotda Sangani.

3 The School Master of Davaliā.

4 The School Master of Ganod.

him. There is such a tree near the station of Shiroi. There is a tamarind tree on the road from Tamnagar to Khantalia which is believed to be the residence of *chithario* Hanumān and receives similar offerings. Another tamarind tree of this description is near Marad and there is a *Khijado* tree on the road between Kālāvad and Vāvadi which is similarly treated.[1]

It is related by some people that in deserts trees are rare and the summer heat is oppressive. To the travellers passing through such deserts, the only place of rest is in the shadow of a solitary tree that is to be met occasionally. In order that no harm be done to such trees, some people have given currency to the belief that a spirit called *māmo* dwells in such trees and expects the offering of a rag and a pice at the hands of every passer by.[1]

Some are of opinion that the *bhuvās*, in order to raise money from the credulous by terrifying them, daub a tree within the limits of each village with the form of a trident, and fix rags to it, stating that it is the abode of a *māmo* or a *pir*. At times they ask their clients to offer certain things to such trees, which they appropriate to themselves.[2]

There is also a belief, that the holy trees that receive offerings of rags from travellers, are the abodes of gods or evil spirits, and are distinguished from other trees of the same species by the epithet of *chithario*. Some people hoist flags on such trees instead of offering rags.

In some places, the *Borādi* (jujube), *Pipal*, *Vad* (banyan) and the sweet basil receive offerings of a pice and a betelnut from travellers, while the *Khijado* and *Bāval* are given rags.[3]

It is stated by some people that the belief in *chithario* pir has grown during the last four hundred years.

Rags are never offered to wells, but it is common to offer them copper coins and betelnuts. Sometimes flags are hoisted near holy wells in honour of the water-goddess Jaldevki. Travellers hoist flags on certain wells and throw copper coins into them in the course of their journey. The origin of this offering is said to be in the desire of travellers to prevent people from committing a nuisance near wells.

Some wells are noted as being the abode of spirits who have the power of effecting certain cures. It is customary to throw a pice in such wells. When a person is bitten by a rabid dog, he goes to a well inhabited by a *vāchharo*, the spirit who cures hydrophobia, with two earthen cups filled with milk, with a pice in each, and empties the contents into the water.

It is a belief among Hindus that to give alms in secret confers a great merit on the donor. Some of the orthodox people, therefore, throw pice into wells, considering it to be a kind of secret charity.

The belief in the practices adopted for transferring disease from one person to another obtains mostly among women, who have recourse to such practices for curing their children.

One of such practices is to lay a suffering child in the cradle of a healthy child. This act is believed to result in transferring the disease of the ailing child to the healthy child. Another practice is that the mother of the sickly child should touch the mother of a healthy child with the object of transferring the disease of her child to the child of the latter. Some believe that the mere contact of an ailing child with a healthy child is sufficient to transfer the malady of the former to the person of the latter. Others maintain that this can be brought about by a mother either by touching the cradle of another

[1] The School Master of Limbdi Taluka.

[2] The School Master of Kolki.

[3] The School Master of Dadvi.

child or by touching the person of another woman. There are others, who hold that the disease of a sickly child can be transferred to another child by feeding the latter with the leavings of the former. There is a further belief that a mother can transfer the disease of her suffering child to the child of another woman by applying the end of her robe to the end of the robe of the latter. In some places, when a child begins to weaken, its mother makes an idol of cow or buffalo dung, and keeps it fixed to a wall of the house, in the belief that the child will be cured slowly as the idol dries. It is stated that instances are actually known of the recovery of children by this process. These methods of transferring disease are called *tuchakās* i. e. mystic methods. As a rule superstitious women practise them on Sundays or Tuesdays, as it is believed, that to be efficacious, they must be practised on these days.

In addition to the *tuchakās* above stated the *utārs*, *dorās*, etc., already described, are used for curing diseases.

Some diseases are attributed to *vir* possession. *Virs* are male spirits fifty two in number. The *bhuvās* or exorcists are believed to have control over them, and are supposed to be able to detect an illness caused by possession by a *vir*. In such cases, the *bhuvās* drive away the evil spirits from the patients by magic incantations, or transfer them to others by waving a certain number of grain seeds round the head of the patient. By another process the *bhuvās* can confine the evil spirit in a glass bottle, which is buried underground.

In order to eradicate a dangerous disease, an *utār* is frequently offered to a dog, in the belief that by eating the *utār* the disease is transferred to the dog.

In some places, diseases of long standing due to spirit possession are cured by employing a *bhuvā*, (exorcist), who, accompanied by others of his order, goes to the patient's house, makes a bamboo bier, waves an *utār* round the patient's head, and lays himself on the bier with the *utār* by his side. The bier is carried to the burning ground by four persons to the accompaniment of the beatings of drums, followed by the exorcists, who throw *bāklāns* (round flat cakes of *juvāri* flour) into the air as the procession moves on. When the party reach the burning ground, the bier is put down, and the *bhuvā*, shaking violently, offers the *utār* to a spirit of the place. He then prostrates himself four times with his face turned towards the four directions and drives a nail into the ground at each turn. Next, the *bhuvā* lets loose a goat or a ram, to which the *vir* in the body of the patient is supposed to be transferred. It is said that the performance of this rite relieves the patient's mind of anxiety regarding the cause of his disease, and he thereafter shows signs of improvement.[1]

When a man is suffering from *ānjani* (a sore or mole on the eye-lid) he goes to another person's house and strikes earthen vessels against his door saying "I have shaken the vessels. May the *ānjani* be with me to-day and with you tomorrow". It is also stated that such a patient goes to the house of a man who has two wives while the latter is asleep, and taps his door uttering the words "*Anjani ghar bhāngani āj mane ane kal tane*" i. e., "May *ānjani*, the breaker of the house, be to-day with me and tomorrow with thee." This process is believed to transfer the disease from the person of the patient to that of the husband of the two wives.

A common method for transferring disease is to wave water round a sick person and give it to another to drink. Similarly, a goblet filled with water is passed round a patient's head and offered to a *bhuvā*, who drinks off the contents.

A belief prevails all over Gujarāt that a disease can be passed from one species of

[1] The School Master of Zinzuwādā.

animals to another, and various practices are adopted to effect this. Generally a *bhuvā* or exorcist arranges the transfer. The *bhuvā*, accompanied by a troupe of dancers and drummers, visits the house of the sick person and, after examining corn seeds *dānās* which have been waved round the patient's head on a night preceding a Sunday or Tuesday, declares that the evil spirit possessing the patient requires a living victim. A cock, goat or a male buffalo is then brought as a substitute for the patient, is waved round him, the tip of its right ear is cut off, and it is offered to the *mātā* or goddess, that is, it is released to stray as it pleases. These goats, etc., are called *mātā's* goats, *mātā's* cocks, or *mātā's* male buffaloes, and are seen wandering about in many villages. Sometimes the goat, etc., is killed before the image of the *mātā* and the *bhuvā* dipping the palms of his hands into its blood, presses them against the doors of every house in the village. In the case of an outbreak of epidemic, the victim is set at liberty beyond the limits of the village affected. It is believed by some people that the animal to which a disease is conveyed in the above manner, dies of its effects.[1]

In some places the patient is supposed to be possessed by a goddess instead of by an evil spirit. A goat, cock or a male buffalo is offered to the goddess in the same way as to an evil spirit.

In some villages, when there is an outbreak of a serious epidemic, it is customary to drive a buffalo beyond the village boundary, with the disease on his back. The back of the buffalo which is chosen for this purpose is marked with a trident in red lead and covered with a piece of black cloth, on which are laid a few grains of *adad* and an iron nail. Thus decorated, the buffalo is driven beyond the limits of the village. It is believed that an animal driven in this way carries the disease wherever it goes.

Very often, the beast to which a disease is transferred is kept tied to a post all its life, with the belief that by so doing the disease remains enchained. Jain teachers confine a disease in a bottle and bury it underground. Sometimes, a disease is passed on to a crow, whose legs are tied to a pillar, thus making it a life-long prisoner.

Once upon a time, when there was an outbreak of cholera in a certain village, a *bāvā* (recluse) happened to arrive on the scene. He caught two rams, made them move in a circle, and left them in the burning ground, where they died, the epidemic disappearing with their death. Hence a belief gained ground that an epidemic of cholera can be expelled by passing it on to two rams or goats.[2]

It is related that, at Gondal, a case of cholera was cured by a Bhangi (sweeper) by waving a cock round the patient's head.[3]

A few years ago there lived in Khākhi Jalia, a village in the vicinity of Kolki, a *Khākhi* (recluse) named Nārandās, who, when laid up with fever, passed on the disease to his blanket, and after a time drew it back to his own person.

[1] The School Master of Dhānk.

[2] The Pathashālā Shastri, Talpur.

[3] The School Mistress of Gondal.

CHAPTER IV.

WORSHIP OF ANCESTORS AND SAINTS.

The spirits of a deceased father, grand father, great grand father, and of a mother, grand mother, and great grand mother, i. e., all the male and female ascendants up to the third degree, receive systematic worship when the *Shrāddha* or funeral ceremonies are performed either on the anniversary of the death of any of them or on the day when the *Nārāyan bali* is performed in such holy places as Gayā, Sidadhapur or Prabhās Pātan. The spirits of those who meet heroic deaths on fields of battle are called *Suropuros*, and pillars are erected in their memory on the spot where they breathed their last. They receive only occasional worship.[1]

The *purvajas* or spirits of deceased ancestors receive worship on the thirteenth or fourteenth day of the dark half of *Shrāvan* (the tenth month of the Gujarāt Hindu year), on the fourteenth of the dark half of *Ashvin*, on the death anniversaries and on days on which the *Shrāddhas*, *tripindis* or *nil parnāvavi* ceremonies are performed. On these occasions, the *pitriyas* (deceased ancestors) are represented by twisted braids of the *durvā* grass (cynodon dactylon)[2]

Purvajas or ancestral spirits descend to the level of ghosts when they are strongly attached to worldly objects. Such spirits often possess the bodies of their descendants, though the necessary *Shrāddhas* are performed for their release. The 13th, 14th and 15th days of the bright half of the months of *Kārtik* and *Chaitra* are the special days for propitiation of departed spirits by their relatives either at home or in holy places, while the whole of the dark half of the month of *Bhādarvā* is devoted to this purpose.* During this fortnight, *shrāddha* is performed in honour of the deceased on the day corresponding to the day of his death, when Brāhmans are feasted. Thus, a person dying on the 5th day of *Kārtik* has his *shrāddha* performed on the 5th day of the *sharādian*. On this occasion, water is poured at the root of the *Pipal*, *tarpan* or offerings of water are made, and *pinds* or balls of rice are offered to the deceased.

Of all the days of the *sharādian* the 13th, 14th and 15th are considered to be of special importance.

The death annivesary of a *pitriya* is called *samvatsari*, *valgo samachari* or *chhamachhari*, when a *shrāddha* is performed and Brāhmans are feasted.

The *pitriyas* are also worshipped on auspicious occasions such as marriages, by the performance of a *shrāddha* called *nāndi*, when *pinds* (balls) of molasses are offered instead of rice. It is considered an act of merit to perform *shrāddha* in honour of the *pitriyas* on the banks of a river or tank at midday on the 8th day of the dark half of a month.

From the 13th to the 15th day of the dark half of *Shrāvan*, after their morning ablutions, orthodox people pour water over the *Pipal*, the *Bābul*, the *Ber* (Zizyphus jujube) and, *durvā* grass, and on those places where cows are known to congregate, in the belief that by so doing the thirst of the spirits of the deceased is quenched. It is also believed that if feasts are given to the relatives of the deceased and to Brāhmans the *pitriyas* are satisfied.

According to some, the *Sharādian* lasts from the full-moon day of the month of

[1] The School Master of Dhānk.

* This period of 15 days is called *Sharādian*.

[2] The School Master of Kotda Sangani.

Bhādarvā to the new-moon day of the same month, that is for a period of sixteen days. The *Shrāddhas* of those who die on the *Punema* or full-moon day of a month are performed on the full-moon day of *Bhādarvā*, and the *Shrāddhas* of those who die on the new-moon day *amavasia* of a month are performed on the *amavasia* of *Bhādarvā*. The 13th day of the dark half of *Bhādarvā* is called *bālā terash* that is childrens' thirteenth. This day is specially devoted to the propitiation of the spirits of children.[1]

On the *Shrāddha* days Brāhmans and relatives of the deceased are feasted, and oblations called *Vāsh*, consisting of rice and sweets, are offered to crows.

On *Āsho Vad* fourteenth, that is, the fourteenth of the dark half of *Āsho*, it is customary to apply red lead to the pillars erected in honour of men that die heroic or noble deaths on fields of battle, to break cocoanuts before them, to light lamps fed with ghi and to offer cooked food to their spirits.[2]

The spirits of those who die with strong attachment to the objects of this world are said to enter the state known as *asur gati* or the path of demons. In this condition the spirit of the deceased possesses the person of one of his relatives and torments the family in which he lived. The members of the family, when worried by his persecutions, engage the services of a *bhuvā* or exorcist, who sets up a wooden image of the tormenting spirit in a niche in a wall of the house. A lamp fed with *ghi* is lighted daily before this image, and in times of trouble, a cocoanut is offered to it in the belief that the spirit can protect the offerers from injuries.

The *pitriyas* or ancestral spirits are propitiated by pouring water over the *Bordi* (jujube), the *Tulsi* (sweet basil) the *Vad* (banyan) the *Pipal* or *durvā* grass (cynodon dactyton) on the 13th, 14th and 15th days of the bright half of *Chaitra* and on the same days of the dark half of *Kārtik* and *Shrāvan*. On *Vaishākh Shud Trij*, that is, on the third of the bright half of *Vaishākh*, which is called *Akhā Trij*, women offer to Brāhmans two earthen jars filled with water and covered with an earthen cup. containing a betelnut, a pice and a *pān* or betel leaf, for the propitiation of the spirits of their deceased ancestors.[3]

For the propitiation of a male spirit a party of Brāhmans is feasted, and for the propitiation of a female spirit three unwidowed married women.[4]

Rajputs, Bharvāds, Ahirs and Kolis set up either a pile of stones or a single stone on the boundary of their village in honour of those among them who die on battle fields. These piles or stones are called *Pālios*. On the *Pālios* are placed engraved images to represent the deceased in whose memory the *Pālios* are erected. Small pillars are also raised in the localities where such persons met their death. On the *Kāli Chaudas* or black fourteenth, that is the fourteenth day of the dark half of *Āsho*, the *Pālios* are daubed with red lead and worshipped with offerings of cocoanuts. Women who have become *sati* receive worship and offerings on the Hindu new year's day.[5]

Spiritual guides such as Shankarāchārya, Vallabāchārya, the *mahārājas* or spiritual heads of the sect called Swāminārāyan, Lālo Bhagat and Talo Bhagat are worshipped by their devotees with offerings of food, garments and cash. In this *Kali Yuga* or iron age, men who are really great are rare, and even if there be some, they are invisible to the faulty vision of the present day degraded mortals. A few come into contact with such holy men by virtue of the good deeds performed by them in their past lives. These are said to attain paradise by this *satsang*[6] (contact with the righteous).

[1] Mr. K. D. Desāi.
[2] The School Master of Luvaria.
[3] The School Master of Jodiā.
[4] The School Master of Lilāpur.
[5] The School Master of Sānka.
[6] The School Master of Dhānk.

Holy men receive personal worship during their life-time. After they are dead, their relics, such as impressions of their footsteps, their photos or busts are worshipped with offerings of sandal paste, flowers, red powder, frankincense, lamps fed with ghi and *ārati* (swingings of lamps)[1]

Every sect of Hindus has a *Mahārāja* or spiritual head, and it is considered meritorious to entertain and worship him on certain special occasions. The *Mahārāja* or *Guru* is received with great *éclat.* His followers form a procession and carry him in a palanquin or a carriage and pair accompanied with music. At the house of the person who invites him, the floor is covered with rich cloth, over which the *Mahārāja* is led to a raised seat specially arranged for the purpose. He is then worshipped by the host with the same details as the image of a god. His feet are washed by *panchāmrita* (five nectars), that is a mixture of ghi, milk, honey, sugar and water, which is sipped by the worshipper and distributed among the followers of the *Mahārāja.* Very often the feet of the *Mahārāja* are washed in water, which is considered as purifying as the *panchāmrita.* Great festivity and rejoicings are observed on this day at the house of the *Mahārāja's* host, where crowds of the *Mahārāja's* followers assemble eager for a sight of him. After spending about half an hour in the house, the *Mahārāja* departs, first receiving valuable presents from the host.

Spiritual guides who claim the power of working miracles are held in high esteem by the people. Some of these guides are said to have control over spiritual beings or to possess their favour. These spirits are supposed to endow them with the power of preparing mystic threads, which, when worn round the waist, neck or arm, cure various diseases.

In the Kadavāsan woods, near the village of Daldi, there lives a *bāvā* called Bhimputi, who is believed to possess miraculous powers. He surprises visitors by his wonderful feats and commands vows from the afflicted by mitigating their sufferings. Every day, before breakfast, the *bāvā* visits seven villages to collect sugar and flour, which he throws in handfuls over every anthill which he meets on his way. This act of charity has established him as a saint, and most of his prophecies are believed to be fulfilled.

A Musalmān named Muhammad Chhail is held in great respect by the people on account of his great magical powers. He is believed to be in the good graces of a *Pir,* who has endowed him with the power of commanding material objects to come to him from long distances, and of breaking them and making them whole again.[2]

Great men of antiquity often command worship as gods. A fast is observed by Hindus on the 9th day of the bright half of *Chaitra,* the birth day of Rāma, whose birth anniversary is celebrated at noon on that day in his temple. On this occasion, all visitors to the temple offer a pice or two to his image and receive his *Prasād,* that is, consecrated food, which consists of a mixture of curdled milk and sugar. The birth of Krishna is celebrated at mid-night on the eighth day of the dark half of *Shrāvan,* when people keep awake for the whole of the night.

The Jains observe a fast for seven days from *Shrāvan Vad Bāras,* that is the 12th day of the dark half of *Shrāvan,* to the 5th day of the bright half of *Bhādarvā,* in honour of Mahāvir Swāmi, one of their spiritual teachers, who is believed to have been born on the 2nd day of the bright half of *Bhādarvā.* This period is known as the *Pajusan,* during which the Jains cause the

[1] The School Master of Ganod.

[2] The School Master of Zinzuvādā.

slaughter-houses and fish markets to be closed and give alms to the poor.[1]

A century ago there lived at Nalkanthā a sage named Bhānsāb. He met a holy death by deep meditations, and a few days after rose up from his grave in his original form. This led him to be classed in the category of great men and to command divine worship.[2]

Vithal, a sage of the Kāthi tribe, is revered in Pāliād. Sāvo, a devotee at Zanzarkā, is worshipped by Dheds. Fehalā a Rajput and Tolat his wife, are enshrined at Anjār, a village in Cutch. Lālo, a Baniā devotee of Sindhāvār, received divine honours in his life-time and his image in Sāyalā is held in great reverence to this day. The *samādh* of Mādhvagar, an *atit* of Vastadi, situated in Unchadi a village in the Dhandhuka taluka in Ahmedābād, is an object of worship. Harikrishna Mahārāja, a Brāhman saint of Chudā, received divine honours at Chudā and the Charotar.[3]

If the souls of the departed ones are condemned to become ghosts, *shrāddha* ceremonies performed by their descendants are said to be efficacious in freeing them from their ghostly existence and relegating them to some other form of life.

The lives of *bhuts* and *pishāchas*, male and female ghosts, are said to extend over a thousand years.[4] *Shrāddhas*, such as the *samāchari* i. e., the death anniversary and *Nārāyanbali* i. e., a *shrāddha* performed in a holy place, emancipate the ghostly spirits from their wretched existence and make them eligible for birth in a better form.[5] Some believe that at the end of their ghostly existence (a thousand years) they take birth in the animal kingdom in the mortal world.[6]

The soul is not said to have finally perished unless it merges into the divine self and attains *moksha* or salvation. The passions and desires of a dying man do not permit his soul ascending beyond a certain stage, where he or she remains as a ghost until the soul is purged of all his or her desires and sins by the performance of funeral ceremonies. For relieving ancestral spirits from the low order of *bhuts* and *pishāchas*, *shrāddhas* are performed by their surviving relatives in such holy places as Prabhās, Gayā and Pindtārak. These ceremonies are known as *Nārāyanbali*, *Nilotsarga* and *saptāha-pārāyan* (recitation of a sacred book for seven consecutive days).[7]

Those persons who die with wicked thoughts still present and their desires not fulfilled, enter the order of evil spirits, from which they are liberated after their desires have been satisfied and their wicked thoughts eliminated.[8]

Bhuts and *pishāchas*-ghosts, male and female—can be prevented from doing harm by recourse to certain processes. For instance, the wife of a Nāgar of Gadhadā became a witch after her death and began to torment the second wife of her husband by throwing her out of bed whenever she was asleep. To prevent this, the husband took a vow to perform a *shrāddha* at Sidhpur in the name of the deceased wife, after the performance of which the ghostly presence stopped harassing the new wife of her husband.[9]

Bhuts and *pishāchas* are believed by some people to be immortal, because they are supposed to belong to the order of demi-gods. In the *Amorkosha*—the well-known Sanskrit lexicon—they are classed with divinities, such

[1] The School Master of Jodia.

[2] The School Master of Lālāpur.

[3] The School Master of Sānkā.

[4] The School Masters of Kotda Sangani and Dadvi.

[5] The School Master of Kotda Sangani.

[6] The School Master of Dadvi.

[7] The School Master of Ganod.

[8] The School Master of Motā Devaliā.

[9] The Deputy Educational Inspector, Gohilvād.

as *guhyaks*, and *sidhas*. The *bhut* is defined as a deity that troubles infants and the *pishācha* as a deity that lives on flesh. *Bhuts* and *pishāchas* are the *ganas* or attendants of Shiva, one of the gods of the Hindu Trinity. They are supposed to be *upadevas* or demi-gods.

Preta is the spirit of a person that dies a sudden or unnatural death with many of his desires unfulfilled. His soul attains emancipation by the performance of a *saptāh*, that is a recitation of the *Bhāgvat* on seven consecutive days. It is described in the *Bhāgvat* that Dhundhumari, the brother of Gokarn, who had become a *preta*, was released from his *preta* existence by the performance of a *saptāh* which his brother caused to be made. The *Garudpurān* mentions that King Babruvāhan emancipated a *preta* by the performance of a *shrāddha*. The *mukti* or salvation of a *preta* is in itself its death. This would prove *pretas* to be mortal.[1]

The span of life of the *bhuts* and *pretas* is very long, but those whose descendants offer them the usual oblations gain their emancipation sooner. There is a *kund* or spring called Zilānand in the vicinity of Jhinjhuvādā, on the banks of which is a temple of Zilakeshwar Mahādev. The performance of the *pitri shrāddha* by the side of this spring is believed to expedite the emancipation of the spirits of the deceased from ghostly life. Every year, on the *Bhādarvā amāvāsya*, that is, the new moon day of the month *Bhādarvā*, a great fair is held on this spot, when people from long distances visit the place to get their relatives exorcised by the *bhuvās* or exorcists.

It is believed, that though *bhuts*, *pretas* and *pishāchas* are immortal, they are scared away by the sound of a European band and of other musical instruments.[2] It is said that all drums and other weird instruments whether European or Indian, have the power of scaring away evil spirits.

An evil spirit called Bābaro had entered the person of the uncle of Māldev the king of Jhālāvād much to the king's annoyance. Māldev offered a stubborn fight to Bābaro, who, unable to cope with Māldev, promised to extend his kingdom over those villages in which he would hang up bunting in one night. It is said that the present extent of the Jāhlwād territories was due to king Māldev's enterprise in hanging up bunting over these territories as asked by Bābaro.[3]

Though at the time of a man's death the faculties may hardly be sound, yet the *vārsanā*—the impressions—left on his mind by his past actions are in themselves good or bad enough to impress him so as to make his departing spirit assume a new form of life in keeping with them. For instance, a man following a particular profession becomes subject to dreams bearing on that profession. When the impression created by his actions in daily life is so deep as to induce dreams, his mind, even after death, leaves to his departing soul an inclination to be engaged in the subject of his mind's last activities. This is *vāsanā*.*

It is a popular saying among Hindus that children inherit the nature of their parents. It is for this reason that high caste Hindus do not utter the names of their eldest sons. There is a further belief that the *Pitriyas* departed from the world with certain desires unfulfilled reappear as descendants of their children to have these desires satisfied.[4]

As the saying goes *Pitā putrena jāyate*, that is a father is born in the form of the

[1] Shāstri Bhāyāvadar Pāthshālā.
[2] The School Master of Todiā.
[3] The School Master of Jodiā.
[4] The School Master of Kotdā Sangani.

* A *vāsanā* is the outcome of a person's good or bad actions. It is not the last desire of a man as supposed by some, but the result of his good or bad actions or rather of the workings of his mind during life. It is believed that, if at the moment of death, a man's mind is fixed on the strong attachment he feels for his children, he is born as a descendant of his offspring.—The School Master of Dhānk.

son, so the *Pitriyas* are born as descendants of their children, or according to the *Bija vrikshanyāya*, as a tree springs from its seed, that is, its offerings, so parents take birth as children of their offspring.[1]

The *Pitriyas*, whose attachment to their children or family or wealth does not die with them, reappear in the same family as descendants. It is also believed that persons dying with debts unpaid with the consciousness that they must be paid, are reborn in this world for the discharge of their obligations.[2]

It is not always that the *Purvajas* reappear in the same family. It is said about the departed spirits, that after undergoing punishment for their sins and enjoying the fruits of their good actions, they come down on earth again as drops of rain, and forming part of the grain which grows on rain water make their way into the wombs of animals and are thus reborn.[3]

On account of the community of their feelings, habits and ideas in previous births, members of different families form different groups. The actions performed in this life keep them bound to one another either as recipients of the return of the obligations given in the past or as givers of fresh obligations. The members of a family stand thus to one another in the relation of debtors and creditors. It is for the discharge of these debts and recovery of dues that several individuals are united in a family. This naturally leads to the members of a family taking birth again in the same family for the proper discharge of debts.

A virtuous child is declared to have been born to return the debts contracted in its past lives, and a vicious one to recover the dues.[4]

When an *atit* or holy man or a recluse dies, his body is interred, and a platform rising waist high from the ground, or a small dome-shaped temple, is built over the spot. This is called a *samādh*. An image of the god Shiva is generally installed in the *samādh*; but sometimes *pādukās* *i. e.* the impressions on stone of the footsteps of the deceased, are installed instead. Instances of the latter are the *pādukās* of Dattātraya, Gorakha and Machchendra Nāth.

Both the *Samādh* and the image of the god Shiva as well as the *pādukās* installed therein, are worshipped by the people, who, in course of time, give currency to the belief that the *Samādh* possesses certain miraculous powers, such as curing long-standing diseases, blessing barren women with children, etc. Offerings are made to the *Samādh* by pious persons and festivals or fairs are held in its honour by the inhabitants of the village in which the *Samādh* is located.[5]

Kabars or tombs raised over the graves of Mahomedan saints or *Pirs* are held in equal reverence both by Mahomedans and Hindus. To these offerings are made, and fairs are held in their honour.

Some *Samādhs* and *Kabars* noted for miraculous powers are given below.

1. *Gorakhnāth* :—The *Samādh* of Gorakhnāth lies on Mount Girnār. It is said that when the word *Salām* is shouted by any one standing on the brink of the hollow wherein the *Samādh* is said to be, the word "*Aleka, Aleka, Aleka*" is heard in response.[6]

2. *Kevaldās* :—The *Samādh* of Kevaldās stands in Susavāv. It is told that, on one occasion, when a festival was being celebrated in honour of the Bāvā Kevaldās, a *nimb* tree (Azadiarchta Indica) overhanging the *Samādh* was transformed into a *mitho Limbdo* (Ailantas excelsa).

3. *The Samādh at Kāngā* :—In the religious house at Kāngā , a village in the Junāgadh State, there lived a *bāvā* given to

1 The School Master of Ganod.
2 The School Master of Dadvi.
3 The School Master of Motā Devaliā.
4 The School Master of Charādwa.
5 The School Master of Ganod.
6 The School Master of Dhānk and the School Mistress of Gondal.

religious austerities. It is said that he took *Samādh** during life. This *Samādh* is said to work miracles at times.

4. Similarly, a *bāvā* in the religious house at Navānagar called *Shāradā Matha* has taken a *Samādh* during life, and his remains and the structure over them have become an object of worship.

5. *The Samādh of Lālā bhakta* :—Lālā bhakta was a native of Sāyolā. He was famous for his piety, and after his death his *Samādh* was deified. It is said in reference to this *Samādh* that a meal of dainty dishes prepared for five or six persons by its side, would satisfy the hunger of a company of fifty, if one happened to arrive there at the time of serving the meal[1].

6. *Dātār† Pir* :—The tomb of this Pir is situated on Mount Girnār. Almost all people in Kāthiāwār and many from Gujarāt offer vows to this Pir.[2]

This Pir is also known by the name of Kālā Yavan.[3] It is believed that he has the power of releasing the chain bonds of a person falsely accused with an offence provided he approaches the *Pir* in chains. The sanctity of this *Pir* is so great that vows in his honour secure to persons desiring male heirs the birth of sons.[4]

7. *Asāmi Pir* :—The tomb of this *Pir* is in Lunār. He is believed to ensure the fulfilment of certain vows made by those who have faith in him.[5]

8. *Devalshā Pir* :—The tomb of this *Pir* is situated at Amarān about seven miles from Todia. Many Hindus perform the first hair-cutting ceremony of their children at the shrine of this *Pir* with an offering of a sweet preparation of ghi, sugar or molasses, and wheat flour. The Muhammadans distribute cooked rice among the Fakirs about this shrine.

A tradition runs that, once seven eunuchs defied the power of this *Pir* saying that they would put no faith in him unless they conceived sons. This they did, and when in terror regarding their approaching confinement, they were told that the children would have to be taken out by cutting their bodies open. The tombs of these seven eunuchs and their sons still stand near the tomb of Devalshā to bear testimony to his glory and miraculous power.[6]

9. *The Kabar of Hāji Karmāni* :—Is situated at Dwārkān and is much respected by both Hindus and Muhammadans.[7]

10. *The tombs of Jesal and Toral* :—These are said to be the tombs of a husband and wife of the names of Jesal and Toral. They are situated in Anjār, a village in Cutch. It is said that originally these tombs were at the distance of twenty-seven feet from one another, but now the distance between them is only 7½ feet. A belief is current that the day of judgment will come when these two tombs meet.[8]

11. *Hāj Pir and Gebānshā Pir* :—The tombs of these *Pirs* are at Mendardā. Vows are offered to the Hāj Pir (Pilgrims saint) with the object of securing a good rainfall after an unusual drought, also for the restoration of stolen property. Vows to the Gebanshā Pir are believed to be efficacious in curing foot diseases of cattle and skin diseases of children.[9]

* A *samādh* is taken during life in the following way.
A deep pit is dug in the ground. The person who wishes to take a *samādh* goes into a deep trance by meditation, and then runs yelling and screaming to the pit, while drums are beaten furiously and a loud din is raised, so that none should hear a possible exclamation or cry from the runner. In the midst of this din the runner leaps into the pit and is covered over with salt and earth. An altar is raised over this spot wtth Shiva's image, which afterwards becomes an object of worship. It is believed that if a word or a cry from the runner is heard while he is taking the leap, the whole village will be destroyed.—Mr. K. D. Desāi.

1 The Pāthshālā Shāstri, Bhāyāvadar.

† Dātār means the great giver or munificent. The *Pir* is so called on account of his power of fulfilling the vows of many.

2 The School Master of Dhānk.

3 The School Master of Movaiya.

4 The School Master of Dhānk and Moti Parabdi.

5 The School Master of Dadvi.

6 The School Master of Dadvi.

7 The School Master of Dadvi.

8 The School Master of Davaliā.

9 The School Master of Mendardā.

12. *Panch or Five Pirs* :—The tombs of these *Pirs* are situated in Dahurā, each of them measuring about twenty-seven feet. A miracle is attributed to these tombs in the phenomenon that they can never be accurately measured, each attempt at measurement giving a different result. Women whose sons die in infancy make vows in honour of the Panch Pirs, and take them to their tombs on their attaining a certain age, where they observe *fakiri** for ten days.[1]

13. *Aulia Pir*† :—The tomb of this *Pir* lies on Mount Girnār. It is believed to possess the miraculous power of stopping the career of galloping horses and bringing them to the ground, and of stupefying the senses of a person who enters the shrine.[2]

14. *Miran Dātār* :—The celebrated tomb of this Pir is in the village of Unjhā near Baroda, where a fair is held every Friday in *Shrāvan*. Persons possessed by evil spirits are said to be cured by visiting this tomb and offering an image of a horse stuffed with cotton, and a cocoanut. People from all parts of Gujarāt and from distant places suffering from physical infirmities, observe vows in honour of this *Pir*. Some wear iron wristlets round their wrists in his honour.[3]

15. *Pir Māhābali* :—The tomb of this *Pir* is situated at Gotarkā near Rādhanpur. Every year a fair is held in honour of this tomb, when the chief Pujāri of the shrine of Varalu goes there, holding in one hand a bayonet with its point touching his breast, and in the other, a cocoanut. It is said that when the Pujāri reaches the third step leading to the entrance of the shrine, the locked doors of the shrine fly open, and the Pujāri throws the cocoanut into the shrine. If the shrine gates do not open of themselves on his approach, the Pujari has to stab himself to death then and there.[4]

16. *Kalu Pir* :—It is said that this *Pir* leads a procession every night, when monstrous kettle-drums are beaten by his phantom followers. On every Friday this procession goes on its rounds, which cover a large area.[5]

Other tombs noted for miraculous powers are those of Gebalshā Pir in Charādwa, of Dariā Pir in Morvi, of Hajarat Pir in Baghdād and of Khojā Pir in Ajmere.[6]

The followers of the tenets of Swāminnārāyān, Vallabhāchārya, Kabir, Shankarāchārya, Rāmānuja, Madhwāchārya, Nimbārk and Talo Bhagat look upon these personages as gods, and worship their images.[7]

Some of the spiritual teachers mentioned above maintained large establishments and made their supremacy hereditary. Their representatives (that is either their heirs or disciples) are looked upon as the embodiments of the same virtues as were concentrated in the founders of the sects. The great teachers are worshipped either in the form of their footprints, their images or their representatives.[8]

The worship of the following Muhammadan Pirs has been adopted by Hindus :—

(1) Dātār Pir in Junāgadh.

(2) Dātār in Rātaiya near Khirāsara.

(3) Gobalsha Pir :—This Pir is noted for curing boils.

* A symbol of servitude of the saint.

† *Aulia* and *Pir*, synonymous terms, the first Arabic, the second Persian. Aulia is the Arabic plural of *wali* which means a saint. In Hindustāni the plural form is used to signify the singular e. g., a single *wali* or saint is often spoken of as an *aulia*. The word *Pir* originally meaning an old man is used in Hindustān in the sense of a saint. Aulia Pir is the Gujarāti for a single or many saints.

1 The School Master of Sultānpur.

2 The School Master of Moti Porabdi.

3 The School Master of Zinzuwādā.

4 The School Master of Surel.

5 The School Master of Jaseluan.

6 The School Master of Charādwā.

7 The School Master of Dhank.

8 Mr. K. D. Desāi.

(4) **Tāg Pir or the live saint near Bhāyāvadar:**—This Pir is believed to have the power of curing enlargement of the spleen. Persons suffering from this disease go to his shrine and distribute dry dates among children. This is supposed to propitiate him and to effect the cure.[1]

(5) Miran Dātār:—The miraculous and curative powers of this Pir are so potent that blind persons are known to have their eye-sight restored and childless persons to have their longings for children satisfied through his favour. Persons possessed by evil spirits are exorcised by merely wearing a ring in his name.[2]

The shrine of this Pir is situated in the village of Unāva in the Gāikwār's territory in North Gujarāt. His Highness the late Gāikwār Khanderāo has fixed solid silver railings round the shrine of this Pir in gratitude for a cure effected by him.

(6) Rāmde Pir:—This Pir has obtained the epithet of Hindva Pir as he is worshipped mostly by the Hindus. He has worshippers in many places, where shrines are erected in his honour and verses and hymns composed and sung in his praise.[3] He is evidently, as his name suggests, one of the first Khoja missionaries who practised teachings more Hindu than Musalmān in order to secure a following among the Hindus.

(7) Hāji Karmāni near Dvārikhān.

(8) The Dāvalsha Pir near Amarān.

(9) The Lakad Pir and the Hussein Pir in the vicinity of Ganod.

(10) Mahābali Dāda Pir:—This Pir is to be found close to the village of Varai. Milk offered to him in his shrine in *indās* (egg-shaped pots) is said to remain fresh for a year. Similarly, the doors of his shrine open of themselves after the lapse of a year.

(11) Mangalio Pir:—This Pir is worshipped at Dadvi.

(12) Moto Pir:—Is worshipped at Khandorana.

(13) Hindva Pir:—This is the Pir of the Khojās in Pirāna near Ahmedābād. He is so called because he is worshipped by the Hindus also.

(14) Bhadiādaro Pir:—Is in the village of Bhādia near Dhorāli.

(15) Ingārāsha Pir and Bālamsha Pir.

(16) Tamialsha and Kāsamsha Pir:—The shrines of these Pirs are on the Girnar hill.[4]

(17) Ganj Pir:—The shrine of this Pir is near Todia. Vows to offer a quarter of a pound of molasses to this Pir are believed to be efficacious in curing persons of fever and children of their ailments.[5]

There is a Pir in the village of Vadhardun near Viramgām. Persons suspected of having committed thefts are conducted in chains before this Pir. It is said that, if the charge be false, the chains break asunder of themselves.[6]

Apart from the respect paid to the Pirs mentioned above, the Hindus hold in great reverence the *tābuts* of the Muhammadans.[7]

[1] The School Master of Devalia.

[2] The School Masters of Dhānk and Vanod.

[3] The School Mistress, Female Training College, Rājkot.

[4] The School Master of Moti Parabadi.

[5] The School Master of Todia.

[6] The School Master of Lilāpur.

[7] Mr. K. D. Desāi.

There are various rural methods in vogue for the cure of barrenness.

One of these is for the barren woman to swallow the navel-string of a new-born child.[8] Another is to partake of the preparation called *kātlān*.[1]

There are two kinds of preparations which go by the name of *kātlān*. One is prepared from seven pieces of dry ginger.[2] The other is a mixture of *suva*,* *sunth* (dry ginger), *gundar* (gum arabic), *gol* (molasses) etc.[3] In order to secure the desired effect, the *kātlān* must be eaten seven times every Sunday or Tuesday seated on the cot of a woman in child-bed.[4]

The longing for a child is also believed to be satisfied by partaking of the food served to a woman, in confinement, sitting on her bed, either on a Sunday or Tuesday.[5]

There is also another preparation which is believed to cause conception. It consists of a mixture of *pitpāpdo* (Glossocardi Boswellia), sugar-cane and butter. In order to be efficacious, it must be taken on seven consecutive days commencing from the fourth day of the monthly menstrual period.[6]

Conception is also believed to be favoured by administering the gum of the *bābul* tree dissolved in milk for three days commencing from the third day of the monthly period.[6]

Some believe that, in order to be effective, this mixture must be taken standing.[7] In some places, seeds of a vegetable plant called *shivalangi* are also administered.[6]

To secure conception, a bit of coral is also eaten, with the face turned towards the sun.[6]

Other preparations taken with the belief that they cause conception are:—

(1) *Harde* (Myrobalan) put in *kansār* (a preparation of wheat flour cooked in water and sweetened with molasses), (2) extract of the fruit called *sārangdha*, (3) *pāras pipalo* (Thespesia populnea) mixed with clarified butter,[8] (4) gum mixed with plantains, (5) juice of the cooked leaves of the *Ārani* (Elaeodendren glaucum),[9] (6) powder of *Nāg kesar* (Messua ferrea) put into milk, and (7) the roots of *Bhong ringdi* (a kind of poisonous plant) mixed with the milk of a cow.[10]

It is also believed that if a barren woman succeeds in carrying away grains of rice from the folds of the upper garment of a pregnant woman, and eats them cooked in milk, her desire for a child is satisfied.[11]

In celebrating the *Simānt* or first pregnancy ceremony of a woman, the pregnant woman is taken for a bath to a dung-hill or to a distance of about thirty yards behind the house. After the bath is over, she returns home walking over sheets of cloth spread on her way. On this occasion her company is coveted by barren women for the purpose of tearing off unseen a piece of her upper garment, as this is believed to bring about conception. It is said that if a woman succeeds in doing this, she conceives, while the victim has a miscarriage.[12]

Some believe that a slight pressure by a childless woman on the upper garment of a pregnant woman is sufficient to bring about the result mentioned above.[13]

[1] The School Master of Dhānk.
[2] The School Master of Chhatrāsa.
[3] The School Master of Uptala.
[4] The School Mistress, Girls' School, Gondal.
[5] The School Master of Sultānpur.
[6] The School Master of Dhānk.
[7] The School Master of Dadvi.
[8] The School Master of Ganod.
[9] The School Mistress of Rājkot, Civil Station Girls' Scohol.
[10] The School Master of Bhayavadar.
[11] The School Master of Sultānpur.
[12] The School Master of Dhānk and Mr. K. D. Desai.
[13] The School Master of Dadvi.

* An ingredient used in preparing spices.

Others hold that a slight blow on the shoulder of a pregnant woman by a childless woman satisfies the desire of the latter for a child.[1]

Conception is also said to be effected by branding children while at play in the streets.[2]

It is believed that this brand, to have efficacy, must be inflicted on a Sunday or Tuesday.[2] The operation is generally performed in the evening with a red-hot needle. It is said that the branded child dies while the branding barren woman conceives a child.[3]

Offering bread to black dogs is also supposed to be a cure for barrenness.

Conception is also favoured by passing under the bier or palanquin holding the corpse of an ascetic or holy man while it is being carried to the cemetery.[4] Some believe that such an ascetic or saint must be a follower of the Jain faith.[5] Others maintain that the desired end can be secured only by wearing round the elbows the grains of rice or coins offered to the bier of a saint on its way to the cemetery.[6]

Other methods practised for the cure of barrenness are as follows:

The barren woman cuts off a lock of the hair of a child-bearing woman and keeps it in her custody.[7]

Some women collect the dust trodden on by a child-bearing woman in an earthen pot and eat it every day till it is exhausted.[7]

Some throw grains of *adad* (Phaseolus mungo) over the bed of a woman in confinement.*

Others daub their foreheads with the blood emitted by a woman in menses.[7]

There are some who pour water in a circle at the village gate on a Sunday or Tuesday, and when in period, partake of the powder of *mindhal* mixed with *lápsi* (coarse wheat flour fried in *ghi* and sweetened with molasses or sugar) seated on the threshold of the house.[8]

Many wear round their necks leaves called *bhojapatras* on which the mystical figure given below is drawn by an exorcist.

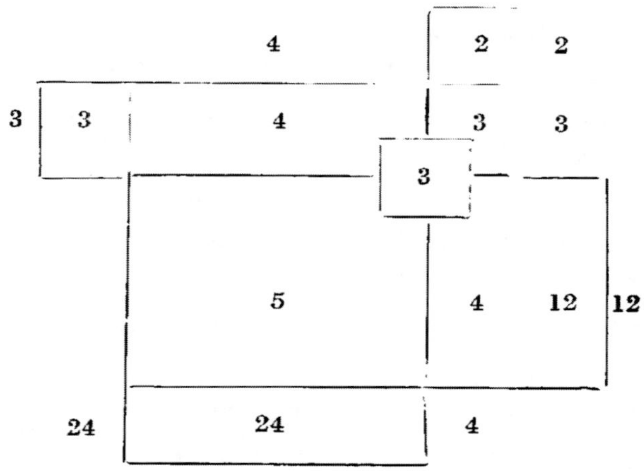

Pieces of paper on which the following *jantra* is written by an ascetic, woven in a string made of five kinds of silk, are also worn round the elbows:—

Swāhā aum rhin kling swāhā.

About a month and a quarter after the delivery of a woman, a ceremony called *zarmān zarvān* is performed, when the woman goes to a neighbouring stream or well to fetch water for the first time after her delivery. Near the stream or well five small heaps of sand are made and daubed with red lead. Next, a lamp fed with *ghi* is lighted, and seven small betelnuts are offered to the

[1] The School Master of Kotda Sangani.
[2] The School Master of Ganod.
[3] Mr. K. D. Desāi.
[4] The School Masters of Kotda Sangani and Chhatrāsa.
[5] The School Master of Jetpur.
[6] The Deputy Educational Inspector, Gohilwād.
[7] The School Master of Vanod.
[8] The School Masters of Dadvi and Chhatrāsa.

* It is for this eason that barren women are not allowed to approach the bed of a woman in child-bed.

stream or well. A cocoanut is then broken, and a part of it is thrown into the water as an offering. Next, the woman fills a jar with the water of the stream or well and returns home, taking with her six out of the seven betelnuts offered to the stream or well. On her way home she is approached by barren women who request to be favoured with one of the betelnuts, as it is believed that swallowing such a betelnut causes conception.[1]

Some believe that only the smallest of the seven betelnuts has the power of producing this result[2]. Others hold that this betelnut must be swallowed on the threshold of a house.[3]

Eating cocoa-kernel and molasses sitting on the threshold of the house on the fourth day of the monthly period is also believed to be a remedy for the cure of barrenness.

Placing a box containing a *kori*, (a small silver coin) on a spot where three roads cross one another is also said to favour conception.[4]

In some places, a black earthen pot containing charcoal and grains of *adad* (Phaseolus mungo) is placed on a spot where two roads cross one another, on a Sunday or Tuesday. On this day the barren woman has to take her meals without salt.[5]

Cutting off a lock of a child's hair and keeping it in custody is also believed to satisfy the longing of a barren woman for a child. This result can also be obtained by securing a piece of a garment of a suckling child.

Some worship daily a cocoanut and a betelnut consecrated with incantations.[6]

Some take a bath on the third day of their period, and stand on the threshold of the house with their hair sprinkled over with *kankotri* (red powder). Next, a *ghi*-fed lamp is offered to the deities, and the devotee prostrates herself before the lamp.[7]

It is also believed that barrenness can be cured by religious vows, by offering alms in propitiation of malignant planets such as Mars, and by reciting the *jap* or incantation called *gopāl santān* to please the deity of that name.[8]

One of the religious vows of this nature is to observe, fasts on twelve consecutive Sundays or Tuesdays. On these days the devotee fixes her gaze on the sun and offers him worship, after which she takes a meal prepared in milk without salt or sugar. [9]

Some hold a recitation of the *chandi kavach* a hundred times through Brāhmans with sacrificial oblations of clarified butter, sesamum seed, *kamod* (a kind of rice), *gugal* (rhododendron), sandal wood and sugar-candy.[10] Others have the story of the *Harivansha* recited on seventeen consecutive days, during which period the devotee (i.e., the barren woman) observes *brahmacharya* that is abstains from sexual enjoyment. This ceremony is believed to exorcise the fiend of barrenness.[10]

Some keep a vow of standing on their legs for the whole day on the fourteenth of the month of *Phālgun* (the fifth month of the Gujarāt Hindu year) and of breaking their fast after worshipping the sacred pyre.[11]

There is another vow called the *Punema* or full-moon day vow, the observance of which is believed to favour the birth of a son.[12]

[1] The School Master of Todia.
[2] The School Master of Mota Devalia.
[3] The School Master of Luvaria.
[4] The School Master of Chhatrāsa.
[5] The School Master of Rājpāra.
[6] The School Master of Khirāsara.
[7] The School Master of Jhinjhuwāda.
[8] The School Master of Dhānk.
[9] The School Master of Kotdā Sangani.
[10] The School Master of Ganod.
[11] The School Master of Todia.
[12] The School Master of Ganod.

Pouring water at the root of, or circumambulating, a *pipal* or *bābul* tree after a bath without removing the wet clothes, is also believed to cause conception.[1]

Some observe the vow of entertaining thirteen Brāhmans and thirteen virgins to a feast, and of setting up Randal Bantva.[2]

Women whose children die in infancy give them opprobrious names such as Khacharo (filth), Ghelo (stupid), Natho, Uko, Ukardo, Bodho, Pujo, Adāvo, Mongho, Tulhi, Tutho, Kadavi, etc. in the belief that by so doing the life of the children is lengthened.[3] The idea is almost Asiatic in extent. Among Musalmāns also such names are given; and even among the Persians and Arabs boys are given such names as Masriequ and Osaid—the Stolen and the Black. Sometimes parents arrange that their childern be actually stolen; and some next of kin, generally the aunt, is made to commit the kindly felony. She afterwards returns the child for a certain amount in cash or clothes. The custom is as old as the scriptures, there being an allusion in the Korān to how the little Joseph was made to steal some garment of his aunt and was claimed as a forfeit by her. Speaking about Levi, the older brothers of Joseph say to the Egyptian soldiers, "If he hath stolen (the king's goblet) verily the brother of his too did (formerly) steal."

Some make a vow of not cutting the hair of their children till they are taken to Ambāji, where their hair is cut for the first time.[4]

Some treat their children as beggars until they attain the age of five years, that is, they are dressed till that age in clothes obtained by begging. Some bore the nose of the child.[4]

[1] The School Master of Chhatrāsa.

[2] The School Master of Khirasara.

[3] The School Master of Ganod.

[4] The School Master of Todia.

CHAPTER V.

WORSHIP OF THE MALEVOLENT DEAD.

The beliefs current as to the cause of dreams are many. One of these is that memory of known facts or incidents heard or seen causes dreams, Dreams are also supposed to be caused by disorders in the brain, by brooding constantly over a particular occurrence, by anxiety or by the perpetration of sinful acts.[1] Those who are indebted to the *pitris* (ancestral spirits) are also said to be troubled by dreams.[2] A hearty meal at night just before going to bed is also supposed to cause dreams.[3]

There are three conditions of human existence, (1) *Jāgriti* that is wakefulness (2) *Swapna* that is dream and (3) *Sushupti* that is sleep. The incidents which impress the mind strongly during wakefulness are reproduced in dreams. Very often thoughts that never occur to our minds strike us in dreams. These are ascribed to the impressions made on the soul during past lives.[4]

It is said that the interpretation of dreams goes by contraries. But at times they are fully borne out. A good dream is an indication of future good, and a bad one of future evil.[5]

There are some persons whose dreams are always fulfilled. Dreams dreamt by persons pure of mind and heart seldom turn out false.

Dreams occurring in the first quarter of the night are believed to be fulfilled in a year, those in the second quarter of the night in six months, those in the third quarter in three months, and those in the last quarter in one month. A dream seen during an hour and a half before daybreak bears fruit in ten days, while that seen just at day-break is realised immediately.[6]

Dreams that occur before midnight are never fulfilled.[7]

If a person has a bad dream, he should go to sleep at once, and not communicate it to any one. If he has a good dream, he should not sleep on that night after its occurrence. Early on the following morning he should communicate it to a preceptor or saint; but if neither be available, he should repeat it into the ears of a cow. A good dream should never be told to a bad or low-minded person.

If a man sleeps after a good dream and has a bad one, the former loses its force while the latter gains ascendancy and comes true.[8]

It is related that Allāuddin the bloody once entered the house of a blacksmith when the latter was asleep dreaming that he saw a treasure trove after having bathed in a stream and drunk a little water. At the same time Allāuddin saw a small insect come

---

1 The School Master of Chhatrāsa.

2 The School Master of Dhānk.

3 The School Master of Dadvi.

4 The School Master of Ganod.

5 The School Master of Dhānk.

6 The School Master of Chhatrāsa.

7 The School Master of Ganod.

8 The School Master of Chhatrāsa.

out of the blacksmith's nostril, drink water from a neighbouring cistern, and return to the place from whence he came. When the dream was over, the blacksmith woke and communicated it to Allāuddin, which enabled the latter to spot the treasure, found by excavating the place where the insect was hidden.[1]

The king Nala was questioned in his sleep several times by an individual unknown to him, "May I come now or later ?" Nala replied "Come now" thinking that if it was misfortune that put him the question, it would be better to get rid of it soon, so that the latter part of life might be passed happily. The questioner proved to be misfortune, and it is related that Nala met many mishaps during his youth.[1]

Similarly, a bad dream dreamt by Harischandra was followed by a series of calamities.[1]

Rāvan, the demon king of Lanka or Ceylon, had a dream in the third quarter of the night that Lanka was destroyed, and the destruction of Lanka followed.[2]

To see or think or experience in dreams the following, as the case may be is considered to be auspicious :—

(1) A cow, (2) a bullock, (3) an elephant, (4) a palace, (5) a mountain, (6) a high peak, (7) the droppings of a bird, (8) ointment, (9) weeping, (10) a king, (11) gold, (12) the crossing of the ocean, (13) a lamp, (14) flesh, (15) fruit, (16) a lotus, (17) a flag, (18) the image of one's favourite god, (19) a saint, (20) a Brāhman, (21) an ancestral spirit, (22) a white snake biting the right side, (23) a flowering tree, (24) climbing a tree, (25) climbing the *Rāyan* (Mimusops hexandra), (26) a woman dressed in white, (27) walking over a layer of lead, (28) lifting a goblet filled with wine, (29) a lion, (30) the goddess of wealth, (31) a garland, (32) driving in a carriage to which an elephant, a lion, a horse or a bullock is yoked, (33) swallowing the disc of the sun or the moon, (34) the hands or feet of a man, (35) worship of a deity, (36) barley. (37) rice, (38) sandal paste, (39) the *Dro* grass (Cynodon Dactylon), (40) the moon, (41) the sun, (42) a goblet, (43) an ocean of milk, (44) jewels, (45) smokeless fire, (46) an image of the god Shiva, Brahma or Ganesh or of the goddess Gauri, (47) a celestial vehicle, (48) the heaven, (49) the *Kalpavriksha* or the magic tree that satisfies all desires, (50) a river in floods, (51) fish, (52) curdled milk, (53) going on a pilgrimage, (54) ornaments, (55) crossing a river, (56) eating the flesh of a man's legs or flowers.[3]

To see in a dream (1) a person leading a life of celibacy, (2) a virgin, (3) a green tree, (4) or students returning from school, is also considered to foretell good fotune.[4]

Similarly, the sight of an unwidowed woman and the thought of the death of any person, in a dream, is believed to bring good luck.[4]

A dream in which one of the following objects is seen is also supposed to be good :—

1. An assemblage of Brāhmans, (2) a gardener, (3) milk, (4) a prostitute, (5) a shield and sword, (6) a musket, (7) a scimitar, (8) an antelope, (9) an unwidowed woman carrying on her head a jar filled with water, (10) a mongoose, (11) a peacock, (12) a woman carrying a child on her waist, (13) newly-washed dry clothes, (14) a costly fan, (15) a man dressed in white clothes.[5]

In a book called *Harit-sanhita* the subject of the influence of dreams on human happiness or misery is fully treated.

The book says :—If the sun, the moon, the congregation of the stars, a lake filled

[1] The School Master of Dhánk.

[2] The School Master of Todia.

[3] The School Master of Chhatrāsa.

[4] The School Master of Ganod.

[5] The Schol Master of Kolki.

with clusters of expanded lotuses, or crossing the sea or a river full of water be seen or experienced in a dream by a man, he attains wealth, happiness and prosperity and relief from diseases.

"If a cow, a horse, an elephant, a king or a flower called *prashasta* is seen in a dream by a sickly person, his illness disappears; if by one laid in sick bed, he is cured; if by one confined in a jail, he is released." [1]

If a child grinds its teeth and weeps in a dream, it indicates liquidation of pecuniary liabilities. One who sees a man die in a dream is blessed with longevity.[2]

A bite by a white snake in a dream is an omen of increase of wealth.[3]

"All black objects except a cow, a horse, a king, an elephant, and fish, seen in a dream, are the precursors of disease and calamity."

"One who sees in a dream his body devoured by crows, herons, camels, serpents, boars, eagles, foxes, dogs, wolves, asses, buffaloes, birds moving in the sky, tigers, fishes, alligators or monkeys, experiences in the immediate future a heavy loss or a terrible disease.[4]

The following objects seen, heard or experienced in a dream are believed to forebode evil :—

1. Cotton, (2) ashes, (3) bones, (4) whey, (5) singing, (6) merriment, (7) laughing, (8) studying, (9) a woman dressed in red, (10) a red mark on the forehead, (11) a *gandharva* or heavenly bard, (12) a demon, (13) a wizard, (14) a witch, (15) a prickly shrub, (16) a cemetery, (17) a cat, (18) vomiting, (19) darkness, (20) a hide, (21) a woman with a bad reputation, (22) thirst, (23) a contest between two planets, (24) fall of a luminous body, (25) a whirlwind, (26) *vishotak* (a disease in which the skin is covered with ulcers) (27) one carrying away one's vehicle, wife, jewels, gold, silver or bell-metal utensils, (28) the breaking of one's own house (29) the drinking of a poisonous liquid.[5]

If in a dream one relishes a dish of sweetmeats, plays upon a musical instrument, or sees a widow dressed in the garment of an unwidowed woman, it is believed to prognosticate evil and bring misfortune.

Similarly, if in a dream, the sleeper marries or hears the crowing of a crow or the bark of a dog, or an owl speak like a man, it portends misfortune [6]

Seeing an auspicious mark, or bathing in or being besmeared with oil, in a dream, is an indication of one's death in the near future. Going to the south riding a he-buffalo, or seeing a widow, brings on misfortune.[7]

If a man in health comes across a corpse in a dream, he apprehends illness. If a patient does the same, he fears death.[8]

It is a common belief that the soul can leave the body temporarily.

When a man feels thirsty in sleep, his soul is supposed to leave the body to drink water, and if it finds the water pots covered, not to return to the body, which is found dead the next morning.* It is for this reason that most people drink water at the time of going to bed.[9]

Shankarāchārya was a life long celibate. Once, in a discussion with the wife of Mandan Mishra, she put to him a question on the subject of the pleasures of married life. To answer the question it was necessary to have the experiences of a married life. To

[1] The Shāstri, Bhāyāvadar Pāthashāla.
[2] The School Master of Todia.
[3] The School Master of Gondal.
[4] The Shāstri, Bhāyāvadar Pāthshāla.
[5] The School Master of Chhatrāsa.
[6] The School Master of Kotda Sangani.
[7] The School Master of Dadvi.
[8] The School Master of Gondal.
[9] The School Master of Dhānk.

* The Musalmān Haditte has it that spirits cannot open closed doors, uncover covered pots, or even remove a piece of cloth if it is spread over a tray or vessel to save its contents from view.

gain these experiences Shankarāchārya's soul left his body and entered the corpse of a king just dead, and enjoyed the pleasures of married life for six months in the company of the queen of the deceased king. It then returned to his body, which was preserved by his disciples according to his instructions, and answered the question put to him by the wife of Mandan Mishra.[1]

It is related that the spirit of the daughter of a black-smith in Luvaria returned to her body two hours after her death, after which she lived for a fortnight.

A similar story is told of a Nāgar Brāhman, who lived for some years after the return of his spirit to his body.[2]

About forty years ago, the corpse of a Kanbi in Lilāpur was carried to the burning ground for cremation, and there his spirit returned to his body. On being asked where he had been, the Kanbi replied that he had been to Dharmarāja, the lord of hell, who told him to go back to his body, saying that his life's thread had not yet ended. It is related that the Kanbi lived for some years after this incident.

Another instance of the soul departing and then returning to the body is that of a Kanbi woman in Lilāpur, whose soul returned to the body after she had been carried to the burning ground. The woman lived for five years after this occurrence.[3]

A Brāhman in Limbdi named Vaijnāth had, by the performance of *yoga*, obtained the power of sending his spirit out of his body and recalling it at pleasure.[4]

The soul of a living being leaves its physical tabernacle during sleep and hovers about. It can go to and return from even the heavenly and infernal regions.

There are eighteen kinds of *siddhis* or accomplishments, one of which is *parakāyāpravesh* or the power of entering the body of another and returning to one's own body at will. The soul cannot exist separated from the body. When a person who revives after death is asked how he returned to life, he declares that he has been carried to the presence of the god of death by his messengers, being mistaken for another bearing the same name and living in the same locality. When such a mistake is detected, the god of death tells the soul of the man concerned that his life's span has not yet ended, and sends it back to the body, which appears to be dead.[5]

Often the soul of a man ascends to his temples, when the man is supposed to be dead although he is alive. In such cases, when the soul descends, the man is supposed to come to life again.

It is believed by some people that if all the desires of a man are not satisfied at the time of his death, his soul leaves the body to satisfy them and subsequently returns to the corpse, whereupon the body revives.[6]

A devotee in his meditative trance can send forth his soul whithersoever he pleases.[7]

It is also believed that the soul of man leaves the body in sleep to enjoy those pleasures which it cannot enjoy in wakefulness.[8]

The popular conceptions of the character and functions of the *bhut* or disembodied soul are as follows :

A ghost has no recognised form. It may assume the form of a human being, a goat, a blaze of fire, a whirl-wind or any other object it pleases.[9]

Some assume a terribly gigantic and fearfully uncouth frame, with big fang-like

1 The School Master of Dhānk.
2 The School Master of Luvaria.
3 The School Master of Lilāpur.
4 The School Master of Ganod.
5 The School Master of Vanod.
6 The School Master of Dadvi.
7 The School Master of Kolki.
8 The School Master of Mojidād.
9 The School Master of Dhānk.

teeth, long matted hair and a height that reaches the sky. At times they assume the form of a child and cry heart-breakingly at a concealed corner of a road. Should a passer-by, out of compassion, try to save it, the supposed infant begins to lengthen its legs to show its benefactor its real and supernatural dimensions. Sometimes it transforms itself into a gigantic and terrible being, taking possession of the man if he becomes afraid.[1]

Some evil spirits manifest themselves as showers of burning charcoal, while some are so forward as to offer their services as guides to strangers from one village to another. Some assume the form of *Bhensāsur*—a demon in the form of a buffalo—said to be a most malignant ghost.[2]

The throat of a ghost is as narrow as the fine end of a needle, and yet it is believed to require a dozen potfuls of water to quench its thirst. It cannot get pure water, as such water is guarded by the god Varuna. It has, therefore, to quench its thirst with such dirty water as it can get. Similarly, it cannot get clean food, and has to satisfy its hunger on human excretions, the droppings of birds and other animals, urine, and the filth of houses.[3]

It is generally believed that evil spirits do not cast shadows. All attempts to catch them prove futile, as they vanish in the form of a flame.[4]

If it is sought to catch hold of a goat-shaped ghost, the goat swells into such a monstrous size that the spectator gets terrified, whereupon the ghost finds an opportunity of disappearing in a flame.

It is believed that ghosts prefer darkness to light and silence to noise. They live on the *Pipal* (Ficus religiosa) or *Shami* (Prosopis spicigera) trees.[5]

A ghost presents itself to the vision of a man by blocking its way in the form of a goat or some other animal.[6]

Ghosts are believed to infest woods, unused wells, cellars and old tanks. They are also found in ruins and cemeteries. As far as possible they keep themselves aloof from mortals; but at times they are visible to human beings, mostly to those destitute of religion and morals. They roam about and terrify people. Sometimes they enter the persons of human beings. Such men either gain in strength, fall sick, or become senseless. The ghosts who possess them make them laugh or work, without being fatigued, with ten times the vigour they originally possessed.[7]

Ghosts keep their persons uncovered, feed upon flesh and blood, sleep during the day, and roam about at night.[8]

Often a large concourse of ghosts meet together and dance, sing and make merry uttering loud and fierce shrieks. A ghost has no back, and has its feet reversed. It keeps away from man, but terrifies him by pelting him with stones from a distance.[9]

On the fourteenth day of the dark half of *Aśhvin* (the twelfth month of the Gujarāti Hindu year) all ghosts are believed to go about playing pranks with poor mortals and possessing them.[10]

The *Navarātra* holidays is the season when ghosts appear in many places.[11]

Ghosts enter corpses or possess human beings and speak through them as a medium. Sometimes they assume their original human form, and often torment people with disease.

[1] The School Master of Kolki.
[2] The School Master of Dadvi.
[3] The School Master of Ganod.
[4] The School Master of Bāntva.
[5] The School Masters of Sānka and Songadh
[6] The School Master of Charādva.
[7] The School Master of Dhānk.
[8] The School Master of Kotda Sangani.
[9] The School Master of Vanod.
[10] The School Master of Kolki.
[11] The School Master of Lilāpur.

They present themselves as animals and pass away in a blaze. They hum in the air without being seen, wrestle with men or carry unseen human beings from one place to another. Some women are believed to conceive by intercourse with male ghosts.[1]

If a man happens to step in the circle described by water round the offering given to a ghost, viz., *utār*, he is possessed by the ghost. A house haunted by a ghost is the scene of great mischief.[2]

Ghosts are said to be most mischievous during the first part of the night. Their fury diminishes with the advance of night.[3]

Ghosts are inimical to human beings, terrify them, and sometimes, assuming the form of a cobra, kill those whom they hated most during life.[4]

They are pleased with offerings of blood.[5]

To throw stones at houses and trees and to set them on fire are their usual pranks.[6]

The ghost called *Jān* manifests itself as a giant, its height reaching the sky. If a man comes under its shadow, he is seized by it and dashed to pieces on the ground. On the contrary, if a man wins its favour, he becomes prosperous. Hence a proverb has been current that "seizing another as by a *jān*" meaning "being attacked by a dire misfortune."*

There is a female ghost called *Chudel*. Its back is covered with flesh, its feet are reversed, its form is hollow and its face handsome like that of a charming woman.[7].

It is said that a woman dying in childbed becomes a *chudel*. Her form is a skeleton behind with the figure of a pretty woman in front.

It is believed that mastery over ghosts can be obtained by dint of incantations or *mantras*. Those who subjugate ghosts in this way have power to command them to do their behests. But the process by which such powers are procured is believed to be beset with dangers, and many lose their lives in so doing.[8]

There is also a belief that a *bhut* or ghost can be brought under control by lopping off a lock of its hair or top knot and keeping it in one's custody.[9]

It is said that this lock ought to be kept inside the right thigh by tearing a hole in the flesh. It is believed that the thigh can be cut open by a hair of the ghost without injury.[10]

The ghost so subjugated should never be kept unemployed; otherwise it oppresses its master.[11]

It is believed that the spirits of deceased persons become ghosts under the following conditions :—

1 If scriptural ceremonies are not performed with the ceremonial offerings of rice balls to the deceased.

2 If the deceased dies with a strong attachment to worldly objects.

3 If the death is unnatural that is, caused by an accident.

All ghosts get absolution by the performance of propitiative ceremonies by their descendants as prescribed in the scriptures.[12]

There are various beliefs current as to the state of the soul after death. The *Garud purān* contains many passages illustrating its movements after it leaves the body. Says the book :—

"When the soul leaves the body it assumes a form as small as a thumb. At this very

1 The School Master of Ganod.
2 The School Master of Dadvi.
3 The School Master of Kolki
4 The School Master of Oman.
5 The School Master of Khirāsara.
6 The School Master of Rājpāra.
7 The School Master of Dhānk.
8 The School Master of Vanod.
9 The School Master of Dadvi.
10 Mr. K. D. Desāi.
11 The School Master of Gondal.
12 The School Master of Ganod.

* The word *Jān* is the plural of the Arabic *jinni*. It has remained as a relic of Arab supremacy and occupation of the Kathiāwār coast just in the beginning of Islām during its first conquests—about half a century after the Prophets' death.

moment it is caught by the servants of Yama while he is crying out ha! ha! looking at its corporal receptacle."

And again:—

"Covering the body of the soul (which suffers intensely) and strangling it forcibly, the servants of the god Yama carry it away just as a culprit is carried by a king's soldiers."

The verses that follow describe the miseries inflicted upon the poor thumb-shaped soul for the sins committed by him during his lifetime. The sinful soul has to undergo similar miseries in hell. From hell it returns to this world guarded by the servants of Yama, to partake of the rice-balls and other articles of food offered by the sons or other relatives. It is then again taken to hell to suffer more miseries and penalties in expiation of past sins. Then it returns once more to receive the offerings of rice-balls made at *shrāddha* ceremonies. If, even after this, any desires remain unfulfilled, it has to continue a wretched existence in the other world.[1]

In a chapter of the *Pretamanjari* of the *Garud Purān* it is stated that the souls of righteous men go to the next world unmolested.[2]

Some people believe that the departing soul assumes a form like a thumb, and remains in that state until relieved by the performance of *shrāddha* by his heirs. It then enters the other world to enjoy the fruits of its good actions. The *Yamapuri* or the city of the god of death is 8,600 *Yōjans*—a *Yōjan* being equal to four miles—to the south of the earth. The lord of this place is Dharmarāja. Yama is his servant, whose duty is to carry the soul from one place to another.[3]

Others maintain that two states await the soul after death according to whether it has performed righteous or sinful acts during life.

The righteous attain to heaven and enter the *Pārshad Vaikunta* of Vishnu. The sinful go to hell or *Yamaloka*.[4]

The sinful souls go to *Yamaloka* and are made to suffer the miseries of twenty-eight *naraks* or hells in proportion to the sins perpetrated by them, after which they return to the earth.

The following are some of the punishments meted out to wicked souls for their sins, in their next lives:—

1 Those who murder Brāhmans suffer from consumption.

2 Those who slaughter cows are born as tortoises.

3 Those guilty of female infanticide suffer from white leprosy.

4 One who kills his wife, as well as a woman guilty of causing abortion, becomes a beggar.

5 Those who commit adultery become impotent.

6 He who seats himself on the bed or seat of his preceptor is affected by skin diseases.

7 Flesh-eaters get a red body.

8 Those who indulge in drink get black teeth.

9 A Brāhman partaking of prohibited food suffers from dropsy.

10 One who eats sweets without sharing them with the by-standers suffers from cancer in the throat.

11 One who offers polluted food to departed spirits suffers from black leprosy.

12 One who disobeys and despises his teacher suffers from wind *apasmār*.

13 One who does not believe in the *shāstras* suffers from enlargement of the spleen or Bright's disease.

14 A perjurer is born dumb.

[1] The Shāstri, Bhāyāvadar Pāthshāla

[2] The School Master of Dhānk.

[3] The School Master of Ganod.

[4] The D. E. Inspector, Hālār.

15 One who does not serve food equally to all the members at a dining table loses one of his eyes.

16 Those who break off a marriage alliance are punished with thick (negro-like) lips.

17 Those who steal books lose their eye-sight.

18 He who kicks a Brāhman becomes lame.

19 A liar becomes a stammerer.

20 Those who listen to contradictory versions of what is generally believed to be true become deaf.

21 One who poisons another becomes a lunatic.

22 One who steals precious metals becomes indigent.

23 An incendiary is punished with a bald head.

24 Meat-sellers meet with misfortunes.

25 One who steals gold has his nails deformed.

26 He who steals food is born a mouse.

27 One stealing corn has to be reborn as a locust.

28 One stealing opium or other poisonous drugs is born a scorpion.

29 One who steals leaves or vegetables is born a peacock.

30 One who enjoys perfumes by stealing them is born a mole.

31 One who steals honey becomes an eagle.

32 One who steals flour, rice., etc. is born a monkey.[1]

The state of the soul after death depends upon a man's good or bad actions in life.

The souls of the righteous leave the body without any trouble. The messengers of the god of death present themselves to these souls in the form of saints and carry them to that part of the heaven which is presided over by their favourite deity, by the eastern, northern, or western gates. They are received there with great respect. Here they enjoy the fruits of their merit, after which they return to this world and are born either in the family of a wealthy virtuous man or in that of a poor Brāhman who has attained the knowledge of God. In this new life they accumulate further merit, in virtue of which they are endowed with a higher spiritual life in the following birth, and so on until they attain final emancipation.

After attaining *moksha* or salvation the soul becomes free from the wheel of birth and rebirth.

To the souls of the sinful, who leave their bodies with a great struggle, the messengers of the god of death present themselves in a terrible form. They are carried to hell by the southern gate, being constantly lashed on the way. There they are relegated to one of the twenty-eight pits (of hell) appropriate to their misdeeds, to suffer retribution for their sins.[2]

The soul is carried to Dharmarāja after it leaves the body. Thence, with the permission of the god, it returns to this world and halts for thirteen days at the threshold of its house. On the thirteenth day an earthen jar filled with water is emptied on a *pipal* tree (Ficus religiosa) after which its connection with this world ceases. Then it returns to the heavenly judge of actions (Dharmarāja), and is again born in the species prescribed by him. The soul of a strictly spiritual being merges into the divine entity and becomes free from birth and rebirth.

Moksha or *Mukti*, that is final emancipation is of two kinds, *sāyujya* or merging into the divine form and *sāmishya* or entering the divine order and living in this state so long as one's merits allow.[2]

Dharmarāja keeps an account of the good and bad actions of all men in his book

[1] The Shāstri, Pāthshāla, Bhāyāvadar.

[2] The School Master of Dhānk.

called *siddhi karan*, and dispenses justice according to it. A man guilty of adultery is sentenced to embrace a redhot image of a woman; one who has slaughtered animals is devoured by those animals; while those who have committed the sin of murdering Brāhmans are relegated to hell for ever.[1]

There are seven rungs to the ladder which leads to the next world. The first is covered with a thick forest. The second bristles with pointed spears. The third is strewn with *gokharu* (a species of thorns). The fourth has piercing blasts. On the fifth runs the river Vaitarna. The sixth is full of red-hot iron. The seventh is covered with deep streams.[2]

After death, the soul has to cross the river Vaitarna (*vide* the fifth rung above) on its way to the next world. Those who have given cows in charity can cross this river without difficulty by holding the tails of the cows, who present themselves to help them.

Those who have given shoes in charity can tread the third step with ease.

The sinful have to walk barefooted on ground studded with pointed spears, and to embrace red-hot iron pillars. It is with the object of avoiding these miseries that people distribute shoes and clothes in charity.[3]

The sinful expiate their sins by passing through a cycle of 8,400,000births. * They have to be born 2,100,000 times in the class of creatures born of eggs, 2,100,000 times in the species of worms produced from sweat, 2,100,000 times from embryonic birth and a similar number of times in the vegetable kingdom.

Those who lack virtue but commit no sins are born in the divine order of a low grade such as the servants of Kuber, the attendants of the god Shiva, Gandharvas, Vaitāls, Brahmarākshasas, Kushmānds and other demigods. Virtuous women are born as goddesses or *devis* or as *apsarās* or celestial songstresses. Those who have performed only a few acts of righteousness enter the ranks of Jakhanis, Kinnaris, Mātrikās, and the maid servants of the goddess Durga.[4]

The souls of the righteous are carried by *Yamadutas* or the messengers of the god of death through five cities, by a route passing through beautiful gardens; while those of the sinful are led barefooted over brambles and pointed spears by roads running through dense forests hidden in pitchy darkness. The latter have also to cross large rivers and pass through streams filled with blood and puss. As they pass, eagles prey upon their bodies and they are bitten by venomous snakes.[5]

The souls of those who have in life performed good actions pass through the sun and assume divine forms; while those of ordinary beings pass through the moon and return to this world.[6]

A sinful soul has to go to *Yamaloka* or hell through sixteen cities. On its way it has to cross the river Vaitarna, which consists of blood mixed with puss. He who has presented a cow to a Brāhman can cross this river with ease. Beyond this river lies a land which is covered with spikes. Those who have given in charity *ashtamah-dān*, that is, sesamum seeds, flour, gold, cotton, salt, clarified butter, milk and sugarcandy, can walk over this ground without being hurt. When the soul has reached Yama or the god of death, the sun and the moon, the ever-living witnesses of human actions,

[1] The School Mistress, Barton Female Training College, Rājkot.

[2] The School Master of Limbdi.

[3] The School Master of Kotda Sangani.

* " Like the green grass on the turf I have often grown and regrown. I have visited 770,000 bodies. ' Maulana Ilaluddin Rumi.

[4] The School Master of Ganod.

[5] The School Master of Vanod.

[6] The School Master of Jetalpur.

testify to its virtues and sins, and it is meted out a punishment appropriate to its sins.[1]

In order that the departed soul may not find its way difficult, his heirs make a gift to a Brāhman of a bedstead, bedding, a lamp, corn, a pair of shoes and other articles, on the thirteenth day after death. This gift is called *seraja*.[2]

One enters the human order after passing through 8,400,000 species of living beings. It is in the human life that one can accumulate merit, and wipe out the influence of past sins.

Those who meet a sudden or violent death, e. g., by being crushed under a falling house, by drowning in a well, by an accidental fall, by a snake bite, etc. enter the order of *bhuts, pretas, pishāchas*, etc., and are said to have gone to *durgati* or to a bad path.[3]

But those who die on a field of battle are believed to attain heaven.[4]

According to another belief, persons dying a violent death have to pass through the same fate, that is, die violently, for the next seven lives.[5]

Their souls are said to be liable to enter the *asurgati* or the order of devils. They are emancipated from this condition by the performance by their descendants of the ceremony called *Nil parnāvavi* or of those ceremonies prescribed in the *Pāl Shāstra*.[6]

It is also believed that such souls after entering the order of ghosts oppress and torment their descendants and relatives.[7]

In the case of suicides, when the crime is proved before the god of death the culprit is hurled into a hell called *Mahāraurava*, where he has to pass a thousand years. After the expiry of this period he is born again into this world, again commits suicide, and again meets the same fate after death. This is repeated seven times, after which he has to pass through 8,400,000 species of animals before again obtaining the human life.[8]

If the suicide be caused by poisoning, the person, in his next life, becomes a serpent; if by drowning or strangling, he becomes a ghost.[9]

Some believe that the souls of persons meeting a violent death enter the order of such ghosts as *Jinni, Māmo*, etc. For their emancipation *shrāddhas* are performed by their descendants. At times these ghosts possess the persons of their nearest relatives, and through this medium declare their desires. If they express a desire to have a *pālio* or pillar erected in their name, one is erected on the spot where they breathed their last. On this pillar is engraved a figure riding a horse, representing the deceased, which is besmeared with red lead or ochre. This representation is worshipped as a deity with offerings of frankincense, cocoanuts and lamps fed with *ghi*.[10]

The *pālio* is called *surdhan*, and is worshipped, especially on the death anniversary of the deceased.[11]

In some castes the *surdhans* are installed in the house of the deceased.[12]

There are various beliefs current as to the way in which spirits enter and leave the body.

According to one belief, when a person gets frightened by the apparition of a ghost, the ghost enters his body through one of the organs, and makes him senseless and violent.[13]

1 The D. E. Inspector, Hālār.
2 The School Master of Dhānk.
3 Mr. K. D. Desāi.
4 The School Master of Charādva.
5 The School Master of Dhānk.
6 The School Master of Kotda Sangani.
7 The School Master of Kolki.
8 The School Mistress, Barton Female Training College, Rājkot.
9 The School Master of Bhāyāvadar.
10 The School Master of Todia
11 The School Master of Songadh.
12 The School Master of Devalia.
13 The School Master of Dhānk.

According to another belief, a ghost, as stated above, takes an airy form and enters the body through any channel through which air can enter the body. It leaves the body by the same route.[1]

There is also a belief that evil spirits enter the body of a man through any part of the body and under their influeuce the person possessed, dances, jumps, foams or sits idle[2].

There is a further belief that a ghost enters the body through the thumb and gets out by the ears.[3]

According to some, a ghost makes its way into the body through the anus and its exit by the same route.[4]

Others maintain that it enters the body through the nostrils and gets out by the same passage.[5]

Some say that it finds an entrance and outlet through the skull.[6]

There are others who are of opinion that the immaterial form of a ghost can find admission into the body by the right side and egress the same way.[7]

It is said that when the body is unclean, a ghost can enter it through any of the organs.[8]

To drive away an evil spirit from the body of a person, a conjuror, Vānjha, Koli Vāghri, Atit, Fakir or other exorcist is engaged to set a *dānklān** and to offer a victim and frankincense to the evil spirit, which is supposed to drive the spirit out by the same route by which it entered the body.†[9]

Another method of driving away an evil spirit from the body is as follows :—

As soon as it is ascertained that a man is possessed by an evil spirit, somebody catches hold of the top-knot of the man or ties it into a knot. Next he is lashed with a whip or chain until the ghost in him cries out "Please don't beat me. I shall leave the body and shall never return." Then the ghost is told that it is a liar, that it said a thousand times that it would leave the body and not return, but it did not do it. No faith, therefore, would be put in its word. After a haggling dialogue of this kind and on the ghost's confirmation of its offer never to return by some satisfactory oath or assurance, the top-knot is unloosed and the ghost disappears.[10]

A third method is to subject the person possessed to the fumes of red chillies or of black wood, or to tie a sacred thread round his elbow.

After one of these processess has been performed to expel the ghost, the victim gives a deep yawn, and it is said that the ghost goes out in the yawn. Next the relieved person is given water to drink, and an exorcist is engaged to take measures to prevent the possibility of the ghost's return.[11]

In a book entitled *Brāhman Nighanta Ratnākar* is described the method of driving away an evil spirit from the body of a man by an offering of *dhup* or frankincense. The *dhup* to be used for this purpose must be made of *gugal*, and it must be offered with honey and clarified butter, repeating the following *mantra* :—

"Amen. Bow to the divine Lord of the evil spirits, the Lord whose teeth, jaws, and

[1] The School Master of Ganod.
[2] The School Master of Pātan Vāo.
[3] The D. E. Inpector, Gohilwād.
[4] The School Master of Luvaria.
[5] The School Master of Bāntva.
[6] The School Master of Rājpāra.
[7] The School Master of Vāla.
[8] The School Master of Ganod.
[9] The School Master of Dhānk.

† If a lock of the hair of the person possessed by an evil spirit be knotted round and round while the exorcist is trying to cast the spirit, it cannot get out.—The School Master of Vanod.

[10] Mr. K. D. Desāi.

* See p. 3.

[11] The School Master of Pātan Vāo.

mouth are fierce, by whose three eyes the forehead is ablaze, whose lustre is marked by irresistible anger, who holds a crescent moon on the forehead and matted hair on the head, whose body is besmeared with ashes; whose neck is adorned by the poison of the fierce lord of the cobras. Oh! may success attend to thee! Oh! Great one! The Lord of spirits! manifest thy form, dance, dance; move, move; tie with a chain, tie; terrify by a neigh, terrify; kill, kill by the adamantine wand; cut, cut off by a sharp weapon; tear off, tear off by the point of a spear; reduce, reduce to atoms by the bludgeon; remove remove, all the evil spirits *Swāha*."[1]

There are various superstitious beliefs entertained by people regarding sneezing.

According to one belief, if a person sneezes face to face with another who is about to begin an auspicious act, such as starting on a journey, decking his person with ornaments, performing a marriage ceremony, and the like, it portends misfortune to the latter; but a sneeze on his right or at his back foretells good. A sneeze in front of a person starting to perform an auspicious act is supposed to mean that a blow has been struck on his forehead, suggesting that the act should be stopped. If, in spite of this warning, the act is commenced, evil consequences are sure to follow.

A sneeze at a man's back confirms the unobstructed fulfilment of the act taken in hand, as it is believed to have patted the man on his back or shoulders in token of approval.

Sneezes on either side, right or left, portend neither good nor evil.

As a rule, sneezes are believed to forebode evil, and it is considered highly unmannerly to sneeze while one is about to begin an auspicious act or start with a good purpose. If, in spite of this etiquette, one sneezes, he excuses himself by saying that he is suffering from cold.[2]

Some people believe that a sneeze in front is an indication of a broil on the road, a sneeze on the left side portends loss of money, one from above is a harbinger of success, one from below foretells danger, while the sneeze of the man who is engaged or is starting on the act contemplated is believed to be very injurious. A sneeze on the right is considered neither good nor bad.[3]

A sneeze in the east causes anxiety, in the south-east foretells happiness, in the south speaks of coming loss, and in the south-west is an indication of good. A sneeze from the west or north-west is considered good, from the north injurious, and from the east auspicious.[4]

Some lines from the sayings of Gorakhrāj run to the effect that a sneeze in the east causes anxiety, one in the south-east inflicts a sound beating, one in the south brings a visitor or guest, one in the south-west subjects the person concerned to a taunt, one in the west bestows a throne or crown, one in the north-west promises sweets or dainties, one in the north foretells good, one in the north-east brings disappointment, while one's own sneeze is so ominous that one should never start out on any business after sneezing.[5]

The beliefs enumerated above relate to sneezes which occur on certain week days. The sneezes which occur on Sundays have the following consequences.

A sneeze from the east is good, one from the south-east points to delay in the fulfilment of one's intended object, one from the south brings in profit, one from the south-west results in death, one from the west in happiness, one from the north-west throws one into the society of good men, one from the north is

[1] The School Master of Bhāyāvadar.
[2] The School Master of Kotda Sangani.
[3] The School Master of Sānka.
[4] The School Master of Kolki.
[5] The School Master of Chharādva.

productive of pecuniary gain, and one from the north-east of general wellbeing.[1]

It is a common belief that if while one is about to commence some act, somebody sneezes once, the act is doomed to fail, and to avoid failure it must be postponed. But if the sneeze is repeated, no harm ensues.[1]

A sneeze by an ailing person is believed to be a sign of his recovery, and more sneezes by the same person are supposed to indicate his complete recovery, even though the symptoms be not favourable.

A sneeze by a cow at the commencement of an auspicious act is supposed to be the worst possible omen, and a sneeze by a cat is proverbially a portent of failure in any act taken in hand at the time.[2]

A yawn is generally believed to be harmless, as it does not foretell either good or evil. Still as sometimes it results in accidental instantaneous death, the elders of a person when he yawns, exclaim, "Be long-lived! Patience! Live long!", and the spiritually disposed repeat the name of the god of their devotion.[3]

Lest spirits may make their way into the body of a person through his mouth when he is yawning, or lest his soul may pass out of it, some people pinch him to stop the yawn while others utter the words "Rām" "Rām" to divert his attention.[4]

In mythological times, Brahma, one of the gods of the Hindu Trinity, once left his body for a time. Some people began to molest the body, when he cried out, "*Rākho! Rākho!*" that is "Keep aloof! Keep aloof!" or "Wait! Wait!". These people came to be called *Rākho** w ich in course of time corrupted into *Rākshasa*. The beings who hold sway over *rākshasas* are called *Mahārākshasas*. In the *Rāmāyan* and other *purāns*, *rākshasas* are represented as feeding on human flesh.[5]

A *rākshasa* is supposed to be sixteen miles in height and to roam about for his prey within a circle with a radius of sixteen miles.[6]

The *Mahārākshasas* are supposed to have their abode in the seas. It is said that they burn or swallow ships sailing thereon.[7]

The *rākshasas* are supposed to number 60,000,000 and the *mahārākshasas* 20,000 Kubera, a *mahārākshasa* is the lord of the *rākshasas*.[8]

It is said that the *rākshasas*, *mahārākshasas* wizards and witches were visible to the human eye during the *tretāyuga*. With the commencement of the present or *kaliyuga* they have become invisible. It is stated in the *Purāns* that during the recitation of the *Surya kavach*, *Saptsasani* or the *Nārāyan kavach*, if the *rākshasas* or *mahārākshasas* fall into or approach the limits circumscribed for them, the recitation proves ineffective.[9]

It is a common belief that there is bitter enmity between the gods and *rākshasas*. The former follow the path of virtue while the latter lead immoral lives devouring Brāhmans and cows, feeding on flesh, and indulging in intoxicating drinks. The habitat of the *rākshasas* is the *pātāl* or nether world, Rāwan being their king.[10]

The exploits of some of the *rākshasas* are described in the *Mahābhārat*, *Bhāgvat* and the *Rāmāyan*. For instance, the misdeeds of Jarāsandh, Ghatotkacha and Hedamba are described in the *Mahābhārat*; those of Kansa, Bānāsur, Pralambāsur, Adhāsur, Dhenukāsur, Kālanemi, Shankāsur and Vritrāsur in the

1 The School Master of Limbdi.
2 The School Master of Jhinjhuwāda.
3 The School Master of Vanod.
4 The School Master of Dhānk.

* This derivation of the word *rākshasa* is obviously fanciful. *Rākshasa* is a Sanskrit word and has no connection with the Gujarāti word *rākho* which itself is derived from the Sanskrit root *raksha* to protect.

5 The School Mastr of Dhānk.
6 The School Master of Bāntva.
7 The School Master of Moti Parabdi.
8 The School Master of Rājpāra.
9 The School Master of Charādva.
10 The School Master of Kotda Sangani.

Bhāgvat ; and those of Rāvan, Kumbhakarna and Indrajit in the *Rāmāyan*.[1]

A *rākshasa* named Tripurāsur conquered the heavens, the earth and the nether regions, and began to annoy the gods. The god Shiva burnt the *rākshasa* to ashes.[2]

The two *rākshasas* Hiranyāksha and Hiranyakashyapu were originally the gate-keepers of Vishnu, one of the gods of the Hindu trinity. Once they affronted Sanatkumār, the son of Brahma, when they were cursed by Vishnu who decreed that they would be born *rākshasas* in three successive lives. In these lives they had to play the part of the enemies of gods and men, and were destroyed by Vishnu as such [2]

A *rākshasa* named Jalandhar is stated to have met his death when the chastity of his wife was violated by the god Vishnu in the disguise of her husband.[3]

Mahārākshasas are also known by the name of *Brahma rākshasas*. A Brāhman dying without imparting all his learning to his disciples or with the guilt of the murder of a Brāhman or a cow on him is believed to enter the order of *Brahma rākshasas* after his death. In this state he possesses a body without a head. A *Brahma rākshasa* is also called *Khavis*.[4] *

In addition to the wizards and witches mentioned above, there are others the names of which are as follows:—

(1) Dākini, (2) Sakini, (3) Kushmānd (4) Zod, (5) Dholio, (6) Pāle Marad, (7) Bhuchar, (8) Khechar, (9) Jalaj, (10) Jakharo, (11) Shikotrum, (12) Ashtabhāro, (13) Chand Chani, (14) Chorosi Kāntini, (15) Jogani, (16) Hathadi, (17) Miyali, (18) Ghānchini, (19) Mochini, (20) Baladi, (21) Molani, (22) Khuntini, (23) Suti, (24) Gavati, (25) Bethi, (26) Ubhi, (27) Avi, (28) Chaurār, (29) Madhu Pavanti, (30) Mānsa Khavanti, (31) Bhāsika, (32) Pratāb, (33) Vira, (34) Vāvānchara, (35) Chorāsi Viru, (36) Nao Narasing, (37) Jaikha, (38) Jutaka, (39) Masida, (40) Gāndharavi, (41) Jami, (42) Asmāni, (43) Mamikula,[5] (44) Zāmpadi, (45) Meladi (46) Balla.[6]

Of the above, the first forty-three together with Chudela or Vantri and Preta are believed by some to be the names of so many *Joganis* or female evil spirits or witches. The remaining are living *Dākans* or witches who are believed to cause illness or even death by their evil eye to those on whom they throw a glance. [7]

Wizards live upon ordinary food, witches on air, while *pretas* require nothing to eat for their maintenance. It is said that their backs and shoulders are covered with filth and emit an offensive odour.[8]

It is generally believed that the spirits of such male members of low unclean castes as die a violent death become *Khavis*.[9] Some believe that *Khavis* or *Khabith* is a Musalmān ghost.[10] Others hold that he is the lord of all ghosts.[11]

Khavis has no head His eyes are located in the chest. He is as tall as a cocoa-palm or bamboo. He roams about holding in one hand a weapon and in the other a lump of flesh. Those over whom his shadow falls are said to fall ill.[12] His appearance is so terrible that a person who sees him for the first time is frightened to death.[13] It is stated that he starts on his excursions after sun-set.[14]

The attendants of the god Shiva known as *Vaitālikas* are said to have no heads.[15] They live in cremation grounds, as they have a

[1] The School Master of Ganod.

[2] The School Master of Lewaria.

[3] The School Master of Upleta.

[4] The School Master of Venod.

* The word *Khavis* comes from the Arabic *Khabith* from the root verb *Khabotha* and means one who has become impure or unholy.

[5] The School Master of Sultānpur.

[6] The School Masters of Khirāsara and Pipalāna.

[7] Mr. K. D. Desāi.

[8] The School Master of Ānandpur.

[9] The School Master of Lilāpur.

[10] The School Master of Khirāsara.

[11] The School Master of Vasāvād.

[12] The School Master of Kotda Sangani.

[13] The School Master of Chhatrāsa.

[14] The School Master of Khirāsara.

[15] The School Master of Ganod.

burning desire to possess the bodies of deceased persons.[1]

A belief runs that the trunk of the evil spirit called *Suropuro*, that is the spirit of one who meets a heroic death, moves about like a *Khavis*.[2]

It is a common belief that evil spirits haunt trees, groves, deserted tanks and woods.[3]

Vetāl roams over burial and cremation grounds, as also *Bhachar, Khechar, Kāl Bhairav* and a number of other ghosts.[4]

The Jimp, Bābaro and some other ghosts reside in fortresses and unoccupied houses and roam about in the burning grounds. *Chudela, Kotda* and *Brahma Rākshasa* make their abodes on the tamarind, *Shami* (Prosopis spicigera), *Bābul* and *Kerado* trees and in deep tanks and wells in deserted places. Their favourite haunts are river banks.[5]

It is stated by some people that the *Chudel, Vantri, Dākan, Jimp, Khavis* and other ghosts generally haunt cremation grounds, fields where battles have been fought, thresholds of houses and latrines and cross roads.[6]

Some declare that ghosts are also to be found in temples in which there are no images and in dry wells.[7]

The ghost *preta* is said to be as tall as a camel, the passage of its throat being as small as the bore of a needle. It is therefore believed to be always wandering about in quest of water.[8]

The evil spirit *Jān* haunts mountains and forests and *Māmo* the centres of filth, while *Vetāl* is found in cremation grounds.[9]

Jān, Brahma Rākshasa and *Khavis* reside in woods, trees, or on mountains, *Khijadio Māmo* lives in the *Khijada* or *Shami* tree and *Amatho Māmo* in a grove of trees. Spirits of high caste people not emancipated from the trammels of birth and rebirth have their abode in the *Pipal* tree.[10]

It is related that once a number of boys, on their return from a tank to which they had gone on a swimming excursion, passed by a *Khijada* tree, when one of them suggested to the others to throw stones at the tree, saying that any one not doing so would fall under the displeasure of God. One of the boys threw a stone at a neighbouring *Bābul* tree with the result that on reaching home he fell ill in a fit of terror. He began to shake and said "Why did you strike me with a stone? I had resorted to the *Bābul* tree from the *Khijado* and you struck me there. I shall not depart until I take your life." Evidently it was the *Khijadio Māmo* who had possessed the boy who spoke the above words; and an exorcist was called who drove him out by the incantation of *mantras*; after which the boy recovered.[11]

It is believed that a woman who dies an unnatural death becomes a *Chudel* and troubles her husband, her successor or co-wife, or her children.[12]

There are three classes of *Chudels*, (1) *Poshi*, (2) *Soshi* and (3) *Toshi*. Those women that have not enjoyed before death the pleasures of this world to their satisfaction enter the order of *Poshi Chudels*. They fondle children and render good service to their widower husbands.

Those women that are persecuted beyond endurance by the members of their families become *Soshi Chudels* after death. They dry up the blood of men and prove very troublesome to the members of the family.

Those women who bear a strong attachment to their husbands enter the order of

[1] The School Master of Gondal.
[2] The School Master of Bāntva.
[3] The School Master of Dhānk.
[4] The School Master of Talpur and Luvaria.
[5] The School Master of Vanod.
[6] The School Master of Dadvi.
[7] The School Master of Kolki.
[8] The School Master of Chhatrāsa
[9] The School Master of Dhānk.
[10] The School Master of Kolki.
[11] The D. E. Inspector, Gohilwād.
[12] The School Master of Dhānk.

Toshi Chudels and bring great pleasure and happiness to their husbands in this life.[1]

Most high caste people, on the death of their first wives, take an impression of their feet on gold leaves or leaf-like tablets of gold and cause their second wives to wear them round their necks.[2] These impresses of feet are called *shok-pagalāns* or mourning foot-prints. Among the lower castes, the hands or the feet of the second wives are tattooed in the belief that this prevents the deceased wife from causing injury to the second wife.[3]

All female spirits called *Pishāchas* or *Dākans* and male spirits called *Virs* or *Bhuts* oppress their descendants.[4]

It is also believed that any male member of a family dying with certain of his desires unfulfilled becomes a *Surdhan* and oppresses the surviving relatives, while a female member troubles others as *Sikoturu* or *Māvadi*.[5]

The spirits of men that fall victims to tigers or other wild animals are believed to enter the ghostly order and wander about until they are relieved from this state by the performance of the prescribed *shrāddha* by some pious surviving relative.[6] These evil spirits live in forests and eat nothing but flesh.[7] If they do not get flesh to eat they eat the flesh of their own bodies.[8] At times they put their relatives to great annoyance by entering their persons. To pacify them, *pālios* are erected in their name, and their images are set up in the square cavities of walls. These images are besmeared with red lead and oil by their descendants on the four-teenth day of the dark half of *Ashvin*. The relief of such spirits is sought by the performance of a *shrāddha* either at Siddhapur or at Gaya.[9]

It is believed that a woman dying in child-bed or menses enters the order of ghosts variously known as *Chudels*, *Vantris* or *Taxamis*. In order that she may not return from the cremation ground, mustard seeds are strewn along the road behind her bier, for a belief prevails that she can only succeed in returning if she can collect all the mustard seeds thus strewn on the way.[10]

In some places, loose cotton wool is thrown over the bier so as to be scattered all along the road to the cemetery. It is believed that the *Chudel* can only return to the house if she can collect all the cotton scattered behind her in one night. This is considered an impossible task, and no fear is therefore entertained of her return after the cotton has been scattered.[11]

To prevent the return of the *Chudel*, some people pass underneath the bier the legs of the cot on which the woman lay in her confinement, while others drive in an iron nail at the end of the street immediately after the corpse has been carried beyond the village boundary.[12]

In some places, the nail is driven into the threshold of the house.[13]

Even after the precautions mentioned above have been taken, to prevent the return of a *Chudel* or *Vantri*, *Shrāddhas* are performed, and a number of Brāhman women feasted on the twelfth and thirteenth day after death to propitiate her as the fear of the mischief done by her is very strong.[13]

A *Chudel* has no shoulders.[14] Any passer by coming across her is asked by her to take her to his home, and if he agrees, she accompanies him, passes the night in his company, and brings his life to a speedy end. In the village of Charādi under the jurisdiction of Dhrānga-

[1] The School Master of Vanod.
[2] The School Master of Jetpur.
[3] The School Master of Songadh.
[4] The School Master of Kotda Sangani.
[5] The School Master of Jhinjhuwāda.
[6] The School Master of Dhānk.
[7] The School Master of Kotda Sangani.
[8] The School Master of Rājpāra.
[9] The School Master of Vanod.
[10] The School Master of Dhānk.
[11] Mr. K. D. Desāi.
[12] The School Master of Vanod.
[13] Mr. K. D. Desāi.
[14] The School Master of Limbdi.

dhra, a Girāsia named Halāji fell into the clutches of a *Chudel* who was driven from his person by the enchantment of a *Jati* on condition that he should not go into the eastern part of the village.[1]

It is believed that a woman can be relieved from the ghostly order of a *Chudel* by the performance of a *shrāddha* at Siddhapur.[2]

There is no belief that the father has to take special precautions at the birth of his child except that care is taken to note the exact time of the child's birth for the purpose of casting its horoscope correctly. An inkstand and pen are also placed in the lying-in-room, as it is believed that the creator writes the destiny of a child as soon as it makes its appearance into the world.[3]

All children born in *Jyeshta Nakshatra. Mula-nakshatra*, or *Yamaghanta* are said to cause the death of their male parent. Such children were left to starve uncared for in forests in olden times; but now-a-days they are kept alive, as certain performances are believed to avert the evil. One such performance is only to see the child after clarified butter has been given in donation. Another is to see its face after it has been bathed with the water collected from eighteen wells in a pot with a thousand holes.[4] In a third, the parents of the child hold in their hands goblets filled with clarified butter, and see their faces reflected in them before the child is presented to the sight of the father.

Such children are named Mulubhāi, Mulchand, Muli or Mulo.

A child born in the month of *Jyestha* prognosticates poverty.[5]

If the birth time of a child happens to fall within the ecliptic period, that is the period of nine hours before an eclipse takes place, as well as in the duration of the eclipse, the father does not see the child before performing certain rites, as to do so is supposed to bring misfortune.[6]

If a man has a child in his twentieth year he does not see the child before he completes it.[7]

If a child is born at a wrong juncture or conjunction of the stars, the father does not see it for twenty-seven days.[8]

A child born on the fourth, fourteenth or fifteenth day of a month is supposed to become a burden to its father.[9]

It is a common belief that a woman in child bed should not see the face of her husband nor he of her.[10]

Women who do not obey the commands of their husbands, who partake of their meals secretly before their husbands,* or violate any of their duties towards their husbands, are believed to enter the order of bats or owls after their death.[11]

According to another belief, men who have been incontinent become owls after death, while such women become bats.[12]

The owls and bats are blind during the day, but they can see corpses and the spirits of the deceased and converse with them in their own tongue.[13]

The spirits of the deceased are supposed to remain in their worldly tenement for twelve days, and owls and bats are supposed to be able to see them at night and talk to them.[14]

1 The School Master of Lilāpur.
2 The School Masters of Dhānk and Vanod.
3 Mr. K. D. Desāi.
4 The School Master of Vanod.
5 The School Mistress, Female Training College, Rājkot.
6 The School Master of Todia.
7 The School Master of Lilāpur.
8 The School Master of Gondal.
9 The School Master of Kolki.
10 The School Master of Devalia.

* This is a point of conjugal etiquette in India. Hindu, and in Gujarāt and the Deccan, Musalmān women, would much rather starve than dine before their husbands.

11 The School Master of Dhānk.
12 The School Master of Vanod.
13 The School Master of Kotda Sangani.
14 The School Master of Chhatrāsā.

One of the beliefs entertained by Hindus about the owl is that none should throw a lump of earth at it, as the owl is believed to pick up the missile and throw it into a well or tank or any sheet of water, with the result that it gradually dissolves and disappears, and simultaneously the body of the person is said to be consumed.[1]

If perchance an owl utters some note perching on the top cross beam of a house on a Sunday or Tuesday night, the owner of the house should pass a dark woollen thread below the cross beam, to which a nude person should give a knot at every screech of the owl. If such a thread be kept in one's anklet, one need have no fear of ghosts nor can he be seen by a *dākan* or witch.

If a person in sleep responds to the call of an owl, he is believed to expire within six months from that date.[2]

If an owl screeches every night for six months on one's house or an adjacent tree, a terror seizes the members of the house that some sure and certain calamity not short of death is imminent.[3]

An owl sitting on the house of a person and screeching is said to be uttering threats or forebodings of calamities and misfortunes, and is believed to foretell the death of some near relative or of a member of the household.[4]

If a miser dies after accumulating vast treasures, his spirit becomes a ghost or a snake and guards his wealth.[5]

According to another belief, a miser dying without an heir becomes a snake to guard his treasure.[6]

It is believed that such treasures are accessible to *batrisas*[7] (those possessed of thirty two accomplishments).

Those persons that die while ousted from the houses built by them become ghosts, and residing in the houses, do not allow any body to live therein, and leave them only when they are demolished.[8]

Some evil spirits guard treasures in the form of drones.[9]

It is related that there is a pond called Lakhota near Jamvādi in Gondal. It contains a treasure guarded by a cobra which tries to bite whosoever attempts to remove it.[10]

The *Janchar*, *Bhuchar*, *Jin* and some other spirits are believed to haunt valleys.[11]

Some believe that those persons that meet their death in valleys become evil spirits and haunt the valleys.[12]

Rakhevālio, *Andhārio*, *Sevālio*, *Sulio* and *Ragatio* are evil spirits that haunt the ruins of magnificent buildings and also valleys.[13]

---

1 Mr. K. D. Desāi.

2 The School Master of Kolki.

3 The School Master of Zinzuvāda.

4 Mr. K. D. Desāi.

5 The School Master of Dhānk.

6 The School Master of Māvaiya.

7 The School Master of Dhānk.

8 The School Master of Vanod.

9 The School Master of Sāyala.

10 The School Master of Gondal.

11 The School Master of Kotda Sangani.

12 The School Master of Vanod.

13 The School Master of Rājpāra.

CHAPTER VI.

THE EVIL EYE AND THE SCARING OF GHOSTS.

The superstitious dread of an evil eye is to be seen mostly among ignorant people, especially among women. If a boy were to fall ill, they say, "Chhotio (the name of the boy) was playing in the house wearing a fine dress and was prattling sweetly, when that wretch came to the house and her evil eye fell on him"[1] or "The boy was eating a dainty dish when that devilish woman came up and her evil eye influenced the boy."[2]

Persons born on a Sunday or Tuesday are generally believed to have an evil eye.[3]

The evil eye causes its victim to vomit what he has eaten in its presence.[4]

If a child weeps all day long, or a person finds his appetite very weak, the evil is attributed to an evil eye.[5]

If milch cattle do not give milk, or if *seva* (vermicelli) *pāpad* (wafer biscuits) pickles, *dudhpāk* (rice cooked in milk and sweetened with sugar) or such other eatables are spoilt, it is believed that the evil eye is at the root of the trouble.[6]

It is believed that the following objects are liable to be influenced by an evil eye:—

(1) Persons having fine glossy hair, fiery eyes, exquisite form, refined gait, fine speech or good handwriting, (2) good sportsmen, (3), pickles, (4) *pāpad* (wafer biscuits), (5) *Seva* (vermicelli), (6) all attractive objects

If a person falls ill after he is praised, he is said to have been a victim of an evil eye.[7]

The precautions taken to evade the influence of the evil eye are as follows:—

(1) When children are dressed and decked with ornaments, a spot is made on their cheeks or near their necks with a black pigment or collyrium, as it is believed that the dark colour is an antidote against the influence of the evil eye.

(2) Some efficacious inscription is engraved on a copper plate, which is suspended round the child's neck.

(3) A bead of *kachakada* is also worn round the neck.

(4) A tiger's nail or tooth is worn round the neck.

(5) An iron ring is worn on the finger.

(6) A lime is worn in the turban or headdress.

(7) An incantation in the praise of Hanumān is written on a piece of paper and put in an anklet which is worn.

(8) A piece of thread of five kinds of silk or cotton spun by a virgin is given seven knots on the fourteenth day of the dark half of *Áshvin* and worn on the person.

(9) In order that sweet meats and other eatables such as *pāpad* (wafer biscuits), pickles, etc., may not be spoilt by an evil eye, a lime, an iron nail or a knife is put into them.

(10) In order that a cot or cradle may not be broken by the influence of an evil eye, a black woollen thread is tied round it.

(11) To prevent *dudhbāk* (rice cooked in milk and sweetened with sugar) from being spoilt, a piece of charcoal is put into the pot in which it is prepared.[8]

While taking one's meal one should avoid the company of an evil-eyed person, but if perchance one happen to be present, a morsel of the food should be thrown behind him or

---

[1] The School Master of Dhānk.

[2] Mr. K. D. Dasāi.

[3] The School Master of Kolki

[4] The School Master of Chhatrāsa.

[5] The School Master of Jetpur.

[6] The School Master of Devalia.

[7] The School Master of Sāyala.

[8] The School Master of Ganod.

set aside on the ground as an offering to the evil eye.[1]

If, in spite of the precautions mentioned above, the influence of the evil eye prevails, the following remedies are adopted to remove its effects:—

(1) The evil eye is fastened or curbed, as they say, by one of the processes described in Chapter III above.

(2) A red-hot charcoal is placed on a dinner plate and covered with an earthen jar. A bowl filled with water is then passed round the head of the patient, emptied over the jar and placed on it with its mouth touching the jar. Next, a scythe is placed over the bowl. The jar, which is heated with the heat of the burning charcoal placed under it produces a hissing sound as soon as it is touched by the water in the bowl, and is said to speak. This process is called *Ghadulo* and is performed after sunset.[2]

In some places, it is a belief that the plate to be used in this process must be of bell-metal, and that over the fire placed in it mustard seeds, chillies and salt must be thrown before it is covered with the earthen jar.[3]

(3) An *utār** or sacrificial offering is taken to the village gate on a Sunday or Tuesday.

(4) Milk is passed three or seven times round the head of the ailing child, poured into a black earthen pot, and offered to a black bitch on a Sunday or Tuesday.[4]

(5) The mother or some other near relative of the child suffering from the effects of the evil eye, puts in a bell-metal cup mustard seed, salt, chillies and seven stones from the village gate, passes the cup thrice round the child's head, puts burning charcoal in the cup, and after it is heated, places it overturned in a bell-metal pot and pours over it water mixed with cowdung, so that the cup adheres to the pot. This sticking of the cup is called *najar chonti gai* (the evil eye has stuck fast) and is believed to cure the child.[5]

(6) An exorcist is engaged to wave a bowl filled with water round the head of the patient. He then drinks off the water, and the patient believes that the disease has been drunk with it.[6]

(7) A handful of salt and chillies is passed thrice round the head of the patient and thrown into the fire. If the chillies burn without giving out fumes of an unpleasant odour, the evil eye is believed to be at the root of the illness.†[7]

(8) A little dust collected from a spot where two roads cross one another, or red lead and oil offered to Hanumān, a red chilly, an iron nail and grains of *adad* (Phaseolus mungo) are packed into a piece of white cotton cloth with a black woollen thread, and tied to the cradle of the suffering child.[8]

(9) A side of a loaf of millet flour is baked by being exposed to fire, clarified butter is applied to this side, and a fine cotton thread is passed round the loaf. Next, the loaf is waved round the head of the ailing child and thrown into fire. If the cotton thread is not burnt by the fire, an evil eye is believed to be the cause of the illness.[8]

Sometimes the loaf is offered to a black dog after it has been waved round the child's head.[8]

(10) If the illness be due to the influence of the evil eye of a woman, she is called in and asked to pass her hand over the child's head.[9]

1 Mr. K. D. Desāi

2 The School Master of Ganod.

3 The School Master of Dhānk.

* See page 3.

4 The School Master of Ganod.

5 The School Master of Vanod.

6 The School Master of Kotda Sangani.

7 Mr. K. D. Desāi.

† This process is generally adopted in cases of milch cattle not giving milk and all other ailments to ascertain the influence of the evil eye.

8 The School Master of Dadvi.

9 Mr. K. D. Desāi.

(11) In order to avoid the effects of the evil eye, when a child returns home from an outside visit, a bowl filled with water is passed thrice round its head and emptied outside the house before it crosses the threshold of the house.[1]

(12) The grains of *Adad*, twigs of the *Thor* (Euphoria nerifolia), salt and dust are passed seven times round the head of a person suffering from the effects of an evil eye, on the threshold of the house, and thrown away.[2]

(13) Grains of *Adad*, twigs of the *Thor*, salt, an iron nail and charcoal are put into an unused earthen pot and taken to the village boundary with a bowl filled with water. The person carrying the pot and bowl should not look behind either on his way to, or on his return from, the village boundary. The pot is placed on the village boundary, and water is poured over it seven times from the bowl.[3]

(14) A loaf baked on one side, with seven grains of *Adad*, seven grains of salt and seven cotton seeds placed over it, is passed seven times round the patient's head and placed on a spot where two roads cross one another. The person carrying the bread should not look behind while carrying it.[4]

Those whose children do not live, or die in infancy, or who get children with difficulty, give them opprobrious names, as it is believed that objects so named, being considered of no value, are left unharmed both by men and by gods.[5]

Some people believe that children so named are considered impure by Fate or Destiny, and consequently not molested by her.[6]

It is believed by some that, as good names attract attention, giving opprobrious names averts the danger of the evil eye.[7]

Some people throw a newly-born child on a dung-hill and take it back, saying that they found it on the dung-hill, with the belief that a child of such low origin cannot be snatched away from them by Fate. Such children are named Punjio, Unkardo or Kacharo meaning 'dung-hill.'

Some children are named Khoto, Amatho or Jutho, all meaning 'false', with the belief that children so named are considered to belong to gods or Fate, and hence cannot be taken away from their parents by the god of death.

Some people exchange their children for sweets, or offer them to others and purchase them back at a nominal price. Others roll them in the dust and name them Dhulio or dust. This is believed to ensure a long life to the children.[8]

In some places, a relative of the child's on the mother's side presents it with a necklace of gold beads shaped like large black ants. When the child attains the age of eight or ten years this necklace is offered to some god or goddess. The child is named Sānkalio as it wears round its neck this *sānkal* or chain, that is, necklace.[9]

It is held by some that children bearing contemptuous names are not affected by magic.[10]

Some weigh the child against corn and give the name of that corn to the child, *e. g.*, 'Kodario'. 'Juvārio'. The corn is then distributed among beggars, which is supposed to ensure a long life to the child.[11]

Some make earthen figures of children, call them *Ila Ili* or *Pithad*, and carry them through the village on the *Holi* day (the full-moon day of *Fālgun*), with the belief that by so doing they ensure a long life to the children.

[1] Mr. K. D. Desāi.
[2] The School Master of Bāntva.
[3] The School Master of Aman.
[4] The School Master of Sāyala.
[5] The School Master of Dhānk.
[6] The School Master of Devalia.
[7] The School Master of Vanod.
[8] Mr. M. M. Rāna, Barton Female Training College, Rājkot.
[9] The School Master of Sultānpur.
[10] The School Master of Moti Khilori.
[11] The School Master of Khirāsara.

It is related that a carpenter's children used to die in infancy, so he named one of his sons 'Pithad' and he lived. Since then, parents whose children do not live name them 'Pithad. Some name their children 'Jivo' that is 'Live' with the hope that they may live long.[1]

The opprobrious and other special spirit-scaring names generally given to boys are as follows :—

NAME.	MEANING.	NAME.	MEANING.
Amatho	Useless	Gobaro[3]	
Jutho	False	Fakiro	Beggar
Kacharo	Refuse	Mafatio	Worthless
Nathu	Tied	Nāgo	Shameless
Punjo	Refuse	Bocho	Coward
Jivo	Live	Bakor	Noise
Kālo	Black	Bow	Name of a demon
Ghelo	Mad	How	Ditto.
Gafal	Stupid	Limbo	Poisonous
Valu or Vāyali	Eccentric	Gānglo	Stony[4]
Sawo or Siwo	Sewed	Bhikhāri or Bhikho	Beggar
Dungar	Hill	Vaigrāi	Recluse
Ado ...	Useless	Amar	Immortal
Bhābho	Worthless	Sidio	Negro-like
Mālo	Bower	Vasto[5]	
Velo	Creeper	Polio or Polo	Hollow
Nāno	Small	Kadavo	Bitter
Khodo	Lame	Bero	Deaf
Oghad	Fool	Dipo	Panther
Hakalo		Vāgh	Tiger
Bhukhan		Cohampalo	Meddlesome
Uko	Dung-hill	Chindharo	Ragged
Lāvo	Parasite	Chiko	
Jino	Small	Chuntho	Ragged
Doso	Old	Jinthro	Ragged
Rāno	Lord (ironical)	Jalo	
Bāvo	Recluse	Davalo	Not loved
Rupo	Handsome (ironical)	Dendo	The croaking of a frog.
Mor ...	Peacock	Dhingo	Fat
Popat	Parrot	Bodo	Bald-headed
Jado	Fastened[2]	Rotal	Womanish
Bodho		Radio	Crying[6]

[1] The School Master of Todia.
[2] The School Master of Dhānk.
[3] The School Master of Ganod.
[4] The School Master of Vanod.
[5] The School Master of Dadvi
[6] The School Master of Kolki.

The contemptuous names given to girls are:—

NAME.	MEANING.
Liri	
Dhori	White
Zini	Small
Punji	Refuse
Kāli	Black
Ful	Light as a flower[1]
Nāthi	
Juthi	False
Jādi	Fat
Monghi	
Jāba[2]	
Kadvi	Bitter
Jivi	Live.
Divi[3]	

Veju, Bhilak, Chichi, Lāghu[4], Mafat useless), Gheli (mad), Panchi[5], Dedki, Kukadi and Zabu.[6]

It is said that in ancient times change of sex could be effected.

Tradition relates that all the children of a certain Solanki king died in infancy, except the last child, a girl. She was dressed in male attire and passed for a boy. When the pretended boy attained marriageable age, he was betrothed to a princess. When the day fixed for the marriage drew near, the king became anxious and went on an hunting expedition to pass the time. On his way back from the hunt he became very thirsty, and quenched his thirst with the water of a pond near which a temple of Bahucharāji stands to this day. His bitch, which was with him, leapt into the pond, and on coming out of the water was found to be transformed into a dog. On seeing this the king brought his daughter and bathed her into the pond with the result that she was transformed into a boy. The king then built a big tank on the spot, which is known by the name of *Mān*.[7]

In a chapter called *Brahmottar Khand* of the *Padma Purān*, which describes the glory of a vow called *Uma Mahesh*, the greatness of observing fasts on Mondays is described at length. Two Brāhman brothers, one dressed as a man and the other as a woman, set out on a journey. Once they halted in a temple of the god Shiva, where lived a woman who had observed the fasts on Mondays. She invited them to dinner, taking them, as they appeared to be, for a man and a woman. The devotion of the hostess was so great that the brother dressed as a woman was actually transformed into a woman while partaking of the meal served to him.[8]

It is related that in ancient times the son of a certain sage once disguised himself as a girl with the result that he was actually changed into a girl. He was thereafter called Mudrālopi and married to the sage Agastya.[9]

The warrior Shikhandi who assisted the Pāndavas in killing Bhishma (who had vowed not to raise his arms against a woman) was at first a girl, and was subsequently transformed into a boy by the boon of the gods.[10]

There is supposed to be a forest of Pārvati in a continent called Ilavrit. Any man visiting it is at once turned into a woman.[11]

A king named Sudyaman visited this forest and was transformed into a woman. It was only after appeasing Pārvati by a sacrifice that he was restored to his original form.[12]

It is believed that in Kamaru Desha or the land of fairies, children are transformed into the opposite sex by the spell of the inhabitants.[13]

[1] The School Master of Dhānk.
[2] The School Master of Ganod.
[3] The School Master of Kolki.
[4] The School Master of Bhāyāvadar
[5] The School Master of Khirāsara.
[6] The School Master of Sānka.
[7] The School Master of Zinzuvāda.
[8] The School Master of Dhānk.
[9] The School Master of Uptela.
[10] The School Master of Ganod.
[11] The School Master of Vanod.
[12] The School Master of Bhāyāvadar.
[13] The School Master of Jetpur.

A belief is current that change of sex can be effected by the performance of the *Shatchandi* or the *prayoga* of Rudra, Bahucharāji, Āshāpuri and Mahākāli.[1]

It is also believed that change of sex can also be effected by the spell of magic.[2]

There is a further belief that *Yogis* by their incantations, and *Mahātmās* by their blessings or curses, can effect a change of sex.[3]

The following things are considered efficacious in protecting oneself against evil spirits:—

(1) A sword, (2) iron,[4] (3) a woollen blanket, (4) fire, (5) a coin in the funeral pyre, (6) a nail of a tiger, (7) a blue thread, (8) the red lead offered to the god Hanumān, (9) a lime consecrated with incantations, (10) five kinds of cotton thread worn round the elbow,[5] (11) blood, (12) corn, (13) frankincense, (14) salt, (15) water, (16) leather, (17) an amulet of iron procured from a well polluted by the death of some one in its water,[6] (18) a garland, the beads of which are made of the wood of the *Ekal ber* (Zizyphus jujuba) (19) The sacred thread worn by Brāhmans,[7] (20) iron nails extracted from a wheel of a cart used for carrying fuel for cremation,* (21) human blood,[8] (22) a costly jewel.

Amulets are generally used as a precaution against the attack of evil spirits or the influence of an evil eye. They are also used to cure diseases. They are made of iron, copper, tin, gold, silver, alloys of precious metals, or leather.

Chithis or pieces of paper on which mystic signs are drawn are put into the amulets and are tied to the forearm with black woollen or silk thread.[9]

In some places, frankincense of *gugal* (Canarium strictum) or *lobān* (olibanum) is offered to the amulets before they are worn.[10]

Amulets are also made of *tād-patras* (palm-leaves). They are tied round the arm with an indigo-coloured cloth.[11]

Dorās or threads are also worn with the same object as amulets. They are generally made of five kinds of silk thread, black wool, or red or black cotton thread. The length of the *dora* must be eight feet, one and a quarter of a cubit or a man's height. They must have three folds and must be twisted seven or twenty-one times. After they are twisted, they are knotted seven, fourteen or twenty-one times, when they become ready for use. An offering of frankincense made of *gugal* or of *lobān* is made to a *dora* before it is worn.[12]

It is believed by some people, that a *chiti* (amulet) or *dora* in order to be effective, must not be touched with water.

The *dora* of the god Kālbhairav at Benares, which is made of silk thread with seven twists, is tied round the wrist of a patient in the belief that it cures illness.

A *janjiro* (black cotton thread with seven knots) of the god Hanumān is worn round the arm with the same belief.

Surakano, that is, twisted iron wire, consecrated by the worshipper of the goddess Machhu, is worn by the Bharvāds round the elbow or the wrist with the belief that it cures wind.

Those people whose children do not live long put silver anklets round their left legs in the belief that by so doing their life is lengthened.[13]

[1] The School Master of Kotda Sangani.
[2] The School Master of Mota Devalia.
[3] The D. E. Inspector, Hālār.
[4] The School Master of Dhānk.
[5] The School Master of Kotda Sangani.
[6] The School Master of Kolki.
[7] The Deputy Educational Inspector, Gohilwād.
* Anklets are made of these nails and worn round the wrist.—The School Master of Zinzuwāda.
[8] The School Master of Vasvad.
[9] The School Master of Kotda Sangani.
[10] The School Master of Dhānk.
[11] The School Master of Gohilwād.
[12] The School Master of Dhānk.
[13] The School Master of Todia.

An amulet made of a piece of cloth is called *dhāga*.[1] It is either a piece of cloth used by a holy man, a piece of cloth containing a mixture of red lead and oil offered to the god Hanumān,[2] or a piece of cloth in which are wrapped up the things put into an amulet. The *dhāga* is either worn round the wrist or suspended from the neck.[3]

Amulets tied to the horns of pet animals such as cows, bullocks, horses, etc., are called *dąmanās*. Sometimes they are also suspended from the necks of these animals. They are made of the hides of sacred animals and are believed to protect the animals against the evil eye, evil spirits and magic.[4]

It is believed by some people that one can escape injury from an evil spirit by seating oneself in a circle or square drawn in and plastered with cowdung,[5]

Others hold that the circle must be drawn with the point of a sword.[5]

Some maintain that the circle cannot be a protective unless it is drawn with enchanted water, milk or sesamum oil.

There are others who are of opinion that the entry of evil spirits into the circle can be prevented only by calling upon God not to allow the evil spirits to enter it.[6]

When an evil spirit is expelled from the body of a person, it is buried underground, a circle of water is made round the spot and an iron nail is driven into the ground, in order that it may be imprisoned there.[7]

If anybody step into such a circle, the evil spirit confined therein takes possession of him, and is thus freed.[8]

To prevent this, evil spirits are generally confined in secluded spots.[9]

As the circle drawn by the point of a sword is a protection against an evil spirit, those who go to the burning ground to propitiate or subjugate evil spirits, seat themselves in such circles while reciting *mantras*.[10]

After entering the circle, some people recite the name of Hanumān, Chandi or Bhairav.[11]

Some people, after seating themselves in the circle, make offerings to the evil spirits, while reciting *mantras*, to propitiate them more easily. The *Kāli chaudas* or the fourteenth day of the dark half of *Ashvin* is considered a suitable day for propitiating or subjugating evil spirits.[12]

There are various superstitious beliefs entertained by people regarding omens.

1. If when leaving the house on a visit or with some definite object in view, a deer crosses one's path from right to left, it is considered a bad omen, while crossing from left to right is considered good. On returning home, this omen is read in the reverse way to that just stated.[13]

2. When starting on a journey, the braying of an ass on the right is a good omen and on the left, evil.[14]

3. If on leaving the house, a man meets an unwidowed woman or a virgin with a jar filled with water on her head, it is an indication that the object of the expedition will be accomplished.[15]

4. While starting on a good errand, if one breathes through the left nostril or comes across a person carrying a basket of eggs, it is a good omen.

5. If at the time of leaving for a visit to another town or village, the position of the moon in the circle explaining the position of stars with reference to one's birth-day stars, be in the rear or on the left of that position, it is a bad omen, but if it be in the front or on the right it is a good omen.

[1] Mr. K. D. Desāi.
[2] The Pathashala Shastri, Jetpur.
[3] The Girl School-Mistress, Gondal.
[4] Mr. K. D. Desāi.
[5] The School Master of Dhānk.
[6] The School Master of Kotda Sangani.
[7] The School Master of Dadvi.
[8] The School Master of Todia.
[9] The School Master of Dadvi.
[10] The School Master of Ganod.
[11] The School Master of Chok.
[12] The School Master of Zinzuvada.
[13] The School Master of Dhānk.
[14] The School Masters of Dadvi and Dhānk.
[15] The School Master of Dhānk.

The moon in front means fulfilment of the intended purpose, on the right, it confers happiness and prosperity, on the back it causes death; and on the left, loss of wealth.

6. The warbling of the bird *bhairav* on the right while going out and on the left while returning is a good omen, but the opposite is bad.[1]

7. A cat or a serpent crossing one's path is ominous of evil; but if either passes on the right, it foretells good.[1]

8. A jackal howling in the evening prognosticates damage by fire to the town or village; its howling at midnight predicts robbery; while in the last part of the night it foretells good.

9. *Kāg-rāshiās* (expounders of the utterances of crows) know the good and bad indications of the croakings of crows.

10. The wailing notes of the bird *Fāvadi* forebode evil.[1]

11. The throbbing of the right eye or side in the case of men and of the left eye or side in the case of women is considered to be a good omen, while the contrary is bad.[1]

12. If the bird *holo* sweeps the roof of one's house continuously for a number of days, a calamity is supposed to be imminent for the inmates of the house.

13. If a dog barks in front of a man it is considered to be a bad omen.[2]

A Brāhman, a cow, fruits, flowers, milk, pearls, jewels, a prostitute, an elephant, an umbrella, meat, fish, a gun, a bayonet, a mirror, a mongoose, a peacock with its plumage expanded, girls singing songs, band-players and a washerman carrying washed clothes are all considered to be good omens, if one comes across them while going out on business.[3]

The sight of a king, an armed man, a Dhed, a Bhangi or a Darji is also considered to be an auspicious omen.[4]

The sight of boys going to or returning from school is a good omen.[5]

A labourer carrying a load of fuel on his head, a corpse in front, a potter carrying earth on his head or on his donkey, a woman carrying her son, a man carrying molasses, are all auspicious omens.[6]

A male monkey or a donkey crying on the right while going out, and on the left while returning home is considered to be a good omen.[7]

Wine and good speech are also considered good omens.[8]

The sight of a herdswoman, a dog scratching its right side, a cuckoo singing on a tree or a black sparrow is a good omen.[9]

Fuel, hides, grass, vegetables, a smoking fire, sesamum oil, molasses, a barren woman, an enemy, a disorderly mob, a woman without the auspicious mark on her forehead, a man besmeared with oil, a eunuch, mud, wet clothes, an ascetic, a beggar, are all considered to be bad omens, if one sees them while going on business.[10]

The sight of dry cow-dung cakes is supposed to be a bad omen.[11]

The sight of a widow or of a corpse* is bad.[12]

Weasels crossing the road, dogs shaking their ears, a man carrying a black earthen vessel, a woman with loose hair, a person carrying clarified butter, a man with gray moustaches, a man having no hair on his chest, a cat-eyed man, a person carrying flour, a Brāhman without the sacred mark on his forehead are all bad omens.[13]

[1] The School Master of Ganod.
[2] The School Master of Vanod.
[3] The School Master of Dhānk.
[4] The School Master of Kotda Sangani.
[5] The School Master of Ganod.
[6] The School Master of Vanod.
[7] The School Master of Dadvi.
[8] The School Master of Bhāyāvadar.
[9] The School Master of Songadh.
[10] The School Master of Dhānk.
[11] The School Master of Kotda Sangani.
[12] The School Master of Ganod.

* The sight of a corpse is a good omen when one sees it on entering a village where he goes on business.

[13] The School Master of Vanod.

The sight of the husk of corn, a man with a medicinal application, or a lunatic, is a bad omen.[1]

The question "*kiān jāo chho*" that is "Where are you going" is a bad omen.[2]

The mixture of whey, mud and cow-dung, a recluse with matted hair, a man spitting, a cough, and a man with the whole of his head shaved are bad omens[3].

Similarly, the sight of a drunkard, *Adad* or cotton seeds is a bad omen.[4]

A bride stumbling on her entry into the bridegroom's house is said to be a bad omen.[5]

A dog scratching its left side with his paws, a man riding a he-buffalo or a donkey, two Baniās, one Musalmān, one male goat, one ox, five she-buffaloes, six dogs, three cows, or seven horses, confronting a man on starting from the house are ominous of evil.[6]

Some numbers are believed to be auspicious and some inauspicious. There is a book on this subject, in which some good or evil is attributed to each number. One who wants to know the result of the undertaking in hand puts his finger on any number in the book, and the expounder of the science, reading the passage bearing on the number, explains how the undertaking will end.[7]

The numbers, 12, 18, 56 and 58 are considered inauspicious.[8]

An odd number is generally believed to be inauspicious. It is for this reason that newly-married girls are not sent to their husbands' house for the first time in any of the odd years of their age. They are also not sent back to their parents' house in an odd year of their age for the same reason.[9]

The numbers 5, 7, 9, 10, 11, 13, 15, and 21 are believed to be lucky while 3, 4, 8 and 12 are considered unlucky.[10]

A belief exists that if a company of three start on a mission, the mission is sure to fail. This has given rise to the proverb "*Tran trikat ane maha vikat*" that is, "Three persons going on an errand meet with great difficulties or danger."[11]

A zero is believed to be inauspicious. In monetary transactions or bargains, therefore, all numbers ending in a zero are avoided. If such numbers are unavoidable, the sign of $\frac{1}{4}$ is placed before them. The number 12 is considered unlucky, to avoid which $11\frac{1}{2}$ is used in its place.[12]

Some people believe that the numbers $1\frac{1}{4}$, 5, 7, 21, 108 and 1,008 are lucky while 12 is unlucky.[13]

It is a belief that in the sales of cattle and certain other things if the price is raised by $1\frac{1}{4}$, it results in good both to the seller and buyer.[14]

It is for this reason that in subscribing to charitable funds people write 401 instead of 400 and so on. But $1\frac{1}{4}$ is preferred to 1 in valuing things. So in all purchases and sales $1\frac{1}{4}$ is added to the actual price of a thing.[15]

The numbers 5 and 7 are believed to be auspicious, because on starting on a journey from the house one is given five betelnuts as a sign of good omen, while in all auspicious ceremonies seven betelnuts are used.[16]

Certain days of the week are considered lucky while others are considered unlucky. It is also believed that certain days are

[1] The School Master of Dadvi.
[2] Mr. K. D. Desāi.
[3] The School Master of Bhāyāvadar.
[4] The School Master of Limbdi.
[5] The School Master of Todia.
[6] The School Master of Songadh.
[7] The School Master of Dhānk.
[8] The School Master of Ganod.
[9] The School Master of Vanod.
[10] The School Master of Dadvi.
[11] Mr. K. D. Desāi.
[12] The School Master of Mota Devalia.
[13] The School Master of Limbdi.
[14] Mr. K. D. Desāi.
[15] The School Master of Todia.
[16] The School Master of Todia.

auspicious for performing certain acts, while others are inauspicious for the performance of the same acts.

Monday, Wednesday, Thursday and Friday are considered lucky, while Tuesday, Saturday and Sunday are believed to be unlucky.[1]

It is a common belief that one should not go in certain directions on certain days ; for doing so results in what is called *dishā-shul* or pain caused by directions.[2]

Going to the north on Sunday, to the west on Tuesday, to the north-west on Monday, to the south-west on Wednesday, to the south on Thursday, to the south-east on Friday and to the east on Saturday is considered ominous of evil.[3]

According to another belief, Sunday and Thursday are inauspicious for going to the south-east ; Monday and Friday, to the south-west ; Saturday and Tuesday, to the north-west and Wednesday to the north-east.[4]

Some people believe that by going to the west on Monday or Saturday one secures the fulfilment of the desired object.[5]

Many hold that the favourableness or otherwise of the days for going in particular directions varies according to the occasion.[6]

The auspicious days for sending a girl to her husband's house are believed to be Monday, Thursday and Friday. Sunday and Tuesday are also considered auspicious for a girl to go to her house, but they are considered very unlucky for her to return to her parents.[7]

It is forbidden to eat *dālia* (baked split gram) on Sunday, but it is favoured on Friday.

Wednesday is considered to be a lucky day for sowing corn, and making purchases of new articles. Thursday is believed to be auspicious for sending a boy to school for the first time.[8]

Wednesday is considered unfavourable for the separation of brothers and sisters, but it is considered a suitable day for their meeting.[9]

It is believed that if a man wears new clothes on Sunday they will be burnt ; if on Tuesday, they will be lost ; if on Wednesday or Saturday, a quarrel with some one is the result.[10]

It is considered auspicious to go to a Chamār or tanner on Sunday, to a prostitute on Monday, to a Kāchhia (vegetable seller) on Tuesday, to a washerman on Wednesday, to a Brāhman on Thursday, to a Bania on Friday and to a barber on Saturday.[11]

The beliefs regarding the lucky and unlucky days of a month are similar to those of the lucky and unlucky days of the week.

According to some, all the days of the bright half of a month are auspicious for performing any good act, while the days in the dark half are considered favourable for perpetrating black deeds.[12]

Some believe that the 1st, 3rd, 5th, 6th, 8th, 10th, 11th, 13th and the full-moon day of a month are auspicious, while the 2nd, 4th, 7th 9th and 14th, whether of the bright or dark half, as well as the new-moon day, are inauspicious.[13]

According to another belief, the 1st, 6th and 11th days of a month are good, the 3rd and 8th are dates of success (that is acts commenced on these days are crowned with success) ; the 5th, 10th and 15th are *purna tithis*, that is, complete days, (meaning that the moon on these days appears full one-third, full two-thirds and completely full) ; while the 2nd, 7th and 12th are auspicious days,

1 The School Master of Dhānk.
2 Mr. K. D. Desāi.
3 The School Master of Sāyala.
4 The School Master of Ganod.
5 The School Master of Vanod.
6 The School Master of Ganod.
7 The School Master of Kolki.
8 The School Master of Bāntva.
9 The School Master of Zinzuvāda.
10 The School Master of Todia.
11 The School Master of Songadh.
12 The School Master of Dhānk.
13 The School Master of Kotda Sangani.

The 4th, 9th and 14th days of a month are inauspicious.[1]

Some hold that if the 1st, 4th, 12th, 14th and 30th day of a month fall on a Saturday they are good; otherwise bad.[2]

The 1st, 13th or 14th day of either the bright or dark half of a month, as well as the full-moon and new-moon day, are considered unfavourable to patients.[3]

The 2nd, 14th and the last day of a month are considered unlucky. Those days on which there is a *panchak*—a grouping of constellations lasting for five consecutive days—are very inauspicious for commencing auspicious acts.[4]

A belief prevails that any one dying in a *panchak* draws five companions to heaven, that is, his death is followed by the death of four others of the same village.[5]

A son born on the full-moon day is believed to turn out brave, but is supposed to forebode evil to the parents.[6]

If a girl is born on the 2nd, 7th or 12th day of a month falling on a Tuesday or Saturday in the *Ashlesha*, *Kritikā* or *Shutbhilla nakshatra*, she loses her husband.[7]

The *Mul nakshatra* falling on the 1st day of a month, *Bharani* on the 5th, *Kritika* on the 8th, *Rohini* on the 9th and *Ashlesha* on the 10th, has an effect like a volcano. A girl born on the 1st, 6th or 11th day of a month falling on a Saturday, Tuesday or Sunday in the *Kritika* or *Mrigshar nakshatra* is like poison. She is supposed to cause the death of herself, her husband, or all the members of her father's family.[8]

Some of the Hindu holidays are considered auspicious for performing certain deeds, while inauspicious for performing certain others.[9]

The ceremonies described below are performed to help the spirit to the other world.

When a man is on the point of death the floor is cowdunged and an offering of sesamum seeds, *Durva* grass (cynadon dactylon) and *Java* (barley) is made to the deities. Next, water of the Ganges or the Jumna is dropped into the mouth of the dying man and the name of Rām is whispered in his ear, as this is believed to turn his consciousness to God and thus facilitate his way to the other world.

When a patient is convinced that his case is hopeless, he distributes money or other valuable articles among Brāhmans, as this is believed to make his way to heaven easy.

When life is extinct, the corpse is placed on the cow-dunged floor and then carried on a bier to the burning ground with the cries of "Shri Rām", "Rām", "*Rām nām satya hai*",* or "Jaya Shri Krishna". In the fuel with which it is burnt is put *Tulsi* (sweet basil) *Pipal* and sandal wood and cocoanuts. The bones and ashes are collected and preserved, to be thrown into the Dāmodar *kund*, (pool of water) at *Gaya* or other holy waters. For three days after death, holy water and milk is offered to the spirit of the deceased. On the 10th, 11th and 12th day after death, on all the days of every month in the first year corresponding to the day of death, and on every anniversary of the death, *Shrāddha* is performed. *Shrāddha* is also performed annually on the day corresponding to the day of death in the dark half of the month of *Bhādrapad*.

The ceremonies mentioned above are believed to make the passage of the soul to the other world easy. For his final emancipation a man must renounce all pleasures of the senses and all egotism.[10]

[1] The School Master of Moti Parabadi.
[2] The School Master of Charādva.
[3] The School Masters of Ganod and Vanod.
[4] The School Master of Kolki.
[5] Mr. K. D. Desāi.
[6] The School Master of Mota Devalia.
[7] The School Master of Limbdi.
[8] The School Master of Zinzuvāda.
[9] Mr. K. D. Desāi.
* "The name of Rām is alone true" meaning all else except God is illusion.
[10] The School Master of Dhānk and Mr. K. D. Desāi.

Giving alms to the poor, holding recitations of the *Bhāgvat*, performing the *Vishnu Yāg*, *Gāyatri-purashcaran* and the *Chāndrāyan vrat* are also believed to make the passage of the soul to heaven easy.[1]

In order that the departing spirit may meet with no obstruction on the way, cows, articles of dress, shoes and food are presented to a Brāhman for one year after death.[2]

Places for offering water to passers by, and houses in which to feed the needy, are also established by well-to-do people with the same object.[3]

The gift of sacks for holding corn, of umbrellas, blankets and bedding to travellers, is also believed to smooth the passage of the soul to heaven.[4]

The performance of the *shrāddhas* and other ceremonies mentioned above is believed to prevent the return of the spirit to this world.[5]

Observing fasts by the survivors of the deceased on the *Rishi Panchami* (the 5th day of the bright half of *Bhādrapad*), the *Jamāshtami* (the eighth day of the dark half of *Shrāvan*) and the *Rāmnavami* (the ninth day of the bright half of *Chaitra*) is also believed to prevent the return of a spirit from heaven. Some worship the *Pipal* with the same object.[6]

Reading the *Garud Purān* for nine days after death is also believed to be a means of preventing the return of the soul to this world.[7]

Some people believe that performing *shrāddha* in sixty-eight holy places secures this end.[8]

Daily offerings of rice and water to the departed spirits also prevent them from revisiting this world.[9]

The same means which are adopted to help the spirit to the other world and to prevent its return also secure its good-will to the survivors.[10]

Persons living on the banks of the Ganges do not burn the dead, but throw the corpses into the holy water of the river.[11]

If a pregnant woman dies in the eighth month of her pregnancy, the foetus is taken out by cutting open the womb and buried, while the woman is burnt.[12]

Corpses of persons dying an unnatural death are burnt in a *Gondaro* (place where the village cows rest) or on the village common, in the belief that by so doing the deceased escapes divine wrath and is freed from rebirth.[13]

When a grave is commenced in a certain spot, the corpse must be buried on that spot, even though the ground be rocky or otherwise unsuitable. As far as possible, the corpses of relatives are buried near one another.[13]

The occasions on which the hair is shaved are as follows:—

1. When a boy attains the age of three years, his head is shaved completely for the first time.

2. At the time of performing *shrāddha* in holy places, the head, except the top-knot, and the moustaches and face must be shaved.

3. On the ninth day after the death of a man, all his male relatives younger than himself have to shave their heads, except the top-knot, and the moustaches and chin.

4. On the day of investing a boy with the sacred thread his head is shaved before the investiture.

5. Amongst high caste Hindus the heads of widows are shaved on the tenth day after the death of their husbands.[14]

---

[1] The School Master of Ganod.
[2] The School Master of Pātanvāv.
[3] The School Master of Khirāsara.
[4] The School Master of Hālār.
[5] The School Master of Dhānk.
[6] The School Master of Kotda Sangani.
[7] Mr. K. D. Desāi.
[8] The School Master of Kolki.
[9] The School Master of Vanod.
[10] The School Master of Dhānk and Mr. K. D. Desāi.
[11] The School Master of Kotda Sangani.
[12] The School Master of Ganod.
[13] The School Master of Chhatrāsa.
[14] The School Master of Dhānk.

6. *Gorjis* or preceptors of the *Atits*, *Shrāvaks* and *Sanyāsis* have to get their heads shaved at the time of entering the order.[1]

7. All the male relatives of the deceased have to get their heads shaved on the ninth day after death.

8. *Atits* and *Bāvās* get the heads of their disciples shaved at the time of admitting them into their order.[2]

9. The preceptors of the Swāmi Nārāyan sect shave off their moustaches every time they shave their heads.[3]

10. At the time of admitting a Jain to the ascetic order of the religion, the hairs of his head are pulled out one by one until the head is completely bald.[4]

11. On the occasion of a man being re-admitted to his own caste, out of which he has been expelled for some breach of caste rules, he has to shave his head and face by way of *prāyaschitta* or atonement.[4]

It is believed that if the head of a widow is not shaved on the tenth day after the death of her husband, his soul is not admitted to heaven, and the funeral ceremonics performed in his honour bear no fruit.[5]

The heads of such widows are shaved on the banks of the Godāvari or at Benarcs or at some other holy place in the neighbourhood.[6]

The spirits of the dead are represented by balls of rice flour or cooked rice, and offerings of water, cotton thread, red powder, *abir* (white scented powder), red lead, sandal paste, frankincense, lamps, sesamum seeds and of the leaves of the *Tulsi*, the tamarind, the *Agathio* or *Agathi* (Sesbania grandiflora) and the *Bhangra*, and the flowers and seeds of the *Java*, are made to them.

The ancestral spirits are also represented by *chats* (twisted braids of the *Durva* grass (Cynodon Dactylon), and to them are offered the *Suran* (Elephant-foot) cooked rice, fried cakes of the flour of *mag* (Phaseolus mungo), rice cooked in milk, etc.[7]

It is believed that the departed spirits are pleased with offerings of *pindas* or rice-balls.[8]

Pindas are also made of wheat flour or molasses. Costly dishes, sesamum seeds, honey, curdled milk, clarified butter, and sugarcandy are also offered to the *manes*.[9]

The *pindas* are generally offered on the 10th, 11th and 12th day after death and on the occasion of performing *shrāddha*.[10]

Rice balls are also offered to crows or thrown into water in the belief that by so offering they reach the spirits of deceased ancestors.[10]

A belief prevails that the messengers of the god of death eat the flesh of the deceased if *pindas* are not offered to them. So, in ancient times, offerings of flesh balls were made instead rice ones.[11]

It is believed that male and female evil spirits such as *bhuts* and *pishāchas* manifest themselves as dogs, notably black dogs, goats, fire, the whirl-wind, snakes or children.[12]

They may assume the form of a he-buffalo, a heifer, a ram, a man, a woman,[13] a lion, a tiger or a cat.[14]

The evil spirit called *jān* is believed to manifest itself as a snake.[15]

The voice of an evil spirit in any of the above forms is heard from a distance, and the nearer the hearer approaches the more it is found to recede.[16]

1 The School Master of Kotda Sangani.
2 The School Master of Ganod.
3 The School Master of Bāntva.
4 The School Master of Uptela.
5 The School Master of Ganod.
6 Mr. K. D. Desāi.
7 The School Master of Dhānk.
8 The School Master of Kotda Sangani.
9 The School Master of Ganod.
10 The School Master of Dadvi.
11 The School Mistress, Girls' school, Civil Station, Râjkot.
12 The School Master of Dhānk.
13 The School Master of Kotda Sangani.
14 The School Masters of Chhatrāsa and Uptela.
15 The School Master of Dadvi.
16 The School Master of Chhatrāsa.

Among Bharvāds and Sonis, seven or nine earthen pots are broken in the house of the deceased on the tenth day after death. The number of the pots varies according to the individual merits of the deceased.[1]

Among some low castes, an earthen pot is broken on the village boundary and another in the burning ground.[2]

Some break an earthen pot at the village gate on their way back from the cemetery after the performance of *shrāddha*.[3]

In some places, the earthen pots placed on the spot where the corpse is laid in the house are broken at the village gate.[4]

In some low castes two earthen pots are placed on the village boundary on the twelfth day after death, and broken by children.[5]

Some carry the funeral fire in a black earthen jar as far as the village gate, where the jar is broken and the fire carried in the hand, by one of the mourners, to the burning ground.[6]

According to some, this breaking of an earthen pot is a symbol indicating that the connection of the deceased with this world has broken or ceased.[7]

Others hold that it indicates the disintegration of the constituents of the body into the elements of which it was formed.[8]

There are others who are of opinion that the messengers of the god of death are satisfied with the breaking of an earthen pot after an offering to them of six rice balls and water.[9]

When a death takes place in a family, a *prāna-poka* or death-wail is raised by the chief mourner, who is joined afterwards by the other relatives.[10]

The *prāna-poka* is believed to open the gates of heaven for the admission of the soul.[11]

Some are of opinion that the object of the death-wail, which begins with "*O māra bhāi* !" that is, "Oh my brother!" or "*O māra bāp* !" that is, "Oh my father!", is that at the moment of death, the soul, by hearing the sound 'Om' may ascend to the *brahmarandhra* or the divine seat of the brain and thus attain salvation.[12]

When the funeral party start with the bier for the burning ground, the women of the house, accompanied by other women of the neighbourhood or village, follow them as far as the village gate, crying and singing funeral dirges. There they stop a while and sing more funeral dirges, keeping time by beating their breasts. They then start to return home, and, on their way, bathe in a tank or well and again mourn for some time before entering the house. The funeral party enter the house after the women and cry aloud for a few seconds. They also cry when the pyre is set on fire.[13]

The mourning of the women continues for thirteen* days after death. They also weep on such holidays as the *Holi*, the *Divāli*, etc., and on the quarterly, six-monthly and the first anniversary *Shrāddha* day.[14]

Male relatives of the deceased wear a white turban as a sign of mourning.[15]

It is generally believed that *bhuts* or evil spirits prove beneficial to those who succeed in securing locks of their hair or subjugate them by incantations or magical rites.[16]

[1] The School Master of Vanod.
[2] The School Master of Dadvi.
[3] The School Master of Gunjar.
[4] The School Master of Bhāyāvadar.
[5] The School Master of Ganod.
[6] The School Master of Hālār.
[7] The School Master of Dadvi.
[8] The School Master of Kotda Sangani.
[9] The School Mistress, Civil Station Girls' School, Rājkot.
[10] The School Master of Dhānk.
[11] The School Master of Gunjār.
[12] The School Mistress of Civil Station Girls'School, Rājkot and the School Master of Todia.
[13] Mr. K. D. Desāi.

* It is believed that the spirit of the deceased returns to its house for thirteen days after death. Hence the period of mourning is thirteen days.—The School Master of Kotda Sangani.

[14] The School Master of Ganod.
[15] The School Master of Todia.
[16] The School Master of Dhānk.

Such spirits generally belong to the class of the *Bavan*, the *Vir*, the *Bābro*, *Māmo*, *Vaitāl*, *Dādamo* and *Yaksha*. Of these, *Māmo*, *Vir*, *Vaitāl* and *Dādamo* prove beneficial through favour, while the rest become the slaves of those who subdue them.[1]

It is believed that *Suro Puro* and *Dādo* favour only their blood relations.[2]

It is related that in building the numerous tanks and temples attributed to Siddhrāj Jaysing, a former king of Gujarāt, he was assisted by the spirit *Bābario* whom he had brought under his control.[3]

A tradition is current that Tulsidās, the celebrated author of the *Rāmāyan* in Hindi and a great devotee of Rām, had secured personal visits from the god Hanumān through the favour of a ghost.

The king Vikram is said to have received great services from the evil spirits *Vaitāl* and *Jāl*.[4]

In a book entitled *Vaitāla Pachisi* it is described how a *bhut* lived on a banyan tree in Ujjain.[5]

It is related that in Rājkot a *bhut* called *hunthia* lived on a banyan tree.[6]

To the east of Kolki there is a tree called *Jāla* which is inhabited by a *māmo*. It is related that the *māmo* frightens persons passing by the tree. Near the school at Kolki there is a *Pipal* on which lives a *sikotarun* who frightens people passing along the road.[7]

Is is related that a *māmo* lived on a *Khijado* tree at the gate of the village Surel. He manifested himself, dressed in white garments, for a period of nearly ten years. Once he frightened several persons out of their senses. It is said that on his being propitiated with an offering of wheaten bread at his abode (the *Khijado* tree), these persons recovered their senses.[8]

The *Habib-Vad* or Habib's banyan tree on the road leading from Māvaiya to Gondal is a favourite haunt of *bhuts*, who frighten and stupefy persons passing by that road.[9]

There is a step-well near Hāmpar under the jurisdiction of Dhrāngadhra which is the resort of a *bhut*. A Girāsia and his wife arrived here one day at midnight. The Girāsia tied his mare to a tree hard by, and went to the well to fetch water for the mare. On his return he found there a number of mares like his own tied to the trees. He therefore smelt their mouths to recognise which of them was his own, but in the flurry caused by the appearance of so many mares, his waist-cloth got entangled, and while mounting his mare he fell down, which frightened him so much that he exclaimed "I am overtaken (by a ghost)" and died.[10]

It is related that in the *Chhāliāchok* at Limbdi, no woman has yet succeeded in reciting a *garabi* (song) in honour of the goddess Mahākāli to the end, as a ghost which lives on the tamarind tree opposite the *chok* (square) is averse to its completion.

There is a house at Porbandar haunted by a ghost, in which none is able to reside.[11]

It is believed that only those trees, the wood of which cannot be used for sacrificial purposes, can be haunted by evil spirits. Such trees are the *Khijado*, the *Bāval*, the *Kerādo* and the tamarind.[12]

Kshetrapāl is believed to be the guardian spirit of fields and *Suropuro* and *Māmado* are believed to protect harvest and cattle.[13]

[1] The School Masters of Vanod and Kotda Sangani.
[2] The School Master of Dadvi.
[3] The School Master of Kolki.
[4] The School Master of Uptela.
[5] The School Master of Dhānk.
[6] The School Mistress of Girls' school, Gondal, and the School Master of Dhānk.
[7] The School Master of Kolki
[8] The School Master of Surel.
[9] The School Master of Māvaiya.
[10] The School Master of Lilāpur.
[11] The School Master of Limbdi.
[12] The School Master of Moti Murad.
[13] The School Master of Kotda Sangani.

It is also believed that the spirit *jakhara* protects crops and cattle.[1]

Māmo and *Dādamo* are also believed by some to be the guardian spirits of crops and cattle.[2]

A belief runs that if a cousin (father's brother's son) becomes a spirit after death, he proves beneficial to the cattle of his relatives.[3]

There are various ways of frightening crying children to silence, one of which is to invoke evil spirits.

When a child continues to cry for a long time, the mother says, " keep quiet, *Bāghada* has come." " Oh *Bāu*, come and take away this child." " *Bābara*, come here. Don't come, my child is now silent." "May *Bāghada* carry you away." These exclamations are uttered in such a tone and with such gestures, that generally the child is at once frightened into silence.[4]

In addition to the spirits mentioned above *Bābaro*, *Chudda*, *Dākana*, *Satarsingo* and other spirits are also invoked to frighten a weeping child to silence.[5]

A *Bāva* or *Bairāgi*, a *Fakir*, a tiger, a dog, a cat or a rat are all presented to the child as objects of terror, and are called one after another to silence it.[6]

1 The School Master of Jetpur.
2 The School Master of Rājpāra.
3 The School Master of Zinzuwāda.
4 Mr. K. D. Desāi.
5 The School Master of Dhānk.
6 Mr. K. D. Desāi.

CHAPTER VII.

TREE AND SERPENT WORSHIP.

Certain trees are considered holy, and they are neither cut nor their wood used as fuel.

The *Pipal* is one of such trees. It is considered to be the incarnation of a Brāhman, and to cut it is considered to be as great a sin as murdering a Brāhman. It is believed that the family of one who cuts it becomes extinct.[1]

Some people believe that the spirits of the deceased do not get water to drink in the next world. The water poured at the root of the *Pipal* on the 13th, 14th and 15th day of the dark half of *Kārtik* and *Shrāvan* and on the 14th day of the bright half of *Chaitra* is believed to reach these spirits and quench their thirst.[2]

Although to cut the *Pipal* is supposed to be a great sin, it is believed that if a corpse is burnt with its wood, the soul of the deceased attains salvation.[3]

The *Vad* or banyan tree is believed to be a representation of the god Shiva.[4] There is a proverb to the effect that one who cuts this tree is punished with the extirpation of his family.[5]

According to another belief, the god Vishnu once slept on this tree.[6]

The *Tulsi* or sweet basil is considered to represent Lakshmi, the wife of Vishnu. It is also related that Krishna wanted to kill the demon Jalandhar, but he could not be killed on account of the merit of the chastity of his wife Vrinda. Krishna, therefore, assumed the form of Jalandhar, violated the chastity of Vrinda, and was thus enabled to kill the demon. Krishna next expressed a desire to marry Vrinda, when she transformed herself into the *Tulsi* plant. It is considered an act of great religious merit to wed Krishna with the *Tulsi*, and this marriage is celebrated every year by all Hindus on the 11th day of the bright half of *Kārtik* otherwise called *Dev Divāli*.

It is considered a great sin to uproot this plant, though no sin attaches to the plucking of its leaves during the day time. The leaves of the *Tulsi* are considered holy and are offered to the image of the god Vishnu and are required in all religious ceremonies.[7]

The *Khijado* or *Shami* tree is also held sacred. When the Pāndavas lost their kingdom in gambling with the Kauravas, the latter promised the former that they would give them back their kingdom if they lived in the forest for twelve years and unknown for one year. After having completed their stay in the forest, the Pāndavas remained unknown for one year in the city of Virāt. During this year they concealed their weapons on a *Khijado* tree. Before taking these weapons, they worshipped the tree. Next took place the great battle of Kurukshetra in which the Pāndavas won a splendid victory. This has given rise to the custom of worshipping the tree on the tenth day of the bright half of *Ashvin* or the *Dasara* day.[8]

It is a common belief that a tree haunted by ghosts should not be cut. So the *Khijado* is not cut, because it is the favourite residence of ghosts.[9]

---

[1] The School Master of Ganod.
[2] The School Master of Todia.
[3] Mr. K. D. Desāi.
[4] The School Master of Dhānk.
[5] The School Master of Moti Parabdi.
[6] The School Master of Todia.
[7] Mr. K. D. Desāi.
[8] Mr. K. D. Desāi.
[9] The School Master of Chhatrāsa.

The *Kadamb* (Anthocephalus cadumba) is considered sacred because it is believed that God Krishna rested under this tree when he took cattle to graze.[1]

The *Limbdo* (Nim tree) is also considered sacred as it represents the god Brahma.[2] Some believe that it represents Jagannāthji.[3]

The *Rudrāksha* is believed to be a representation of the god Shiva. It is therefore considered a sin to cut it. Garlands of *Rudrāksha* beads are worn round the neck by the devotees of Shiva.

The leaves of the *Bel* (Aegle marmelos) are offered to the god Shiva as they are supposed to be liked by him. It is also considered a sin to cut this tree.[4]

The *Karan* (Mimuspos hexandra) is believed to be a representation of Shiva. A grove of the *Karan* trees is supposed to be inhabited by natural powers called *Mātās* and to cut a *Karan* is supposed to bring disaster to the cutter.[5]

Tke *Maravo* (Marjoram) is considered sacred by Musalmāns. They dip its leaves into oil and rub them against the face of a corpse.[6]

There is a temple of Bhimnāth Mahādev near Baravāla in the shade of an ancient *Jāl* tree. The worshipper at the temple, a wealthy man, once thought of erecting a grand temple over the image, but he was prevented from doing so by the god appearing in his dream and telling him that he preferred to live under the tree.[7]

Under a *Jāl* tree near Dhandhuka there is a shrine of Bhimnāth Shankar who is known as Bhimnāth Jālvālo after the tree.[8]

There is a *Sakhotia* tree near Kutiāna, which is supposed to be the abode of a snake deity.[9]

Near Rājkot in Kāthiāwār there is a tree called *Gāndu* or mad. vows in honour of which are said to cure children of bronchites.[10]

In the village of Vadāl near Bhiyāl in the Junāgadh State there is a banyan tree called *Lāl Vad* said to have sprung from the sticks of a *Vad* (banyan) used as tooth brushes by Lāl Bāva, a preceptor of the Vaishnav school. A silver staff and silver umbrella belonging to Lāl Bāva are kept near this tree, which is visited and worshipped by the followers of the preceptor.[11]

It is related that in this *Lāl Vad* there is an opening through which the virtuous can pass to the other side, but not the sinful.[12]

There are two banyan trees near Anandpur, one of which is called *Bhut-vad* or the banyan tree of the evil spirits, as it is supposed to be inhabited by ghosts. The other is called *Visalvad*, because a devotee named Visaman Bhagat lived under this tree.[13]

There is a branch of the followers of Kabir called *Khijāda Panth*. They worship the *Khijāda* or *Shami* in their temples.[14]

There is a belief that the sanctity attached to the *Pipal* tree has been the act of the god Krishna. This tree is invested with a sacred thread.[15]

According to tradition, Krishna breathed his last under a *Pipal* tree.[16]

It is related that once blood gushed forth from a *Pipal* tree when it was cut. Thenceforward it came to be regarded as a Brāhman and it is no longer cut.[17]

There is a *Pipal* tree in the village of Prāchi near Prabhās Pātan, vows in whose honour are believed to favour childless persons with children.[18]

It is described in the *Purānas* that Sāvitri, the daughter of King Ashupati, lost her husband within a year after her marriage. The death took place under a banyan tree, by worshipping which, Sāvitri succeeded in revi-

[1] The School Master of Todia.
[2] The School Master of Zinzuvāda.
[3] The School Master of Dadvi.
[4] The School Master of Vanod.
[5] The School Master of Kolki.
[6] The School Master of Dadvi.
[7] The School Master of Dhānk.
[8] The School Master of Kolki.
[9] The School Master of Dhānk.
[10] The School Master of Dhānk.
[11] The School Master of Bhāyāvadar.
[12] The School Master of Uptela.
[13] The School Master of Anandpur.
[14] The School Masters of Ganod and Khirāsara.
[15] The School Master of Dhānk.
[16] The School Master of Kolki.
[17] The School Master of Chhatrāsa.
[18] The School Master of Limbdi.

ving her husband. Since then women perform a vow called *Vat Sāvitri Vrat* on the 13th, 14th and 15th days of the bright half of *Jetha* by observing a fast and worshipping and circumambulating the banyan tree.[1]

There is a legend that in mythological times a woman named Vrinda was cursed to be a plant for infidelity to her husband. She became the *Tulsi* (sweet basil), which is held sacred by Hindus, and worshipped by women.[2]

On the top of the hill in the village of Jasdan there are two tall trees called 'mad trees'. As the fruits of these trees resemble the face of a saint, they are considered divine and worshipped with offerings of red lead, oil and cocoanuts.[3]

Amongst Rajputs, during the marriage ceremony, the bride has to walk four times round the sacrificial fire in the company of the bridegroom. Two of these turns are generally taken with a wooden blade called *Khāndu*.[4]

When a girl loses her betrothed twice in succession, she is married to a *Pipal* tree before being betrothed for the third time.[5]

If the betrothed husband of a girl dies before the celebration of the marriage, she is married to a *Pipal* or *Ankda* (a poisonous plant) in the belief that the danger of death will fall on the tree, and that the next husband of the girl will survive.[6]

If a man loses two wives one after the other, he is married to a *Shami* tree before he is married again, and his third marriage is called the fourth.[7]

In some places, such a man is married to a *Bordi* (Zizyphus Jujuba) instead of a *Shami*.[8]

In some places, if a man's wives do not live, his next wife is married to an *Ankdi* plant before her marriage with him.[9]

A belief prevails that an insane maiden is cured of her insanity if married to the field god Kshetrapāl.[10]

If a girl attains puberty before marriage, she is married to a *Pipal* tree. A girl with congenital deformities is also married to a *Pipal* tree[11]

It is generally believed that if a betrothed girl touches red lead, she is carried away by Kshetrapāl.[12]

The belief that Kshetrapāl carries away the bride from the marriage altar is so common, that a stone representing the god is placed on the marriage altar and touched by the bridal pair at every turn round the sacrificial fire.[13]

If this is not done, disastrous consequences follow, to avert which, that portion of the marriage ceremony in which Kshetrapāl is propitiated has to be performed a second time.[14]

Disagreement between husband and wife soon after marriage is attributed to the wrath of Kshetrapāl. To bring about a reconcilation between them, they are taken to a triangular field and married there to please the god.[15]

All Hindus worship the snake. The day especially devoted to its worship is the fifth day of the bright half of *Shrāvan*, which is called *Nāg panchami*. In some places *Nāg panchami* is observed on the 5th day of the dark half of *Shrāvan*. On this day an image of a snake is made of cowdung or earth, or its picture is drawn on the wall.

The image is worshipped as a deity, and *kulera*, a mixture of wheat, oat or rice flour, clarified butter, and sugar or molasses is offered to it. After worship, the members of the household take their meal and eat *kulera*, cocoanuts and cucumbers. Only one meal is taken on this day by men and women.[16]

1 The School Master of Limbdi.
2 The School Master of Ganod.
3 The School Master of Jasdan.
4 The School Masters of Dhānk and Dadvi.
5 The School Masters of Dhānk and Māvaiya.
6 The School Master of Ganod.
7 Mr. K. D. Desāi.
8 The School Master of Dhānk.
9 The School Master of Khirāsara.
10 The School Master of Dhānk.
11 The School Master of Vanod.
12 The School Master of Chhatrāsa.
13 The School Masters of Uptela and Limbdi.
14 The School Master of Zinzuvāda.
15 The School Master of Kotda Sangani.
16 The Schoolmistress, Barton Female Training College, Rajkot.

The *Nāg panchmi* is observed as a *vrat* or vow, generally by women. They do not take any meal on this day, but live only on *kulera*. On this day, her Highness the Mahārāni of Baroda, mounted on an elephant, goes in procession to the woods to worship an ant-hill. The pipers who accompany the procession blow their pipes, and allured by the sound, the snakes come out of their holes, when they are worshipped and fed with milk.[1]

Women do not pound, grind or sift corn on the *Nāg panchami* day, and all people try to see a snake.

It is obligatory in some families to offer a cocoanut to the Nāgdev (snake god) on the *Nāg panchami* day.[2]

In some places, the likeness of the snake is engraved on a stone or copper plate and worshipped. In others, it is drawn on a piece of paper which is affixed to the wall.[3]

In many places there are temples dedicated to snake gods. These gods are known by various names. Some of the temples with the names of the gods installed in them are given below :—

1. The temple of Sarmālio Nāg at Arani Timba near Bikāner.

2. The temple of Ragatio Nāg midway between Kanāza and Vanthali in the Junāgadh State.

3. The temple of Charmālio Nāg at Chokdi near Chuda. Vows of offering sweets are made to this Nāg by persons bitten by snakes, who visit the temple, hold the sweets before the image of the god, distribute them among the visitors, and are in return presented with cotton thread which they wear round the neck.

This god is also reputed to have the power of blessing childless persons with offspring. The offerings concerned consist of cradles, which are presented to the god after the wished for object has been fulfilled.

4. The temple of Vāsuki Nāg near Thāngadh. This Nāg is supposed to be a servant of the god Shiva. An old snake with gray moustaches is said to live in this temple. He drinks milk at the hands of visitors. Many vows are made in honour of this snake god.

5. The temple of Khambhadio Nāg at Khāmbhada.

6. The temple of Nāg Mandal at Dadvi.

7. The temple of Bhujia Nāg at Bhuj.

8. The temple of Shimalia Nāg near Jadeshvar in the neighbourhood of Jetpur.

9. The temple of Fulia Nāg near Jopanāth.

10. The temple of Malodaro Nāg at Malod.

11. The temple of Charmālio Nāg at Chudia.

12. The temple of Chhatrāsia Nāg in Chhatrāsa.

13. The temple of Monapario Nāg at Monpar near Chital.

14. The temple of Ashāpāl at Nanadiya in the Bantva State.

15. The temple of Khodiāl Nāgini at Khokharda in the Junāgadh State.

16. The temple of Gondalia Nāg at Gondal.

It is related that there were once divine snakes in the royal fort of Jodia. When a pair (male and female) of these snakes were found killed, the heinous act was atoned for by the bodies of the snakes being buried and a temple erected over the grave. The male snake of this pair is known as Nāg Nāth or the Lord of Snakes.

According to others, Nāg Nāth was a big white snake with gray moustaches. He once waylaid a milkman of the royal household, forced him to put down the milkpot he was carrying, drank the milk and went away. This snake is believed to be divine.[4]

[1] The School Master of Khirāsara.
[2] The School Master of Sānka.
[3] The School Master of Dhānk.
[4] The School Master of Jodia.

The god Shiva is supposed to wear a snake round his neck like a garland of flowers. So, in all temples of Shiva, an image of a snake is installed behind the idol of the god with his hood spread over the idol.[1]

In ancient times dead snakes were buried and temples and altars were erected over their graves. An image of the dead snake was engraved on the altar.[2]

There is a shrine dedicated to Chāndalia Nāg on the bank of the river Palavo on the road from Mota Devalia to Tramboda. It is visited by a sect of beggars called Nāg-magas. The Nāg-magas beg wealth of the snake god, and it is said, that he bestows it on them. They are never seen begging from any body else.[3]

In the *Purānas*, the Shesh Nāg, the Takshak Nāg, Pundarik, Kāli Nāg and Karkotak Nāg are described as gods. In modern times, Sarmālio, Bhujo and Gadhio are believed to be as powerful as gods, and vows are observed in their honour.[4]

Dhananjaya, Pushkar and Vāsuki are also considered to be very powerful.[5]

Takshak is believed to have drunk the nectar of immortality.[6]

A tradition is current that god Vishnu sleeps on the Shesha Nāg in the Milky Ocean. This snake is believed to have a thousand mouths and to support the earth on its hood.[7]

It is described in the *Purānas* how King Parikshit was bitten by Takshak Nāg and King Nala by Karkotak Nāg. King Nala became deformed owing to the bite, but he could assume his original form by wearing a special dress, through the favour of Karkotak.

Vāsuki Nāg was wrapped round the Māndār mountain, which was used as a churning handle by the gods and demons to churn the ocean for the recovery of the fourteen jewels from the ocean.[8]

It is a common belief that treasures buried underground are guarded by snakes.

Generally a miser dying without an heir is supposed to be born as a snake after his death, to guard his hoarded money.

It is believed by some people that on the establishment of a new dynasty of kings after a revolution, a snake makes its appearance to guard the accumulated wealth of the fallen dynasty.[9]

It is also believed that a rich man dying with his mind fixed on his wealth is born as a snake, to guard the wealth.[10]

There is a further belief that one who collects money by foul means and does not spend it, is born as a snake in his next life to guard his buried treasure.[11]

There is still another belief that a man who buries his treasure in a secret place becomes a snake after death, to guard the treasure.[12]

The beliefs mentioned above have given rise to the impression that places where big snakes are found are sure to have treasure trove concealed in them.[13]

It is believed that the snake guarding the treasure of his previous life does not allow anybody to remove it, and bites any one who attempts to do so.[14]

If in spite of this, a man succeeds in seizing the treasure by force or by the power of *mantras* or incantations, it is believed that he leaves no heirs to use it.[15]

A belief is also current that such guardian snakes allow those persons to take away the treasures guarded by them if they are destined to possess them.[16]

[1] The School Master of Ganod.
[2] The School Master of Jodia.
[3] The School Master of Mota Devalia.
[4] The School Master of Dhānk.
[5] The School Master of Ganod.
[6] The School Master of Vanod.
[7] The School Master of Ganod.
[8] The School Mistress, Barton Female Training College, Rājkot.
[9] The School Master of Dhānk.
[10] The School Master of Kotda Sangani.
[11] The School Master of Charādva.
[12] The School Master of Khirāsara.
[13] The School Master of Ganod.
[14] The School Master of Vanod.
[15] The School Master of Songadh.
[16] The School Master of Sonka.

To the south of Kolki there is a site of a deserted village. It is believed to contain a buried treasure which is guarded by a snake with white moustaches. This snake is seen roaming about the place.[1]

It is related that a Brāhman once read in an old paper that there was a treasure buried under a *Shami* tree in Deola. He communicated the information to the Thākor of Dhrol who secured the treasure by excavating the place. The Brāhman went to worship the spot, but was buried alive. The Thākor buried the treasure in his castle, but the Brāhman, becoming a snake, guarded the treasure and allowed none to touch it. All attempts to dig it up were frustrated by attacks of bees and the appearance of a snake.

A Kshatriya named Dev Karan, while the foundation of his house was being dug, found a treasure guarded by a snake. He killed the snake by pouring boiling oil over it and secured the treasure.

A Kunbi of Malia, while digging a pit for storing corn, found a large vessel filled with costly coins guarded by a snake. He killed the snake and secured the vessel.[2]

There are many practices in vogue to render the poisonous bite of a snake ineffective.

If the man bitten by a snake be bold, he cuts off the bitten part.

Some have the bitten part branded.

Those who have no ulcer in the mouth suck the poison, and spit it out.

The powder of the fruit of the *Nol Vel* is also administered with water.

Sometimes emetics and purgative medicines are given.

A mixture of pepper and clarified butter is also believed to be efficacious.[3]

Other remedies for the cure of snake bite, are as follows:—

The patient is made to wear a cotton thread in the name of Charmālia Nāg, Sharmalia Nāg, or Vasangi Nāg, and certain observances, as stated above, are promised to the snake deity.[4]

The ends of peacock feathers are pounded and smoked in a *chilum* (clay pipe) by the patient.[5]

A *moharo* (stone found in the head of a snake supposed to be a cure for snake poison) is applied to the wound caused by the bite. It absorbs the poison, and on being dipped into milk, transfers the poison to the milk.

Thus it can be used any number of times.[6]

There is a Girāsia in Lakhtar who is believed to cure patients suffering from snake poison. As soon as a person is bitten by a snake, one of the garments worn by him is taken to the Girāsia, who ties it into a knot and this cures the patient.[7]

There is a *Bāva* in Rajpāra, a village near Anandpur. He and all the members of his family are reputed to be able to cure snake-bites. When a person is bitten by a snake, he or a friend goes to the *Bāvā's* house and informs him or any member of his family of the occurrence. The *Bāva* or the person who receives the intimation folds into a knot a garment of the informant, which he afterwards unfolds. As soon as this is done, the patient is in great pain, loses his senses, is seized with convulsions and tells why the snake bit him. Thereupon the relatives of the patient implore the pardon of the snake, which is granted on condition that the patient should give alms to the poor.[8]

[1] The School Master of Kolki.

[2] The School Master of Todia.

[3] The School Master of Dhānk.

[4] The School Master of Kotda Sangani.

[5] The School Mistress, Barton Female Training College, Rājkot.

[6] The D. E. Inspector, Hālār.

[7] The School Master of Lilāpur.

[8] The School Master of Anandpur.

In some places, *Bhagats* or devotees of Mātāji are invited to dinner along with a number of exorcists, who are generally Rabāris. After they have assembled at the house of the patient, they start out in a procession headed by one who holds in his hand a bunch of peacock feathers, to bathe in a river. On their way to and back from the river they sing songs in praise of the goddess to the accompaniment of drums and other musical instruments. After their return from the river, the whole party are treated to a feast, which is supposed to cure the patient of the effects of the snake-bite.[1]

Some people believe that snakes, like evil spirits, can enter the bodies of human beings. Such persons, when possessed, are supposed to have the power of curing snake-bites.[2]

Every village has an exorcist who is a specialist in curing the effects of snake-bites. When a person is bitten by a snake the exorcist is at once sent for. He gives the patient *Nim* leaves and pepper to chew, to determine the extent of the effect of the bite. Next he asks one of those present to bathe and bring water in an unused earthen jar. He then recites incantations, and sprinkles water from the jar over the body of the patient. If this does not counteract the effects of the poison, he throws red-hot pieces of charcoal at the patient, when the snake speaks through the patient and states that he bit the patient because he committed a certain offence, and that he will leave him if certain offerings are made. After he has ceased speaking, the patient begins to shake and to crawl about like a snake, and is then cured. If the man be doomed to death, the snake would say, "I have bitten him by the order of the god of death, and I will not leave him without taking his life."[3]

Sometimes the exorcist fans the patient with branches of the *Nim* tree, reciting *mantras*, and thereupon the patient becomes possessed by the snake and declares the cause of his offence.

Some exorcists present a magic epistle or charm asking the snake that bit the patient to be present. The snake obeys the call, and appears before the exorcist. The latter then asks the snake to suck the poison from the wound of the patient, which is done by the snake, and the patient is then cured.[4]

In some places, the exorcist ties up the patient when the snake tells the cause of the bite. Next the exorcist calls on the snake to leave the body of the patient, who then begins to crawl about like a snake and is cured.

On some occasions, the exorcist slaps the cheek of the person who calls him to attend the patient. It is said that the poison disappears as soon as the slap is given.[5]

Some exorcists take a stick having seven joints and break them one by one. As the stick is broken, the patient recovers, his recovery being complete when the seventh joint is broken.[6]

It is believed that the Dhedas are the oldest worshippers of *Nāgs* or snakes. When a person is bitten by a snake, he is seated near a Dheda, who prays the snake to leave the body of the patient. It is said that in some cases this method proves efficacious in curing the patient.[7]

It is stated that exorcists who know the *mantra* (incantation) for the cure of snake-bites must lead a strictly moral life. If they touch a woman in child-bed or during her period the *mantra* loses its power. This can be regained through purification, bathing, and by reciting the *mantra* while inhaling the smoke of burning frankincense. Some

[1] The School Master of Dhānk.
[2] The School Master of Dadvi.
[3] The School Master of Dhānk.
[4] The Schaol Master of Chhatrāsa.
[5] The D. E. Inspector, Hālār.
[6] The School Master of Songadh.
[7] The School Master of Sānka.

exorcists abstain from certain kinds of vegetables and sweets, e. g., the *Mogri* (Rat-tailed raddish) *Julebi* (a kind of sweet) etc. They have also to abstain from articles of a colour like that of a snake.[1]

A belief prevails that there is a precious stone in the head of the snake. Such stones are called *mohors*. They are occasionally shown to the people by snake-charmers, who declare that it is very difficult to procure them.

It is stated that on dark nights snakes take these *mohors* out of their head and place them on prominent spots in order to be able to move about in the dark by their light.[2]

It is believed that snakes give these *mohors* to those who please them. If one tries to take a *mohor* by force, the snake swallows it and dissolves it into water.[3]

As stated above, the *mohor* has the property of absorbing the poison from snake-bites.

It is because a snake is believed to hold a precious stone in its head that it is called *manidhar*, that is, holder of a jewel.[4]

It is believed by some people that the *mohor* shines the most when a rainbow appears in the sky.[5]

According to the *Purānas* the *pātāl* or nether world is as beautiful as heaven. It is inhabited by *Nāgs* or snakes in human form. The *Nāg* girls are reputed to be so handsome that an extraordinarily beautiful girl is commonly likened to a *Nāg* girl.

It is believed that in ancient times inter-marriages between *Nāgs* and human beings were common.[6]

It is a common belief that Kshetrapāl, the guardian snake of fields, married human brides. So, to propitiate him, his image is installed on the marriage altar, and the bride takes three turns round it when walking round the sacrificial fire with the bride-groom.[7]

According to the *Purānas*, king Dasharath married a *Nāg* girl Sumitra.[8] Similarly Indrajit, the son of Rāvan, the Lord of Lanka or Ceylon, married a *Nāg* girl.[9]

At times snakes are seen in houses. They are believed to be the guardians of the houses, and worshipped with offerings of lamps fed with ghi. After worship, the members of the family pray to the snake, "Oh snake ! Thou art our guardian. Protect our health and wealth. We are thy children and live in thy garden."[10]

Some people believe that the spirits of deceased ancestors, on account of the anxiety for the welfare of progeny, become snakes and guard the house.[11]

1 The School Mistress, Barton Female Training College, Rājkot
2 The School Master of Dhānk.
3 The School Master of Chhatrāsa.
4 Mr. K. D. Desāi.
5 The School Master of Kolki.
6 The School Master of Vanod.
7 The School Master of Kolki.
8 The School Mistress, Civil Station Girls' School, Rājkot.
9 The School Master of Zinzuvāda.
10 The School Master of Vanod, and Mr. K. D. Desāi.
11 The School Master of Sāyala.

CHAPTER VIII.

TOTEMISM AND FETISHISM.

The worship of totems is not known to prevail in Gujarāt, but the names of persons and clans or families are occasionally derived from animals and plants.

Instances of names derived from animals are given below :—

	NAME.		ANIMAL FROM WHICH DERIVED.
1.	Hāthibhāi	...	*Hathi*—an elephant.
2.	Vāghajibhāi	...	*Vāgh*—a tiger.
3.	Nāgjibhāi	...	*Nāg*—a snake.
4.	Popatbhāi	...	*Popat*—a parrot.
5.	Morbhāi	...	*Mor*—a peacock.
6.	Chaklibhat	...	*Chakli*—a sparrow.[1]
7.	Kido ...	...	*Kidi*—an ant.
8.	Mankodia	...	*Mankoda*—a black ant
9.	Tido ...	...	*Tid*—a locust.[2]
10.	Hansrāj	...	*Hansa*—a goose.
11.	Vinchi* ...	...	*Vinchi*—a female scorpion.
12.	Olo ...	...	*Olo*—a species of bird.
13.	Ajo ...	...	*Aja*—a goat.
14.	Mena* ...	...	*Mena*—a species of bird.[3]

The *Kāli Parāj* or aboriginal tribes in Gujarāt give such names as Kāgdo (crow), Kolo (Jackal), Bilādo (cat), Kutro (dog) to their children according as one or other of these animals is heard to cry at the time of birth.[4]

The following are instances of names derived from plants :—

	NAME.		PLANT OR TREE FROM WHICH DERIVED.
1.	Gulāb † ...	...	*Gulāb*—the rose.
2.	Ambo ...	...	*Ambo*—the mango.
3.	Tulsibāi*	...	*Tulsi*—the sweet basil
4.	Tulsidās	...	Ditto.
5.	Kesharbāi*	...	*Keshar*—Saffron.
6.	Galālbāi*	...	*Galāl*—Red powder.[5]
7.	Bili* ...	...	*Bili*—Aegle marmelos
8.	Dudhi* ...	...	*Dudhi*—Pumpkin.
9.	Lavengi*	...	*Laveng*—Clove.
10.	Mulo ...	...	*Mulo*—Raddish.
11.	Limbdo	...	*Limbdo*—The *Nim* tree.
12.	Mako ...	...	*Maki*—Maize.[6]
13.	Champo	...	*Champa*—Michelia Champaca.[7]

Instances of family or clan names derived from trees and animals are as follows :—

	NAME.		DERIVATION.
1.	Untia ...	...	*Unt*—camel.
2.	Gadheda	...	*Gadheda*—An ass.
3.	Dedakia ...	...	*Dedako*—A frog.
4.	Balada ...	...	*Balad*—An ox.
5.	Godhani ...	...	*Godho*—A bull.
6.	Bhensdadia	...	*Bhensa*—A buffalo.
7.	Ghetiya ...	...	*Gheta*—A sheep.
8.	Sāvaj ...	...	A species of wild animals.[8]
9.	Kakadia ...	...	Kakadi—cucumber.[9]

[1] The School Master of Dhānk.

[2] The School Master of Kotda Sangani.

[3] The School Master of Kolki.

[4] The School Master of Hālār.

[5] The School Master of Dhānk.

[6] The School Master of Dadvi.

[7] The School Master of Kolki.

[8] The School Master of Dhānk.

[9] The School Master of Kotda Sangani.

* These are female names.

† Both male and female.

The cow, the she-goat, the horse, the deer, peacock, the *Tilad* or singing sparrow, the goose, the *Nāg* or snake, the eagle, the elephant and the male monkey are believed to be sacred by all Hindus. Of these, the greatest sanctity attaches to the cow. Her urine is sipped for the atonement of sins. The cow is also revered by the Pārsis.[1]

The mouth of the she-goat and the smell of the horse are considered sacred.[1]

An elephant is considered sacred, because when the head of Ganpati was chopped off by Shiva, the head of an elephant was joined to his trunk.[2]

The peacock is considered sacred on account of its being the conveyance of Sarasvati, the goddess of learning.[2]

A male monkey is held holy, because it is supposed to represent the monkey god Māruti.[2]

Some sanctity attaches to the rat also, as it is the conveyance of the god Ganpati. He is called *Māma* or maternal uncle by the Hindus.[3]

The pig is held taboo by the Musalmāns.[4]

Brāhmans, Baniās, Bhātiās, Kunbis, Sutārs and Darjis abstain from flesh and liquor.[5]

Some Brāhmans and Baniās do not eat *tādiās* (fruit of the palm tree) as they look like human eyes.[6]

Some Brāhmans abstain from garlic and onions. Some do not eat *Kodra*"(punctured millet).[7]

The *masur* (Lentil) pulse is not eaten by Brāhmans and Baniās, because, when cooked, it looks red like blood.[8]

The Humbad Baniās do not eat whey, milk, curdled milk and clarified butter.[9]

The Shrāvaks abstain from the *suran* (Elephant foot), potatoes and roots that grow underground.[10]

Mahomedans abstain from the *suran*, because "*su*" the first letter of the word *suran* is also the first letter of their taboo'd animal the pig.[11]

There are some deities associated with the worship of animals. These animals, with the deities with whom they are connected, are given below.

1. *Pothio* or the bull is believed to be the vehicle of god Shiva. In all temples of Shiva its image is installed, facing the image of Shiva in the centre of the temple.

2. *Sinha* or the lion is believed to be the vehicle of Pārvati, the consort of Shiva. The lion is also connected with the demon planet *Rāhu*.

3. *Hansa* the goose is associated with Brahma the creator.

4. *Gadhedo* the ass is believed to be connected with Shitala, the goddess of small pox

5. *Undar* the mouse is the conveyance of Ganpati.

6. *Mor* the peacock is the conveyance of Sarasvati, the goddess of learning. The peacock is also associated with Kārtik Swāmi.

7. *Garud* the eagle is the conveyance of the god Vishnu.

8. *Pādo* the male buffalo is the conveyance of Devis or goddesses.

9. *Ghodo* the horse is the conveyance of the Sun. The horse is also associated with the planet *Guru* or Jupiter and *Shukra* or Venus.

10. *Mrig* the deer is supposed to be the conveyance of the Moon as well as of *Mangal* or Mars.

[1] The School Master of Dhānk.
[2] The School Master of Todia.
[3] The School Master of Mota Devalia.
[4] The School Master of Kotda Sangani.
[5] The School Master of Kotda Sangani.
[6] The School Master of Vanod.
[7] The School Master of Zinzuvāda.
[8] The School Master of Songadh.
[9] The School Master of Pātanvāv.
[10] The School Master of Vāla.
[11] The School Master of Songadh.

11. *Balad* the ox is connected with Mars and *Shani* or Saturn.

12. *Hāthi* the elephant is supposed to be the conveyance of Indra. It is also connected with *Budha* or Mercury.

13 The tiger is the conveyance of the goddess Ambāji.

The animals mentioned above are worshipped along with deities and planets with whom they are associated[1].

It is generally believed that the earth is supported by a tortoise. So, whenever the goddess earth or Prithvi is worshipped, the tortoise is also worshipped.[2]

In the temples of the *Mātās* cocks and hens, and in the temple of Kāl Bhairav, dogs, are worshipped.[3]

For the propitiation of goddesses and evil spirits, male goats, he-buffaloes and cocks are sacrificed.[4]

In his first incarnation, the god Vishnu was born as a fish, in the second as an alligator, and in the third as a boar. For this reason the images of these animals are worshipped.[5]

All the gods, goddesses and spirits mentioned in the preceding pages are represented by idols made of stone, metal or wood. In addition to stone idols of gods there are certain stones which are considered to represent gods and worshipped as such. Some of these stones are described below.

All the stones found in the river Narbada are believed to represent the god Shiva and worshipped.

There is a kind of stone found in the river Gandaki which is smooth on one side and porous on the other. It is either round or square and about five inches in length. This stone is called *Shāligrām* and is believed to represent the god Vishnu. It is kept in the household gods and worshipped daily.

There is another kind of hard, white, porous stone found near Dwārka. It is also worshipped along with the idol of Vishnu.

Sometimes tridents are drawn with red lead on stones to represent goddesses.[6]

There is a tank near the Pir in Kutiāna in which bored stones are found floating on the surface of the water. These stones are considered sacred.[7]

Certain stones are considered sacred on account of their supposed curative properties. One of such stones is called *Pāro*. It is believed to be efficacious in curing rheumatism.[8]

There is also a kind of red stone which is supposed to cure skin diseases.[9]

Each of the nine planets is supposed to be in touch with a stone of a particular colour. For instance, the stone in touch with *Shani* or Saturn is black, and that with *Mangal* or Mars is red. These stones are bored, and set in rings which are worn by persons suffering from the influence of these planets.

A kind of stone called *Akik*, found in abundance in Cambay, is considered sacred by the Mahomedan saints, who wear garlands made of beads carved out of these stones.[10]

In ancient times human sacrifices were offered on certain occasions. Now-a-days, in place of a human being, a cocoanut or a *Kolu* (Cucurbita maxima) is offered. At the time of making the offering, the coco'anut is plastered with red lead and other holy applications and covered with a silk cloth. The *Kolu* is offered by cutting it into two pieces with a stroke of a knife or sword.[11]

[1] The School Master of Dhānk.
[2] The School Master of Vanod.
[3] The School Master of Vanod.
[4] The School Master of Dadvi.
[5] The School Master of Bāntva.
[6] The School Master of Ganod.
[7] The School Master of Devalia.
[8] The School Master of Chhatrāsa.
[9] The School Master of Jetpur.
[10] The School Master of Zinzuvāda.
[11] The School Master of Kotda Sangani, Zinzuvāda and Gohelwād.

Sometimes an image of the flour of *Adad* is sacrificed in place of a human being.[1]

This sacrifice is generally made on the eighth or tenth day of the bright half of *Ashvin*.

In place of human blood, milk mixed with *gulāl* (red powder) and molasses is offered.[2]

In ancient times, when a well was dug, a human sacrifice was made to it if it did not yield water, with the belief that this would bring water into the well. Now-a-days, instead of this sacrifice, blood from the fourth finger of a man is sprinkled over the spot.[3]

It is also related that in ancient times, when a king was crowned, a human sacrifice was offered. Now-a-days, instead of this sacrifice, the king's forehead is marked with the blood from the fourth finger of a low caste Hindu at the time of the coronation ceremony.[4]

There are a few stones which are supposed to have the power of curing certain diseases. One of such stones is known as *Ratvano Pāro*. It is found at a distance of about two miles from Kolki. It is marked with red lines. It is bored and worn round the neck by persons suffering from *ratawa*[5] (a disease in which red spots or pimples are seen on the skin).

There is another stone called *Suleimani Pāro* which is supposed to have the power of curing many diseases.[6]

There is a kind of white semi-circular stone which is supposed to cure eye diseases when rubbed on the eyes and fever when rubbed on the body.[7]

Sieves for flour and corn, brooms, *sambelus* or corn pounders, and ploughs are regarded as sacred.

Sieves are considered sacred for the following reasons.

1. Because articles of food such as flour, grain, etc., are sifted through them.[8]

2. Because, on auspicious occasions, when women go to worship the potter's wheel, the materials of worship are carried in a sieve.

3. Because the fire used for igniting the sacrificial fuel is taken in a sieve, or is covered with a sieve while it is being carried to the sacrificial altar.[9]

4. Because at the time of performing the ceremony when commencing to prepare sweets for a marriage, a sieve is worshipped.[10]

5. Because, in some communities like the Bhātiās, the bride's mother, when receiving the bridegroom in the marriage booth, carries in a dish a lamp covered with a sieve.[11]

The flour collected by Brāhmans by begging from door to door is supposed to be polluted. But it is considered purified when it is passed through a sieve.[12]

The *sambelu* is considered so sacred that it is not touched with the foot. If a woman lie down during day time, she will not touch it either with her head or with her foot.

One of the reasons why it is considered sacred is that it was used as a weapon by Baldev, the brother of the god Krishna.

A *sambelu* is one of the articles, required for performing the reception ceremony on a bridegroom's entering the marriage *pandal*.[13]

It is believed that a fall of rain is expedited by placing a *sambelu* erect in a dish when there is a drought.[14]

Among Shrigaud Brāhmans, on the marriage day, one of the men of the bridegroom's party wears a wreath made of a *sambelu*, a broom and other articles. Some special marks are also made on his forehead. Thus adorned, he

[1] The School Master of Hālār.
[2] The School Master of Kotda Sangani.
[3] The School Master of Devalia.
[4] The School Master of Todia
[5] The School Master of Kolki.
[6] The School Master of Dhānk.
[7] The School Master of Jetpur.
[8] The School Master of Dhānk.
[9] The School Master of Dadvi.
[10] The School Master of Aman.
[11] The School Master of Todia.
[12] The School Master of Lilāpur.
[13] The School Master of Dhānk.
[14] The School Master of Zinzuvāda.

goes with the bridegroom's procession and plays jokes with the parents of both the bride and bridegroom. His doing so is supposed to bless the bridal pair with a long life and a large family.[1]

On the marriage day, after the ceremony of propitiating the nine planets has been performed in the bride's house, in some castes three, and in others one *sambelu*, is kept near the spot where the planets are worshipped. Next, five unwidowed women of the family hold the *sambelus* and thrash them five or seven times on the floor repeating the words "On the chest of the ill-wisher of the host." The *sambelus* are bound together by a thread.[2]

If a woman has to take part in an auspicious ceremony on the fourth day of her monthly period, she is made to thresh one maund of rice with a *sambelu*. Her fourth day is then considered as the fifth* and she becomes eligible for taking part in the ceremony.[3]

The plough is considered sacred, because it is the chief implement for cultivating the soil. It is worshipped on the full-moon day of *Shrāvan* which is known as a *Balev* holiday, the worship being called *Grahan-pujan*.[4]

Some people consider the plough sacred because Sita, the consort of Rām, was born of the earth by the touch of a plough.[5] Others hold it sacred as it was used as a weapon by Baldev, the brother of the god Krishna.

On account of the sanctity which attaches to the plough, it forms part of the articles, with which a bridegroom is received in the marriage *pandal* by the bride's mother.[6]

It is related that king Janak ploughed the soil on which he had to perform a sacrifice. Hence it has become a practice to purify with a plough the spot on which a sacrifice is to be performed.[7]

In some places, on the *Balev* day, a number of persons gather together near a pond, and each of them fills an earthen jar with the water of the pond. Next, one of the party is made to stand at a long distance from the others with a small plough in his hands. The others then run a race towards the latter. He who wins the race is presented with molasses and a cocoanut.[8]

It is customary among Brāhmans to perform the worship known as *Baleviān* after the performance of a thread ceremony. In Native States, the prime minister and other State officials and clerks join the ceremony, the principal function of the ceremony being performed by the prime minister. In villages, this function is performed by the headman of the village. The party go in procession to a neighbouring village or a pond where an earthen image of Ganpati besmeared with red lead is installed on a red cloth two feet square. Near this image are installed the nine planets, represented by nine heaps of corn, on each of which is placed a betelnut. This is called the installation of *Baleviān*. A plough about two feet in length is kept standing near the *Baleviān* with its end buried in the ground. The prime minister or the village headman worships the plough, after which, four Kumbhārs or potters wash themselves, and holding four jars on their heads, run a race. Each of the Kumbhārs is named after one of the four months of the rainy season. He who wins the race is presented with the plough. The expenses of the ceremony are paid from the State treasury or the village fund.[9]

According to a popular saying, a broom should not be kept erect or trampled under foot. This indicates that brooms are held sacred.

1 The School Master of Zinzuvāda.
2 The School Master of Todia.
3 The School Master of Lilāpur.
4 The School Masters of Dhānk and Kotda Sangani.
5 The School Master of Ganod.
6 The School Master of Dadvi.
7 The School Master of Lilāpur.
8 The School Master of Zinzuvāda.
9 The School Master of Todia.
* Among Hindus women in menses are considered impure for four days.

When a newly-born infant does not cry, the leaves of a broom are thrown into the fire and their smoke is passed over the child. It is said that this makes the child cry.[1]

Some people consider brooms sacred, because they are used in sweeping the ground[1] (that is the earth, which is a goddess).

In some places, children suffering from cough are fanned with a broom.[2]

In some castes, a broom is worshipped on the marriage day.[3]

Many people deny any sanctity to a broom. A belief is common that if a man sees a broom the first thing after getting up in the morning, he does not pass the day happily.[4]

Some believe that if a broom be kept erect in the house, a quarrel between the husband and wife is sure to follow. There is also a belief that if a person thrashes another with a broom, the former is liable to suffer from a gland under the arm.[5]

Fire is considered to be a deity by all Hindus. In all sacrifices, fire is first ignited with certain ceremonies of worship.[6] In all Brāhman families, every morning before breakfast, a ceremony called *Vaishvadeva* is performed, in which fire is worshipped and cooked rice is offered to it.[7]

The *Agnihotris* keep a constant fire burning in their houses and worship it thrice a day, morning, noon and evening[8].

The Pārsis consider fire so sacred that they do not smoke. Neither do they cross fire. In their temples called *Agiāris* a fire of sandal wood is kept constantly burning. It is considered a great mishap if this fire is extinguished.[8]

Fire is specially worshipped on the *Holi* day, that is the full-moon day of the month of *Fālgun*.[9]

Other special occasions on which it is worshipped are the thread ceremony, the ceremony of installing a new idol in a temple, the first pregnancy ceremony, and the ceremony performed at the time of entering a new house.[10]

Fire is also worshipped in *Mahārudra*, *Vishnuyāg*, *Gāyatripurascharan*, *Nilōtsarga*, *Vāstupujan*, *Shatachandi*, *Lakshachandi*, and the sacrifices performed during the *Navarātra* and on the *Dasara* day.[11]

Fire is considered to be the mouth of God, through which he is supposed to receive all offerings.[12]

The offerings made to fire generally consist of clarified butter, cocoanuts, sesamum seed, the *Java*, chips of the wood of the *Pipal* and the *Shami*, curdled milk and frankincense.[13]

The fire to be used for sacrifices and *agnihotras* is produced by the friction of two pieces of the wood of the *Arani*, [14] the *Pipal*, the *Shami* [15] or the bamboo while *mantras* or incantations are being recited by Brāhmans.[16]

1 The School Master of Dhānk.
2 The School Master of Kolki.
3 The School Master of Songadh.
4 The School Master of Limbdi.
5 The School Master of Todia.
6 The School Master of Dhānk.
7 The School Masters of Dhānk and Vanod.
8 The School Master of Kalavad and Mr. K. D. Desāi
9 The School Masters of Ganod and Dhānk.
10 The School Master of Dadvi.
11 The School Masters of Ganod and Kalavad and Mr. K. D. Desāi.
12 The School Master of Todia.
13 The School Master of Wala.
14 The School Masters of Dadvi and Dhānk.
15 The School Master of Jetpur.
16 The School Master of Aman.

CHAPTER IX.

ANIMAL WORSHIP.

The following animals are considered sacred and worshipped by the Hindus.

1. The cow :—is regarded as the holiest of animals. She is worshipped on the fourth day of the dark half of *Shrāvan* which is known as *Bol Choth*;* and a vow is observed by women in her honour on the fifteenth day of *Bhādarva.* It is known as *Gautrad Vrat.* On this day women do not eat wheat, milk, clarified butter and the whey of a cow.[1]

The sanctity which attaches to the due to the belief that in her body reside thirty three crores of gods.[2]

2. The horse :—The horse is believed by some people to be the last incarnation of God. It is also believed to represent Vāchhado, the deity who cures hydrophobia.[3]

Some people believe the horse to be a celestial animal. It is said that in ancient times it had wings, traces of which are believed to be still visible in its knees.

Of the fourteen jewels obtained by the gods and demons by churning the ocean, one was a horse with seven mouths. Hence the horse is considered divine.[4]

The horse is worshipped on the *Dasara* day.[5]

3. The elephant :—The elephant is considered divine because it is the vehicle of Indra, the lord of gods, and because its head was fixed on the trunk of Ganpati, the son of Pārvati and Shiva. It is believed by some people that vows to offer cocoanuts to an elephant are efficatious in curing fever.[6]

At the time of celebrating a coronation ceremony an elephant is worshipped. There is a tradition that in ancient times the coronation waters were poured over the king by a she-elephant.[7]

4. The lion :—The lion is considered sacred because it is believed to be the lord of the beasts of the forest and the vehicle of goddesses.[4]

5. The tiger :—The tiger is worshipped with Vāgheshvari Māta as it is believed to be her vehicle.

6. The she-buffalo :—Some sanctity attaches to the she-buffalo, as it is believed that a she-buffalo was given in dowry to a *Nāg kanya* (snake girl) by her father.[8]

To atone for a great sin a she-buffalo decked with a black wreath, iron, red lead and marks made with the flour of *adad* is presented to a Brāhman.[9]

7. The donkey :—Is believed to be the vehicle of the goddess of small-pox.[10]

It is also believed that the god Brahma had formerly five mouths, one of which was like that of a donkey.[11]

8. The dog :—The dog is believed to have divine vision and to be able to see the messengers of the god of death. Some believe that in its next life a dog becomes a man.[12]

The dog is also believed to be the vehicle of Kāl Bhairav and is worshipped along with his image.[13]

Some people offer bread to dogs in the belief that they will bear witness to their merits before God[14].

---

[1] The School Master of Dhānk.
[2] The School Master of Kotda Sangani.
[3] The School Master of Devalia.
[4] The Deputy Educational Inspector, Gohelwād.
[5] The School Master of Ganod.
[6] The School Master of Chhatrāsa.
[7] The School Master of Todia.
[8] The School Master of Chhatrāsa.
[9] The School Master of Moti Marad.
[10] The School Master of Chhatrāsa.
[11] The School Master of Moti Parabdi.
[12] The School Master of Chhatrāsa.
[13] The School Master of Aman.
[14] The School Master of Limbdi.

* See pp. 48-49.

9. The goat:—is worshipped by the Bharvāds when they worship the goddess Machhu.[1]

10. The cat:—is worshipped in the belief that by so doing a man can win over his opponents.[2]

11. The bear:—is considered by some people to be a holy animal because the god Krishna married Jāmbuvanti, the daughter of Jāmbuvant, the heroic bear who assisted Rāma.[3]

12. Fish:—are considered sacred because they are supposed to carry the food (*pindas*) to the *manes* offered (in water) at the *shrāddha* ceremony.[4]

13. Alligators:—are worshipped in a pond at Magar Pir, near Karāchi.[5]

14. The crows:—are worshipped because they are supposed to represent *rishis*.[6]

Some people believe that crows were formerly *rishis*. They are supposed to have divine vision, and food offered to them is believed to reach deceased ancestors.

A loaf is cut into three parts. One of them is designated *kāl* (ordinary), the second *dukāl* (famine), and the third *sukāl* (plenty). Next they are offered to a crow. If the crow takes away the *kāl*, it is believed that the crops in the following year will be normal; if it takes away the *dukāl* a famine is apprehended in the following year, and if the *sukāl*, it is believed that the crops will be plentiful.[7]

15. The goose:—is supposed to be the vehicle of the goddess Sarasvati. It is believed that its worship ensures success in any enterprise. If a goose is seen in a dream, it is considered to be a very good omen.[8]

A goose is believed to be endowed with the power of separating milk from water. It is supposed to feed on rubies. It is found in lake Mān in the Himālayās.[9]

16. The cock:—is considered holy as it is believed to be the vehicle of the goddess Bahucharāji.[10]

17. The hen:—is worshipped on the last Sunday of the month of *Jeth*.[11]

18. The parrot:—is worshipped by singers desiring to improve their voice. It is also worshipped by dull persons desirous of improving their intellect.[12]

---

1 The School Master of Aman.
2 The School Master of Todia.
3 The Deputy Educational Inspector of Gohelwād.
4 The School Master of Chhatrāsa.
5 The School Master of Dadvi.
6 The School Master of Kolki.
7 The School Master of Todia.
8 The School Master of Todia.
9 The School Master of Chhatrāsa.
10 The School Master of Luvaria.
11 The School Master of Aman.
12 The School Master of Todia.

CHAPTER X.

WITCHCRAFT.

Dākans are of two kinds, human and of the order of ghosts.[1]

Girls born in the *Ashlesha nakshatra* on the *bij* or second day of a month, in the *Kritika nakshatra* on the seventh day of a month and in the *Shatabhigha nakshatra* on the twelfth day of a month, are believed to be human *dākans*. They cause the death of their husbands, and their evil eye injures all things and individuals that come under its influence.[2]

Women who die in child-bed, meet an untimely death or commit suicide, become *Dākans* or *Chudels* after death.[2]

Some people believe that women of such low castes as Kolis, Vāghris and Chārans become *Dākans*. High caste *Dākans* are rare.[3]

A ghostly *Dākan* dresses in fine clothes and decks her person with ornaments. But she does not cover her back, which is horrible to look at. It is so frightful that any one happening to see it dies of horror.[4]

Ghostly *Dākans* trouble only women. When possessed by them, the latter have convulsive fits, loose their hair, and cry out without any reason.[5]

A ghostly *Dākan* lives with a man as his wife, brings him dainties and turns the refuse of food into flesh and bones. The man gradually becomes emaciated and ultimately dies.[6]

It is believed that generally a Dākan kills a man within six months.[7]

The *Dākans* do not allow calves to suck, cattle to give milk, and healthy persons to enjoy sound health. Sometimes they cause cattle to yield blood instead of milk.[8]

A *Dākan* by virtue of her powers, can ascend to the sky. She lives upon the flesh of corpses.[9]

A *Dākan* can assume any form she likes. She appears as a cat, a buffalo, a goat or any other animal. She can swell and shrink her body at will. Her feet are reversed.[10]

Dākans haunt trees, cemeteries, deserted tanks, mines or other desolate places.[11]

They also haunt ruins and places where four roads meet.[12]

---

1 The School Master of Dhānk.
2 The School Master of Ganod.
3 The School Master of Gondal.
4 The School Master of Sultānpur.
5 Mr. K. D. Desāi.
6 The School Master of Vanod.
7 The School Master of Dadvi.
8 The School Master of Moti Khilori.
9 The School Master of Ganod.
10 Mr. K. D. Desāi.
11 The School Master of Dhānk.
12 The School Master of Ganod.

CHAPTER XI.

GENERAL.

Various ceremonies are performed by cultivators at the time of ploughing the soil, sowing, reaping and harvesting. These ceremonies differ in details in different localities.

In all places, an auspicious day for ploughing and sowing is fixed in consultation with an astrologer. On the day when ploughing is to be commenced, the front court yard of the house is cowdunged and an auspicious figure called *Sathia** is drawn on it with the grains of *juvāri*.[1]

A dish called *kansār* is prepared, and served to all members of the family at the morning meal. Their foreheads are marked with red powder, and a pice and betelnut are offered to the household gods. Hand-spun cotton threads marked at intervals with red powder are then tied round the plough and to the horns of the bullocks which are to be yoked to the plough.[2]

Next, the farmer stands waiting at the front door of his house for good omens,[3] and when a few are seen, sets out for his field.

In some places, the foreheads of the bullocks are daubed with red lead, clarified butter is applied to their horns, and they are fed with molasses.[4]

In others, a betelnut is placed over the *Sathia* and given to the person who first meets the farmer on leaving his house.[5]

In some localities again, the farmer holds the plough over the *Sathia*, touching it with the end, eats a morsel of molasses, and bows to the *Sathia* before starting.[6]

As a rule, seed is not sown on Saturdays or Tuesdays. Wednesday is believed to be the most favourable day for this purpose.[7]

Sowing is commenced from that corner of the field which has been pronounced by the astrologer to be the best for the operation.[8]

Sunday is believed to be the most auspicious day for reaping.[9] While reaping, a part of the crop is offered to the image of Kshetrapāl and to other village deities. In order to secure a good harvest, sweets are offered to the village gods on the eighth or tenth day of the bright half of *Ashvin* or on the second day of the bright half of *Kārtik* which is called *Ananakuta*.[10]

No crop is brought into the house before a part of it has been offered to the local deities.[11]

When juice is to be extracted from sugarcanes, the mill is first worshipped. In the shed erected for storing the jars of molasses, an image of Ganpati is installed, and worshipped before placing the jars in the shed.[12]

The first jar of molasses and two bits of sugar cane are offered to the local deities.[13]

Before reaping cotton, offerings are made to the village gods.[14]

When a cow or she-buffalo is about to calve a packet containing a few pebbles or cowries, the *mali* (red lead) from the image of Hanumān, dust collected from a place where four roads meet, and grains of *Adad*, are tied to its horns by an indigo-coloured thread, in the belief that this protects the animal from the effects of the evil eye.[15]

To guard cattle against an attack of small-pox, women observe a vow called *Shili Sātem* on the seventh day of the bright half of *Shrāvan*.[16]

---

1 The School Master of Chhatrāsa.
2 The School Master of Vanod.
3 The School Master of Devalia.
4 The School Master of Kotda Sangani.
5 The School Master of Jetpur.
6 The School Master of Jetpur.
7 The School Master of Ganod.
8 Mr. K. D. Desāi.
9 The School Master of Jodia.
10 The School Master of Movaiya.
11 The School Masters of Zinzuvāda and Devalia.
12 The School Master of Luvaria.
13 The School Master of Bhāyāvadar.
14 The School Master of Kotda Sangani.
15 The School Master of Kotda Sangani.
16 The School Master of Vanod.
* See p.14 *Supra*.

To prevent a tiger from attacking cattle, a circle of the flour of *charonthi* is drawn round them by an exorcist reciting *mantras* or incantations. If a tiger tries to enter this protected area its mouth at once becomes swollen.[1]

In some places, salt heated over the fire of the *Holi* is put into the food given to the cattle in the belief that this protects them from disease.[2]

Instead of salt, some people give cattle leaves of castor-oil plants roasted over the fire of the *Holi*.[3]

In some places, on the *Divāli* holiday, a torch and a rice pounder are placed in the cattle shed, and the cattle are made to cross them one by one. This process is believed to protect them from disease.[4]

A ceremony called the *Doro* of Mahādev is also performed in the month of *Shrāvan* to proteet cattle against disease.[5]

Vows in the honour of Ashpāl or Nāgdev are also observed for the protection of cattle.[6]

In the *Hasta nakshatra* during the monsoon, when there is a thunder storm, a *sāmbelu* (rice pounder) is struck seven times against the main cross beam of the house in the belief that the sound thus produced destroys insects.[7]

To scare the insects called *itidio*, vows are observed in honour of the Itidio Pir.[8]

In order that insects and worms may not spoil the corn stored in a granary or in earthen jars, the ashes of the fire of the *Holi* or leaves of the *nim* tree are mixed with it.

To prevent insects from spoiling wheat, *bājari* and *juvāri*, mercury and ashes are put into them, while it is believed that gram cannot be eaten by insects if it is mixed with dust from a place where three roads meet.[9]

To drive away insects, a ceremony called *Adagho Badagho* or *Mariyun* is performed on the *Divāli* holiday. It is as follows :—

One man holds a lighted torch in his hand, and another an earthen jar, which he beats with a small stick. The two men pass through every nook and corner of the house and the cattle-shed crying "*Adagho* may go, *Badagho* may go", that is, "May troubles and diseases disappear; may bugs, serpents, mice, scorpions, mosquitoes and other insects die out." Next they proceed, repeating the same words, through the streets to the village boundary, where the torch, the earthen jar and the stick are thrown away, thus ending the ceremony.[10]

In order to secure sunshine and favourable weather, oblations are offered to the local deities, sacrificial offerings are made and bunting is suspended from the doors of temples.[11]

In order to secure a favourable rainfall, a grand festival is observed on an auspicious day. On this day all agricultural work is stopped and *megh laddus* (sweet balls called *megh* or cloud) are eaten by the people.[12]

In some places, for the protection of the crops, a thread charmed by the incantations of an exorcist is passed round the hedge of the field.[13]

For the protection of crops of gram, wheat and sugar-cane against injury by rats, a ceremony called *Dādh Bāndhavi* is performed, in which a thread over which incantations have been repeated by an exorcist is passed round the crop, and an image of Ganpati is installed and worshipped with offerings of sweet balls of wheat flour.[14]

---

[1] The School Master of Chok.
[2] The School Master of Devalia.
[3] The School Master of Chhatrāsa.
[4] The School Master of Jetpur.
[5] The School Master of Pātan Vāv.
[6] The School Master of Moti Marad.
[7] The School Master of Kotda Sangani.
[8] The School Master of Pātan Vāv.
[9] The School Master of Sānka.
[10] Mr. K. D. Desāi.
[11] The School Master of Kotda Sangani.
[12] The School Master of Vanod.
[13] The School Master of Dhānk.
[14] The School Master of Ganod.

In some places, the ceremony of *Dādh Bāndhavi* is performed somewhat differently. Instead of passing a thread round the field, the exorcist walks round the field repeating incantations, holding in his hand a pot containing fire, over which is placed a pan containing *Gugal*. This ceremony is generally performed for the protection of sugar-cane crops against the attacks of jackals. It is believed that an animal entering the field after the performance of this ceremony has its *dādh* (gums) stiffened.[1]

Silence and secrecy are considered essential in working mystic lore, for it is a belief that if learnt openly such lore loses its power.[2]

The ceremony for obtaining command over Kāl Bhairav is performed in perfect silence at midnight on the *Kālichaudas*, that is the fourteenth day of the dark half of *Ashvin*.[3]

Silence and secrecy are also essential in the ceremonies which are performed for subjugating such evil spirits as Meldi and Shikotar and Mātās.[4]

When Vaishnavas make offerings to their gods, the doors of the shrine are closed.

The initiating ceremonies of the Shakti Panthis and Margi Panthis are also performed in close secrecy.[5]

The Shrāvaks have to observe perfect silence at the time of performing the *Shāmag Padakamanu*[6] (a form of devotion to god).

Some people observe a vow of keeping silent while taking their meals either for life or during the monsoon.[7]

There are various legends current among the people regarding the origin of the *Holi* holiday. The chief versions are as follows:—

1. In ancient times there lived a demoness named Dhunda who preyed upon children. Her misdeeds caused great misery to the people, who went to Vasishtha, the preceptor of Rāma, and implored him to tell them of some remedy for the mischief wrought by the demoness. Vasishtha told them to light a pyre in honour of the goddess Holika, which he said, would consume the demoness. The people accordingly lighted a huge fire, into which the demoness was driven by boys who led her to the spot by abusing her and troubling her in many ways. She was reduced to ashes by the fire, and the people were saved.[8]

2. A demon named Hiraniāksha had a sister named Holika and a son named Prahlād. Hiraniāksha bore great enmity to Rāma, while Prahlād was his devotee. Hiraniāksha did not like his son's devotion to Rāma, and told him several times to give it up, and even threatened to take his life. But Prahlād did not swerve an inch from the path of his devotion. At last, being desperate, Hiraniāksha decided to kill him, and entrusted his sister with the mission. Holika raised a big pile of cow-dung cakes, set it on fire, and seated herself on the pile, taking Prahlād in her lap. But through the grace of Rāma, Prahlād escaped uninjured while Holika was reduced to ashes.

3. A demoness called Dhunda had obtained a boon from Shiva to the effect that she would not meet her death during any of the three seasons of the year, either by day or by night. At the same time she was warned to beware of injury from children between sunset and nightfall at the commencement of a new season. To prevent any possibility of injury from children, she began to destroy them by preying upon their bodies. This caused a great panic among the people, who went to Vasishtha and asked his advice as to how to kill the demoness. He advised them to kill her in the way

[1] The School Master of Chhatrāsa.

[2] The School Master of Kotda Sangani.

[3] The School Master of Vanod.

[4] The School Master of Dadvi.

[5] The School Master of Devalia

[6] The School Master of Limbdi.

[7] The School Master of Ganod

[8] The School Masters of Dhānk and Ganod.

described in legend No. I above, and she was killed accordingly.[1]

4. The Govardhan mountain had two sisters named Holi and Divāli. Holi was a woman of bad conduct while Divāli's character was good. Although unchaste, Holi boasted that she was chaste, and once, to prove her chastity, she threw herself on to a big fire. She could not bear the pain caused by the flames, and began to scream aloud, when people beat drums, abused her, and raised such a din that her screams became inaudible. Hence the custom of using abusive language and reciting abusive verses during the *Holi* holidays. Govardhan could not bear the disgrace attached to his sister's reputation. So he threw himself into the fire and met his death without uttering a word of pain. This has given rise to the custom of throwing into the *Holi* fire the cow-dung image of Govardhan, which is installed during the *Divāli* holidays.[2]

On the *Holi* day sweet dishes are prepared and taken with the morning meal. Some women observe a vow on this day, and dine once only in the evening, after worshipping the *Holi* fire with an offering of a cocoanut and walking seven times round it.[3]

In some places, on the day preceding the *Holi*, which is known as *Kamala Holi*, sweet stuffed cakes are prepared, and on the *Holi Punema* day vermicelli is eaten.[4]

The fuel for the *Holi* fire is generally collected by boys. At about two in the afternoon on the *Holi* day a party of boys goes from house to house and receive five to fifteen cow-dung cakes from each household. These cow-dung cakes are bored, and strung on strings.[5]

The fuel thus collected is heaped at the village boundary or the end of the street. All the male residents of the village or street meet at the spot, a pit is dug, and earthen pots filled with wheat, gram and water mixed together are placed in the pit and covered with cow-dung cakes. Next, the headman of the village or the leading resident of the street worships the pile with the assistance of a Brāhman priest. After worship, the pile is lighted, at the time fixed by an astrologer,* by a low caste Hindu, generally a Bhangi or Kotwāl, as Hindus of good caste consider it a sin to kindle the *Holi* fuel. The Bhangi or Kotwāl receives a few dates and cocoanut kernel for this service.[6]

The offerings thrown into the *Holi* fire generally consist of fried *juvāri* grain, fried gram and cocoanuts. Flowers of mango trees and tender mango fruits are also thrown into the *Holi* fire. It is believed that newly married pairs, by worshipping the *Holi* fire, are blessed with long life, prosperity, and the birth of children. After the principal ceremony is over, they worship it one by one with the ends of their upper garments tied in a knot, and walk seven times round the fire with their hands folded, the husband leading the wife.[7]

Infants dressed in gay clothes and decked with garlands of dry dates and bits of cocoanut kernel are also taken to the *Holi* fire by their parents. The latter worship the *Holi* Māta and walk four times round the fire, taking the children in their arms. Next they offer cocoanuts to the goddess, which are either thrown into the fire or distributed among those present.[8]

Women whose children die in infancy observe a vow of remaining standing on the *Holi* day. When the *Holi* is lighted they worship the fire, after which they may sit down and take their

[1] The School Mistress, Barton Female Training College, Rājkot.

[2] Mr. K. D. Desāi.

[3] The School Master of Vanod.

[4] The School Master of Moti Khiroli.

[5] The School Masters of Dhānk and Songadh.

* This is generally in the evening or an hour or two after nightfall.

[6] The School Masters of Zinzuvāda and Moti Marad.

[7] The School Masters of Dhānk and Vanod.

[8] The School Master of Chhatrāsa.

meal. It is believed that the observance of this vow ensures long life to children.[1]

Although the *Holi* itself falls on the full-moon day of *Fālgun* the rejoicings connected with it commence from the first day of that month. The principal feature of the rejoicings consists in indulging in indecent and vulgar songs and language. Vulgar songs or *fāgs* in honour of the goddess Holi are also sung. Songs are composed abusing each caste, and sung addressing passers by, by groups of boys who have full license during the *Holi* holidays to indulge in all sorts of pranks and abuses.

Some make wooden blocks with engravings of vulgar and indecent words, dip them in coloured water, and press them on the clothes of passers by.

Others make naked idols of mud, and place them on the tops of houses.[2]

The day following the *Holi* is known as *Dhul Pādavo* or *Dhuleti*. On this day people indulge in the throwing of cow-dung, black pigments, urine, mud, coloured water and red powder.[2]

In some places, on the *Dhuleti* day, a game is played with a cocoanut. The players form themselves into two parties and stand opposite to one another. Midway between them is placed a cocoanut. Each party tries to take away the cocoanut, and prevents the other from so doing by throwing stones and cow-dung cakes. The party which succeeds in taking away the cocoanut wins the game.[3]

Amongst Dheds, Kolis, Rāvals and other low castes a post of the wood of the tamarind tree is planted in the ground and surrounded by women holding whips and cords in their hands. A party of men run to the women to drive them away and take possession of the post. The women prevent them from doing so by striking them with all their might with the whips and cords in their hands. This struggle commences at 10 A. M. on the *Dhuleti* day and continues till one o'clock in the morning on the following day. At last the men succeed in carrying away the post, thus ending the game.[4]

In some places, a man is tied to a bier as if he were a corpse, and carried on the shoulders of four men to the post of tamarind wood, followed by a party of men and women wailing aloud, to the great merriment of the crowd assembled near the post to witness the struggle described above.[5]

Sometimes contests are held between two parties of boys in singing vulgar songs. The contest commences by one of the parties singing a song. The other party responds to it by singing another song, which is generally more indecent than the song sung first. The contest goes on like this, and the party which fails to respond to its rival is said to be defeated.[5]

The immoral practices described above are only to be seen among low caste people, and even their women take part in these practices.

The women of higher castes wear rich clothes and ornaments on the *Dhuleti* day, and sing songs in their houses. At times they throw coloured water and red powder at each other.[6]

In big temples a festivity called *Ful Dol* is observed, in which water coloured with the flowers of the *Khākhra* (Butea frondosa) is thrown by the party assembled, and *kundaliās* or indecent songs are sung in a loud voice.[7]

In some temples, holy songs are sung at night and prayers are held. At the end, fried *juvāri*, gram and sweets are distributed as the grace of God.[8]

The boys who take an active part in the *Holi* celebrations are known as *geraiyās* or *holiās*. For two or three nights before the *Holi* they steal fuel for the *Holi* fire and beat and abuse

1 The School Master of Todia.
2 The School Master of Songadh.
3 The School Master of Kolki.
4 The School Masters of Zinzuvāda and Todia.
5 The School Master of Todia.
6 The School Mistress, Barton Female Training College, Rājkot.
7 The School Master of Luvaria.
8 The School Master of Todia.

those who try to prevent them from so doing. They also recite coarse songs and play with dirt and mud freely. Parties of them go from shop to shop and obtain by force dates and fried gram.[1]

At midnight of the *Holi* day a bower is erected in the centre of the village with bits of broken earthen vessels and cocoanut shells. A fool, generally a son-in-law of some low caste Hindu in the village, is induced, by the promise of dates and cocoanut kernel, to dress in a coat on which are drawn naked pictures. A garland of worn out shoes is tied round his neck and he is mounted on a donkey. He is then called *Vālam* and taken from the bower through the village accompanied with music and crowds of people, who utter in a loud voice coarse and vulgar expressions as the procession moves on. At times they play jokes with the *Vālam*, and give him blows on the head with their fists.[2]

In some places, this procession is called *Vālama Vālami* and is celebrated on the night preceding the *Holi*. Two poor stupid persons are dressed as bride and bridegroom, the latter in a ridiculously grotesque dress. They are married on the following morning, when vulgar songs are sung. The *Vālam* and *Vālami* are represented by two naked idols, made of rags, of a man and a woman. They are carried through the village in a noisy procession and married on an altar of black earthen vessels. They are then placed erect on two wooden posts side by side.[3]

In some villages, a large stone is placed in a spacious compound in the centre of the village, and broken earthen vessels are suspended over it with cords from the wooden bower erected over the stone. An ass is brought to the spot, and a fool decked with a garland of worn out shoes is mounted on it with his face turned towards the tail of the ass. He holds the tail of the ass in his hands as reins and is carried in procession through the village to be brought back to the bower and married to another fool, dust, ashes and water being freely used in the service.[4]

In some localities naked images of a husband and wife are set in a cart and taken through the village accompanied with music, the crowd singing indecent songs all the way long.[5]

On the *Holi* holiday children are presented with *harda* (garlands of balls made of sugar) by their relatives and the friends of their families.[6]

The *Holi* fire is extinguished by women on the morning of the following day. The earthen vessels containing wheat and gram which are put into the pit of the *Holi* before the fire is lighted are then taken out. The grain is cooked by the fire of *Holi*, and is called *Ghugari*. It is distributed among the villagers, the belief being that those who eat it are protected against disease by the goddess of the *Holi*.[7]

There are many other superstitious beliefs held by people in connection with the *Holi*.

According to one belief, those who expose themselves to the heat of the *Holi* fire keep good health during the ensuing year. According to some, this can be secured by eating sugar-cane heated over the fire. *Juvāri* stems heated over the fire are given to cattle with the same object.[8]

Some believe that if salt heated over the *Holi* fire is given to cattle it protects them against epidemics.[8]

Virgins take home a little of the *Holi* fire and light five cow-dung cakes with it in the

[1] The School Master of Pātan Vāv.

[2] The School Masters of Ganod, Vanod and Dhānk.

[3] The School Master of Kolki.

[4] The School Mistress, Barton Female Training College, Rājkot.

[5] The School Master of Todia.

[6] The School Master of Songadh and Mr. K. D. Desāi

[7] The School Master of Pātan Vāv.

[8] The School Master of Songadh.

courtyard of their house. When the cakes are burnt, the ashes are removed and the spot is purified with a plaster of cow-dung. Next, they draw some auspicious figures on the spot and worship them for a number of days in the belief that this ensures good health to their brothers.[1]

Among Gujarāt Hindus no special ceremonies are performed when a girl attains puberty, except that on the third or fifth day she is bathed by an unwidowed woman and dressed in green or saffron-coloured robes. She is given rice in milk, sweetened with sugar, and is presented with a piece of green satin.[2]

In some places, the girl is bathed on the fourth day and given *kansār* to eat. She then bows to her mother-in-law and makes her a present of half a rupee. The mother-in-law blesses her and presents her with a bodice cloth.[3]

After the bath, a mark with red powder is made on her forehead and she is taken to the temple of the family deity.[4]

In some places, the red powder mark is made under the girl's right arm in the belief that this ensures to her the birth of many children.[5]

In some localities the girl is bathed on the third day, dainty dishes are served her, and she is presented with a cocoanut by each of her kinsfolk[6]

In some castes, when a girl attains puberty, a feast of cooked rice and molasses is given to the caste people. In other castes, pieces of cocoanut kernel are distributed among children, and the girl is presented with a robe and bodice by her parents-in-law.[7]

In some castes, a girl is not allowed to cook before she attains puberty.[8]

No ceremonies are performed when a boy attains puberty, probably because in the case of boys the change is not so marked as in the case of girls.

1 The School Master of Khirāsara.
2 The School Master of Dhānk.
3 The School Master of Vanod.
4 The School Master of Dadvi
5 The School Master of Chok.
6 The School Mistress of Barton Female Training College, Rājkot.
7 The School Master of Chhatrāsa.
8 The School Master of Uptela.

FOLK
LORE
NOTES

FOLK
LORE
NOTES

Vol. I — Gujarat
Vol. II — Konkan

Compiled from Materials Collected by
A.M.T. Jackson

Vol. II
FOLKLORE OF KONKAN
R.E. Enthoven

ISBN : 978-93-5324-425-5 (Set)
ISBN : 978-93-5324-427-9 (HB)
First Published, 1915 (Vol. II)
Published, 2020

Published by

Facsimile Publisher
12 Pragati Market
Ashok Vihar, Ph-2
Delhi-110052
E-mail: books@facsimilepublisher.com

Printed at: G. Print Process, Delhi.

Folklore of Gujarat
Author: A.M.T. Jackson

FOLK LORE NOTES

VOL. II—KONKAN

COMPILED FROM MATERIALS COLLECTED BY

THE LATE A. M. T. JACKSON, INDIAN CIVIL SERVICE

R. E. ENTHOVEN, C.I.E., I.C.S.

BRITISH INDIA PRESS, MAZGAON, BOMBAY

1915

TABLE OF CONTENTS.

CHAPTER I.

Nature Powers.

CHAPTER II.

The Heroic Godlings.

CHAPTER III.

Disease Deities.

CHAPTER IV.

The worship of Ancestors and Saints.

CHAPTER V.

The Worship of the malevolent dead.

FOLKLORE OF THE KONKAN.

CHAPTER I.

NATURE POWERS.

THE worship of minor local deities is connected with such low castes as Guravas, Bhopis, Marátha Kunbis, Dhangars, Wághes, Murlis, Mahárs and Mángs in the District of Kolhápur. It is believed by the Bráhmans that once an image is consecrated and worshipped, it should be worshipped uninterruptedly every day, and he who neglects to worship such an image daily incurs the sin of *Brahma-hatya* or Bráhman-murder. For this reason Bráhmans generally do not worship minor local deities. In former times Bráhmans who worshipped these deities were excommunicated by their caste-men. Such *Pujáris* were compelled to wear a folded *dhotur* or waist cloth, and were forbidden to put on the *gandh* or sandal paste mark in straight or cross lines. They were allowed to put on the *tila* or circular mark of sandal paste. Another reason why Bráhmans are not the *Pujáris* or worshippers of such deities is that Bráhmans cannot accept or partake of the *Naivedya* offering of cooked food, fowls, etc., made to them. Lower class people can partake of such offerings, and are therefore generally the worshippers or ministrants of minor local deities.

At Palshet in the Ratnágiri District, there are two *grámdevis*, viz., Jholái and Mhárjái, and the *pujáris* of these deities are respectively a Gurav and a Mahár.[1] The *pujáris* of goddesses are generally men of the lower castes. The guardian goddesses of the villages of Pule, Varavade, Nandivade, and Rila have Kunbis as their *pujáris*; while the *pujáris* of the goddesses Mahálakshmi, Bhagvati, Mahákáli, and Jogái are generally chosen from the Gurav caste.[2] In the Konkan the Ráuls (Shudras) are the *pujáris* of the deities Vithoba, Ravalnáth and Bhaváni; the Ghádis are the *pujáris* of the deities Sáteri and Khavaneshwar; while the deities Mahádev and Máruti are worshipped by *pujáris* belonging to the Gurav caste.[3] The goddesses Makhajan and Jakhmáta at Sangameshwar in the Ratnágiri District are worshipped by *pujáris* who belong to the Gurav and Bhoi castes respectively. The god Ganpati at Makhnele has for his *pujári* a Wáni. The *pujáris* of the temple of Shiva at Lánje in the Ratnágiri District are Wánis.[4] It is said that the *pujári* of Pundárik at Pandharpur is a Kiráta (fisherman) by caste.[5]

The *pujári* of the goddess Narmáta at Sidgad in the Thána District is a Koli; whilst the *pujáris* of Kánoba, Khandoba, and Vetál are of the lower castes.[6] The goddesses Mahálakshmi of Kolvan and Vajreshvari have their *pujáris* chosen from the lower castes.[7] The *pujáris* of Jari-Mari, Mhasoba, Bahiroba, Cheda and other deities which are said to prevent contagious diseases, are always men of the lower castes.[8]

The *pujáris* of the guardian goddesses of the villages Petsai, Dasgaum and Nizámpur are a Mahár, a Kumbhár or potter, and a Marátha, respectively.[9] The *pujári* of the

[1] School Master, Palshet, Ratnágiri.
[2] School Master, Adivále, Ratnágiri.
[3] School Master, Parule, Ratnágiri.
[4] School Master, Makhnele, Ratnágiri.
[5] School Master, Rájápur, Ratnágiri.
[6] School Masters, Ágáshi and Arnála, Thána.
[7] School Master, Málád, Thána.
[8] School Master, Shahápur, Thána.
[9] School Master, Dasgaum, Kolába.

guardian goddesses of Chaul in the Kolába District belongs to the lower castes.[1] The goddess Mángái has always a Mahár as her *pujári*.[2] Everyday the god Shiva is required to be worshipped first by a *pujári* of the Gurav caste. The *pujári* of Bahiri, a corruption of the word Bhairav, one of the manifestations of Shiva, is a man belonging to the lower castes. Similarly the *pujáris* of Bhagavati, Bhaváni, Ambika, Kálika, Jákhái, Jholái, Janni, Kolhái, Vadyájái, Shitaládevi, Chandika, etc., are persons belonging to lower castes.[3]

It is considered by the Hindus very meritorious and holy to worship the Sun; and by Bráhmans the Sun is considered to be their chief deity. The *Gáyatri Mantra* of the Bráhmans is a prayer to the Sun-god or the Savita Dev, and the Bráhmans offer *arghya* or oblations of water to the Sun thrice a day. Those who want health, wealth and prosperity propitiate the Sun-god by prayers and ceremonies. The *Ratha Saptami* is considered to be the principal day for special worship and festivities in honour of the Sun-god. On this day, on a low wooden stool, is drawn, in red sandal paste, a figure of the Sun in human shape seated in a chariot drawn by seven horses, or by a horse with seven faces. This figure is then placed in the sun-shine, and it is then worshipped by offering it *arghya* or spoonfuls of water, red powder, red flowers mixed with red sandal paste, camphor, incense and fruits. Some people kneel down while offering the *arghyas* to the Sun. These *arghyas* are either three or twelve in number. Some persons make a vow not to eat anything unless they have worshipped the Sun and performed the twelve *Namaskaras* by falling prostrate and bowing with folded hands twelve times, and at each time repeating one of the twelve names of the Sun.*

In the Ratnágiri District some people worship the Sun on the Sundays of the month of *Shrávan*. A ceremony held on the *Rathasaptami* day, *i.e.*, the 7th day of the bright half of *Mágh*, is deemed a special festival in honour of the Sun-god. On that day people draw, on a small wooden stool, an image of the Sun, seated in a chariot drawn by seven horses, and worship it with great reverence. Milk is then boiled on a fire made of cow-dung cakes in front of the household *Tulsi* plant. If the milk overflows to the east, it is believed that there will be abundance of crops, but if it flows to the west it is taken as a sign of the near approach of famine.[4] The Sun-god is also worshipped on the following occasions, *e.g.*, *Trikal*, *Gajaccháya*, *Ardhodaya*, *Mahodaya*, *Vyatipát*, *Makar-Sankránt*, *Kark-Sankránt* and the Solar eclipse.[5] Though there are few temples dedicated to the Sun, the village of Parule has the honour of having one called "the temple of Adi-Náráyan." Non-Bráhmanical classes are not seen worshipping the Sun in this district, despite the fact that the Sun is said to be the embodiment of the three principal deities of the Hindus.[6]

The people of the Thána District believe that the *Swastika* is the central point of the helmet of the Sun, and a vow called the *Swastika Vrata* is held in its honor. A woman who observes this vow, draws a figure of the *Swastika* and worships it daily during the *Cháturmás* (four months of the rainy season), at the expiration of which she gives a Bráhman a golden or silver plate with the sign of the Swastika upon it.[7] Another vow named *Dhanurmás*, common to all districts in the Konkan, requires a person to complete his daily rites before sun-rise, and to offer a

[1] School Master, Chaul, Kolába.
[2] School Master, Akola, Kolába.
[3] School Master, Poladpur, Kolába.
* These twelve names are :—1 Mitra, 2 Ravi, 3 Surya, 4 Bhanu, 5 Khaga, 6 Pushne, 7 Hiranyagarbha, 8 Marichi, 9 Aditya, 10 Savita, 11 Arka, 12 Bhasker.
[4] School Master, Phonden.
[5] School Master, Devarukh.
[6] School Master, Parule.
[7] School Master, Anjur.

preparation of food called *Khichadi* to the Sun-god. The observer of this vow then partakes of the food, regarding it as a gift from that god. This is either done for one day or repeated for a month till the *Dhanu-Sankránt.*[1] On the *Somavati-Amávásya* day (the 15th day of the dark half of a month falling on Monday), and the *Kapiláshasthi* day, the Sun is held in especial reverence.[2] A curious story is narrated regarding the offering of *Arghya* to the Sun. It is said that the Sun rejoices at the birth of a Bráhman, and gives 1,000,000 cows in charity, believing that the *Arghya* which the Bráhman will offer later on will devour his foes, one drop of the *Arghya* killing 1,000 of them*. The repetition of the *Gáyatri-mantra* 108 times a day is supposed to release a Bráhman from the debt of 1,000,000 cows owed in this way to the Sun. [3] The *Yoga-Sutras* of Pátanjali however prohibit a man from looking at the setting Sun, though the sin thus incurred is made amends for by the offering of *Arghya* to that god. [4] It is interesting to note that women do not grind corn on the *Ratha-Saptami* day. [5]

Women bow down to the Sun on the 11th, 12th, 30th or 40th day after their delivery; but Kunbi women generally worship that god on the 7th day.[6] On this occasion some women show a churning handle† to the Sun-god and offer him some grains of rice.[7]

The *Swastika* is considered so holy in the Konkan that it is always drawn on the *Antarpat*; and at the time of the *Punyáha Wachan* ceremony which precedes a Hindu wedding, a *Swastika* drawn in rice is worshipped.[8] The principal deities of the Hindus, whenever they are invoked on special occasions, are seated on the *Swastika.*[9] The people of the Ratnágiri District worship the *Swastika,* regarding it as the symbol as well as the seat of the Sun-god.[10]

By some the *Swastika* is regarded as the foundation-stone of the universe[11] and is held to be the symbol of the god Shiva, and not of the Sun.[12]

The conception of Kunbi is said to have taken place by the influence of the rays of the Sun.[13]

The *Swastika* is considered as an emblem of peace and prosperity, and for this reason Bráhman women draw a figure of the *Swastika* in front of their houses. [14] The custom of moving round such sacred objects as the Banyan, the *Pipal*, the *Tulsi* or sweet basil plant, the *Umbar*, the *Avala* (Phylanthus emblica), etc., is prevalent in the district of Kolhápur. There are no cases recorded in which women after child-birth are exposed to the Sun. But on the 12th day after her delivery, the mother puts on new bangles and new clothes; cocoanuts, betel-nuts and leaves, grains of rice, plantains and grains of wheat are placed in her lap. She then comes out and bows to the Sun. Wealthy persons on this occasion perform a *homa* sacrifice in their houses by kindling the holy fire and feeding Bráhmans. No one in this district believes that conception is caused, or is likely to be caused, by exposure to the rays of the Sun.

The Hindu women of the Konkan walk round *Pipal*, *Tulsi*, and *Umbar* trees every Saturday and on the *Somavati-amávásya* day, *i.e.*, the 15th day of the dark half of a month when it falls on Monday.[15] Sometimes, however, women make a vow to walk round a

1 School Master, Vasind.
2 School Master, Málád.
3 School Master, Málád.
4 School Masters, Agashi and Arnala.
5 School Master, Padaghe.
* 33,000,0000 demons are said to be born every day to impede the journey of the Sun.
6 School Master, Chaul, Kolába.
7 School Master, Nevare, Ratnágiri.
8 School Master, Mithbáv, Ratnágiri.
9 School Master, Makhanele, Ratnágiri.
10 School Master, Pendhur, Málvan, Ratnágiri.
11 School Masters, Agáshi and Arnála.
12 School Masters, Chauk, Karjat, Kolába.
13 School Masters, Chauk, Karjat, Kolába.
14 Rao Saheb Shelke.
15 School Master, Malgund, Ratnágiri.
† The churning handle or rod is called in Maráthi *Ravi*, which is one of the names of the Sun.

temple or a sacred tree one-hundred thousand times; and for the fulfilment of this vow they walk round the temple or tree for about seven or eight hours every day. If they find it difficult to make up the number of rounds themselves, they ask their near relations to assist them in their undertaking.[1]

The Moon is worshipped by the Hindus on the 2nd of the bright half of every month. On this day it is considered very lucky to see the moon, and many people, particularly the lower classes, pull out threads from the clothes they wear, and offer them to the moon, saying "O! God, accept these old clothes of ours and be pleased to give us new ones in their stead." Some people worship the moon on the *Sankasti Chaturthi* 4th day of the dark half of every month; and such people will not eat anything until they have seen and worshipped the moon on that day. The moon is not worshipped on the *Ganesh Chaturthi* day that is, the 4th of the bright half of the month of *Bhádrapad*, as it is considered very unlucky to see the moon on that night. It is firmly believed that any one who sees the moon on the *Ganesh Chaturthi* day even by accident will be falsely accused of theft or some other crime. In order to avoid this, people who have accidently seen the moon, throw stones at the houses of their neighbours, and if the neighbours abuse them in return, the mischiefmakers consider themselves freed by the abuse from the sin of having looked at the moon on a forbidden night.

The spots on the surface of the moon are believed by some to be the *rath* or chariot of the god. Others think that they are lunar mountains; but many believe that the spots are the visible signs of the stain on the character of the moon-god due to his having outraged the modesty of the wife of his *guru*, the god Brahaspati or Jupiter. In the *Puráns* it is stated that on one occasion, a dispute arose between the moon and Brahaspati or Jupiter about the wife of Brahaspati, each of them claiming to be the cause of her conception. Subsequently a son was born who was named Budha (Mercury). Brahaspati's wife, on being asked who was the father of the child, named the moon. Thereupon Brahaspati cursed the moon for his adultery. The spots on the surface of the moon are said to be the effect of this curse.

The moon-god is believed to distribute nectar through his rays, and therefore this deity is said to have the power of removing diseases and restoring human beings to health. The moon is the king of herbs, and all trees, plants, etc., thrive owing to the influence of the moon. Sometimes people place at night, figs, plantains, sugarcane and other eatables in the moonlight and eat them early in the morning; and it is said that those who do so improve in health. The practice of drinking the moon's rays does not prevail in the Kolhápur district. But people occasionally dine in the moon light.[2]

On a full moon day people perform the special worship of their chosen deity. On the full moon of the month of *Kártika* temples are illuminated, and on the full moon day of *Mágha*, raw corn such as wheat, *bájri*, etc., is cooked and offered to the household and other deities.* On this day are also performed the special rites and ceremonies that are required in connection with the *Kula-devatás* or family gods or goddesses. On the full moon day of *Fálguna* the *Holi* fire is kindled and worshipped. In certain families the full moon of *Chaitra* is considered auspicious for making offerings to family deities. On the full moon day of *Shrávan* is observed the feast of Cocoanut day, and on this day Bráhmans put on new sacred threads. The full moon is considered by the *Sanyásis* or ascetics an auspicious day for shaving their heads.

1 School Master, Phonde, Ratnágiri.

2 Rao Sahib Shelke.

* In the Konkan the *Navánna Purnima* or full moon day of new food is observed in the month of *Ashwina*. This is, no doubt, due to the difference in the season of the harvest.

On the new moon day the *Pitras* or Manes are worshipped. Lighted lamps are worshipped on the new moon day, of *Ashádha*. In the Kolhápur State this is called *Tadali* new moon day, and in the Konkan it is called *Divali* new moon day. On the new moon day of *Ashwin*, Lakshmi the goddess of wealth is worshipped. All special ceremonies for the propitiation of the *Bhutas* or evil spirits are usually performed on the new moon day. The *Dwitiya* or 2nd day of every month is considered sacred to the moon, and on this day the moon is worshipped; while the *Chaturthi* is considered sacred to the god Ganapati, and on the Cháturthi of Bhádrapada a special festival is held in honour of the god Ganpati. [1]

On the 15th day of the bright half of the month of *Ashwin* people put milk in the rays of the moon for some time, and then, after offering it to the moon, they drink it. Drinking milk in this way is called drinking the rays of the moon. [2] On the *Sankránt Chaturthi* day and on that *Chaturthi* which immediately follows the *Dasara* holiday, people draw an image of the moon and worship it. [3] In the Ratnágiri district several conflicting theories are held regarding the spots on the surface of the moon. Some believe that the spot observed on the moon is a tamarind tree in which that god has stationed himself; others hold that the spot is the reflection of a deer which is yoked to the chariot of the moon.[4]; while many more believe that it has been occasioned by the hoof of the horse of King Nala. Some say that the spot on the surface of the moon represents a *Pipal* tree and a cow fastened to the roots of the tree; others on the authority of Hindu mythology suppose that God created *Madan* (cupid) from the essence taken from the body of the moon and hence the moon-god has spots on his body.[5] In the *Mahábhárat* it is stated that on the surface of the moon is reflected the island of Sudarshan on this earth, together with some trees and a great hare, the bright part being nothing but water.[6] The spot on the surface of the moon is considered by some a deer which the god has taken on his lap.[7] Some believe that Yashoda, the mother of Krishna, after waving an earthen dish round the face of Krishna, threw it at the sky. It struck the moon and thereby the spots on the surface of the moon were caused. Nectar is supposed to have been derived from the rays of the moon; and in some sacred books it is stated that the Chakora bird (Bartavelle Partridge) drinks the rays of the moon.[8]

The people of the Thána District hold similar notions regarding the spots on the surface of the moon. It has been said by some that the portion in question represents mud, while others say that the moon has been disfigured owing to a curse from a sage. [9] Some people say that the spots are due to the moon being cursed by his preceptor Brahaspati with whose wife the moon-god had connection. Being unable to bear the pain of the spots, the moon, it is said, propitiated his preceptor, who directed him to bathe in the Bhima river to alleviate the agony. Accordingly the pain was assuaged, and the part of the river where the Moon-god bathed thus came to be called *Chandra bhága*. [10] Some persons suggest that the spots are a *Pipal* tree with two deer feeding upon it from two sides[11]. Others hold that the spots on the surface of the moon are due to its having been kicked by a deer which, when pursued by a hunter, was refused shelter. [12]

1 Rao Saheb, Shelke.
2 School Master, Ibhrámpur.
3 School Mster, Gaumkhadi, Rájápur.
4 School Master, Adivare, Rájápur.
5 School Master, Dábhol, Ratnágiri.
6 School Master, Ratnágiri.
7 School Master, Ubhádánda, Vengurla.
8 School Master, Ratnágiri.
9 School Master, Murbád.
10 School Master, Vásind, Sáhápur.
11 School Master, Wáda.
12 School Master, Edvan, Máhim.

The people of the Thána District believe that the rays of the moon influence conception. [1]

In the Kolába District, to sit in an open place on a moon-light night, is regarded as drinking the rays of the moon. [2] The elongated part of the orb of the moon pointing towards the north or the south is supposed to forebode scarcity or abundance, respectively.[3]

It is a common belief that the moon should not be seen on the *Ganesh Chaturthi* day, *i.e.*, the 4th day of the bright half of *Bhádrapad.*

Looking at the moon continuously for a short time on every moon light night is said to keep one's sight in good order.[4]

If the *Amâvásya* falls on Monday, Bráhman women of the Thána District walk round a *Tulsi* plant or a Pipal tree and make a vow to a Bráhman.[5]

In the Kolába District a special ceremony is held in honour of minor goddesses on the 8th day of a month. The following things are avoided one on each of the fifteen *tithis* respectively :—
Kohala (pumpkin) *dorli* (Solanum indicum,) salt, sesamum, sour things, oil, *úvale* (Emblic myrobalan), cocoanuts, *bhopala* (gourd), *padval* (snake-gourd), *pávte* (Dolichos Lablah) *masur* (Lens esculenta) brinjal, honey, gambling. [6]

The people observe a fast on the 13th (*Pradosha*) and the 14th day (*Shivarátra*) of the dark half of every month.[7] On the 15th day of the bright half of *Chaitra*, a fair is held in honour of the guardian deity of a village, and hens, goats, etc., are offered as a sacrifice.[8]

The following are days of special importance.

Gudhi-pádva, i.e., the first day of the bright half of *Chaitra*:—This being the first day of the year, *gudhis* and *toranas* are hoisted in front of every house and are worshipped.[9]

Bháu-bij :—On the 2nd day of the bright half of *Kártik* every sister waves round the face of her brother a lamp, and makes him a present. [10]

The ceremony on the *Bháu-bij* day has come into vogue on account of Subhadra having given a very pleasant bath to her brother Krishna on that day. The Court of Yama is also said to be closed on that day, since he goes to his sister; and consequently persons who die on that day, however sinful they may be, are not supposed to go to *Yamaloka i. e.*, hell.[11]

Akshya Tritiya:—On the third day of the bright half of *Vaishákh* cold water and winnowing fans are distributed as tokens for appeasing the *Manes* of ancestors. On this day is also celebrated the birth of the god Parashurám.[12]

Ganesh Chaturthi:—On the 4th day of the bright half of *Bhádrapad*, an earthen image of Ganpati is worshipped and a great ceremony is held in his honour.[13] The fourth day of the bright half of every month is called *Vináyaka-Chaturthi*; while that of the dark half is called *Sankasti-Chaturthi*. On the *Vináyaka-Chaturthi* day, people fast the whole day and dine the next day; while on the *Sankasti Chaturthi* day, they fast during the day time and dine after moon-rise.[14] That *Sankasti Chaturthi* which falls on Tuesday is considered the best.[15]

1 School Master, Kalyán, No. 1 and School Master, Padaghe, Bhivandi.
2 School Master, Chidhran, Kolába.
3 School Master, Polådpur.
4 School Master, Chauk, Kolába.
5 School Master, Anjur, Thána.
6 School Master, Chauk, Kolába.
7 School Master, Polådpur.
8 School Master, Polådpur, Kolába
9 School Master, Basani, Ratnágiri.
10 School Master, Basani, Ratnágiri.
11 School Master, Pendur, Málvan, Ratnágiri
12 School Master, Basani, Ratnágiri.
13 School Master, Basani, Ratnágiri.
14 School Master, Malgund, Ratnágiri.
15 School Master, Ubhádánda, Vengurla.

Nágpanchami:—On the 5th day of the bright half of *Shrávan*, pictures of serpents and snake holes are worshipped.[1]

Champá-Shashti:—On the 6th day of the bright half of *Márgashirsha*, some ceremony relating to the family-deity is performed.[2]

Ratha-Saptami:—On the 7th day of the bright half of *Mágh*, the sun is worshipped and milk is boiled until it overflows.[3]

Gokul-Ashtami:—On the 8th day of the dark half of *Shrávan* the birth of the god Krishna is celebrated.[4]

Ráma-Navami:—On the 9th day of the bright half of *Chaitra* the birth of the god Ráma is celebrated.[5]

Vijayádashmi :—On the 10th day of the bright half of *Ashvin* people cross the boundary of their village and distribute *sone* (leaves of the *Shami* and *Apta* trees). It is a popular belief that a work commenced on this day is sure to end well. Weapons are also worshipped on this day.[6]

Ekádashi:—On the 11th day of *Ashádh* and *Kártik* a special fast is observed. People also fast on the 11th day of each month. A man who dies on this auspicious day is supposed to go to heaven.[7] Sometimes the *Ekádási* falls on two consecutive days; in which case the Smártas observe the first, while the Bhágvats observe the second.[8]

Wáman-dwádashi:—On the 12th day of the bright half of *Bhádrapad* Wáman is worshipped and one or twelve boys are adored, being held to represent Wáman. The marriage of the *Tulsi* plant is sometimes celebrated on this day.[9]

Dhana-Trayodashi:—On the 13th day of the dark half of *Ashvin*, Lakshmi, the goddess of wealth is worshipped.[10]

Narak-Chaturdashi :—On the 14th day of the dark half of *Ashvin*, the demon Narakásur was killed. In consequence, on this day people take their bath before sun-rise, break *Karinta* (a fruit), regarding it as a demon, and apply its seeds to their heads.[11]

Nárali Paurnima :—On the 15th day of the bright half of *Shrávan*, people worship the sea and throw into it a cocoanut.[12]

Wata-Paurnima :—On the 15th day of the bright half of *Jyestha*, women whose husbands are alive fast the whole day, and worship the *Wata*-tree.[13]

On the 15th day of the bright half of *Ashvin*, people keep themselves awake the whole night and amuse themselves in a variety of ways. On the 15th day of the bright half of *Kártika* houses are illuminated. This day is called *Tripuri-Paurnima*. On this night people illuminate with earthen lamps all temples in the village, but particularly the temple of Shiva. This is done in commemoration of the triumph of the god Shiva over the demon Tripurásura. The full-moon day of the month of *Mágha* is called *Chudi Paurnima*. On this night people light *chudies* torches and with them slightly burn certain flowers, trees and plants. The full-moon day of the month of *Fálguna* is called the *Holi* or *Holi-Paurnima* and is the biggest holiday of the lower class Hindus. On this night the Hindus kindle the Holi-fire and worship it.[14] On the 15th day of the bright half of *Ashvin* people eat grain of the new harvest. On the full-moon day of *Shrávan* they perform the *Shrávani* ceremony and give a lamp in charity. On the full-moon day of the month of *Chaitra*, *Vaishakha* and *Márgashirsha*, the births of Máruti, Narasimha and Dattátraya respectively are celebrated.[15] The Kunbis of the Ratnágiri District believe that

[1] School Master, Basani, Ratnágiri.
[2] School Master, Basani, Ratnágiri.
[3] School Master, Basani, Ratnágiri.
[4] School Master, Basani, Ratnágiri.
[5] School Master, Basani, Ratnágiri.
[6] School Master, Basani, Ratnágiri.
[7] School Master, Basani, Ratnágiri.
[8] School Master, Málgund, Ratnágiri.
[9] School Master, Basani, Ratnágiri.
[10] School Master, Basani, Ratnágiri.
[11] School Master, Basani, Ratnágiri.
[12] School Master, Basani, Ratnágiri.
[13] School Master, Basani, Ratnágiri.
[14] School Master, Bandivade Budruk, Ratnágiri.
[15] School Master, Pendur, Ratnágiri.

on the 15th or full-moon day of *Pausha*, the Hindu gods go out hunting and that they return from their hunting expedition on the full-moon day of the month of *Mágha*. During this period the Kunbis abstain from worshipping their gods.[1]

Amávásya:—On the 15th day of the dark half of every month, oblations are given to the *Manes* of the dead.[2] The commencement of a good deed, journey to a distant place, and the ploughing of land are postponed on the no-moon day of a month.[3] Sanyásis are enjoined to get their beard shaved on the *Páurnima* and *Amávásya* days only.[4]

People do not set out on a journey on the following *tithis*, regarding them as *rikta* (unfruitful or inauspicious):—

Chaturthi, *Navami* and *Chaturdashi*.[5]

The Chándráyana Vrata:—Widows fast on the no-moon day of a month. They are required to regulate their diet in such an increasing proportion that on the next full moon day they should have a full meal. The reverse process follows for a fortnight after, so that they observe an absolute fast on the following no-moon day.[6]

People have various ideas about the cause of the eclipses of the sun and the moon. Some say that the sun and the moon are superior deities, and that the demons Ráhu and Ketu who belong to the caste of Mángs attempt to touch them and to devour them. Others believe that the planets Ráhu and Ketu stand in the path of the Sun and the Moon and thereby darkness is caused on the earth. It is believed that about 5 hours before the commencement of the obscuration, in the case of the Sun and about 4 hours in the case of the Moon, the *Vedha* or malign influence of the monsters begins and during the period till the whole eclipse is over a strict fast is observed. At the commencement of the eclipse, as well as at its close, people bathe. Some sit on a low wooden stool with a rosary in their hands repeating the names of the gods, or the *gáyatri* or some of the *mantras*. But those who want to acquire the art of magic or witch-craft or the power of removing the evil effects of snake-poison, or scorpion sting, go to a lonely place on the riverside, and there standing in water repeat the *mantras* taught to them by their *guru* or teacher. People give alms to Mahárs and Mángs on this occasion, and therefore persons of this class go about the streets saying loudly "Give us alms and the eclipse will be over" *De dán suté girán*.

A strict fast is observed on an eclipse day, but children and pregnant women who cannot bear the privation are given something to eat under a *sike*. The eclipse time is so inauspicious that children and animals born at that time are considered unlucky.[7] Sometimes an eclipse cannot be observed owing to the intervention of clouds. On that occasion the people of the Konkan resort to the following expedient in order to ascertain whether the luminary is eclipsed or not. They take a potful of water and hold in it a *musal*. If it stands in the pot unsupported it is regarded as indicative of the existence of an eclipse. Mángs, Mahárs, etc., are supposed to be the descendants of Ráhu and Ketu; and for this reason gifts are made to them in charity on an eclipse day.[8]

The people of the Thána District believe that corn grows abundantly in a year that witnesses many eclipses.[9]

The popular cause of an eclipse in the Kolába district, is the *Girha*, a minor deity which is said to wander through the sky and swallow the Sun and the Moon when

1 School Master, Anjarle, Ratnágiri.
2 School Master, Bašani, Ratnágiri.
3 School Master, Pendur, Ratnágiri.
4 School Master, Rájápur, Ratnágiri.
5 School Master, Adivare, Ratnágiri.
6 School Master, Ubhádánda, Ratnágiri.
7 School Master, Khetwádi, A.V. School, Bombay.
8 School Master, Khetwadi, A.V. School, Bombay.
9 School Master, Padaghe, Thána.

they cross his path.[1] Besides the mythological story regarding the cause of an eclipse, the people of the Ratnágiri District also believe that the *Girha* throws his shadow on the sun and the moon, when he comes to demand his dues from them.[2] The Konkan villagers, on an eclipse day, strike barren trees with a pestle,[3] in order that they may bear fruits and flowers. A barren woman is also beaten with the same motive. Similarly many other superstitious beliefs are connected with an eclipse. Pregnant women are not allowed to see the eclipse of the sun or the moon, nor are they to engage in cutting, sewing, etc. as this is believed to be injurious to the child in the womb.[4] The eclipse time is supposed to be the most suitable to learn *mantras* or incantations.[5] The *mantris* also mutter incantations during an eclipse in a naked condition.[6] The people who believe that the eclipses are caused by the influence of the planets *Ráhu* and *Ketu* offer prayers to *Ráhu* on the lunar eclipse day and to Ketu on the solar eclipse day.[7]

The planets and stars are worshipped by the Hindus. It is believed that a person who is to die within six months cannot see the polar star. From the movements of the planets past and future events of one's career are foretold by Bráhman and other astrologers. And as it is believed that man's good and bad luck are dependant upon the influence of the planets, offerings of various kinds are made and sacrifices performed for securing the favour of the *Navagrahas* or the nine planets. In order to avert the effect of the evil influence of certain planets people sometimes wear rings of those precious stones which are supposed to be the favourites of the planets.

The rainbow is called *Indra dhanushya* or the Indra's bow, and it is believed that if the rain-bow appears in the east, it indicates the coming of more rain, and if it appears in the west it is a sure sign of the close of the monsoon.

The milky way is believed to be the heavenly Ganges. Well known tradition relates how Wáman (the 5th incarnation of Vishnu) went to Bali the king of the lower regions and asked him to give him land measuring three feet only. The king consented, whereupon the god Wáman enlarged his body to such an extent that by his one footstep he occupied the whole earth and by the second he occupied heaven. Upon this the god Brahma worshipped the foot of the god Vishnu which was in heaven, and from that foot sprang the heavenly Ganges which flows in heaven and is called Dudha Ganga or the milky Ganges.

The worship of stars and planets is in vogue among Konkan Hindu families of the higher castes. The polar star in particular is seen and worshipped by the bride and the bridegroom after the ceremony at the marriage altar is over.[8] A very interesting story is connected with the polar star. By the great power of his penance the sage Vishvámitra despatched king Trishanku to Heaven, but the gods hurled him down. Thereupon Vishvámitra became enraged and began to create a new heaven. Hindu mythological books say that he thus created the sages Vashista, Angiras, Pulah, Pulastya, Rutu, Atri, and Marichi, and stationed Trishanku in the sky. The *Nava-grahas* or the nine planets are worshipped before the commencement of all important ceremonies.[9] A cluster of seven stars called the *Sapta-rishis* are worshipped by men at the time of the *Shrávani* ceremony, while women worship them on the 5th day of the bright half of

[1] School Master, Poládpur, Kolába.
[2] School Master, Masuri, Ratnágiri.
[3] School Master, Kalse, Ratnagiri.
[4] School Master, Vijayadurg, Ratnágiri.
[5] School Master, Makhanele, Ratnágiri.
[6] School Master, Ubhádánda, Ratnágiri.
[7] School Master, Makhanele, Ratnágiri.
[8] School Master, Makhanele, Ratnágiri.
[9] School Master, Devarukh, Ratnágiri.

Bhádrapada. [1] These *Sapta-rishis* are said to have been created by the God Brahma from his own body; and teaching them the four Vedas, he handed them over to them and asked them to regulate the affairs of the world.[2]

Some people of the Ratnágiri District believe that the rain-bow is the bow used by Ráma, the hero of the Rámáyana. Its appearance on the east is regarded by them as symptomatic of the approach of rain, while its appearance on the west is equivalent to the departure of rain.[3]

The short duration of the rain-bow is held to indicate an excessive fall of rain while its long duration forbodes a scarcity of rain. [4] The appearance of the rain-bow on a river is supposed to indicate the approach of rain, while its appearance on a mountain means the departure of rain.[5] Of the two bows of which the rain-bow seems to be composed, the larger is believed to belong to Ráma, and the smaller to Lakshman. [6] Since the God Indra is supposed to send rain, the *Indradhanushya* (the rain-bow) is regarded as a sign of the advent of rain.[7]

By some Hindus it is believed that the milky way is a heavenly river which is a favourite bathing place of the gods.[8] Others suppose it to be a branch of the celestial Ganges which is said to have been brought down upon this earth by king Bhagiratha.[9] Some persons, however, believe that since the great sage Agastya is said to reside at Rámeshwar in the southern direction, the Ganges (the milky way) runs through the sky to the south in order to bathe him. Sometimes the milky way is believed to be a white cloud.[10]

On the authority of the Mahákála Nirván Tantra, some people of the Thána District believe that a person who cannot get a view of the polar star will die within six months; while others substitute the *Arundhati* star for the polar star and determine the duration of life of a diseased person by the same process. [11]

The people of the Thána District believe that the rain-bow is caused by the accumulation of moisture in the air.[12] The rain-bow is said to consecrate the region over which it appears [13]. The appearance of the rain-bow in the morning is supposed to forbode the approach of rain.[14]

Some people of the Kolába District believe that the holy persons such as Káshyapa, Arundhati and other sages, who lived on this earth in ancient times are seen shining in the sky by the sacred lustre of their powers.[15] Hindu women worship the planets Budha and Guru (Mercury and Jupiter) in the month of Shravan.[16]

The *Sapta-rishis* are somewhere called *Khatale* and *Bájale* (cot)[17]. The rain-bow is held by some to be the symbol of Ráma and Lakshman, who visit the world in that form with the view of watching its proceedings. Others, however, believe that it represents God Indra who assumes that form to see how his orders are executed by his subordinates.[18] The rain-bow is said to foretell good if it appears either at the beginning or end of the rainy season, while its appearance at any other time is supposed to forbode evil.[19]

[1] School Master, Makhanele, Ratnágiri.
[2] School Master, Pendur, Ratnágiri.
[3] School Master, Basani, Ratnágiri.
[4] School Master, Makhanele, Ratnágiri.
[5] School Master, Navare, Ratnágiri.
[6] School Master, Adivare, Ratnágiri.
[7] School Master, Malgund, Ratnágiri.
[8] School Master, Kankavli, Ratnágiri.
[9] School Master, Makhanele, Ratnágiri.
[10] School Master, Basani, Ratnágiri.
[11] School Master, Agáshi and Arnála, Thána.
[12] School Master, Rai, Thána.
[13] School Master, Badlapur, Thána.
[14] School Master, Mokhada, Thána.
[15] School Master, Chaul, Kolába.
[16] School Master, Kasu, Kolába.
[17] School Master, Vavasi, Kolába.
[18] School Master, Chaul, Kolába.
[19] School Master, Vavanje, Kolába.

Hindus regard the earth as one of their important deities and worship it on various occasions. It is enjoined upon Bráhmans to worship it daily at the time of their *Sandhya* rite, as well as while performing the *Shrávani* ceremony.[1] The people of the Ratnágiri District pray to the earth as soon as they leave their bed in the morning.[2] The earth is required to be worshipped at the time of laying the foundation-stone of a house, as well as at the time of bringing into use a newly built house.[3] Since it is held unholy to sleep on the bare ground, those whose parents die, sleep on a woollen cloth on the ground till their parents anniversary is over.[4] Wanprastas, Sanyásis, and Bráhmans are required to sleep on the ground.[5] Some pious men sleep on the bare ground during the *Cháturmás* (the four months of the rainy season),at the expiry of which they present a bed to a Bráhman.[6] It is enjoined upon a prince to sleep on the bare ground on the eve of the coronation day.[7]

Widows and women are required to sleep on the ground during their monthly courses. Women whose husbands are away are also to do the same.[8] In the Ratnágiri District *Katkaris*, on the day on which they wish to be possessed by a particular deity or spirit, are required to sleep on the earth.[9] When people are on the point of death, they are made to lie on blades of darbha grass placed on the earth.[10] The performer of a sacrifice as well as one who has observed a vow are to sleep on the ground.[11] The following articles should not be allowed to touch the earth, viz ; pearls, the *Shaligram* stone, an image of the god Vishnu, the *linga* of Shiva, a conchshell, the sacred thread of a Bráhman, flowers intended for worship, basil leaves, and Govardan.[12]

The following lines are repeated in the morning before setting foot to the ground[13]:—

O Goddess! who is clothed (surrounded) by the sea, whose breasts are mountains, and who is the wife of Vishnu, I bow down to thee; please forgive the touch of my feet. O Goddess Earth! who art born by the power of Vishnu, whose surface is of the colour of a conch shell and who art the store house of innumerable jewels, I bow down to thee.

Some women of the Thána District worship the earth daily during the *Cháturmás* (four months of the rainy season), at the end of which they give a Bráhman a piece of land or the money equivalent of it[14]. Persons who perform a particular rite, *e. g.*, the *Solásomavár-vrata* (a vow observed on sixteen successive Mondays) are required to sleep on the bare ground.[15] At the sowing and harvest time, farmers appease the earth by offering it cocoanuts, fowls, rice mixed with curd, etc.[16] The blood of a king and the balls of rice given to the *manes* of the dead are not allowed to touch the ground. People convey to a distant place the water of the Ganges, without placing it on the ground.[17]

The earth is required to be worshipped before taking a portion of it for sacrificial purposes.[18] A vessel containing water over which incantations have been repeated is not allowed to touch the ground.[19] On the 15th day of the bright half of *Ashvin* every farmer prepares some sweetmeats in his house, and takes them to his farm. There he gathers five

1 School Master, Nevare, Ratnágiri.
2 School Master, Kasba, Sangameshwar, Ratnágiri.
3 School Master, Adivare, Ratnágiri.
4 School Master, Pendhur, Ratnágiri.
5 School Master, Devarukh, Ratnágiri.
6 School Master, Málgund, Ratnágiri.
7 School Master, Ratnágiri.
8 School Master, Vijayadurg, Ratnágiri.
9 School Master, Chiplun, Ratnágiri.
10 School Master, Kankava, Ratnágiri.
11 School Master, Masure, Ratnágiri.
12 School Master, Chiplun. Ratnágiri.
13 School Master, Khetwadi, A. V. S., Bombay.
14 School Master, Anjur, Thána.
15 School Master, Rai, Thána.
16 School Master, Shahápur, Thána.
17 School Master, Bhuvan, Thána.
18 School Master, Chauk, Kolába.
19 School Master, Vavanje, Kolába.

stones, worships them, and offers the sweetmeats to the earth. Afterwards he takes a portion of the food and scatters it over the farm. His family then gather there and take a hearty meal. In the evening the person who carried the food to the farm, picks up some grains of barley and puts them into a basket. On return home the grains are thrown over the house.[1]

Various conflicting notions are entertained regarding thunder and lightning. The people of the Ratnágiri District believe that the clouds are animals that roar. When these animals emit water it bursts forth on account of the circular motion of the winds called Chanda and Munda. This bursting is supposed to produce thunder and lightning.[2] Somewhere thunder and lightning are said to be the signals given by the god Indra, to birds, beasts, etc., of the setting in of the rainy season.[3] Some people believe that the god Indra sends rain through his elephants who, being excited, make a noise like thunder.[4]

Others regard the thunder as the roaring of the elephant of the gods, while sucking sea-water. The thunder is also believed to be the roaring of the god Varuna, the king of the clouds.[5] The boys of the Ratnágiri District believe that thunder is a sign of the wedding ceremonies performed in the heavenly houses of the gods.[6] Some Mahomedans believe that an angel called Mekail has control over the rain. To cause a fall of rain Mekail strikes the clouds with a whip of lightning. The clouds then utter a cry, and this is the cause of thunder.[7] Some people of the Thána District believe that there are big stones in the sky which strike against each other owing to the force of the wind, and produce thunder. The dashing of these stones against each other also generates lightning.[8]

In the Kolába District it is believed that thunder is the military band of the king of clouds and lightning is his banner.[9] Lightning is said to be produced by the fighting of celestial elephants; while thunder is heard when they pour out water.[10] Some people think that thunder is the noise of the feet of the elephants (clouds) that give rain; lightning is also said to be generated from their foot fall.[11] The clouds are supposed to be the messengers of gods, lightning being the manifestation of Divine power. The gods are said to confine these messengers from the *nakshatra* of Ardra to the *nakshatra* of Hasti, in which latter *nakshatra* they again begin to roar.[12]

Thunder is supposed to take place when the god Indra draws his bow; while lightning is said to be produced when the same god strikes his adamant against a mountain.[13]

In the Ratnágiri District it is believed that earthquake occurs whenever the thousand headed Shesha shakes its head.[14] It is said that at one time a demon named Gayásur became very troublesome, and all the gods held him down by standing on his body. Thereupon the demon requested all the gods to remain on his body for ever. Occasionally this Gayásur shakes his body and this causes the earthquake.[15] Some people believe that the earth trembles of its own accord when sins accumulate upon it.[16] Others hold that the earthquake takes place in the hollow parts of the earth.[17] Some people, however, believe that since the earth floats upon water, it naturally quakes at times.[18]

[1] School Master, Akol, Kolába.
[2] School Master, Pendur, Ratnágiri.
[3] School Master, Kasba, Sangameshwar, Ratnágiri.
[4] School Master, Makhanele, Ratnágiri.
[5] School Master, Masure, Ratnágiri.
[6] School Master, Basani, Ratnágiri.
[7] School Master, Chiplun, Ratnágiri.
[8] School Master, Anjur, Thána.
[9] School Master, Varsai, Kolába.
[10] School Master, Chaul, Kolába.
[11] School Master, Varsai, Kolába.
[12] School Master, Poládpur, Kolába.
[13] School Master, Chauk, Kolába.
[14] School Master, Chiplun, Ratnágiri.
[15] School Master, Palspot, Ratnágiri.
[16] School Master, Pendur, Ratnágiri.
[17] School Master, Murbád, Thâna.
[18] School Master, Bhuvan, Thána.

The Hindus being element worshippers naturally hold in reverence certain rivers, ponds, etc. In the Ratnágiri District the spring at Rájápur, called the *Rájápurchi Ganga* is considered very sacred. It flows from the roots of a Banyan tree. There are fifteen *Kundas* or ponds, and the principal *Kunda* always remains filled with water. On occasions a big *játra* fair is held and people from distant places come to bathe and worship at the spring.[1] Some people believe that many of the lakes, springs, etc., situated in the Kolhápur State are sacred.[2] A spring or rivulet that flows to the east is considered specially sacred. It is called a *Surya-Vansi* spring, and it is considered meritorious to bathe in it.[3] In the village of Kunkauli in the Ratnágiri District if a person is bitten by a snake or other poisonous reptile, no medicine is administered to him, but holy water brought from the temple of the village goddess is given to him to drink, and it is said that the patient is thus cured.[4] The water fall at Maral near Devarkuha, where the river *Bán* takes its rise, is held sacred.[5] At Shivam in the Ratnágiri District the people use the *tirtha* of a deity as medicine for diseases due to poison. They say that it is the sole remedy they apply in such cases.[6] There are ponds at Manora in the Goa State, and Vetore in the Sávantwádi State, the water of which is used as medicine for the cure of persons suffering from the poison of snakes, mice, spiders, and scorpions.[7] When a well is dug, the people call a Bráhman priest to consecrate it. The Bráhman takes cow's urine, milk, curds, ghi, sandle paste, flowers, basil leaves, and rice, and mixes them with water, and after repeating sacred *mantras* over the water, throws the mixture into the well. After this ceremony, the people are at liberty to drink water from the well.[8]

Before a well is dug, an expert is consulted to ascertain the place where a spring flows. A well is then dug, after offering a sacrifice to the spirits and deities that happen to dwell at that spot. A dinner is given to Bráhmans after the well is built.[9] A golden cow is often thrown into a newly built well as an offering to the water deities.[10] There is a well at Mandangad, the water of which serves as medicine to cure the poison of snakes and other reptiles.[11]

It is believed that there is a class of wicked water nymphs called *Asara* who generally dwell in wells, ponds, or rivers, far from the habitation of men. Whenever these nymphs come across a lonely man or woman entering a well, pond, etc., they carry that person under water. The village of Mith-Báv in the Ratnágiri District is a well-known resort of these Asarás, and many instances are given by the villagers of persons being drowned and carried off in the river by these wicked nymphs. A tank in the village of Hindalem in the same district has a similar reputation.[12] The people of the Konkan believe that water nymphs are sometimes seen in the form of women near wells, rivers, and ponds.[13] Some say that the water nymphs and water spirits confer objects desired by worshippers if they are propitiated by prayers.[14]

There are seven *kundas*, ponds, at Nirmal in the Thána District, forming a large lake. This

[1] School Master, Ratnágiri.
[2] School Master, Phonde, Ratnágiri.
[3] School Master, Wanhavli, Ratnágiri.
[4] School Master, Bandivade, Budruk, Ratnágiri.
[5] School Master, Makhanele, Ratnágiri.
[6] School Master, Masure, Ratnágiri.
[7] School Master, Ubhádánda, Ratnágiri.
[8] School Master, Mith-Báv, Ratnágiri.
[9] School Master, Basani, Ratnágiri.
[10] School Master, Masure, Ratnágiri.
[11] School Master, Basani, Ratnágiri.
[12] School Master, Mith-Báv, Ratnágiri.
[13] School Master, Malgund, Ratnágiri.
[14] School Master, Devarukh, Ratnágiri.

lake is said to have been formed from the blood of the demon Vimalásur. At Sháhápur there is a holy spring of hot water under a *Pipal* tree. It is called *Ganga.*[1] There are *kundas*, pools, of hot water in the *Vaitarna* river in the Thána District, in which people bathe on the 13th day of the dark half of *Chaitra*.[2] There are also springs of hot water on the bank of the Surya river at Vajreshvari and at Koknere, in the Thána District.[3] A handful of corn, if thrown into the hot water *kundas* at Tungar, is said to be boiled at once.[4] It is held holy to bathe in the *kundas*, of hot water that are situated in the rivers Tánsa and Bánganga in the Thána District.[5] The water of a well which is drawn without touching the earth or without being placed upon the ground is given as medicine for indigestion. Similarly the water of seven tanks, or at least of one pond, in which lotuses grow is said to check the virulence of measles, small-pox, etc.[6] A bath in a certain tank in the Mahim *taluka* is said to cure persons suffering from the itch, and water purified by repeating incantations over it is also said to be a good remedy for the same disease.[7]

The water of a tank or a well is supposed to be wholesome to a person of indifferent health, if given to him to drink without placing it upon the ground.[8] Some people believe that the water of the Ganges is so holy and powerful that if bows are thrown into it they are instantly reduced to powder.[9] The repair of lakes, caravansaries, temples, etc., is held more meritorious than their actual erection.[10] It is enjoined upon a man to perform a certain rite if he wishes to relinquish his right of ownership over a well or tank, and after this rite is performed, it can be utilized for public purposes. But no ceremony is required to be performed if a well is dug for the benefit of the public.[11]

The people of the Thána District believe that water nymphs reside in every reservoir of water.[12] Some people, however, believe that the water nymphs dwell in those lakes in which lotuses grow. These nymphs are said to do harm to children and young women, especially when they set out for a walk accompanied by their brother Gavala. They are unusually dangerous.[13] The people worship the images of the following seven water nymphs or *apsaras*, viz., Machhi, Kurmi, Karkati, Darduri, Jatupi, Somapa and Makari.[14]

The following places are said to be inhabited by water spirits:—the channel of Kalamba, the tanks of Sopara and Utaratal and the lake called Tambra-tirtha at Bassein [15]. Water nymphs are supposed to drown a person who tries to save another fallen into water.[16] A species of small men named *Uda*, otherwise called water-spirits, are said to dwell in water and subsist on fishes.[17] The spirits called Khais and Mhashya are supposed to reside in water.[18]

The river Sávitri in the Kolába District takes its rise near Mahábaleshwar and is considered very sacred. The following traditionary account is given of its origin. The god Brahma had two wives, Sávitri and Gáyatri. A dispute having arisen between them, they both jumped over a precipice. Sávitri assumed the form of a river and fell into the sea near Bánkot. Gáyatri, on the other hand, concealed herself in the river Sávitri and manifested herself as a spring near Harihareshwar in the Janjira State.[19] A man is

[1] School Masters, Agáshi and Arnála, Thána.
[2] School Master, Murbád, Thána.
[3] School Master, Málád, Thána.
[4] School Master, Anjur, Thána.
[5] School Master, Wáda, Thána.
[6] School Masters, Agáshi and Arnála, Thána.
[7] School Master, Anjur, Thána.
[8] School Master, Saloli, Thána.
[9] School Masters, Agáshi and Arnála, Thána.
[10] School Master, Kinhavali, Thána.
[11] School Master, Rái, Thána.
[12] School Master, Khativali, Thána.
[13] School Masters, Agáshi and Arnála, Thána.
[14] School Master, Murbád, Thána.
[15] School Masters, Agáshi and Arnála, Thána.
[16] School Master, Bhuvan, Thána.
[17] School Masters, Wáda, Thána.
[18] School Master, Sháhápur, Thána.
[19] School Master, Poládpur, Kolába.

said to be released from re-birth if he takes a bath in the *kund* (pond) named Katkale-tirtha near Násik.[1] Bows are said to be reduced to powder if thrown into a certain *kund* at Uddhar-Rámeshwar in the Sudhagad taluka.[2] *Kupotsarga* is defined to be the digging of a well for the benefit of the public and abandoning one's right of ownership over it.[3]

A pond near Khopoli in the Kolába district is held very sacred. The following story is related in connection with it. The villagers say that the water nymphs in the pond used to provide pots for marriage festivities if a written application were made to them a day previous to the wedding. The pots were, however, required to be returned within a limited time. But one man having failed to comply with this condition, they have ceased to lend pots. Another interesting story is associated with the same pond. It is as follows. A man had fallen into the pond and was taken to the abode of the nymphs. He was, however, returned by them after a few days on the understanding that he would be recalled if he spoke of what he had seen there. One day he communicated to the people the good things that he enjoyed there, and to the surprise of all he was found dead immediately after.[4] Water nymphs are said to reside in a pond at Varsai in the Kolába district. Consequently persons that are held unclean, *e.g.*, women in their monthly course, etc., are not allowed to touch it. The nymphs of the same lake were once said to lend pots on festive occasions.[5] It is said that the water nymphs used to provide ornaments for marriage and other ceremonies, if returned within a prescribed period. But some people having failed to return them, they ceased to lend them.[6]

A spirit called Girha is supposed to reside in water. It is said to make mischief with man in a variety of ways by enticing him into deep water.[7] The Jakrin is said to be a deity residing in water.[8] Persons drowned in water are believed to become water-spirits, and to trouble innocent passers-by.[9]

A mountain near the village Pule, in the district of Ratnágiri is held sacred on account of the residence of the god Ganpati at that place. For this reason people walk round the mountain and worship it. Tradition says that Ganpati was at first at Gule in the Ratnágiri district, but on account of the sanctity of the place being violated by some wicked persons the god transferred his residence to Pule. At Gule there is still a very beautiful temple of Ganpati, though it is now in a dilapidated condition.[10] The cave of the sage Much-kund near Machal on the Sahyádri mountain is considered sacred. In the Konkan it is not held sinful to ascend a mountain or a hill, though to sit upon its summit is considered sinful.[11] The hill of Mirya near Ratnágiri is considered sacred. This hill is believed to be a particle (*miri*) of the mythological mountain Dronagiri.[12]

A hill near Dhárávi in the Thána District is consecrated by the temple of a goddess upon the top. This goddess is said to preserve ships at sea, and people are occasionally possessed by her. It is said that a Roman Catholic priest met instantaneous death on having insulted her.[13]

The hill of Mahálakshmi in the Dahánu táluka is held sacred. The villagers consider it dangerous to ascend this hill.[14] On the hill of the same name is a temple of the goddess Jivadhani, who is said to preserve children from small-pox. The following

1 School Master, Chauk, Kolába.
2 School Master, Wavasi, Kolába.
3 School Master, Varsai, Kolába.
4 School Master, Khopoli, Kolába.
5 School Master, Wavasi, Kolába.
6 School Master, Chauk, Kolába.
7 School Master, Chaul, Kolába.
8 School Master, Akol, Kolába.
9 School Master, Vavasi, Kolába.
10 School Master, Basani, Ratnágiri.
11 School Master, Bándivade, Budruk, Ratnágiri.
12 School Master, Málgund, Ratnágiri.
13 School Masters, Agáshi and Arnála, Thána.
14 School Master, Dahánu, Thána.

story is told in connection with the goddess. A person in need of money used to place before her image as large a heap of flowers as he wanted gold, stating that he would return the gold when he had done with it. He used then to go home and return on an appointed day for the gold, which was sure to be found where he had placed the heap of flowers. Once a man failed to return the gold, and thenceforth the goddess withheld her bounty. There is no door to the temple of this goddess. It is only through a hole in a big stone that one can have a view of her image. Sweet scent is said to be continually emitted from this hole. The goddess is said to have fastened the door of her temple for the following reason. One day the goddess was walking at the foot of the hill at night. A cowherd who happened to be there was bewitched by her matchless beauty and fell a prey to evil desire. He pursued her to the top of the hill, when the goddess, divining his motive, fastened the door of her temple with a prodigious stone. On the same hill is a cattle shed in which fresh cow-dung is said to be always found. This place being inaccessible to cows and other quadrupeds, the people believe that the goddess keeps a cow of her own.[1]

The hill of Tungar is consecrated by the temple of a certain goddess upon it. There is also a very famous hill near Arnála, called the hill of Buddha. This hill was once the seat of a king belonging to the weaver caste. Recently a pond was discovered upon it, in which was found a stone-box containing a begging-pot and a diamond. A great fair is held annually on the hill of Motmávali near Bandra in the Thána district. The devotees of the deity are Hindus, Parsis, and Christians. It is said this goddess was once worshipped by Hindus only. A Bráhman is the *pujári* of the *Pir* on the hill of Bába Malang near Kalyán. It is said that the *Pir* has declared that no Moslem *pujári* should worship him. The Hindus and Moslems worship him alike.[2]

Bráhmans do not cross the top of a mountain without stopping for a short time before ascending the summit.[3]

At a short distance from Chaul in the Kolába District is a hill dedicated to the god Dattatraya, in whose honour a great fair is held annually. The following story is told in connection with this hill. In ancient times a Bráhman used to practise austerities on this hill near a *Tulsi* plant (the place on which the present temple stands). He used to spend the whole day there, but returned home at nightfall. On his way home fearful scenes were often presented to him, and in his dreams he was asked not to go there any more. But the Bráhman was obdurate. He persisted in his resolution to practise austerities for a number of years, and at last succeeded in obtaining a personal interview with the god Dattatraya, who commanded him to bow down to his feet (*páduka*). From that time pious men live on this hill and offer their prayers to the god Dattatraya. Nearly four hundred steps have been constructed for the ascent of this hill, and additional steps are being built every year. Here also are some springs of pure water. It is worth while to note that the *pujári* of this god is a Shudra by caste.[4] On the north-east side of the hill dedicated to the god Dattatraya stands the temple of the goddess Hingláj. To the north of this temple are four caves, while to the west is a deep den resembling a well, through which a lane appears to have been dug. This is said to be the road excavated by the Pándavas to enable them to go to Kási.[5] At a distance of

[1] School Masters, Agáshi and Arnála, Thána.
[2] School Masters, Agáshi and Arnála, Thána.
[3] School Master, Umbargaum, Thána.
[4] School Master, Chaul, Kolába.
[5] School Master, Chaul, Kolába.

two miles from Akóla in the Kolába District is a hill called Mallikárjun. This is said to be a small stone fallen from the mythological mountain Dronagiri. This hill is said to contain many medical herbs.[1] The hill at Kankeshwar near Alibág is held sacred, and tradition says that in ancient times it had golden dust upon it.[2] A cave at Ambivali near Karjat in the Kolába district consists of seven rooms, one of which is spacious enough to accommodate five hundred persons. In the same *taluka* there is another cave at Kondhavane.[3]

The gods Indra and Varuna are supposed to send rain; but it is believed that the god Shiva in chief has the power of causing the fall of rain, and for this reason whenever there is a scarcity of rain people pour water over the *linga* of Shiva until the whole *linga* is submerged.[4] In order that there should be a fall of rain, some people besmear the *linga* of the god Shiva with cooked rice and curds.[5] In the Ratnágiri District, whenever there is a scarcity of rain, people go to the place known as Parashurám Kshetra, and there pray to the god Parashurám to send rain.[6] Sacrifices are also offered to Indra, the god of rain, in order that there should be plenty of rain. Some believe that there are certain *mantris* or enchanters who by the power of their *mantras* are able to prevent the fall of rain.[7]

In the Ratnágiri District the following ceremony is performed by the lower castes such as Kunbis, etc., to avert drought. All the male villagers assemble together at an appointed place, and there they select one of them as their *Gowala-deva.* All of them then go about in the village from house to house. The owner of every house sprinkles water over the assembly, and curds and butter-milk over the body of the Gowala-deva. They are also given some *shidha* consisting of rice, pulse, vegetables, etc. After visiting most of the houses in the village, the assembly headed by the Gowala-deva go to the bank of a river. Here they cook the food, offer it first to the Gowala-deva and then partake of the remainder as a *prasád* from the Gowala-deva.[8] Some people make an image of the sage *Shringarishi* for the purpose of causing the fall of rain.[9] Others make an image of Dhondal-deva in order that there should be plenty of rain.[10] Sometimes people repeat *mantras* addressed to Parjanya (rain) so that rain should fall.[11] The goddess Navachandika is worshipped in order that there should be rain. The *Kunbis* perform a peculiar rite for checking the fall of rain. They ask a person born in the months of *Jyestha, Ashádh, Shrávan* or *Bhádrapad* to fetch some rain-water in an *alu* leaf, and this is fastened to the eaves of thatched houses by means of a string. Note that, if this rite is to be performed in the month of *Jyestha,* a person born in that month only is required and no other; and so forth.[12] In order to check an excessive fall of rain the villagers sometimes ask a boy to take off his clothes and then to catch rain-water in the leaves of the *alu* plant. The leaves containing the water are then tied to the eaves of the house.[13] The people say that during the rule of the Peshwás there was a class of *mantris* who had the power of causing a failure of rain.[14] To check the fall of rain, some people ask naked boys to throw burning

[1] School Master, Akol, Kolába.
[2] School Master, Sasavane, Kolába.
[3] School Master, Chauk, Kolába.
[4] School Master, Mith Bav, Ratnágiri.
[5] School Master, Málvan, Ratnágiri.
[6] School Master, Anjarle, Ratnágiri.
[7] School Master, Kankavli, Ratnágiri.
[8] School Master, Phonde, Ratnágiri.
[9] School Master, Chiplun, Ratnágiri.
[10] School Master, Nevare, Ratnágiri.
[11] School Master, Ratnágiri.
[12] School Master, Ubhádánda, Ratnágiri.
[13] School Master, Bándevade, Budruk, Ratnágiri.
[14] School Master, Málvan, Ratnágiri.

coals into the rain water.[1] *Irale* (a protection against rain, made of the leaves of trees) is kept in the rain upside down, the goddess Holika is worshipped, the boughs of the *Avali* tree are conveyed to a place where four roads meet and stones are heaped over it, and eaves of thatched houses are beaten by boys who do not wear clothes, all these being done by the villagers with a view to preventing an excessive fall of rain.[2]

The people of the Thána District believe that distinct deities preside over distinct seasons, *e.g.*, Mars presides over the spring (Vasant), Venus over summer (Grishma), the moon over autumn (Varsha), Mercury over *sharat*, Saturn over winter (Hemant and Shishir).[3] When the people are in need of rain they say to the god of rain "Let us have plenty of rain tomorrow and we will give thee, Oh! God of rain! rice mixed with curd." The same offer is made to the god of rain even when they do not want it. In order that there should be no scarcity of rain, some people perform the rites of *Laghu-rudra* and *Mahá-rudra*.[4] The following measure if adopted is said to cause rain. The villagers go from house to house with boughs of the *Limb* tree on their heads, and water is then poured upon them by the inmates.[5] The fall of rain is supposed to cease if a person born in the month of *Fálgun* extinguishes burning coals in rainwater when his garments have been removed.[6]

Some stones are supposed to have influence over rain fall. There is a big stone at Varasai in the Kolába District on which are drawn certain images. The people believe that it rains hard if this stone is held straight, and then swung to and fro.[7] Some people perform the following rite known as the *Dhondiljagya*. They ask a person of the Kaikádi or Vadar caste to remain naked and break the string round his waist. A small image of black earth is made and placed upon his head. The boy then conveys the image from house to house in the village. A woman in each house sprinkles water over the image while the boy dances saying "*Dhondil gajya, Páus gajya.*" It is believed that it rains in the direction in which the water sprinkled falls. A person who accompanies the boy gathers corn at every house. A dinner is then prepared, and the people of the caste to which the boy belongs, partake of it heartily. It is also said that making water in a standing posture causes the fall of rain.[8] The god Rámeshwar at Chaul in the Kolába District is said to have control over rain. In the temple of this god there is a *parjanya-kund* (pond) which is opened after performing a sacred rite, if there be a scarcity of rain. There are also other *kundas* in the temple, viz., *Váyu-kund* and *Agni-kund*, but no occasion has yet arisen to open them.[9] Some people believe that the god Agni regulates the seasons[10].

Eaves of thatched houses are cleansed with a brush made from the leaves of cocoanut trees in order that a fall of rain should be prevented.[11]

The ceremonies of Haritálika, Rishi-Panchami, Vata-Sávitri, Vaná-Shasthi, Mangalá-Gouri, Shital-Saptami are to be performed by women alone.[12] Similarly, the ceremonies of Mahálakshmi, Vasubáras, Shivá-mutha, and a rite on the Makar Sankrant day are performed by women exclusively.[13]

[1] School Master, Dábhol, Ratnágiri.
[2] School Master, Basani, Ratnágiri.
[3] School Masters, Agáshi and Arnála, Thána.
[4] School Master, Murbad, Thána.
[5] School Master, Dahánu, Thána.
[6] School Master, Padaghe, Thána.
[7] School Master, Nágothana, Kolába.
[8] School Master, Akol, Kolába.
[9] School Master, Chaul, Kolába.
[10] School Master, Apte, Kolába.
[11] School Master, Khetwadi, A.V.S., Bombay.
[12] School Master, Málvan, Ratnágiri.
[13] School Master, Málgund, Ratnágiri.

The rite of *Rishi-Panchami* is performed on the 5th day of the bright-half of *Bhádrapad* to make amends for sins committed without knowledge. On this day women go to a river, a well, or some other sacred place, cleanse their teeth with the leaves of the *Aghâda* plant, and take baths with something on the head. They then take some stones from that place and worship them as *Rishis*. On the conclusion of the worship, they partake of fruits. On the *Vrata-Sávitri* day women worship a banyan tree or its boughs. The ceremony falls on the 15th day of the bright half of *Jyesta*.[1] On the *Haritálika* day *i.e.*, the 3rd day of the bright half of *Bhádrapád*, women make images of earth of Párvati and her two friends and worship them and fast the whole day. The observance of this rite contributes to their good fortune. Even girls of tender years observe this fast. The worship of Mangalá-Gauri is a ceremony performed by married girls for five successive years on every Tuesday of the month of *Shrávan*. Similarly, the goddess Mahálakshmi is worshipped on the 8th day of the bright half of *Ashvin*. On the *Makar Sankránt* day women worship a *sugad* * and present it to a Bráhman.[2] The *Shiva-mutha* consists of a handful of corn offered to the god Shiva by married girls on every Monday in the month of *Shrávan*.[3]

The worship of Shadananda and the Holika Devi and the ceremonies of *Shrávani*, *Shráddha* and *Antyesti* are performed by men alone.[4]

In some families of non-Bráhmans on a particular day, especially on the full-moon day of *Ashvin*, the host and the hostess put off their clothes and perform certain family rites.[5]

The women of the Thána District fast the whole day on the 12th day of the dark half of *Ashvin*. At night they worship a cow, give in charity a calf, and then take their meal. It is to be noted that this ceremony called the *Vasu-dwádasi* is performed by women who have children. On the *Haritálika* day some women live on the leaves of a *Rui* tree.[6]

On the *Somavati-Amávásya* day women worship a *Pipal* tree and offer it a hundred and eight things of one kind.[7] Women desirous of having a son perform a certain rite at midnight, without clothing.[8] If one wishes to have a son, one has to go through a ceremony called the *Hanumán* in a naked state.[9]

The god Kálbhairav is worshipped by a naked person on the *Narka-Chathurdasi* day (14th day of the dark half of *Ashvin*). Those learning the dark lore, e. g., *muth márane*, are also required to remain naked while studying it. They learn this lore on an eclipse day on the bank of a river.[10] The rite called *Somaya* is performed by the host when his clothes are off his body. On a certain Monday in the month of *Shrávan* a lamp of wheat flour is prepared and burned by adding ghi. This lamp is regarded as a deity, and is worshipped solemnly. During the performance of this ceremony as well as the preparation of the requisite food, the host and the hostess are required to remain naked.[11]

[1] School Master, Ubhádánda, Ratnágiri.

* Two earthen pots tied face to face, one of which containing some corn and red and yellow powders.

[2] School Master, Basani, Ratnágiri.

[3] School Master, Malgund, Ratnágiri.

[4] School Master, Málvan, Ratnágiri.

[5] School Master, Makhanele, Ratnágiri.

[6] School Master, Anjur, Thána.

[7] School Master, Badlapur, Kalyan.

[8] School Master, Bhuvan, Thána.

[9] School Master, Bhuvan, Thána.

[10] School Master, Tale, School No. I, Kolába.

[11] School Master, Poládpur, Kolába.

The Swayambhu (unartificial) *linga* of the god Shiva is supposed to have influence over the fall of rain.[1]

The people of the Thána District believe that the following ceremony causes a fall of rain. Stones are taken out of a pool and worshipped. They are then carried to every house in the village, and water is poured upon them by the inmates.[2] There is a temple of the god of clouds at Viranáth in the Thána District.[3]

The appearance of a comet is regarded by the Hindus as symptomatic of a coming evil, *e.g.*, a big war, a great famine, or a terrible contagious disease spreading itself throughout the length and breadth of a country.[4] Some persons think that comets and shooting stars bode evil to the king.[5]

Whenever a great person or a very holy man is about to be born, it is believed that he alights on the earth in the shape of a shooting star. Sometimes a big star falls on the earth, and thereby a noise like that of thunder is produced. When this happens, people believe that a great Rája or a holy saint whose merit has been exhausted is going to be born on earth.[6] The following verse from the *Mrichhakatika Nátak* supports the view in accordance with which orthodox people in the Konkan avoid looking at shooting stars:—

इंद्रधनुष्य आणि गोप्रसूति । नक्षत्रांची अधोगति सत्पुरुषांची प्राणविपत्ति ॥ पाहूं नये साचार ॥ *i.e.*,

The following four things, *viz.*, the rainbow, the fall of shooting stars, the delivery of a cow, and the death-struggle of saints or holy men should not be looked at.[7] It is generally believed by Hindus that a child will immediately be born in the house towards which shooting stars are directed.[8]

1 School Master, Devarukh, Ratnágiri.

2 School Master, Badlapur, Thána.

3 School Masters, Agashi and Arnála, Thána.

4 School Master, Mith Bav, Ratnágiri.

5 School Master, Nivare, Ratnágiri.

6 School Master, Mith Bav, Ratnágiri.

7 School Master, Thána.

8 School Master, Kolába.

CHAPTER II.

THE HEROIC GODLINGS.

In the Konkan the deities of the Hindus are divided into the following five classes, *viz* :—

(1) The *Grámadevatás* or Village deities,

(2) The *Sthánadevatás* or Local deities,

(3) The *Kuladevatás* or Family deities,

(4) The *Ishtadevatás* or Chosen deities, and

(5) The *Wástudevatás* or *Grihadevatás*, that is, the class of deity which presides over the house and is established at the time of the housewarming or *Wástu* ceremony.

The principal *Gráma-devatás* are Hanumán or Máruti, Kálika, Amba, Wághoba, Chedoba, Mhasoba, Bahiroba or Bhairav, Ganesh, Vira, Mhálsa or Maha Lakshmi, Chámunda, Vetál, Khandoba Malhári Jogái, Bhawáni, and Wágeshwari and Shiva. In most villages the chief village god is Máruti or Hanumán, whose temple is situated at the entrance of the village. Máruti is considered to be an *avatár* or incarnation of Shiva, and is held in great reverence by all classes. A festival or *jatra* is held in honour of Hanumán on the bright half of the month of *Chaitra*. On this occasion the temple is decorated with ever-greens, and flowers, the stone image of the god is newly painted or covered with red lead and oil, and garlands of the *Rui* (Gigantic snake wort) flowers are placed round the neck of the image, cocoanuts, plantains, betel-nuts and leaves are offered to the god, camphor is lighted and waved round the image, incense is burnt, cooked food and sweets are offered, and money presents are made. Every worshipper brings with him some oil, red-lead or *Cendur*, a cocoanut, a *vidá-supári*, i.e., two betel leaves, one betel-nut and a copper coin, and a garland of *Rui* flowers. These are given to the temple ministrant, who offers a part of the oil and red lead to the deity, places the garland round the deity's neck, and, breaking the cocoanut into pieces, gives a piece or two to the devotee as the *prasád* or favoured gift of the deity. Saturday is the sacred day of the monkey god Máruti. Every Saturday fresh oil and red lead are offered to the god by the devotees. The *Pujáris* in most of the temples of Máruti are Guravs, Ghádis, Maráthas or Gosávis.

Every Saturday in the month of *Shrávan* (August), called the *Sampat Shaniwár* or the wealth-giving Saturday a special *puja* or worship is performed in the temples of Máruti in Bombay as well as in the Konkan. On this day people fast the whole day and dine in the evening, after offering the god Hanumán or Máruti a preparation of rice and pulse called *khichadi* and cakes made of *udid* flour called *vade.*[1]

There is no village in the Konkan which has not the honour of having a temple of the god Máruti. Máruti is supposed to guard the village against evils of all kinds. Care is therefore taken to build the temple of Máruti at the outskirts of the village.[2] There is a tradition that at the time of leaving the Dandaka forest (the present Maháráshtra), Ráma asked Máruti to reside therein. It is for this reason, the people say, that every village in the Konkan and on the Gháts has a temple of Máruti.[3] The god Máruti is worshipped in the village of Wásind on Tuesdays and Saturdays.[4] In former days it was customary to establish an image of the god Máruti in a newly built castle or fort.[5] Hanumán, the son of Anjani and the wind or Márut, is known for his loyalty to his master

---

[1] School Master, Khetwadi, Bombay.
[2] School Master, Devgád, Ratnágiri.
[3] School Master, Kamathipura, Bombay.
[4] School Master, Washind, Thána.
[5] School Master, Umela, Thána.

and for his bravery. In days gone by he utilized his strength for the protection of Saints, Rishis, Bráhmans and cows, and for this merit he was elevated to the rank of a Hindu god. Every Hindu village or locality is supposed to possess at least one temple of the god Máruti, and in Maháráshtra Máruti is the guardian of every village. He is a *Brahmachari*, or bachelor and is one of the seven heroes who are believed to be *chiranjivis* or immortals.* Máruti is supposed to be the originator of the *Mantra-Shástra*, by the study and repetition of which one obtains strength and superhuman power. Women desirous of getting children go to the temple of Máruti, and there burn before his image lamps made of wheat flour and filled with ghi. The image of Hanumán is represented in temples in two ways, that is (1) Víra Hanumán or Warrior Hanumán, (2) Dása-Hanumán or servant Hanumán. The former is found in a temple consecrated to the worship of the god Hanumán alone, whereas the latter is found in a temple dedicated to the worship of the god Ráma.[1] Since Máruti is the god of strength, gymnasts tie an image of Máruti to their wrists, and they also consecrate an image of Máruti in their gymnasiums. The number eleven is said to be dear and sacred to him because he is believed to be an incarnation of the eleven Rudras. The birth day of the god Máruti which falls on the 15th of the bright half of *Chaitra*, called the *Hanumán Jayanti* day, is celebrated in the Kolhápur District with great reverence. Those who wish to have a son draw the figure of Máruti on a wall in red-lead, and worship it daily with sandal paste, flowers and garlands of *Rui*. Others burn lamps made of wheat flour before the image of the god. Persons who are under the evil influence of the planets, and especially of the planets Saturn, worship the god Hanumán on Saturdays in order to propitiate the planets. On this day they make wreaths of the leaves and flowers of the *Rui* plant and adorn his neck with them. They also offer him *udid* (Phaseolus radiatus) and salt. The story told of Máruti is that Anjani his mother pleased the god Shiva with her penance, and when the god asked her to claim a boon, she requested that Shiva himself should be born as her son. Shiva therefore took birth in her womb and manifested himself as Hanumán or Máruti[2].

The Local deities are generally found in special localities or sacred places called *Kshetras* or *Punya sthánas*. Thus the god Ráma at Násik, Vithoba at Pandharpur, Krishna at Dwárka, Mahálakshmi at Kolwan, Wágreshwari at Nirmal (Thána), Mharloba in the Ratnágiri, Shitala devi at Kelwa Máhim, and Khandoba or Khanderái at Jejuri.

Khanderái is said to be an incarnation of the god Shiva. Khanderái killed the demon Mani-Malla who was devastating the earth, and he is therefore called Mallári or Malhári. Kunbis and lower class Hindus in the Konkan as well as in the Deccan occasionally make a vow to the god Khandoba that if their desire is fulfilled they will offer their first born male or female child to the service of the god. The male child thus dedicated to Khandoba is called Wághya and the female is called Murali. The Wághya and Murali do not engage in any business, but maintain themselves by begging in the streets in the name of the god Khanderái. Though they are not actually married, the Wághyás and Muralis live as husband and wife, and their progeny are also called Wághyas and Muralis. They repeat the sacred cry *jai khanderáyácha Elkot*, and give to people *bel-bhandár* of Khanderái consisting of the sacred *Bel* leaves and turmeric powder. The god Khanderái is the family deity of some Deshasth Bráhmans, who perform a family rite

* The Hindus believe that there are seven heroes who can never die, *i. e.*, 1 Ashwattháma, 2 Bali, 3 Vyása, 4 Hanumán, 5 Bibhíshana, 6 Kripáchárya and 7 Parashurám. The Sanskrit text is:—

अश्वत्थामा बलि व्यासो हनुमंतो बिभीषणः । कृपाचार्यः परशुरामस्सप्तैते चिरजीविनः ॥

1 School Masters, Agáshi and Arnála, Thána.

2 School Master, Samangad, Kolhápur.

called *Tali bharane* तळी भरणें on every *purnima* or full moon day. The rite is as follows :—

A *tali* or plate is filled with cocoanuts, fruits, betel nuts, saffron, turmeric or *bel-bhándár*, etc. Then a pot is filled with water, and on its mouth a cocoanut is placed. This cocoanut, with the pot, is then worshipped with flowers, sandal paste, etc., a lighted lamp filled with ghi is put in the same place, and the *tali* is waved thrice round the pot, which is supposed to contain the god Khandoba. Five persons then lift up the cocoanut with the *tali* and place it three times on the pot, repeating each time the words *Elkot* or *Khande ráyácha Elkot*. The cocoanut is then broken into pieces, mixed with sugar or *jágri*, and is distributed among friends and relations as *prasád*. On this occasion, as well as on the occasions of all *Kuladharmas*, that is, the days fixed for performing the special worship of the family goddess or family god of each family, the ceremony called the *Gondhal* dance is performed. On the same occasion another ceremony called *Bodan* is performed by the Deshasths and by the Chitpávans. It is as follows:—An image of the family deity is placed in a pot or plate called *támhan*, and it is then bathed in the *panchámrit*, that is, the five holy things, *viz.*, milk, curds, ghi, honey and sugar. Sandal-paste is offered to it as well as flowers, lighted lamps and some sweets and incense. Five women whose husbands are alive then prepare five lamps of wheat flour called *Kuranandi* and wave them thrice round the face of the goddess or god, as the case may be. All the lamps are then placed in the plate or *támhan* in which the deity is kept, and the *panchámrita* and other materials of worship and food and sweet cakes are mixed together. Occasionally one of the five women becomes possessed with the spirit of the *kula-devi* or family deity, and confers blessings on the members of the family for their devotion. It is believed that those families which fail to perform periodically the *Bodan*, *Tali* and *Gondhal* ceremonies in honour of their tutelary deity are sure to suffer, from some misfortune or calamity during the year.[1] The local deities chiefly worshipped at Chaul, Kolába District, are Hingláj, Jakhmáta, Bhagawati, Champáwati, Mahikáwati, and Golamba-devi. At the sowing and reaping times, people of the lower castes offer fowls and goats to these deities, and Bráhmans offer cocoanuts.[2] The local deity of the village Wávashi near Pen in the Kolába District is said to possess the power of averting evil, and is accordingly held in great respect by the people of many villages in the District. Every third year a great fair is held, and a buffalo is sacrificed to the goddess on the full moon day of the month of *Chaitra*. The *Pujári* of this goddess is a Gurav.[3] Another celebrated *Sthána-deva* in the Kolába District is Bahiri-Somajai of Khopoli. It is believed that a person suffering from snake-bite is cured without any medicine if he simply resides for one night in the temple of this goddess. Sacrifices of goats, fowls and cocoanuts are made to this goddess at the time of sowing and reaping. The *Pujáris* of this deity are known as Shingade Guravs.[4] The worship of the local deity Bápdev is much in favour among the villages of Apta and the surrounding places. At the times of sowing and reaping, offerings of fowls, goats and cocoanuts are made to Bápdev through the *Pujári*.[5] The worship of the local deities Kolambái, Bhawáni, and Giroba is prevalent in the Chauk villages.[6] To the *Gráma-devi* of the village of Tale every third year a buffalo is sacrificed, and at an interval of two years goats are offered.[7] The deities Shiva and Kálkái are worshipped with great reverence at Bakavali in the Ratnágiri District.[8]

1 School Master, Poládpur, Kolába.
2 School Master, Chaul, Kolába.
3 School Master, Wávshi, Kolába.
4 School Master, Khopoli, Kolába.
5 School Master, Apta, Kolába
6 School Master, Chauk, Kolába.
7 School Master, Tale, Kolába.
8 School Master, Bakavali, Ratnágiri.

In many villages of the Ratnágiri District the goddess Pandhar is considered to be the *Gaon-devi* or the chief goddess of the village. The *Pujári* is generally a Gurav or Maráthá Kunbi. On every full moon day cocoanuts are offered, and on the occasions of sowing and reaping, goats and fowls are sacrificed to this deity.[1] At Devgad there is a temple of the goddess Gajábái on the sea shore. The *Pujári* of this goddess is a man of the Ghádi caste. On the first day of the bright half of the month of *Márgashirsh* (December) special offerings of goats, fowls and cocoanuts are made by the villagers.[2] The deities Ravalnath, Máuli, Vetál, Rámeshwar and Hanumân are usually worshipped in most villages in Ratnágiri. The villagers in the Ratnágiri District have great faith in their local deities, and before undertaking any important business they obtain the consent or take the omen of the deity. This ceremony is known as *kaul ghálne* and it is performed as follows :—Two betel nuts or flowers are taken and one of them is placed on the right side of the deity and the other on the left side. The worshipper then bows before the deity and requests her to let the nut on the right side fall first if the deity is pleased to consent, if not, to let the nut on the left side fall first. Naturally one of the two nuts falls first, and they interpret this as either consent or dissent as the case may be. The villagers have so much faith in this *kaul* that they make use of this method of divination to ascertain whether sick or diseased persons will recover or die. Special sacrifices are offered to these local deities whenever an epidemic like cholera occurs.[3] In the Ratnágiri District, at many places, there are *Swayambhu* or natural *lingas* of the god Shiva, and over these places temples are built. The *Pujáris* of these temples are generally Jangams or Lingayat Guravs. No animal sacrifices are made at these shrines.[4] At a short distance from the village of Makhamle there is a temple of the god Shiva called Amnáyeshwar. The following legend is narrated in connection with this temple:—The place where the present temple stands once abounded with *Amani* trees and formed a pasture for cattle. The cow of a certain man of the village daily used to go to graze at this place. The cow used to give milk twice, but one day she gave milk only once, and thereafter she continued to give milk only once a day. The owner therefore asked the *Gavali* or cowherd to ascertain the cause of this sudden change. One day the cowherd noticed that the cow allowed her milk to drop upon a stone. At this the cowherd was so enraged that he struck the stone with his scythe so hard that it was cloven in two and blood gushed forth. He hurriedly repaired to the village and related this wonderful phenomenon to the people. The villagers came to the spot, and decided to build a temple to the god Shiva over the stone. One part of the stone is in this temple and the other part was taken to the village of Kalamburi, where another temple was built over it.[5] In the Sangameshwar village the Bráhmans also worship the images of the local goddesses Chandukái, Jholái and Sunkái. In the Konkan the deities Náráyan, Rawalnáth, Manli, Datta, Vetál and Shiva are worshipped everywhere.[6] The following legend is told about the deity Vetál, the leader of the ghosts:—In the Sáwantwádi State there is a temple of Vetál in the village of Ajgaon.[7] As part of his worship it is considered necessary to offer to this deity a pair of shoes every month. The people believe that after a few days the shoes become worn out. The inference drawn from this by the people is that at night the god Vetál goes out walking in the new shoes.[8] In the village of Khed

[1] School Master, Ratnágiri.
[2] School Master, Devgad, Ratnágiri.
[3] School Master, Parule, Ratnágiri.
[4] School Master, Poladpur, Kolába.
[5] School Master, Malgund, Ratnágiri.
[6] School Master, Makhamle, Ratnágiri.
[7] School Master, Sangameshwar, Ratnágiri.
[8] School Master, Kámáthipura, Bombay.

in the Ratnágiri District, a buffalo is offered to the goddess Rcdjái on the full moon day of *Chaitra* every third year. [1] At Náringre offerings of cocoanuts, etc. are made to the deities Bhávakái, Chala, etc. on the 1st of the month of *Márgashirsha*. [2] The Schoolmaster of Ibrampur states that one of the following deities is the *grámadevata* of every village in the Ratnágiri District *viz*: Chandkái, Varadhan, Khem, Bahiri, Kedár, Vággaya, Antaral, Manaya, Salbaya and Vághámbari. A procession in their honour takes place in the months of *Chaitra* and *Fálgun*. The *Pujáris* are generally either Guravs or Marátha Kunbis. A ceremony called *Palejatra* is performed in the sowing season, while the *Dhal-jatra* is performed at the harvest time. At these fairs fowls, cocoanuts, goats, fruits, etc. are offered to these deities.[3] At Málwan on the no-moon day of *Shrávan* (August) local deities and ghosts are propitiated by offering to them goats, fowls, etc.[4] At Pálset in the Ratnágiri District, the god Parashurám is the most important deity especially for Chitpávans. He exterminated the Kshatriyas twenty-one times, and having no space for himself and his Bráhmans, he asked the sea to provide him with new land. On meeting with a refusal, Parashurám became enraged and was about to push the sea back with his arrow, when, at the instigation of the sea, a black-bee *(bhunga)* cut the string of his bow, and the arrow only went a short distance. The people say that the space thus recovered from the sea came to be called Konkan.[5] At Anjarle there are two local goddesses Sawanekarin and Bahiri. Offerings of goats and fowls are made to them in the months of *Márgashirsha* (December) and *Fálgun* (March). Sometimes liquor and eggs are also offered. Offerings can be made on any day except Monday and *Ekádashi*, Tuesdays and Sundays being considered most suitable.[6] At Ubhádánda in the Ratnágiri District, Ravalnáth and Bhutanáth are held in great reverence. They are believed to be incarnations of the god Shiva. The *Pujáris* are generally Guravs, Ghádis, Ráuls and Sutárs.[7] The following goddesses which are popular in the Ratnágiri District are believed to be incarnations of the goddess Durga, *viz*. Navala-devi, Vághur-devi, Jakha-devi and Kálkái.[8] At Maral in the Ratnágiri District there is a *swayambhu* or natural *linga* of the god Shiva. It is called Maheshwar, and in its honour a fair is held on the *Sankránt* day.[9] The chief local deity of the Dahánu taluka, Thána District, is Mahálakshmi. She has seven sisters and one brother, two of the sisters being the Pangala-devi at Tárápur and the Delavadi-devi at Ghivali. Goats and fowls are offered to the Pangala-devi on the *Dasara* day. Her *Pujári* is a Gurav. It is said that the goddess Delwadi used to receive her garments from the sea, but now this is no longer the case though it is still believed that the incense which is burnt before her comes floating from Dwárka.[10] In the village of Edwan there is a goddess called Ashápuri, who used to supply her devotees with whatever they wanted. The devotee was required to besmear with cow-dung a plot of ground in the temple, and to pray for the things wanted by him. The next day, when he came to the temple, he found the desired things on the spot besmeared with cow-dung.[11] At Mángaon the *Pujári* of the local goddess is either the Pátil or the Madhavi of the village.[12] In the village of Dahigaon cocoanuts are offered annually to the village Máruti, and fowls and goats to the other local deities, in order that the village may be protected against danger and disease.[13] It is believed that any

---

1 School Master, Dábhol, Ratnágiri.
2 School Master, Náringre, Ratnágiri.
3 School Master, Ibrámpur, Ratnágiri.
4 School Master, Málwan, Ratnágiri.
5 School Master, Palset, Ratnágiri.
6 School Master, Anjarle, Ratnágiri.
7 School Master, Ubhádánda, Ratnágiri.
8 School Master, Masure, Ratnágiri.
9 School Master, Sákharpe, Ratnágiri.
10 School Master, Dahánu, Thána.
11 School Master, Edwan, Thána.
12 School Master, Mángaon, Thána.
13 School Master, Dahigaon.

Bráhman who acts as the *Pujári* of the god Shiva will find his family exterminated, and for this reason Bráhmans do not act as *Pujáris* in the temples of Shiva.

In a few temples of goddesses like Jakhái etc. the *Pujári* is of the Mahár caste.[1] A great fair is held in honour of the goddess Vajrá-bái or Vajreshwari near Nirmal in the month of *Kártika* (November). The *Pujári* of the goddess is a Gosávi of the Giri sect. The worship of Bhimasena is not prevalent in the Konkan, but the hero Bhima, like Máruti, is held in reverence by the gymnasts. Bhima is not worshipped, but a work called the *Bhima-stavaráj* is read at the bed of a dying man in order that he may obtain salvation. At Ashirgad there is a *gumpha* or cave of Ashwatháma, a hero of the Mahábhárata, and it is said that a noise is heard coming from the cave on the full moon day.[2]

Wherever a village is founded, it is customary to establish a village deity as the guardian of the village. The deities chosen are Máruti, Káli, Chandkái, Varadani, etc. In the Konkan, goddesses are preferred, and on the Ghats generally Máruti is preferred. Certain ceremonies are performed for consecrating the place to the deity, and sometimes the deity is called after the village as Marleshwar[3] etc. By many lower class people the goddess Pondhar is often selected as the guardian of a new village. At Shahpur, if the newly founded village is to be inhabited by high class Hindus, the deities Máruti and Durga are selected as *gráma-devatas,* but if it is to be inhabited by lower class people, then such deities as Mhasoba, Chedoba, Jákhái, etc. are chosen.[4] In the Bassein and Sálsette tálukas the following deities *viz.* Máruti, Chedá, Chandkái, and Shiva, are chosen as village deities. Cheda is represented by a long piece of wood or stone besmeared with red-powder, and is placed on the outskirts of the village. No Bráhman is necessary for establishing a Cheda. The *Pujári* is generally a Kunbi or Máli, and he establishes the deity by offering it a goat or fowls and cocoanuts.[5] Sometimes the guardian deity of a new settlement is decided upon by a *Kaul.* Two or three names of deities are selected, betelnuts or flowers are placed on the sides of the guardian deity of the neighbouring village and that deity in whose name the betelnut falls first is chosen as the deity of the new village.[6] At Chaul, the deity called Bápdev is very popular among the lower classes. It is represented by a big stone fixed on mortar and besmeared with red-powder. When it is established for the first time in a village, a Bráhman is required to make the first *púja* or worship, but after this it is worshipped by a *Pújári* of a lower caste.[7] The Mahars in the Kolába District select the ghost-deity called Jhaloba as the guardian deity of a new settlement.[8] In many cases the deity of their former village or of the neighbouring village [9] is named by a Bhagat or exorcist, who becomes possessed.[10]

In the Konkan every village farm is supposed to be under the guardianship of the minor godlings, the majority of which are called *Bhuta-Devatás* or ghostly godlings. In some cases the field guardians are also the Bráhmanic godlings like Máruti and Shiva. To the Bráhmanic guardians of the field, cocoanuts and flowers are offered at the sowing and reaping seasons, and to the rest, fowls, cocoanuts, and sometimes goats, are offered. The higher classes feed one or two Bráhmans in order to propitiate the deities of the fields; and for the propitiation of the minor deities of the field

[1] School Master, Bhiwandi, Thána.
[2] School Master, Agashi, Arnáia, Thána.
[3] School Master, Agashi, Thána.
[4] School Master, Malgund, Ratnágiri.
[5] School Master, Shahápur, Thána.
[6] School Master, Agáshi, Thána.
[7] School Master, Medhe, Kolába.
[8] School Master, Chaul, Kolába.
[9] School Master, Akol, Kolába.
[10] School Master, Masure, Ratnágiri.
[11] School Master, Shiroshi, Thána District.

the lower classes perform a rite called *Dalap*. This rite is performed by a man of the Gurav, Ghádi, or Rául, caste by sacrificing to the field deity a goat or fowls and cocoanuts. The *pujári* repeats prayers for a good harvest, and then distributes portions of the offerings among the people assembled there for witnessing the rite.[1] In the Ratnágiri District on the no moon day of *Jeshta* people assemble in the temple of the village deity and perform a rite called *Gárháne* in order that they should have a good crop, that their village may be free from diseases, and that their cattle may be protected. A similar rite is performed on the first day of the bright half of the month of *Márgashirsha* (December), and on this occasion sometimes a goat or sheep is sacrificed at the boundary of the village.[2] In order that there should be a good harvest, the villagers of Kankaoli worship on certain days from the month of *Kártika* (November) to the month of *Shimga* (March) the minor deities of the field by offering them fowls, cocoanuts, etc.[3] At Achare (Ratnágiri) some people worship the god of the clouds on the day on which the *Mriga-shirsha* constellation begins, and they believe that thereby plenty of rain is ensured for the season.[4] For good harvests and for the protection of their cattle, the villagers of Achare pray to the *Gráma-devata* in the month of *Jeshta* (June), and then go in procession from the temple of the village deity to the boundary of the village, where they sacrifice a cock and offer some cooked rice with a burning wick upon it, to the deity that presides over the fields and harvests.[5] In the village of Palset of the Ratnágiri District the goddess Khema is worshipped by the villagers to obtain good crops, and for the protection of their cattle. The *Púja* or special worship takes place on the full-moon day of *Márgashirsha* and on this occasion the sacred *Gondhal* dance is also performed.[6] In certain villages of the Ratnágiri District, for obtaining good harvest, people worship the godling Maháþurush at the beginning of the sowing and reaping operations, and offer the deity fowls, cocoanuts and cooked rice.[7] In the village of Málwan, at the sowing and reaping seasons, the villagers usually make offerings of fowls and cocoanuts and goats to the guardians of the fields, but Bráhmans and such Kunbi farmers as do not eat flesh make offerings of cooked rice mixed with curds.[8] At Ubhádánda village, in order to secure a good harvest and for the protection of the cattle, the villagers worship the spirit godlings called *Sambandhas* and perform the rite called *Devachár*.[9] At Kochare, annual prayers are offered to the godling called Gavat-dev for the protection of the village cattle.[10] In the Devgad taluka people believe that some deity resides in every farm or in every collection of fields, and that good or bad harvests are caused as the deity is pleased or displeased.[11] In order that there should be plenty of rain and that the cattle should be protected, the villagers of Málgund assemble in the temple of the village deity and offer prayers on the full moon day of *Fálgun* (March) and on the 1st day of the bright half of *Márgashirsh*.[12] In the Kolába District, for the protection of cattle and for good crops, prayers are offered to the god Bahiri and the ghosts Khavis and Sambandh.[13]

At Chauk in the Kolába District the villagers perform a special *púja* or worship of the god Krishna in order that the village cattle may be protected.[14] At Casawani a fair called *pále jatra* is held in the month of

[1] School Master, Parule, Ratnágiri.
[2] School Master, Adivare, Ratnágiri.
[3] School Master, Kankaoli, Ratnágiri.
[4] School Master, Achare, Ratnágiri.
[5] School Master, Masure, Ratnágiri.
[6] School Master, Palset, Ratnágiri.
[7] School Master, Basani, Ratnágiri.
[8] School Master, Malwan, Ratnágiri.
[9] School Master, Ubhádánda, Ratnágiri.
[10] School Master, Kochare, Ratnágiri.
[11] School Master, Devgad, Ratnágiri.
[12] School Master, Malgund, Ratnágirl.
[13] School Master, Khopoli, Kolába.
[14] School Master, Chauk, Kolába.

Bhádrapad (September) in order that the villagers may have a good harvest, and that their cattle may be protected against tigers and disease.[1] At Akol, on the day which follows the *Ganesh-Chaturthi*, people throw parched rice over their fields and houses so that the rats may not run over them.[2] At Málád in the Thána District, for the protection of cattle, the god Wághoba is worshipped at night on the 12th of *Ashwin* which is called the *Wágh-báras*.[3] In some villages of the Thána District the deity Wághoba or Wághya is worshipped on the 12th day of the dark half of *Kártik*. On that day the cowherds collect a quantity of milk and prepare a kind of food known as *Khir* by mixing *jágri* and cooked rice. They then proceed to the stone image of the deity in the jungle, and besmear it with new red-lead or *shendur*. They pour a portion of the sweet milk over the stone, and offer prayers for the protection of their cattle. They then partake of the remaining milk.[4] At Agáshi and other neighbouring villages, before the fields are ploughed, the villagers assemble and collect a certain sum of money, with which they buy goats, fowls, red-powder, cocoanuts and parched grain. A goat and some cocks are then sacrificed to the spirits residing in the cemeteries and at the boundary of the village. Cocoanuts besmeared with *gulál* red powder are also offered to these ghost godlings. A goat decorated with garlands and red powder is then made to walk round the village three times at night, accompanied by the villagers, who throw *láhya* parched rice while passing. This rite is called *Siwa Bándhane* or binding the boundary, and is supposed to protect the village crops and cattle. No farmer dares to sow his seed unless this rite has been performed. After this rite has been performed, every farmer appeases his family deity *i.e.* Khandoba, Bahiroba, Kankoba, etc., by performing a ceremony at home called *Deopan* or *Devaśki*, which relates to the worship of ancestors. Most of the farmers regard one of their dead ancestors as their chief deity, and represent him in their house by a cocoanut. They do not enter on any new business without first offering prayers to this cocoanut, and they also believe that they can bring evil upon their enemies by simply cursing them before the deified cocoanut. The only materials generally required for the worship of this cocoanut are red powder, incense and flowers. On rare occasions, goats and fowls are sacrificed. It is believed that the ancestor in the cocoanut likes to be worshipped by the wife or husband (as the case may be) of the person represented by the cocoanut. Some farmers, in addition to the cocoanut, worship a stick or cap of their ancestor along with the cocoanut, and offer prayers for the protection of their cattle, for good rain and harvest, and also for the destruction of their enemies.[5]

[1] School Master, Sasawani, Kolába.

[2] School Master, Akol, Kolába.

[3] School Master, Málád, Thána.

[4] School Master, Bhuwan, Thána.

[5] School Master, Agáshi, Thána District.

CHAPTER III.

DISEASE DEITIES.

At Vengurla, in the Ratnágiri District, when epidemic diseases prevail, the people of the village assemble and prepare a basket in which are placed cooked rice, cocoanuts, lemons, wine, red flowers and *Udid* (Phaseolus radiatus) grain. The basket is then carried out of the village along with a cock or a goat, and deposited outside the village boundary. To carry this basket, a person belonging to the Mahar caste is generally selected. The people of the next village similarly carry the basket beyond their village limits; and it is finally thrown into the sea. It is believed that if the basket of offerings to the disease-deities is carried from one village to another, it is sure to bring the disease with it. Great care is therefore taken to throw the offerings into the sea. In cases of small pox a feast is given to women whose husbands are alive. In some cases boiled rice is mixed with the blood of a cock, and on the rice is placed a burning black cotton wick in a cocoanut shell with a little oil in it. The whole is then carried beyond the village boundary and thrown away.[1] In the village of Mitbáv in the Ratnágiri District, epidemic diseases like cholera, small pox, plague, etc., are supposed to come from disease deities, and in order to avoid the danger of such diseases the people of the village go to the temple of the village deity and pray for protection. The special form of worship on such occasions is the *Kaul* i.e., asking a favour from the deity. When an epidemic of plague broke out for the first time at Sangmeshwar, the people of the village at once proceeded to worship the village deity; but a few cases of plague occurred, even after worshipping the village goddess *Jákhmáta*. When the people went to the temple and asked the reason why the plague continued, it was announced by the deity through the temple ministrant that she was helpless in the case of plague, and desired the people to worship the god Shiva, thereby signifying that the village deity has limited powers, and that the power of averting great evils lies with Shiva the god of destruction.[2] In the Devgad Taluka of the Ratnágiri District in epidemic diseases like cholera, etc., the usual ceremony, *i.e.*, the *Paradi* (disease-scaring basket) is performed. A basket containing boiled rice, red powder, red flowers, lemons, betel nuts, betel leaves, etc., is prepared, and on that rice is kept a burning cotton wick dipped in oil. The basket is then carried beyond the village boundary along with a goat having a red flower garland round its neck. The goat is set free at the outskirts of the village. In cases of small pox, married women whose husbands are alive are worshipped with turmeric powder, cocoanuts, flowers, etc., and incense is kept burning in the house. The deity of small pox is also specially worshipped for a number of days. It is represented by a brass or copper *lota* with a cocoanut placed over it. This process is called *mánd bharane* *i.e.* arranging the materials of worship. The girls in the house sing songs in praise of the small pox deity. It is believed that in this way the severity of the disease is reduced.[3]

[1] School Master, Ubhádánda, Ratnágiri.

[2] School Master, Mitbáv, Ratnágiri.

[3] School Master, Fonda, Ratnágiri.

In the Sangameshwar taluka of the Ratnágiri District, when epidemic diseases prevail, the people of the village assemble in the temple of the village deity, offer a cocoanut to the goddess, and ask for a *Kaul* (omen). After receiving the *Kaul* they pray for mercy. It is believed that if the *Kaul* is in favour of the people the diseases will disappear.[1] At Achare in the Málwan taluka of the Ratnágiri District it is believed that epidemic diseases such as cholera, small pox, etc., are caused by the anger of the deities *Jari* and *Mari*; and in order to satisfy those deities animal sacrifices are offered at the time of their worship. There are no other deities who cause such diseases.[2] At Vijayadurg in the Ratnágiri District, in cases of small pox, the child suffering from the disease is made to sleep on a silk garment *Sovalen*. Flowers are thrown upon the patient's body, and are given to him to smell. Incense is burnt in the house. On the seventh day from the beginning of the disease, the child is first bathed in milk and then in water. Black scented powder called *Abir* is thrown on the body. After two or three days an image representing the deity is made of flour, which is worshipped, and a feast is given to Bráhmans and unwidowed women.[3]

At Basani in the Ratnágiri District the disease of small pox is averted by a Bráhman worshipping the goddess *Shitala*. Bráhmans are also worshipped, and a feast is given to them. In cases of cholera and the other epidemic diseases the village deity is worshipped and sacrifices are made to her.[4]

At Kochare in the Vengurla taluka of the Ratnágiri District, a woman whose husband is alive is made to represent the goddess *Jari Mari*, and is worshipped with flowers, red powder *Kunku* and black ointment *Kájal*. She is given a feast of sweet things; and rice and cocoanuts are put into her lap by another woman whose husband is alive. She is then carried in procession through the village with beating of drums and the singing of songs. This is similar to the *Paradi* procession, which is also common in that District.[5]

At Navare in the Ratnágiri District, in cases of small pox, the diseased child and the person into whose body the small pox deities called *Báyás* enter, are worshipped with *Abir* black scented powder, flower garlands, &c.[6]

At Pendur in the Málwan taluka of the Ratnágiri District the wrath of the female deities or *Mátrikás* is supposed to be the cause of epidemic diseases, and these *Mátrikás* are accordingly worshipped for their pacification.[7]

At Chaul in the Kolába District the god Shankar is worshipped by Bráhmans when epidemic diseases prevail in a village. The worship consists in repeating *Vedic* hymns. The nine planets are also propitiated by sacrifices of boiled rice, etc. There is a famous temple of the goddess Shitala at Chaul where the deity is worshipped by Bráhmans, who recite *Vedic* hymns, whenever small pox prevails in the village. The *mantras* of the goddess and the Shitala *Ashtaka* are also repeated in the *Pauránic* style. The women walk round the temple every day as long as the signs of the disease are visible on their children. The goddess is worshipped with turmeric and red powders, and clothes and fruits are given to her. The *Kaul* ceremony is also practised in this District. It is worth noticing that even Musalmáns ask for a *Kaul* from this goddess. The days fixed for *Kaul* are :—Sunday, Tuesday, Thursday and Friday. The morning hours are considered specially auspicious

[1] School Master, Sangmeshwar, Ratnágiri.
[2] School Master, Achare, Ratnágiri.
[3] School Master, Vijaydurg, Ratnágiri.
[4] School Master, Basani, Ratnágiri.
[5] School Master, Kochare, Ratnágiri.
[6] School Master, Navare, Ratnágiri.
[7] School Master, Pendur, Ratnágiri.

for the *Kaul*. There is another temple at Chaul, of the goddess Shri Golába *Devi*. This goddess is also worshipped when other epidemic diseases prevail in the village. *Saptáha* i.e. continuous worship for seven days is also performed in honour of the deity. The gardeners (*Mális*) of the village worship this deity every Tuesday morning with cocoanuts gathered from every house in the village. This temple is being repaired at present.[1]

When epidemic diseases prevail in the village of Poladpur of the Kolába District the god Shiva is worshipped by continuously pouring water over the deity's head or *linga*. Sacrifices of fruits and animals are also offered to the village deity. Where there is a temple of the deity Mári or Mahámári, the deity is worshipped through a Bráhman, and sacrifices of cocks and goats are offered to her. The deity named Shitala is worshipped in cases of small pox.[2]

At Vávashi in the Pen taluka of the Kolába District, in cases of epidemic diseases, the people of the village invoke the god Shiva, and holy fires called *homa* are kindled in honour of that god. Sacrifices of boiled rice are also offered to the deity. For averting small pox the deity Shitala is invoked by the *mantras* called *Shitala Astaka*. For averting fevers the gods Shankar and Vishnu are also worshipped.[3]

At Medhe in the Rohe taluka of the Kolába District the god Shiva is worshipped in order to avert an epidemic, and Hanumán is worshipped to avert fevers.[4]

At Málád in the Salsette taluka of the Thána District, when an epidemic prevails in a village, the goddess *Navachandi* is worshipped and the *Homa* is kindled in her honour. On the last day of worship a goat is set free as a sacrifice to the deity. The *Bali* i. e., the offering of boiled rice, and the goat are taken beyond the boundary of the village, and handed over to the people of the neighbouring village, who follow the same procedure, and at last both the sacrifices are thrown into the sea. The goat generally dies, as it does not get water and food till it reaches the sea.[5]

In the village of Anjur in the Thána District, in cases of long standing fevers the Bráhmans observe the ceremony called *Udak Shanti* or propitiation by water. It is as follows:— An earthen pot filled with water is placed on the ground. On the top of the pot is placed a round plate in which the image of the god Brahmadev the son of Vishnu is consecrated. Four Bráhmans sit on the four sides of the pot and repeat their Vedic hymns. These four Bráhmans are supposed to be the four mouths of the god Brahmadev. It is believed by the people that by performing this ceremony the fever is made to disappear.[6]

At Rái in the Thána District some people believe that malarial fevers are averted by placing secretly a small stone on the head of the god Hanumán.[7]

In the Kolhápur District the nine planets are worshipped in the house to ward off diseases such as cholera, small pox, fevers, etc. The goddess Laxmi is worshipped in order to avert small pox, the worship being generally performed in a garden or a grove of mango trees, when parched rice, cocoanuts and lemons are offered to her. The people assembled at the spot partake of the food. To avert fever, the people perform a certain ceremony ordained in the *Shástras*. If the sick person is supposed to be under the evil influence of the planet Saturn, the planet is invoked by repeating the

1 School Master, Chaul, Kolába.
2 School Master, Poladpur, Kolába.
3 School Master, Vávashi, Kolába.
4 School Master, Medhe, Kolába.
5 School Master, Málád, Thána.
6 School Master, Anjur, Thána.
7 School Master, Rái, Thána.

mantras, and worshipped with the usual offerings. Garments such as a *Sári* and a *Choli* are offered to the goddesses Mári and Kálubái. When an epidemic disease such as cholera prevails in a village, the people of the village instal the deity Margai at a place where four roads meet, and worship her for seven or eight days with much ceremony. Every one brings offerings of cocoanuts, lemons, *ambil* or conjee, cooked rice and curds, etc. with the beating of drums to offer to the deity. After worshipping the goddess in this manner for eight successive days they sacrifice a *Bali* of a he-buffalo before her. The deity is then put upon a bullock cart and carried through the village with the beating of drums and much ceremony, to be thrown away beyond the village boundary along with the offerings.[1]

Epidemic diseases are not attributed to witchcraft at Devgad in the Ratnágiri District. It is believed that they are caused by the accumulated sins of the people.[2] In the Dápoli taluka of the Ratnágiri District epidemic diseases are attributed to witchcraft by low caste people. The power of averting such diseases lies in the hands of the village deities. They are therefore propitiated by the sacrifices of cocks, goats, and cocoanuts.[3] At Poládpur in the Kolába District, epidemic diseases are sometimes attributed to witchcraft by low caste people. Persons well versed in the *mantras* of evil spirits are called Bhagats or exorcists. Some of them keep evil spirits at their command. The poor people believe that what these exorcists foretell is sure to occur. It is believed that the spirit dwells on the tongue of these exorcists. When these spirits are hungry, they are let loose in the village by the sorcerers for the destruction of the people, thus causing an epidemic. When a spirit is to be destroyed, the people of the village assemble in a mob and attack the sorcerer, a small quantity of blood is taken from his tongue and water from the earthen pot of a Chámbhár is poured upon it. It is believed that by so doing the spirit is permanently destroyed and the sorcerer either forgets all his *mantras* or they become ineffective. The spirit is called *tond bhut*, and it sometimes troubles even animals.[4]

At Chauk in the Karjat taluka of the Kolába District, the people believe that the devotees of the Mári deity bring on epidemic diseases by the use of their *mantras*, and in order to satisfy them, offerings are made to the deity Mári which are taken by the devotees or Bhagats.[5] At Váde in the Thána District epidemic diseases are attributed to witchcraft. There are some women who are supposed to bring on, or at least foster, the growth of such diseases by their evil *mantras*. Such women are threatened or punished by the people, and sometimes they are even driven out of the village.[6] In the village of Anjur of the Thána District, if a man vomits blood accidently and falls ill, or dies, it is believed to be due to the act of *Muth Márane*, that is, the throwing of a handful of rice over which incantations have been repeated. If there be any sorcerer in the village who has learnt the same incantations, he alone is able to return the *Muth* to the sorcerer who first used it.[7] At Shirgaum in the Umbergaon taluka of the Thána District, when epidemic diseases prevail in the village, the people of the village take a turn round the village in a body and kill a buffalo. A *Bali* or offering of boiled rice, cocoanuts, cocks and goats is also offered to the deities that cause epidemic diseases.[8]

1 Rao Saheb Shelke, Kolhápur.
2 School Master, Mitbáv, Ratnágiri.
3 School Master, Anjarle, Ratnágiri.
4 School Master, Poladpur, Kolába.
5 School Master, Chauk, Kolába.
6 School Master, Váde, Thána.
7 School Master, Anjur, Thána.
8 School Master, Umbergaon, Thána.

When cattle disease breaks out in a village the people of the Devagad taluka in the Ratnágiri District generally prevent the healthy cattle from mixing with the diseased, and the people of the neighbouring villages take precautions against using the milk, etc. of the diseased cattle. At such times the cattle of the village in which the disease breaks out are prohibited from entering the neighbouring villages.[1] At Ubhádánda in the Ratnágiri District, the deity named Maha Gira is worshipped in connection with cattle diseases. At some places a feast is given to Bráhmans, and in certain villages of this District a man is painted like a tiger, carried out of the village and bathed in a river. It is believed that this is one of the remedies for averting cattle diseases.[2] At Fonda in the Ratnágiri District, when cattle disease breaks ut, a goat or a cock is sacrificed at the temples of the village deity.[3] In some villages of the Málwan taluka the deity Bráhman is worshipped.[4] At Basani in the Ratnágiri District the gods of the Mahars as also the village deity are worshipped in connection with the cattle diseases.[5] At Vávashi in the Kolába District when cattle disease prevails in a village, a pig is killed and buried on the border of the village. A sweet oil lamp in the shell of a crab or a lobster is kept burning in the cowshed. River or sweet water fishes are boiled in water, and the water is given to the animals to drink. The owner also cleans the cowshed and burns sulpher, camphor, dammer and other disinfectants.[6] At Varsai in the Pen taluka of the Kolába District a *Kaul* is taken from the village deity to prevent cattle diseases, that is, the village deity is consulted through the temple ministrant, who acts as the spokesman of the oracle.[7] At Medhe in the Rohe taluka of the Kolába District the village deity Bahiroba is worshipped in connection with cattle diseases. The diseased animals are minutely examined, and the affected part of their body is branded with a red hot iron.[8] In the village of Umela of the Thána District the village deity is worshipped and sacrifices are offered to her. Milk from the affected villages is prohibited, and vegetables are not fried in oil during the prevalence of the disease in the village.[9] At Kolhápur, the people make vows to the god, and ashes from the temples are brought and applied to the forehead of the cattle. Cotton strings are tied to the feet or the neck of the cattle in the name of the god. They also make vows to the deities Tamjái and Wághjái, and offer to them eyes made of silver, a new cloth, a fowl or a goat, when their animals are cured of the disease.[10]

In the Devgad taluka of the Ratnágiri District, in cases of malarial fevers pieces of certain kinds of herbs are fastened together with black cotton strings, and tied round the arm or neck of the person suffering from the disease. Sacred ashes are put in a copper amulet and the amulet is tied in the manner above described.[11] At Fonda in the Ratnágiri District, in addition to herbs and copper amulets, peacock feathers in black cotton strings are tied to the arms of the persons suffering from malarial fevers, etc.[12] At Vengurla in the Ratnágiri District, in fevers like malaria, black strings of cotton are tied round the arm or neck, and certain secret *mantras* are repeated at the time. It is believed that the power of the *mantras* is lost if they are disclosed to the public.[13] At Murud in the Dápoli taluka of the Ratnágiri District the *mantras* of the god Narsinh, the fourth incarnation of Vishnu, are repeated for the exorcism of diseases.[14] In the Dápoli taluka people who want to get rid of their diseases tie a copper amulet to their arms. The *mantras* that are repeated on such occasions are kept secret. There are at present

1 School Master, Mitbáv, Ratnágiri.
2 School Master, Ubhádánda, Ratnágiri.
3 School Master, Fonda, Ratnágiri.
4 School Master, Bándivade, Ratnágiri.
5 School Master, Basani, Ratnágiri.
6 School Master, Vavashi, Kolába.
7 School Master, Varsai, Kolába.
8 School Master, Medhe, Kolába
9 School Master, Umela, Thána.
10 Rao Saheb Shelke, Kolhápur.
11 School Master, Mitbáv, Ratnágiri.
12 School Master, Fonda, Ratnágiri.
13 School Master, Ubhádánda, Ratnágiri.
14 School Master, Murud, Ratnágiri.

some persons in the Anjarle village who give such amulets and charms.[1] In the Chiplun taluka of the Ratnágiri District the following articles are used for averting diseases:—Copper amulets, black cotton strings, and holy water over which certain *mantras* have been repeated by the exorcist.[2] At Poladpur in the Kolába District, black cotton strings are tied round the arm in cases of malarial fevers. Some *mantras* are repeated in cases of pain in the right or left side of the body. Besides the *mantras* some signs and figures are drawn on birch leaves, and tied round the arm or the neck of the patient. Women who wish to have children wear such black cotton strings and copper amulets.[3] At Vávashi in the Kolába District *mantras* are in vogue for the exorcism of diseases such as liver and spleen affections. For exorcising eye diseases black cotton thread is tied to the ear.[4] At Chauk in the Karjat taluka of the Kolába District, ashes are applied to the body of the sick person after repeating certain *mantras* over them.[5] At Málád in the Thána District, for exorcising diseases caused by evil spirits, certain letters of the *Nrisinha mantra* are written on a birch leaf, and the leaf is tied round the arm of the sick man with a copper amulet. In order to drive out the evil spirit permanently, the god Nrisinha is worshipped, and sacred fire is kindled to propitiate the deity. For the worship of Nrisinha the ministrant required must be a regular devotee of Nrisinha, and he must also be a *Panchákshari* i.e. one who knows the *mantras* of evil spirits.[6] In the village of Shirgaon in the Máhim taluka of the Thána District, in addition to copper amulets and black threads of cotton, *mantras* of Musalmán saints or *pirs* are in vogue for exorcising disease.[7] At Kolhápur, the higher classes perform the religious ceremony called *Anushthán* to propitiate Shiva, the god of destruction, in order to avert disease, and also make vows to the same deity. The lower classes offer cocoanuts, fowls or a goat. They sometimes go to the exorcist for ashes in the name of the god, and apply them to the forehead of the diseased person. Copper amulets and cotton strings given by the exorcist are also tied round the neck of the sick person.[8]

At Adivare in the Ratnágiri District the following practices are adopted for driving out evil spirits that cause disease. Incense is burnt before the exorcist, drums are beaten, and then the exorcist takes a burning wick in his hand and frightens the diseased person by striking the ground with a cane or a broom of peacock feathers. He also cries out loudly. He then draws out the evil spirit from the body of the diseased person, and puts it in a bottle, which is either carried out of the village and buried under ground near a big tree or is thrown into the sea.[9] In the Sangameshwar taluka of the Ratnágiri District, the process of exorcising is sometimes accompanied by dancing and loud cries. The person who suffers from evil spirits is taken to *Narsoba's Wádi* in the Kolhápur State where patients are believed to find a cure.[10] In the Devgad taluka of the Ratnágiri District the exorcist, when possessed, does not dance as at other places, but freely uses abusive epithets to drive out the evil spirits; and on such occasions the threats are repeated loudly by the exorcist.[11] In the Dápoli taluka of the Ratnágiri District, dancing is used in exorcism. While dancing, the exorcist makes a show of different kinds of fits. They are similar to those made by a person suffering from hysteria. He also stands and sways his body to and fro for some time, then assumes a serene and quiet attitude, and begins to cry out loudly.[12] There are some sorcerers at Dásgaon in the Kolába District, who dance and cry out loudly in order to drive out the evil spirits from the body of the diseased.[13] At Málád in the Thána District dancing is used

[1] School Master, Anjarle, Ratnágiri.
[2] School Master, Ibhrampur, Ratnágiri.
[3] School Master, Poladpur, Kolába.
[4] School Master, Vavashi, Kolába.
[5] School Master, Chauk, Kolába.
[6] School Master, Málád, Thána.
[7] School Master, Shirgaon, Thána.
[8] Ráo Sáheb, Shelke, Kolhápur.
[9] School Master, Adivare, Ratnágiri.
[10] School Master, Sangmeshwar, Ratnágiri.
[11] School Master, Fonde, Ratnágiri.
[12] School Master, Anjarle, Ratnágiri.
[13] Schoolmaster, Dásgaon, Kolába.

in exorcism. The following is a description of one of these dances. Songs of the deity which is to be summoned on the occasion are sung along with the music of the *Tál* (a kind of cymbal) and the beating of drums called *Ghumat*. The *Ghumat* is an earthen jar, the lower and upper ends of which are covered over with leather. The man in whose body the deity is to make its appearance takes his bath and sits by the side of a small prayer carpet called *Asan*. A small quantity of rice (about a *ser*) is put in front of the carpet, and a copper pot filled with water is placed on the rice. The musicians begin to strike their instrument with a loud clash, and the exorcist's body begins to shake. The shaking of the body is a sure indication of his being spirit-possessed. He then sits upon the carpet and begins to throw grains of rice into the coppe pot containing water, gives out the name of the particular spirit with which he is possessed, and the cause for which it has attacked the patient. He then explains the measures and rites by which the spirit can be driven out. The people abide by his directions, and the patient is thus cured.[1]

At Padghe in the Thána District, when an evil spirit is to be driven out from the body of the patient, the latter is asked to hold in his mouth a betelnut or a lemon. After some time, the betelnut or the lemon is put into a bottle, the bottle is then tightly corked and buried underground. A copper pot is filled with water, and the diseased person is asked to hold the pot upside down. If the water runs out it is believed that the spirit has disappeared.[2]

In the village of Edwan of the Thána District, dancing is practised in cases of spirit possession, but it is resorted to among the lower castes only. While dancing, the sorcerer cries out loudly, and throws grains of *Udid* (Phaseeolus radiatus)on the body of the diseased person[3] after repeating certain *mantras*. This rit is styled *Bhárani* or the process of charming.

At Kolhápur, dancing is not used in exorcism, but the people suffering from evil spirits sometimes dance and cry out loudly. Some of them loose their hair while dancing, and even strike their heads. Some quarrel like combatants, and some of them try to make speeches like orators. There is a temple of the god Shri Dutta at Narsinhwádi in the Kolhápur State, to which people suffering from evil spirits are brought for a cure. These people cry out loudly when the palanquin of the *Swámi Maharaj* is carried through the village, and spirits usually quit the bodies of their victims at this ime, for it is said that they cannot bear the proximity of the *Swámi Maháráj*. Patients are also cured by residing in the village for a certain period. On this account the village of Narsobáchiwádi is considered very holy. A big festival is celebrated in this village annually on the twelfth day of the dark half of *Ashwin* (October). Feasts are given to the Bráhmans, the expenses being borne by the Kolhápur State.[4]

In the Sangameshwar taluka of the Ratnágiri District, the *Bhagat* or exorcist is respected by the lower caste people. His duties are to ask a *kaul* from the deity on behalf of the people and to alleviate their sufferings. His appointment is hereditary, the clever member of the family generally following the profession of his father.[5] In the Devgad taluka of the Ratnágiri District, low class people are afraid of sorcerers because they might injure them if they are offended. They therefore are careful not to cause them displeasure. There, the profession of a sorcerer or exorcist is not hereditary. Any one who learns the wicked *mantras* after attending regularly the burial and burning grounds for some days becomes an expert, and may follow the profession.[6] In the Málwan taluka of the Ratnágiri District the chief function of the village sorcerer is to worship the village deity. All kinds of gifts and presents intended for the deity are made through him. His profession is hereditary

1 School Master, Málád, Thána.

2 School Master, Padghe, Thána.

3 School Master, Edwan, Thána.

4 Rao Saheb Shelke, Kolhápur.

5 School Master, Sangameshwar, Ratnágiri.

6 School Master, Mitbáv, Ratnágiri.

and he is much respected by the ignorant people[1]. At Fonda in the Ratnágiri District the exorcist is not appointed, but one who can satisfactorily interpret or explain to the village deity the sufferings of the people is generally selected.[2]

In the Vengurla taluka of the RatnágiriDistrict, the chief function of the village sorcerer is to find remedies for the cure of persons suffering from evil spirits. His position among the people of the low classes is considered high. He follows the hereditary profession of a sorcerer, and generally the eldest son succeeds his father.[3]

At Chidhran in the Panwel taluka of the Kolába District, Bhutes, a caste of beggars, are the devotees of a goddess. Some of them are called *Bhagats*. *Devrishis* are very rare. The difference between a *Devrishi* and a *Bhagat* is as follows:—A *Devrishi* removes the evil spirits by simply repeating the *mantras* while the *Bhagat* removes them by bringing the evil spirit into his own body and by dancing, etc.[4]

At Chaul in the Kolába District, Bhutes go begging in the morning every day for the first nine days of the month of *Ashwin* (October). On the tenth day the Bhutya is given a pice from every house. These Bhutes are devotees of the goddess Shakti. At Sasawane in the Kolába District the village sorcerer comes to beg every day and is given rice, etc., but during the first nine days of the bright half of *Ashwin* (October) he is given copper coins.[5] At Anjur in the Thána District the devotee of a particular god is called *Bhagat*, and one who knows how to summon or eject evil spirits is called Bhutya. A Devrishi is a person who knows the *mantras* for warding off the great evil spirits such as *Brahma Rákshasa*, *Brahma Samband*, etc. These three classes are respected only for performing their respective duties, and not otherwise.[6]

At Kolhápur, the sorcerer is never appointed. His functions are to ask a *kaul* from the deity, to pray for the welfare of the people, and explain to them what he sees in his dreams. He holds no position in higher society, but the poor people who believe in him are afraid of him. Sorcerers are generally very cunning; they frighten poor people, and obtain from them presents and gifts for their maintenance.[7]

In the Vengurla taluka of the Ratnágri District red flags are hoisted on Banyan, *Pipal*, and *Umbar* trees, and on certain occasions offerings of coins and cocoanuts are made. It is believed that when the three kinds of trees happen to grow together, *i.e.*, close to each other, near a well or on the bank of a river, the god Datta resides there, but such cases are very rare. These trees are supposed to be the haunts of the *Munja* spirit, and therefore copper coins waved round the persons suffering from evil spirits are thrown underneath them. There are no sacred wells in this taluka.[8] In the Dápoli taluka of the Ratnágiri District, the Banyan and *Pipal* trees are worshipped. The former is worshipped by women on the full moon day of the month of *Jestha* (June) and on the no moon day when it falls on Monday. On these occasions a cotton thread is tied round the tree, and offerings of glass beads, cocoanuts, fruits, etc., are made. These trees are also worshipped with offerings of copper coins, etc.[9] In the Dápoli taluka, there is a certain place between the two villages of Anjarla and Harnai where persons passing by that side throw one or two stones, causing thereby a heap of stones there. It is believed that by doing this the person who throws such stones gets rid of his itch. This place

[1] School Master, Bándiwade, Ratnágiri.
[2] School Master, Fonda, Ratnágiri.
[3] School Master, Ubbádánda, Ratnágiri.
[4] School Master, Chidran, Kolába.
[5] School Master, Sasawane, Kolába.
[6] School Master, Anjur, Thána.
[7] Ráo Sáheb Shelke, Kolhápur.
[8] School Master, Ubbádánda, Ratnágiri.
[9] School Master, Bankavli, Ratnágiri.

is called Girjoba. Hands and feet made of wood are also offered by persons who make vows to do so when their hands or legs are affected by any disease.[1] At Ibhrampur in the Ratnágiri District offerings of cotton thread, copper coins, and fruit are made to Banyan and *Pipal* trees on the full moon day of the month of *Jestha* (June) and on every Saturday in the month of *Shráwan* (August).[2]

At Vavanje in the Panwel taluka of the Kolába District, offerings of coins, etc., to sacred trees are made at the time of *Parwani* (a festival). For instance, when the no moon day falls on Monday, the women worship the *Pipal* tree, and on the full moon day of *Jestha* (June) they worship the Banyan tree. The custom prevails of the worship of a well by women after their delivery. A woman, after completing the period of her confinement or ceremonial impurity, is taken to a well, from which she has to bring home water, and is required to worship the well with the following materials, *viz* :— cotton thread, copper coins, cocoanuts and such other fruit as can be had on the occasion.[3] At Varsai in the Pen taluka of the Kolába District, offerings of cotton cloth, copper coins, cocoanuts, betelnuts and plantains are made to the Banyan, *Pipal,* and *Umbar* trees, and also to holy wells. The *Pipal, Tulsi,* and *Umbar* trees are worshipped daily by women in this district, while the Banyan is worshipped on the full moon day of Jestha (June). The materials of worship are :— rice, fruits, water, sandalpaste, flowers, mangoes and jack fruits.[4]

At Málád in the Thána District, the Banyan tree is worshipped by women of the *Dwijas*, i.e., of the twice born castes, on the full moon day of the month of *Jestha*. Copper or silver coins and fruit are offered to the tree These offerings are taken by the Bráhman priest, who explains to them the modes of worship. The Bráhman priest is also given some money as a gift. This *Vrata,* i.e., vow, is observed by women by fasting for three successive days, from the 13th to the 15th day of the bright half of *Jestha* (June). The *Pipal* tree is worshipped daily by some men and women of the Bráhman caste. Women walk round this tree for a hundred and eight times or more daily. Some persons hold a thread ceremony for the Pipal tree in order to obtain a son, and worship the tree for a certain period. It is worshipped with fruit and copper coins. Wooden cradles are also offered to the tree. Wells are worshipped on auspicious days such as *Parwani* by women of the upper castes.[5] At Padghe in the Thána District the Banyan tree is worshipped on the full moon day of *Jestha*, and the *Pipal* is worshipped every Saturday in the month of *Shráwan* (August). The *Pipal* tree is not worshipped before the performance of its thread ceremony, and its thread ceremony is not performed till the tree bears at least one thousand leaves.[6]

At Kolhápur, the Banyan and *Pipal* trees are considered very holy, and offerings of rags, coins, etc., are made to them. It is a custom among the Hindu women to worship the Banyan tree on the full moon day of *Jestha*. Offerings of cloth and fruit are made to this tree, and copper or silver coins are given as *dakshana*. Some women make a small model in gold, silver, or copper of the Banyan tree or of its leaf, and present it to the Bráhman priest along with a present of money. All these rites are required to be strictly performed as enjoined in the *Shástras*.[7]

1 School Master, Anjarle, Ratnágiri.
2 School Master, Ibhrampur, Ratnágiri.
3 School Master, Vavanje, Kolába.
4 School Master, Varsai, Kolába.
5 School Master, Málád, Thána.
6 School Master, Padghe, Thána.
7 Ráo Sáheb Shelke, Kolhápur.

At Nágothane in the Kolába District, it is believed that men who are well versed in the *mantras* of witchcraft and sorcery sometimes transfer diseases from one person to another.[1] Vaccination is believed to be a method of transferring disease to other persons.[2]

At Málád in the Thána District a method of transferring disease from one person to another is in practice among the *Shudras*. It is as follows :—A woman without a child cuts secretly a little piece from the garment of a woman who has children. She then burns the piece, puts the ashes into water, and the mixture is then drunk by the barren woman. It is believed that, by so doing, the evil spirit of the disease that is troubling the barren woman is transferred to the other who has children. The barrenness of the first woman then disappears, and she begets children. It is said that if the second woman comes to know of the mischief before using that garment, she discontinues the use of the same, and no harm is done to her.[3]

In the Umbergaon taluka of the Thána District the methods of transferring disease are called *Muth Márane* i. e., a bewitched lime is sent to the person to whom the disease is to be transferred. Various *mantras* are also secretly repeated with the object of transferring the disease to an enemy.[4]

At Kolhápur, there are no methods of transferring disease to other persons, but it is said that the following ceremony is practised in the case of persons suffering from swollen glands. Rice, *Udid* grain etc. are tied in a yellow cloth, and three knots are made in it. This is then kept for one night under the pillow of the diseased person. It is taken out the next morning and thrown away at a place where three roads meet. It is then supposed that the person who steps on the bundle first is attacked with the disease, and the one for whom the rite is performed is cured.[5]

At Devgad taluka in the Ratnágiri District it is believed that evil spirits are fond of things like a cock, cocoanuts, boiled rice, etc., and when a person considers himself attacked by evil spirits, these things are waved round his body and thrown away at some distance from his residence. This is generally done in the evening, but if necessary it can be done at any time. The person who goes to throw these things away is prohibited from looking behind. The things required for a *bali*, i. e., oblation, on such occasions are boiled rice, red powder, and an oil lamp made of black cotton wick.[6]

In the Vengurla taluka of the Ratnágiri District, when a person is suffering from any disease for a long time, and when ordinary medicines prove to be ineffective, a goat or a cock is waved round the body of the patient, and are then put beyond the village boundary or taken away by the sorcerer. While performing this rite, the man must repeat certain *mantras*.[7]

At Fonda in the Ratnágiri District, the use of scapegoats is resorted to in cases of persons supposed to have been attacked by evil spirits. Curds and boiled rice are waved round the body of the diseased person and thrown away at a distance from the house. In some cases it is said that the cock which is waved round the body of the sick person dies instantaneously.[8]

In the Málwan taluka of the Ratnágiri District the scapegoat (often a cock) is waved

[1] School Master, Nágothane, Kolába.
[2] School Master, Navare, Ratnágiri.
[3] School Master, Málád, Thána.
[4] School Master, Shirgaon, Thána.
[5] Ráo Saheb Shelke, Kolhápur.
[6] School Master, Mitbáv, Ratnágiri.
[7] School Master, Ubhádánda, Ratnágiri.
[8] School Master, Fonde, Ratnágiri.

three times round the sick person and thrown into the street. The man who goes to throw it away is prohibited from looking behind. Burnt cowdung ashes are thrown out of the door after the man has left the house, and the door is closed at once.[1]

In the Dápoli taluka, cocoanuts, curds, boiled rice, turmeric powder, red powder, cocks etc. are waved round the body of the sick person and taken beyond the village boundary or to a big tree supposed to be haunted by evil spirits, and in some cases these things are thrown away where four roads meet.[2]

In the Rájápur taluka of the Ratnágiri District scapegoats are used by the low caste people, while Bráhmans use cocoanuts, boiled rice and copper coins.[3] At Kálse in the Ratnágiri District eggs, cocks, goats, etc. are used as scapegoats. These things are waved round the body of the patient, and taken beyond the village limits or far from the residence of the sick person. For this rite a man from the Ghádi, Gurav, Rával, or Máhar caste is invited at night, and he is paid in cash for his services.[4]

At Ibhrampur in the Ratnágiri District, the cocks and goats used for driving out evil spirits from the body of the patient are not thrown away, but are eaten by the exorcist.[5]

At Navre in the Ratnágiri District, hens are used to extract the poison of snake bites from the body of the sufferer. In cases of evil spirits alone, cocoanuts, cocks and goats are used as scapegoats.[6]

At Dásgaon in the Kolába District, a *Paradi* (basket) containing black glass beads, bangles, turmeric and red powders, sweetmeat of five sorts, flowers, cocoanut, a burning scented stick, and rice, is waved three times round the body of the patient, and thrown away outside the village.[7]

At Kolhápur, the use of fowls, goats, limes, cocoanuts, copper coins, dry chillies and salt is in vogue, not only in cases of sick persons, but also when a person performs a feat such as bending an iron bar, or doubling with his hands a silver coin, or winning a victory in wrestling. The articles are then waved round him and thrown away in order that he may not suffer from an evil eye. Among the rich the same rite is performed on ordinary occasions such as leaving a house, starting on a journey etc. In cases of illness it is specially performed in the evening, and the articles are thrown away at the outskirts of the village, or by the side of a well.[8]

1 School Master, Bandivade, Ratnágiri.
2 School Master, Anjarla, Ratnágiri.
3 School Master, Adivare, Ratnágiri.
4 School Master, Kálse, Ratnágiri.
5 School Master, Ibhrampur, Ratnágiri.
6 School Master, Navre, Ratnágiri.
7 School Master, Dásgaon, Kolába.
8 Rao Sáhib, Shelke, Kolhápur.

CHAPTER IV.

WORSHIP OF ANCESTORS AND SAINTS.

In the Konkan, especially among the lower classes, a strong belief prevails regarding the mortality of the spirits of the dead and of their re-appearance or re-birth in their children. And for this reason, as well as for protection against evil, the dead ancestors are worshipped.

The custom regarding the worship of ancestors prevailing at Kálshe in the Ratnágiri District is as follows:—The worship of ancestors is called *Shráddha* (anniversary). It is performed on the no moon day of every month, on the date of the death of the person every year, and also on the same date of the dark half of the month of *Bhádrapada* (September). Among the Bráhmans, Bráhman priests are invited, worshipped, and are given a feast, after worshipping balls of boiled rice as representing the dead ancestors. The special materials used for worship are sesamum and barley grain. The same custom prevails among non-Bráhmans with the exception that the balls are made of rice flour and not of boiled rice. To partake of the food on such occasions, the lower classes invite married persons of their own caste. The anniversary day of *Sádhus* and *Mahants*, i.e. saints, is called *Punya tithi* i.e. the day of merit.

It is commonly believed that spirits are mortal. The life of the deceased remains in the spirit condition until the sins which he may have committed are washed away by the good deeds of his descendants. There is no belief that one spirit dies and another takes its place, but it is believed that the ancestors are sometimes reborn in the same family.[1]

At Ubhádánda in the Vengurla taluka of the Ratnágiri District ancestors are worshipped every year on the same date of the month (according to the Hindu calendar year) on which the person died, by performing a *Shráddha* rite. They are also worshipped on the same date in the second half of *Bhádrapada* (September) every year. This is by a rite called *Mahálaya Shráddha*. On both these occasions Bráhmans are invited, and the worshipping ceremony is performed by repeating the *mantras*. After the ceremony, all the invited guests men and women partake of food.

Sádhus are worshipped after washing their feet with sandal paste, flowers, cocoanuts and gifts of money.

It is believed that evil spirits undergo a transformation after a lapse of twelve years. The practice of giving the names of ancestors to children is common, and it is due to the belief that the spirits of the dead are reborn in children in the same family.[2]

At Pendur in the Ratnágiri District the ancestors are worshipped on the last day of every Hindu calendar month. This monthly worship is called *Darsha Shráddha*. The annual anniversay of the *manes* is celebrated by the ceremony called the *Sámvatsarik Shráddha*. If any ancestor has died after becoming a recluse or *Sanyási*, his body is

---

[1] School Master, Kálse, Ratnágiri.

[2] School Master, Ubhádánda, Ratnágiri.

buried, and a tomb called a *samádhi* is erected over it; and his descendants, instead of performing the annual *Shráddha*, worship the tomb of the recluse every day. It is believed that the spirits take a different form after the lapse of seven generations. The belief that the spirits of the dead are reborn in the same family prevails among the people of this district. The following measures are adopted for the purpose of identification. When a person dies in a family, a basil or *bel* leaf is placed on a certain part of the body, or some familiar sign is made in sandal paste; and when a child is born in the family, its body is carefully examined to ascertain whether there are any signs on the body of the child such as were made on the dead body of the ancestor. If the same sign appears to the satisfaction of the members of the family, it is believed that the dead person has been reborn in the same family.[1]

At Navare in the Ratnágiri District Bráhmans are invited, worshipped and given a feast in honour of ancestors. *Sádhus* and *Mahants*, or saints, are worshipped by giving them the same honour accorded to the family deities.[2]

At Basani in the Ratnágiri District the anniversary day of saints is observed by the performance of a *Bhajan*, which consists in singing the good deeds of saints and in offering prayers. It is believed that spirits are mortal, but they do not die like ordinary human beings. They cease to exist as spirits as soon as the period of their release is over. The spirits obtain absolution by visiting certain holy places.[3]

At Dabhol in the Ratnágiri District the people believe that the souls of ancestors are reborn in children in the same family if some of their desires remain unfulfilled at the time of their demise.[4]

At Shiravde in the Ratnágiri District ancestors are worshipped every year by performing the rites called *tarpan*, which consist in offering oblations of holy water, sesamum, barley grains and repeating prayers. The *tarpan* is observed on the very date of the month in which the person died. The procedure of worshipping the Hindu saints is similar to that of the other deities. Owing to the belief that the spirit of the dead are reborn in children in the same family the name of the grandfather is given to the grandson.[5]

At Náringre in the Ratnágiri taluka ancestors are worshipped by inviting Bráhman priests, and worshipping them with sandal paste and flowers. These Bráhmans are supposed to represent the father, grandfather and great grandfather of the worshipper.[6]

At Bándivade in the Ratnágiri District the leaves of the herb called *pudina*, (a good medicine for worms) sesamum, and *darbha* grass are required for the worship of ancestors. The man who worships the ancestors has to turn his sacred thread from the right hand to the left.[7]

At Anjarle in the Ratnágiri District *Mahants* and *Sádhus* are worshipped in their lifetime like family deities, and their tombs are worshipped after their death.[8]

At Fonde in the Ratnágiri District ancestors are worshipped by making balls of boiled rice on their anniversary day. The balls are supposed to take the place of the dead parents, and they are worshipped with sandal paste and flowers, and by burning incense and lighting a lamp of clarified butter. Betelnuts and leaves, cocoanuts and *Dakshina* (presents of money) are given to them. People also bow before them.

[1] School Master, Pendur, Ratnágiri.
[2] School Master, Navare, Ratnágiri.
[3] School Master, Basani, Ratnágiri.
[4] School Master, Dabhol, Ratnágiri.
[5] School Master, Shiravde, Ratnágiri.
[6] School Master, Náringre, Ratnágiri.
[7] School Master, Bándivade, Ratnágiri.
[8] School Master, Anjarle, Ratnágiri.

Mahants and *Sádhus* are worshipped by washing their feet, sandal paste is applied to their body, and they are garlanded with flowers. Cocoanuts, a piece of cloth and a gift in coins are given to them according to the means of the giver. It is said that spirits can remain as spirits for about a thousand years.[1]

At Vijayadurg in the Ratnágiri District the method of worshipping ancestors is as follows:—In some cases elderly parents as well as a grandfather and great grandfather are also worshipped, their feet are washed with water, and the water is accepted as *tirth* or holywater. While worshipping the *Mahants* and *Sádhus*, or saints, water is poured on their right hand, and they are worshipped with sandal paste and flowers, and given a *dakshana* or gifts of money according to one's means and will. The *pádukas*, or foot prints, of saints are worshipped after their death.[2]

At Mitbáv in the Ratnágiri District holy persons such as Sanyásis are worshipped after their death by performing their anniversary ceremony every year. It is believed that spirits are mortal. Evil spirits such as *munjas*, etc., undergo a kind of transformation, and it is believed that this occurs at places like Narsoba's Wádi.[3]

At Devgad in the Ratnágiri District ancestors are worshipped on their anniversary days, the *manes* being represented by pieces of *Darbha* grass and balls of boiled rice.[4]

At Poladpur in the Kolába District a person whose father is alive but who has lost his mother's father, has to perform the *Shráddha* of that grandfather on the 1st day of the bright half of *Ashwin* (October). This *Shráddha* is called *Duhitra*. A person who has lost his wife has to perform the *Shráddha* for that wife on the 9th day of the dark half of the month of *Bhádrapada*. This day is called *Ahev Navami*. These different sorts of *Shráddhas* are observed only by the high class Hindus. The lower classes worship their ancestors on the last day of the month of *Bhádrapada* by preparing a ball of boiled rice or flour, and putting it out for the crows to eat. It is believed that spirits are mortal. The ceremony called *Narayan Nagabali* is performed when it is believed that the spirit of an ancestor is giving trouble to the family. When this rite is performed, the spirit is saved and the ailment ceases. It is believed that the spirits of the dead are sometimes reborn in children in the same family, and in such cases the names of the ancestors are given to their children by the people.[5]

At Khopoli in the Karjat taluka of the Kolába District the form of worship of ancestors is similar to that of the ordinary Hindu deities. In the case of the worship of the deities the person performing the worship has to sit with his face towards the east, while at the worship of the ancestors he has to sit with his face towards the south.[6]

At Chaul in the Kolába District, the tombs of *Sanyásis*, i.e. ascetics and *Sádhus* are worshipped on their anniversary days, and a great fair is held in their honour. The other ancestors are worshipped by the *shráddha* rites. The anniversary of the founders of the different sects is observed by their followers by a *bhajan*, i. e. singing songs in their own style and exhibiting the different insignia and flag of the sect as advised by their founders.[7]

The people of Chidhran in the Kolába District believe that the period for which the soul has to remain in the spirit state depends

[1] School Master, Fonde, Ratnágiri.
[2] School Master, Vijayadurg, Ratnágiri.
[3] School Master, Mitbáv, Ratnágiri.
[4] School Master, Devgad, Ratnágiri.
[5] School Master, Poladpur, Kolába.
[6] School Master, Khopoli, Kolába.
[7] School Master, Chaul, Kolába.

upon the sins of the person, or the wishes which remained unfulfilled during his life time. It is not that all the spirits of the dead are reborn in children. The rebirth depends upon the good or bad deeds of the deceased. However, if the nature of any child suggests the nature of any dead person in the family, it is assumed that the spirit of the deceased has returned to the family.[1]

At Nágothane in the Pen taluka of the Kolába District some of the communities worship small images called *tánks* on the anniversary of their ancestors' death; among the *Shudras* food is given to the crows on the last day of *Bhádrapad*. The custom of giving a grandfather's name to the grandson prevails largely, and is due to the belief that the spirits of the dead are sometimes reborn in the same family.[2] It is also said that in some of the Hindu communities, if a child cries continuously, ashes are applied to its forehead in the name of one of the ancestors in the family; and if the child sleeps quietly or stops crying, the name of that ancestor is given to it.[3]

At Shirgaon in the Thána District, the worship of ancestors is performed on the day of the father's death, every year. On any auspicious occasion the rite called *Nándi shráddha* is performed at the beginning of the ceremony. It is believed that evil spirits or ghosts have to remain in the ghostly state for about one thousand years, or at least until one of the descendants in the family goes to a holy place like *Káshi* (Benares) and there performs the *shráddha* rites of his ancestors.[4]

At Málád in the Thána District, the worship of ancestors is performed on the day of the father's death every month till the completion of one year by inviting Bráhmans and giving them a feast. This is done among Bráhmans only. The other communities worship their ancestors by performing the rite called *Chata Shráddha* and by giving *Shidha*, i.e. rice pulse, vegetables and ghi to Bráhman priests. A feast is then given to their castemen.[5]

At Kolhápur, ancestors, *Mahants* and *Sádhus* are worshipped by the rites known as the Puranic ritual, that is, no Vedic *mantras* are repeated while performing these rites. It is a common belief in this province that the soul of the person who has committed a murder, or has incurred debt and enmity, is obliged to repay the debt by being born again as a servant or in some other subordinate capacity of the debtor.[6]

The tombs of the Hindu and Mahomedan saints are considered holy, but they are not supposed to possess miraculor powers.[7] The following is a list of saints who have been deified and worshipped by the people of the Ratnágiri District. (1) Mukundráj, (2) Dnyándev, (3) Tukárám, (4) Eknáth (5) Námdev, (6) Rámdás, (7) Akkalkotche Swámi, (8) Ranganáth, (9) Dev Mámlatdár (10) Kabir, (11) Kamál, (12) Nipat Niranjan, (13) Tulshidás, (14) Pundalik, (15) Vashistha, (16) Dattátraya, (17) Sohiroba, (18) Gorakshanath, (19) Purnanáth.

At Shiroda in the Ratnágiri District a practice prevails of making vows to the tombs of women who burnt themselves as *Satvis*. Vows are also made to the Musalman Pirs, and offerings are often made in fulfilment of such vows.[8]

At the fort of *Vishálgad* there is a tomb of a Pir (saint). It is usual to make a vow to

1 School Master, Chidhran, Kolába.
2 School Master, Nágothane, Kolába.
3 School Master, Vavanje, Kolába.
4 School Master, Shirgaon, Thána.
5 School Master, Málád, Thána.
6 Rao Saheb Shelke, Kolhápur.
7 School Master, Pendur, Ratnágiri.
8 School Master, Shiroda, Ratnágiri.

worship this Pir with fetters on one's legs, and it is believed that, at the time of worship, the chains break off.[1]

There is at Dahibáv in the Ratnágiri District a tomb of a Hindu saint named *Shri Anand Murti,* to which the people of that locality make vows when severe calamities befall them, and it is believed that the saint listens to their prayers.[2]

When a Bráhman assumes the garb of a recluse or *Sanyási,* he is considered by the people as sacred as a Hindu god, and is worshipped with great reverence, provided he abides by the rules contained in the *shastras.*[3]

There is a tomb of a Pir at Báwa Málangad in the Panwel taluka of the Kolába District, where the people make vows to the Pir, and it is believed that the Pir fulfils their wishes. Hindu saints such as Rámdás, Dnyáneshwar, Námdev are held in great honour in this District.[4]

There is a temple of *Nágoba* at Avas in the Kolába District where persons suffering from snake-bite, if carried to the temple while still alive, are said to be cured.[5]

At Kawad in the Bhiwandi taluka of the Thána District there is a tomb of a *Brahmáchari* named *Sakhárám Báva* who has been deified by the people of that District. A great fair is held at the tomb every year.[6]

The following instance is given of a miracle at the tomb *Sakhárám Báva* of Kawad. A man suffering from fits showed an inclination to go to Kawad to read *Guru Charitra* for seven successive days. He was taken to that place accordingly. After his arrival, he continued to suffer from these fits in the morning and evening at the time of the worship at the tomb. Once during the fits he said that he would be free from the disease if Rs. 200 were spent in giving a feast to the Bráhmans at Páli. The relatives of the sufferer agreed to arrange accordingly, and instantly the man put his head on the *Samádhi* (tomb) and threw himself on his back. He came to his senses after ten minutes, and from that time he was completely cured. A feast was then given to the Bráhmans at Páli, and Rs. 200 were spent over it as promised. Another instance of miracular power is cited, and that is of the priest of the goddess *Mahaluxmi* of Kolwan. This priest goes up and hoists the flag of the goddess on a steep hill which no other person can climb, and it is believed that he can do this only when the spirit of the goddess enters his body.[7]

At Umbergaon in the Thána District there is a miracle-working tomb of a saint called the Dátár "Pir." Sakhárámbáva of Angaon Kawad, a Hindu saint, is held in high honour in this village.[8] At this place it is also believed that some of the Pirs walk round the village at night, and their tombs are said to be seen in motion. The Dátár Pir is worshipped even by the Hindus of that locality.[9]

At Shirosi in the Murbád Taluka of the Thána District, Sakhárámbáva of Kawad, Dev Mámlatdár, Chandirámbuva of Khed, Narayanbuva of Nanuri, the *Swámi* of Akkalkot, the *Swámi* of Kumbhar Peth at Kolhápur, and the Dandekerbuva of Rájápur are the principal saints held in honour by the people.[10]

At Mánikpur in the Thána District it is said that a bright light or flames emanate from certain tombs of Musalman saints.[11]

[1] School Master, Sakharane, Ratnágiri.
[2] School Master, Náringre, Ratnágiri.
[3] School Master, Adivare, Ratnágiri.
[4] School Master, Chauk, Ratnágiri.
[5] School Master, Akshi, Kolába.
[6] School Master, Váda, Thána.
[7] School Master, Padghe, Thána.
[8] School Master, Dahánu, Thána.
[9] School Master, Umbergaon, Thána.
[10] School Master, Shirosi, Thána.
[11] School Master, Mánikpur, Thána.

At Umela in the Thána District it is said that flames and smoke are given out from the tombs of certain Mahomedan saints situated in the locality. These flames appear and disappear very suddenly.[1]

In the Kolhápur District people believe that the *Samádhi* of Swámi Anandmúrti, who was a disciple of Raghunath Swámi of Bhramanál, shakes on the *Shiwarátri* day, that is the 13th of the dark half of *Mágha*, and on the Rámanawami day *i. e.* the 9th of the bright half of *Chaitra*, at the time of the worship called *Bhajan*. Among the tombs held most sacred by the Hindus of the Konkan may be mentioned the following *viz*: Bhujang Swámi of Lokapur, Rámdás Swámi, the *Samádhi* of Shri Shankaráchárya at Shirgaon, Chintaman Swámi of Murgud, and the *Samádhi* of Mangalmúrti Morya at Chinchwad near Poona. All these *Swámis* were *Brahmacháris* or bachelors, and they spent their lives in the service of God and preached virtue and morality to the masses. These *Samádhis* are of two kinds: (1) of saints after death, and (2) of saints on the point of death. The third kind is called *Jal Samádhi*, i.e. immersion in water, but no tomb of the latter kind is to be found in this Province. It is said that, if a lime is placed above the *Samádhi* of Bhujanga Swámi, it begins to shake at the time of the *Arti* ceremony. The present disciple of Bhujanga Swámi sits in (*Samádhi*) meditation continuously for four to eight days. There prevails a belief at Kolhápur that the *swámi* whose body is buried in the tomb at Chinchwad is still alive. Some years ago when the present disciple of the Chinchwad *Swámi* was anxious to take *Samádh*, he had a dream in which the *swámi* in the tomb told him that he was still living in that *Samádhi*, and that therefore there was no need for his disciple to take *Samádh*. He was thus obliged to forego the project. The Peshwas of Poona, who were staunch devotees of the Chinchwad *swámi*, and by whose favour they were raised to a position of social equality among the Deccan Bráhmans, granted an *Inam* of some villages for the maintenance of this *Samádhi*, and the British Government have allowed the descendants of the *swámi* to retain the *Inam*. The following are the principal Musalman saints who have been deified in the Kolhapur District:—

(1) *Bába Jamál*, (2) *Ghod Pir*, (3) *Bara Imám*, (4) *Avachit Pir*, (5) *Buran Sáheb* and (6) *Mira Sáheb* of *Miraj*. All these Pirs have been supplied with annual grants of money by the Kolhápur State.[2]

At Ubhádánda in the Vengurla taluka of the Ratnágiri District some Hindus have adopted the worship of Mahomedan saints. Mahomedan Pirs are worshipped in the month of *Moharram*. On these occasions Hindus beg in the town in the disguise of *Fakirs*, and the alms thus obtained are offered to the Pir. They make offerings of water to the Pirs, while the *tábuts* are being carried to the sea for immersion. But this practice is being slowly discontinued.[3]

At Bándivade in the Ratnágiri District Hindus offer cocoanuts and *khichadi* to the Pirs at the time of the *Moharram*, and at some places a lamp is kept burning every Monday in honour of a Pir.[4]

At Kálbádevi in the Ratnágiri taluka there is a tomb of a Musalmán saint who is worshipped by the Hindus. Similarly there is a Pir at *Gaonkhádi* in the Rájápur taluka who is held in reverence even by high caste Hindus.[5]

At Ade in the Dápoli taluka of the Ratnágiri District there is a tomb of a Musalman saint which is worshipped by the Hindus including the Bráhmans. The building and also the mosque in that village have been repaired from contributions obtained from high class Hindus.[6] Many Hindus of Devagad in the Ratnágiri District worship Musalman saints. Occasionally they offer cocoanuts to *tábuts*, and throw red powder over them. They also make vows to the Pirs.[7]

1 School Master, Umela, Thána.

2 Ráo Sáheb Shelke, Kolhápur.

3 School Master, Ubhádánda, Ratnágiri.

4 School Master, Bandivade, Ratnágiri.

5 School Master, Basani, Ratnágiri.

6 School Master, Murud, Ratnágiri.

7 School Master, Devagad, Ratnágiri.

There are two Pirs at Vijayadurg who are worshipped by the Hindus. The same practice prevails at Rájápur and Khárepátan.[1]

At Chauk in the Karjat taluka of the Kolába District some Hindus worship Pirs. The members of the *Ketkar* family of Chauk are the *Pujáris* or ministrants of the Musalmán saint known as *Báva Málangad*. This shows that even Bráhmans worship Musalmán saints.[2]

The tomb of *Bavá Málangad* situated in the Kolába District is worshipped first by a Bráhman and then by Musalmáns. The Bráhman worshipper performs this task more for the pecuniary benefit which he derives from the worship than from faith in the divinity of the Pir.[3]

At Poladpur in the Mahád taluka of the Kolába District there are no instances of Musalmán saints being worshipped by Hindus, but persons wishing to have children make vows to Pirs, and children born by the favour of such Pirs are required to assume the robe of a *Fakir* during the *Moharram* festivities.[4]

The practice of worshipping such saints exists at Khopoli in the Kolába District. Persons in trouble, or desirous of getting children, make vows to the saint Imám Hussein, and when their desires are fulfilled they dress themselves as *Fakirs* and beg at certain places during the *Moharram* festivities.[5] A certain Lakshman Gangádhar Joshi of Rewdanda in the Kolába District is the *Mujáwar* (priest or ministrant) of a Musalman saint *Chánsewalli* and he holds an *Inám* in connection with his office of *Mujáwar* of the saint's *Darga*.[6]

At Akshi in the Kolába District there is a tomb of a Pir which is worshipped by lower class Hindus such as *Kolis, Mális* and *Bhandáris*.[7]

The Hindus of Bhuwan in the Murbád taluka of the Kolába District worship the Pir of the locality. It is said that the cultivators of the village once lost their cattle, and that a *Fakir* attributed the loss to the rage of the Pir. Since that time they are careful to worship the saint, and the result is that there has been no disease among their cattle. They offer *Malinda* i. e. bread and *jágri*, to the Pir every Thursday.[8]

The Hindu inhabitants of Málád in the Thána District sprinkle water over the roads by which the *tábuts* are to pass, and allow their children to pass beneath the *tábuts*. Some throw sweetmeat on the *tábuts*, and distribute the same to the poor.[9]

At Shirgaon in the Máhim taluka of the Thána District some Hindus make vows to the local Pir and take part in the *tábut* procession. They pour water over the feet of the *tábut* bearers, and throw *abir* (black scented powder) and flowers on the *tábuts*. They also distribute to the *fakirs Malinda*, or *Khichadi*.[10]

The *Mujáwar* (priest) of the saint *Walli Amir Shaha* of Shahápur in the Thána District is a Marátha by caste.[11]

In the Kolhápur District Pirs are held in great reverence by Hindus. They make vows to the Pirs in order to get a son, and when their object is fulfilled they offer a preparation of *Til* (sesamum) and sugar called *Rewadi*, and other sweets called *Chonge, Malinda* and *Pedhe* at the time of *Moharram*. They also give *Fakiri* to their sons in the *tábut* season. Some of them even bring a *tábut* and *Nál sáheb* to their houses, and spend much money on them for illuminations, etc. They dance from one *Nálpir* to the other saying that the *Nalpir* has entered their bodies. While going through the streets they cry out very loudly the words '*Yalli Dhulla*'. The holiday of the *Moharram* is obsereved for ten days. On the tenth day the *tábuts* and the *Nálpirs* are taken

[1] School Master, Vijaydurg, Ratnágiri.
[2] School Master, Chauk, Kolába.
[3] School Master, Chidhran, Kolába.
[4] School Master, Poladpur, Kolába.
[5] School Master, Khopoli, Kolába.
[6] School Master, Chowl, Kolába.
[7] School Master, Akshi, Kolába.
[8] School Master, Bhuwan, Thána.
[9] School Master, Málád, Thána.
[10] School Master, Shirgaon, Thána.
[11] School Master, Shirosi, Thána.

to the river for the purpose of immersion. While returning home from the river with the bundle of the *Patka* of *Nálpir* on their heads they cry out loudly the following words: "*Alabidáyo ála bidásha ya Husan bani alidosháke sultán albida*". On the third day after the immersion of *tábuts* into the river, the Pirs devotees kill a goat in the name of their patron Pir and make a preparation of the goat's flesh called *Konduri*.[1]

The following rites are in vogue for the cure of barrenness in the village of Dábhol in the Ratnágiri District.—(1) Walking round the *Pipal* tree daily; (2) Observing a fast for sixteen successive Mondays; (3) Performing the worship of Shiva after observing the aforesaid fast.[2]

At Kálshe in the Málwan taluka of the Ratnágiri District a barren woman is required to walk round a *Pipal* tree every day in the morning, and if the barrenness be attributed to the disfavour of any deity or the attack of an evil spirit, the same deity or the evil spirit is invoked and worshipped by the woman herself, or through a medium who knows the appropriate mode of worship.[3]

To steal an earthen image of the God *Ganpati*, to make a cross or a *Swástika* on the bodies of children with marking nut, and the worship of the god *Máruti* or some other powerful deity at midnight in the no moon by a barren woman, after divesting herself of her clothes, are rural methods for the cure of barrenness observed at Anjarle and other places in the Dápoli taluka of the Ratnágiri District.[4]

At Bándivade in the Ratnágiri District copper amulets and black cotton strings are used to cure barrenness. Some people make vows to a particular deity, and some perform the rite of *Nágabali*.[5]

To walk round *Pipal* and *Umbar* trees, to circumambulate the temple of a particular deity, and to make vows to that deity, to recite or have recited the holy scripture *Harivansha*, are methods in practice for cure of barrenness at Achre in the Málwan taluka of the Ratnágiri District.[6]

At Vijayadurg in the Ratnágiri District, it is believed that beating a woman at the time of an eclipse is one of the surest methods of curing barrenness. Some people give charity, observe fasts, worship certain deities and make vows to them to obtain children.[7]

At Ubhádánda in the Ratnágiri District, stealing the idol of Krishna when it is being worshipped on the 8th day of the dark half of *Shráwan* (August), the birth day of the god Krishna, and putting a cocoanut or a betelnut in its place is believed to be the best method of curing barrenness.[8]

At Chauk in the Kolába District, the same plan of stealing the idol of the god Krishna is observed as a cure for barrenness. But here the idol is returned with great pomp, and replaced in its original place after the birth of a child. The godlings *Hanumán* and *Bawan Vir* are also worshipped for the cure of barrenness.[9]

At Poladpur in the Kolába District the favourite method of curing barrenness is to obtain copper amulets and black or red cotton strings from a Fakir.[10]

The following are the methods in vogue for the cure of barrenness at Khopoli in the Kolába District.

(1) To inquire from a sorcerer the cause of barrenness, and then to perform the rites mentioned by him.

(2) To use copper amulets and cotton strings taken from a *Mántrik* i. e., one well versed in the *mantras*.

[1] Ráo Sáheb Shelke, Kolhápur.
[2] School Master, Dábhol, Ratnágiri.
[3] School Master, Kalshe, Ratnágiri.
[4] School Master, Anjarle, Ratnágiri.
[5] School Master, Bándivade, Ratnágiri.
[6] School Master, Achre, Ratnágiri.
[7] School Master, Vijayadurg, Ratnágiri.
[8] School Master, Ubhádánda, Ratnágiri.
[9] School Master, Chauk, Kolába.
[10] School Master, Poladpur, Kolába.

(3) To walk round the *Tulsi* (basil) plant or the *Pipal* or Banyan tree daily in the morning after worshipping it.

(4) To feed another woman's child, or to give milk to a child.[1]

At Náta in the Kolába District, a woman wishing to have a child is required to strike with a knife the Jack, the Tamarind, and the *Chámpa* trees during an eclipse. It is believed that by so doing the woman will bear a child, and the trees will also bear flowers and fruits.[2]

At Medhe in the Roha taluka of the Kolába District, the following methods are in vogue for the cure of barrenness:—

(1) To worship the god Shiva and to observe fasts on Mondays.

(2) To worship the god Ganpati and to observe fasts on *Sankasthi chaturthi* i. e., the fourth day of the dark half of every month.

(3) To walk round the temple of *Máruti* and *Pipal* and *Umbar* trees every day, in the morning.[3]

At Padaghe in the Bhiwandi taluka of the Thána District, images of Ráma and Krishna are put into the lap of a barren woman on their respective birthdays *i. e.*, the 9th day of the bright half of *Chaitra*, and the 8th day of the dark half of *Shráwan*. Cocoanuts are also placed in her lap with these images.[4]

At Mánikpur in the Thána District the goddess *Shitala* is worshipped by women to cure barrenness. They observe fasts, and go to the temple of the goddess bare-footed with their hair loose and throwing milk on their path. They offer to the goddess wooden cradles and children's toys in fulfilment of their vows.[5]

At Shirgaon in the Máhim taluka of the Thána District, it is said that the repetition of the *mantra* "*Santán Gopál jáy*" is resorted to as a cure for barrenness.[6]

At Wáde in the Thána District, women make vows even to minor deities such as Chedoba to get rid of barrenness. They also use copper amulets and cotton strings procured from a sorcerer well versed in the use of *mantras*.[7]

At Dahigaon in the Thána District the worship of the god Shri Satya Náráyan is held to cure barrenness. Some women also distribute to the poor *jágri* equal to the weight of a child.[8]

At Dehari in the Murbád taluka of the Thána District, the village deity Dehari Máta is invoked and worshipped by women for the cure of barrenness.[9] In the Kolhápur District, the help of the family deities and of the household deities is invoked. Women take turns round the Banyan, *Pipal* and *Umbar*, trees. Some make vows to the gods, and perform certain propitiatory rites as well as the *Náráyan Nágabali*. It is believed that the children do not live long if a member of the family has killed a snake, or if the funeral rites of a person in the family have remained unperformed. The following ceremony is known as *Náráyan Nágabali*. A snake is made from the flour of *Rála* (panic seed), and another made of gold is put into it. It is then burnt like a dead body. All the ordinary funeral rites are performed. After performing the eleventh day rites, *homa*, i.e., sacred fire, is kindled at night time, and after keeping vigil for the whole night, milk and a *dakshana* are given to Bráhmans. A feast is given to eleven Bráhmans on that day. On the twelfth day sixteen Bráhmans are fed, and on the thirteenth, five Bráhmans are given a feast, after performing the *Shráddha* rites. On the fourteenth day, again, a feast is given to about 100 to 500 Bráhmans according to the means of the host. It is believed that, after the performance of these rites, the soul of the deceased reaches heaven, and there is an end to the troubles and misfortunes of the family.[10]

1 School Master, Khopoli, Kolába.
2 School Master; Náta, Kolába.
3 School Master, Medhe, Kolába.
4 School Master, Padaghe, Thána.
5 School Master, Mánikpur, Thána.
6 School Master, Shirgaon, Thána.
7 School Master, Wáde, Thána.
8 School Master, Dahigaon, Thána.
9 School Master, Dehari, Thána.
10 Ráo Sáheb Shelke, Kolhápur.

CHAPTER V.

THE WORSHIP OF THE MALEVOLENT DEAD.

At Ubhádánda in the Ratnágiri District the following dreams are believed to be lucky and propitious. To swim through the river or sea, to rise to the sky, to see the Sun, the Moon and the other planets, to eat meat, to bathe in blood, and to eat rice and curds. It is also believed that the sight of white objects in dreams foretells success in any work or undertaking that may be in view. A deity, a Bráhman, a king, a married woman decked with ornaments, a bullock, a mountain, trees full of fruits, climbing the *Umber* tree, a looking glass, meat and flowers, if seen in dreams, are good omens. Climbing the *Palas* tree, *Warul* i. e. an ant heap, the bitter lime tree, to marry, to use red clothes or red flower garlands, to eat cooked meat, to see the sun and the moon without lustre, and to see shooting stars during dreams, are said to be bad omens. [1]

At Mitbáv in the Devgad taluka of the Ratnágiri District dreams are believed to be caused by indigestion and restlessness. To embrace a dead body in a dream, to see troubled waters, to dine heartily, are said to be bad omens. Feasting friends and receiving gifts from them are said to be good omens.[2]

At Fonde in the Ratnágiri District dreams are said to indicate things that have happened, or are about to happen in the near future. All white substances other than cotton, salt, and bones, are considered auspicious, and all black substances excepting a lotus, a horse, an elephant, and a deity are considered inauspicious.[3]

At Ibhrampur in the Chiplun taluka, horrible dreams are good omens, while pleasing dreams indicate approaching calamities.[4]

At Pendur in the Ratnágiri District it is believed that dreams foretell future events. It is believed that the dream will prove correct and effective if the person dreaming has asked three questions and received three answers in his dream. Those dreams which are caused through cold are called *Jalap*. They are generally false dreams, and no good omens are derived therefrom.[5]

At Basani in the Ratnágiri District it is believed that the ancestors who take interest in the welfare of their descendants appear in dreams and foretell future events, so that the dreaming person may take the needful precautions for the prevention of future calamities.[6]

At Kálse in the Málwan taluka of the Ratnágiri Distri .t it is believed that dreams in the last part of the night. *i. e.*, just before daybreak, and in which great men are seen, generally prove effective. If anybody sees himself married in a dream it is supposed that he will hear of the death of some relative.[7]

At Chauk in the Kolába District it is believed that, when calamities are threatened, the guardian deity of the family as well as the dead ancestors appear in dreams and give warnings of the coming calamities.[8]

---

1 School Master, Ubhádánda, Ratnagiri.
2 School Master, Mitbáv, Ratnágiri.
3 School Master, Fonde, Ratnágiri.
4 School Master, Ibhrampur, Ratnágiri.
5 School Master, Pendur, Ratnágiri.
6 School Master, Basani, Ratnágiri.
7 School Master, Kálse, Ratnágiri.
8 School Master, Chauk, Kolába.

The people of Poladpur in the Kolába District believe in dreams; and when some of their deities appear in dreams and give them advice or directions, they are careful to follow them. Sometimes even evil spirits appear in dreams, and advise the people to do certain things to avert calamities. People who have faith in such spirits act according to their wishes, and if they fail to do so, trouble is sure to follow.[1]

The people of Khopoli in the Kolába District believe that if a person sees in a dream, the dead body of a near relative, it indicates that the person whose corpse was seen in the dream will live long.[2]

At Birwadi in the Kolába District it is believed that if a person sees a snake in a dream, a son will be born to him; if he sees a hell, he is sure to get wealth. If he sees gold, it is a sure sign of losing wealth. Again, if a person sees himself taking his meals in a dream, it indicates that his death is nigh at hand.[3]

At Málád in the Thána District, omens are derived from dreams. In case of bad dreams the god Vishnu is remembered, and the gods Shankar and Máruti are also worshipped.[4]

At Belápur, wood, cowdung cakes and turbid water, if seen in dreams, foretell calamities. White clothes, beautiful flowers, and food containing sweetmeat are considered auspicious.[5]

At Murbád in the Thána District it is believed that all black things, and white things such as ashes, are inauspicious when seen in dreams, but a black cow, white flowers, and pearls are auspicious. Considering the four parts of the night, the dreams that occur in the first part prove effective within one year, that of the second part within six months, that of the third within three months, and of the fourth within one month, and those caused at daybreak are realized immediately.[6]

At Kolhápur, dreams are believed to be caused through some mental derangement or bodily disorder. It is customary to derive omens from dreams, but their nature greatly depends upon the different times at which these dreams occur. The dreams caused in the latter part of the night, *i. e.* just before daybreak, are believed to come true.[7]

At Ubhádánda in the Vengurla taluka it is believed that the soul of a person leaves the body temporarily during his sleep; hence it is said that no changes or marks of colour, etc. should be made on the body of a person during sleep, because it is believed that, while returning, the soul identifies the body, and if it is satisfied with the marks of the body it enters it; otherwise it might not return.[8]

At Adivare it is believed that only Hindu saints and ascetics, after deep and devout meditation, are capable of removing the soul from the body. It is believed that their souls go to heaven during that period and return at pleasure. At present there are no such *sádhus* in the district.[9]

Many Hindus in the Ratnágiri District believe that the soul goes to drink water at night, and therefore keep a pot filled with water at their sleeping place.[10]

The people of Chaul in the Kolába District do not consider it possible ordinarily for the soul to leave the body, but they state that the Swámi of Alandi, who died in or about the year 1886, used to remove his soul from the body by means of *Yoga*.[11]

At Kolhápur, it is believed that the soul leaves the body temporarily at night when a person is asleep.[12]

---

1 School Master, Poládpur, Kolába.
2 School Master, Khopoli, Kolába.
3 School Master, Birwadi, Kolába.
4 School Master, Málád, Thána.
5 School Master, Belápur, Thána.
6 School Master, Bhuwan, Murbád, Thána.
7 Rao Sâheb Shelke, Kolhápur.
8 School Master, Ubhádánda, Ratnágiri.
School Master, Adivare, Ratnágiri.
10 School Master, Kalshe, Ratnágiri.
11 School Master, Chaul, Kolába.
12 Ráo Sáheb Shelke.

At Bankavali in the Dápoli taluka, it is believed that ghosts or evil spirits have the form of a human being, but their feet are turned backwards. They can assume any form they choose. Their character is ordinarily to trouble the people, but when satisfied they are said to prove friendly. The following story is narrated of a person who went to reside in one of the villages of the Konkan. His wife was first attacked by a ghost called Girha. The Girha troubled him much by playing mischief in his house, *viz*: by taking away eatables or by mixing dirt in his food. At night he used to divest the couple of their clothes, and on one occasion an ornament was removed by the spirit from the person of the wife. Tired of these annoyances, the man left the village and went to reside at a distance, when, to the astonishment of the public, it happened that the ornament which was lost at the old village was restored to the man's wife while she was asleep in the new village, and nobody knew who brought it there. All this was believed to be the work of the Girha.[1]

At Ubhádánda in the Vengurla taluka people believe that a *Bhut* is fierce in aspect and very troublesome, but when its wishes are complied with, it becomes harmless. The *Bhuts* reside in jungles, burial or cremation grounds, old trees, sacred groves and deserted houses. They assume all sorts of shapes and forms. Sometimes they appear very tall, and they can instantly assume the shape of a dog, a cat, a tiger, or any other animal. Some ghosts are even seen fishing on the banks of rivers.[2]

At Mitbáv in the Devgad taluka it is believed that the souls of those who die with their wishes unfulfilled take the form of a *Bhut*. They enter the bodies of people. Any woman who is attacked by the *Bhut* of a Pir becomes able to speak in the Hindi language although it may not be her mother tongue. When a child or a person is suffering from the attacks of a spirit, incense is burnt, and it at once begins to tell the whereabouts of the spirit and the reason why the person has been attacked. He is then asked to state what he wants, and when the things which the spirit wants are offered, it goes away.[3] Spirits are generally invisible.

The spirits that belong to the class of malignant *Bhuts* are of a ferocious appearance: but those that belong to the class of friendly *Bhuts* possess bodies like human beings.[4]

At Náringre in the Devgad taluka, it is believed that spirits are cruel by nature and have no shadow, that they are capable of taking any form they like, and can perform miracles.[5] At Pendur it is believed that *Bhuts* eat chillies, and that they do not speak with human beings. Spirits are said to remove and conceal their victims for a certain period of time.[6] At Vijayadurg, a *Bhut* is considered to be of mean character. People perform certain rites to bring it under subjection. Their actions are always contrary to nature. When a person begins to cry, dance, to eat forbidden things etc. he is said to be attacked by a *Bhut*. When there is enmity between two persons, the one who dies first becomes a *sambandh* and troubles his living enemy.[7] At Basani, there is a belief that there are two kinds of spirits. Some aim at the welfare of the people, and others are always troublesome. As they have no regular form they cannot easily be recognised. They can change their forms at any time.[8]

The character of a *Bhut* is to trouble people and to take revenge on an old enemy. A person attacked by a spirit speaks incoherently and acts like a mad man. In such cases the leaves of the herb *satáp* are used.

1 School Master, Bankavali, Ratnágiri.
2 School Master, Ubhádánda, Ratnágiri
3 School Master, Mitbáv, Ratnágiri.
4 School Master, Ibbrampur, Ratnágiri.
5 School Master, Náringre, Ratnágiri.
6 School Master, Pendur, Ratnágiri.
7 School Master, Vijayadurg, Ratnágiri.
8 School Master, Basani, Ratnágiri.

The leaves are pounded and put under the patient's nose. In a few minutes, the person who is possessed by the spirit begins to speak.[1]

The people of Chauk in the Kolába District believe that the main function of a *Bhut* is to frighten people, to beat them, and to make them perform unpleasant tasks and thereby to obtain food from them.[2] At Poládpur it is believed that if a person is able to bring a *Bhut* under his control he can make it do every kind of work for himself.[3] The people of Akshi believe that kindling fire without any reason and throwing stones at certain houses are the main functions of *Bhuts*.[4] At Vávashi in the Pen táluka, it is believed that *Bhuts*, while walking, never touch the earth but always move through the air, and that they have no shadow.[5] The old men of Shirgaum in the Máhim taluka advise young children not to respond to the call of anybody at night unless the person calling is an acquaintance. For such calls are sometimes those of an evil spirit.[6]

In the Kolhápur District, it is believed that the character of a *Bhut* is like that of a human being. When a person is attacked by a spirit, a great change is observed in his language and actions. He begins to speak in the language of the *Bhut* by which he is attacked. If the ghost is of the female sex, the person speaks the language of females. It is believed that the souls of those who have been murdered or tortured assume the form of a spirit known as *Sambandh*, and trouble the murderer or the torturer, by entering his body. It is said that in some cases the spirit does not leave the body of such a person till he dies, thus exacting revenge for his past misdeeds.[7] In Khopoli in Ratnágiri it is said that the cow which is given to a Bráhman while performing the funeral rites of a dead person helps him to reach heaven. He gets there by catching hold of her tail. There are three paths to the other world. They are *Bhaktimárga*, *Karmamárga*, and *Yogamárga*. The *Karmamárga* is believed to be superior to all.[8] At Málád, a belief prevails that the path to the other world is through the Himálayas. While going through the mountains of the Himálayas, souls find happiness or sorrow according to their actions in life-time. The people also believe that the soul returns every month on the date of the man's death to accept *Kágvás* i. e. cooked food given to the *manes*, and reaches heaven at the end of one year.[9] At Dahigaum in the Murbád taluka, it is customary among the Hindus to smear with cow dung the place from which a dead body has been removed to the burning ground. The place is then covered with rice flour, and is hidden under a basket, an oil-lamp being kept burning near by. The persons who accompany the corpse return home to look at the lamp, and it is believed that the soul of the deceased will pass to any creature or species of which footprints are seen on the rice flour.[10]

At Kolhápur it is believed that the soul of a person after death attains that state to which he aspires at the last moment before his death. Virtuous persons who die without any desire reach heaven and remain there in the form of the stars, where they are believed to enjoy the happiness of heaven. Some of them are sent to this world when they wish to return. Sinners are said to reach hell in consequence of their misdeeds, but some remain in this world in the form of *Bhuts*.[11]

1 School Master, Chawl, Kolába,
2 School Master, Chauk, Kolába.
3 School Master, Poládpur, Kolába.
4 School Master, Akshi, Kolába.
5 School Master, Vávashi, Kolába.
6 School Master, Shirgaum, Thána.
7 Ráo Sáheb Shelke, Kolhápur.
8 School Master, Khopoli, Kolába.
9 School Master, Málád, Thána.
10 School Master, Dahigaon, Thána.
11 Râo Sâheb Shelke, Kolhápur.

The people of Achare in the Málwan taluka believe that the souls of persons who die by accident return to the same caste, and have to remain there till the expiry of an appointed period.[1]

The people of Chauk believe that persons dying a sudden or violent death leave wishes unfulfilled, and are therefore compelled to remain in this world in the form of *Bhuts*.[2]

At Rái in the Sálsette taluka it is believed that the souls of those dying a sudden or violent death attain salvation according to their deeds in lifetime, but it is a current belief that those committing suicide take the form of a ghost, and those who die on battlefields attain eternal salvation.[3]

At Kolhápur, it is believed that the souls of those who die violent deaths do not attain salvation, but are turned into ghosts.[4]

The people of Ubhádánda in the Vengurla taluka believe that *Bhuts* do not possess visible human forms. They can assume any shapes they like, but there is a common belief that the hands and feet of *Bhuts* are always turned backwards.[5]

The most favourable times for spirits to enter human bodies are midday, midnight and twilight.[6] Women in delivery as well as those in their menses are most liable to be attacked by spirits.[7] It is generally believed that persons adorned with ornaments are attacked by spirits, especially in cases of women and children. Again, a common belief prevails in the Konkan that persons, and particularly ladies, decked with flowers and ornaments are more liable to be attacked by spirits than others.[8] The people of Fonda are of opinion that spirits generally enter and leave human bodies through the organ of hearing, while the people of Náringre hold that the hair is the best way for spirits to enter.[9] The residents of Ibhrámpur state that the mouth and the nose are the favourite channels for spirits entering human bodies.[10] At Mitbáv it is believed that spirits attack people in the throat, and generally only those persons who are uncleanly in their habits are liable to be attacked. There are no special ways for entering human bodies.[11] At Chaul a belief prevails that spirits enter the body when a person is suffering from any disease or when he is frightened.[12]

In the Konkan, people attempt to find good or bad omens in sneezing. It depends upon the time and the position or standing of the person who sneezes. If a sick person sneezes it is presumed that he will recover from his illness within a very short period, but if the sneezing is caused by the use of tobacco or snuff, no good or bad omens are drawn.[13] Sneezing at the time of conversation or when contemplating any particular task or business is held to be inauspicious. Hence if anybody sneezes at the beginning of a task, or at the time of starting out on any such task, the time is unfavourable. Yawning is said to be caused by a relative or friend remembering the person who yawns.[14] In ancient times happiness and calamities were foretold by a voice from the sky, and in modern days they are expressed by sneezing. People have much faith in sneezing, and often inquire whether it is a good or bad omen to sneeze at the beginning of any work or undertaking.[15]

If a man sneezes with his face towards the west, it is considered auspicious. If a man sneezes while contemplating any task or business, the sneezing is considered inauspicious.

[1] School Master, Achare, Ratnágiri.
[2] School Master, Chauk, Kolába.
[3] School Master, Rái, Thána.
[4] Ráo Saheb Shelke, Kolhápur.
[5] School Master, Ubhádánda, Ratnágiri.
[6] School Master, Anjarle, Ratnágiri.
[7] School Master, Rai, Thána.
[8] School Master, Bándivade, Ratnágiri.
[9] School Master, Fonde, Ratnágiri.
[10] School Master, Ibhrámpur, Ratnágiri.
[11] School Master, Mitbáv, Ratnágiri.
[12] School Master, Chawl, Kolába.
[13] School Master, Pendur, Ratnágiri.
[14] School Master, Ubhádánda, Ratnágiri.
[15] School Master, Bándivade, Ratnágiri.

Sneezing at the time of taking food *i. e.* while at meals, while sleeping, and while sitting on a praying carpet is considered auspicious. Sneezing with one's face turned towards the north, the south, and the east is also unlucky.[1]

In the case of Bhagats and exorcists yawning is considered to indicate that the disease will disappear.[2]

In the Konkan it is believed that sneezing and yawning indicate the call of death, and therefore it is customary among the Hindus to snap the thumb and the middle finger at the time of yawning, and to repeat the words *Shatanjiva i. e.* Live for hundred years, at the time of sneezing.[3] Sneeziug on a threshold is believed to forebode evil.[4]

At Kolhápur, people believe that sneezing and yawning forebode evil, and the practice is to repeat the following words at the time of sneezing and yawning, viz, *Shatanjiva i. e.* Live a hundred years, and also to repeat the name of *Rám*, while snapping the thumb and finger (*chutaki*). In the case of a person suffering from a serious illness, sneezing is supposed to indicate a cure. If a woman sneezes while a man speaks, it is lucky, and if a man sneezes it is unlucky. The reverse is the case in respect of females.[5]

In the Konkan, Rákshasas, or malevolent spirits, are believed to be very cruel. These evil spirits are held in great fear, and people try to avoid giving them offence. It is supposed that to cause displeasure to these demons may bring about death. With a view to propitiate them, offerings of cocks and goats are made to them every year regularly on fixed days.[6] If a woman gives birth to a child which is extraordinary or horrible in size and appearance, it is believed to be a demon reborn. Such a child is supposed to bring bad luck to the family.[7] The Konkan people believe that in former days Rákshasas, or malevolent demons, used to be tall, ugly, black, with long and loose hair, big teeth, and with their foreheads painted with red lead, or *shendur*. They could assume any form they liked, were powerful, and could fly in the air. They were fond of human flesh.[8] The people of Khopoli believe that Khavis is the ghost of an African *Sidhi*. This spirit is very malevolent, and exorcists find it very difficult to bring it under control. A strong belief prevails in the Konkan districts that those attacked by the spirits of non-Hindus are beyond cure.[9]

According to the belief of the people in the Kolhápur District, *Brahma Rákshasa* is one of the most powerful spirits. It takes up its abode in the sacred Pipal tree, and when it attacks a person, little hope is entertained of his delivery from its grasp.[10]

The following are the principal malignant spirits of the Konkan.

(1) Vetál, (2) Brahmagraha, (3) Sambandhas, (4) Devachár, (5) Munja, (6) Khavis, (7) Girha, (8) Chetak, (9) Zoting, (10) Vir, (11) Cheda, (12) Mhasoba, (13) Jákhin or Alwant, (14) Lávsant, and (15) Hadal.

(1) Vetál is believed to be the King of Spirits.[11] Vetál is considered to be a deity and not an evil spirit. It enters into the body of an exorcist and helps him to drive away other evil spirits.[12]

(2) Brahmagraha is the ghost of a Bráhman well versed in the *Vedas*, but who is over proud of his education.[13]

1 School Master, Khopoli, Kolába.
2 School Master, Chawl, Kolába.
3 School Master, Vavanje, Kolába.
4 School Master, Umbergaon, Thána.
5 Ráo Saheb Shelke, Kolhápur.
6 School Master, Ubhádánda, Ratnágiri.
7 School Master, Fonde, Ratnágiri.
8 School Master, Adivan, Ratnágiri.
9 School Master, Khopoli, Kolába.
10 Ráo Saheb Shelke, Kolhápur.
11 School Master, Anjarle, Ratnágiri.
12 School Master, Shirgaon, Thána.
13 School Master, Ubhádánda, Ratnágiri.

(3) Sambandha is the spirit of a person who dies without an heir, and whose funeral rites have not been performed by any member of his family. It troubles the members of the family, but when invoked through a *Bhagat* it becomes harmless, and even favourable to the family.[1] It is the spirit of a covetous person or a *sanyási* who dies with his desires unfulfilled.[2] It does not allow anybody to enjoy his wealth, and takes revenge on an enemy till death ensues. It haunts trees, wells and unoccupied houses.[3]

(4) Devachár is the spirit of a Shudra who dies after his marriage.[4] These (Devachar) spirits are said to reside on the four sides of a village. The spirits which reside in burial or cremation grounds, on river banks, and in old trees are said to be subordinate to these. Cocoanuts, plantains, sugar, cocks and goats must be given annually to gain their favour.[5]

(5) Munja is the spirit of a Bráhman boy who dies immediately after his thread ceremony, but before the final ceremony called *Sod-munj* is complete. It does not greatly affect its victim but simply frightens. When it attacks, it is difficult to drive out. It is cast out only when the patient makes a pilgrimage to a holy shrine.[6] It resides in a Pipal tree or in a well.

(6) Khavis is the spirit of a Musalmán or a non-Hindu.[7] It is also the spirit of a Mahár or a Máng.[8]

(7) Girha is the ghost of a person who dies by drowning, or of a murdered person.[9] Girha is not very powerful, and obeys the orders of the exorcists. It only frightens and troubles people.[10] It lives by the water side, and deceives persons at night by calling them by their names and leading them into false paths. It often troubles people while crossing rivers or creeks at night, and leads them to places where the water is very deep. It is said that the spirit Girha becomes the regular slave of a person who takes possession of the hair of its head, and gives him anything that he requires. It requests the person to return its hair, but this should not be given under any circumstances. For, if the Girha gets back its hair all sorts of misfortunes will befall the man.[11]

(8) Chetak is the ghost of a person of the Kunbi or Shudra caste.[12] This spirit is also known as *Dáv.*

(9) Zoting is the ghost of a man belonging to the Khárvi or Koli caste[13] It is also said to be the ghost of a Musalmán.[14]

(10) Vir is the ghost of an unmarried person belonging to the Kshatriya community.[15] It is also said to be the ghost of a Rajput or a *Purbhaya* (Pardeshi.)

(11) Cheda is the ghost of an unmarried Mahár. It resides on mountains, in jungles, and the outskirts of the village.[16] Cheda attacks domestic animals. It haunts fields and farms, and resides at public places where the *Holi* fires are annually kindled. To avoid being troubled by it, people offer annual sacrifices of fowls and goats.[17]

(12) Mhasoba is the lord of the ghosts, and is equal in might to Vetál.[18]

(13) Jákhin or Alwant. Jákhin is the ghost of a woman who has a husband alive. Alwant is believed to be the spirit of a woman dying at childbirth or during her menses.

1 Ráo Saheb Shelke, Kolhápur.
2 School Master, Basani, Ratnágiri.
3 School Master. Cháuk, Kolába.
4 School Master, Ubhádánda, Ratnágiri.
5 School Master, Khopoli, Kolába.
6 School Master, Anjarle, Ratnágiri.
7 Rao Saheb Shelke, Kolhápur.
8 School Master, Chowl, Kolába.
9 School Master, Khopoli, Kolába.
10 School Master, Shirgaon, Thána.
11 School Master, Anjarle, Ratnágiri.
12 School Master, Bankavli, Ratnágiri.
13 Ráo Saheb Shelke, Kolhápur.
14 School Master, Basani, Ratnágiri.
15 School Master, Basani, Ratnágiri.
16 School Master, Shirgaon, Thána.
17 School Master, Anjarle, Ratnágiri.
18 School Master, Shirgaon, Thána.

It resides at burial or cremation grounds. Persons attacked by this spirit are taken to Narsoba's Wádi or Gángápur, which are celebrated as shrines for the removal of malignant spirits.[1]

(14) Lávsat is the ghost of a widow. It generally resides in burial and burning grounds, and attacks domestic animals and their calves. It is also said to tear clothes and eat corpses.[2]

(15) Hadal or Hedali is the ghost of a woman who dies within ten days of childbirth or during her menses. It is supposed to be an evil spirit, but it can be kept in check by the use of a cane. It attacks all sorts of persons, but leaves them as soon as it is beaten.[3]

This spirit is also known as *Dákan* in the Kolhápur district.[4] Satavi is the ghost of a woman. It troubles women in childbirth, and kills their children on the 5th or 6th day after their birth.[5] Shákini is the ghost of an unmarried girl. Talkhámba is the ghost of an unmarried Shudra or a person from the low castes.[6] The people of Vijayadrug believe that one who hates and troubles the Bráhmans and speaks ill of their religious duties becomes a *Brahma Sambandha* after death.[7] At Poládpur in the Kolába District the ghost *Bápa* is represented by a stone painted with red lead and oil and placed at the boundary of a field. It is the guardian of the field, and protects the owners' interests. Offerings are made to it annually. If the annual offerings are neglected, it troubles the owner of the field. It also troubles others when disturbed.[8]

The spirits known as *Kálkáiche Bhut* and *Bahirobáche Bhut* are not troublesome. When they favour any person, he enjoys health and happiness for a period of twelve years. But after that period he is ruined.[9] In addition to the varieties of malignant spirits already described, the following spirits are known at Shirgaon in the Máhim taluka of the Thána District. They are—*Hirwa, Wághoba, Asarás, Gángud, Saitán* and *Chaitannadya*. The spirit known as *Hirwa* requires the offerings of a bow and an arrow, *bháng, bájri* bread, and a *chatni* of garlic. The *Wághoba* haunts jungles and troubles domestic animals. Cocoanuts and lamps of ghi are offered to it. *Asarás* are the deities that dwell in water. They infest the wells and ponds and attack women and children at noon time and in the evening. Red lead, cocoanuts, flowers, parched rice (*láhya*) and *nádápudi* are given to them.[10]

At Ibhrámpur in the Ratnágiri District it is said that the evil spirit Zoting goes about headless.[11]

The people of Medhe in the Rohe taluka believe that the spirit known as *Girha*, which resides in water, goes about headless.[12]

At Shirgaon in the Máhim taluka it is believed that the spirit *Hirwa* goes about headless. It troubles human beings and animals. The sea and the jungle are its places of abode. To avoid being troubled by it, *bháng*, cocoanuts, fowls are given to it.[13]

The people of Dahigaon in the Murbád taluka believe that the *Bhut* known as *Peesa* goes about headless.[14]

Some evil spirits haunt trees such as the *Pipal*, *Bábhul* and *Adulsa*. Some have their haunts on a public road where three streets meet, or in a dirty place, some haunt old houses, and the rest prefer to reside in burial and burning grounds.[15]

---

1 School Master, Ubhádánda, Ratnágiri.
2 School Master, Chauk, Kolába.
3 School Master, Khopol, Kolába.
4 Rao Saheb Shelke, Kolhápur.
5 School Master, Chauk, Kolába.
6 School Master, Basani, Ratnágiri.
7 School Master, Vijayadurg, Ratnágiri.
8 School Master, Poládpur, Kolába.
9 School Master, Khopoli, Kolába.
10 School Master, Shirgaon, Thána
11 School Master, Ibhrampur, Ratnágiri.
12 School Master, Medhe, Kolába.
13 School Master, Shirgaon, Thána.
14 School Master, Dahigaon, Thána.
15 Ráo Saheb Shelke, Kolhápur.

Many spirits dwell in burial or cremation grounds. Among them are Vetál, Jákhin, Khavis, Kháprya, Zoting, Dáv, Girha, Alavat and Lávsat.[1]

The spirits Munja and Sambandh are said to reside near houses and old trees that produce sweet smelling flowers. The spirits Devchár and Chálegat are said to reside at the four corners or the boundary of a village.[2]

It is believed that all kinds of spirits assemble at night at the funeral ground when a body is burnt or buried.[3]

The evil spirits known as *Khavis*, *Zoting* and *Kafri* are said to dwell on mountains and in jungles ; while the others named *Sambandha*, *Jákhin*, *Hadal* and *Lávsat* are said to reside on trees.[4]

Munja resides in the *Pipal* tree. *Sambandha* dwells in the Banyan, *Pipal* and *Umbar* trees. It is supposed to be a guardian of buried treasure.[5]

At Murbád in the Thána District, it is believed that an evil spirit known as *Hadal* infests the tamarind trees.[6]

In the Kolhápur District it is believed that the ghosts of persons dying on battlefields infest mountains and jungles, and the evil spirit known as *Sambandh* infests trees.[7]

Generally in the Konkan, and specially in the Ratnágiri District, young mothers and their children are supposed to be liable to the attacks of the spirits *Satávi, Avagat, Alavant, Jákhin, Devchár* and *Chálegat*.[8]

At Khopoli in the Kolába District it is believed that a young mother and her child are generally attacked by the spirit of the dead wife of her husband, or by a *Hadal* or *Lávsat*. The spirit that attacks a woman during her childbirth is difficult to drive out. The spirits are always afraid of cleanliness, and therefore, where there is cleanliness, there is very little fear of their attacks[9].

The people of Shirgaon believe that the fiend known as *Hedli* attacks a young mother and her child. The *Bhutya*, or the sorcerer, makes use of his cane and of the dirty incense known as *Nurkya Uda*, and compels her to speak and to ask for what she wants. Sometimes she speaks and asks for the things required. Boiled rice and curds, and oil with red lead are given to her. When she leaves the body, the person becomes insensible for a short time.[10]

The fiend known as *Hadal*, and other evil spirits of the female sex, generally attack a young mother and her child. They are generally attacked by these fiends on a public cross road where three roads meet, or under a *Bábhul* tree, and also at wells.[11]

At Ubhádánda in the Vengurla taluka it is believed that those who are killed by tigers or other wild beasts are born as kings in the next generation.[12] On the other hand the people of Bankavli are of opinion that those who suffer death at the hands of tigers and other wild beasts are turned into spirits. The spirit of a person killed by a tiger is called *Vághvir*.[13]

At Achare it is believed that persons killed by lions and tigers attain salvation, while those killed by inferior beasts go to hell.[14]

The people of Ibhrámpur believe that unmarried persons killed by tigers or other wild beasts take the form of a ghost. Males become *Girhas* and females become *Jákhins* and *Lávsats*.[15]

[1] School Master, Mitbáv, Ratnágiri.
[2] School Master, Fonde, Ratnágiri.
[3] School Master, Ibhrampur, Ratnágiri.
[4] School Master, Ibhrampur, Ratnágiri.
[5] School Master, Chauk, Kolába.
[6] School Master, Murbád, Thána.
[7] Ráo Sáheb Shelke, Kolhápur.
[8] School Master, Achare, Ratnágiri.
[9] School Master, Khopoli, Kolába.
[10] School Master, Shirgaon, Thána.
[11] Ráo Sáheb Shelke, Kolhápur.
[12] School Master, Ubhádánda, Ratnágiri.
[13] School Master, Bankavli, Ratnágiri.
[14] School Master, Achare, Ratnágiri.
[15] School Master, Ibhrampur, Ratnágiri.

At Pendur it is believed that persons killed by tigers and other wild beasts become *Brahma Rákshasa*. The same form is assumed by those who die by accident. A murdered man becomes a *Devachár*.[1]

In the District of Kolhápur a belief prevails that the spirits of those killed by tigers or other wild beasts assume the form of ghosts. It is also believed that persons who die before they are married do not attain salvation, and therefore it is considered inauspicious among the Hindus to remain unmarried. This is the real reason why the majority of the Hindus marry their children at an early age.[2]

The ghost of a woman dying in childbirth or during her menses assumes the form of *Alwant*. For the purpose of preventing the dead woman turning into a ghost the following device is adopted. The corpse, instead of being burnt as usual, is buried underground, and four iron nails are fixed at the four corners of the spot on which the body is buried, and plants bearing red flowers are planted thereon.[3]

At Bankavli it is believed that the ghost of a woman dying in childbirth or during her menses assumes the form of *Jákhin*, while the people of the Kolhápur District believe that it assumes the form of *Hadal*.[4]

The special precautions that a father has to take at the birth of a child are:—

To arrange for a suitable place or a room provided with the materials required for the occasion, and to ensure the correct moment for the birth of the child. No person other than a midwife is allowed to enter the room for the first ten days. A pot is kept filled with water and a twig of the *nim* tree in the entrance of the house, and all persons entering the house have to wash their feet with this water. A knife or some other sharp weapon is kept under the bed of the woman in order that the mother and her child may not be attacked by a spirit.[5]

The chief reason for ensuring the correct moment for the birth is that, if the birth takes place at an unlucky hour, special rites are necessary for averting the evil effects. These rites consist in the recitation of certain holy *mantras* and in giving presents of money, sessamum, *jágri*, clarified butter, etc., to the Bráhmans and alms to the poor.[6]

At Medhe in the Rohe taluka, it is customary for the father to throw a stone in a well, a pond, or a river at the birth of his son, and then to look at the face of the child.[7]

An owl is considered to be a bird of such evil repute that, in all parts of the Konkan, it is considered necessary to perform expiatory rites when an owl perches on the roof. If these rites are not performed, it is firmly believed that some evil will befall the members of the family. Various omens are drawn from the cries of the bird *Pingla*, and these cries are known as *Kilbil*, *Chilbil* and *Khit Khit*.[8]

If an owl sits on the roof of a house, it is a sure sign of coming death to a member of the family.[9]

At Devgad in the Ratnágiri District the sound of a bat or an owl is considered inauspicious, and indicates the death of a sick person in the house.[10]

At Chauk an owl is said to have some connection with spirits. Its sound at night indicates the approaching death of a sick person in the house. One variety of the owl called the *pingla* is supposed to foretell future events by its movements and cries, while the bat is considered an inauspicious bird, and its appearance forebodes coming evil.[11]

[1] School Master, Pendur, Ratnágiri.
[2] Ráo Sáheb Shelke, Kolhápur.
[3] School Master, Ubhádánda, Ratnágiri.
[4] School Master, Bankavli, Ratnágiri.
[5] Ráo Sáheb Shelke, Kolhápur.
[6] School Master, Pendur, Ratnágiri.
[7] School Master, Medhe, Kolába.
[8] School Master, Shirgaon, Thána.
[9] School Master, Adivare, Ratnágiri.
[10] School Master, Devgad, Ratnágiri.
[11] School Master, Chauk, Kolába.

At Umbergaon people do not throw stones at an owl. For it is considered that the owl might sit and rub the stone, and that the person throwing it will become weak and wasted as the stone wears away.[1]

The people of Kolhápur do not believe that there is any connection between the bat or owl and the spirits of the dead, but they believe that, if an owl cries out in the evening or at night, it indicates the death of a sick person in the family. This applies also to the sound of a single *pingla*, but the sound of a pair of *pinglas* is considered auspicious.[2]

It is generally believed that old unoccupied houses are haunted by evil spirits. Persons who wish to inhabit such houses first perform the *Vástu shánti* ceremony, and give a feast to Bráhmans. In former times, in the districts that were ruled by the Portuguese, religious persecution prevailed. To escape from these persecutions, people were compelled to leave their houses unprotected. Before leaving their houses, they used to bury their treasure in the ground, and on that spot a human being or an animal was sacrificed in order that the spirit of the dead should hover about the place, and prevent strangers from coming.[3]

The evil spirits which haunt ruins and guard buried treasures and old forts are known as *Mahápurush*, *Khavis*, *Brahma Rákshasa* and *Sambandh*.[4]

If there be any buried treasure in an old unoccupied house, the owner of the treasure remains there in the form of a ghost. If the treasure be near the temple of a deity, it is supposed to be under the guardianship of that deity.[5]

At Vijayadurg it is believed that a person who builds a house in the days of his prosperity and does not survive to enjoy it, becomes a Sambandh. He remains in that house in the form of a ghost, and troubles every one who comes to stay there, excepting the members of his family. A man who buries his treasure underground becomes a ghost after death, comes back to watch his treasure, and troubles those who try to remove it.[6]

Unoccupied houses are generally haunted by evil spirits. At certain forts in the Konkan where battles were fought, the souls of those slain in the battles are said to have assumed the forms of spirits, and to keep a watch over the forts.[7]

In the Kolhápur District there is a village Nigve beyond the river Panch Ganga at a distance of three miles from Kolhápur, where the soul of a person named Appáji Kulkarni has assumed the form of a *Sambandh* and guards the buried treasures in his house. When anybody tries to dig up the buried money, the ghost enters the body of his daughter-in-law and begins to dance and cry out loudly, and does not allow any one to touch his treasure. It is also said that he strikes the ground with his stick at night. Another similar instance is cited in the case of the village of Latvade in the Shirol Peta, where Bápujipant Kulkarni continues to guard his house after death. He does not allow anybody to live in the house, and if any one is bold enough to sleep there at night, the spirit of Bápuji appears and throws him out of the house. The house is therefore uninhabited at present. His wife has adopted a son, but he has to live in another village Vadange.[8]

[1] School Master, Umbergaon, Thána.

[2] Ráo Sáheb Shelke, Kolhápur.

[3] School Master, Ubhádánda, Ratnágiri.

[4] School Master, Adivare, Ratnágiri.

[5] School Master, Pendur, Ratnágiri.

[6] School Master, Vijayadrug, Ratnágiri.

[7] School Master, Poládpur, Kolába.

[8] Ráo Sáheb Shelke, Kolhápur.

CHAPTER VI.

THE EVIL EYE AND THE SCARING OF GHOSTS.

Hindus generally believe in the effects of the evil eye. If an accident befall any thing of value, or it undergoes any sudden change, it is said to be due to the effects of an evil eye. In order to escape from the influence of an evil eye, people begin the use of incantations and charms on a Sunday, Wednesday, or Thursday and finish them on the third or the fifth day. Small children, domestic animals, and beautiful objects are generally liable to be affected by an evil eye.

The following are some of the methods of evading the effects of an evil eye.

1st.—Dry chillies are waved round the body of the affected person and thrown into the fire, and if they do not thereupon make a loud noise, it is said that the effects of an evil eye are averted.

2nd.—Mustard seed and salt are waved round the face of a child and then thrown into the fire.

3rd.—Alum is waved round the child and then thrown into fire. The piece of alum thus thrown is sometimes believed to be changed into the form of a man or a woman. From this, conjectures are made as to the sex of the person by whose evil eye the patient is affected. The form or the figure is then broken by a toe of the left foot of the patient, and dry chillies, garlic, hair, rubbish from the house and salt are mixed in the alum powder. The mixture is waved round the patient three times and then thrown into fire. Meanwhile the sorcerer repeats the names of all persons, things and evil spirits suspected by him. After this performance has been repeated three times, the fire is deposited in a public place where three roads meet.

4th.—If the evil eye is believed to be that of a ghost, the sorcerer mutters some words to himself, waves ashes round the affected child, and blows them in the air.

5th.—The evil eye of a tiger is removed from an affected animal in the following manner. An oil lamp is burnt in the eye of a dead tiger and the lamp is waved round the animal by a Mahár. The Mahár is given a loaf prepared from eight kinds of grain.

6th.—Copper amulets and black cotton strings charmed by a sorcerer are also tied round the neck or arms of the patient. [1]

When a child is to be removed from one village to another, rice is scattered at the boundary of the village, at the bridges, rivers, creeks, etc, that are crossed during the journey. Cocoanuts are waved round the child and thrown away at the boundary of the village and at places supposed to be haunted by ghosts. Before entering a house in a new village, a small quantity of boiled rice, bread,

[1] School Master, Ubhádánda, Ratnágiri.

or grains of rice are waved round the child and thrown away. It is believed that, when black ointment is applied to the eyes, cheeks, or forehead of a child, there is no fear of its being affected by an evil eye. This also depends on the position of the stars at the birth of a child. If anybody sees a beautiful thing and praises it, there is a chance of its being affected by an evil eye. It is believed that children, animals, trees, and even wood and stones, are apt to be affected by an evil eye. In order to avoid injury from an evil eye, cocoanut shells or a shoe are tied on a conspicuous part of a tree or a creeping plant, black beads known as *Vajrabuttu* are tied round the necks of children, and *cowries* and black beads are tied round the necks of animals. Even grown up persons are affected by an evil eye. When a man is very ill or frequently becomes unconscious, cocoanuts, fowls and boiled rice are waved round him and thrown away.[1]

When the effects of an evil eye cannot be removed by ordinary methods, the evil influence is said to have entered through the bones, '*Hádi drusta padali*.' In order to remove it people bring the bone of an animal in the evening, and after besmearing it with oil and turmeric powder, wash it in hot water. It is dressed in a yellow cloth, and black and red ointments are applied to it. It is then waved round the affected person, and thrown away in some public place where three roads meet.[2]

For evading the effects of an evil eye, salt, mustard seed, hair, garlic, dry leaves of onions, dry chillies, and seven small stones from the road are put on the fire. The fire is then waved round the body of the affected person and thrown away. Charmed black cotton strings are turned over the burning incense and tied round the arm or the neck. Charmed ashes from the temples of certain deities are also applied to the forehead of the affected person.[3]

At Ibhrámpur in the Ratnágiri District, it is believed that a person whose eyes have come under the influence of evil stars possesses the power of the evil eye. Ashes are taken on a mango leaf, and charmed with the *mantras* or incantations for an evil eye, and then they are applied to the forehead of the affected person.[4]

The people of Poladpur in the Kolába District believe the effects of an evil eye to be as follows. A healthy child becomes sickly and cries, a man may suffer from indigestion or loss of appetite, a cow or a she-buffalo yielding plenty of milk suddenly ceases to give milk or gives blood in place of it, a good image is disfigured or broken, and even stones are shattered to pieces by the effects of an evil eye.

The following devices are used to ward off such evil effects. A black mark is made on the forehead of children. Black beads called *Drustamani*, and *Vajrabuttu* are tied round their necks. Marking nuts and cowries tied with a black thread are fastened round the necks of animals. A little black spot is marked on an image. A worn out shoe or a sandal is tied to the fruit-yielding trees. Salt and mustard seed are waved thrice round the face of a child repeating "*Ishta mishta konyá pápinichi drushta*" and thrown into the fire. Some people roll a cotton thread round a curry stone, wave it three times round the patient, and then put it into the fire; if the thread burns, the evil eye is held to have been removed. If the evil eye be on the food, three morsels of food are first raised to the mouth, and then thrown into the fire. Sacred ashes are applied to trees and creeping plants to remove the effects of an evil eye.[5]

The people of Khopoli in the Kolába District believe that the evil eye can be diverted from living creatures only, and not from inanimate things such as a stone or an earthen image. Sacred ashes are applied to the forehead of the suffering child by

[1] School Master, Mitbàv, Ratnágiri.
[2] School Master, Anjarle, Ratnágiri.
[3] School Master, Achare, Ratnágiri.
[4] School Master, Ibhrampur, Ratnágiri.
[5] School Master, Poladpur, Kolába.

repeating the *Rám raksha stotra, i. e,* the protecting praises of Ráma, the seventh incarnation of Vishnu. Among Bráhmans, rice grains are waved thrice round the face of a child and put into water. The water is then thrown away. Even flowers are waved round the faces of small children in the evening and thrown away.[1]

At Chauk in the Karjat taluka of the Kolába District, some people wave the left shoe thrice round the body of the affected person for the purpose of evading the effects of an evil eye. A red hot iron bar is also cooled in water mixed with turmeric powder.[2]

At Shirgáon in the Máhim taluka of the Thána District water is drawn in a brass or a copper pot in the evening, and turmeric powder, rice, and any other edible articles on which the evil eye has fallen are put into it. Twentyone date leaves, each of them with a knot, are then waved round the body of the affected person and thrown into the water pot, burning coals being dropped into the mixture. The pot is then waved thrice round the body of the affected person, and kept in a corner of the bedroom for one night, with a basket, a broom, and a sandal or an old shoe placed on the top. It is then thrown away in the morning in some public place where three roads meet. If the water becomes red, it is supposed that the evil eye has been removed.[3]

The effects of an evil eye are sometimes visible on the face of a child in the form of small red pustules. The appearance of such pustules is called *Chák padane.*[4]

If a person is affected by an evil eye at the time of taking his meals, he loses his appetite. He also becomes weaker day by day. One of the modes of removing these evils is to wave fresh date leaves three times round the face of the affected person, and to throw them into water. Some people take water in a copper plate and extinguish in it burning sticks of the tamarind tree, after waving them round the body of the affected person.[5]

At Khárbáv in the Bassein taluka of the Thána District, five pieces of broken tiles are made red hot and put into water in which a little quantity of all the cooked food in the house has been mixed. Turmeric powder is also put into it. A pen knife or some other iron instrument is then turned five times in the water. A winnowing basket and a broom are waved thrice round the face of the affected person, and placed over the water pot.[6]

At Dahánu in the Thána District, two big stones, of which one has been waved round the face of a person affected by an evil eye, are struck one against the other. If the stone breaks, it is believed that the evil effect has been removed. Cowdung is mixed with water in a brass or a copper plate, and dust from a public road, hair, and burning black cotton cloth are put into another small vessel. This vessel is then waved round the person, and placed upside down over the mixture of cowdung. If it sticks to the brass plate, this is supposed to be due to the evil eye.[7]

The people of Kolhápur believe in the effects of an evil eye. A child suffering from an evil eye turns pale and thin, and suffers from headache. To avoid these effects, elderly women make a mark with lamp black on the face or brow of the child. Boiled rice and curds, and bread and oil are also passed round the face of a child, and thrown into a public road.[8]

Generally, in the Konkan districts, opprobrious names are given to children when they are sickly, always crying, and weak, or when they are short lived. These names are

[1] School Master, Khopoli, Kolába.
[2] School Master, Chauk, Kolába.
[3] School Master, Shirgaon, Thána.
[4] School Master, Padghe, Thána.
[5] School Master, Malád, Thána.
[6] School Master, Khárbáv, Thána.
[7] School Master, Dahánu, Thána.
[8] Ráo Sáheb Shelke, Kolhápur.

Marya, Rodya, Kerya, etc. It is believed that children improve in health when called by such opprobrious names.[1]

Opprobrious names such as *Dhondu, Kondu, Keru,* are given to children in families in which the first children are shortlived. But their real names are different. The names of the wellknown arithmetician Keru Nána Chhatre and his son Kondopant Chhatre are examples of opprobrious names.[2]

Among high class Hindus, the first son is not generally called by his real name, but by one of the opprobrious names given above.[3]

Children are sometimes weighed with shoes or sandals, and also with cowdung. In some cases, their nostrils are bored, especially the right one.[4]

Hindus generally call their children by the names of their deities and ancestors, and they attribute the premature death of their children to their own misbehaviour towards such ancestors, or to their having abused them; they fear that such abuse or misbehaviour has offended the ancestors. To avoid their displeasure and the consequent death of their children, the people give opprobrious names to their next born such as *Dagadya, Dhondya, Gundya, Dandya Kerya, Ukirdya, Kondya, Lobhya,* etc. The custom of tattooing one side of the body of females also prevails in the Kolhápur District, especially in cases where the children in a family are shortlived.[5]

In the *Puránas* there are instances of males being transformed into females, and females into males. For example, the female Amba was transformed into a male called Shikhandi and the male Nárad was transformed into a female. Arjuna, the third brother of the Pándavas is said to have changed his sex, and turned into Bruhannada.[6]

In the *Shivlilamruta*, a book pertaining to the god Shiva, in the chapter of Simantini, it has been described how a man was turned into a woman.[7]

At Kolhápur, there are no instances known of a change of sex. The goddess Yallamma has a high reputation in this district for making a change in the habits and deportments of men and women, especially among low caste people. It is believed that the curse of this goddess has the power of destroying the virility of males, whereupon they behave like females. Many instances of this type can be seen at the fair of the goddess Yallamma, which is held in *Márgashirsha* (December); men dressed in women's clothes and vice versa are often seen at this fair.[8]

In Western India, iron nails are generally used when any spirit is to be buried in the ground. Other metals, such as gold, silver, and copper, are sometimes offered to the ghosts. The blood of fowls and goats is also offered to them. When incense is burnt before a sorcerer, the spirit enters into his body. Water is charmed and sprinkled over the body of a person attacked by an evil spirit. Rice and *udid* grains are required for exorcising spirits. Red powder *Pinjar*, turmeric powder, black ointment *kájal*, lemons, *Narakya Wuda* a kind of incense, betel-leaves, betelnuts, cocoanuts, mango leaves, *Nirguḍi* leaves, and pieces of cloth are also used for the same purpose.[9]

Cane sticks are used by people as a protection against evil spirits. A stick cut from the tree known as *Pándhri* is also used as protection. Charmed black cotton strings are tied to the wrist, arm or neck. If a man is very much afraid of a ghost, he repeats the name of the monkey god Máruti or any other deity that may be favourable to his family.[10]

[1] School Master, Mitbáv, Ratnágiri.
[2] School Master, Anjarle, Ratnágiri.
[3] School Master, Bhayándár, Thána.
[4] School Master, Dahánu, Thána.
[5] Ráo Sáheb Shelke, Kolhápur.
[6] School Master, Ibrahmpur, Ratnágiri.
[7] School Master, Murbád, Thána.
[8] Ráo Sáheb Shelke, Kolhápur.
[9] School Master, Basani, Ratnágiri.
[10] School Master, Mitbáv, Ratnágiri.

The blood of fowls and goats is used as a protection against ghosts and *Devachárs*, and also against witchcraft. Charmed water is waved round the person affected by an evil spirit, and thrown away. Rings, amulets, and anklets made of metals of five kinds are put on the hands and legs of children to ward off the effects of evil spirits.[1]

It is customary among certain people to apply spittle to the sandalpaste mark on the forehead of a man, and to the red *Kunku* mark on the forehead of an unwidowed woman. It is considered to be a protection against evil spirits.[2]

The beak of an eagle, a stick cut from a tree known as *Pándhri*, a cane having three joints, and the root of a shrub called *Shrávad*, which has white leaves, are used as protection against evil spirits.[3]

At Pendur in the Málwan taluka of the Ratnágiri District it is believed that an iron stick held in the hand is a protection against evil spirits.[4]

At Chauk in the Karjat taluka of the Kolába District, pictures of certain deities are tattooed on the body for the purpose of protection against evil spirits. It is also believed that evil spirits run away when salt and garlic are thrown into fire as they cannot bear the smoke of burning garlic.[5]

At Medhe in the Rohe taluka, when the dead body of a woman dying within ten days of her delivery is taken out of the house for burial, an iron horseshoe is driven into the threshold of the house, and grains of *Náchani* are scattered in the street while the corpse is being carried to the burial ground.[6]

At Bhuwan in the Murbád taluka some people tie a square piece of leather to the necks of their children as protection against evil spirits.[7]

At Rái, a custom prevails of putting coral necklaces on children as a protective against evil spirits.[8]

Iron nails and horseshoes are driven into the threshold or on to the door of a house on the full moon day or the last day of the Hindu calendar month at evening time, to prevent the entrance of evil spirits. Dirty localities being considered to be haunts of evil spirits, people living in such localities burn incense in their houses every day. While exorcising evil spirits the sorcerers throw charmed *Udid* grains and *Ràle* panic seeds on the body of the diseased, or place these things below his bed. Rings made of metals of five kinds,—iron, copper, brass, silver and gold—are charmed on an eclipse day, and worn by people. Red lead and cowries are tied to the necks or feet of animals as protection against evil spirits. The spirits that haunt buried treasures are pacified by the blood of fowls and goats when digging up such treasures.[9]

Certain *mantras* are written on a paper, and the paper is tied to a black cotton string, or the paper is put into a copper amulet, and then tied to a black cotton string. The black cotton string with the amulet is then tied round the arm or the neck of a person attacked by evil spirits, or suffering from malarial fevers. These *mantras* are never disclosed to anybody.[10]

Nádádora is a black cotton thread having seven or nine knots with a charmed paper in one of these knots. The thread is first held over burning incense, and then tied round the neck or the arm of the diseased. Sunday is generally chosen for attaching these threads.[11]

[1] School Master, Ubhádanda, Ratnágiri.
[2] School Master, Bándivade, Ratnágiri.
[3] School Master, Fonde, Ratnágiri.
[4] School Master, Pendur, Ratnágiri.
[5] School Master, Chauk, Kolába.
[6] School Master, Medhe, Kolába.
[7] School Master, Bhuwan, Thána.
[8] School Master, Rái, Thána.
[9] Ráo Sáheb Shelke, Kolhápur.
[10] School Master, Bándivade, Ratnágiri.
[11] School Master, Kálse, Ratnágiri.

At Poladpur in the Kolába District, there lived a sorcerer who used to give such amulets and charmed threads. He placed about ten or twelve copper rings or amulets in a copper plate kept in the sun. While thus exposed to the sun, these amulets were continuously watched by the sorcerer for some two hours, repeating certain *mantras*.[1]

At Málád in the Thána District, copper amulets and charmed black cotton threads in the name of Kál Bhairav, an incarnation of the god Shiva, are used as protective against evil spirits. They are tied to the arms or the neck of the diseased on an eclipse day, on the last day of the Hindu calendar month, or on a Tuesday, Wednesday and Saturday.[2]

At Kolhápur, the use of amulets is generally resorted to by people suffering from the attacks of evil spirits or from malarial fevers. The sorcerer who exorcises the evil spirits writes certain *mantras* on a paper, or draws certain symbols and repeats the *mantras* over them. The paper is then wrapped in an amulet made of copper or silver, and fastened to a cotton thread. This amulet is tied round the arm or the neck of the diseased. Before tying it to the arm or the neck, it is once held over burning incense.[3]

A sacred circle is frequently used as a protection from spirits. The sorcerer draws a circle on the ground, with his stick, and the following articles are put inside it. Cocoanuts, lemons, red lead, and a *Kohala* gourd. Fowls are also sacrificed to this circle. The filling in of this circle is called *mánda bharane* by the exorcists.[4]

Rice or *Udid* grain, and ashes charmed by *mantras*, are scattered round a certain area of land, or are given to a person supposed to be affected by evil spirits. The spirits cannot enter a place charmed in this manner. They are also scattered round the place supposed to be haunted by evil spirits in the belief that neither evil spirits nor snakes can transgress the boundary thus marked by a sorcerer.[5]

Formerly sages and saints used to make such sacred circles round their residence, repeating certain *mantras*, for their protection from evil spirits. It is believed that the spirits cannot enter or leave these enchanted circles. They used to bury bottles containing such spirits at the boundaries of these circles. There are many such places in the Kolhápur District, such as Buránsáheb of Brahmapuri, the Sádhubuwa of Panhála, and Bábu Jámál at Kolhápur.[6]

It is a general belief among all classes of Hindus in the Bombay Presidency that Saturday is an unlucky day, and in some places Friday and Tuesday are also considered inauspicious.

Sunday is considered as an ordinary day. Monday, Wednesday and Thursday are believed to be auspicious or lucky days.

It is said that a thing suggested or thought of on Friday cannot be carried out successfully.[7]

Sowing seed and watering trees is strictly forbidden on Sunday. It is believed that trees do not bear well if watered on Sundays.[8]

Tuesday and Friday are considered unlucky days for beginning a new task. Wednesday and Saturday are said to be inauspicious for visiting another village.[9]

The numbers 2, 6 11, and zero are believed to be lucky, 4, 5, 10 and 8 are unlucky, and 1, 3, 7 and 9 are considered as middling or moderate.

The figure zero is by some considered inauspicious.[10]

The numbers 5, 7, 9 are said by some, to be auspicious. and 1, 3, 11 and 13 inauspicious.[11]

Odd numbers are auspicious, and even numbers are said to be inauspicious.[12]

1 School Master, Poladpur, Kolába.
2 School Master, Málád, Thána.
3 Ráo Sáheb, Shelke, Kolhápur.
4 School Master, Bándivade, Ratnágiri.
5 School Master, Ubhádánda, Ratnágiri.
6 Ráo Sáheb Shelke, Kolhápur.
7 School Master, Ubhádánda, Ratnágiri.
8 School Master, Basani, Ratnágiri.
9 School Master, Khopoli, Kolába.
10 School Master, Rái, Thána
11 School Master, Bándivade, Ratnágiri.
12 Ráo Sáheb Shelke, Kolhápur.

The following are generally held to be auspicious omens :—

While going on any business, to come across an unwidowed woman, a cow, Bráhmans, a five-petaled flower, or a pot filled with water ;[1] the throbbing of the right eyelid and of the right arm of a man, and of the left eyelid of a woman ; a Bráhman coming in front with a cup and a spoon in his hand after taking his bath ;[2] the appearance of a peacock, the *Bháradwáj* or the blue jay, and the mongoose, especially when they pass on the left side of the person going on business.[3]

The following are considered to be auspicious when seen within a hundred paces of a person starting on business :—

Bráhmans, unwidowed women, boiled food, meat, fishes, milk, any kind of corn, the bird *Chásha* or the blue jay, passing by the left side, the appearance of the moon in front, a person coming across one's path with vessels filled with water, and a married couple. a cow with its calf, images of god, cocoanuts and other fruits, the mother, white clothes, the sound of a musical instrument, a horse, an elephant, curds, flowers, a lighted lamp, a jackal, a spiritual preceptor, a public woman, a Mahár, a washerman coming with a bundle of washed clothes, and a marriage procession.[4]

The following objects and persons are generally believed to be inauspicious :—

Oil, buttermilk, a couple of snakes, a monkey, pig, and an ass, firewood, ashes and cotton, a person with a disfigured nose, a man dressing his hair in the shape of a crown, red garlands, wet clothes, a woman wearing red cloth, an empty earthen vessel, a Bráhman widow, a *Brahmachári* and an unmarried Bráhman[5], a widow, a bare-headed Bráhman, a cat going across the path, a dog flapping his ears, meeting a barber with his bag, a beggar, sneezing, or the asking of a question at the time of departure, waiting, meeting a person with an empty vessel,[6] howling of dogs and jackals, a pair of crows playing on the ground, and a lighted lamp extinguished by its fall on the ground.[7]

While plans or proposals are being made, it is considered inauspicious if any one sneezes or the sound of a lizard is heard.[8] Meeting a person of the depressed classes whose touch is pollution, or a Bráhman who accepts funeral gifts, is considered inauspicious.[9] Meeting a woman who is in her menses, a mourner, a buffalo, a snake and a *diwad* are considered inauspicious.[10] An iron vessel or an iron bar, cow dung cakes, salt, grass, a broom, a vulture, and a washerman bringing with him dirty clothes are also considered to be inauspicious omens.[11]

Among the Hindus in Western India, for the purpose of helping the spirit to go to heaven safely, and for securing its goodwill towards the survivors, after death ceremonies called the *Shráddhas* are generally performed. Some perform these ceremonies once a year in the month of *Bhádrapada*, and others perform them twice or thrice i.e. on the anniversary day of the deceased as well as in the dark half of *Bhádrapada*, which is generally known as the *manes'* fortnight (*pitru paksha*).[12]

The funeral solemnities performed from the 1st to the 14th day from the death of the deceased are as described below :—

On the first day, at the time of burning the dead body, a plot of ground is purified by repeating certain *mantras*, and the corpse is then placed on it. Before setting the funeral pile on fire, balls of boiled rice or wheat flour are put on the face, the forehead, arms and the chest of the corpse. Such balls are placed

[1] School Master, Ubhádánda, Ratnágiri.
[2] School Master, Khopoli, Kolába.
[3] School Master, Achare, Ratnágiri.
[4] School Master, Mitbáv, Ratnágiri.
[5] School Master, Achare, Ratnágiri.
[6] School Master, Ubhádánda, Ratnágiri.
[7] School Master, Khopoli, Kolába.
[8] School Master, Mitbáv, Ratnágiri.
[9] School Master, Anjarle, Ratnágiri.
[10] School Master, Pendur, Ratnágiri.
[11] Ráo Sáheb Shelke, Kolhápur.
[12] School Master, Devgad, Ratnágiri.

on the body of the deceased only when death has taken place on an unlucky day, or when there is an unlucky conjunction of stars. The son, or some other near relative, of the deceased generally performs these rites with the help of a Bráhman priest. On the third day he goes to the burning place, collects the ashes of the deceased, and throws them into the sea. On this occasion he is accompanied by the relatives of the deceased. Rich persons who are able to go to Benares keep the bones of their deceased parents and throw them into the Ganges at Prayága near Benares after performing certain *Shráddhas* there. The giving of oblations continues daily till the tenth day. The oblations of the tenth day are called *Das Pinda.* The rites of the eleventh day are called *Ekotistha.* On the eleventh day the person performing the rites has to change his sacred thread, after sipping a little cow's urine. Cooked food is prepared at the place where the rites of the eleventh day are performed, and Bráhmans are fed there, or at least thirty-two mouthfuls of cooked food are offered to the sacred fire. A big ball of boiled rice is put before the sacred fire or near the Bráhmans taking their meals. This ball is then thrown into the sea. A male calf is branded, worshipped and let loose. This calf is called *Vasu,* and is considered sacred by the villagers. On the 11th day, special ceremonies for propitiating the eight *Vasus* and the eleven *Rudras* are performed, and gifts of a plot of ground, a cow, cooking vessels, various kinds of corn, golden images, silver and copper coins, clothes, shoes, umbrellas, bedding, etc. are given to the Bráhmans collected there. On the 13th day after death a feast is given to 13 or more Bráhmans and the other relatives. *Navakádán,* i.e., the gift of a ship and *Gopradán* i.e., of a cow and a calf, are also given to the Bráhmans on the understanding that they will help the soul of the dead while crossing the river Vaitarna.[1]

Water mixed with *til* or sesamum seed, sandalpaste, and oblations of boiled rice are given daily to the *manes* to secure their good-will towards the survivors.[2]

At Bankavli in the Dápoli taluka of the Ratnágiri District, in order to prevent the soul from assuming the form of a ghost, there is a custom of tying a piece of *Gulvel,* a species of moonseed, or the seed of a vegetable known as *Máthbháji,* round the neck of the corpse before burning it. It is also believed that, by doing this, the soul is prevented from troubling the survivors.[3]

At Poladpur in the Kolába District, some villagers drive an iron nail into the head of the corpse before it is taken to the funeral ground. They believe that, in consequence, the soul of the deceased will not turn into an evil spirit. Some people scatter grain on the road while the corpse is being carried to the cremation ground.[4]

Among the Hindus in the Konkan, as well as in the Deccan, dead bodies are generally burnt, but under the following circumstances they are buried.

Persons dying of small pox, women dying in childbirth or during their menses, children dying within six months from their birth, and *Sanyásis* are buried. The bodies of persons suffering from leprosy are necessarily buried.[5] Among Lingáyats the bodies are always buried. Certain *mantras* are repeated while burying or burning the dead body. While burying, cocoanuts and certain kinds of grain are thrown into the grave, and after covering the dead body with salt, the grave is filled up with earth and stones.[6] While burning, the dead body is placed on the funeral pile with its head to the north and feet towards the south. *Tulsi* wood, sandal-wood, and *Bel* wood are kept on the pile before placing

1 Ráo Sáheb Shelke, Kolhápur.

2 School Master, Bándivade, Ratnágiri.

3 School Master, Bankavli, Ratnágiri.

4 School Master, Poladpur, Kolába.

5 School Master, Ubhádánda, Ratnágiri.

6 School Master, Ibbrampur, Ratnágiri.

the dead body over it. Cocoanuts and camphor cakes are placed on the body, and it is set on fire. Among the Lingáyats and Gosávis the dead are buried. Before burying, the Lingáyats have to take a written order from their priest, the Ayya or Jangam. The paper is then tied to the neck of the deceased, and the body is placed in a bag made of new cloth, the head being allowed to remain out of the bag. *Bhasma* or ashes, salt and camphor are also put into the bag along with the corpse, which is then buried. The Jangam repeats *mantras* when the body is in the grave. No such written order is necessary for the burial of Gosávis. A cocoanut is broken on the head of the corpse at the time of burying it. Among high class Hindus the corpse is carried to the funeral ground in a bier made of bamboos. Among the Lingáyats a gaily dressed frame called *Makhar* is prepared on the bier, and the body is dressed with clothes and head dress and seated in the *Makhar*. Some of them carry the dead body in a bag made of blanket. There is a custom of keeping foot-prints on the spot where a *Sanyási* is buried, and they are daily worshipped by the people.[1] Among the Káthawatis of Thána and Kolába districts the dead body is first buried, and after a few days the skeleton is taken out of the grave and then burnt as usual.[2] Among the high class Hindus the moustaches are shaved at the death of parents paternal uncle and elder brother. Among the Shudras it is not necessary to shave.[3] Persons who have lost their parents have to perform certain funeral rites or *Shráddhas* when they visit holy places such as Benáres, Prayág, Ayodhya and Násik, and they have to shave their moustaches at all these places before performing the funeral rites.[4] Moustaches are also shaved as a penance for certain sins. The *Agnihotri*, i.e., one who preserves perpetual fire in his house for worship, has to get himself shaved every fortnight.[5]

Among high class Hindus boiled rice is daily offered to the dead after a portion has been thrown into the fire, the remainder being given to the crows. The portion thrown in the fire is called *Vaishvadev*, and that which is given to the crows is called *Kágwás*. Among other Hindus it is given on the last day of *Bhádrapada* and on the date of the father's death, annually.[6] Oblations of boiled rice are given to the dead every day, on the last day of the Hindu calendar month, on the date of a person's death every month, on the same date of the dark half of *Bhádrapada* every year. These oblations are put out of the house before taking the meals. It is believed that the ancestors come down in the form of crows to partake of these offerings.[7] Oblations of cooked food are also offered to a cow, and considered thus to be received by the dead. They are especially given to the crows annually in the dark half of *Bhádrapada* on the date of the deceased's death.[8] After the corpse has been carried to the funeral ground, an oil lamp containing one cotton wick is kept on the spot where the deceased expired. The flame of the lamp is directed towards the south as it is believed that the soul goes to heaven by the south. A ball of boiled rice and a little quantity of water or milk is kept daily for the first ten days near the lamp while repeating the name of the deceased and of the *gotra* to which it belonged. The lamp is taken out of the house on the 11th day.[9]

Hindus believe that impurity attaches to all the things in the house in consequence of the death of a person in that house. All those things which can be purified by washing are washed and taken back, while things like

[1] Ráo Sáheb Shelke, Kolhápur.
[2] School Master, Mokhade, Thána.
[3] School Master, Mitbáv, Ratnágiri.
[4] Ráo Sáheb Shelke, Kolhápur.
[5] School Master, Khed, Ratnágiri.
[6] School Master, Kelwá-Máhim, Thána.
[7] School Master, Ubhádánda, Ratnágiri.
[8] School Master, Devgad, Ratnágiri.
[9] Ráo Sáheb Shelke, Kolhápur.

earthen pots, cooked food, etc. are thrown away, special care being taken to break these pots, so that they may not be used again. Even the walls of the house are white washed.[1] The earthen pots that are required for the funeral rites of the dead are all broken. One which is required for boiling water to bathe the corpse is broken when the body is carried to the funeral ground. Of the rest, one is broken at the funeral pile after the son has passed thrice round the pile with an earthen vessel filled with water. It is believed that birds and animals drinking water out of these vessels would be infected by disease, and this is the reason why these pots are broken. The mourners who use earthen vessels during the mourning break them at the end of the mourning period.[2] Among the Agris of Chaul in the Kolába District, all earthen vessels in the house are broken on the eleventh day after a death in the family, the chief reason assigned for this act being that the wishes and desires of the deceased might lurk in the earthen vessels and cause trouble to the inmates of the house.[3]

All the members of the family of the dead have to observe mourning for ten days. They are purified on the eleventh day after taking a bath and sipping *Panchgavya*, or the five products of the cow. The son of the dead person, or one who performs the funeral rites of the dead is purified on the twelfth day after completing the rites of *Sapindi*. A man in mourning does not touch those who are not in mourning. If anybody touches him, both of them have to take a bath. The son of the deceased or, in the absence of a son, any male member belonging to the family is entitled to perform the funeral rites of the dead. These rites are performed during the first twelve days, beginning from the first day or from the 3rd, 5th, 7th or the 9th. One who performs these rites has to sleep on the ground during these twelve days. A person hearing of the death of a member of his family within the first ten days from the date of the death, becomes free from that mourning on the eleventh day. If he happens to hear it within one month of the death, he has to observe it for three days and after one month he has to observe it for one day only.[4] The son, or one who performs the funeral rites of the deceased has to sleep on the ground, and has to take his meals only once a day till the end of the 13th day. He takes his bath in cold water. Sweet things are not prepared in the house during the days of mourning. During the period of mourning, every morning, a Bráhman comes to the mourner's house and recites some passages from the *Garud Purána*, which relates to the state of the soul after death. On the eleventh day the house is besmeared with cowdung, and cow's urine is sprinkled in the house. All the clothes are washed. Mourning is not observed in the case of a death of a *Sanyási*, and the Lingáyats do not observe any kind of mourning[5].

The brother of the deceased, his son, grandson and all the members belonging to the family, have to observe the mourning for ten days. The married daughter of the deceased has to observe it for three days. From the fifth or sixth generation in the same family, it is observed for three or one day only.[6] In case of the death of a wife's parents, the husband has to observe mourning for three days. During the mourning days people do not worship the gods or go to the temples. Milk is also prohibited during the mourning period. The mourners are not to touch anybody except the members of their family.[7]

On the thirteenth day the sons and other members of the family are taken out to visit the temple of any deity by the people assembled

[1] School Master, Ubhádánda, Ratnágiri.
[2] Ráo Sáheb Shelke, Kolhápur.
[3] School Master, Chowl, Kolába.
[4] School Master, Ubhádánda, Ratnágiri.
[5] Ráo Sáheb Shelke, Kolhápur.
[6] School Master, Mitbáv, Ratnágiri.
[7] School Master, Vavanje, Kolába.

for the purpose. It is believed that after going to the temple on the 13th day, the sons and the other members of the family are at liberty to go out of the house.[1]

At Kolhápur it is believed that the deities Etalái and Kálkái of the Konkan districts keep with them evil spirits as their servants. These servant spirits obey the orders of these deities. Some people in this district go to the temples of these deities and request them to lend them the services of these spirit servants. It is considered very lucky to secure the help of these spirits. The temple ministrant then requests the deity to give a *Kaul* or omen. For this purpose, the temple ministrant calls on the deity to enter his body, and when he is possessed by the spirit of the deity, he allows the applicant to take with him one of the deity's servants for a fixed period. The Gurav, or the ministrant, then explains to the person the period for which the spirit servant is given, and the amount of the annual tribute required to be given to the deity for the use of her servant. He also gives him a cocoanut and sacred ashes. The applicant then returns home, believing that the spirit servant will follow him, and from that time he prospers. This spirit servant is called *Chetuk*, and it can be seen only by the person in whose charge it is given by the Gurav.[2]

At Achare in the Ratnágiri District, the spirit of a Bráhman well versed in the *Vedas* is called Mahápurusha and it is said to be benevolent. It haunts *Pipal* and *Umbar* trees.[3]

At Murbád in the Thána District, the spirit known as Vetál, the king of evil spirits, is considered to be benevolent.[4]

The spirits known as Mahápurush haunts the *Pipal* and *Umbar* trees. Avagat the ghost of a widow haunts the *Avali* (Phyllanthus emblica) tree. Alavant, the ghost of a woman dying at childbirth or during her menses, lives in the *Nágchámpa, Surang* and the *Kájra* trees. Devachár, Sambandh, Munja, Zoting, Khavis and Khápra reside in trees and plants.[5]

The people of Kolhápur believe that the spirits known as Bramhasambandh, Brahma Rákshasa, and Khavis reside in trees.[6]

The spirits known as Devchár and Chálegat are considered to be the special protectors of crops and cattle.[7]

The people of Ubhádánda in the Ratnágiri District believe that the village deities and the Devachárs are the special protectors of crops and cattle. Offerings of fowls and cocoanuts are made to them annually.[8]

At Kochare in the Ratnágiri District, the spirit known as Viswáti is believed to be the special protector of crops and cattle.[9]

The people of the Kolába District consider that the spirits known as Mhashya, Khavis, and Bándav are the protectors of crops and cattle.[10]

At Dahánu in the Thána District, the spirit Cheda is believed to be the guardian of crops and cattle.[11]

The people of Kolhápur believe that the deities of the fields protect the crops and cattle. Those who are in possession of the *Chetuk*, or the servant spirit, are sure to find their crops and cattle protected by this servant spirit.[12]

Evil spirits are not usually invoked to frighten children, but occasionally the names of goblins such as Bágulbáwa, Bowáji, Gosávi etc. are mentioned to scare them.[13]

[1] School Master, Málád, Thána.
[2] Ráo Sáheb Shelke, Kolhápur.
[3] School Master, Achare, Ratnágiri.
[4] School Master, Murbád, Thána.
[5] School Master, Achare, Ratnágiri
[6] Ráo Sáheb Shelke, Kolhápur.
[7] School Master, Fonde, Ratnágiri.
[8] School Master, Ubhádánda, Ratnágiri.
[9] School Master, Kochare, Ratnágiri.
[10] School Master Varsai, Kolába.
[11] School Master, Dahánu, Thána.
[12] Ráo Sáheb Shelke, Kolhápur.
[13] School Master, Achare, Ratnágiri.

CHAPTER VII.

TREE AND SERPENT WORSHIP.

Groves of mango trees are considered to be sacred as they have a pleasing appearance, and afford grateful shelter against the heat of the day. It is a general belief among Hindus that trees from which such pleasure and protection are derived must naturally be the abode of the gods. There are many such groves in Satára. During the spring season people go to these groves and worship the trees. The Hindus have a general prejudice against cutting living trees which yield fruits, and it is considered specially inauspicious to cut the following trees :—

Umbar, Vad or Banian tree, *Pipal, Saundad* or *Shami, Palus, Bel, Rui, Avali* and the *Tulsi* plant, for it is believed that these trees are the abode of deities, *e.g.* the god Dattátraya resides under the *Umbar* tree, the goddess Párvati on the Banian tree, and the god Vishnu resides near the *Tulsi* plant. The god Brahma, the creator of the world, is found in the *Pipal* tree. The plantain tree is also considered to be sacred. While gathering a bunch of plantains, the tree is first cut before the bunch. It is considered inauspicious to gather the bunch without so doing.[1]

There are certain groves at Ubhádánda in the Vengurla taluka of the Ratnágiri District which are supposed to be haunted by *Devachárs*, and are therefore not cut by the people.[2]

The people of Ibhrámpur in the Chiplun taluka consider it inauspicious to cut the *Vad* and *Pipal* trees of which the thread ceremonies have been performed. After the thread ceremony of these trees is over, a stone platform is raised around them.[3]

At Fonde in the Devgad taluka, it is considered inauspicious to cut the trees and the groves that surround the temple of a village deity, for they are believed to belong to that deity.[4]

At Padghe in the Thána District, the trees which are supposed to have been haunted by evil spirits such as *Sambandh, Munja, Devachár*, etc. are not generally cut by the people through fear of these spirits. When any tree is cut down, the custom is to keep a stone at the root of the tree in order that the place may no longer be affected or haunted by the spirit in the tree.[5] There are certain families who do not burn *Pipal, Khair*, or *Shiwani* wood. They believe that the burning of these trees causes harm to their families. It is said that the burning of the *Apta* tree causes the breeding of the insect known as *Gochadi*, i. e. the cattle or dog louse.[6]

There is an *Awdumbar* tree of the god Dattátraya at Bhillawadi, and a big Banian tree near the *math* of the Lingáyat *swámi* named Kadappa near Kolhápur, which are worshipped by the people of the neighbouring villages. The *Saundad* tree, better known as *Shami*, is worshipped once a year on the *Dasara*, the 10th day of the bright half of *Ashwin* (October). It is said that Ráma, the seventh incarnation of Vishnu, kept his arms on the *Shami* tree during his fourteen years' exile, and took them back again when he marched upon Lanka or Ceylon to kill Ráwan, the demon king of Ceylon. While going to Lanka he bowed to the *Shami* tree, and as he was successful in his undertaking, the Maráthás used to start for a campaign on the

[1] Ráo Sáheb Shelke, Kolhápur.
[2] School Master, Ubhádánda, Ratnágiri.
[3] School Master, Ibhrámpur, Ratnágiri.
[4] School Master, Fonde, Ratnágiri.
[5] School Master, Padghe, Thána.
[6] School Master, Dahigaon, Thána.

Dasara day after worshipping the *Shami* tree, and distributing its leaves among their friends calling it *Suwarn* or gold. This is said to be the origin of the festival of *Dasara*. A species of the tamarind tree called *Gorakh Chinch* is said to be connected with the Hindu saint Gorakhnáth. For this reason this tree is worshipped by the people. A great fair is held every year at Battis Shiråle in the Satára District, which is situated at a distance of about ten miles from Kolhápur.[1]

The *Pipal*, the *Umbar*, the *Vad* or Banian tree, and the *Tulsi* plant are worshipped by Hindus in general. The *Apta* tree is worshipped by Hindus on the *Dasara* day, and its leaves are distributed under the name of *sone*, or gold, among their friends and relatives.[2]

At Medhe in the Roha taluka of the Kolába District, there is a tree *Vehala* (Beleric myrobalan) which is believed to be connected with the local deity Mhasoba. It is considered to be a sacred tree, and nobody dares to cut it or to touch it with the feet.[3]

At Shirgáon in the Máhim taluka of the Thána District there is a *Ránjani* tree on the bank of a tank called Khambále, which is said to be connected with the deity Brahma; and therefore no branch of that tree is cut by the people. It is considered harmful to cut the tree.[4]

At Gánagápur in the Kolhápur District, there is a *Vad* tree connected with the saint Kabir. It is called *Kabirvad*. There is also an *Awdumbar* tree connected with the god Dattátraya, and known as *Dattátraya Awdumbar*.[5]

The *Umbar*, *Pipal*, *Vad*, and the *Tulsi* plant are considered to be sacred, and are respected by Hindus. The following are some of the legends about their sacredness.

Umbar—When the god Vishnu in his fourth incarnation, called Narsinh, i.e. half man and half lion, tore into pieces the body of the demon named Hiranyakashipu with his claws, he felt a burning sensation of the poison from the body of that demon, which was assuaged by thrusting his hands into the trunk of the *Umbar* or *Awadumbar* tree.[6]

In order that they may get the auspicious sight of a deity early in the morning, Hindus generally plant the *Umbar* and *Tulsi* trees in front of their houses, and worship them daily. The juice of the root of the *Umbar* has a cooling effect, and hence it is freely used in cases of measles or itch. Its sap is also used as medicine for swellings. It is very pleasant to sit under the shade of this tree, and as it is believed that the god Dattátraya resides beneath this tree, it is held very sacred by the Hindus.[7]

Pipal—The *Pipal* tree is considered very sacred because it is believed that the god Brahma resides in the roots, the god Vishnu in the trunk, and the god Shiva on the top of this tree. Persons who make a particular vow or have any objects to be fulfilled worship the *Pipal* tree, and walk round it several times every day.[8] The evil spirits *Sambandh*, *Devachár*, *Munja*, and *Vetál* haunt the *Pipal* tree. These spirits are considered to be the servants of the god Shiva. It is also believed that persons who worship and walk round this tree daily are not affected by those spirits. The *Pipal* tree is specially worshipped at dawn on Saturday as it is considered that the gods Brahma, Vishnu, and Mahesh or Shiva happen to be there at that time.[9]

1 Ráo Sáheb Shelke, Kolhápur.
2 School Master, Shiravade, Ratnágiri.
3 School Master, Medhe, Kolába.
4 School Master, Shirgaon, Thána.
5 School Master, Umele, Thána.
6 School Master, Fonde, Ratnágiri.
7 Ráo Sáheb Shelke, Kolhápur.
8 Ráo Sáheb Shelke, Kolhápur.
9 School Master, Ubhádánda, Ratnágiri.

Vad or the Banian tree—A prince named Satyawán died of snakebite under the *Vad* tree. His wife named Sávitri, who was very chaste and dutiful, requested Yama, the god of death, and succeeded in securing from him the life of her husband Satyawán. As the prince Satyawán returned from the jaws of death under the *Vad* tree, this tree was specially worshipped by her, and it is therefore believed that Sávitri has ever since then been responsible for the practice of worshipping the *Vad* tree by women for the purpose of securing a long life to their husbands.[1] It is also believed that the god Vishnu takes shelter under the *Vad* at the time of the general destruction of the world. The worship of this tree is similar to that of the other deities, and women take turns around it at the close of the worship or *puja*.[2]

The *Tulsi* plant is worshipped daily by the Hindus in general, and women in particular, by keeping the plant near their houses. The god Vishnu is worshipped particularly by the leaf of this plant.[2] The *Tulsi* plant is considered by the people to represent the goddess Luxmi, the wife of Vishnu. Hindu women will not take their meals before worshipping the *Tulsi* plant daily in the morning. It is also said that the god Vishnu, in his eighth incarnation called Krishna, had loved Vrunda, the wife of a demon. After her death she was burnt, but on her burning ground there grew the *Tulsi* plant. As Krishna loved Vrunda very dearly, he began to love this plant also, and hence the image of Bál Krishna, or the god Vishnu, is married to this plant every year on the 12th day of the bright half of *Kártik* (November).[3] As it is also believed that the god Vishnu resides in the *Tulsi* plant, the worship of this plant is equivalent to the worship of the god Vishnu.[4]

Besides the above mentioned trees, the *Palus* (Butea frondosa), the *Bel*, a tree sacred to god Shiva, and the *Shami* (Prosopis spicigera), a tree sacred to god Ganpati the son of Shiva, are considered to be holy by the Hindus.[5]

A common custom among Hindus is for a person who has lost his two wives and wishes to marry a third, to be first married to a *Rui* plant, and then to the actual bride. His marriage with the *Rui* plant is considered as a third marriage. After the marriage, the *Rui* plant is cut down and buried, and thus the marriage with the third bride is considered to be a fourth marriage. The marriage with the *Rui* plant has been adopted in the belief that the third wife is sure to die unless the spirit of the deceased is made to enter the *Rui* plant.[6]

When a girl is born under the influence of inauspicious planets which may be harmful to her husband, she is first married to a tree or an earthen pot, and then to the bridegroom. The marriage with the earthen pot is called *Kumbhaviváha*, or the pot-wedding. It is believed that, by observing this practice, the danger to her husband is avoided. The danger passes to the tree to which she is first married.[7]

Among the lower classes in the Thána District[8] a poor man unable to marry owing to his poverty is first married to a *Rui* plant and then to a widow. This marriage with a widow is called *pát lávane*. This remarriage of a widow among the lower classes is generally performed at night, and under an old mango tree. It is never performed in the house. A widow who has remarried cannot take part in any auspicious ceremony such as a marriage, etc.[8]

At Vankavli in the Ratnágiri Disrtict there is a custom among the low class Hindus of a woman who has lost her second husband and wishes to marry for the third time, first marrying a cock, *i.e.*, she takes the cock in her arms at the time of her marriage with the third husband.[9]

Persons who have no children make a vow to Khandoba at Jejuri that the firstborn, male or female, shall be offered to him. The females, offered in fulfilment of such vows are called

[1] Ráo Sáheb Shelke, Kolhápur.
[2] School Master, Mitbáv, Ratnágiri.
[3] School Master, Dahánu, Thána.
[4] School Master, Ubhádánda, Ratnágiri.
[5] School Master, Devgad, Ratnágiri.
[6] School Master, Mitbáv, Ratnágiri.
[7] School Master, Khopoli, Kolába.
[8] School Master, Edwan, Thána.
[9] School Master, Vankávli, Ratnágiri.

Muralis. They are married to the god Khandoba, and have to earn their livelihood by begging in villages. A male child thus offered to the god is called a *Vághya*.[1]

There is a custom of offering children to the deities Yallamma and Khandoba in fulfilment of vows made in order to get a child. The child is taken to the temple of these deities, accompanied with music. The temple ministrant asks the child to stand on a wooden board on a heap of rice in front of the deity, and puts into its hands a *paradi*—a flat basket of bamboo, tying to its neck the *darshana* of the deity. A female child is married to the dagger—*Katyár*—of the deity. When once this ceremony has been performed, parents abandon their rights to such children. When these children come of age, the males can marry but the females cannot. The latter earns her livelihood begging *jogava* in the name of the goddess Amba with a *paradi* in her hand. A male child offered to the goddess Yallamma is called *jogata*, and a female, *jogatin*. Children dedicated to the goddess Máyáka are called *Jogi* and *Jogin*. Children offered to *Firangái* and *Ambábái* are called *Bhutya* (male) and *Bhutin* (female).[2]

In the Konkan districts there is a class of women known as Bhávinis who are said to be married to *Khanjir*, *i.e.*, a dagger belonging to the god. They are also called *deva yoshita*, *i.e.*, prostitutes offered to the god. They have no caste of their own. They retain the name of the caste to which they originally belonged, such as Maráthe Bhávini, Bhandári Bhávini, Sutár Bhavini, etc. The following account is given of the origin of the sect of Bhávinis. A woman wishing to abandon her husband goes to the temple of a village deity at night, and in presence of the people assembled in that temple she takes oil from the lamp burning in the temple, and pours it upon her head. This process is called *Deval righane*, *i.e.*, to enter into the service of the temple. After she has poured sweet oil from the lamp upon her head, she has no further connection with her husband. She becomes the maid servant of the temple, and is free to behave as she likes. Daughters of such Bhávinis who do not wish to marry, undergo the process of *shesa bharane*, and follow the occupation of their mothers. The sons of the Bhávinis have an equal right to the property of their mother, but any daughter who marries a lawful husband loses her share in the property of her mother. A Devali follows the occupation of blowing the horn or cornet, and is entitled to hold the torches in the marriage ceremonies of the people in the village. Many of them learn the art of playing upon the tabour—*mrudunga*—and are useful to *Kathekaris*, *i.e.*, those who recite legends of the gods with music and singing. Some of them become farmers while others are unoccupied.

Bhávinis follow the occupation of a maid-servant in the temple, but their real occupation is that of public women. They are not scorned by the public. On the contrary, they are required to be present at the time of a marriage to tie the marriage-string—*Mangalsutra*—of a bride, for they are supposed to enjoy perpetual unwidowhood—'*Janma suwásini*.' Some of the houses of Bhávinis become the favourite resorts of gamblers and vagabonds. In the absence of a daughter, a Bhávini purchases a girl from a harlot, and adopts her as her daughter to carry on her profession.[3]

Snakes are believed to be the step-brothers of the gods. They reside under the earth and are very powerful. The snake is considered to be very beautiful among creeping animals, and is one of the ornaments of the god Shiva. An image of a snake made of brass is kept in the temple of the god Shiva, and worshipped daily along with the god. There is a custom among the Hindus of worshipping *Nága*, *i.e.*, the cobra, once a year on the *Nága panchami* day, *i.e.*, the fifth day of the bright half of *Shráwan* (August). Images of snakes are drawn with sandalpaste on a wooden board or on the walls of houses,

[1] School Master, Palshet, Ratnágiri.
[2] Ráo Sáheb Shelke, Kolhápur.
[3] School Master, Kálshe, Ratnágiri.

and worshipped by Hindu women on this day. *Durva* grass, sacred to Ganpati, parched rice *láhya*, legumes *kadadan*, and milk are offered to this image. Some people go to the snakes, abode *Várul*—an ant-hill—on this day to worship the snake itself, if they happen to catch sight of it.[1]

It is said that at Battisa Shiràle in the Belgáum District the real *Nága* comes out of its abode below the earth on this day, and is worshipped by the people. Milk and *láhya*, parched rice, are put outside the house at night on this day with the intention that they may be consumed by a snake. Hindus do not dig or plough the earth on *Nága panchami* day. Even vegetables are not cut and fried on this day by some people.[2]

Earthen images of snakes are worshipped by some people in the Konkan districts on the *Nága panchami* day. The *Nága* is considered to be a Bráhman by caste, and it is believed that the family of the person who kills a snake becomes extinct. The cobra being considered a Bráhman, its dead body is adorned with the *jánawe*, and then burnt as that of a human being. A copper coin is also thrown into its funeral pile.[3]

At certain villages in the Deccan a big earthen image of a snake is consecrated in a public place on the *Nága panchami* day, and worshipped by Hindus in general. Women sing their songs in circles before this image while men perform *tamáshás* by its side. In fact, the day is enjoyed by the people as a holiday. The snake is removed next day, and an idol in the form of a man made of mud is seated in its place. This idol is called Shirálshet, who is said once to have been a king and to have ruled over this earth for one and one-fourths of a *ghataka*, *i. e.*, for half an hour only. This day, is observed as a day of rejoicing by the people.[4]

The names of the snake deities are Takshaka, Vásuki and Shesha. Their shrines are at Kolhápur, Nágothane, Prayaga, Nágadeváchi Wádi and Subramhanya. A great fair is held every year at Battisa Shiràle on the *Nága panchami* day.[4]

There is a shrine of a snake deity at Sávantwádi. The management of the shrine is in the hands of the State officials. It is believed that a real snake resides therein.[5]

There is a shrine of a snake deity at Awás in the Alibág taluka of the Kolába District, where a great fair is held every year on the 14th day of the bright half of *Kártik* (November). It is said that persons suffering from snakebites recover when taken in time to this temple.[6]

It is said that a covetous person who acquires great wealth during his life-time and dies without enjoying it, or without issue, becomes a snake after death, and guards his buried treasures. At Kolhápur there was a *Sáwkár*—money-lender—named Kodulkar who is said to have become a snake, and to guard his treasures. In the village of Kailava in the Panhála petha of the Kolhápur District there is a snake in the house of a Kulkarni, who scares away those who try to enter the storehouse of the Kulkarni.[7]

It is a general belief among the Hindus that snakes guard treasures. It is said that there are certain places guarded by snakes in Goa territory. Persons who were compelled to abandon Portuguese territory owing to religious persecutions at the hands of the Portuguese buried their treasures beneath the ground. Those who died during exile are said to have become *bhuts* or ghosts, and it is believed that they guard their buried treasures in the form of snakes.[8]

The Hindus generally believe that the snakes who guard buried treasures do not allow any one to go near them. The snake frightens those who try to approach, but when he wishes

1 School Master, Mitbáv, Ratnágiri.

2 School Master, Kálshe, Ratnágiri.

3 School Master, Khopoli, Kolába.

4 Ráo Sáheb Shelke, Kolhápur.

5 School Master, Pendur, Ratnágiri.

6 School Master, Apte, Panwel, Kolába.

7 Ráo Sáheb Shelke, Kolhápur.

8 School Master, Ubhádánda, Ratnágiri.

to hand over the treasure to anybody he goes to that person at night, and tells him in a dream that the treasure buried at such and such a place belongs to him, and requests him to take it over. After the person has taken possession of the treasure as requested, the snake disappears from the spot.[1]

It is said that a snake which guards treasure is generally very old, white in complexion, and has long hair on its body.[2]

Hindus worship the image of a snake made of *Darbha* grass or of silk thread on the *Anant Chaturdashi* day, *i.e.*, the 14th day of the bright half of *Ashwin* (October), and observe that day as a holiday. Legends of the exploits of the god are related with music and singing on this day.[3]

A snake festival is observed in the Nágeshwar temple at Awás in the Kolába District on the night of the 14th day of the bright half of *Kártika* (November). Nearly four hundred devotees of the god Shankar assemble in the temple, holding in their hands *vetra-sarpa* long cane sticks with snake images at their ends. They advance dancing and repeating certain words, and take turns round the temple till midnight. After getting the permission of the chief devotee, they scatter throughout the neighbouring villages with small axes in their hands, and cut down, and bring from the gardens, cocoanuts, plantains, and other edible things that are seen on their way. They return to the temple after two hours, the last man being the chief devotee called *Kuwarkándya*. The fruits are then distributed among the people assembled at the temple. Nobody interferes with them on this day in taking away cocoanuts and other fruits from the village gardens. On the next day they go dancing in the same manner to the Kanakeshwar hill with the snake sticks in their hands.[4]

In the Deccan no special snake festivals like those described above are celebrated. But in the temples devoted to snake deities, on the full moon day of *Kártik*, which is sacred to the snake deity, the deity is worshipped with special pomp, and the crests of the temples are illuminated on that night.[5]

The village cures for snakebite are :—

1. The use of charmed water and the repetition of *mantras* by a sorcerer.

2. The use of certain roots and herbs as medicines.

3. The removal of the sufferer to the neighbouring temple.

4. Branding the wound with fire.

5. The drinking of soapnut juice, or of water in which copper coins have been boiled by the patient, who is thus made to vomit the snake poison.[6]

In the Deccan a person suffering from snakebite is taken to a village temple, and the ministrant is requested to give him holy water. The deity is also invoked. Thus keeping the person for one night in the temple, he is carried to his house the following day if cured. The vows made to the deity for the recovery of the person are then fulfilled. There is one *turabat*, a tomb of *Avalia* a Mahomedan saint, at Panhála where persons suffering from snakebite are made to sit near the tomb, and it is said that they are cured. In some villages there are enchanted trees of *Kadulimb* where persons placed under the shade of such trees are cured of snakebites. Some people tie a stone round the neck of the sufferer as soon as he is better, repeating the words *Adi Gudi Imám* the name of a Mahomedan saint. After recovery from snakebite the person is taken to the mosque of the *Adi Gudi Imám Sáheb*, where the stone is untied before the tomb, and *jágri* equal to the weight of the stone is offered. A feast is also given to the *Mujáwar* or ministrant of the mosque. There is at persent a famous enchanter—*Mántrika*—at Satára who cures persons suffering from snakebite. It is said that he throws charmed water on the body of the sufferer, and in a few minutes the snake

[1] School Master, Chawk, Kolába.
[2] School Master, Basani, Ratnágiri.
[3] School Master, Pendur, Ratnágiri.
[4] School Master, Chawl, Kolába.
[5] Ráo Sáheb Shelke, Kolhápur.
[6] School Master, Jambivali, Kolába.

begins to speak through the victim. The sorcerer enquires what the snake wants.. The snake gives reasons for biting the person. When any thing thus asked for by the snake is offered, the victim comes to his senses, and is cured. There are many witnesses to the above fact.[1]

At Mitbáv in the Ratnágiri District chickens numbering from twenty to twenty-five are applied to the wound caused by the snakebite. A chicken has the power of drawing out the poison from the body through the wound, but this causes the death of the chicken. The remedy above described is sure to be successful if it is tried within three hours of the person being bitten. There are several other medicines which act on the snakebite, but they must be given very promptly. There are some men in this village who give charmed water for snake or any other bites. Many persons suffering from snakebite have been cured by the use of *mantras* and charmed water.[2]

Water from the tanks of Vetávare in the Sávantwádi State and Mánjare in Goa territory is generally used as medicine for snakebite. It is believed that by the power of *mantras* a snake can be prevented from entering or leaving a particular area. This process is called '*sarpa bándhane*'. There are some sorcerers who can draw snakes out of their holes by the use of their *mantras*, and carry them away without touching them with their hands.[3]

At Adivare, in the Rájápur taluka, roots of certain herbs are mixed in water and applied to the wound caused by the snakebite, and given to the sufferer to drink.[4]

At Náringre in the Ratnágiri District, persons suffering from snakebite are given the juice of *Kadulimb* leaves, and are kept in the temple of Hanumán. The feet of the deity are washed with holy water, and the water is given to the victim to drink.[5]

A snake is believed to have a white jewel or *mani* in its head, and it loses its life when this jewel is removed. This jewel has the power of drawing out the poison of snakebite. When it is applied to the wound, it becomes green, but when kept in milk for sometime, it loses its greenness and reverts to its usual white colour. It gives out to the milk all the poison that has been absorbed from the wound, and the milk becomes green. This jewel can be used several times as an absorbent of the poison of snakebite. The green milk must be buried under ground, so that it may not be used again by any one else.[6]

It is believed that an old snake having long hair on its body has a jewel in its head. This jewel is compared with the colours of a rainbow. The snake can take this jewel from its head at night, and search for food in its lustre. Such snakes never come near the habitation of human beings, but always reside in the depth of the jungle. This species of snake is called *Deva Sarpa, i. e.*, a snake belonging to a deity. It is related that a snake was born of a woman in the Kinkar's house at Tardál in the Sángli State, and another one in the Gabale's house at Kolhápur.[7]

1 Ráo Sáheb Shelke, Kolhápur.
2 School Master, Mitbáv, Ratnágiri.
3 School Master, Ubhádánda, Ratnágiri.
4 School Master, Adivare, Ratnágiri.
5 School Master, Náringre, Ratnágiri.
6 School Master, Kálshe, Ratnágiri.
7 Ráo Sáheb Shelke, Kolhápur.

CHAPTER VIII.

TOTEMISM AND FETISHISM.

The worship of totems, or *Devaks,* prevails among Hindus in Western India. The term *Devak* is applied to the deity or deities worshipped at the beginning of a thread or a marriage ceremony. The ceremony is as follows: A small quantity of rice is put into a winnowing fan, and with it six small sticks of the *Umbar* tree, each covered with mango leaves and cotton thread. These are worshipped as deities. Near the winnowing fan is kept an earthen or copper vessel filled with rice, turmeric, red powder, betelnuts, sweet balls made of wheat flour, ghi and sugar ; and on the top of the vessel is a small sprig of mango and a cocoanut covered with cotton thread. This vessel is also worshipped as a deity, and offerings of sweet eatables are made to it. After the worship of this vessel, the regular ceremony of. *Punyáhavachana* is performed. Twenty-seven *Mátrikás*, or village and local deities, represented by betelnuts are consecrated in a new winnowing fan or a bamboo basket. Seven *Mátrikás* are made of mango leaves, six of which contain *durva* grass, and the seventh *darbha* grass. Each of them is bound with a raw cotton thread separately. They are worshipped along with a *Kalasha* or a copper *lota* as mentioned above. This copper *lota* is filled with rice, betelnuts, turmeric, etc., a sprig of mango leaves is placed on the *lota,* and a cocoanut is put over it. The *lota* is also bound with a cotton thread. Sandalpaste, rice, flowers, and *durva* grass are required for its worship. An oil lamp called *Arati* is waved round the *devak,* the parents, and the boy or the girl whose thread or marriage ceremony is to be performed. A *Suwásini* is called and requested to wave this *Arati,* and the silver coin which is put into the *Arati* by the parents is taken by her. The father takes the winnowing fan and the mother takes the *Kalasha,* and they are carried from the *mandap* to the *devak* consecrated in the house. A lighted lamp is kept continually burning near this *devak* till the completion of the ceremony. After completion of the thread or marriage ceremony the *devak* is again worshipped, and the ceremony comes to an end. The deity in the *devak* is requested to depart on the second or the fourth day from the date of its consecration. No mourning is observed during the period the *devak* remains installed in the house.

Among Maráthás and many of the lower classes in the Ratnágiri District the branch of a *Vad, Kadamba,* mango, or an *Apta* tree is worshipped as their *devak* or *kul.*[1]

Some Maráthás have a sword or a dagger as their *devak,* which is worshipped by them before commencing the ritual of the marriage ceremony.[2]

The family known as Ráne at Náringre in the Davagad taluka of the Ratnágiri District, and the families known as Gadakari and Jádhava at Málwan, consider the *Vad* or Banian tree as their *devak,* and do not make use of its leaves. In the same manner, some people consider the *Kadamba* tree sacred to their family.[3]

There are some people among the Hindus in Western India whose surnames are derived from the names of animals and plants, such as *Boke, Lándage, Wágh, Dukre, Káwale, Garud More, Mhase, Rede, Keer, Popat, Ghode, Shelár, Gáyatonde, Wághmáre, Shálunke, Bhende, Padwal, Wálke, Apte, Ambekar, Pimpalkhare, Kelkar* and *Kálke.*

The Hindus believe that a cow, a horse, and an elephant are sacred animals. The cow is treated with special respect by the Hindus

---

[1] School Master, Adivare, Ratnágiri.
[2] School Master, Kálshe, Ratnágiri.
[3] School Master, Achare, Ratnágiri.

in general, and the bull by the Lingáyats and oilmen. The milk, the urine, and the dung of a cow are used as medicines, and they are also given as offerings to the god in sacrifices.

The Shelár family considers the sheep as their *devak*, and they do not eat the flesh of a sheep. The Shálunke family respects the *Shálunki* or sparrow. People belonging to the More family do not eat the flesh of a peacock as they consider it to be their *devak*.[1]

The Bhandáris whose surname is Padwal do not eat the vegetable of a snake-gourd or *Padwal*.[2]

Hindus do not eat the flesh of the animal respected by them, and those who offer any fruit to their *guru* as a token of respect do not eat that fruit in future. Some Hindus do not eat onions, garlic and the fruit of a palm tree. The fruit of a tree believed to be the *devak* of a family is not eaten by the members of that family.

The families of Ráva and Ráne do not take their food on the leaf of a *Vad* or Banian tree as they consider it to be their *devak*.[3]

There are some Hindu families in the Kolába District who believe that their *kul* or totem consists of the tortoise and the goat, and they do not eat the flesh of such animals. A certain community of the *Vaishyas* or traders known as Swár believe that a jack tree or *Phanas* is their *kul*, and they do not use the leaves of that tree.[4]

It is believed among the Hindus that the deity *Satwái* protects children for the first three months from their birth. The deity is worshipped on the fifth day from the birth of a child, and if there occurs any omission or error in the worship of that deity, the child begins to cry, or does not keep good health. On such occasions the parents of the child make certain vows to the deity, and if the child recovers, the parents go to a jungle, and collect seven small stones. They then besmear the stones with red lead and oil, and worship them along with a she goat in the manner in which the vow was promised to be fulfilled.[5]

The horse is connected with the worship of the god Khandoba because this animal is sacred to that deity, being his favourite vehicle. For this reason all the devotees or *Bhaktas* of Khandoba take care to worship the horse in order that its master, the god Khandoba, may be pleased with them.

It is well known that the cow is considered as most sacred of all the animals by the Hindus, and the reason assigned for this special veneration is that all the deities dwell in the cow.

The *Nandi*, or a bullock made of stone, consecrated in front of the temple of Shiva, the *Vágh* or a tiger at the temple of a goddess and cows and dogs in the temple of Dattátraya are worshipped by the Hindus.

The mouse, being the vehicle of Ganpati the god of wisdom, is worshipped by the people along with that god.

In the Konkan cattle are worshipped by the Hindus on the first day of *Kártika*, and they are made to pass over fire.

The mountains having caves and temples of deities are generally worshipped by the Hindus. The Abucha Pahád, the Girnár, the Panchmadhi, the Brahmagiri, the Sahyádri, the Tungár, the Jivadancha *dongar*, the Munja *dongar* at Junnar, the Tugábáicha *dongar*, the Ganesh Lene, and the Shivabai are the principal holy mountains in the Bombay Presidency.

Mount Abu, known as the Abucha Pahád, is believed to be very sacred, and many Hindus go on a pilgrimage to that mountain.

Hills are worshipped at Ganpati Pule and Chaul. At Pule there is a temple of the god Ganpati, the son of Shiva, and at Chaul in the Kolába District there is a temple of the god Dattátraya.

[1] School Master, Anjarle, Ratnágiri.
[2] School Master, Achare, Ratnágiri.
[3] School Master, Fonde, Ratnágiri.
[4] School Master, Chauk, Kolába.
[5] Ráo Sáheb Shelke, Kolhápur.

The place which produces sound when water is poured over it is considered to be holy, and is worshipped by the people.

In the Deccan, hills are worshipped by the people on the *Narak chaturdashi* day in *Dipawáli*, 14th day of the dark half of *Ashwin* (October). The legend of this worship is that the god Shri Krishna lifted the Govardhan mountain on this day, and protected the people of this world. A hill made of cowdung is worshipped at every house on the *Narak chaturdashi* day.[1]

Stones of certain kinds are first considered as one of the deities, or as one of the chief heroes in the family, and then worshipped by the people. Many such stones are found worshipped in the vicinity of any temple.

A stone coming out of the earth with a phallus or *lingam* of Shiva is worshipped by the Hindus. If such a *lingam* lies in a deep jungle, it is worshipped by them at least once a year, and daily, if practicable, in the month of *Adhikamás*, an intercalary month which comes every third year.[2]

The red stones found in the Narmada river represent the god Ganpati, and are worshipped by the people.

A big stone at Phutaka Tembha near Murud in the Ratnágiri District is worshipped by the people, who believe it to be the monkey god Hanumán or Máruti. All the stone images of gods that are called *Swayambhu* or self-existent are nothing but rough stones of peculiar shapes. There are such *swayambhu*—natural-images—at Kelshi and Kolthare in the Ratnágiri District.[3]

There is a big stone at Palshet in the Ratnágiri District which is worshipped as *Kálikádevi*.[4]

Stones are sometimes worshipped by the people in the belief that they are haunted by evil spirits. We have for example a stoen called *Mora Dhonda* lying by the seashore at Málwan in the Ratnágiri District. It is supposed to be haunted by *Devachár*.[5]

The stones which are once consecrated and worshipped as deities have to be continually worshipped, even when perforated. The small, round, white stone slab known as *Vishnupada*, which is naturally perforated, is considered to be holy, and is worshipped daily by the Hindus along with the other images of gods. The holes in this slab do not extend right through.[6]

It is considered inauspicious to worship the fractured images of gods, but the perforated black stone called *Sháligrám*, taken from the Gandaki river, is considered very holy, and worshipped by the people. For it is believed to be perforated from its very beginning. Every *Sháligrám* has a hole in it, even when it is in the river.[7]

Broken stones are not worshipped by the people. But the household gods of the Bráhmans and other higher classes which are called the *Pancháyatan*—a collection of five gods—generally consist of five stones with holes in them.[8]

No instances of human sacrifices occur in India in these days, but there are many practices and customs which appear to be the survivals of human sacrifices. These survivals are visible in the offerings of fowls, goats, buffaloes, and fruits like cocoanuts, brinjals, the *Kohále* or pumpkion gourd and others.

Human sacrifices are not practised in these days, but among the Karháda Bráhmans there is a practice of giving poison to animals in order to satisfy their family deity. It is said that they used to kill a Bráhman by giving him poisoned food.

It is believed that the people belonging to the caste of Karháda Bráhmans used to offer human sacrifices to their deity, and therefore nobody relies on a Karháda Bráhman in these

[1] Ráo Sáheb Shelke, Kolhápur.
[2] School Master, Medhe, Kolába.
[3] School Master, Anjarle, Ratnágiri.
[4] School Master, Palshet, Ratnágiri.
[5] School Master, Kálshe, Ratnágiri.
[6] School Master, Mokháde, Thána.
[7] Ráo Sáheb Shelke, Kolhápur.
[8] School Master, Kálshe, Ratnágiri.

days. There is a proverb in Maráthi which means that a man can trust even a *Kasái* or a butcher but not a Karháda.

As they cannot offer human sacrifices in these days, it is said that during the *Navarátra* holidays, *i. e.*, the first nine days of the bright half of *Ashwin* (October), they offer poisoned food to crows, dogs and other animals.[1]

At Kálshe in the Málwan taluka of the Ratnágiri District, the servants of gods, *i.e.*, the ministrants or the Bhopis of the temple prick their breast with a knife on the *Dasara* day, and cry out loudly the words '*Koya*' '*Koya*'. No blood comes from the breast as the wound is slight. This appears to be a survival of human sacrifice.[2]

In the Bombay Presidency, and more especially in the Konkan districts, fetish stones are generally worshipped for the purpose of averting evil and curing diseases. In every village stones are found sacred to spirit deities like Bahiroba, Chedoba, Khandoba, Mhasoba, Zoting, Vetál, Jakhái, Kokái, Kalkái and others. The low class people such as Mahárs, Mángs, etc., apply red lead and oil to stones, and call them by one of the above names, and ignorant people are very much afraid of such deities. They believe that such deities have control over all the evil spirits or ghosts. It is said that the spirit Vetál starts to take a round in a village on the night of the nomoon day of every month, accompanied by all the ghosts. When any epidemic prevails in a village, people offer to these fetish stones offerings of eatables, cocoanuts, fowls an' goats.

There is a stone deity named Bhávai at Kokisare in the Bávada State, to whom vows are made by the people to cure diseases. As the deity is in the burning ground, it is naturally believed that this is the abode of spirits.[3]

At Achare, in the Málwan taluka of the Ratnágiri District, the round stones known as *Kshetrapál* are supposed to possess the power of curing diseases, and are also believed to be the abode of spirits.[4]

At Adivare, in the Ratnágiri District, there is a stone named *Mahár Purukha* which is worshipped by the people when cattle disease prevails, especially the disease of a large tick or the cattle or dog louse.[5]

At Ubhádánda, in the Ratnágiri District, there are some stones which are believed to be haunted by Vetál, Bhutnáth, Rawalnáth and such other servants of the god Shiva, and it is supposed that they have the power of curing epidemic diseases. People make vows to these stones when any disease prevails in the locality.[6]

The Hindus generally consider as sacred all objects that are the means of their livelihood, and, for this reason, the oilmen worship their oil-mill, the Bráhmans hold in veneration the sacred thread—*Yadnopavit*,—and religious books, the goldsmiths consider their firepots as sacred, and do not touch them with their feet. In case any one accidently happens to touch them with his foot, he apologises and bows to them.

It is believed by the Hindus that the broom, the winnowing fan, the *páyali*—a measure of four *shers*, the *Samai* or sweet-oil lamp, a metal vessel, fire and *Sahán* or the levigating slab should not be touched with foot.

The metals gold, silver, and copper, the King's coins, jewels and pearls, corns, the *Sháligrám* stone, the *Ganpati* stone from the Narmada river, conch-shell, sacred ashes, elephant tusks, the horns of an wild ox (*Gava*), tiger skin, deer skin, milk, curds, ghi, cow's urine, *Bel*, basil leaves or *Tulsi*, cocoanuts, betelnuts, and flowers are considered as sacred by the Hindus, and no one will dare to touch them with his foot.

[1] School Master, Chawk, Kolába.
[2] School Master, Kálshe, Ratnágiri.
[3] School Master, Fonde, Ratnágiri.
[4] School Master, Achare, Ratnágiri.
[5] School Master, Náringre, Ratnágiri.
[6] School Master, Ubhádánda, Ratnágiri.

Hindus worship annually on the *Dasara* day the arms and all the instruments or implements by which they earn their livelihood. The corn sieve, the winnowing basket, the broom, the rice-pounder, the plough, the *Awuta* or wood bill, and other such implements are worshipped on this day. The agriculturists respect their winnowing fans and corn sieves, and do not touch them with their feet.

In the Kolhápur District all the instruments and implements are worshipped by the people one day previous to the *Dasara* holiday. This worship is called *Khándepujan*. They also worship all agricultural instruments, and tie to them leaves of *Pipal* and mango trees.[1]

A new winnowing fan is considered to be holy by the Hindus. It is filled with rice, fruits, cocoanuts and betelnuts, and a *Khana*—a piece of bodicecloth—is spread over it. It is then worshipped and given to a Bráhman lady in fulfilment of certain vows, or on the occasion of the worship of a Bráhman *Dampatya* or married pair.

The broom is considered to be holy by the Hindus. Red powder—*Kunku*—is applied to a new broom before it is taken into use. It should not be touched with the feet.

At Rewadanda, in the Kolába District, some people worship a wood-bill or *Koyata* on the 6th day from the birth of a child. The rice-pounder, or *Musal*, is worshipped by them as a *devak* at the time of thread and marriage ceremonies.[2]

Fire is considered to be holy among the high class Hindus. It is considered as an angel that conveys the sacrificial offerings from this earth to the gods in heaven. It is considered as one of the Hindu deities, and worshipped daily by high class Hindus. A Bráhman has to worship the fire every day in connection with the ceremony *Vaishwadeva*—oblations of boiled rice and ghi given to the fire. It is also worshipped by the Hindus on special religious occasions.

Fire is worshipped at the time of *Yadnas* or Sacrifices. Sacrifices are of five kinds. They are—

Devayadna, *Bhutayadna* or *Brahmayadna*, *Rishiyadna* or *Atithiyadna*, *Pitruyadna* and *Manushyayadna*. The offerings of rice, ghi, firewood, *Til* or sesamum, *Java* or barley, etc., are made in these *yadnas*. It is also worshipped at the time of *Shrávani* or *Upákarma*—the ceremony of renewing the sacred thread annually in the month of *Shrávan*.[3]

Among the lower classes fire is worshipped on the *Mahálaya* or *Shráddha* day. They throw oblations of food into the fire on that day.

The fire produced by rubbing sticks of the *Pipal* or *Shevari* tree is considered sacred, and it is essentially necessary that the sacred fire required for the *Agnihotra* rites should be produced in the manner described above.

Agnihotra is a perpetual sacred fire preserved in *Agnikunda*, —a hole in the ground for receiving and preserving consecrated fire. A Bráhman, who has to accept the *Agnihotra*, has to preserve in his house the sacred fire day and night after his thread ceremony, and to worship it three times a day after taking his bath. When an *Agnihotri* dies, his body is burnt by the people who prepare fire by rubbing sticks of *Pipal* wood together.[4]

There are some Bráhmans who keep the fire continuously burning in their houses only for *Chátarmás* or four months of the year. The fire which is preserved and worshipped for four months is called "*Smárta Agni*."[5]

[1] Rao Sáheb Shelke, Kolhápur.
[2] School Master, Rewadanda, Kolába.
[3] School Master, Ibhrámpur, Ratnágiri.
[4] School Master, Adivare, Ratnágiri.
[5] School Master, Anjur, Thána.

CHAPTER IX.

ANIMAL WORSHIP.

The following animals, birds and insects are respected by the Hindus :—The cow, bullock, she-buffalo, horse, elephant, tiger, deer, mouse, goat, ants and alligators; and among the birds the following are held sacred.—Peacock, swan, eagle and *kokil* or cuckoo.

Of all the animals the cow is considered to be the most sacred by Hindus. It is generally worshipped daily in the morning for the whole year, or at least for the *Chátturmás* or four months beginning from the 11th day of the bright half of *Ashádha* to the 11th day of the bright half of the month of *Kártika*; and a special worship is offered to it in the evening on the 12th day of the dark half of *Ashwin* (October).

The cow is believed to be the abode of all the deities and *rishis.* It is compared with the earth in its sacredness, and it is considered that when it is pleased it is capable of giving everything required for the maintenance of mankind, and for this reason it is styled the *Káma Dhenu* or the giver of desired objects. It is said that a person who walks round the cow at the time of its delivery obtains the *punya* or merit of going round the whole earth. The cow is even worshipped by the god Vishnu.

The cow is considered next to a mother, as little children and the people in general are fed by the milk of a cow. Some women among high class Hindus take a vow not to take their meals before worshipping the cow, and when the cow is not available for worship, they draw in turmeric, white or red powder the cow's foot-prints and worship the same. At the completion of the vow it is worshipped, and then given as a gift to a Bráhman. It is considered very meritorious to give a *Gopradán*—a gift of a cow along with its calf, to a Bráhman. The sight of a cow in the morning is believed by all Hindus to be auspicious.

The bullock is respected by the people as it is the favourite vehicle of the god Shiva, and is very useful for agricultural purposes. The *Nandi* or bull is worshipped by Hindus. The bullock is specially worshipped on the 12th day of the bright half of *Kártika.* When performing the funeral rites of the dead, a bull is worshipped and set free. The bull thus set free is considered sacred by the people, and is never used again for agricultural or any other domestic purposes.

In order to avoid calamities arising from the influence of inauspicious planets, Hindus worship the she-buffalo, and offer it as a gift to a Bráhman. The she-buffalo is compared with the *Kál Purusha* or the god of Death, the reason being that Yama is believed to ride a buffalo. The Bráhman who accepts this gift has to shave his moustaches and to undergo a certain penance. The cowherds sometimes worship the she-buffalo. As it is the vehicle of Yama, the buffalo is specially worshipped by people when an epidemic occurs in a village. In certain villages in the Konkan districts the buffalo is worshipped and sacrificed on the same day.

The horse is the vehicle of the deity Khandoba of Jejuri. It is worshipped on the *Vijaya Dashami* or the *Dasara* holiday as in former days, on the occasion of the horse sacrifice or *Ashwamedha.*

The elephant is the vehicle of the god Indra and is specially worshipped on the *Dasara* day. It is also believed that there are eight sacred elephants posted at the eight directions. These are called *Ashtadik-Pálas, i.e.*, the protectors of the eight different directions, and they are worshipped along with other deities on auspicious ceremonial occasions, like weddings, thread-girding, etc.

The deer and the tiger are considered to be holy by Hindus, and their skins are used by Bráhmans and ascetics while performing their austerities. The deer skin is used on the occasion of thread girding. A small piece of the deer skin is tied to the neck of the boy along with the new sacred thread.

The mouse, being the vehicle of the god Ganpati, is worshipped along with that deity on the *Ganesh Chaturthi* day, the fourth day of the bright half of *Bhádrapada*.

The goat is believed to be holy for sacrificial purposes. It is worshipped at the time of its sacrifice, which is performed to gain the favour of certain deities.

The ass is generally considered as unholy by the Hindus, and its mere touch is held to cause pollution. But certain lower class Hindus like the Lonáris consider it sacred, and worship it on the *Gokul Ashthami* day (8th day of the dark half of *Shráwan*).

The dog is believed to be an incarnation of the deity Khandoba, and it is respected as the favourite animal of the god Dattátraya. But it is not touched by high class Hindus.

It is considered a great sin to kill a cat.

All domestic animals are worshipped by the Hindus on the morning of the first day of *Márgashirsha* (December).

On this day the horns of these animals are washed with warm water, painted with red colours, and a lighted lamp is passed round their faces. They are feasted on this day as it is considered to be the gala day (*Diváli* holiday) of the animals.

Hindus consider it meritorious to feed ants and fish, and to throw grain to the birds. Ants are fed by the people scattering sugar and flour on the ant-hills. It is believed that, by feeding the ants with sugar or flour, a person obtains the *Punya* or merit of *sahasrabhojan, i.e.*, of giving a feast to a thousand Bráhmans.

Alligators are worshipped as water deities by the Hindus.

The peacock is the favourite vehicle of Saraswati, the Goddess of Learning, and it is therefore respected by the people.

The swan is the vehicle of Brahma, the god of creation.

The eagle is the vehicle of the god Vishnu, and is a favourite devotee of that deity. It is therefore held sacred by Hindus.

The cuckoo or *Kokil* is believed to be an incarnation of the goddess Párwati. This bird is specially worshipped by high caste Hindu women for the period of one month on the occasion of a special festival called the festival of the cuckoos, or *Kokila vrata*, which is held in the month of *Ashádha* at intervals of twenty years.

The crow is generally held inauspicious by Hindus, but as the *manes* or *pitras* are said to assume the form of crows, these birds are respected in order that they may be able to partake of the food offered to the dead ancestors in the dark half of *Bhádrapada* called *Pitrupaksha*.

It is necessary that the oblations given in performance of the funeral rites on the tenth day after the death of a person should be eaten by the crow. But if the crow refuses to touch these oblations, it is believed that the soul of the dead has not obtained salvation; and hence it is conjectured that certain wishes of the dead have remained unfulfilled. The son or the relatives of the dead then take water in the cavity of their right hand, and solemnly promise to fulfil the wishes of the dead. When this is done, the crow begins to eat the food.

The harsh sound of a crow is taken as a sure sign of an impending mishap.

The dog, cat, pig, ass, buffalo, rat, *bhálu*, an old female jackal, lizard, and the birds cock, crow, kite, vulture, owl, bat, and *pingla* are considered as unholy and inauspicious by Hindus.

CHAPTER X.

WITCHCRAFT.

Chetak is an art secretly learnt by women. It is a form of the black art. A woman well versed in the *mantras* of *chetak* can do any mischief she chooses. She can kill a child or turn any person into a dog or other animal by the power of her incantations. The *Chetakin* can remove all the hair from the head of a woman, or scatter filth, etc. in a person's house, make marks of crosses with marking nuts on all the clothes, or play many other such tricks without betraying a trace of the author of the mischief. The *chetakins* are able to mesmerize a man and order him to do anything they want. A *Chetakin* or witch cannot herself appear in the form of an animal.

They follow revolting forms of ceremonies. All witches who have learnt the black art meet at night once a month on the *Amavásya* day or no moon day of every month, at a burning ground outside the village. On such occasions they go quite naked, and apply turmeric and red powders to the body and forehead. While coming to the cremation ground they bring on their heads burning coals in an earthen pot called *Kondi*. At this meeting they repeat their *mantras*, and take care that none are forgotten. After completing the repetition of the *mantras*, they go round the village and return to their respective houses. They have no special haunts or seasons.

In the Kolhápur District the woman who is in possession of a *chetak* is called *chetakin*. The *chetak* is said to abide by her orders. It is believed to bring corn and other things from houses or harvesting grounds. It is seen only by its mistress the *chetakin*. The belief that the *chetakins* can turn a person into the form of an animal does not prevail in this district. They do not wander from one place to another. The *chetakin* has to go once a year to the temple of the deity from whom the *chetak* has been brought, and to pay the annual tribute for the use of that *chetak* or servant spirit.[1]

There are no witches in the Ratnágiri District. It is said that there are some at Kolwan in the Thána District. They are generally found among Thákars. Some of them come to the Ratnágiri District, but though no one can tell anything about their powers, ignorant people are very much afraid of them.[2] It is believed that they can turn persons into animals by means of their incantations. The person once charmed by their *mantras* is said to blindly abide by their orders. It is also believed that they can ruin anybody by their magic.

There are no witches at Rái in the Thána District. The woman who can influence evil spirits to do harm to others is called a *Bhutáli*. It is said that the *Bhutális* assemble at the funeral ground in a naked state on the full-moon day and on the *Amávásya*, or the last day of every month, to refresh their knowledge of the black art.[3]

A witch has dirty habits and observances. The chief sign for detecting a witch or *chetakin* is a foam or froth that appears on the lips of

[1] Ráo Sáheb Shelke, Kolhápur.
[2] School Master, Anjarle, Ratnágiri.
[3] School Master, Rái, Thána.

her mouth when she is asleep. The only means to guard against her witchcraft is to remain on friendly terms with her, and not to hurt her feelings on any occasion. People generally keep a watch over the actions of a woman who is suspected to be a witch, and if she is found practising her black art, and is caught red-handed, people then pour into her mouth water brought from the shoe-maker's earthen pot or *kundi*. It is believed that, when she is compelled to drink such water, her black art becomes ineffective.[1]

In the Thána District it is believed that the skin round the eyes of a witch is always black, her eyes have an intoxicated appearance, her nails are generally parched and have a darkish colour, and the lower portions of her feet seem to be scraped. When any sorcerer gives out the name of such a *Bhutáli*, she is threatened by the people that, should she continue to give trouble in the village, her own black art or another spirit would be set against her; and she then ceases to give trouble.[2]

There are some sorcerers in the Thána District who can move a small brass cup or *váti* by the power of their magic. They can detect a witch by the movement of this vessel. When the brass vessel or *váti* reaches the house of a witch, it at once settles upon the witch's head. She is then threatened by the people that she will be driven out of the village if found practising her black art.[3]

In the Kolhápur District, when the people come to know of the existence of a witch in their village, they take special precautions at the time of harvest. They arrange to harvest a different kind of grain to the one selected for harvesting by the witch. After some time they go to the field of the witch, and discover whether there is a mixture of grain in her field. If they are convinced of the fact, they take further precautions. In order to avoid being troubled by the *chetak*, they keep an old, worn out shoe or sandal and a charmed copper amulet under the eaves at the main door of their houses, or make crosses with marking nut on both sides of a door. At some places *chunam* spots or circles are marked on the front of a house, the object being to guard against the evil effects of the *chetak's* tricks.[4]

[1] School Master, Khopoli, Kolába.

[2] School Master, Rái, Thána.

[3] School Master, Padghe, Thána.

[4] Ráo Saheb Shelke, Kolhápur.

CHAPTER XI.

GENERAL.

Offerings of cocoanuts, fowls or goats are annually made to the spirits that guard the fields. They are generally made at the time of beginning a plantation or the harvesting of a crop. When making these offerings, the farmers pray to the god to give prosperous crops every year. They prepare their cooked food in the field on the first harvesting day and offer it as *naivedya* (god's meal) along with the above mentioned offerings.[1]

At Bándivade in the Ratnágiri District, while commencing the sowing of crops the farmers worship a certain number of bullocks made of rice floor and then throw them into the pond or river adjoining the fields. On other occasions, offerings of cocoanuts and fowls are sacrificed to the deities that protect the fields. Some people give a feast to the Bráhmans at the end of the harvesting season.[2]

Ceremonies in connection with ploughing, etc., are not observed for all the lands. But fields which are supposed to be haunted by evil spirits are worshipped at the time of ploughing, and the evil spirits are propitiated, cocoanuts, sugar, fowls or goats are offered to the local deities or *devachárs*. There is a custom of worshipping in the fields the heaps of new corn at the time of harvest, and this custom generally prevails in almost all the Konkan districts.[3]

At Fonde in the Ratnágiri District the *Shiwar* generally composed of boiled rice mixed with curds is kept at the corner of a field at the time of reaping the crops. The *Shiwar* is sometimes composed of the offerings of fowls and goats.[4] This ritual is also known by the name *Chorawa*.[5]

At Dásgáv in the Kolába District, there is a custom of carrying one onion in the corn taken to the fields for sowing and placing five handfuls of corn on a piece of cloth before beginning to sow the corn. At the time of *Láwani* or plantation of crops a fair called *Palejatra* is held by the people, and every farmer breaks a cocoanut in the field at the time of plantation or *lávani* of crops. At the time of harvesting it is customary with many of the cultivators in the Konkan to place a cocoanut in the field and to thrash it by the first bundle of crop several times before the regular operation of thrashing is begun. At the close of the harvest the peasants offer cocoanuts, fowls or a goat to the guardian deity of the field.[6]

At Váda in the Thána District the ploughs are worshipped by the farmers on Saturday and then carried to the fields for ploughing. At the time of harvesting, the wooden post to which the bullocks are tied is worshipped by them and at the close of the harvest the heap of new corn is worshipped and cocoanuts are broken over it.[7]

In the Kolhápur District the farmers worship the plough before beginning to plough the land. At the time of sowing the corn they worship the *Kuri* an implement for sowing corn. At the time of *Ropani* or transplanting the crops they split a cocoanut, and worship the stone consecrated by the side of the field after besmearing it with red powders, and make a vow of sacrificing a goat for the prosperity of their crops. At the time of harvesting they also worship the heap of new corn and after giving to the deity offerings of cocoanuts, fowls or goats they carry the corn to their houses.[8]

In the Konkan districts the village deity is invoked to protect the cattle. People offer fowls and cocoanuts in the annual fair of a village deity, and request her to protect their cattle and crops. They have to offer a goat or buffalo to the deity every third year, and to hold annual fairs in her honour. The procession of *bali* is one of the measures adopted for averting cattle diseases.[9]

---

1 School Master, Khopoli, Kolába.
2 School Master, Bándivade, Ratnágiri.
3 School Master, Devgad, Ratnágiri.
4 School Master, Fonde, Ratnágiri.
5 School Master, Ubhádánda, Ratnágiri.
6 School Master, Dásgáv, Kolába.
7 School Master, Váda, Thána.
8 Ráo Sáheb Shelke, Kolhápur.
9 School Master, Khopoli, Kolába.

When there was scarcity of rain the Hindus formerly invoked Indra, the god of rain, by means of *Yadnyas* or sacrifices, but such sacrifices are now rarely performed as they are very costly. The general method of ensuring rainfall in these days is to drown the *Lingam* of the god Shiva in water and to offer prayers to that deity.[1]

The following rural rites are intended to ensure sunshine and to check excessive rain. A man born in the month of *Fálgun* (March) is requested to collect rain water in the leaf of the *Alu* plant, and the leaf is then tied to a stick and kept on the roof of a house. Burning coals are also thrown into rainwater after passing them between the legs of a person born in the month of *Fálgun*.[2]

In order to protect the crops from wild pig the people of Umbergáon in the Thána District post in their fields twigs of *Ayan* tree on the *Ganesh Chaturthi* (fourth day of the bright half of *Bhádrapada* or September) day every year.[3]

In the Kolhápur District the deities Tamjái Tungái, and Wághái are invoked by the villagers for the protection of cattle. When the cattle disease has disappeared the people offer cocoanuts and other offerings to these deities. The potters and the Chudbude Joshis observe the following ceremony for causing rainfall. A *lingam* or phallus of Shiva made of mud is consecrated on a wooden board or *pát*, and a naked boy is asked to hold it over his head. The boy carries it from house to house and the inmates of the houses pour water over the phallus. The Bráhmans and the high class Hindus pour water on the *lingam* at the temple of the god Shiva continuously for several days. This is called *Rudrábhisheka*. It is a religious rite in which eleven Bráhmans are seated in a temple to repeat the prayers of the god Shiva.

In order to scare noxious animals or insects from the fields, the owners of the fields throw charmed rice round the boundaries of their fields. The figure of a tiger made of dry leaves of sugarcane is posted at a conspicuous place in the fields for protecting the crops of sugarcane.[4]

Great secrecy is required to be observed on the occasion of the special *puja* of Shiva which is performed on the first day of the bright half of the month of *Bhádrapada* (September). This rite is called *Maunya vrata* or silent worship, and should be performed only by the male members of the family. On this day all the members of the family have to remain silent while taking their meals. Women do not speak while cooking, as the food which is to be offered to the god must be cooked in silence.[5]

Newly married girls have to perform the worship of Mangala Gauri successively for the first five years on every Tuesday in the month of *Shráwan* (August), and it is enjoined that they should not speak while taking their meals on that day. Some people do not speak while taking their meals on every Monday of *Shráwan*, and others make a vow of observing silence and secrecy at their meals every day. All Bráhmans have to remain silent when going to the closet and making water.[6]

Certain persons observe silence at their meals during the period of four months (*Cháturmás*) commencing from the 11th day of the bright half of *Ashádha* (July) to the 11th day of the bright half of *Kártik* (November). Certain classes of Hindus observe the penance of secrecy in the additional month that occurs at the lapse of every third year.[7]

Silence is essential at the time of performing certain austerities such as *Sandhya*, worshipping the gods, and the repetition of the *Bráhma Gáyatri mantra* and other such *mantras*. Secrecy is specially observed when a disciple is initiated by his *Guru* or spiritual guide with the sacred *mantras* or incantations.[8]

Secrecy and silence are essential when learning the *mantras* on snakebite, on evil eye and the evil spirit of Vetál. All followers of the Shákta

[1] School Master, Fonde, Ratnágiri.

[2] School Master, Náringre, Ratnágiri.

[3] School Master, Umbergáon, Thána.

[4] Ráo Sáheb Shelke, Kolhápur.

[5] School Master, Chinchani, Thána.

[6] School Master, Dahánu, Thána.

[7] School Master, Dábhol, Ratnágiri.

[8] School Master, Fonde, Ratnágiri.

sect must worship the goddess (Durga) very secretly. Silence is also observed by people in welcoming to their homes and worshipping the goddess Párvati or Gauri in the bright half of *Bhádrapada* every year.[1]

At Váde in the Thána District, one day previous to the planting of rice crops the farmer has to go to his field even before day break with five balls of boiled rice, cocoanuts and other things. There he worships the guardian deity of the field and buries the balls of rice underground. He has to do it secretly and has to remain silent during the whole period. He is also forbidden to look behind while going to the field for the purpose.[2]

Secrecy and silence are observed when performing the rites of *Chetuks* and evil spirits or ghosts. Widow remarriages among the lower classes are performed secretly. The pair wishing to be remarried is accompanied by a Bráhman priest and the marriage is performed apart from the house. The priest applies red lead (*Kunku*) to the forehead of the bride and throws grains of rice over their heads and a stone mortar or *páta* is touched to the backbone of the bride. The priest then turns his face and walks away silently.[3]

The *Holi* is a religious festival. It is annually celebrated in memory of the death of Kámdev the God of Love who was destroyed by the god Shankar on the full moon day of *Fálgun* (March). The object of this festival appears to have been a desire to abstain from lust by burning in the *Holi* fire all vicious thoughts and desires. As a rule, females do not take any part in this festival.

In the Konkan districts the annual festival of *Holi* begins from the fifth day of the bright half of *Fálgun* (March). Boys from all the localities of a village assemble at a place appointed for the *Holi*. The place appointed for kindling the *Holi* is not generally changed. The boys then go from house to house asking for firewood, and bring it to the *Holi* spot. They arrange the firewood and other combustible articles around the branch of a mango, betelnut or a *Sáwar* tree in the pit dug out for the purpose and then set it on fire. After kindling the sacred fire they take five turns round the *Holi* accompanied with the beating of drums and raise loud cries of obscene words. After this they play the Indian games of *Atyápátya* and *Khokho* and occasionally rob the neighbouring people of their firewood and other combustible articles. At the close of these games they daub their foreheads with sacred ashes gathered from the *Holi* fire. They consider these ashes especially auspicious and carry them home for the use of the other members of their families. This process is continued every night till the close of the fullmoon day. Elderly persons take part in this festival only during the last few days.

On the fullmoon day all the males of the village, including old men, start after sunset for the *Holi* spot, collecting on their way pieces of firewood from all the houses in the locality and arrange them in the manner described above. After having arranged the *Holi*, the officiating priest recites sacred verses and the *puja* is performed by the *mánkari* of the village. This *mánkari* or *pátil* is either the headman or some other leading person of the village and to him belongs the right of kindling the *Holi* fire first. Some persons kindle a small *Holi* in front of their houses and worship it individually, but they can take part in the public *Holi*. In the towns the *Holis* of different localities are kindled separately while in small villages there is only one for every village.

At Vijaydurg in the Ratnágiri District a hen is tied to the top of a tree or a bamboo placed in the pit dug out for kindling the *Holi* fire. The fowl tied to the top of the bamboo is called *Shit*. A small quantity of dry grass is first burnt at the bottom of this tree when the Mahárs beat their drums. The *Shit* (fowl) is then removed from the tree after it is half burnt and taken by the Mahárs. The *Holi* fire is then worshipped and kindled by the Gurav. Worshipping and kindling the *Holi* and taking the *Shit* (fowl) are considered as high honours. Occasionally quarrels and differences arise over this privilege and they are decided by the village *Panch*.[4]

[1] School Master, Chauk, Kolába.

[2] School Master, Váde, Thána.

[3] Ráo Sáheb Shelke, Kolhápur.

[4] School Master, Poladpur and Vijaydurg.

After the kindling of the *Holi* the people assembled there offer to the *Holi* a *Naivedya* (god's meal) of *poli*—a sweet cake made of *Jagri*, wheat flour and gram pulse. Cocoanuts from all the houses in the village are thrown into this sacred fire. Some of these cocoanuts are afterwards taken out of the sacred fire, cut into pieces, mixed with sugar and are distributed among the people assembled as *prasád* or favoured gift. Lower classes of Hindus offer a live goat to the *Holi*, take it out when it is half burnt and feast thereon.

On the night of the fullmoon day and the first day of the dark half of *Fálgun*, the people assembled at the *Holi* fire wander about the village, enter gardens and steal plantains, cocoanuts and other garden produce. Robbery of such things committed during these days is considered to be pardonable. Some people take advantage of this opportunity for taking revenge on their enemies in this respect.

The fire kindled at the *Holi* on the fullmoon day is kept constantly burning till the *Rangpanchami* day *i. e.*, fifth day of the dark half of *Fálgun*. Next morning *i. e.*, on the first day of the dark half of *Fálgun*, the people boil water over that fire and use it for the purpose of bathing. It is believed that water boiled on the sacred fire has the power of dispelling all the diseases from the body. People go on dancing in the village and sing songs for the next five days. They generally sing *Lávanis*, a kind of ballad, during this festival. Among these dancers a boy is dressed like a girl and is called *Rádha*. This *Rádha* has to dance at every house while the others repeat *Lávanis*.

The second day of the dark half of *Fálgun* is called *Dhulvad* or dust day when people start in procession through the village, and compel the males of every house to join the party. They thus go to the *Holi* fire and raise loud cries of obscene words throwing mud and ashes upon each other. They afterwards go to the river or a pond to take their bath at noon time and then return to their houses. The third day of the dark half is also spent like the previous one with a slight difference which is that cow dung is used instead of mud. This day is called *Shenwad* day. On the fourth day the Dhunda Rákshahasin (a demon goddess) is worshipped by the people, and the day is spent in making merry and singing obscene songs called *Lávanis*. The fifth day of the dark half is known as *Rangpanchami* day and is observed by the people in throwing coloured water upon each other. Water in which *Kusumba* and other colours are mixed is carried in large quantity on bullock carts through the streets of a city and sprinkled on the people passing through these streets. On this day the sacred fire of the *Holi* is extinguished by throwing coloured water over it. This water is also thrown upon the persons assembled at the *Holi*. The money collected as *post* during this period is utilised in feasting and drinking.

At Ibhrampur in the Ratnágiri District the image of cupid is seated in a palanquin and carried with music from the temple to the *Holi* ground. The palanquin is then placed on a certain spot. The place for thus depositing the image of the god is called Sáhán.[1] At Náringre there is a big stone called *Holdev* which is worshipped by the people before kindling the *Holi* fire.[2] After the kindling of the sacred fire the palanquin is lifted from the *Sáhán*, and turned round the *Holi* fire with great rejoicings. The palanquin is then carried through the village and is first taken to the house of a *Mánkari*, and then from house to house during the next five days. The inmates of the houses worship the deity in the palanquin and offer cocoanuts and other fruits and make certain vows. The palanquin is taken back to the temple on the fifth day of the dark half of *Fálgun* when on its way *gulál* or red powder is thrown over the image and on the people who accompany it.[3]

Among high class Hindus the thread girding ceremony of a boy is performed when he attains puberty. The girls are generally married a an early age, and when a girl attains puberty, sugar is distributed among the friends and relatives of her husband. She is then seated in a *Makhar*—a gaily dressed frame. Dishes of sweets which are brought by the girl's

[1] School Master, Ibhrampur, Ratnágiri. [2] School Master, Náringre, Ratnágiri.
[3] School Master, Ibhrampur, Ratnágiri.

parents and the relatives of her husband are given to her for the first three days. She takes her bath on the fourth day accompanied by the playing of music and the beating of drums. Sweetmeats in dishes are brought by the relatives till the day of *Rutushanti* (the first bridal night). The *Garbhádán* or *Rutushánti* ceremony is one of the sixteen ceremonies that are required to be performed during the life of every Hindu. This ceremony is performed within the first sixteen days from the girl's attaining her puberty, the 4th, 7th, 9th, 11th and the 13th being considered inauspicious for this purpose. While performing this ceremony the following three rites are required to be observed. They are *Ganpatipujan* or the worship of the god *Ganpati*, *Punhyáhavachan* or the special ceremony for invoking divine blessings and *Navagrahashánti* the ceremony for propitiating the nine planets. The ritual of this ceremony is as follows :—

The husband and the wife are seated side by side on wooden boards to perform the above three rites. The *Kadali pujan* or plantain tree worship is performed by the pair. The sacred fire or *Homa* is required to be kindled. The juice of the *Durwa* grass is then poured into the right nostril of the bride by her husband. This is intended to expel all diseases from the body of the girl and to secure safe conception. They are then seated in a *Makhar*, and presents of clothes, ornaments etc., are made by the parents of the girl and other relatives. After this the husband fills the lap of the girl with rice, a cocoanut, five betelnuts, five dry dates, five almonds, five plantains and five pieces of turmeric. The girl is then carried to a temple accompanied by the playing of music. A grand feast is given to the friends and relatives at the close of this ceremony.

The Hindus generally make various kinds of vows in order to procure offspring or with some other such object, and fulfil them when they succeed in getting their desire. The following are the different kinds of vows made. They offer cocoanuts, sugar, plantains and other fruits, costly new dresses and ornaments to the deities, and give feasts to Bráhmans. Special ceremonies called *Laghurudra* and *Mahárudra* in honour of Shiva the god of destruction are also performed. Sweetmeats such as *pedhas* etc. are offered to the gods in fulfilment of vows. Some people make vows to observe fasts, to feed Bráhmans, and to distribute coins and clothes to the poor ; while others hang *torana*-wreaths of flowers and mango leaves—on the entrance of the temple, and hoist flags over it. Rich people erect new temples to different Hindu deities. Some observe fasts to propitiate the goddess Chandika and worship her during *Navarátra* the first nine days of the bright half of *Ashvin* (October) and others offer fowls and goats to their favourite deities. Women make it a vow to walk round the *Audumbar* or *Pipal* tree, and to distribute cocoanuts, sugar, jagri, copper or silver equal to the weight of their children.

Vows are made by people with the object of securing health, wealth and children and other desired objects such as education, etc. They are as follows :—

Performing the worship of Shri Satya Náráyan, offering clothes and ornaments to the temple deities, hanging bells, constructing a foot path or steps leading to the temple of the special deity.[1] Vows are also made to obtain freedom from disease or such other calamities. When any person in the family becomes ill or when a sudden calamity befalls a family an elderly member of the family goes to the temple of a deity and makes certain vows according to his means, fulfilling them as soon as the calamity or disease has disappeared.[2]

Vows are usually to perform acts of benevolence. These consist in distributing cocoanut mixed in sugar, giving feasts to Bráhman priests, observing fasts on Saturday, Tuesday and Sunday, offering clothes and ornaments to deities, building new temples and guest houses (*dharmshálás*), digging out new wells and in distributing clothes and food to the poor.[3]

At Khopoli in the Kolába District, people who have no children or whose children die shortly after birth make a vow to the Satwái deity whose temple is at a short distance from Khopoli. The vow is generally to bring the child to the *darshana* (sight) of the deity and

[1] School Master, Fonde, Ratnágiri. [2] School Master, Bankavli, Ratnágiri.
[3] School Master, Vijaydurg, Ratnágiri.

to feed five or more (married) Bráhman pairs. Such vows are fulfilled after the birth of a child. Some worship the god Satya Náráyan on a grand scale and others propitiate the god Shiva by the ceremony of *Abhisheka* (water sprinkling).[1] Some offer nails made of gold or silver to the goddess Shitala after the recovery of a child suffering from small pox. Eyes and other parts of the body made of gold and silver are also occasionally offered in fulfilment of vows. People abstain from eating certain things till the vows are fulfilled.[2]

Vows are made in times of difficulties and sorrow. The person afflicted with sorrow or misfortune prays to his favourite deity and promises to offer particular things or to perform special ceremonies, and fulfils his vows when his desired objects are attained. The ceremonies commonly observed for these purposes are the special *pujás* of Satya Náráyan and Satya Vináyak. Native Christians make their vows to their saints and Mot-Mávali (Mother Mary) in the taluka of Salsette.[3]

There is a shrine of the god Shankar at Kanakeshwar a village on the sea side two miles from Mitbáv in the Ratnágiri District. Many years ago it so happened that a rich Mahomedan merchant was carrying his merchandise in a ship. The ship foundered in a storm at a distance of about two or three miles from Kanakeshwar. When the vessel, seemed to be on the point of sinking the merchant despairing of his life and goods, made a vow to erect a nice temple for the Hindu shrine of Kanakeshwar if he, his vessel and its cargo were saved. By the grace of God the vessel weathered the storm and he arrived safely in his country with the merchandise. In fulfilment of this vow he erected a good temple over the shrine of Shri Shankar at Kanakeshwar, which cost him about rupees six thousand. This temple is in good condition to the present day. Many such vows are made to special deities. When the people get their desired objects they attribute the success to the favour of the deity invoked, but when their expectations are not fulfilled they blame their fate and not the deity.[4]

In the Konkan districts there are some persons who practise black art of several kinds such as *Chetak*, *Járan*, *Máran* and *Uchátan*. *Chetak* is a kind of evil spirit brought from the temple of the goddess Italái of the Konkan districts. It is brought for a fixed or limited period, and an annual tribute is required to be paid to the goddess for the services.

Another kind of black art widely practised in the Konkan districts is known by the name of *Muth márane*. In this art the sorcerer prepares an image of wheat flour, and worships it with flowers, incense, etc. A lemon pierced with a number of pins is then placed before the image. The sorcerer begins to pour spoonfuls of water mixed with *Jagri* on the face of the image, and repeats certain *mantras*. Meanwhile, the lemon gradually disappears and goes to the person whose death it is intended to secure. The person aimed at receives a heavy blow in the chest and at once falls to the ground vomitting blood. Sometimes he is known to expire instantaneously. The charmed lemon, after completing its task returns to the sorcerer, who anxiously awaits its return, for it is believed that if the lemon fails to return some calamity or misfortune is sure to occur to him. For this reason the beginner desiring to be initiated into the mystery of this black art has to make the first trial of his *mantras* on a tree or a fowl.

Females are also initiated into the mysteries of *Jádu* or black art. Such women are required to go to the burning ground at midnight in a naked state, holding in their hands hearths containing burning coals. While on their way they untie their hair, and then begin the recital of their *mantras*. There they dig out the bones of buried corpses, bring them home, and preserve them for practising black art.

There is a sect of Hindus known as Sháktas who practise the black art. The Sháktas worship their goddess at night, make offerings of wine and flesh, and then feast thereon.

1 School Master, Khopoli, Kolába.
2 School Master, Poladpur. Kolába.
3 School Master, Bassein, Thána.
4 School Master, Mitbáv, Ratnágiri.

APPENDIX.

GLOSSARY OF VERNACULAR TERMS OCCURING IN VOLUMES I AND II.*

A.

ABIL: A kind of incense.
ABIR: White scented powder.
ADACHH: Red cotton yarn.
ADÁD: Lentils.
ADAGHO BADAGHO: A ceremony performed to drive away insects.
ADHÁSUR: Name of a demon.
ADHIKAMÁS: Intercalary month.
ADI-NARÁYAN: A name of Vishnu.
ADO: Useless.
ADULSA: Name of a medicinal plant.
AGÁR: Excreta.
AGASTYA: Name of a sage; name of a constellation.
AGATHI: A tree, Sesbania Grandiflora.
AGATHIO: *See* Agathi.
AGHÁDA: Name of a plant.
AGHORI: A sect of Hindus.
AGIÁRI: Fire temple of the Pársis.
AGNI: Fire; the deity presiding over fire.
AGNICHAR: An order of evil spirits living in fire.
AGNIHOTRA: A perpetual sacred fire preserved in a hole in the ground for receiving and preserving consecrated fire.
AGNIHOTRI: One who keeps an Agnihotra.
AGNIKUNDA: A hole in the ground, or an enclosed space, on the surface, or a metal square-mouthed vessel, for receiving and preserving consecrated fire.
AGNI-SANSKÁR: The rite of setting fire to a corpse.
AGRI: Name of a caste or an individual of it.
AHALYA: The wife of the sage Gautam.
AHEVA NAVAMI: The ninth day of the dark half of *Bhádrapad*.
AHI: Name of a demon.
AHIR: A caste of shepherds.
AHUTI: A handful of rice, ghi, sesamum, etc., cast into fire, water, upon the ground etc, as an offering to the deities.
AIRÁVAT: Name of the elephant of Indra; the elephant presiding over the east.
AJA: A goat.
AJAMO: Lingusticum ajwaen.
AKÁSH: The sky.
AKÁSH-GANGA: The milky way.
AKHAND SAUBHÁGYA: Perpetual unwidowhood.
AKIK: A kind of stone.
AKHÁ TRIJ: The third day of the bright half of *Vaishákh*.
AKSHAYA TRITIYA: *See* Akhá Trij.
ALAWÁNA: A sort of shawl.
ALWANT: A spirit of a woman dying in childbirth or during menses.
ALU: An esculent vegetable.
ALUNDA: Name of a vow.

* The terms given below are as they are used by the common people in popular parlance in which form they are given in the text. They will therefore not be found to be grammatically correct in all cases Again, only such meanings of the terms are given as apply in the context.

AMANI : A kind of tree.
AMAR : Immortal.
AMATHO : Useless.
AMATHO MÁMO : An order of ghosts.
AMÁVÁSYA : The last day of a month.
AMBA : Name of a goddess.
AMBIL : Conjee.
AMBO : Mango.
AMNÁYESHWAR : A name of the god Mahádev.
ANAGH : Name of a vow.
ANAGODHA : *See* Anagh.
ANANT CHATURDASHI : The fourteenth day of the dark half of *Bhádrapad* sacred to Vishnu.
ANDHÁRIO : An order of ghosts.
ANGIRAS : Name of a sage.
ANJALI : Palmful.
ANJAN : Soot used as collyrium.
ANJANI : Mother of Máruti.
ÁNJANI : A sore or mole on the eye-lid.
ANKADA : Namo of a poisonous plant.
ANNADEVA : The god presiding over food.
ANNAKUTA : The eighth or tenth day of the bright half of *Ashvin* or the second day of the bright half of *Kártik* when sweets are offered to gods.
ANNAPURNA : The goddess presiding over food.
ANTARAL : Name of a deity.
ANTARAPAT : The piece of cloth which is held between the bride and bridegroom at the time of a Hindu wedding.
ANTYESHTI : Funeral rites.
ANURÁDHA : Name of a constellation.
ANUSHTHÁN : Performance of certain ceremonies and works in propitiation of a god.
APASMÁR : Epilepsy.
APSARA : Certain female divinities who reside in the sky and are the wives of the Gandharvas. They are sometimes represented as the common women of the gods.
APTA : Name of a tree.
ARANI : Elaeodendren glaucum.
ARATI : The ceremony of waving (around an idol, a *guru*, etc.,) a platter containing a burning lamp.
ARDHODAYA : Half-risen state of a heavenly body.
ARDRA ; Name of a constellation.
ARGHYA : A respectful offering to a god or a venerable person consisting of various ingredients or of water only.
ARJUNA : The third of the five Pándava brothers.
ARUNDHATI : Wife of Vasishtha ; name of a star.
ASARA : A water nymph.
ASAN : A prayer carpet.
ASHÁDH : The fourth month of the Deccani Hindu and the ninth month of the Gujarát Hindu calendar year.
ASHÁPURI : Name of a goddess.
ASHLESHA : Name of a constellation.
ASHO : A corrupted form of *Ashvin.*
ASHAPATI : Name of a mythological king.
ASHTABHÁRO : An order of ghosts.
ASHTADALA : Eight-cornered.
ASHTA-DIK-PÁLA : Protectors of the eight different directions.
ASHTAKA : A hymn consisting of eight verses.

ASHTAMAHÁDÁN : A gift consisting of eight kinds of articles.

ASHTÁVASU : A class of divine beings eight in number.

ASHVIN : The seventh month of the Deccani Hindu and the twelfth month of the Gujarát Hindu calendar year.

ASHVINI : Name of a constellation.

ASHVINI KUMÁR : The twin sons of the sun by his wife Sanjnya in the form of a mare. They are famous as heavenly physicians.

ASHWAMEDHA : Horse sacrifice.

ASHWATTHÁMA : The only son of Drona, the military preceptor of the Kauravas and Pándavas.

ASMÁNI : An order of ghosts.

ASO : A corrupted form of *Ashvin.*

ASOPALAVA : Name of a tree.

ASUR GATI : The path of the demons.

ATIT : A class of religious beggars.

ATLAS : A kind of cloth.

ATRI : Name of a sage.

ATYÁPÁTYA : Name of an out-door game played in the Deccan.

AVAD-MÁTA : Name of a goddess.

AVAGAT : An order of ghosts.

AVAGATI : Fallen condition.

AVALIA : A Muhammadan saint.

AVALA : Name of a tree.

AVATÁR : An incarnation of Vishnu.

AVI : An order of ghosts.

AVLI : Name of a tree.

AWDUMBAR : A tree, Ficus glomerata.

AWUTA : Wood bill.

AYAN : Name of a tree.

B.

BÁBARO : An order of ghosts.

BÁBHUL : Acacia arabica.

BÁBRIO : *See* Bábaro.

BÁBRO : *See* Bábaro.

BABRUVÁHAN : Name of a demon ; a son of Arjuna.

BÁBUL : Acacia arabica.

BÁDHA : Impending evil.

BÁGHADA : Name of an evil spirit.

BÁGULBÁWA : Name of a goblin.

BAHIRI : Name of a goddess.

BAHIRI-SOMJAI : Name of a goddess.

BAHIROBA : Name of a minor deity.

BAHIROBÁCHE BHUT : An order of ghosts.

BÁJA : Dish.

BÁJALE : A wooden cot.

BÁJAT : A wooden stool.

BAJÁNIA : A cast of tumblers or an individual of it.

BAKA : Name of a demon; name of a sage.

BÁKLA : A small round flat cake of dry boiled beans.

BÁKLÁN : *See* Bákla.

BAKOR : Noise.

BÁLA TERASH : The 13th day of the dark half of *Bhádrapad.*

BALAD : An ox.

BALADI : An order of ghosts.

BALDEV : Name of the brother of Krishna, the eighth incarnation of Vishnu

BALEV : The full moon day of *Shrávana.*

BALEVA : *See* Balev.

BALEVIÁN : A kind of worship.

BALI : Name of a mighty demon, the lord of the nether world or *pátál*; an oblation; a victim offered to any deity; name of a procession.

BALIDÁN : Offering of a victim.

BALLA : An order of ghosts.

BÁNÁSUR : Name of a demon.

BANDHÁI-JAVAN : Name of a cattle disease.

BANIA : A trader.

BÁPA : Name of a guardian spirit of fields.

BÁPDEV : *See* Bápa.

BARANESHWAR MAHÁDEV : A name of Mahádev.

BÁRAS : The twelfth day of the bright or dark half of a month.

BÁRVATIA : An outlaw.

BATÁSA : A kind of sweetmeat.

BATRISA : A man possessed of thirty-two accomplishments.

BATUK : Name of a minor deity.

BÁU : A word used to frighten children; a goblin.

BÁVA : A term of respectful compellation or mention for an ascetic or religious teacher.

BÁVAL : *See* Bábul.

BÁVO : *See* Báva.

BAYA : Name of a deity presiding over small-pox.

BÁWAN VIR : Name of a minor deity.

BECHRA MÁTA : Name of a goddess.

BEDA : Name of a tree.

BEL : Aegle Marmelos.

BEL-BHANDÁR : Leaves of the Aegle Marmelos and the turmeric powder that are kept on an idol.

BER : Jujube tree.

BERO : Deaf.

BETHI : An order of ghosts.

BHÁBHO : Worthless.

BHÁDARWA : *See* Bhádrapad.

BHÁDRAPAD : The sixth month of the Deccani Hindu and the eleventh month of the Gujarát Hindu calendar year.

BHAGAT : An exorcist.

BHAGIRATH : Name of an ancient king of the solar dynasty who is said to have brought down the Ganges from heaven to the earth.

BHÁGVAT : Name of one of the eighteen *purános*.

BHAGVATI : Name of a goddess.

BHAGWÁN : An epithet of Vishnu; of Shiva.

BHAGWATI : *See* Bhagvati.

BHAIRAV : A name of an inferior manifestation of Shiva.

BHAJAN : Repeating the name of a god as an act of worship; hymns or pieces or verses sung to a god.

BHAKTIMARGA : Path of devotion.

BHÁLU : An old female jackal.

BHANDÁRI : A caste of Hindus.

BHÁNG : Hemp water.

BHANGI : A scavenger; name of the caste of scavengers.

BHANGRA : A kind of tree.
BHARANAI : Name of a goddess.
BHARANI : Name of a constellation.
BHÁRANI : The process of charming.
BHARATA : Name of a brother of Ráma the seventh incarnation of Vishnu.
BHARVÁD : A caste of shepherds.
BHÁSIKA : An order of ghosts.
BHASMA : Holy ashes.
BHASMÁSUR : Name of a demon.
BHÁUBIJ : The second day of the bright half of *Kártik*.
BHAVÁI : Name of a stone deity.
BHÁVAKÁI : Name of a goddess.
BHAVÁNI : A name of the goddess Párvati.
BHÁVIN : A caste of female temple servants who are prostitutes by profession.
BHAWÁNI : *See* Bhaváni.
BHENSA : A she-buffalo.
BHENSÁSUR : A demon in the form of a he-buffalo.
BHIKHÁRI : A beggar.
BHIKHO : A beggar.
BHIL : A partly Hindu, partly animistic tribe.
BHIMA : The second of the five Pándava brothers.
BHIMA-AGIÁRAS : The eleventh day of the bright half of *Jyeshtha*.
BHIMASENA : *See* Bhima.
BHIMNÁTH MAHÁDEV : A name of Shiva.
BHIMNÁTH SHANKAR : A name of Shiva.
BHISHMA : Son of Shántanu and the river Ganges and grand-uncle of the Pándavas and Kauravas.
BHOGAVA : Village boundary.
BHOI : A caste of fishermen and palanquin-bearers.
BHOJAPATRA : A palm-leaf.
BHOLÁNÁTH : A name of Shiva.
BHONG RINGDI : Name of a poisonous plant.
BHOPALA : Gourd.
BHOPI : The person that officiates in the temples of village deities.
BHUCHAR ; An order of ghosts hovering over the earth.
BHUNGA : A black bee.
BHUSHUNDAKÁK : Name of a sage.
BHUT : An evil spirit.
BHUTA : *See* Bhut.
BHUTA-DEVATA : A ghostly godling.
BHUTÁLI : A woman who can influence evil spirits to do harm to others.
BHUTE : Plural of Bhutya : *See* Bhutya.
BHUTIN : A female member of an order of devotees of the goddess Bhaváni.
BHUTNÁTH : Name of an evil spirit.
BHUTYA : A male member of an order of devotees of the goddess Bhaváni.
BHUVA : A male exorcist.
BHUVI : A female exorcist.
BIBHISHANA : Brother of Rávana, the demon king of Lanka or Ceylon.
BIJ : The second day of the bright or dark half of a month.
BIJAVRIKSHANYÁYA : The maxim of seed and shoot. The maxim takes its origin from the mutual relation of causation that exists between seed and shoot, and is applied to cases in which two objects stand to each other in the relation of both cause and effect.
BILÁDO : A cat.

BILI : *See* Bel.
BINDU : A drop.
BOCHO : A coward.
BODAN : A ceremony in which curds, milk, boiled rice, fried cakes, etc., are mixed up together and presented in oblation to the goddess Mahálakshmi by a company of at least five married women and one virgin.
BODO : Bald-headed.
BOL CHOTH : The fourth day of the dark half of *Shrávan.*
BORÁDI : The Jujube tree.
BOTERUN : A complete cessation of rain for seventy-two days.
BOWÁJI : *See* Báva.
BOW : *See* Báu.
BRAHMA GRAHA : Ghost of a Bráhman.
BRAHMA : The first god of the Hindu Trinity.
BRAHMABHOJ : A feast to Bráhmans.
BRAHMACHARYA : Celibacy.
BRAHMACHÁRI : One who has taken a vow to lead a celibate life.
BRAHMAHATYA : The murder of a Bráhman.
BRÁHMAN : The sacerdotal caste of Hindus or an individual of it.
BRÁHMANA-VARUNA : The appointment of duly authorised Bráhmans to perform religious ceremonies.
BRAHMARANDHRA : The aperture supposed to be at the crown of the head, through which the soul takes its flight on death.
BRAHMA RÁKSHASA : *See* Brahma Sambandh.
BRAHMA SAMBANDH : The ghost of a Bráhman that in his life time possessed high attainments, and a haughty spirit.
BRIHASPATI : Name of the preceptor of the gods.
BRUHANNADA : The name assumed by Arjuna when residing at the palace of Viráta.
BUDHA : Mercury.
BUDDHI : Name of a wife of Ganpati.

C

CENDUR : Red lead.
CHÁDA : Rent.
CHAITANNADYA : An order of ghosts.
CHAITRA : The first month of the Deccani Hindu and the sixth month of the Gujarát Hindu calendar year.
CHAKLI : A sparrow.
CHÁK PADANE : Appearance of red pustules on the face supposed to be caused by the influence of an evil eye.
CHAKORA : A bird, Bartavelle Partridge.
CHÁLA : Name of a deity.
CHÁLEGHAT : An order of ghosts.
CHAMÁR : A caste of tanners.
CHAMPA : Michelia champaca.
CHAMPÁ-SHASHTI : The sixth day of the bright half of *Márgashirsha.*
CHAMPÁVATI : Name of a goddess.
CHANA : Gram.
CHANDA : Name of a kind of wind.
CHAND CHANI : An order of ghosts.
CHANDAN : Sandal wood.
CHANDIKA : Name of a goddess.
CHANDI KAVACH : A hymn in honour of the goddess Chandi or Durga.
CHANDIPÁTH : Recitation of a hymn in honour of the goddess Chandi or Durga.
CHANDKÁI : Name of a goddess.

CHANDRA: The moon.
CHANDRAMANDAL: The disk of the moon; the lunar sphere.
CHÁNDRÁYAN VRAT: Name of a vow.
CHARAK: Excreta.
CHÁRAN: A caste of genealogists and bards.
CHARANÁMRIT: Water in which the feet of a spiritual guide have been washed.
CHARMARIA: Name of a snake deity.
CHARONTHI: A kind of flour.
CHASHA: The Blue jay.
CHAT: An image of *darbha* grass at *Shráddha* when the required Bráhman is not present
CHATA SHRÁDDHA: A *shráddha* in which a *chat* represents a Bráhman.
CHÁTURMÁS: The period of four months commencing from the tenth day of the bright half of *Ashádh* and ending with the tenth day of the bright half of *Kártik*.
CHATURTHI: The fourth day of the bright or dark half of a month.
CHAURÁR: An order of ghosts.
CHEDA: Ghost of a person of the Kunbi or Shudra caste or an unmarried Mahár.
CHEDOBA: Name of a spirit deity.
CHELA: A disciple.
CHELAN: An oblation to a Máta or goddess.
CHETAK: A kind of black art.
CHETAKIN: A witch.
CHETUK: A spirit servant.
CHHAMACHHARI: Death anniversary.
CHHIPA: A caste of calico-printers.
CHHOGALA: Celebrated, Great.
CHHOGALO: With a tail.
CHILBIL: Notes of the *Pingala* bird.
CHILUM: A clay pipe.
CHINDHARO: Ragged.
CHIRANJIVA: Immortal.
CHITHI: A piece of paper on which mystic signs are drawn; an amulet.
CHITHARIA: Ragged.
CHITI: *See* Chithi.
CHITPÁVAN: A caste of Bráhmans also known as Konkanasth.
CHITRA: Name of a constellation.
CHOK: A square.
CHOLA: Dolichos Sinensio.
CHOLI: A bodice.
CHONGE: A kind of sweet.
CHORÁSI KÁNTINI: An order of ghosts.
CHORÁSI VIRU: An order of ghosts.
CHORAWA: A ceremony performed at the time of reaping.
CHOTH: The fourth day of the bright or dark half of a month.
CHUDBUDE JOSHI: A caste of fortune-tellers.
CHUDEL: An order of female ghosts.
CHUDELA: *See* Chudel.
CHUDI: A torch.
CHUDI PAURNIMA: The full-moon day of the month of *Mágh*.
CHUNADI: A kind of cloth worn by females.
CHUNTHO: Ragged.
CHUNVÁLIA KOLI: A tribe of Kolis.
CHURAMA: Sweet balls of wheat flour fried and soaked in ghi.
CHUTAKI: Snapping the thumb and finger.
COHAMPALO: Meddlesome.

D

DÁDAMO : An order of ghosts.
DÁDAMOKHODIÁR : Name of a field deity.
DÁDH : A molar tooth.
DÁDH BÁNDHAVI : To deprive of the power of eating by a charm or spell.
DÁDO : An order of ghosts.
DÁKAN : A witch ; an order of ghosts.
DÁKINI : *See* Dákan.
DÁKLA : A spirit instrument in the form of a small kettle-drum.
DAKSHA : A celebrated *Prajápati* born from the thumb of Brahma.
DAKSHA PRAJÁPATI : *See* Daksha.
DAKSHANA : A gift of money made to Bráhmans.
DÁL : Name of a sect of Hindus.
DALAP : A ceremony performed for the propitiation of the minor deities of the fields.
DÁLIA : Baked split gram.
DÁMANA : An amulet tied to the horns of a pet animal.
DAMPATYA : A married pair.
DÁNA : Corn seed.
DÁNDA : The bat at the game of trap-stick.
DÁNKLA : *See* Dákla.
DÁNKLA BESWÁN : The installation of a *dánkla*.
DÁNKLÁN : *See* Dákla.
DARBHA : A sacred grass ; Cynodon Dactylon.
DARDURI : Name of a water nymph.
DARGA : A Muhammadan place of worship.
DARJI : A caste of tailors.
DASHA : Influence.
DARSHA SHRÁDDHA : A *shráddha* to the manes on every new moon day.
DASARA : The tenth day of the bright half of *Kártik*.
DASHARATHA : Son of Aja and father of Ráma.
DAS PINDA : The oblations collectively to the manes of a deceased ancestor which are offered daily from the first day of his decease until the tenth, or which are offered together on the tenth : also the rite.
DÁTAN : Wooden sticks for brushing the teeth.
DATTA : Name of a god.
DATTÁTRAYA : *See* Datta.
DÁV : An order of ghosts.
DEDAKO: A frog.
DEHARI MÁTA : Name of a goddess.
DELAVADI DEVI : Name of a goddess.
DENDO : The croaking of a frog.
DEOPAN : Ceremonies and observances in propitiation of a god.
DESHASTHA : A caste of Bráhmans found in the Deccan.
DEVA : A god.
DEVACHÁR : Spirit of a Shudra who dies after his marriage.
DEVAHUTI : Name of the mother of the sage Kapil.
DEVAK : A term for the deity or deities worshipped at marriages, thread investitures etc. ; a totem.
DEVAKI : Mother of Krishna.
DEVAL : A temple.
DEVAL RIGHANE : Entering into the service of the temple.
DEVALI : The male offspring of a Bhávin.
DEVALO : Not loved.

DEVARSHI : A dealer with gods and devils : one that summons, exorcises them, etc.
DEVA SARPA : A snake belonging to a deity.
DEVASKI : The annual ceremonies in honour of the tutelar divinity of a village.
DEVA YOSHITA : A woman offered to a god.
DEV DIVÁLI : The eleventh day of the bright half of *Kártik*.
DEVI : A goddess.
DEVIPANTH : A sect of the worshippers of the goddess Durga.
DHÁGA : An amulet made of a piece of cloth.
DHAL-JATRA : A ceremony performed at the time of harvest.
DHAMA : A name of Hanumán.
DHANA : Coriander.
DHANANJAYA : Name of a snake.
DHANA-TRAYODASHI : The thirteenth day of the dark half of *Ashvin*.
DHANGAR : A caste of shepherds.
DHANISHTHA : Name of a constellation.
DHANU : Sagittarius.
DHANURMÁS : The period during which the sun is in Sagittarius.
DHANU-SANKRÁNT : Transit or passage of the sun through Sagittarius.
DHÁRÁVADI : A stream of milk.
DHARMARÁJA : The god of death.
DHARMASHÁLA : A rest house.
DHARMASHÁSTRA : The code of body of Hindu law.
DHARMASINDHU : Name of a work treating of Hindu law.
DHED : An impure caste of Hindus.
DHEDVÁDA : The ward or place occupied by the Dhed caste.
DHINGO : Fat.
DHOBI : A caste of washermen.
DHOL : A drum.
DHOLIO : An order of ghosts.
DHONDILGAJYA : Name of a rite performed for securing rainfall.
DHORI : White.
DHOTAR : Waist cloth.
DHUL PÁDAVO : The first day of the dark half of *Fálgun*.
DHRUVA : The son of Uttánapáda. He was a great devotee of the god Vishnu. The solar star.
DHULETI : *See* Dhul Pádavo.
DHULWAD : *See* Dhul Pádavo. The day of throwing dust after the burning of the *Holi*.
DHUNDA : Name of a demon goddess.
DHUNDA RÁKSHASIN : *See* Dhunda.
DHUNDHUMARI : Name of a mythological personage.
DHUNI : The smoke-fire of an ascetic over which he sits inhaling the smoke.
DHUPA : Frankincense.
DIGAMBARA : Name of a goddess.
DIPO : Panther.
DISHA-SHUL : Pain caused by directions.
DIVÁLI : A festival with nocturnal illuminations, feastings, gambling, etc. held during the concluding day of *Ashvin* and the first and second day of *Kártik*.
DIVÁSA : The fifteenth day of the dark half of *Ashádh*.
DIWAD : A serpent of a large but harmless species.
DODKA : One hundredth part of a rupee.
DOKADO : A ball of molasses and sesamum seed cooked together.
DORA : Piece of a string ; a magic thread.
DORLI : Solanum indicum.
DOSO : Old.

DRO : A kind of sacred grass.

DRONA : Son of Bháradvája, by birth a Bráhman but acquainted with military science which he received as a gift from Parashurám. He instructed the Kauravas and Pándavas in the use of arms.

DRUSTAMANI : A kind of black beads.

DUDHA : Milk.

DUDHPÁK : Rice cooked in milk and sweetened with sugar.

DUG-DUDIOON : *See* Dákla.

DUHITRA : *Shráddha* performed by a grandson to propitiate his maternal grandfather.

DUKÁL : Famine.

DUNDUBHI : A kettle-drum.

DUNGAR : A hill.

DURBÁR : The court of an Indian Chief.

DURGA : Name of a goddess.

DURGATI : Fallen condition.

DURVA : A kind of sacred grass.

DURYODHANA : The eldest of the Kaurava brothers.

DWIJA : A twice-born. A Bráhman, a Kshatriya or a Vaishya, whose investiture with the sacred thread constitutes, religiously and metaphorically a second birth.

DWITIYA : The second day of the bright or dark half of a month.

E

EKÁDASHI : The eleventh day of the bright and dark halves of a month.

EKAL PER : Zizyphus jujuba.

EKÁNTARIO : Intermittant fever.

EKOTISHTA : The rites performed on the eleventh day after death.

ETALÁI : Name of a goddess.

F

FÁG : A vulgar song.

FÁGAN : A corrupted form of Fálgun. *See* Fálgun.

FAKIR : A Muhammadan mendicant.

FAKIRI : Alms given to *Fakirs* in the *Muharram.*

FAKIRO : A beggar.

FÁLGUN : The twelfth month of the Deccani Hindu and the fifth month of the Gujarát Hindu calendar year.

FÁVADI : Name of a bird.

FIRANGÁI : Name of a goddess.

FUL : A flower.

FUL DOL : A festival in which coloured water is thrown.

G

GADHEDA : A donkey.

GADHEDO : *See* Gadheda.

GADHERIMÁTA : Name of a goddess installed to protect a fortress or a street.

GAFAL : Stupid.

GAGANACHAR : An order of ghosts moving in the etherial regions.

GAGARBEDIUN : A piece of leather thong or a piece of black wood on which mysticspells have been cast.

GAJÁBÁI : Name of a goddess.

GAJACHHAYA : A festival—the day of the new moon of *Bhádrapad* the moon being in the *Hasta* constellation.

GALÁL : Red powder.

GANA : A troop of demigods considered as Shiva's attendants.
GANAGOR : Name of a vow.
GANDHARVA : A celestial musician ; a class of demigods who are considered to be the singers of gods.
GÁNDIVA : Name of the bow of Arjuna.
GÁNDU : Name of a tree.
GANDH : Sandal paste.
GANESH CHATURTHI : The fourth day of the bright half of *Bhádrapad* celebrated as the birthday of Ganesh.
GANESHIO : A hook-shaped instrument used by thieves in boring holes through walls.
GANGA : The river Ganges.
GANGÁJAL : Water of the Ganges.
GANGIGOR : Name of a vow.
GÁNGLO : Stony.
GÁNGUD : An order of ghosts.
GÁNJA : Hemp flower.
GANPATI : The son of Shiva and Párvati. He is the deity of wisdom and the remover of difficulties and obstacles.
GANPATIPUJAN : The worship of Ganpati.
GÁNTHIA : A preparation of gram flour.
GAON-DEVI : Village goddess.
GARABI : A song in propitiation of a goddess.
GARBHADÁN : The marriage consummation ceremony.
GÁRHÁNE : Supplication to an idol.
GARUD : The eagle.
GARUD PURÁN : Name of a *purán*.
GÁTRÁD : Name of a goddess.
GAU : A measure of distance equal to 1⅔ miles.
GAUTAM : Name of a sage.
GAVA : A wild ox.
GAVALI : A caste or herdsmen.
GAVATDEV : Name of a godling.
GAVATI : An order of ghosts.
GAYÁSUR : Name of a demon.
GÁYATRI : Name of a daughter of Brahma.
GÁYATRI MANTRA : A sacred verse from the Vedas held specially sacred and repeated by every Bráhman at his morning and evening devotion. The verse is in honour of the sun.
GÁYATRI PURASCHARAN : A form of devotion requiring the recitation of the *Gáyatri mantra* a hundred thousand times with certain symbolic ceremonies.
GÁYATRIPURASCHAVACHAN *See* Gáyatripurascharan.
GEDI : A bat.
GEDI-DÁNDA : An outdoor game played by boys.
GERIA : A boy who takes an active part in the *Holi* festival.
GHÁDI : An exorcist. A caste of temple ministrants or an individual of it.
GHADI : A measure of time equal to twenty-four minutes.
GHADULO : A process for removing the effects of the evil eye.
GHÁNCHINI : An order of ghosts.
GHÁNDHARAVI : An order of ghosts.
GHÁNI : That quantity of oil seeds which is put in at one time to be crushed in an oil mill.
GHÁT : Steps on the side of a river or tank leading to the water.
GHATOTKACHA : Name of a demon.
GHELI : Mad.

GHELO : Mad.

GHELUN : Mad.

GHERÁYALA : Eclipsed.

GHETA : A sheep.

GHODO : A horse.

GHUGARI : Grain boiled whole, i.e. unsplit and unhusked.

GHUMAT : A sort of musical instrument—an earthen vessel, pitcher-form, covered over at the larger mouth with leather.

GHUNA : A mysterious watery pit.

GIDOTÁN : Name of a creeper.

GILLI-DÁNDA : A play amongst boys, trapstick.

GIRÁSIA : A Rajput landholder.

GIRHA : A water demon. Applied to Ráhu or to an eclipse in general, solar or lunar.

GIRI : An order or individual of it among *Gosávis*.

GOCHADI : Cattle or dog louse.

GODHO : A bull.

GOKARN : Name of a mythological king.

GOKHALO : A niche in the wall.

GOKUL : The name of the village at which Krishna was brought up.

GOKHARU : A species of thorns.

GOKUL-ASHTAMI : The eighth day of the dark half of *Bhádrapad* celebrated as the birthday of Krishna.

GOL : Molasses.

GOLÁBA : Name of a goddess.

GOLAMBÁDEVI : Name of a goddess.

GOMUKH : Mouth of a cow.

GONDARO : Place where the village cattle rest.

GONDHAL : A kind of religious dance.

GOOLVEL : A kind of creeper.

GOPÁLSANTÁN : Name of an incantation.

GOPRADÁN : Gift of a cow with its calf to a Bráhman.

GOR : A priest.

GORA : A black earthen vessel filled with curds.

GORADIA : A name of Hanumán.

GORÁIN : A married unwidowed woman.

GORAKHA : Name of a saint.

GORAKH CHINCH : A kind of tree.

GORJI : A preceptor.

GORAKHRÁJ : Name of a saint.

GOSÁVI : An ascetic.

GOTRA : A section of a caste having a common ancestor.

GOURI-PUJAN : The worship of the goddess Gouri, a festival observed only by women.

GOUTRAD : A vow in honour of the cow lasting from the eleventh day to the fifteenth day of the bright half of *Bhádrapad*.

GOUTRÁL : Name of a vow.

GOVARDHAN : A celebrated hill near Mathura. A large heap of cow dung or of rice, vegetables, etc. made on the first day of the bright half of *Kártik* in imitation of the mountain.

GOWALÁ-DEVA : Name of a deity connected with rain-fall.

GRAHA : A planet.

GRAHANA : An eclipse.

GRAHAN-PUJAN : The worship of the plough on the full-moon day of *Shrávan*.

GRAHA-SHÁNTI : A ceremony in propitiation of the planets.

GRÁMADEVATA : A village goddess.

GRÁMA-DEVI : A village goddess.

GRIHADEVATA : The diety which presides over the house.
GRISHMA-RITU : The summer.
GRIVA : Name of a deity.
GUDHI : A pole, wrapped around with a cloth, a mango sprig, etc., erected on the first day of the year before the house-door.
GUDHI-PÁDVA : The first day of the bright half of *Chaitra*, the new year's day of the Deccani Hindus.
GUHYAK : An order of semi-divine beings.
GULÁB : A rose.
GUGAL : Balsamodendron.
GUJAKALPA : Name of a medicinal preparation.
GULÁL : Red powder.
GUMPHA : A cave.
GUNDAR : Gum arabic.
GURAV : A caste of temple ministrants or an individual of it.
GURU : A religious preceptor ; Jupiter.
GURU CHARITRA : Name of a sacred book.

H.

HADAL : Ghost of a woman who dies within ten days of childbirth or during menses.
HADALI : *See* Hadal.
HÁJ : A pilgrim.
HAJÁM : A caste of barbers or an individual of it.
HALÁHAL : A sort of deadly poison produced at the churning of the ocean.
HANSA : A goose.
HANUMÁN : Name of a deity in the form of a monkey. He was a great devotee of Ráma.
HANUMÁN-JAYANTI : The full-moon-day of *chaitra* celebrated as the birthday of Hanumán.
HAR : A name of Shiva.
HARDA : A garland of balls made of sugar.
HARDÁS : One who performs *Kathás* that is relates stories of Hindu deities to the accompaniment of music.
HARDE : Myrobalan.
HARI : A name of Vishnu.
HARISCHANDRA : Name of a mythological king.
HARITÁLIKA : The third day of the bright half of *Bhádrapad* on which images of Párvati made of earth are worshipped by women.
HARIVANSHA : Name of a *purán*.
HASTA : Name of a constellation.
HATHADI : An order of ghosts.
HÁTHI : An elephant.
HAVAN : A sacrificial offering.
HEDAMATIO : A name of Hanumán.
HEDAMBA : Name of a giantess.
HEDLI : An order of ghosts.
HEMANT-RITU : Winter.
HIDIMBA : Name of a giantess.
HIJADA : A eunuch.
HINGLÁJ : Name of a goddess.
HIRANYAKASHIPU : Name of a demon.
HIRANYAKASHYAPU : Name of a demon.
HIRANYÁKSHA : Name of a demon.
HIRWA : An order of ghosts.
HOL : Name of a goddess.
HOLI : A festival held at the approach of the vernal equinox. The pile arranged to be kindled at the festival.

HOLIA: A boy who takes an active part in the *Holi* celebrations.

HOLIKA: Name of a goddess.

HOLO: A species of birds.

HOMA: A sacrifice.

HOMAHAVAN: A formation expressing comprehensively or collectively, the several acts and points appertaining to oblation by fire: also any one indefinely of these acts and points.

HOW: Name of a demon.

HUMBAD: A caste of Vániás or an individual of it.

HUTÁSHANI: The pile arranged to be kindled at the festival of *Holi*.

I.

INA: An egg.

INÁM: A gift.

INDA: An egg-shaped vessel.

INDRA-DHANUSHYA: A rain-bow.

INDRAJIT: Name of a demon.

INDRAMAHOTSAVA: A festival celebrated in honour of the god Indra.

IRALE: A protection against rain made of the leaves of trees.

ISHTADEVATA: A chosen deity.

ITIDIO: A species of insects.

J.

JÁDI: Fat.

JADO: Fastened.

JÁDU: The black art.

JÁGRAN: The fifteenth day of the bright half of *Ashádh*.

JÁGRITI: Wakefulness.

JAIKHA: An order of ghosts.

JÁKHÁI: Name of a minor goddess.

JAKHANI: An order of semi-divine beings.

JAKHÁI-DEVI: Name of a minor goddess.

JAKHARA: Name of a minor goddess.

JAKHARO: An order of ghosts.

JÁKHIN: Spirit of a woman whose husband is alive.

JAKHMÁTA: Name of a minor goddess.

JAKRIN: Name of a deity residing in water.

JÁL: An order of ghosts; name of a tree,

JALACHAR: An order of evil spirits living in water.

JALADEVI: Water-goddess.

JALAJ: An order of ghosts.

JALA-JATRA: The ceremony of submerging the image of Shiva.

JALANDHAR: Name of a demon.

JALAP: A dream caused by cold.

JALDEVKI: Water-goddess.

JALOTSAVA: A water festival.

JAMBUVANT: One of the generals of Rama's army at the siege of Lanka or Ceylon.

JAMBUVANTI: The daughter of Jambuvant.

JAMI: An order of ghosts.

JÁN: An order of ghosts.

JANAK: A king of Mahila, the foster-father of Sita.

JÁNAWE: A sacred thread.

JANGAM: A Lingáyat priest.

JANHU: Name of a mythological king.

JANJIRO: A black cotton thread with seven knots.

JANMÁSHTAMI : The eighth day of the dark half of *Shrávan* celebrated as the birth-day of Krishna.
JANMA-SUWÁSINI : A woman who is perpetually unwidowed.
JANNI : Name of a minor goddess.
JANTRA : A mystical arrangement of words.
JAP : Repeating prayers in a muttering manner.
JAP-MÁL : A rosary.
JÁRAN : A kind of black art.
JARÁSANDH : Name of a demon.
JARI : Name of a goddess.
JARI-MARI : A goddess presiding over an epidemic or pestilential disease.
JATA : Matted hair.
JATRA : A fair.
JATUPI : Name of a sage.
JAVA : Barley.
JAVÁLA : Tender wheat plants.
JETHA : The eighth month of the Gujarát Hindu calendar year.
JHAPAT : A sudden encounter.
JHOLÁI : Name of a goddess.
JIMP : An order of ghosts.
JINNI : An order of ghosts.
JINO : Small.
JINTHRO : Rugged.
JIREN : Cumin-seed.
JIVADHANI : Name of a goddess.
JIVI : Live.
JIVO : Live.
JOGÁI : Name of a goddess.
JOGANI : A female harpie.
JOGATA : A male child offered to the goddess Yallamma.
JOGATIN : A female child offered to the goddess Yallamma.
JOGAVA : Begging in the name of the goddess Amba.
JOGI : A male child offered to the goddess Máyáka.
JOGIN : A female child offered to the goddess Máyáka.
JUÁRI : A kind of corn.
JULEBI : A kind of sweet.
JUTHI : False.
JUVÁRI : A kind of corn.
JYESHTHA : The third month of the Deccani Hindu and the eighth month of the Gujarát Hindu calendar year. Name of a constellation.
JYOTISH-SHÁSTRA : The science of astronomy.

K.

KABAR : A tomb raised over the grave of a Muhammadan saint.
KABIR : Name of a celebrated saint.
KACHA : The son of Brihaspati, the preceptor of gods.
KACHAKADA : A kind of bead.
KACHARO : Refuse.
KACHBI : Rainbow.
KÁCHHIA : A caste of vegetable sellers.
KADADAN : Legumes.
KADALIPUJAN : Plantain tree worship.
KADAMB : Authocephalus cadumba.

KADVI : Bitter.

KADAVO : Bitter.

KADULIMB : Melia Azadirachta.

KÁFRI : An order of ghosts.

KÁGDO : A crow.

KÁGRÁSHIA : An expounder of the utterances of crows.

KÁGVA : Cooked food offered to the manes.

KAITABHA : Name of a demon.

KÁJAL : Collyrium.

KÁJRA : A kind of tree.

KAKADI : A cucumber.

KÁKBHUSHUNDI : Name of a sage.

KALASH : A jar.

KALASHI : A weight of corn.

KÁLANEMI : Name of a demon.

KALASIO : A bowl.

KÁLI : Name of a goddess.

KÁLIKA : Name of a goddess.

KÁLKÁICHE BHUT : An order of ghosts.

KÁLI CHAUDAS : The fourteenth day of the dark half of *Ashvin.*

KALINGI : Daughter of the king of the Kalingas.

KÁLI PARAJ : A name applied collectively to the aboriginal tribes of Gujarát.

KÁLIYA NÁG : Name of a mythological snake.

KALI YUGA : The fourth age of the world according to the Hindu scriptures.

KÁLO : Black.

KÁLO VA : Name of a cattle disease.

KALPAVRIKSHA : A fabulous tree granting all desires.

KÁL BHAIRAV : A name of Mahádev.

KÁL PURUSHA : The god of death.

KÁLUBÁI : Name of a minor goddess.

KALYÁN : Welfare.

KÁMA DHENU : A heavenly cow granting all desires.

KAMALA HOLI : The fourteenth day of the bright half of *Fálgun.*

KÁMAN : A kind of black art of bewitching a person.

KAMANDALU : A gourd.

KÁMDEV MAHÁDEV : A name of Mahádev.

KAMOD : A kind of rice.

KANAKNÁTH : A name of Mahádev.

KANKOTRI : Red powder.

KÁNOBA : Name of a minor deity.

KANSA : King of Mathura, maternal uncle of Krishna.

KANSÁR : Coarse wheat flour cooked in water or ghi and sweetened with molasses or sugar.

KANYA : A girl ; Virgo.

KAPHAN : The cloth in which a corpse is wrapped.

KAPIL : Name of a sage.

KAPILÁSHASTHI : A day on which synchronize six particulars—the day, Tuesday ; the month, *Bhádrapad ;* the date, the sixth of the dark fortnight ; the *Nakshatra*, Rohini ; the *Yog*, Vyatipát ; the *Mahánakshatra*, Hasti.

KAPILASHETE : *See* Kapiláshasthi.

KARAN : A kind of tree.

KARHÁDA : A caste of Bráhmans found in the Deccan.

KARKA : Cancer.

KARKATA : Name of a water nymph.
KARKATI : *See* Karkata.
KARKOTAK : Name of a snake.
KARMAMÁRGA : The path of action.
KÁRTIK : The eighth month of the Deccani Hindu and the first month of the Gujarát Hindu calendar year.
KÁRTIKEY : Son of Shiva, the commander of the army of the gods.
KÁSADA : A kind of sacred grass.
KASÁI : A butcher.
KASATIA : Name of a god.
KASATIA-GÁNTH : Tying the knot of Kasatia, a vow observed in the name of the god Kasatia.
KÁSHI : Benares.
KÁTHAWATI : Name of a tribe.
KATHEKARI : A narrator of the legends of the gods.
KÁTHI : Name of a tribe.
KÁTKARI : Name of a tribe.
KÁTLÁN : A kind of medicinal preparation.
KATYÁR : A dagger.
KAUL : The rice, betelnuts, etc., stuck upon an idol when it is consulted.
KAUL GHÁLNE : To consult a deity by *kaul.*
KAURAVA : The patronymic of the descendants of Kuru, but usually applied to the sons of Dhritaráshtra.
KAUSTUBHA : Name of a celebrated jem obtained at the churning of the ocean and worn by Vishnu.
KAVANESHWAR : A name of Mahádev.
KÁYA : Body.
KEDÁR : Name of a deity.
KERÁDO : A kind of tree.
KESHAR : Saffron.
KESHAVA : A name of Krishna.
KETU : In astronomy, the ninth of the planets; in mythology, a demon.
KHABITH : An order of ghosts.
KHAD-KHADYA-BESÁDVI : A ceremony performed by exorcists to propitiate their favourite goddesses.
KHADI : Red or green earth.
KHAGACHAR : An order of ghosts roaming in the sky.
KHAIR : Acacia catechu.
KHAIS : A species of water spirits.
KHAJÁDA PANTH : A sect of Hindus.
KHÁKHARA : A kind of tree.
KHÁKHI : A sect of Hindus.
KHAL : The passage in the *Shivalinga* (phallus of Shiva).
KHANA : A bodice cloth.
KHÁNDE PUJAN : Worship of arms.
KHANDERÁI : A name of the deity Khandoba.
KHANDOBA : Name of a deity.
KHANJIR : A dagger.
KHÁPARI : A kind of cattle disease.
KHÁPRYA : An order of ghosts.
KHÁRAVA : A disease of cattle in which the hoofs are affected.
KHÁRVA : A caste of fishermen and sailors or an individual of it.
KHARVI : *See* Khárva.
KHÁTALE : A cot.

KHATRI : A caste of weavers.
KHAVÁS: A caste of Hindus.
KHAVIS : An order of ghosts.
KHETALO : Name of a snake deity.
KHETRVA : A field.
KHEM : An order of ghosts.
KHICHADI : A preparation of rice and pulse cooked together.
KHIJADIO : The *Shami* tree, Prosopis spicigera
KHIJADO : *See* Khijadio.
KHIJADO MÁMO : An order of ghosts.
KHILI : A peg.
KHIR : Rice cooked in milk and sweetened with sugar.
KHIT KHIT : Notes of the *Pingla* bird.
KHODIÁR MÁTA : Name of a goddess.
KHODO : Lame.
KHODO MÁMO : Name of a minor deity.
KHOJA : A class of Musalmáns.
KHOKHO : An outdoor game played in the Deccan.
KHUNTINI : An order of ghosts.
KIDI : An ant.
KILBIL : Notes of the *Pingla* bird.
KINKHÁB : Silk worked with gold and silver flowers, brocade.
KINNARI : An order of semi-divine beings.
KIRÁTA : A fisherman.
KISHORDÁS : A name of Hanumán.
KODRA : Punctured millet.
KOHALA : Pumpkin.
KOKÁI : Name of a goddess.
KOKIL : A cuckoo.
KOKILA VRATA : The festival of cuckoos which is held in the month of *Ashádh* after a lapse of twenty years.
KOLAMBÁI : Name of a goddess.
KOLHÁI : Name of a goddess.
KOLI : A primitive tribe of Hindus common in the Bombay Presidency.
KOLO : A jackal.
KOLKÁI : Name of a goddess.
KOLU : Cucurbita maxima.
KONDI : A kind of earthen pot.
KONDURI : A preparation of mutton.
KORI : A new garment ; an unused earthen jar ; a small silver coin.
KOTHALI : Reticule.
KOTWAL : Name of an untouchable caste of Hindus.
KOYATA : A wood bill.
KRISHNA : The eighth incarnation of Vishnu.
KRITIKA : Name of a constellation.
KRIYA BHAUDÁI : Name of a deity.
KSHATRIYA : The warrior class, the second of the fourfold divisions of Manu.
KSHETRA : A holy place.
KSHETRAPÁL : The guardian spirit of fields ; a kind of stone.
KUBER : The lord of wealth, the regent of the north and the king of the *Yakshas* and *Kinnaras*.
KUKAD VEL : A kind of creeper.
Kul : A totem ; a clan.
KULA-DEVATA : Family deity.
KULA-DEVI : Family goddess.

KULADHARMA : A special worship of the family god or goddess of each family.
KULATHI : A kind of corn.
KULERA : A mixture of wheat, oat or rice flour, clarified butter and sugar or molasses.
KULKARNI : A village accountant.
KUMBHA : Aquarius.
KUMBHAKARN : Name of a demon.
KUMBHÁR : A caste of potters.
KUMBHÁRAN : A woman of the Kumbhár caste.
KUMBHAVA : Name of a cattle disease.
KUMBHAVIVÁHA : Marriage with an earthen jar.
KUNBI : A cultivator.
KUND : A pond ; a pit ; a sacred pool.
KUNDALAN : A kind of magic circle.
KUNDALI : An astrological diagram of the position of planets at any particular time
KUNDALIA : A name of Hanumán.
KUNDI : A shoe-maker's earthen pot.
KUNKU : Red powder.
KUNTI : The first wife of Pandu.
KUPOTSARGA : Digging a well for the benefit of the public—and abandoning one's right of ownership over it.
KURANANDI : Wheat flour lumps used in the ceremony of the *Bodan*.
KURI : An implement for sowing corn.
KURMI : Name of a water nymph.
KURUKSHETRA : The extensive plain near Delhi, the scene of the great battle between the Kauravas and Pándavas.
KUSHMÁND : An order of demi-gods.
KUSUMBA : The dye prepared from the dried flowers of the Kusumba (Carthamus tinctorius).
KUTRO : A dog.

L.

LÁDU : A sweet ball.
LAGHURUDRA : A rite in honour of the god Shiva.
LÁHYA : Parched rice.
LAKSHACHANDI : A recitation in honour of the goddess Párvati.
LAKSHAMANA : Brother of Ráma.
LAKSHMI : The goddess of wealth.
LÁLA HARDEV : Name of a minor local deity.
LÁLO : Name of a field deity.
LÁLO BHAGAT : Name of a saint.
LÁMANDIVO : An iron lamp.
LAMLAN : A branch of black magic.
LANKA : Ceylon.
LÁPSI : Coarse wheat flower fried in ghi and sweetened with molasses or sugar.
LAVENG : Clove.
LÁVANI : A kind of ballad ; plantation.
LÁWANI : Plantation.
LÁVO : A Parasite.
LÁVSANT : A ghost of a widow.
LIMDO : A tree, Alantas excelsa.
LIMBO : Poisonous.
LINGA : Phallus.
LINGAM : *See* Linga.
LINGÁYAT : An individual of the Lingáyat religion whose chief object of worship is Shiva.

LOBÁN : Olibanum.
LOBHÁN : Incense powder.
LOTA : A water pot.
LUVÁNA : A caste of traders.
LUXMI : *See* Lakshmi.

M.

MACHCHENDRA NÁTH : Name of a saint.
MACHHI : Name of a water nymph.
MÁCHHO : Name of a goddess.
MACHHU : *See* Máchho.
MADALIUN : A hollow bracelet.
MADAN : Cupid.
MADHAVI : A village headman.
MADHU : Name of a demon.
MADHU PAVANTI : An order of ghosts.
MADHWACHARYA : Name of a great saint who founded a sect of Vaishnavism.
MAFAT : Useless.
MAFATIO : Useless.
MAG : A grain, Phaseolus mungo.
MÁGH : The eleventh month of the Deccani Hindu and the fourth month of the Gujarát Hindu calendar year.
MAGHA : Name of a constellation.
MAGHALO : A lamp of mud covered with leaves to represent the god of rain.
MAHÁBHÁRAT : Name of an epic of the Hindus.
MAHÁDEVA : A name of Shiva.
MAHA GIRA : Name of a minor deity.
MAHÁKÁLI : Name of a goddess.
MAHÁKÁLI NIRVÁN TANTRA : Name of a work on Tantric philosophy.
MAHÁLAKSHMI : Name of a goddess; Name of a ceremony in which the goddess is worshipped on the eighth day of the bright half of *Ashvin.*
MAHÁLAYA SHRÁDDHA : A *shráddha* performed in the dark half of *Bhádrapad* in propitiation of ancestors.
MAHÁMÁRI : Cholera goddess.
MAHANT : A saint.
MAHÁPURUSH : An order of civil spirits.
MAHÁR : An unclean caste of Hindus.
MAHÁR PURUSHA : A kind of stone.
MAHÁRÁJA : A term of respectful compellation applied to kings, religious heads, saints, etc.
MAHÁRÁKSHASA : A class of demons.
MAHÁRUDRA : A sacrifice in honour of Shiva.
MAHÁRAURAVA : A kind of hell.
MAHÁSHIVARÁTRI : The fourteenth day of the dark half of *Mágh,* a fast day in honour of Shiva.
MAHÁTMA : A saint.
MAHÁTMYA : Greatness.
MAHESHA : A name of Shiva.
MAHESHVAR : A name of Shiva.
MAHI : Name of a demon.
MAHIKAWATI : Name of a goddess.
MAHODAYA : Name of a festival.
MAIDAN : A plain.
MAKARA : Capricornus.
MAKARI : Name of a water nymph.
MAKHAR : A gaily dressed up wooden frame.

MAKI : Maize.
MÁLÁR : A musical mode.
MALHÁRI : A name of Kandoba.
MALI : Red lead.
MÁLI : A caste of gardeners or an individual of it.
MALINDA : A sweet preparation of wheat flour fried in ghi.
MALIN : Unclean.
MALLÁRI : A name of Khandoba.
MÁLO : A bower.
MAMIKULA : An order of ghosts.
MÁMO : An order of ghosts ; a maternal uncle.
MANAYA : Name of a deity.
MANDAL : A group.
MANDALU : A circle.
MANDAN MISHRA : Name of an ancient scholar.
MANDAP : A bower.
MÁNDA BHARANE : Filling in a magic circle as a protection from spirits.
MÁNEK-STAMBHA : The auspicious post of the marriage bower.
MÁNG : An unclean caste of the Hindus.
MÁNGÁI : Name of a goddess.
MANGAL : Mars.
MANGALÁ-GOURI : A ceremony performed by married girls for five successive years on every Tuesday of the month of *Shrávan.*
MANGALÁRATI : Moving a lighted lamp round an idol.
MANGALSUTRA : The lucky thread worn by married women.
MANI : A jewel ; name of a deity.
MANIDHAR : A snake.
MANI MALLA : Name of a demon.
MÁNKARI : The person entitled to certain honours and presents at village assemblies.
MANKODA : A black ant.
MÁNSA KHAVANTI : An order of ghosts.
MANTRA : An incantation; a magic spell.
MANTRA-SHÁSTRA : The science of incantations.
MANTRI : An exorcist.
MÁNTRIK : An exorcist.
MANUSHYACHAR : An order of ghosts moving among men.
MÁRAN : A branch of black magic.
MÁRGA : A path ; course.
MARGÁI : Name of a goddess.
MÁRGASHIRSHA : The ninth month of the Deccani Hindu and the second month of the Gujarát Hindu calendar year.
MARGI : A sect of Hindus.
MARGI PANTHI : A follower of the Margi sect.
MARI : Name of a goddess.
MARICHI : Name of a sage.
MARIYUN : A ceremony for driving away insects.
MARVO : Marjoram.
MASUR : Lentil.
MASIDA : An order of ghosts.
MÁTA : A goddess.
MÁTÁJI : *See* Máta
MÁTA ASHTAMI : The eighth day of the *navarátra.*
MÁTARI : Name of a goddess.
MATH : A monastery.

MÁTHBHÁJI : A kind of green vegetable.
MÁTI : Earth.
MÁTRIKA : A mother; an order of semi-divine beings.
MÁULI : Name of a goddess.
MAUNYA VRATA : A vow of silence.
MÁVADI : Ghost of a woman dying with certain desires unfulfilled.
MÁYA : Illusion.
MÁYÁKA : Name of a goddess.
MEDA : Marrow.
MEDINI : The earth.
MEGH : A cloud.
MEGHARÁJA : The god of rains.
MEGHLADDU : A sweet ball of wheat flour fried in ghi.
MEHULO : *See* Maghalo.
MEKAIL : Name of an angel.
MELADI : An order of ghosts.
MELDI : *See* Meladi.
MELI VIDYA : Sacrilegious art.
MENA : A kind of bird.
MERU : Name of a mythological mountain.
MESHA : Aries.
MHÁLSA : Name of a goddess.
MHÁRJÁI : Name of a goddess.
MHARLOBA : Name of a deity.
MHASHYA : A species of water spirits.
MHASOBA : Name of a village deity; lord of ghosts.
MIANA : A class of Musalmáns.
MINA : Pisces.
MINDHAL : A kind of fruit.
MIRI : Particle.
MITHUN : Gemini.
MIYALI : An order of ghosts.
MOBHARA : A hollow stone used for threshing corn.
MOCHI : A caste of shoe-makers.
MOCHINI : An order of ghosts.
MOGRI : Rat-tailed raddish.
MOHAN : A branch of black magic.
MOHINI : A fascinating woman.
MOHARO : The stone found in the head of the snake.
MOHOR : *See* Moharo.
MOKSHA : Salvation
MOLANI : An order of ghosts.
MOTÁKAT : Name of a vow.
MOR : A peacock.
MORIA : An earthen bowl.
MOT MÁVALI : Mother Mary.
MOTUDUKH : A kind of cattle disease.
MOVA KHARAVA : Name of a cattle disease.
MRIG : A deer; name of a constellation.
MRIGÁNKA : The moon.
MRIGA TONCHANA : The moon.
MRITYUNJAYA : Name of an incantation.
MUCHKUND : Name of a sage.
MUJÁVAR : A sweeper of a mosque devoutly or piously fixed to it

MUKTI : Salvation.
MUL : Name of a star.
MULO : Raddish.
MUNDA : A kind of wind.
MUNGESHWAR MAHÁDEV : A name of Shiva.
MUNGI MÁTA : Name of a goddess ; dumb mother.
MUNJA : Spirit of Bráhman boy who dies immediately after his thread ceremony.
MURALI : A flute.
MURDUNGA : Tabour.
MURLI : *See* Murali.
MUSAL : A rice pounder.
MUTH : The fist.
MUTH MÁRANE : Throwing of a handful of rice over which incantations have been repeated; sending a bewitched lemon to a person to whom a disease is to be transferred or who is to be killed.
MUVA-KESHIBI : A kind of cattle disease.

N

NÁCHANI : A kind of grain.
NÁDÁPUDI : A coloured cord with a small parcel containing incense, red powder, etc.
NÁDÁSÁDI : A cord and a robe.
NÁG : A snake ; a species of semi-divine beings half man half serpents in form.
NÁGA : *See* Nág.
NÁGABALI : A propitiatory offering to snakes.
NÁGAR : A caste of Bráhmans found in Gujarát.
NÁGCHÁMFA : A flower tree, Alpinia mutans.
NÁGDEV : The snake god.
NÁGKANYA : A snake girl.
NÁG KESAR : Messua Ferrea.
NÁGMAGA : A class of beggars who worship the snake.
NÁGNÁTH : Name of a snake deity.
NÁG PANCHAMI : The fifth day of the bright half *Shrávan*, a holiday in honour of the snake deity.
NÁGO : Shameless.
NÁGOBA : The snake deity.
NÁGVEL : A kind of creeper.
NAIVEDYA : An offering of some eatable to an idol.
NAKSHATRA : A star ; a constellation.
NALA : Name of a mythological king.
NÁLPIR : Name of a *pir* or Mahomedan saint.
NÁL SÁHEB : A familiar name for the bearer, in the Muharam, of the Tabut-pole which terminates at the top in a *nál* or horse-shoe member.
NAMAN : Oil poured over the image of Hanumán.
NAMASKÁR : Reverential or respectful address or salutation.
NANDA : the adoptive father of Krishna.
NANDARÁJ : Name of a mythological king.
NANDI : A bull.
NÁNDI SHRÁDDHA : A *Shráddha* to the names, preliminary to any joyous occasion.
NÁNO : Small.
NAO NARASING : An order of ghosts.
NARA : Name of a sage.
NÁRAD MUNI : Name of a divine sage.
NARAK : Hell.
NARAK-CHATURDASHI : The fourteenth day of the dark half of *Ashvin*.
NÁRALI PAURNIMA : The cocoanut holiday, the fifteenth day of the bright half of *Shrávan*.
NARASIMHA: An incarnation of Vishnu in the form of half lion half man.

NÁRÁYAN : Name of a sage.
NÁRÁYANA BALI : A sacrifice in propitiation of evil spirits.
NÁRÁYAN KAVACH : A hymn in honour of Vishnu.
NÁRÁYAN NÁGABALI : A kind of offering.
NÁREL-PURNIMA : *See* Nárali Paurnima.
NARGUDIKALPA : A kind of medicinal preparation.
NARKYA UDA : A kind of incense.
NARSINHA : *See* Narsimha.
NARSINHA MEHTA : A celebrated saint of Gujarát.
NÁTAK : A drama.
NATHU : Tied.
NAVACHANDI : Name of a sacrifice.
NAVAGRAHA : The nine planets.
NAVAGRAHASHÁNTI : A ceremony in propitiation of the nine planets.
NAVAKÁDÁN : Gift of a ship.
NAVALÁ-DEVI : Name of a goddess.
NAVAMUTHIUM : A preparation of nine handfuls of wheat.
NAVARÁTRA : The first nine days of the month of *Ashvin* held sacred to Durga.
NAVATERI : A game of nine and thirteen.
NEHADO : A hamlet of Bharváds or shepherds.
NIAR : A kind of rice grown without ploughing.
NILOTSARGA : A kind of *Shráddha.*
NILOTSAVA : *See* Nilparván.
NILPARVÁN : A ceremony in propitiation of the spirits of deceased ancestors.
NIRGUDI : A kind of plant.
NIRMALA : Name of a goddess.
NOL VEL : A kind of creeper.
NRISINHA MANTRA : An incantation in honour of Nrisinha.
NYÁSA : Gesture.

O

OGHAD : A fool.
OKARINU : Vomitting ; a kind of sheep disease.
OLO : A species of birds.
OMKÁR MANDHÁTA : Name of a god.

P

PÁDO : A he-buffalo.
PÁDUKA : Impressions of feet on stones.
PADVAL : Snake-gourd.
PADWAL : *See* Padval.
PAJUSAN : A holiday of Jains.
PALAS : A tree, Butea frondosa.
PALEJATRA: A ceremony performed at the sowing season.
PALE MARAD : An order of ghosts.
PÁLIO : A pillar. A tomb erected on the grave of a person who dies on a field of battle.
PALUS : *See* palas.
PÁN : A betel leaf.
PANCHAK : Grouping of constellations lasting for five days.
PANCHAKSHARI : An exorcist.
PANCHÁMRITA : A mixture of milk, curds, sugar, ghi and honey.
PANCHARATNA : Five kinds of precious things, *viz.,* gold, silver, copper, coral and pearls.
PANCHAYATAN : The five deities, Shiva, Vishnu, Surya, Ganpati and Devi.
PANCH-DEVA : *See* Pancháyatan.

PANCHGAVYA: A mixture of the five products of the cow.
PANCHOPACHÁR: The presenting in oblation to an idol of five articles.
PÁNDAVA: A term applied to the five sons of Pandu.
PANDHAR: Name of a goddess.
PANDIT: A scholar.
PÁNDHRI: A kind of tree.
PÁNGALÁ-DEVI: Name of a goddess.
PANOTI: Certain peculiar conjunctions of planets; name of a goddess.
PÁPAD: Wafer biscuits.
PARADI: A disease-scaring basket; a basket.
PARAKÁYÁPRAVESH: Entering the body of another.
PARASHU: An axe.
PARDESHI: A term applied to men from Upper India, usually low caste.
PARJANYA: Rain.
PARJANYA-SHÁNTI: A ceremony performed to secure rainfall.
PARMÁR: A clan of Rajputs.
PÁRO: A kind of stone.
PARSHAD VAIKUNTHA: Name of a heavenly region.
PÁRTHISHWAR: Lord of the earth; a god.
PÁRVATI: The consort of Shiva.
PARWANI: A festival.
PASHUCHAR: An order of ghosts moving among beasts.
PASHUPATÁKA: A weapon of Shiva.
PASTANA: The being disposed for use—vessels, etc. for idol worship.
PÁT: A low wooden stool; marriage with a widow.
PÁTÁL: The nether world.
PÁTHA: Recitation.
PÁTIL: A village headman.
PATIT-PÁVAN: Purifier of the fallen.
PATKA: A head scarf.
PÁTLA: A low wooden stool.
PÁT LÁVANE: To marry a widow.
PAURÁNIC: As prescribed in the *puránas*.
PAUSH: The tenth month of the Deccani Hindu and the third month of the Gujarát Hindu calendar year.
PÁVAIYA: A sect of goddess worshippers.
PÁVTE: A kind of grain.
PEDHE: A kind of sweets.
PEDI: A small heap or *lápsi*.
PEESA: An order of ghosts.
PENDA: A kind of sweets.
PETTOD: A kind of cattle disease.
PHÁLGUN: The twelfth month of the Deccani Hindu and the fifth month of the Gujarát Hindu calendar year.
PHANAS: The jack fruit.
PIDHAN ÁRATI: The ceremony of substituting night ornaments on an idol for the costly ornaments of the day.
PILUDI: A kind of tree.
PIND: A rice ball.
PINDA: *See* Pind.
PINGLA: A species of birds.
PINJAR: Red powder.
PIPAL: A tree, Ficus religiosa.
PIPALESHWAR MAHÁDEV: A name of Shiva.

PIR : A Muhammadan name for a saint.
PIRAS PIPALO : Thespesia populwa.
PISHÁCHA : An evil spirit.
PITAR : A spirit of a deceased ancestor.
PITHI : Turmeric powder.
PITPÁPDO : Glossocardi Boswellia.
PITRA : Manes.
PITRI : An ancestral spirit.
PITRI SHRÁDDHA : A *Shráddha* in propitiation of the ancestral spirits.
PITRRIYA : A deceased ancestor.
PITRU PAKSHA : Manes' fortnight, the dark half of the month of *Bhádrapad*.
POHOR : A measure of time equal to three hours.
POLIO : Hollow.
POLO : Hollow.
PONDHAR : Name of a goddess.
POPAT : A parrot.
POSHI : A class of *chudels*, an order of ghosts.
POTHIA : An exorcist ; the bull of Shiva.
POTHIO : A bull.
PRÁCHETAS : A patronymic of Manu.
PRADAKSHINA : Circumambulation.
PRADOSHA : The thirteenth day of the dark half of a month.
PRALHÁD : The son of the demon Hiranyakashipu. He was a great devotee of Vishnu.
PRALAMBÁSUR : Name of a demon.
PRÁNA : Life.
PRÁNA-POKA : Death wail.
PRASÁD : Consecrated food.
PRASTHÁNA : *See* Pastana.
PRATÁB : An order of ghosts.
PRÁYASCHITTA : Penance.
PRAYOGA : Performance ; experiment.
PRETA : A goblin; spirit of a person dying a sudden or accidental death.
PUDINA : Mentha Sativa.
PUJA : Worship.
PUJÁRI : A worshipper.
PUJYA : Deserving to be worshipped.
PULAP : Name of a sage.
PULASTYA : Name of a sage.
PUNARVASU : Name of a constellation.
PUNDARIK : Name of a mythological snake.
PUNEMA : The full moon day of a month.
PUNJI : Refuse.
PUNJO : Refuse.
PUNYÁHA WACHAN : A particular ceremony performed on festive occasions.
PUNYA STHÁNA : A holy place.
PUNYA TITHI : The death anniversary of a *Sanyási* or saint.
PURÁN : The name of a certain class of sacred books ascribed to Vyása and containing the whole body of Hindu mythology.
PURBHAYA : A term applied to persons from Upper India.
PURNÁHUTI : An offering into the fire of a handful of rice, ghi, cocoanuts and some other articles.
PURNIMA : *See* Paurnima.
PURNA TITHI : A complete day.
PURUSHOTTAM : Intercalary month.
PURVÁBHÁDRAPADA : Name of a constellation.

PURVÁ-FÁLGUNI : Name of a constellation.
PURVAJA : An ancestor.
PURVÁSHÁDHA : Name of a constellation.
PUSHKAR : Name of a snake.
PUSHYA : Name of a constellation.

R

RABÁRI : A caste of shepherds.
RÁDHA : A man dressed in woman's clothes as a dancer ; name of a sweetheart of Krishna.
RADIO : Crying.
RÁFDA : A kind of jujube tree.
RAGATIO : An order of ghosts.
RÁHU : A demon with the tail of a dragon whose head was severed from his body by Vishnu. The head and tail, retaining their separate existence, were transferred to the planetary heavens, and became, the first, the eighth planet, and the second (Ketu) the ninth.
RAINÁDEVI : Name of a goddess.
RÁJÁH : A king.
RÁJAYAJNA : A kind of sacrifice.
RÁJBÁI MÁTA : Name of a goddess.
RÁJBHOG ARATI : The ceremony of offering dainties and cooked food to the gods.
RAJPUTANI : Wife of a Rajput ; a Rajput woman.
RÁKHADI : A piece of silk thread.
RAKHEVÁLIO : An order of ghosts.
RÁKSHASA : A demon.
RÁLA : Panic seed.
RÁLE : Panic seed.
RAMALASHÁSTRA : The science of divining by means of figures or lines and dice.
RÁMANAVAMI : The ninth day of the bright half of *Chaitra* celebrated as the birth day of Ráma.
RÁMÁNUJA : Name of a great saint and philosopher who founded a sect of Vaishnavism.
RÁMÁYANA : An epic poem by Válmiki describing the exploits and adventures of Ráma.
RÁMCHANDRA : A name of Ráma.
RÁMESHWAR : A name of Shiva.
RÁMNÁTH : Name of a deity.
RÁNDAL : Name of a goddess who presides over child-birth.
RÁNDHAN CHHETHA : The cooking sixth, the sixth day of the dark half of *Shráwan*.
RANGPANCHAMI : The fifth day of the dark half of *Phálgun* on which coloured water is thrown.
RÁNJANI : A kind of tree.
RANNA DEVI : Name of a goddess who presides over child-birth.
RÁNO : A Lord.
RÁSHI : Signs of the Zodiac.
RATANVO PÁRO : A kind of stone.
RATANWA : A kind of skin disease.
RATH : A charriot.
RATHA SAPTAMI ; The seventh day of the bright half of *Mágh*.
RATNA : A jewel.
RATNESHWAR MAHÁDEVA : A name of Shiva.
RÁUL : A caste of Hindus or an individual of it.
RÁVAL : *See* Rául.
RAVALNÁTH : Name of a spirit ; name of a village deity.
RÁVAN : Name of the demon king of Lanka or Ceylon.
RAVI : The sun.
RAWALNÁTH : *See* Ravalnáth.
RÁYAN : A tree, Mimusops hexandra.
REKHA : A line.

RELA : A stream.
REVATI : Name of a constellation.
REWADI : A preparation of sesamum and sugar.
RIKTA : Unfruitful, inauspicious.
RISHI PUNCHAMI : The fifth day of the bright half of *Bhádrapad*.
RITU : A season.
ROHINI : Name of a constellation.
ROPANI : Transplanting.
ROT : A loaf prepared from eight kinds of grain.
ROTAL : Womanish.
RUDRA : An order of semi-divine beings.
RUDRÁBHISHEKA : The ceremony of pouring water in a constant stream over the image of Shiva for eleven consecutive days and nights.
RUDRÁKSHA : A tree sacred to Shiva, Eleocarpus ganitrus.
RUDRÁKSHA MÁLA : A rosary of 108 beads of the *rudráksha* wood.
RUDRAYÁG : A sacrifice in honour of the god Shiva.
RUI : A tree, calotropis gigantea.
RUPO : Handsome.
RUTU : Name of a sage.
RUTUSHÁNTI : The marriage consummation ceremony.

S

SABHA : A meeting.
SÁDÁSÁTI PANOTI : A *panoti* extending over seven years and a half.
SÁDHAN : Accomplishment.
SÁDHU : A saint.
SAGAR : A king of the Solar race, an ancestor of Ráma.
SAHÁN : A levigating slab.
SAHASRABHOJAN : Feeding a thousand Bráhmans.
SAITÁN : An order of ghosts.
SAIYED : A name for Musalmáns directly descended from the Prophet.
SAKHARADO : A kind of disease.
SAKHOTIA : Name of a tree.
SAKINI : An order of ghosts.
SÁKSHI : Witness.
SALÁM : The word used in salutation by and to Muhammadans and other people not Hindu.
SALBAYA : Name of a deity.
SAMACHARI : The death anniversary
SAMÁDH : The edifice which is erected over the burial-place of a *Sanyási* or saint ; deep and devout meditation.
SAMÁDHI : *See* Samádh.
SAMAI : A brass lamp.
SÁMÁNYA PUJA : Ordinary worship.
SAMBANDHA : Spirit of a Bráhman who dies without an heir and whose funeral rites have not been performed.
SÁMELU : A log of wood.
SÁMISHYA : Entering the divine order.
SAMPAT SHANIWAR : Wealth-giving *Shaniwár*, a Saturday in the month of *Shrávan*.
SAMUDRA : The sea.
SAMVAT : A year.
SAMVATSAR : A year ; A period of three cycles of twenty years each, that is sixty years.
SAMVATSARI : Death anniversary.
SÁMVATSARIK SHRÁDDHA : The yearly *Shráddha*.
SANATKUMAR : One of the four sons of Brahma.

SANCHAL : A kind of salt.

SANDHYA : The morning, noon or evening prayers of a Bráhman.

SANDHYA ÁRATI : Offerings of Milk, sugar and cakes to the gods in the evening.

SANIPÁT : Delirium.

SÁNKAL : A chain.

SANKAR : A stone.

SANKASTI CHATURTHI : The fourth lunar day of every dark fortnight.

SANKRÁNT : Transit or passage of the sun or a planet from one sign of the zodiac into another.

SANKRÁNTI : *See* Sankránt.

SANYÁSI : The Bráhman of the fourth order, the religious mendicant.

SAPINDI : The offering of a ball of rice, etc., to the spirit of a deceased relative, commonly on the twelfth day after his decease.

SAPTÁHA : A perusal or reading through of a *purán* or other sacred book in seven consecutive days.

SAPTÁHA-PÁRÁYAN : *See* Saptáha.

SAPTA-RISHI : Ursa Major (the seven stars of which are supposed to be the seven great saint Marichi, Atri, Angiras, Pulastya, Pulaha Kratu and Vasishtha.)

SAPTA SANI : Name of an incarnation.

SÁRANGDHA : A kind of fruit.

SARASVATI : The goddess of learning.

SÁRI : A robe.

SARPA BÁNDHANE : A process by which a snake can be prevented from entering or leaving a particular area.

SARVASÁKSHI : The observer of all things.

SATÁP : A kind of tree.

SATARSINGO : Name of a goblin.

SÁTEM : The seventh day of the bright or dark half of a month.

SÁTERI : Name of a goddess.

SÁTHARA : The place in the house where a corpse is placed.

SATHIA : An auspicious figure drawn on the floor.

SATSANG : Contract with the righteous.

SATVÁI : Name of a goddess ; the ghost of a woman.

SATYA NÁRÁYAN : Name of a deity ; a vow of that name.

SATYA VINÁYAK : A name of a Ganpati ; a vow of that name.

SATYAWÁN : Name of a mythological king.

SAUDÁMINI : The lightning.

SAUNDAD : The *Shami* tree, Prosopis spicigera.

SÁVAJ : A wild animal.

SAVÁPÁTI : Weighing about six pounds and a quarter.

SAVITA : The sun.

SÁVITRI : A mythological woman celebrated for her devotion to her husband.

SAWANEKARIN : Name of a goddess.

SÁWAR : A kind of tree.

SÁWKÁR : A money-lender.

SÁVO : Sewed.

SÁYUJJA : Merging into the divine form.

SER : A measure of weight.

SERAJA : A kind of gift.

SEVA : Vermicelli.

SEVAK : A disciple, a follower.

SEVAKA : *See* Sevak.

SHADÁNADA : Name of a goddess.

SHAKARIO : Name of a cattle disease.

SHÁKINI : An order of ghosts.

SHÁKTA MÁTA: Name of a goddess.
SHAKTI: The energy or active power of a deity personified as his wife; as Párvati of Shiva.
SHAKTIMÁTA: Name of a goddess.
SHAKTI-PANTHI: A follower of the Shakti or Shákta sect that is those who worship a divine energy under its feminine personification.
SHAKTIYÁG: A sacrifice in honour of Shakti.
SHÁLIGRÁM: A sacred stone supposed to represent Vishnu.
SHÁLUNKI: A species of singing birds.
SHANI: Saturn.
SHANGÁR ARATI: The ceremony of taking off the idols night garments and putting on others for the day.
SHANKARÁCHÁRYA: The designation of the celebrated teacher of the Vedánt philosophy.
SHANKÁSUR: Name of a demon.
SHANKHÁSUR: Name of a demon.
SHANKHINI: An order of ghosts.
SHÁNTANU: A king of the lunar race who married *Ganga* and Satyavati.
SHARÁDIAN: The dark half of the month of *Bhádrapad*.
SHÁRANG: The bow of Vishnu.
SHARAD PUNEMA: The full-moon day of *Ashvin*.
SHARAD-RITU: The Autumn.
SHÁSTRA: Scripture.
SHATACHANDI: An incantation in honour of the goddess.
SHATANJIVA: Live for a hundred years.
SHATATÁRAKA: Name of a constellation.
SHATCHANDI: An incantation in honour of the goddess Chandi.
SHES BHARANE: Name of a ceremony.
SHENDUR: Red lead.
SHESH NÁG: The snake of one thousand hoods who supports the earth.
SHEVARI: A kind of tree.
SHIKHANDI: Amba born as the daughter of Drupada. She was given out to be, and brought up as, a male child.
SHIKHAR: Top.
SHIKOTAR: Name of a goddess.
SHILI: Stale.
SHILI SÁTEM: The stale seventh, the seventh day of the dark half of *Shrávan*.
SHIRÁLSHET: Name of an ancient Váni or trader who became a king, and reigned three and a half *ghatika* (a measure of time).
SHISHIR-RITU: The cold season.
SHIT: The fowl tied to the top of the bamboo planted in the pit of the *Holi* fire.
SHITALA ASTAKA: A hymn in praise of the goddess Shitala.
SHITALÁI-PUJAN: A holiday observed by women.
SHITALÁDEVI: The small-pox goddess.
SHITALA MÁTA: *See* Shitaládevi.
SHITAL-SAPTAMI: *See* Shili Sátem.
SHIVA: The third god of the Hindu Trinity.
SHIVALANGI: Name of a plant.
SHIVÁ-MUTHA: A vow in which handfuls of corn are offered by married girls to the god Vishnu on every Monday in the month of *Shrávan*.
SHIVARÁTRA: The fourteenth day of the dark half of every month sacred for the worship of Shiva.
SHIVARÁTRI: *See* Shivarátra.
SHIWANI: A kind of tree.
SHIWAR: An offering of boiled rice mixed with curds; an offering of a goat or fowl.
SHLOKA: A stanza, a verse.
SHODASHOPACHÁR: The sixteen ways of doing homage.

SHOKA-PAGLÁN : Morning foot prints.
SHRÁVAD : A kind of shrub.
SHRÁVAK : A term applied to the members of the Jain religion.
SHRÁVAN : The fifth month of the Deccani and the tenth month of the Gujarát Hindu calendar year.
SHRÁVANI : The ceremony of renewing the sacred thread.
SHRAWANA : Name of a constellation.
SHRI DUTTA : Name of a deity.
SHRINGÁR ÁRATI : *See* Shangár árati.
SHRINGHI : Name of a sage.
SHRI SATYA NÁRÁYAN : Name of a deity.
SHUDDHA : Pure; the bright half of a month.
SHUDRA : The last of the four-fold divisions of Manu.
SHUKAMUNI : Name of a sage.
SHUKRA : Venus.
SIDDHA : An order of semi-divine beings.
SIDDHA PURUSHA : A magician.
SIDDHI : Accomplishment ; the acquisition of supernatural powers; name of a wife of Ganpati.
SIDDHI KARAN : Name of a book in which Dharmarája keeps an account of the good and bad actions of men.
SIDHA : Uncooked articles of food.
SIDIO : Nigro-like.
SIKAN : A sling.
SIKE : A sling.
SIKOTARU : *See* Sikoturu.
SIKOTURU : Ghost of a woman dying with certain desires unfulfilled.
SIMÁNT : The first pregnancy ceremony.
SINDHÁVÁR : Name of a goddess.
SINDUR : Red lead.
SINHA : A lion ; Leo.
SINHIKA : The mother of Ráhu.
SITA : The consort of Ráma.
SIWA BÁNDHANE : Binding the boundary-name of a ceremony.
SIWO : Sewn.
SMÁRTA AGNI : The fire which is kept constantly burning and worshipped during the *Cháturmás*.
SOD-MUNJ : The ceremony of loosening the *munja* (string) from the loins of a Bráhman.
SOLANKI : Name of a clan of Rajputs.
SOLA SOMVÁR-VRATA : A vow observed on sixteen successive Mondays.
SOMAPA : Name of a water nymph
SOMAVATI-AMÁVÁSYA : The fifteenth day of the dark half of a month falling on Monday.
SOMAGA : Name of a religious ceremony.
SONI : A caste of goldsmiths or an individual of it.
SORRO : Sulphuret of antimony.
SOSHI : Name of a class of *chudels*.
SOVALEN : A silk garment.
SPHATIKA MANÍ : A crystal stone.
STAMBHAN : A branch of black magic.
STHÁNA : Locality.
STHÁNA-DEVA : A local deity.
STHÁNADEVATA : *See* Sthána-deva.
STHÁPAN : Installation.
SUD : The bright half of a month.
SUDARSHAN : *See* Sudarshan chakra.
SUDARSHAN CHAKRA : The discus of Vishnu.

SUDHA : Nectar.
SUDHAKAR : The moon.
SUDYAMAN : Name of a mythological king.
SUGAD : A little earthen vessel.
SUKÁL : A plentiful harvest.
SULIO : An order of ghosts.
SULEIMÁNI PÁRO : A kind of stone.
SUMARIA GANESH : A name of Ganpati.
SUNA : Unoccupied.
SUNAKU : A kind of cattle disease.
SUNKÁI : Name of a goddess.
SUNTH : Dry ginger.
SUPADUN : A winnowing fan.
SURA : Liquor.
SURAKANO : Twisted iron wire.
SURAN : Amorphophallus campalatus (elephant foot).
SURANG : A kind of tree.
SURDHAN : Ghost of a male member dying with certain of his desires unfulfilled.
SURMO : *See* Sorro.
SUROPURO : A spirit of one who meets death on a field of battle.
SURYA : The sun.
SURYA KAVACH : A hymn in honour of the Sun.
SURYA-VRAT : A vow in honour of the Sun.
SUTAKI : One ceremonially impure on account of the death of a relative.
SUTÁR : A caste of carpenters or an individual of it.
SUTI : An order of ghosts.
SUTTEE : A woman who burns herself on the funeral pyre of her husband.
SUVA : An ingredient used in preparing spices.
SUWARN : Gold.
SUWÁSINI : An unwidowed woman.
SWÁMI : A lord, a term applied to saints.
SWÁMI MAHÁRÁJ : An epithet of Dattátraya or Shri Dutta.
SWÁMINÁRÁYAN : A sect of Hindus.
SWAPNA : A dream.
SWARGA : Heaven.
SWASTIKA : A kind of mystical figure.
SWÁTI : Name of constellation.
SWAYAMBHU : Self-existent.
SWAYAMVAR : A maiden's choice marriage.

T.

TÁDIA : A fruit of the fan-palm.
TADULI : The full moon day of Ashádh.
TAKSHAK : Name of a snake.
TÁL : A kind of cymbal.
TALABDIA KOLI : A sub-division of the Koli tribe.
TALKHÁMBA : A ghost of an unmarried Shudra.
TALI : A plate.
TALI BHARANE : A rite performed in honour of the god Khandoba.
TALO BHAGAT : Name of a great saint.
TAMÁSHA : A diverting exhibition ; a show, play, farce, mock-fight, etc.
TÁMHAN : A flat saucer-like metal plate.
TAMJÁI : Name of a goddess.
TANYATUN : Lightning.

VÁNZIAPANA : Barrenness.
VARADANI : Name of a goddess.
VARADHAN : Name of a deity.
VARÁH : A boar.
VARÁHA-SANHITA : Name of a book.
VARSHÁ-RITU : The rainy season.
VÁRUL : The white ant-hill.
VÁSANA : Desire.
VASANTAPANCHAMI : The fifth day of the bright half of *Mágh.*
VASANT-RITU : The spring.
VÁSH : An oblation of rice and sweets offered to crows.
VASHIKARAN : A branch of black magic.
VASHISHTHA : Name of a sage.
VÁSTU : A religious rite performed on entering a new house.
VÁSTDEVATA : The guardian spirit of dwelling places.
VÁSTUN : *See* Vástu.
VÁSTUPUJAN : *See* Vástu.
VASU : A bull-calf or bull branded and set at liberty.
VASUBÁRAS : The twelfth day of the bright half of *Ashvin.*
VASUDEVA : Name of the father of Krishna.
VASU-DWÁDASI : *See* Vasubáras.
VÁSUKI : Name of a snake.
VÁSTU SHÁNTI : *See* Vástu.
VATA-SÁVITRI VRAT : Name of a vow observed by women on the full moon day of *Jyeshtha.*
VÁTI : A small metal cup.
VÁTKI : *See* Váti.
VÁV : A reservoir of water; a tank.
VÁYALI ; Eccentric.
VÁYU : Wind; the deity presiding over the wind.
VÁYUSUTA : A name of Máruti.
VEDA : Name of the scriptures of the Hindus.
VEDATRAYI : The three vedas, Rik, Yajus and Sáma.
VEDHA : Malign influence.
VEDIC : Relating to the Vedas; as enjoined in the Vedas.
VEHALA : A tree, Beleric Myrobalan.
VELAN : A stick.
VELO : A creeper.
VETAL : The lord of ghosts; name of a village deity.
VETRASARPA : A cane stick with an image of a snake at its end.
VIDÁ-SUPÁRI : Betel nut and leaves.
VIDYUT : Lightning.
VAJAYADASHAMI : The tenth day of the bright half of *Ashvin.*
VIJLI : Lightning.
VIKRAM : Name of a king.
VIMÁN : A celestial car.
VINÁYAK-CHATURTHI : The fourth day of the bright half of every month.
VINCHI : A female scorpion.
VIR : A male fiend; ghost of an unmarried Kshatriya.
VIRA : An order of ghosts ; name of a village deity.
VISHA : Poison.
VISHÁKHA : Name of a constellation.
VISHESHA PUJA : Special worship.
VISHI : A cycle of twenty years.
VISHNU : The second god of the Hindu Trinity.

VISHNUSAHASRANÁMA : A book containing the thousand names of Vishnu.
VISHNUYÁGA : A sacrifice in honour of Vishnu.
VISHOTAK : Name of a disease.
VISHVÁMITRA : Name of a sage.
VISHWARUPA : That exists in all forms, an epithet of Vishnu.
VISHWESHWAR : A name of Shiva.
VISWÁTI : An order of ghosts.
VITHOBA : Name of a god.
VISUCHIKA : Name of a cholera goddess.
VIVÁNCHARA : An order of ghosts.
VRAT : A vow.
VRIKODARA : Wolf-bellied, an epithet of Bhima.
VRINDA : Name of the wife of Jalandhar, a demon.
VRISCHIKA : Scorpion.
VRISHABHA : Taurus.
VRITRASÁR : Name of ademon.
VRUNDA : *See* Vrinda.
VYATIPÁT : The seventeenth of the Astrological *Yoga* (the twenty-seventh part of a circle measured on the plane of the Ecliptic).

W.

WAD : The banyan tree.
WÁDI : An enclosed piece of meadow-field or garden ground.
WÁGH-BÁRAS : The twelfth day of *Ashvin.*
WÁGHE : Male children offered to the god Khandoba.
WÁGHESHWARI : Name of a village goddess.
WÁGHJAI : Name of a deity.
WÁGHOBA : An order of ghosts.
WÁGRESHWARI : Name of a village goddess.
WÁGHYA : Name of a deity ; a male child offered to the god Khandoba.
WÁMAN-DWÁDASHI : The twelfth day of the bright half of *Bhádrapad.*
WÁNI : A trader ; a general name for all castes of traders *i. e.*, banyas.
WÁNPRASTA : A Bráhman in the third order of his life ; a hermit in general.
WÁRUL : An ant-hill.
WATA : The Banyan tree.
WATA-PAURNIMA : The full moon day of *Jyeshtha.*
WUDA : Incense,

Y.

YADNA : *See* Yajna.
YADNOPAVIT : The sacred thread worn by Bráhmans.
YADNYA : *See* Yajna.
YAJAMÁN : A host ; a person performing a sacrifice.
YAJNA : A sacrifice.
YAKSHA : A class of demi-gods, attendant on Kubera and employed in guarding his treasures.
YAKSHINI : A female Yaksha ; a fairy.
YALLAMMA : Name of a goddess,
YAMA : The God of death.
YAMADUTA : A messenger of the god of death.
YAMAGHANTA : A *Yog* or conjunction of times, viz., a Sunday-falling upon the second day of the bright or dark half of a month ; a Friday falling upon the third lunar day, etc., etc.
YAMALOKA : The region of Yama.
YAMAPURI : The city of the god of death.
YANTRA : A mystical formula or diagram.

YOGA: Religious and abstract meditation.
YOGA MÁRGA: The path of meditation.
YOGA-SUTRA: Name of a work by Pátanjali containing aphorisms of the science of Yoga.
YOGAVÁSHISTHA: Name of a work on philosophy.
YOJAN: A measure of distance equal to eight miles.
YUDHISHTHIR: An epithet of Dharma, the eldest of the Pándava brothers.

Z

ZÁMHÁDI: A female spirit guarding the village gates.
ZAMPAHADI: An order of ghosts.
ZANZARKA: Name of a goddess.
ZANZIRA: A kind of magic incantation.
ZÁR: Fever.
ZARMÁN ZARVÁN: A ceremony in which a woman fetches water for the first time after delivery.
ZILAKESHWAR: A name of Mahádeva.
ZINI: Small.
ZOD: An order of ghosts.